T0178152

Lecture Notes in Computer Science 14362

Founding Editors

Gerhard Goos
Juris Hartmanis

The series Lecture Notes in Computer Science (LNCS), including its subseries Lecture Notes in Artificial Intelligence (LNAI) and Lecture Notes in Bioinformatics (LNBI), has established itself as a medium for the publication of new developments in computer science and information technology research, teaching, and education.

LNCS enjoys close cooperation with the computer science R & D community, the series counts many renowned academics among its volume editors and paper authors, and collaborates with prestigious societies. Its mission is to serve this international community by providing an invaluable service, mainly focused on the publication of conference and workshop proceedings and postproceedings. LNCS commenced publication in 1973.

George Bebis · Golnaz Ghiasi · Yi Fang ·
Andrei Sharf · Yue Dong · Chris Weaver ·
Zhicheng Leo · Joseph J. LaViola Jr. · Luv Kohli
Editors

Advances in Visual Computing

18th International Symposium, ISVC 2023
Lake Tahoe, NV, USA, October 16–18, 2023
Proceedings, Part II

 Springer

Editors
George Bebis
University of Nevada Reno
Reno, NV, USA

Yi Fang
New York University
New York, NY, USA

Yue Dong
Microsoft Research
Beijing, China

Zhicheng Leo
University of Maryland
Collage Park, MD, USA

Luv Kohli
InnerOptic Technology
Hillsborough, NC, USA

Golnaz Ghiasi
Google Research
Mountain View, CA, USA

Andrei Sharf
Ben-Gurion University
Be'er Sheva, Israel

Chris Weaver
The University of Oklahoma
Norman, OK, USA

Joseph J. LaViola Jr.
University of Central Florida
Orlando, FL, USA

ISSN 0302-9743   ISSN 1611-3349 (electronic)
Lecture Notes in Computer Science
ISBN 978-3-031-47965-6   ISBN 978-3-031-47966-3 (eBook)
https://doi.org/10.1007/978-3-031-47966-3

This Springer imprint is published by the registered company Springer Nature Switzerland AG
The registered company address is: Gewerbestrasse 11, 6330 Cham, Switzerland

Paper in this product is recyclable.

Preface

It is with great pleasure that we welcome you to the proceedings of the 18th International Symposium on Visual Computing (ISVC 2023), which was held in Lake Tahoe (October 16–18, 2023). ISVC provides a common umbrella for the four main areas of visual computing including vision, graphics, visualization, and virtual reality. The goal is to provide a forum for researchers, scientists, engineers, and practitioners throughout the world to present their latest research findings, ideas, developments, and applications in the broader area of visual computing.

This year, the program consisted of seven keynote presentations, eleven oral sessions, one poster session, six special tracks, and three tutorials. We received close to 120 submissions for the main symposium from which we accepted 43 papers for oral presentation and 15 papers for poster presentation. A total of 25 papers were accepted for oral presentation in the special tracks from 34 submissions.

All papers were reviewed with an emphasis on the potential to contribute to the state of the art in the field. Selection criteria included accuracy and originality of ideas, clarity and significance of results, and presentation quality. The review process was quite rigorous, involving three independent double-blind reviews followed by several days of discussion. During the discussion period we tried to correct anomalies and errors that might have existed in the initial reviews. Despite our efforts, we recognize that some papers worthy of inclusion may have not been included in the program. We offer our sincere apologies to authors whose contributions might have been overlooked.

We wish to thank everybody who submitted their work to ISVC 2023 for review. It was because of their contributions that we succeeded in having a technical program of high scientific quality. In particular, we would like to thank the keynote speakers, the program chairs, the steering committee, the international Program Committee, the special track organizers, the tutorial organizers, the reviewers, the sponsors, and especially the authors who contributed their work to the symposium. We would like to express our appreciation to Springer for sponsoring the best paper award again this year.

We sincerely hope that ISVC 2023 offered participants opportunities for professional growth.

September 2023

George Bebis
Yue Dong
Yi Fang
Golnaz Ghiasi
Luv Kohli
Joseph J. LaViola Jr.
Zhicheng Leo
Andrei Sharf
Chris Weaver

Organization

Steering Committee

Bebis George (Chair)	University of Nevada, Reno, USA
Coquillart Sabine	Inria, France
Klosowski James	AT&T Labs Research, USA
Kuno Yoshinori	Saitama University, Japan
Lin Steve	Microsoft, China
Lindstrom Peter	Lawrence Livermore National Laboratory, USA
Moreland Kenneth	Oak Ridge National Laboratory, USA
Nefian Ara	NASA Ames Research Center, USA
Tafti Ahmad P.	University of Pittsburgh, USA

Area Chairs

Computer Vision

Fang Yi	New York University, USA
Golnaz Ghiasi	Google Brain, USA

Computer Graphics

Dong Yue	Microsoft, China
Sharf Andrei	Ben-Gurion University, Israel

Virtual Reality

Kohli Luv	InnerOptic Technology, Inc., USA
LaViola Joseph	University of Central Florida, USA

Visualization

Liu Zhicheng (Leo)	University of Maryland, USA
Weaver Chris	University of Oklahoma, USA

Publicity Chair

Ali Erol   Eksperta Software, Turkey

Tutorials and Special Tracks Chairs

Hand Emily   University of Nevada, Reno, USA
Tavakkoli Alireza   University of Nevada, Reno, USA

Awards Chairs

Sun Zehang   Apple, USA
Amayeh Gholamreza   Tesla, USA

Web Master

Isayas Berhe Adhanom   University of Nevada, Reno, USA

Program Committee

Nicoletta Adamo-Villani   Purdue University, USA
Emmanuel Agu   Worcester Polytechnic Institute, USA
Touqeer Ahmad   Blackmagic Design, USA
Kostas Alexis   Norwegian University of Science and Technology,
                                     Norway
Usman Alim   University of Calgary, Canada
Amol Ambardekar   Microsoft, USA
Soheyla Amirian   University of Georgia, USA
Mehdi Ammi   LIMSI-CNRS, France
Naga Surya Sandeep Angara   National Institute of Health, USA
Zahra Anvari   University of Texas at Arlington, USA
Mark Apperley   University of Waikato, New Zealand
Antonis Argyros   Foundation for Research and
                                     Technology – Hellas, Greece
Vijayan K. Asari   University of Dayton, USA
Aishwarya Asesh   Adobe, USA
Vassilis Athitsos   University of Texas at Arlington, USA
Melinos Averkiou   University of Cyprus, Cyprus

George Baciu	Hong Kong Polytechnic University, China
Abdul Bais	University of Regina, Canada
Nikos Bakalos	National Technical University of Athens, Greece
Peter Balazs	University of Szeged, Hungary
Selim Balcısoy	Sabancı University, Turkey
Reneta Barneva	SUNY Fredonia, USA
Paola Barra	Università di Napoli Parthenope, Italy
Ronen Barzel	Drawbridge Labs, UK
Anil Ufuk Batmaz	Concordia University, Canada
George Bebis	University of Nevada, Reno, USA
Jan Bender	RWTH Aachen University, Germany
Bedrich Benes	Purdue University, USA
Ayush Bhargava	Facebook, USA
Harsh Bhatia	Lawrence Livermore National Laboratory, USA
Sanjiv Bhatia	University of Missouri, St. Louis, USA
Ayan Biswas	Los Alamos National Laboratory, USA
Dibio Borges	Universidade de Brasília, Brazil
David Borland	University of North Carolina at Chapel Hill, USA
Nizar Bouguila	Concordia University, Canada
Thierry Bouwmans	University of La Rochelle, France
Jose Braz Pereira	EST Setúbal/IPS, Portugal
Valentin Brimkov	Buffalo State College, USA
Wolfgang Broll	Ilmenau University of Technology, Germany
Gerd Bruder	University of Central Florida, USA
Chris Bryan	Arizona State University, USA
Tolga Çapin	TED University, Turkey
Sek Chai	Latent AI, Inc., USA
Jian Chang	Bournemouth University, UK
Sotirios Chatzis	Cyprus University of Technology, Cyprus
Cunjian Chen	Michigan State University, USA
Zhonggui Chen	Xiamen University, China
Yi-Jen Chiang	New York University, USA
Isaac Cho	Utah State University, USA
Amit Chourasia	University of California at San Diego, USA
Tommy Dang	Texas Tech University, USA
Aritra Dasgupta	NYU, USA
Jeremie Dequidt	University of Lille, France
Daljit Singh Dhillon	Clemson University, USA
Sotirios Diamantas	Tarleton State University, Texas A&M System, USA
Alexandra Diehl	University of Konstanz, Germany
John Dingliana	Trinity College Dublin, Ireland

Ralf Dörner	RheinMain University of Applied Sciences, Germany
Yue Dong	Microsoft Research Asia, China
Gianfranco Doretto	West Virginia University, USA
Anastasios Doulamis	Technical University of Crete, Greece
Shengzhi Du	Tshwane University of Technology, South Africa
Meenal Dugar	Penn State University, USA
Soumya Dutta	Los Alamos National Laboratory, USA
Achim Ebert	University of Kaiserslautern, Germany
Parris Egbert	Brigham Young University, USA
Mohamed El Ansari	Moulay Ismail University, Morocco
El-Sayed M. El-Alfy	King Fahd University of Petroleum and Minerals, Saudi Arabia
Alireza Entezari	University of Florida, USA
Ali Erol	Sigun Information Technologies, UK
Mohammad Eslami	University of Pittsburgh, USA
Yi Fang	New York University, USA
Matteo Ferrara	University of Bologna, Italy
Nivan Ferreira	Universidade Federal de Pernambuco, Brazil
Francesco Ferrise	Politecnico di Milano, Italy
Robert Fisher	University of Edinburgh, UK
Gian Luca	Foresti University of Udine, Italy
Ioannis Fudos	University of Ioannina, Greece
Issei Fujishiro	Keio University, Japan
Radovan Fusek	VŠB-Technical University of Ostrava, Czechia
Marina Gavrilova	University of Calgary, Canada
Krzysztof Gdawiec	University of Silesia in Katowice, Poland
Golnaz Ghiasi	Google Research, USA
Daniela Giorgi	ISTI – CNR, Italy
Deeptha Girish	University of Cincinnati, USA
Wooi-Boon Goh	Nanyang Technological University, Singapore
Minglun Gong	University of Guelph, Canada
Laurent Grisoni	University of Lille, France
David Gustafson	Kansas State University, USA
Felix Hamza-Lup	Georgia Southern University, USA
Emily Hand	University of Nevada, Reno, USA
Brandon Haworth	University of Victoria, Canada
Subhashis Hazarika	SRI International, USA
Eric Hodgson	Miami University, USA
Jing Hua	Wayne State University, USA
Muhammad Hussain	King Saud University, Saudi Arabia
Ahmed Hussein	University of Guelph, Canada

Kei Iwasaki	Saitama University, Japan
Ming Jiang	Lawrence Livermore National Laboratory, USA
Soon Ki Jung	Kyungpook National University, South Korea
Sungchul Jung	Kennesaw State University, USA
Ho Chuen Kam	Chinese University of Hong Kong, China
Takashi Kanai	University of Tokyo, Japan
Konstantinos Karydis	University of California, Riverside, USA
Garrett Kenyon	Los Alamos National Laboratory, USA
Edward Kim	Drexel University, USA
Hyungseok Kim	Konkuk University, South Korea
James Klosowski	AT&T Labs Research, USA
Luv Kohli	InnerOptic Technology, Inc., USA
Stefanos Kollias	National Technical University of Athens, Greece
Takashi Komuro	Saitama University, Japan
Dimitrios Kosmopoulos	University of Patras, Greece
Michael Krone	University of Tübingen, Germany
Arjan Kuijper	TU Darmstadt, Germany
Deepanjan Kundu	Meta Platforms, USA
Yoshinori Kuno	Saitama University, Japan
Hung La	University of Nevada, USA
Yu-Kun Lai	Cardiff University, UK
Robert Laramee	Swansea University, UK
Joseph LaViola Jr.	University of Central Florida, USA
Robert R. Lewis	Washington State University, USA
Frederick Li	University of Durham, UK
Xin Li	Texas A & M University, USA
Kuo-Chin Lien	Layer AI, USA
Chun-Cheng Lin	National Yang Ming Chiao Tung University, Taiwan
Stephen Lin	Microsoft Research Asia, China
Peter Lindstrom	Lawrence Livermore National Laboratory, USA
Hao Liu	KLA Corporation, USA
Shiguang Liu	Tianjin University, China
Zhicheng Liu	Georgia Institute of Technology, USA
Manuel Loaiza	Universidad Católica San Pablo, Peru
Ines Lohse	University of Pittsburgh, USA
Leandro Loss	QuantaVerse, USA, ITU, USA, ESSCA Shanghai, China
Jörn Loviscach	Fachhochschule Bielefeld (University of Applied Sciences), Germany
Aidong Lu	UNC Charlotte, USA
Brendan Macdonald	NIOSH, USA

Giuseppe Placidi	University of L'Aquila, Italy
Kevin Ponto	University of Wisconsin-Madison, USA
Jiju Poovvancheri	University of Victoria, Canada
Nicolas Pronost	Université Claude Bernard Lyon 1, France
Lei Qi	Iowa State University, USA
Hong Qin	Stony Brook University, USA
Christopher Rasmussen	University of Delaware, USA
Emma Regentova	University of Nevada, Las Vegas, USA
Guido Reina	University of Stuttgart, Germany
Erik Reinhard	InterDigital, France
Banafsheh Rekabdar	Portland State University, USA
Hongliang Ren	National University of Singapore, Singapore
Theresa-Marie Rhyne	Consultant, USA
Eraldo Ribeiro	Florida Institute of Technology, USA
Peter Rodgers	University of Kent, UK
Sudipta Roy	Jio Institute, India
Isaac Rudomin	Barcelona Supercomputing Center, Spain
Filip Sadlo	Heidelberg University, Germany
Punam Saha	University of Iowa, USA
Naohisa Sakamoto	Kobe University, Japan
Kristian Sandberg	Computational Solutions, Inc., USA
Nickolas S. Sapidis	University of Western Macedonia, Greece
Fabien Scalzo	Pepperdine University, USA
Thomas Schultz	University of Bonn, Germany
Andrei Sharf	Ben-Gurion University of the Negev, Israel
Puneet Sharma	UiT-The Arctic University of Norway, Norway
Timothy Shead	Sandia National Laboratories, USA
Mohamed Shehata	University of British Columbia, Canada
Gurjot Singh	Fairleigh Dickinson University, USA
Vineeta Singh	University of Cincinnati, USA
Alexei Skurikhin	Los Alamos National Laboratory, USA
Pavel Slavik	Czech Technical University in Prague, Czechia
Jack Snoeyink	University of North Carolina at Chapel Hill, USA
Fabio Solari	University of Genoa, Italy
Paolo Spagnolo	National Research Council, Italy
Jaya Sreevalsan-Nair	IIIT Bangalore, India
Chung-Yen Su	National Taiwan Normal University, Taiwan
Changming Sun	CSIRO, Australia
Guodao Sun	Zhejiang University of Technology, China
Zehang Sun	Apple Inc., USA
Carlo H. Séquin	University of California, Berkeley, USA
Ahmad Tafti	University of Pittsburgh, USA

Jules-Raymond Tapamo	University of KwaZulu-Natal, South Africa
João Manuel R. S.	Tavares University of Porto & INEGI, Portugal
Michael Teti	Los Alamos National Laboratory, USA
Daniel Thalmann	École Polytechnique Fédérale de Lausanne, Switzerland
Holger Theisel	Otto-von-Guericke University, Germany
Yuan Tian	Innopeak Tech Inc., China
Mehmet Engin	Tozal University of Louisiana at Lafayette, USA
Stefano Tubaro	Politecnico di Milano, Italy
Georg Umlauf	HTWG Konstanz, Germany
Serestina Viriri	University of KwaZulu-Natal, South Africa
Chaoli Wang	University of Notre Dame, USA
Cuilan Wang	Georgia Gwinnett College, USA
Yijing Watkins	Pacific Northwest National Laboratory, USA
Chris Weaver	University of Oklahoma, USA
Kin Hong Wong	Chinese University of Hong Kong, China
Tien-Tsin Wong	Chinese University of Hong Kong, China
Kui Wu	LightSpeed Studios, USA
Wei Xu	Brookhaven National Laboratory, USA
Goshiro Yamamoto	Kyoto University, Japan
Yasuyuki Yanagida	Meijo University, Japan
Xiaosong Yang	Bournemouth University, UK
Hsu-Chun Yen	National Taiwan University, Taiwan
Zeyun Yu	University of Wisconsin-Milwaukee, USA
Xiaoru Yuan	Peking University, China
Xenophon Zabulis	FORTH, Greece
Jiri Zara	Czech Technical University in Prague, Czechia
Wei Zeng	Xi'an Jiaotong University, China
Dimitris Zermas	Sentera, USA
Jian Zhang	Bournemouth University, UK
Mengyang Zhao	Dartmouth College, USA
Jianmin Zheng	Nanyang Technological University, Singapore
Chenyang Zhu	Simon Fraser University, Canada
Ying Zhu	Georgia State University, USA

Additional Reviewers

Aliniya, Parvaneh
Bhattacharya, Arindam
Chen, Ho-Lin
Golchin, Bahareh
Gong, Minglun
Iqbal, Hasan
Loizou, Marios
Mohamed, Abdallah

Nykl, Scott
Ramesh, Subhash
Randhawa, Zaigham
Sheibanifard, Armin
Shu, Ziyu
Wang, Meili
Zaveri, Ram
Zgaren, Ahmed

Keynote Talks

Machine Learning for Scientific Data Analysis and Visualization

Han-Wei Shan

The Ohio State University, USA

Abstract. In this talk, I will discuss our recent developments on using machine learning for scientific data analysis and visualization, with special focuses on visualization surrogates and compact representations for scientific data. I will first discuss how to construct visualization surrogates that can help streamline the visualization and analysis of large-scale ensemble simulations and facilitate the exploration of their immense input parameter space. Three different approaches for constructing such visualization surrogates: image space, object space, and hybrid image-object space approaches will be discussed. Then I will discuss how neural networks can be used to extract succinct representations from scientific data for rapid exploration and tracking of features. The use of geometric convolution to represent 3D particle data, and how regions of interest can be used as important measures for more efficient latent generation will be discussed.

Speaker Bio-Sketch: Han-Wei Shen is a Full Professor at The Ohio State University, and currently serves as the Editor-in-Chief of IEEE Transactions on Visualization and Computer Graphics. He is a member of IEEE VGTC Visualization Academy, and was the chair of the steering committee for IEEE SciVis conference from 2018-2020. His primary research interests are visualization, artificial intelligence, high performance computing, and computer graphics. Professor Shen is a winner of National Science Foundation's CAREER award and US Department of Energy's Early Career Principal Investigator Award. He received his BS degree from Department of Computer Science and Information Engineering at National Taiwan University in 1988, the MS degree in computer science from the State University of New York at Stony Brook in 1992, and the PhD degree in computer science from the University of Utah in 1998. From 1996 to 1999, he was a research scientist at NASA Ames Research Center in Mountain View California.

Estimating the Structure and Motion of Biomolecules at Atomic Resolutions

David Fleet

University of Toronto & Google DeepMind, Canada

Abstract. One of the foremost problems in structural biology concerns the inference of the atomic-resolution 3D structure of biomolecules from electron cryo-microscopy (cryo-EM). The problem, in a nutshell, is a form of multi-view 3D reconstruction, inferring the 3D electron density of a particle from large sets of images from an electron microscope. I'll outline the nature of the problem and several of the key algorithmic developments, with particular emphasis on the challenging case in which the imaged molecule exhibits a wide range of conformational variation (or non-rigidity). Through single particle cryo-EM, methods from computer vision and machine learning are reshaping structural biology and drug discovery. This is joint work with Ali Punjani.

Speaker Bio-Sketch: David Fleet is a Research Scientist at Google DeepMind (since 2020) and a Professor of Computer Science at the University of Toronto (since 2004). From 2012–2017 he served as Chair of the Department of Computer and Mathematical Sciences, University of Toronto Scarborough. Before joining the University of Toronto, he worked at Xerox PARC (1999–2004) and Queen's University (1991-1998). He received the PhD in Computer Science from the University of Toronto in 1991. He as awarded an Alfred P. Sloan Research Fellowship in 1996 for his research on visual neuroscience. He received research paper awards at ICCV 1999, CVPR 2001, UIST 2003, BMVC 2009, and NeurIPS 2022. In 2010, with Michael Black and Hedvig Sidenbladh he received the Koenderink Prize for fundamental contributions to computer vision that withstood the test of time. In 2022, with Ali Punjani, he received the Paper of the Year Award from the Journal of Structural Biology for work on cryo-EM. He served as Associate Editor of IEEE Trans PAMI (2000–2004), as Program Co-Chair for CVPR (2003) and ECCV (2014), and as Associate Editor-In-Chief for IEEE Trans PAMI (2005–2008). He was Senior Fellow of the Canadian Institute of Advanced Research (2005–2019), and currently holds a Canadian CIFAR AI Chair. His current research interests span computer vision, image processing machine learning and computational biology.

Curriculum Learning and Active Learning, for Visual Object Recognition when Data is Scarce

Daphna Weinshall

Hebrew University of Jerusalem, Israel

Abstract. Deep learning protocols typically involve the random sampling of training examples by way of SGD. We investigated alternative paradigms, based on the empirical observation that the value of data points changes with time and network proficiency. In this talk I will start with curriculum learning, where by strategically arranging the learning data to present simpler concepts before more complex ones, networks can accelerate their understanding of the easier concepts, resulting in faster convergence and enhanced overall performance. I will then discuss active learning, where one deals with the annotation of data within a predetermined annotation budget. The objective is to select the data instances for annotation that will yield the greatest improvement for the learner. Surprisingly, our findings challenge traditional active learning strategies, which typically assume a high budget. We demonstrate that when the budget is low, it is more beneficial to prioritize annotating a small number of examples that represent the easiest and most typical instances within the data. This stands in contrast to the conventional approach, which suggests selecting examples from the hardest and most atypical portion of the data distribution.

Speaker Bio-Sketch: Daphna Weinshall is a professor of Computer Science at the Hebrew University of Jerusalem, Israel. She acted as a visiting professor at MIT and NYU, and a visiting researcher at IBM Research NY, NECI Research Lab NJ, and Philips Research NY. Dr Weinshall served as an area chair on the program committees of NeurIPS, CVPR, ICCV, ECCV and IJCAI, and on the editorial boards of IEEE PAMI, CVIU and MVA. Additionally, she served as a panel chair or panel member on a number of prestigious grant evaluation committees, including the advance ERC Grants evaluation panel in computer science. Her undergraduate degree in mathematics and computer science is from Tel Aviv University, and she received her M.S. and Ph.D. in statistics (population genetics) from Tel Aviv University. Her recent work is focused on developing and expanding methodologies for deep learning in dynamical settings, including pioneering work on curriculum learning and active learning.

Have We Solved Image Correspondences?

Kwang Moo Yi

University of British Columbia, Canada

Abstract. Finding correspondence across images is a fundamental task in computer vision, which recently, as in many areas of computer vision, have been revolutionized by deep learning. In this talk, I will talk about the state of research in finding correspondence across images, and whether this long-standing problem is actually solved. I will follow the historical trend in how the correspondence problem was tackled in our community, focusing on its application to camera pose estimation with sparse correspondences. Specifically, I will discuss how point cloud networks and deep networks with specific architectural considerations have played a key role in initial breakthroughs, and how they have now become "transformer-ized". I will finally talk about the potential of using large-scale pre-trained models for the correspondence problem, and end with some thoughts on the future of correspondence research.

Speaker Bio-Sketch: Kwang Moo Yi is an assistant professor in the Department of Computer Science at the University of British Columbia (UBC), and a member of the Computer Vision Lab, CAIDA, and ICICS at UBC. Before, he was at the University of Victoria as an assistant professor. Prior to being a professor, he worked as a post-doctoral researcher at the Computer Vision Lab in École Polytechnique Fédérale de Lausanne (EPFL, Switzerland), working with Prof. Pascal Fua and Prof. Vincent Lepetit. He received his Ph.D. from Seoul National University under the supervision of Prof. Jin Young Choi. He also received his B.Sc. from the same University. He serves as area chair for top Computer Vision conferences (CVPR, ICCV, and ECCV), as well as Machine Learning (NeurIPS and AAAI). He is part of the organizing committee for CVPR 2023.

Visual Content Manipulation by Learning Generative Models

Jiebo Luo

University of Rochester, USA

Abstract. Visual content manipulation involves modifying or re-synthesizing an input image such that the output follows a guidance input, such as a target layout, semantic clues, or new attributes. However, even with the development of deep generative models, visual content manipulation is challenging because it typically requires transferring visual patterns in a non-rigid fashion. Moreover, unsupervised learning schemes are often required to learn models without image-guidance data pairs. I will focus on how to: 1) design model architectures and mechanisms for visual pattern transfer, 2) design unsupervised learning schemes for learning from unpaired data, and 3) improve the fidelity of the generated content. Specifically, I will present research results on a range of manipulation tasks including pose-guided transfer, example-guided image synthesis, semantic local editing, image completion, and structure-guided inpainting.

Speaker Bio-Sketch: Jiebo Luo is the Albert Arendt Hopeman Professor of Engineering and Professor of Computer Science at the University of Rochester. His research focuses on computer vision, NLP, machine learning, data mining, social media, computational social science, and digital health. He has authored nearly 600 papers and over 90 U.S. patents. Prof. Luo is also an active member of the research community: a Fellow of NAI, ACM, AAAI, IEEE, IAPR, and SPIE, Editor-in-Chief of the IEEE Transactions on Multimedia (2020–2022), as well as a member of the editorial boards of the IEEE Transactions on Pattern Analysis and Machine Intelligence (2006–2011), IEEE Transactions on Multimedia (2004–2009, 2013–2016), IEEE Transactions on Circuits and Systems for Video Technology (2010–2012), IEEE Transactions on Big Data (2018-), Pattern Recognition (2002–2020), ACM Transactions on Intelligent Systems and Technology (2015-present), and so on. In addition, he served as an organizing or program committee member for numerous technical conferences sponsored by IEEE, ACM, AAAI, ACL, IAPR, and SPIE, including most notably program co-chair of the 2010 ACM Multimedia Conference, 2012 IEEE Conference on Computer Vision and Pattern Recognition (CVPR), 2016 ACM Conference on Multimedia Retrieval (ICMR), and 2017 IEEE International Conference on Image Processing (ICIP).

Lights, Camera, Animation! Adaptive Simulation Methods for Training and Entertainment

Paul Kry

McGill University, Canada

Abstract. Physics-based simulations are a critical part of computer animation. This talk will provide a brief overview of new adaptive reduced methods that use rigid motion to speed up interactive and offline simulations of real-world phenomena. This includes merging rigid bodies at contacts, and rigidifying elastic bodies and shells when they are not deforming. The main challenge how to inexpensively identify when and where parts of a reduced system need more degrees of freedom. Applications and future directions will be discussed.

Speaker Bio-Sketch: Paul G. Kry received his B.Math. in computer science with electrical engineering electives in 1997 from the University of Waterloo, and his M.Sc. and Ph.D. in computer science from the University of British Columbia in 2000 and 2005. He spent time as a visitor at Rutgers during most of his Ph.D., and did postdoctoral work at Inria Rhône Alpes and the LNRS at Université René Descartes. He is currently an associate professor at McGill University. His research interests are in physically based animation, including deformation, contact, motion editing, and simulated control of locomotion, grasping, and balance. He co-chaired ACM/EG Symposium on Computer Animation in 2012, Graphics Interface in 2014, and served on numerous program committees, including ACM SIGGRAPH, ACM/EG Symposium on Computer Animation, Pacific Graphics, and Graphics Interface. He is currently an associate editor for Computer Graphics Forum, and for Computers and Graphics. He heads the Computer Animation and Interaction Capture Laboratory at McGill University. Paul Kry is currently the president of the Canadian Human Computer Communications Society, the organization which sponsors the annual Graphics Interface conference. Starting September 2016 Paul Kry served a 3-year term as a director at large on the ACM SIGGRAPH executive committee.

Beyond the Specs: A Computational and Human-Centered Approach to Wearability in AR/VR

Laura Trutoiu

Meta Reality Labs, USA

Abstract. In the rapidly evolving landscape of AR/VR, 'wearability' emerges as a potentially critical aspect that can shape the future of this technology and ensure broad adoption. This talk introduces a framework for 'wearability' in AR/VR. We will go outside of the usual technical specifications like field of view or latency to consider elements of user experience, comfort, and aesthetics, all tied to human factors considerations. Furthermore, the talk will touch on how bringing a computational data-driven approach to human factors like simulation and modeling can speed up development and insights. Drawing from my industry experiences, I'll advocate for bringing more multidisciplinary expertise and collaboration to the development of next-generation wearable, AR/VR technology. Finally, I'd like the audience to consider what would it take to make AR/VR fully inclusive and wearable for everyone?

Speaker Bio-Sketch: Laura Trutoiu currently leads a multidisciplinary team at Meta's Reality Labs, using her background in computer graphics and robotics to tackle complex system issues. Her work focuses on bringing a computational lens to human factors and design of AR/VR headsets. Her team integrates data science, user research, hardware design, and modeling to optimize the form factor of wearables, and bridge the digital and physical worlds. Previously, Laura was a Senior Computer Scientist at Magic Leap's Advanced Technology office in Seattle, where she prototyped next generation wearable spatial computers. She earned her PhD from the Robotics Institute at Carnegie Mellon University, and her research spanned several industry labs including Disney Research, Industrial Light and Magic, and Max Planck Institute for Biological Cybernetics. In the early days of Oculus Research, she developed the first proof of concept for face-to-face communication in head-mounted displays with realistic facial animations for avatars.

Contents – Part II

Applications

Object Detection and Recognition

Deep Learning

Posters

Contents – Part I

Video Analysis and Event Recognition

**ST: Innovations in Computer Vision & Machine Learning for
Critical & Civil Infrastructures**

ST: Generalization in Visual Machine Learning

Computer Graphics

Medical Image Analysis

Biometrics

Autonomous Anomaly Detection in Images

Virtual Reality

A Pilot Study Comparing User Interactions Between Augmented and Virtual Reality

Adam S. Williams[1]([✉])(iD), Xiaoyan Zhou[1], Anil Ufuk Batmaz[2], Michel Pahud[3], and Francisco Ortega[1]

[1] Colorado State University, Fort Collins, CO, USA
AdamWil@Colostate.edu
[2] Concordia University, Montreal, QC, Canada
[3] Microsoft Research, Redmond, WA, USA

Abstract. Immersive Analytics (IA) and consumer adoption of augmented reality (AR) and virtual reality (VR) head-mounted displays (HMDs) are both rapidly growing. When used in conjunction, stereoscopic IA environments can offer improved user understanding and engagement; however, it is unclear how the choice of stereoscopic display impacts user interactions within an IA environment. This paper presents a pilot study that examines the impact of stereoscopic display choice on object manipulation and environmental navigation using consumer-available AR and VR HMDs. Our observations indicate that the display can impact how users manipulate virtual content and how they navigate the environment.

Keywords: Augmented Reality · Virtual Reality · Immersive Analytics · User Interaction

1 Introduction

Augmented reality (AR) and virtual reality (VR) head-mounted displays (HMDs) can offer many benefits over a standard desktop workspace, including, increased immersion, accessible data display, and improved user engagement [19, Chapter 1]. Three-dimensional (3D) data visualization environments, also called immersive analytics (IA) environments, often leverage the benefits of stereoscopic displays in attempts to improve user understanding of the represented data [21]. If users understand how the choice of AR/VR HMDs can impact their workflow in IA environments they can make a deliberate choice to align the HMD type with their intended tasks.

To leverage prior work in IA that was done using VR-HMDs when developing for AR-HMDs, a more in-depth understanding of how interactions differ between AR and VR displays must be established. Towards that goal, this preliminary work observes how people interact with, navigate, and manage virtual content in

G. Bebis et al. (Eds.): ISVC 2023, LNCS 14362, pp. 3–14, 2023.
https://doi.org/10.1007/978-3-031-47966-3_1

a single IA environment across two types of stereoscopic displays. By taking the focus off of the correctness of user interactions or answers, and by placing limited constraints on users, this work observes how differences may manifest between these devices. In this paper, we do not aim to compare VR vs AR, instead, we want to open conversations around IA use in different types of HMDs. We hope that this work generates a starting point for future larger and more controlled HMD comparisons.

2   Related Work

Researchers have started to shed light on this area by examining how users manage virtual content in VR IA environments [2]. Much of the work that has used AR for IA tasks has done so with a focus on "situated analytics" [8]. Situated analytics is when an AR display shows information that is tied to real world objects, such as showing nutrition information in a virtual panel for a real world food item [6]. Recent work has started to examine how different devices can be used in conjunction for IA tasks. Such work has demonstrated uses cases for AR + mobile devices [16] and AR + large screen displays [3]. Other work has found that AR + tablet use improve user understanding of data [12].

However, most work in IA has been conducted using VR-HMDs alone [8]. There has been minimal work examining IA use in AR HMDs and even less that looks at how the choice of stereoscopic display impacts user interactions in IA environments. Works that have compared across display types often do so at a granular level; comparing object manipulations alone [15], visualization understanding [27], or mode switching between display types (i.e., 2D to 3D) [24]. This preliminary work is positioned to start conversations around how display choice may impact user interactions with and within IA environments.

3   Methods

Twelve volunteers participated in this between-subjects AR-VR IA environment interaction comparison study. VR sessions used an HTC Vive Eye Pro with a 110° field of view[1]. The Vive was connected to a Windows 10 computer with 32 GB of RAM, an Intel i9-9900k CPU (3.60 GHz), and an Nvidia GeForce 2080ti. The AR sessions were deployed to and run on a Microsoft Hololens 2, which has 52° field of view[2]. The IA system was developed using Unity version 2019.2.18f1, the MRTK version 2.5.1, Vuforia version 9.6.3, and the Immersive Analytics Toolkit (IATK) [5]. Video was collected using a web camera and recordings from the rendered environment. The system collected log data for all events. These results are being reported as Observational trends. With the small sample size for each group, significance tests are not reported.

---

[1] https://www.vive.com/us/product/vive-pro/.
[2] https://www.immersiv.io/blog/hands-on-hololens-2-review.

In both AR and VR participants would load and manipulate a 3D scatter plot that represented cereal nutrition information (e.g., grams of fat). In addition to the scatter plot, a control station and a trash area were provided. The participant could place these objects anywhere they wished; however, the objects always initially loaded on the table where the participants were seated. The control station had buttons to load annotations, change the visualization's color mapping, and change the axes mappings. Annotations were always loaded above the control station at a point that was marked by a small semi-transparent sphere. The annotations provided were details on demand (DoD), a mean/median plane (centrality plane), a text entry box, and two highlight volumes (Fig. 1). Participants could delete annotations by moving them to the trash area, which was a plane that read "move annotations here to delete them".

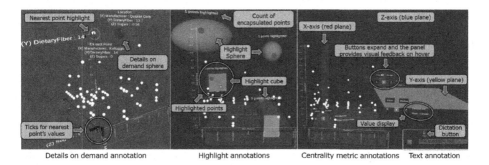

Fig. 1. All available annotations placed on the 3D scatter plot. The annotations and annotation features are labeled in the figure.

In both groups, a ray-cast technique was used to interact. In VR, a Vive controller was used to move the ray-cast, and selection was achieved by pressing a button. In AR, the ray-cast extended from one's hand, and selection was triggered by pinching. Only the HMD and the ray-cast technique used were different between the two groups. The difference in ray-casting was due to the types of tracking technologies available on the devices. The Hololens 2 does not natively support a position tracked controller and the Vive does not natively support hand tracking. All objects apart from the DoD and centrality plane annotations could be scaled or rotated by using the ray-cast to select and interact with handles at the corners and sides of the object respectively. Translation was accomplished by selecting the objects anywhere apart from the handles and moving the ray-cast. All manipulations had unique visual and audio feedback. For example, when translating an object a user would hear a chime on selection and the object would turn to a semi-transparent red. On release the object would return to it's original color and a similar chime would play.

3.1   Procedure and Task

Participants would arrive at the lab and were asked to sit at a round table. Participants first gave informed consent and completed a demographics survey. After completing the pre-study forms, participants were told about the experiment at a high level and donned either an AR or VR HMD and began the study tasks. While in the IA environment, participants first completed a training session that covered how to interact with the visualization (i.e., the scatter-plot), trash tool, and annotation/visualization control station. Participants were asked to place these virtual objects where they would be comfortable interacting with them, acknowledging that object placement could be changed at any time. They were then told how to change the dimension mappings on the visualization (i.e., changing the x-axis) and the five provided annotation tools were explained.

After training, participants were instructed to navigate the visualization, interact with the tools, and generate questions about the data that could be asked to other users. These questions were recorded as part of the video taken during the study. This process (phase one) lasted 15 min or until the participant asked for the next phase to be started. Phase two consisted of a 15-minute session where the researcher would ask questions about the dataset. Phase two ended once a participant answered all questions, when 15 min had elapsed, or when a participant requested to end the session. Some examples of the questions asked during phase two are "What manufacturer has the fewest cereals represented", "What is the highest sugar content contained in the scatter-plot", and "Which manufacturer or manufacturers have the largest portion of their cereals containing lower than average fat". After the experiment, participants removed the HMD and completed a 0–100 scale NASA Task Load Index (TLX) to measure their perceived workload [10].

3.2   Participants

Twelve participants were randomly split into two groups. Matching the participant count of other works in this field [1] can help to increase comparability across literature [18]. All participants confirmed that they were comfortable interacting with 2D scatter-plot charts and had normal or corrected to normal vision. The VR group consisted of 5 females and 1 male with an average age of 21.5 years and a standard deviation (SD) of 3.99. All VR participants were right-handed. Five VR participants had used an AR HMD for 30 min or less prior to this experiment and two indicated that they played VR games. One participant played VR games 3 h a week and one played them 1 h a week. The AR group was made up of 5 males and 1 female (age 25 years, SD 4.78). Four AR participants were right-handed, and three had used an AR HMD for 30 min or less before this experiment and two played VR games for 1 h a week. This gender imbalance was caused by participant session cancellations and new participant recruitment mid-way through data collection and difficulties recruiting participants during the COVID-19 pandemic. No participants reported a gender outside of male and female.

4   Results

With the limited sample size and the confounding variables encountered as a result of using two headsets this work is not reporting tests of significance as part of its results. Where it would have been appropriate to report tests of significance, they were computed, with most returning p-values greater than 0.05. In a future full study these tests will be reported. For this work, we hope that the observational findings and indications of user interaction styles captured by the data reported will provide insights into how using these devices may differ and can build a starting point for conversations around this topic.

4.1   Time Spent in Environment

The AR group spent more time training and less time in the rest of the experiment (Fig. 2). The reduced time in the environment was caused by participant request to end phase one and/or phase two early. The three AR group participants that were least able to navigate the environment exhibited similar tendencies. These three persons took nearly twice as long as the top three performers to complete the training session (mean 16:43 min compared to 9:03) and spent less time in both phases, often stopping all interactions with the visualization towards the end of each phase. The first portion of the training sessions covered how to use the "pinch" gesture interaction for AR users and the controller for VR participants. The pinch gesture took more time to learn than the controller, which could account for some of the differences in training time between the two conditions. All participants had to successfully interact using either the controller or the pinch gesture prior to starting the study.

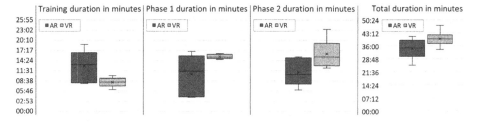

Fig. 2. Times that participants spent in different portions of the experiment by device condition

The VR group had less deviation in their times and did not have anyone request to end a phase early. Participants in the VR group finished the training phase in 8:14 min on average, whereas the AR group took 12:53 min on average. Interestingly, two VR group participants chose to stay in the environment for longer than 15 min during the second phase, staying instead for 23:18 and 17:56 min.

8 A. S. Williams et al.

4.2 Experimental Tasks

AR participants were much more likely to stop interacting with the visualization during phase 1. Only two participants in either device condition generated questions. In the AR group, these participants generated 9 and 4 questions whereas in the VR group, they created 1 and 4 questions.

During phase two, AR participants answered an average of 5.83 questions out of 11 total (SD 2.67), whereas in VR, participants answered an average of 9.5 questions (SD 1.26). The top three performers from the AR group in isolation answered an average of 8.33 questions (SD 1.25). The three less preferment AR participants answered 3, 3, and 4 questions. In VR, all participants continued to answer questions until the end of the session or until 11 questions were asked. For both groups these numbers represent how many questions were answered by the participant, either correctly or incorrectly.

4.3 Participant Interactions

The visualization always began as a .42-meter cube. Participants were able to resize the visualization at any time. Most participants only resized the visualization a few times at the beginning of a session. The VR group used larger scatter plots than the AR group, with an average visualization size of .588 m (SD .191) compared to .502 m (SD .085) (Fig. 3 A). The largest visualization was in the VR group, with a scale of 1.01 m. People across the VR condition tended to sit further back from the visualization and kept their hands closer to their bodies. The AR condition could see the desk in front of them, and all AR participants placed the visualization on that desk. No participants commented on the field of view being a contributing factor to their interactions in the environment.

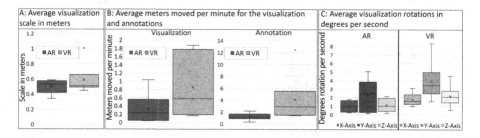

Fig. 3. Box-plots from left to right: Average visualization scale (A), Average meters moved (B), Average rotations made (C)

On average, the VR group moved the visualization more per minute of the experiment than the AR group (Fig. 3 B). The VR group moved the visualization an average of .859 m per minute (SD .716) where the AR group only moved the visualization .334 m per minute (SD .344). Annotations were also moved more by the VR group with an average movement of 4.05 m per minute (SD 3.832) and 1.198 m per minute (SD .55), respectively.

In this environment, an x-axis rotation is pitch, a y-axis rotation is yaw, and a z-axis rotation is roll. Rotations about the x-axis were the least performed rotation with a mean of .97 (SD .71) degrees/second (Deg/Sec) for the AR group and 1.76 Deg/Sec (SD .76) for the VR group (Fig. 3 C). Rotations about the z-axis were the next least used rotation at 1.11 Deg/Sec (SD .78) for the AR group and 2.18 Deg/Sec (SD 1.30) for the VR group. The most performed rotation was yaw or rotating the visualization about the y-axis. In AR participants performed slightly fewer yaw rotations with an average of 2.31 Deg/Sec (SD 1.92) compared to 3.89 Deg/Sec (SD 2.32) for the VR group. In addition to the differences in rotations, VR participants were observed moving their head and upper body to view the data from different angles more frequently than participants in the AR condition. In both groups, ray-cast movement during selection and natural jitters in arm movement caused inaccuracies in selection.

4.4 Observations

Participants using the VR-HMD typically set a larger visualization and placed it without regard to the real-world, often placing it further away from themselves than the AR group. That placement resulted in VR participants interacting with the visualization from a greater distance. In AR participants would place the visualization on the desk in front of them. Once placed, they would interact with it closely, often holding their hands near the visualization.

Apart from the visualization's scale and placement differences, there were differences in how VR users managed or navigated their virtual space. One such difference is that members of the VR group were the only ones who moved the annotation station from their left, where it was generated, to their right. With all VR participants and 4 of the 6 AR participants being right-handed, it was interesting that only a few participants in the VR condition chose to move the system's most interacted with the tool to their dominant side. Additionally, and opposite to our original expectations, VR users were more likely to move around to view the data from different angles, e.g., they did not walk around, but they did stand, lean, and move their upper bodies. This was in contrast to the AR users, who were more likely to rotate or move the visualization.

4.5 NASA TLX

There were limited differences between AR and VR conditions for frustration (38.33 AR vs 36.67 VR) and overall workload (55.42 AR vs 52.08 VR). These low scores for frustration and overall workload are interesting when considering the differences in interaction techniques between the two devices. These scores imply that the selection technique (i.e., button vs pinch) and the ray-cast movement type (i.e., controller vs hand) did not contribute to widely varied frustration scores. The physical demand was more varied and slightly higher for the AR group than the VR group (mean of 46.67 AR vs 30.83 VR). This could be excepted as VR controllers can be used with less movement than mid-air gestures. VR participants perceived that they were using more mental and total effort than the AR group (VR mean 81.67 SD 14.63, AR mean 59.17 SD 18.12). This difference might have been contributed to by the difference in engagement between the two groups where the VR group interacted with the environment more fully and for longer than the AR group.

5   Discussion

This preliminary work has taken the approach of not focusing on the correctness of interactions, questions, or answers. Instead, this work focused on how participants navigated and interacted with the immersive environments. This work chose not to impose question time limits on participants and allowed them to request new questions when they were stuck. These design choices were made in order to maximize participants' sense of agency during the study. Giving participants more control over how they chose to interact with the environment allowed this work to observe how those interaction choices would manifest. With limited prior work examining how stereoscopic display type impacts user interactions, these findings can help inspire future IA use, research, and development.

5.1   Task Completion Time

VR participants spent more time on average in the environment than the AR group. VR participants also completed the training more quickly than AR participants. These training times reflect the amount of time it took the participant to interact with each tool in the system, suggesting that VR participants picked up tools and features of this environment more readily.

Increased time spent in the environment may also be related to VR participants' immersion. VR users could not see the outside world, only the virtual environment, causing them to focus more on the tasks given. This additional focus may be reflected in the differences between the AR and VR NASA TLX mental effort scores. It is unclear why AR participants interacted with the system less, even among the participants that were skilled at using the ray-casts. It might be that seeing the real world kept them from getting fully immersed.

5.2   Interaction Strategies

Over the experimental sessions, several interesting themes in user behaviors were noted. In AR participants were more likely to place the visualization on the table they were seated at. This placement strategy could be leveraged by incorporating passive haptic feedback into the table. In VR participants were more likely to physically move around the visualization, often leaning in or around to view data from different angles. The increased physical activity in VR along with the use of larger visualizations could be tapped into to encourage more interactive IA experiences, such as ones that would require large visualizations or "data physicalization" [17].

5.3   IA Experiment Design Guidelines

Introducing people to this IA environment utilizing stereoscopic displays was difficult [9]. Participants needed interactive training sessions and live interactions with the system before they were able to perform the experimental tasks. Even by the end of the sessions, participants often commented that the system was unfamiliar to them. IA researchers should plan on performing multiple sessions with participants. Ideally, there should be an initial training session where participants become familiar with the environment and interactions used. At a later point, participants could return to complete the experiment. Using this design, researchers could observe how quickly the interaction techniques are remembered by users, providing insights on any differences in retention between the devices. If multiple sessions are not an option, recruiting for prior VR experience may be beneficial as it could help participants more quickly acclimate to the environments and interactions used.

The participants in this study gained a better understanding of the system when they were actively interacting with the system during training, suggesting that researchers might want to avoid video-based instructions in favor of more interactive means of instruction. Moreover, VR-HMDs may be better suited for training. The VR participants were more engaged with the system, interacting more with each tool and the visualization. This was indicated by the lower training times and increased performance of the VR participants. Training participants on the system in VR can tap into that engagement and help reduce the difficulty of learning the system for new users.

6   Limitations

This preliminary work represents early observational results on how users interacted in the same environment given two different HMDs. We specifically chose the two most common HMDs that were used in IA studies [9,14], e.g., HoloLens was previously used in molecular visualization [22], urban analytics [4], for remote collaboration [7], to visualize bird movement [23], and HTC Vive was previously used to evaluate time-space cubes [25], interactive learning for earth science [20], and for animal movement visualization [13]. Both devices are also assessed in terms of usability and received high scores [11,25,26]. That two different HMDs were used introduced a number of confounding variables which can better controlled for in future work. These confounding variables include differences in field of view, device color display, display brightness, and ray-casts.

Additionally, with the confounding variables, gender imbalance, and limited sample-size per group we have chosen not to report tests of significance here. For the sections of this work where tests of significance could be run, they were, with most returning p-values that were greater than 0.05. This limits the work presented here but provides an opportunity for future studies to dive into specific areas of user interaction difference while holding the confounding variables encountered here constant between the devices used.

7 Future Work

This work shows indications of differences between AR and VR IA system use. A more in-depth examination of the differences in time spent in environment and observed levels of participant engagement between AR and VR displays would help better guide future device selection for IA use. To further hone in on the extent and specifics of these differences future work can use a single headset that provides both video pass-through (i.e., AR) and VR modes. Such a headset would eliminate confounds caused by differences in the stereoscopic displays themselves. That headset would provide control over the field-of-view, color display, display brightness, and interaction techniques used in the study.

The AR participant's reduced time spent in the environment and/or their lower levels of engagement might have been influenced by their seeing the real world. Future work could further investigate that impact or compare the impact of different working environments on device preference and how the use of different visualizations (i.e., 2D charts) changes user behavior.

8 Conclusion

This preliminary work is one of the first studies in IA to compare participant interactions and navigation between AR and VR HMDs using the same virtual environment. This study found that not all participants in AR were able to interact successfully in the system, potentially causing those participants to perform poorly and spend less time in the environment. These difficulties may have stemmed from struggles in understanding how to select and navigate content in the environment and a lessened sense of immersion caused by seeing the real world. With those difficulties encountered early on, these AR participants became disengaged with the system, interacting less with it, and answering fewer questions about it. AR participants also spent longer in the training phase but less time in the other study phases.

There were observed differences in how participants in AR compared to those in VR navigated, interacted with, arranged, and understood virtual content. In VR participants were more immersed in the environment, leading to the increased time spent in the system, more interactions with the virtual content, and an increased ability to answer questions about the data presented. These VR participants also more fully utilized the space provided in the virtual environment, moving objects further away from themselves, and placing them with less concern for their position relative to the real world.

Acknowledgements. This work was supported by the National Science Foundation (NSF) awards 2327569, 2238313, 2223432, 2223459, 2106590, 2016714, 2037417. This work was also supported by the Defense Advanced Research Projects Agency (DARPA) award HR00112110011 and the Office of Naval Research (ONR) award N00014-21-1-2949.

References

1. Batmaz, A.U., Machuca, M.D.B., Pham, D.M., Stuerzlinger, W.: Do head-mounted display stereo deficiencies affect 3D pointing tasks in AR and VR? In: 2019 IEEE Conference on Virtual Reality and 3D User Interfaces (VR), pp. 585–592 (2019). https://doi.org/10.1109/VR.2019.8797975
2. Batmaz, A.U., Mutasim, A.K., Stuerzlinger, W.: Precision vs. power grip: a comparison of pen grip styles for selection in virtual reality. In: 2020 IEEE Conference on Virtual Reality and 3D User Interfaces Abstracts and Workshops (VRW), pp. 23–28. Atlanta, GA (2020). https://doi.org/10.1109/VRW50115.2020.00012
3. Büschel, W., Lehmann, A., Dachselt, R.: MIRIA: a mixed reality toolkit for the in-situ visualization and analysis of spatio-temporal interaction data. In: Proceedings of the 2021 CHI Conference on Human Factors in Computing Systems. CHI 2021, Association for Computing Machinery, New York, NY, USA (2021). https://doi.org/10.1145/3411764.3445651
4. Chen, Z., Qu, H., Wu, Y.: Immersive urban analytics through exploded views. In: Workshop on Immersive Analytics: Exploring Future Visualization and Interaction Technologies for Data Analytics. Phoenix, AZ (2017)
5. Cordeil, M., et al.: IATK: an immersive analytics toolkit. In: 2019 IEEE Conference on Virtual Reality and 3D User Interfaces (VR), pp. 200–209 (2019). https://doi.org/10.1109/VR.2019.8797978
6. ElSayed, N.A., Thomas, B.H., Marriott, K., Piantadosi, J., Smith, R.T.: Situated analytics: demonstrating immersive analytical tools with augmented reality. J. Vis. Lang. Comput. **36**, 13–23 (2016). https://doi.org/10.1016/j.jvlc.2016.07.006
7. Farouk, P., Faransawy, N., Sharaf, N.: Using HoloLens for remote collaboration in extended data visualization. In: 2022 26th International Conference Information Visualisation (IV), pp. 209–214. IEEE (2022). https://doi.org/10.1109/IV56949.2022.00042
8. Fonnet, A., Prié, Y.: Survey of immersive analytics. IEEE Trans. Visual. Comput. Graph. **27**(3), 2101–2122 (2019). https://doi.org/10.1109/TVCG.2019.2929033
9. Fonnet, A., Prie, Y.: Survey of immersive analytics. IEEE Trans. Visual Comput. Graph. **27**(3), 2101–2122 (2019)
10. Hart, S.G., Staveland, L.E.: Development of NASA-TLX (task load index): results of empirical and theoretical research. In: Hancock, P.A., Meshkati, N. (eds.) Human Mental Workload, Advances in Psychology, vol. 52, pp. 139–183. North-Holland, USA (1988). https://doi.org/10.1016/S0166-4115(08)62386-9
11. Hoppenstedt, B., et al.: Applicability of immersive analytics in mixed reality: usability study. IEEE Access **7**, 71921–71932 (2019)
12. Hubenschmid, S., Zagermann, J., Butscher, S., Reiterer, H.: Stream: exploring the combination of spatially-aware tablets with augmented reality head-mounted displays for immersive analytics. In: Proceedings of the 2021 CHI Conference on Human Factors in Computing Systems. CHI 2021, Association for Computing Machinery, New York, NY, USA (2021). https://doi.org/10.1145/3411764.3445298
13. Klein, K., et al.: Fly with the flock: immersive solutions for animal movement visualization and analytics. J. R. Soc. Interface **16**(153), 20180794 (2019)
14. Kraus, M., et al.: Immersive analytics with abstract 3D visualizations: a survey. In: Computer Graphics Forum, vol. 41, pp. 201–229. Wiley Online Library (2022)
15. Krichenbauer, M., Yamamoto, G., Taketom, T., Sandor, C., Kato, H.: Augmented reality versus virtual reality for 3D object manipulation. IEEE Trans. Visual Comput. Graph. **24**(2), 1038–1048 (2018). https://doi.org/10.1109/TVCG.2017.2658570

16. Langner, R., Satkowski, M., Büschel, W., Dachselt, R.: MARVIS: combining mobile devices and augmented reality for visual data analysis. In: Proceedings of the 2021 CHI Conference on Human Factors in Computing Systems. CHI 2021, Association for Computing Machinery, New York, NY, USA (2021). https://doi.org/10.1145/3411764.3445593

17. Lee, B., Brown, D., Lee, B., Hurter, C., Drucker, S., Dwyer, T.: Data visceralization: Enabling deeper understanding of data using virtual reality. IEEE Trans. Visual Comput. Graph. **27**(2), 1095–1105 (2021). https://doi.org/10.1109/TVCG.2020.3030435

18. MacKenzie, I.S.: Chapter 5 - designing HCI experiments. In: MacKenzie, I.S. (ed.) Human-Computer Interaction, pp. 157–189. Morgan Kaufmann, Boston (2013). https://doi.org/10.1016/B978-0-12-405865-1.00005-4

19. Marriott, Kim, et al.: Just 5 questions: toward a design framework for immersive analytics. In: Immersive Analytics. LNCS, vol. 11190, pp. 259–288. Springer, Cham (2018). https://doi.org/10.1007/978-3-030-01388-2_9

20. Masrur, A., Zhao, J., Wallgrün, J.O., LaFemina, P., Klippel, A.: Immersive applications for informal and interactive learning for earth science. In: Proceedings of the Workshop on Immersive Analytics, Exploring Future Interaction and Visualization Technologies for Data Analytics, pp. 1–5 (2017)

21. Mota, R.C.R., Rocha, A., Silva, J.D., Alim, U., Sharlin, E.: 3De interactive lenses for visualization in virtual environments. In: 2018 IEEE Scientific Visualization Conference (SciVis), pp. 21–25. Berlin, Germany (2018). https://doi.org/10.1109/SciVis.2018.8823618

22. Müller, C., et al.: Interactive molecular graphics for augmented reality using HoloLens. J. Integr. Bioinform. **15**(2), 20180005 (2018)

23. Nim, H.T., et al.: Design considerations for immersive analytics of bird movements obtained by miniaturised GPS sensors. In: VCBM, pp. 27–31 (2017)

24. Seraji, M.R., Stuerzlinger, W.: HybridAxes: an immersive analytics tool with interoperability between 2d and immersive reality modes. In: 2022 IEEE International Symposium on Mixed and Augmented Reality Adjunct (ISMAR-Adjunct), pp. 155–160 (2022). https://doi.org/10.1109/ISMAR-Adjunct57072.2022.00036

25. Wagner Filho, J.A., Stuerzlinger, W., Nedel, L.: Evaluating an immersive space-time cube geovisualization for intuitive trajectory data exploration. IEEE Trans. Visual Comput. Graph. **26**(1), 514–524 (2019)

26. Wenk, N., Penalver-Andres, J., Buetler, K., Nef, T., Müri, R.M., Marchal-Crespo, L.: Effect of immersive visualization technologies on cognitive load, motivation, usability, and embodiment. Virtual Reality **27**(1), 307–331 (2023)

27. Whitlock, M., Smart, S., Szafir, D.A.: Graphical perception for immersive analytics. In: 2020 IEEE Conference on Virtual Reality and 3D User Interfaces (VR), pp. 616–625. Atlanta, GA, USA (2020). https://doi.org/10.1109/VR46266.2020.00084

Synthesizing Play-Ready VR Scenes with Natural Language Prompts Through GPT API

Lazaros Rafail Kouzelis[1]([✉]) and Ourania Spantidi[2][ID]

[1] Cyprus University of Technology, Limassol, Cyprus
lc.kouzelis@edu.cut.ac.cy
[2] Eastern Michigan University, Ypsilanti, USA
ourania.spantidi@emich.edu

Abstract. In visual computing, 3D scene generation stands as a crucial component, offering applications in various fields such as gaming, virtual reality (VR), and architectural visualization. Creating realistic and versatile virtual environments, however, poses significant challenges. This work presents a novel methodology that leverages the capabilities of a widely adopted large language model (LLM) to address these challenges. Our approach utilizes the GPT API to interpret natural language prompts and generate detailed, VR-ready scenes within Unity3D. Our work is also inherently scalable, since the model accepts any database of 3D objects with minimal prior configuration. The effectiveness of the proposed system is demonstrated through a series of case studies, revealing its potential to generate diverse and functional virtual spaces.

Keywords: Scene Generation · Virtual Reality · AI-driven 3D Design

1 Introduction

In today's digital age, visual computing plays a pivotal role in bridging the gap between human intuition and digital understanding. The realm of 3D scene generation, as a subset of visual computing, has experienced significant progress, continually evolving to meet the diverse needs of various industries, including entertainment, architecture, and virtual reality (VR).

The field of 3D scene generation has grown substantially, but traditional methods still often involve manual environment design or the use of procedural scene populating algorithms [2,5,9]. More recent techniques have employed machine learning models such as graph neural networks [14], which can capture complex dependencies but often involve extensive computational resources. Moreover, many existing works require laborious manual annotation of scenes and data [5], a time-consuming process that limits scalability.

This paper introduces a novel solution for intuitive 3D scene generation, especially benefiting non-technical users who can describe scenes in natural language. We leverage the power of natural language processing (NLP) via a widely

G. Bebis et al. (Eds.): ISVC 2023, LNCS 14362, pp. 15–26, 2023.
https://doi.org/10.1007/978-3-031-47966-3_2

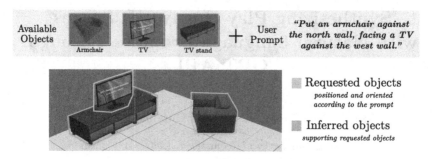

Fig. 1. Brief overview of the capabilities of the proposed system.

adopted large language model (LLM) which is the GPT API[1]. This AI-driven method removes the need for user-initiated model training and complex tasks, thereby increasing accessibility and reducing resource demands. It translates simple natural language text into 3D scenes, as shown in Fig. 1. The main contributions of this work are as follows: (1) we introduce a novel approach for generating 3D scenes using natural language prompts via the GPT API integrated into Unity3D, (2) we demonstrate through multiple case studies the ability of the system to generate functional, detailed, and VR-ready scenes from simple textual instructions, and (3) we evaluate the effectiveness and efficiency of our approach and highlight its unique advantages.

2   Related Works

Leveraging automated systems to synthesize scenes has been a recurring subject in computer graphics. There have been many works that include learning from large databases, natural language processing, and other related approaches towards plausible scene generation, each with its own merits and shortcomings.

Synthesis Using Text-Based Techniques.
A recurring method in these works is the employment of *scene graphs*, "a data structure that describes the contents of a scene" [6]. First, a scene database is annotated with relevant tags, such as object categories, and then a graph is created, that describes object attributes and relationships. Chang et al. [3] used knowledge of view-centric spatial relationships acquired from existing scenes to then arrange objects in new scenes, also adding implicitly required objects, such as supporting surfaces. While their method creates plausible environments, it falls short in a navigation context, since the spatial relationships are based on a single view. In [9] the authors worked on expanding upon the concept of scene graphs, by utilizing a *semantic scene graph*. They annotated a large database in order to extract intricate relationships among objects in the scene, enabling object clustering and more diverse spatial relationships. Although this work

---
[1] https://chat.openai.com/.

adds more depth and context to the scene, it is limited by its inability to parse ambiguous prompts, arbitrary positioning, and object duplication.

A different method, employed by the authors in [4], utilizes a mixed model approach to scene synthesis. First, they extract object existence and configuration probability data from existing scenes, and then new scenes are built starting from larger supporting objects, to smaller supported ones. Kermani et al. [7] worked with a similar model, first extracting data from annotated images, then generating scenes that took into account the entire room (including walls) during building. User testing showed a preference for results from this work, due to a perceived holistic approach to the synthesized scene. This methodology appears to be further improved in [2], where the authors introduced *content chunks*, populating the scene using clusters of related objects instead of single objects or pairs.

The human factor, such as actions taken in the scene and navigation, plays an important role in realistic scene generation. There are works that take this into consideration, such as [8], where the authors opted to use *action graphs* that describe primarily an action that will be taken with an object, grouped together with a human pose and surrounding objects. This results in realistic scenes, but still fails to account for human ergonomics and unpredictability. Yu et al. [15] focused on alleviating this issue by creating a system that takes into account more specific requirements, such as the viewing frustum for an armchair near a television. This is a novel approach to object configurations, but user testing still showed a preference for human-created scenes.

These works can create generally plausible scenes. However, the results often reveal their synthesized nature, largely due to the rigid constraints set during construction. Furthermore, the models employed in them do not adequately produce complex or activity-enhanced layouts.

Synthesis Using Image-Based Techniques. Another approach that could maintain a high degree of scene plausibility is by synthesizing scenes by also using images as prompts. In [13], the authors use a combination of motion recognition, extracted from the user's webcam, natural language prompts (either typed or spoken), and sketch recognition, to populate and manipulate scenes and object placement. Their results seem promising, but the resulting scenes are rudimentary. Fu et al. [5] presented a more complex method to synthesize scenes based on user prompts, by utilizing activity-associated object relationship graphs and floor plan layout masks. Their system shows strong results with big volumes and large objects, but does not show understanding of clutter and smaller objects.

Large Language Model-Powered Scene Synthesis. The aforementioned works generally require some preprocessing, usually on a large visual database, in order to teach their algorithms to recognize object relationships and configurations. This can be bypassed by utilizing a Large Language Model (LLM), that can offer reasonable knowledge in interior design tasks [1]. As presented by NVidia [10], an LLM such as the GPT API by OpenAI [11], can be used to translate a generic user prompt to plausible scene configurations. A construction script then selects appropriate models and their spatial relationships. However, this approach still requires initial room definition and user-specified objects. Moreover, it lacks the ability to adjust object orientation based on human activity clusters like dining areas. As far as we know, this is the only work generating ready-to-use scenes in this category.

Our work is harnessing the power of the GPT API to transform a simple, generic user prompt into a detailed scene description. Since the GPT API performs well in simple tasks [12], we are confident that it can expand on a prompt describing a room with realistic results. In contrast to synthesis using text- and image-based techniques, an LLM offers results without the need for prior model training on databases.

We also offer the possibility of using a local object database, rather than relying on curated public databases. The lack of a dependency and semantic graph also enables object positioning that is not limited by rigid relational constraints. Finally, our system can also work on existing scenes, iterating to add more objects to synthesize a scene that is not only plausible but also takes into account the human factor, such as activities and pathing.

3 Methodology

Our methodology employs a streamlined process using an advanced language model for selecting and positioning 3D objects in Unity3D scenes. Utilizing the GPT API, this approach simplifies and improves virtual 3D object manipulation. Figure 2 outlines the method, which we detail here, focusing on the generation and interpretation of spatial and object data.

3.1 Spatial and Object Data Preparation

In this phase, we create two key data sets: one for the Unity3D scene plane and another for the available 3D objects. These data sets are the backbone of our GPT API-driven method for object selection and placement, ensuring system adaptability across varying scene dimensions and object types.

Users can set scene boundaries in Unity3D by drag-and-dropping a plane object. We then extract key attributes from this plane, such as size, center, and corner locations. Each plane wall is identified by a string indicating its cardinal direction and extent, from point (X, Y, Z) to point (X', Y', Z'). A challenge was enhancing the equation for GPT's spatial understanding. Adding the option for global cardinal directions in the API request improved object placement.

Our framework utilizes a robust and flexible database of prefabs - reusable game objects that include 3D models along with their associated properties and behaviors.

To maintain the consistency and functionality of the database, newly incorporated prefabs must adhere to the established naming conventions. This essentially ensures that the scalability of our database is entirely user-friendly and efficient. As long as new furniture items are appropriately named, they can be

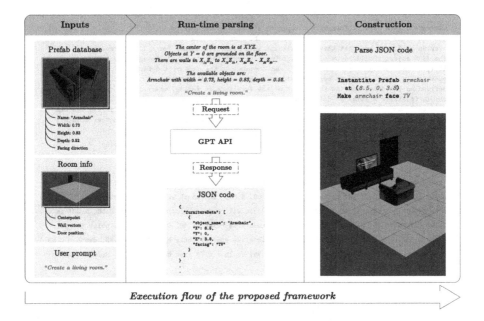

Fig. 2. An overview of the proposed methodology.

instantaneously integrated into the scene-generation process without any computational overhead.

Our methodology relies on real-time parsing and prompt generation, setting it apart from approaches requiring offline preprocessing [5]. The framework dynamically interprets the prefab database, extracting real-time dimensions for each furniture item from their mesh renderer component's bounds. This prevents object overlap by recording width, depth, and height.

3.2 Engaging the GPT API

Establishing the Request Parameters. The first step with the GPT API involves crafting a well-structured request sent via HTTP POST. The API is designed to interpret a series of directives that guide the model's output. We specifically use the *chat completions* feature, as described in the GPT API documentation[2]. Conversations in the API can be divided into two roles: *system* and *user*. The role of *system* is assigned the introductory message: "You are a smart 3D space generator expert". This categorization establishes a context for the AI and serves as a guide throughout the conversation. The role of *user* is where we formulate our request string which uses the information of the 3D world as described in Sect. 3.1. We draw inspiration from the AI Room Generator Extension in [10] to construct our request. Similar to this work, we will be asking for

---

[2] https://platform.openai.com/docs/api-reference/chat/create.

```
Generate a JSON file of furniture placements within a given area.
You must take into account the dimensions of the furniture and the area, ensuring items do not
overlap or float, and that they are oriented in a realistic manner for a living room setup.
The JSON object should be named furnitureData and must contain the following keys: object_name,
X, Y, Z, and facing. object_name, X, Y, and Z represent the name of the furniture, and their
position in the 3D space in terms of width, height, and depth respectively. ''facing'' is
defined as the direction the front part of the furniture is facing, where facing towards the
origin (positive X-axis) is defined as ''north'', away from the origin (negative X-axis) is
''south'', and similarly for ''west'' (positive Z-axis) and ''east'' (negative Z-axis). You can
use combinations such as south-west etc, or select to face towards the name of another chosen
piece of furniture (for instance, a ''Chair'' can face a ''Table'').

The furniture must be correctly positioned on the floor, not floating or overlapping.
```

```
The center of the area you are working with is (9.99, 0.00, 4.00). The north wall expands from
point (12.49, 0.00, 2.40) to point (12.49, 0.00, 5.60). The south wall expands from point (7.49,
0.00, 2.40) to point (7.49, 0.00, 5.60). The east wall expands from point (7.49, 0.00, 2.40) to
point (12.49, 0.00, 2.40). The west wall expands from point (7.49, 0.00, 5.60) to point (12.49,
0.00, 5.60). The available furniture and their sizes are: Armchair has width = 0.73, depth = 0.83,
and height = 0.52. CoffeeTable has width = 0.35, depth = 0.78, and height = 0.27. Sofa has width =
0.73, depth = 1.84, and height = 0.52.
```

```
By default, when Y=0 all objects are grounded on the floor. Be mindful of the furniture sizes
so as they do not overlap. If you want to use more than once instance of a furniture item, start
adding underscores and an increasing number in the second instance ("Table", "Table_2", etc).
```

```
The door is at (12.49, 0, 4) and should not be obstructed.
```

```
Create a living room.
```

```
Remember, you only generate the JSON code as asked.
```

Fig. 3. A sample API request.

the generation of a JSON file that will include the following keys: *object_name*, *X, Y, Z*, and *facing*.

We then establish preliminary constraints and provide further specifics regarding the Unity3D environment. We emphasize instructions concerning spatial orientation.

Next, we dynamically parse the database prefabs and the user-selected plane defining the room. As outlined in Sect. 3.1, we can obtain real-time dimensions for each furniture item. For the room area, we store its center location and points for its four walls, assuming each room has only four walls. Door positions are also recorded, if available. Figure 3 provides an API request example.

In this API request, grey content is static and unchanging, while blue content is generated in real-time. User input, shown in red, is brief but triggers extensive operations, as seen in the example "Create a living room". This blend of predetermined, hard-coded elements, and adaptable components generated in real-time, facilitates the seamless adaptability to changes in the scene.

```
{
  "furnitureData": [
    {
      "object_name": "Armchair",
      "X": 8.5,
      "Y": 0,
      "Z": 3.8,
      "facing": "north"
    },
    {
      "object_name": "Sofa",
      "X": 10.0,
      "Y": 0,
      "Z": 3.8,
      "facing": "south"
    }
  ]
}
```

Fig. 4. Returned JSON code by the GPT API.

A typical example of the returned JSON is shown in Fig. 4. This object contains an array of furniture data, where each entry corresponds to an individual piece. The "object_name" field acts as a key to access the corresponding prefab from our object database. Once retrieved, the prefab is instantiated within the Unity scene at the position specified by the X, Y, and Z values.

In terms of object orientation in the JSON code, we used the "facing" key from the GPT API output. The facing direction of each object is determined by the vector between a _FRONT component and its position relative to the object pivot. We developed a Blender plugin to automatically add the _FRONT component to each object in the prefab database. This extra attribute greatly enhances realistic placement and spatial relationships.

For instance, if the GPT model's output indicates that a given furniture item should face another object, our system orients the objects appropriately by rotating them based on this direction vector. If the GPT API selects an object to face cardinal directions, we leverage the _FRONT component to align the object to global directions.

Augmenting Existing Scenes with Additional Elements. One of the distinctive features of our system lies in its capacity to refine pre-existing scenes by integrating additional elements. Leveraging the information derived from the spatial layout and orientation of existing furniture within a scene, our system forms a comprehensive request to the GPT API, incorporating new elements.

As detailed earlier in Sect. 3.2, the finalized API request is a fusion of *predetermined constraints, dynamically-generated information* during run-time, and the *user's specific requests*. In the process of scene enhancement, our system parses all objects present in the Unity3D scene, collecting their positions and orientations. This data is then transformed into a formatted string and integrated into the final GPT API request as part of the *dynamically-generated information*. The *user's request* pertains to the specific new elements the user wishes to introduce into the scene (e.g., new pieces of furniture, decorations, etc.). ·

This feature is crucial for two reasons: it enables dynamic, ongoing scene development and effectively addresses a GPT API limitation - not maintaining context between requests. To overcome this, we input real-time parsed context from the existing scene, eliminating the need to resend past prompts. This approach allows users to not just build a scene from scratch, but also to refine and adapt it over time to meet evolving needs. The result is a more interactive and adaptive design experience, encouraging an intuitive space for experimentation.

4   Results and Discussion

Our evaluation is based on the incorporation of the GPT-4 API[3] into the Unity3D platform (2021.3.8.f1 LTS). The VR avatar used in our case studies was sourced from the UltimateXR toolkit[4]. All 3D models utilized in this study were modeled by the authors in Blender 3.20 and textured using Adobe Substance 3D Painter. The complete list of objects available to the GPT API is the following: *Armchair, basket, bed, bookshelf, candles, chair, coffee table, desk lamp, dresser, floor lamp, laptop, nightstand, notepad, office chair, sofa, table, tv, tv stand, vase.*

4.1   Generating Basic Scenes

Case Study 1: Creating a Living Room from Scratch. Figs. 5a and 5b show the first-person perspective and the top view of the generated scene when the user provided the prompt "Create a living room". It is evident that the GPT API was able to select multiple pieces of furniture that are appropriate for a living room setup. Notably, the layout respects practical considerations such as ensuring free access through the entrance. It also respects all the constraints that were hard-coded in the initial request as described in Sect. 3.2.

Case Study 2: Integrating a Dining Area into an Existing Living Room. In this case study, we use an already generated room, in this case, the previously generated living room, and parse the existing objects in the scene at run-time. This capability obviates the need to relay the entire history of requests

---

[3] https://platform.openai.com/docs/guides/gpt.

[4] https://www.ultimatexr.io/.

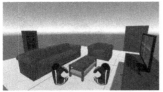

(a) Case Study 1: first-person perspective   (b) Case Study 1: top view

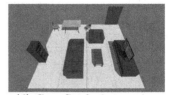

(c) Case Study 2: first-person perspective   (d) Case Study 2: top view

Fig. 5. (Top) scenes generated by generic prompt "Create a living room". (Bottom) augmented scene with additional prompt "Try to fit in a dining area".

to the GPT API, making it more efficient. Specifically, the only input from the user, in this case, is "Try to fit in a dining area". The resulting layout, depicted in Figs. 5c and 5d, showcases how the GPT API resourcefully incorporated a compact dining area into the layout. The dining setup, composed of a table and two chairs, was adeptly situated in a previously unoccupied space, demonstrating the system's ability to intelligently augment existing arrangements.

4.2   Combining Multiple Room Functions

(a) Case Study 3: first-person perspective   (b) Case Study 3: top view

Fig. 6. The generated room for the user prompt "Create a bedroom. Also, incorporate an office area".

The third case study demonstrates the capability of our framework to concurrently manage multiple room functions, specifically combining a bedroom and an office area within the same space. The user's instruction to the system was: "Create a bedroom. Also, incorporate an office area". The key challenge here was to create a harmonious layout that would integrate these two distinct

(a) [14]-generated living room

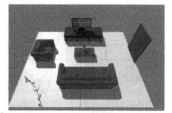
(b) Proposed framework living room

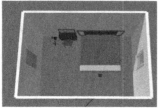
(c) [14]-generated bedroom

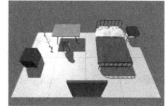
(d) Proposed framework bedroom

Fig. 7. Case Study 4: Comparison with the work in [14] from elaborate prompts. (Top row) Living room scenes. (Bottom row) Bedroom Scenes.

functions seamlessly, without compromising on the functionality and comfort of either area.

As seen in Fig. 6, the the proposed system successfully generated a cohesive scene that integrates both functions. Notably, the system's choices extended beyond merely generating appropriate primary furniture, such as a bed, desk, and office chair. It further enhanced the scene's realism and functionality by adding detailed decorative and utility items. This includes a notepad and a laptop on the desk, candles on the nightstands, and a vase on the dresser. This level of detail underscores the system's ability to generate comprehensive and realistic multi-functional spaces. The richness and precision of the item selection by the GPT API can be attributed to the thoroughness of the information provided for each piece of furniture in the initial request. For instance, precise height parameters included in the original object data allowed for the correct placement of items on the desk, contributing to the overall spatial coherence of the scene.

4.3 Detailed Scene Creation

Case Study 4: Advanced Control over Furniture Placement. In this case study, we replicated queries from [14], focusing on two specific prompts. In this work, the authors employed a contextual completion method for expanding a basic user prompt, which is then converted to a scene graph and finally to a complete scene. Figures 7a and 7b show results for "Create a living room. A coffee table is in front of a sofa. A TV stand is opposite the coffee table". However, as demonstrated in Fig. 7b, our proposed system extends beyond the given instructions to enrich the living room scene. While obeying the user's directive to place a sofa, coffee table, and TV stand, our framework also adds an armchair, situates a TV on the stand, positions a vase on the coffee table, and locates a floor lamp in a room corner. This highlights our system's skill in extrapolating additional context from minimal user directions.

Similar observations can be made for the bedroom scene that was generated by the prompt "A dressing table is in front of a chair. A bed is next to the dressing table". Figure 7c shows the generated scene by the work in [14], which precisely arranged the objects according to the provided spatial instructions. The scene generated by our proposed framework is shown in Fig. 7b. As our current object database lacks a "dressing table", the system substituted it with a simple "table". In addition, it enhanced the scene by incorporating a nightstand and a dresser to create a fuller bedroom scene. Consequently, our system, powered by the GPT API, demonstrates an ability to adjust the selected objects based on the furniture available, showcasing its adaptability. Also noteworthy is the fact that GPT API's spatial understanding infers space between object clusters, to allow for human navigation.

4.4   Discussion and Future Directions

Our proposed framework performs reasonably well in creating plausible scenes, even from a short prompt. However, we identified certain limitations that warrant consideration. We observed that the model struggles with incorporating clutter on multi-level objects, such as bookshelves, even with supporting surfaces indicated. Furthermore, some objects don't naturally have a *front* direction, which sometimes confused the system.

Additionally, populating vertical spaces proved difficult (such as walls). While this could be solved by enriching the initial prompt, we noticed that adding more instructions can occasionally lead to issues in the user prompt parsing step. We are confident that these limitations can be eased as the GPT API is improved and refined, allowing for more efficient prompts with deeper inference capabilities.

The application of the GPT API in this framework demonstrates an ability to interpret and execute both explicit and implicit instructions. As seen in the case studies, it accurately placed objects based on specified guidelines, but it also introduced additional objects to create more functional and realistic spaces. This evidences an underlying understanding of spatial relationships and an ability to infer and execute user intent, even when not explicitly stated. These results are promising, and open up avenues for further development. While we observed some issues, the constant improvements to the GPT API can eventually lead to a more refined prompt that allows for genuinely impressive output, such as expansive open worlds and immersive, complex environments.

5   Conclusion

This work showcases the potential of integrating GPT API and Unity3D for generating VR-ready scenes using natural language. Our method simplifies virtual environment creation, considering human ergonomics and movement, and broadens participation in content creation for interactive experiences. This is a step towards democratizing VR environment design. As the technology evolves, we expect AI technologies like GPT API to revolutionize virtual design and immersive experiences.

References

1. Bahrini, A., et al.: ChatGPT: applications, opportunities, and threats. In: 2023 Systems and Information Engineering Design Symposium (SIEDS), pp. 274–279 (2023)
2. Balint, J.T., Bidarra, R.: A generalized semantic representation for procedural generation of rooms. In: Proceedings of the 14th International Conference on the Foundations of Digital Games, pp. 1–8 (2019)
3. Chang, A., Savva, M., Manning, C.D.: Learning spatial knowledge for text to 3D scene generation. In: Proceedings of the 2014 Conference on Empirical Methods in Natural Language Processing (EMNLP), pp. 2028–2038 (2014)
4. Fisher, M., Ritchie, D., Savva, M., Funkhouser, T., Hanrahan, P.: Example-based synthesis of 3D object arrangements. ACM Trans. Graph. (TOG) **31**(6), 1–11 (2012)
5. Fu, Q., Chen, X., Wang, X., Wen, S., Zhou, B., Fu, H.: Adaptive synthesis of indoor scenes via activity-associated object relation graphs. ACM Trans. Graph. (TOG) **36**(6), 1–13 (2017)
6. Johnson, J., et al.: Image retrieval using scene graphs. In: Proceedings of the IEEE Conference on Computer Vision and Pattern Recognition, pp. 3668–3678 (2015)
7. Kermani, Z.S., Liao, Z., Tan, P., Zhang, H.: Learning 3D scene synthesis from annotated RGB-D images. In: Computer Graphics Forum, vol. 35, pp. 197–206. Wiley Online Library (2016)
8. Ma, R., Li, H., Zou, C., Liao, Z., Tong, X., Zhang, H.: Action-driven 3D indoor scene evolution. ACM Trans. Graph. **35**(6) (2016)
9. Ma, R., et al.: Language-driven synthesis of 3D scenes from scene databases. ACM Trans. Graph. (TOG) **37**(6), 1–16 (2018)
10. NVIDIA Omniverse: ChatGPT and GPT-4 for 3D Content Generation. NVIDIA Developer Blog (2023). https://medium.com/@nvidiaomniverse/chatgpt-and-gpt-4-for-3d-content-generation-9cbe5d17ec15
11. OpenAI: GPT-4 technical report (2023)
12. Qin, C., et al.: Is ChatGPT a general-purpose natural language processing task solver? arXiv preprint arXiv:2302.06476 (2023)
13. Wickramasinghe, W., De Saram, P., Liyanage, C., Rangika, L., Ranathunga, L.: Virtual reality markup framework for generating interactive indoor environment. In: 2017 IEEE 3rd International Conference on Engineering Technologies and Social Sciences (ICETSS), pp. 1–6. IEEE (2017)
14. Yang, X., Hu, F., Ye, L.: Text to scene: a system of configurable 3D indoor scene synthesis. In: Proceedings of the 29th ACM International Conference on Multimedia, pp. 2819–2821 (2021)
15. Yu, L.F., Yeung, S.K., Tang, C.K., Terzopoulos, D., Chan, T.F., Osher, S.J.: Make it home: automatic optimization of furniture arrangement. ACM Transactions on Graphics (TOG)-Proceedings of ACM SIGGRAPH 2011, v. 30, (4), July 2011, article no. 86 30(4) (2011)

Emergent Individual Factors for AR Education and Training

Brendan Kelley[1]([✉]), Anil Ufuk Batmaz[2], Michael Humphrey[1],
Cyane Tornatzky[1], Rosa Martey[1], and Francisco Ortega[1]

[1] Colorado State University, Fort Collins CO, USA
brendan.kelley@colostate.edu
[2] Concordia University, Quebec H3G 1M8, Canada

Abstract. As augmented reality (AR) has continued to expand the technology has seen integration into education and training practices. This study uses a comparative approach to address the question *does prior experience provide for stronger knowledge retention on mobile augmented reality compared to other training and education modalities?* A total of 33 participants were assigned to one of three training modalities (AR, paper manual, or online video). Once the training task was completed, they were tested on their knowledge retention from the experience via a 10-question quiz. While results from this study do not indicate AR provides for a better learning experience than other modalities several results point to the importance of individual characteristics.

Keywords: Augmented reality · mobile AR · training · education · user preference

1 Introduction

A variety of factors can impact the successful integration of emergent technologies into educational practices. Changing political, social, or environmental factors may affect the adoption and uptake of these technologies, such as the COVID-19 pandemic accelerating the hybridization of education on university education [20], as well as technological advancement. New opportunities afforded by emergent technologies, such as mixed reality, or more specifically for this study, Augmented Reality (AR), also help to enable these changes in education practices. While the integration of emerging technologies has proven beneficial, many elements of AR merit further exploration when applied to educational practices, including the tangible affordances of different AR forms, the challenges with integration, and how the technology supports the education process. To this end, this study sought to address the question *does prior experience provide for stronger knowledge retention on mobile augmented reality compared to other training and education modalities?* The results of this work suggest that a "one size fits all" or a generalized approach to education modalities may not be

G. Bebis et al. (Eds.): ISVC 2023, LNCS 14362, pp. 27–38, 2023.
https://doi.org/10.1007/978-3-031-47966-3_3

an ideal approach. Instead, it may be beneficial and necessary to explore individual characteristics (such as learning style, prior experiences, etc.), preferences, and differences that impact education experiences presented through variable modalities.

1.1 AR Training and Education

The expansion of commercially available mixed reality technologies has already led to integration attempts with education and training practices at a variety of different levels, such as children's education, professional assembly tasks, and electronic device repair. For instance, Jung et al. used an Xbox Kinect v2 to educate youth on proper responses to crisis situations (i.e. flooding, fires, earthquakes, etc.) [10]. In this system, a Kinect sensor detected the user's position and posture (limb placement and orientation) and then rendered crisis-related graphics onto a live video feed of the user. Afterwards, users were given prompts on how to react properly to the current situation. This allowed for a more responsive and interactive experience [10].

Professional training has also seen the adoption of mixed reality technologies, such as a recent study exploring the use of AR for engine assembly tasks [22]. For instance, in Werrlich et al.'s study [22], two different HMD-based AR systems were tested (one with four levels of training complexity and another with the same levels of complexity and an additional post-training quiz). Participants were asked to follow along with their assigned training to complete the assembly task. While the study did not produce any AR to non-AR comparative results, it does provide insights into best practices for designing mixed reality training as participants who took more time to complete the training were able to immediately recall more information, and the post-training quiz did not create a higher perceived workload among participants [22]. The application of AR technologies into professional assembly tasks is becoming increasingly common [2,5,14].

Other hands-on trainings have seen the adoption of mixed reality technologies, such as vocational education [5] or electronics repair [11]. In Dayadag et al.'s study, students used an AR HMD that utilized a mobile phone for computation to learn about basic information technology tasks such as crimping ethernet cables [5]. The latter study [11] used AR to present the disassembly instructions of a Playstation 3 console; an often required step in repairing hardware defects and failures. It then compared the results and experience of the AR mode to users utilizing a paper document. Participants using the AR modality exhibited greater knowledge improvement than the paper group [11], which would be expected as increased interactivity has been demonstrated to improve overall engagement with content [21].

Several studies discussed here include completion time as a metric along with performance metrics (i.e. quiz performace) [14,22]. In both academic and professional settings it is important to consider time commitments from both the individual and the institution. An individual user will only have so much time to devote to training before they will need to begin working and institutions have expectations for how long an individual will take to train. If there are little to no tangible benefits to using a particular modality but it requires a larger time commitment to complete it may not be beneficial to adopt and integrate that modality. However there may be other factors such as cost of training, external support, personalization, etc. that can offset time commitment costs.

1.2   External Factors on Training and Education

While there is strong evidence to suggest that proper integration of emerging technologies, e.g., mixed reality [5,11,14,22], can provide various benefits to the education and training process, there exist several challenges with the integration process. First and foremost, it is important to consider "technology as embedded in other social developments"[4]. Any technological advancement and subsequent adoption (or rejection) of that technology can be deeply affected by factors outside of educational practices. These may include economic constraints, cultural expectations, individual characteristics, or shifts in social developments [4]. Essentially there may not be a viable one size fits all approach.

The prior knowledge of the users also affects the training performance. A recent study compared the use of an AR application and a paper manual for both familiar and unfamiliar tasks for car mechanics [9]. Each participant was tasked with completing both wiper change (unfamiliar) and bumper replacement (familiar) using either the AR application or the paper manual. Results from this study "strongly suggest that routine has much more influence on the way car mechanics conduct a familiar task than the support medium" [9, p. 287]. Similarly, a study on performance during a medical simulation game also found that prior knowledge significantly impacted user performance [12]. However, Richter et al. showed that the cognitive load of the users were reduced for learning processes when individuals had prior knowledge regarding the content [18]. All of which may also impact the overall engagement from individuals [6]. Essentially, the prior knowledge of the users has an impact on their performance in training systems.

The use of emerging technologies for education further suffers from modality familiarity as a mediating factor in addition to content familiarity. In addition to finding that routine is a significant factor in task completion, researchers also found that AR modalities take longer for individuals to complete [9]. This may be due to the novelty of the technology as participants "were curious how [the task] would look like" [9, p. 287]. Other studies have also suggested that the medium used to engage with content can act as a potential barrier to access and engagement [15]. This phenomenon should improve as technologies develop, as further development would not only provide improved experiences [13] but also provide increased exposure and practice [9].

While AR may provide benefits for spatial content, it may not be suited for all content or all learning styles. In passive learners, the technological affordances of mixed reality have been found to potentially harm the education process, whereas active learners were found to benefit from the increased interactivity, presence, and embodied consideration [19]. Different types of knowledge engagement (identification, elaboration, planning, or execution) may also affect the overall engagement of individuals [17]. In essence, differences in the task being taught, the individual, and the modality used may impact the overall education experience.

With emerging technologies such as AR, modality differences may be even more pronounced. This is in part due to a potential lack of familiarity [9], but also due to subtle differences in execution. There exists a wide array of not only AR hardware (i.e. HMD vs. mobile), but also software implementation. The inclusion of different interactive techniques and responses, which are often a product of designer choice, provide different affordances, which in turn affect the education process [1]. This becomes especially challenging with the constant advancement and flux of AR technology. As such, it is important to consider not only potential individual differences but also technical nuances when exploring emerging technology education.

This study aims to address the question *does prior experience provide for stronger knowledge retention on mobile augmented reality compared to other training and education modalities?* by comparing post-training quiz results among three different modalities (AR, paper manual, and online video). A mobile AR (AR using smartphone devices) application was developed for the purposes of this study. This study was also conducted in the Nancy Richardson Design Center (RDC); a non-lab setting. This increases the ecological validity of the study by exposing participants to a setting that more accurately resembles actual training conditions. Many prior studies on AR training and education utilized laboratory settings where every factor can be controlled, however when applying these technologies outside of academic research settings there are numerous uncontrollable factors (i.e. noise level, other individuals, lighting, etc.) that are present in this study. Additionally this study includes both expert and novice participants. Each of these aspects provides novelty over prior studies and takes well documented approaches to AR development and explores them in an applied setting comparable to what a student or worker may experience as AR becomes more commonplace.

2   Methodology

To explore the limitations and benefits of mobile AR training in comparison to other training modalities and address the guiding research question, an experimental approach is used. This experiment used a 3 (modalities: online video, paper, AR) by 2 (task familiarity: prior experience and no prior experience) design with an additional variable for only the AR training (AR familiarity: prior AR experience, and no prior AR experience). Participants began by completing a presurvey to collect demographic information and their prior experience with both the machine being trained (a Roland LEF-300 UV printer) and AR. They were then assigned to one of the three training modalities and used their assigned mode to complete the material loading procedure on the LEF-300 UV printer.

During this training task students were timed using a stopwatch for consistency. While it is possible to use the proprietary AR software developed for this training to time, there was not a feasible way to use the same timer for the paper or video modality. After their training was completed, participants took a post-survey which contained both a knowledge test quiz consisting of 10 questions derived from the certification test already in place at the RDC as well as NASA task load index scales (TLX) [7,8]. This is in line with previous work that also used a comparative experimental approach for AR and non-AR training modalities [2,3,9,16,22]. The paper manual and online video used for this study were already developed by the RDC. Additionally, the quiz used as part of the post-survey is used for lab user certification in the RDC facilities. This allows for comparison against actually implemented training materials and practices that are comparable to other lab and fabrication center training approaches.

A total of 33 participants were recruited for this study (15 female, 18 male) with an average age of 24.64 (SD=5.8). Of these participants, 5 had prior experience with the LEF-300 UV printer. In total, 16 participants had experience with other specialty printers (any printer that prints on non-paper material or paper larger than 11" by 17"). Unfortunately due to the "in the wild" nature of this experiment it was not possible to find participants with the same level of experience to develop a full factor design. Additionally expertise among participants with prior experience may vary widely (i.e. even among 50 trained surgeons their actual experience will vary) and was self reported potentially leading to greater variability.

2.1 Apparatus

For this study, a software was developed in partnership with the center. It is a mobile AR application that is compatible with both Android and iOS (Apple) operating systems so long as the installed device supports either ARCore or ARKit (Android and Apples' respective AR software development kits (SDK)). The application, titled the Augmented Reality Assistant or ARA, was built using the Unity game engine and the Vuforia AR Plugin, which allows for robust AR functionality without extensive development requirements. While the application can be applied to a variety of training content, this study chose to focus on task training, where users were guided through the loading procedure of a Roland LEF-300 UV printer.

After opening the application, users chose the desired module from a menu screen. For the purposes of this study, only two modules were available: 1) a brief tutorial module that informs the user on how to use this specific application and 2) the LEF-300 training module. Once a module was selected, the user saw a live video feed from the front of their devices facing camera(s). They then scanned an image target with the camera (see Fig. 1), which spawns the AR objects into the environment. These virtual objects were anchored to the image target and the user's relative position.

From now on, we refer to the primary virtual object users interact with as "quest steps." These objects consisted of informative text, spatially aware highlights, and decorative user interface elements. The text reflected the current step the user was on and provided guidance for the completion of that step.

Fig. 1. The Augmented Reality Assistant (ARA)

The semi-transparent highlights encompassed the area or part of the machine that the user would interact with to complete the step. In addition to these elements, there were also two navigation buttons; one labeled "prev" and one labeled "next." As their labels suggest, the "prev" button returned the user to the previous step, and the "next" button advanced to the next step. Once the user was on the last step, the "next" button transitioned into an "exit" button and returned participants to the main menu. Additionally, they can return to the main menu using the "x" button anchored on the screen.

3   Results

3.1   Time Results

Time results were significant for modality (F(2,32)= 13.803, p<.001) based on ANOVAs run with the Python 3 Scipy package. Examination of QQ plots showed a normal distribution of the data. Further power analysis revealed a large effect size for time results (d = 1.24) with an alpha of 0.05. To achieve a power of 0.8 a total of 24 participants with groups of n = 8. Participants using the AR modality took the most amount of time to complete the task averaging 789 s for completion (*Standard Deviation (SD)* = 219 s). The paper manual took the second most amount of time with an average of 519 s for completion (*SD*= 144 s). At an average completion time of 312 s (*SD*= 81 s), the video training took the least amount of time. We did not observe a significant difference for prior mobile AR experience impact on·the training time; however, prior HMD AR experience did provide a statistically significant impact on the training time (F(1,31)= 5.41, p<0.05) .

3.2   Quiz Results

While the AR modality did produce slightly higher average quiz scores (AR: 7.67 out of 10 *SD*=1.50) than either the paper manual (paper: 6.91 out of 10 *SD*=1.97) or the video (video: 7.0 out of 10 *SD*=1.29) an ANOVA demonstrated that these differences were not statistically significant (F(2,32)=0.69, p>0.05). Power analysis of the quiz data showed a small effect size (d = .2) requiring groups of n = 156 with a power of .7 for statistically significant results

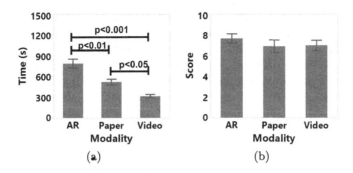

Fig. 2. Training Time (Left) and Quiz Scores (Right)

to emerge. Prior experience with other forms of specialty printers (i.e. any printer that prints on material other than paper or larger than 11in by 17in) did not have a statistically significant impact on the training experience; however, prior experience with the Roland LEF-300 UV printer, which was used for the training task, did have a statistically significant impact on quiz scores ($F(1,31)=4.68$, $p<0.05$) (Fig. 2).

3.3   NASA-TLX

The results of the NASA-TLX scores were given in Table 1. The video modality was rated as the most mentally demanding followed by the AR then paper modality. However the video modality was rated as the least physically demanding with AR being the most. Additionally the video modality was rated as the most rushed with followed by the AR modality and then the paper manual. Participants felt the most successful with the AR and paper manual with AR reported as 5.17 and paper slightly higher with a value of 5.45 for feeling of success. The video was rated as 4.2 for feelings of success. Both the AR and video trainings were ranked as having a 3.0 for workload compared to the lower score of 1.72 for the paper manual. Both the paper and AR manual had a lower rating for frustration than the video.

Table 1. Nasa TLX Results (1–7 Scales)

Measure	AR	Paper	Video
Mental Demand	3.33 ($SD= 1.56$)	2.36 ($SD= 1.12$)	3.9 ($SD= 1.66$)
Physical Demand	2.0 ($SD= 1.21$)	1.27 ($SD= 0.47$)	1.2 ($SD= 0.42$)
Pacing	1.83 ($SD= 0.72$)	1.45 ($SD= 1.51$)	2.2 ($SD= 0.92$)
Success	5.17 ($SD= 1.64$)	5.45 ($SD= 1.29$)	4.2 ($SD= 0.92$)
Workload	3.0 ($SD= 1.13$)	1.72 ($SD= 0.94$)	3.0 ($SD= 1.49$)
Frustration	2.16 ($SD= 0.94$)	1.91 ($SD= 1.22$)	2.6 ($SD= 1.84$)

An additional Pearson's R test was conducted on the NASA-TLX measures and quiz scores (see Table 2). All values except for success ratings were negatively correlated with quiz scores. Thus the higher the reported mental demand, physical demand, pacing, workload, or frustration the lower the quiz score, however these were not significantly significant. The only statistically significant correlation was between reported perceptions of success and knowledge scores but in a positive direction. So as users reporting of success increases their score would also increase.

Table 2. Nasa TLX and Quiz Scores

Measure	Quiz Score Correlation
Mental Demand	−0.02
Physical Demand	−0.12
Pacing	−0.03
Success	0.44*
Workload	−0.14
Frustration	−0.05

Note. * $p < .05$

4 Discussion

In this paper, we investigated if the prior knowledge of the training has an effect across different modalities. While this study did not produce results to exhibit an AR superiority over other modalities for education and training, the results point to a greater area of exploration for human-computer interaction studies. The impact of individual characteristics can be seen in the influence of prior experience with the trained machine on quiz scores. In our study, once an individual possesses knowledge of how to use the device, further information, regardless of the presentation of that information, becomes insignificant. This notion is in line with previous studies that found a routine and prior experience to be a mediating factor [9]. Another example of individual differences affecting the training is the impact of prior AR HMD experience on the training time. This effect, however, was not measured or present in prior studies, such as [2,3,9,16, 22]. Additionally, the effect of AR HMD experience is not intuitively predicted, as this study and training task utilize *mobile* AR, which has several differences in, such as form factor (hand-held device vs head-mounted) and interaction techniques (touch screen vs controller/hand tracking). This was an intentional choice due to the greater accessibility of mobile AR compared to HMD AR as more individuals have access to AR ready mobile devices than expensive AR HMDs.

The Nasa TLX results indicate a higher reported mental demand with the video modality. This is most likely due to the lack of direct interaction with the trained machine requiring more cognitive resources. The AR application was rated as having the highest physical demand, which is unsurprising given the physical demands of interacting with a mobile phone. The higher reported feeling of success with both the AR and paper modality over the video training may indicate a benefit for directly interacting with the training device. While both AR and video had the same reported workload these may be due to different interaction requirements, with AR requiring more physical resources and video requiring more cognitive.

These results may point to deeper individual considerations. While this study did not explicitly inquire about the education or occupational experience of its participants, one of the main recruitment channels primarily targeted computer science students. As such, those with prior AR head-mounted display (HMD) experience may have other pertinent computing experience that influenced the training experience. This potential deeper connection may also be exemplified by the positive correlation between perceived success and quiz scores. The more confident an individual felt with their training session, the better they typically performed regardless of modality. This also poses our new research question: **what makes an individual feel more or less confident during the training experience?** Since these results are independent of the modality used, there may be other identifiable characteristics at play. It may also be the case that different characteristics support success with different modalities.

This work was limited in several ways. First the use of an "in the wild" setting for the experiment introduces factors outside of our control. Included in this is the prior experience and expertise of the participants due to the method used to collect participant data (presurvey and postsurvey separate with no indicators to link these two surveys together). Additionally the sample size of 33 (with 11 for each modality) may be too small to fully capture trends.

5   Future Work

To clearly understand the complex interplay between an individual and different training modalities, further study is necessary with a larger research program. As with any design-related study, such as the one presented here, there are various adjustments and changes to the AR interface, interactions, and content that can be implemented. Additionally, other related technologies, such as virtual reality, can also be of interest to the education and training field. This study was also particularly interested in mobile AR usage due to accessibility considerations (namely cost), but there may be benefits to using an AR HMD that warrants further exploration. However, these changes would still take a generalized or "one size fits all" approach to the topic. Instead, more consideration must be put on the end user in conjunction with the technology.

To this end, future work may consider including questionnaire items related to learning characteristics, personality traits, or other related psychological concepts. However, this may not be feasible for all studies, especially if other measures are already being administered that pertain to the topics of interest. Instead, it may be prudent to develop studies that specifically engage with individual characteristics in relation to technological considerations. For instance, a study may use only a single modality (i.e. AR, VR, video, paper, etc.) but administer measures to identify traits, characteristics, or experiences that make an individual more likely to succeed using that modality. Or a study may use multiple modalities but then allow a participant to choose which training modality to use for the trained task. Subsequent measures would then be taken on not only performance (i.e. quiz score, accuracy, time, etc.) but also on their choice, traits, characteristics, and experiences to determine how their choice aligns with their experience and them as an individual. Most important, measuring metacognition. All these topics reveal new research questions for our future studies. It is often the case with comparative training or education studies, such as the one presented here, that the end goal is to determine which modality works best for a general population. While this is a useful pursue, it does not take into account that different individuals learn differently [17,19].

By exploring these individual factors in conjunction with technological components, a greater understanding of how we interact with computers, how we learn with computers, and how computers affect us can be achieved. Often there is a focus on determining which modality, solution, or technology works best for a wide audience (which is an important and useful exploration to undertake), but this focus can often overlook important aspects pertaining to the human side of human-computer interaction. Additionally, careful attention to the end user in such a manner may open up possibilities for accessible computing via a greater understanding of marginalized groups and their unique attributes and needs.

6 Conclusion

We analyzed how different prior knowledge of the individuals affects training performance in AR training systems in an applied non-lab setting. A comparative study with 33 participants who were randomly assigned to either an AR, paper manual or online video training was conducted. While the modality did not affect the follow-up quiz scores based on available data several unexpected results indicate the importance of considering individual characteristics, experiences, and traits in addition to the computing technology used, such as their prior experience with the training content and perceived performance.

Acknowledgements. The authors of this paper would like to thank the Nancy Richardson Design Center for their assistance in conducting this research. This study was partially supported by ONR grants N00012-21-1-2949, N00014-21-1-2580, and N00014-23-1-2298.

References

1. Bakkiyaraj, M., Kavitha, G., Sai Krishnan, G., Kumar, S.: Impact of augmented reality on learning fused deposition modeling based 3D printing aug-

mented reality for skill development. Mater. Today Proc. **43**, 2464–2471 (2021). https://doi.org/10.1016/j.matpr.2021.02.664, https://linkinghub.elsevier.com/retrieve/pii/S2214785321018174

2. Büttner, S., Prilla, M., Röcker, C.: Augmented reality training for industrial assembly work - are projection-based AR assistive systems an appropriate tool for assembly training? In: Proceedings of the 2020 CHI Conference on Human Factors in Computing Systems, pp. 1–12. ACM, Honolulu HI USA (2020). https://doi.org/10.1145/3313831.3376720

3. Chien, C.H., Chen, C.H., Jeng, T.S.: An interactive augmented reality system for learning anatomy structure, p. 6. Hong Kong (2010)

4. Cloete, A.L.: Erratum: technology and education: challenges and opportunities. HTS Theologiese Stud. Theological Stud. **73**(3), 1 (2017). https://doi.org/10.4102/hts.v73i3.4899, http://www.hts.org.za/index.php/HTS/article/view/4899

5. Dayagdag, C.V., Catanghal, R.A., Palaoag, T.D.: Improving vocational training in the Philippines using AR. In: Proceedings of the 8th International Conference on Informatics, Environment, Energy and Applications - IEEA 2019, pp. 253–257. ACM Press, Osaka, Japan (2019). https://doi.org/10.1145/3323716.3323755, http://dl.acm.org/citation.cfm?doid=3323716.3323755

6. Dong, A., Jong, M.S.Y., King, R.B.: How does prior knowledge influence learning engagement? The mediating roles of cognitive load and help-seeking. Front. Psychol. **11**, 591203 (2020). https://doi.org/10.3389/fpsyg.2020.591203

7. Hart, S.G.: Nasa-Task Load Index (NASA-TLX); 20 Years Later. HUMAN FACTORS AND ERGONOMICS SOCIETY 50th ANNUAL MEETING p. 5 (2006)

8. Hart, S.G., Staveland, L.E.: Development of NASA-TLX (Task Load Index): results of empirical and theoretical research. In: Advances in Psychology, vol. 52, pp. 139–183. Elsevier (1988). https://doi.org/10.1016/S0166-4115(08)62386-9, https://linkinghub.elsevier.com/retrieve/pii/S0166411508623869

9. Hoffmann, C., Büttner, S., Prilla, M., Wundram, K.: Impact of augmented reality guidance for car repairs on novice users of AR: a field experiment on familiar and unfamiliar tasks. In: Proceedings of the Conference on Mensch und Computer, pp. 279–289. ACM, Magdeburg Germany (2020). https://doi.org/10.1145/3404983.3405594

10. Jung, S.U., Cho, H., Jee, H.K.: An AR-based safety training assistant in disaster for children. In: SIGGRAPH ASIA 2016 Posters, pp. 1–2. ACM, Macau (2016). https://doi.org/10.1145/3005274.3005318

11. Lam, M.C., Sadik, M.J., Elias, N.F.: The effect of paper-based manual and stereoscopic-based mobile augmented reality systems on knowledge retention. Virtual Reality (2020). https://doi.org/10.1007/s10055-020-00451-9

12. Lee, J.Y., Donkers, J., Jarodzka, H., van Merriënboer, J.J.: How prior knowledge affects problem-solving performance in a medical simulation game: using game-logs and eye-tracking. Comput. Hum. Behav. **99**, 268–277 (2019). https://doi.org/10.1016/j.chb.2019.05.035, https://linkinghub.elsevier.com/retrieve/pii/S074756321930216X

13. McKnight, R.R., Pean, C.A., Buck, J.S., Hwang, J.S., Hsu, J.R., Pierrie, S.N.: Virtual reality and augmented reality-translating surgical training into surgical technique. Current Rev. Musculoskeletal Med. **13**(6), 663–674 (2020). https://doi.org/10.1007/s12178-020-09667-3

14. Nguyen, D., Meixner, G.: Gamified augmented reality training for an assembly task: a study about user engagement, pp. 901–904 (2019). https://doi.org/10.15439/2019F136, https://fedcsis.org/proceedings/2019/drp/136.html

15. Okhovati, M., Sharifpoor, E., Aazami, M., Zolala, F., Hamzehzadeh, M.: Novice and experienced users' search performance and satisfaction with web of science and Scopus. J. Librarianship Inf. Sci. **49**(4), 359–367 (2017). https://doi.org/10.1177/0961000616656234

16. Pérez-López, D., Contero, M.: Delivering educational multimedia contents through an augmented reality application: a case study on its impact on knowledge acquisition and retention. Turkish Online J. Edu. Technol. **12**(4), 10 (2013)

17. Quinlan, C.L.: Use of schema theory and multimedia technology to explore preservice students' cognitive resources during an earth science activity, p. 26 (2019)

18. Richter, J., Scheiter, K., Eitel, A.: Signaling text-picture relations in multimedia learning: the influence of prior knowledge. J. Educ. Psychol. **110**(4), 544–560 (2018). https://doi.org/10.1037/edu0000220

19. Sari, R.C., Warsono, S., Ratmono, D., Zuhrohtun, Z., Hermawan, H.D.: The effectiveness of teaching virtual reality-based business ethics: is it really suitable for all learning styles? Interactive Technology and Smart Education ahead-of-print(ahead-of-print) (2021). https://doi.org/10.1108/ITSE-05-2021-0084

20. Skulmowski, A., Rey, G.D.: COVID-19 as an accelerator for digitalization at a German university: establishing hybrid campuses in times of crisis. Hum. Behav. Emerg. Technol. **2**(3), 212–216 (2020). https://doi.org/10.1002/hbe2.201

21. Sundar, S.S., Xu, Q., Bellur, S., Oh, J., Jia, H.: Beyond pointing and clicking: how do newer interaction modalities affect user engagement? In: Proceedings of the 2011 Annual Conference Extended Abstracts on Human Factors in Computing Systems - CHI EA 2011, p. 1477. ACM Press, Vancouver, BC, Canada (2011). https://doi.org/10.1145/1979742.1979794

22. Werrlich, S., Nguyen, P.A., Notni, G.: Evaluating the training transfer of head-mounted display based training for assembly tasks. In: Proceedings of the 11th Pervasive Technologies Related to Assistive Environments Conference, pp. 297–302. ACM, Corfu Greece (2018). https://doi.org/10.1145/3197768.3201564

Segmentation

ISLE: A Framework for Image Level Semantic Segmentation Ensemble

Erik Ostrowski[1(✉)] and Muhammad Shafique[2]

[1] Institute of Computer Engineering, Technische Universität Wien (TU Wien),
Vienna, Austria
`erik.ostrowski@tuwien.ac.at`
[2] eBrain Lab, Division of Engineering, New York University Abu Dhabi (NYUAD),
Abu Dhabi , United Arab Emirates
`muhammad.shafique@nyu.edu`

Abstract. One key bottleneck of employing state-of-the-art semantic segmentation networks in the real world is the availability of training labels. Conventional semantic segmentation networks require massive pixel-wise annotated labels to reach state-of-the-art prediction quality. Hence, several works focus on semantic segmentation networks trained with only image-level annotations. However, when scrutinizing the results of state-of-the-art in more detail, we notice that they are remarkably close to each other on average prediction quality, different approaches perform better in different classes while providing low quality in others. To address this problem, we propose a novel framework, ISLE, which employs an ensemble of the "pseudo-labels" for a given set of different semantic segmentation techniques on a class-wise level. Pseudo-labels are the pixel-wise predictions of the image-level semantic segmentation frameworks used to train the final segmentation model. Our pseudo-labels seamlessly combine the strong points of multiple segmentation techniques approaches to reach superior prediction quality. We reach up to 2.4% improvement over ISLE's individual components. An exhaustive analysis was performed to demonstrate ISLE's effectiveness over state-of-the-art frameworks for image-level semantic segmentation.

Keywords: Semantic Segmentation · Weakly Supervised · Ensemble · Deep Learning · Class Activation Maps

1 Introduction

Generating high-quality semantic segmentation predictions using only models trained on image-level annotations would enable a new level of applicability. The progress of fully supervised semantic segmentation networks has already helped provide many useful tools and applications. For example, in autonomous and self-driving vehicles [1,2], remote sensing [3], facial recognition [4,5], agriculture [6,7], and in the medical field [8,9], etc. The downside of those fully supervised semantic segmentation networks (FSSS) is that they require copious amounts of

G. Bebis et al. (Eds.): ISVC 2023, LNCS 14362, pp. 41–52, 2023.
https://doi.org/10.1007/978-3-031-47966-3_4

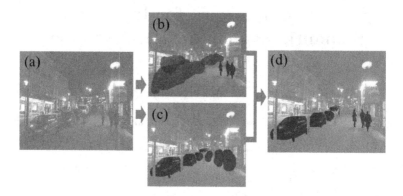

Fig. 1. The idea of our Framework: (a) Input image, (b) prediction of a method that is good with person segmentation and bad with cars, (c) prediction of a method good with car segmentation and bad with persons, (d) prediction of ISLE, combining the strengths of the two methods.

pixel-wise annotated images. Generating such a training set is very tedious and time-consuming work. For instance, one image of the Cityscapes dataset, which contains street scenes from cities that require many complex objects to be annotated, takes more than an hour of manual user-driven labour [10]. Furthermore, medical imaging and molecular biology fields require the knowledge of highly qualified individuals capable of interpreting and annotating the images.

Therefore, to reduce the time and resources required for generating pixel-wise masks, a wide range of research works focus on developing approaches that focus on weaker kinds of supervision. In this work, we will focus on weak supervision in the form of image-level labels. Image-level labels give the least amount of supervision for semantic segmentation but are the easiest to acquire.

Several works already focus on image-level semantic segmentation techniques, and they consistently reach better and better high scores. Most works are based on Class Activation Maps (CAMs) [11]. CAMs localize the object by training a DNN model with classification loss and then reusing the learned weights to highlight the image areas responsible for its classification decision. Most image-level segmentation approaches aim to improve the CAM baseline by adding additional regularizations to the classification loss or refining the CAM mask afterward. As more methods emerge for improving CAM quality, state-of-the-art is usually compiled of regularizations, after-the-fact refinements, or combinations of both. However, when analyzing multiple image-level segmentation techniques on a class-by-class basis, we observed that the differences between them vary significantly on specific classes, although those methods generate predictions that reach comparable scores on average.

Therefore, we are proposing our ISLE framework. In our framework, we combine the pseudo-labels of multiple image-level segmentation techniques based on the respective class scores to generate a superset of pseudo-labels, combining the upsides of multiple different approaches. Figure 1 visualizes the gains possible by our ISLE framework in comparison to its components. The detection of edges of objects is a major weakness in Image-level based semantic segmentation and many state-of-the-art methods tried to address this problem. We noticed that they achieve their goal to some degree. Namely, in certain objects, a specific method achieves remarkable results, but also scores under average with different objects. Hence, our ISLE framework addresses the problem of insufficient object border detection, by applying state-of-the-art only in scenarios, where their individual approach is suited best. We perform extensive experiments on the PASCAL VOC2012 dataset [12] to prove the effectiveness of our framework in various experimental settings and compare them with a range of state-of-the-art techniques to illustrate the benefits of our approach. The **key contributions** of this work are:

1. Our novel ISLE framework improves the prediction quality of segmentation masks by combining state-of-the-art pseudo-labels on a class-by-class basis.
2. Our ISLE framework is not limited by the number or approach of any image-level guided segmentation frameworks to combine their pseudo-labels. Since the ISLE is only used for generating pseudo-labels, it will not add more computations for inference predictions.
3. We present detailed ablation studies and analysis comparing the results of ISLE to state-of-the-art methods on the VOC2012 dataset to evaluate our method's efficacy and the improvements achieved using our framework.
4. The complete framework is open-source and accessible online at https://github.com/ErikOstrowski/ISLE.

2   Related Work

In this section, we provide a discussion of the current state-of-the-art in semantic segmentation using image-level supervision.

AffinityNet [13] trains a second network to learn pixel similarities, which generates a transition matrix combined with the CAM iteratively to refine its activation coverage. PuzzleCAM [14] introduces a loss, that subdivides the input image into multiple parts, forcing the network to predict image segments that contain the non-discriminative parts of an object. CLIMS [15] trained the network by matching text labels to the correct image. Hence, the network maximizes and minimizes the distance between correct and wrong pairs, respectively, instead of just giving a binary classification result. PMM [16] used Coefficient of Variation Smoothing to smooth the CAMs, which introduces a new metric, that highlights the importance of each class on each location, in contrast to the scores trained from the binary classifier. Furthermore, they employed Pretended Underfitting, which improves training with noisy labels, and Cyclic Pseudo-mask to iteratively trains the final segmentation network with its predictions. DRS [17] aims to improve the image's activation area to less discriminative areas. Kim et al. [17] achieve this by suppressing the attention on discriminative regions, thus guiding the attention to adjacent regions to generate a complete attention map of the target object.

Table 1 lists all the twenty classes of the VOC2012 dataset and shows, which state-of-the-art method achieves the best result on specific classes. We observe that PMM has the best result in only two of the twenty classes, DRS in three, CLIMS has the best result in seven, and PuzzleCAM in eight classes.

Table 1. Highest score per VOC2012 class on each component of ISLE.

Class	PMM	DRS	CLIMS	Puzzle
Bus	✓	✗	✗	✗
Car	✓	✗	✗	✗
Bottle	✗	✓	✗	✗
Chair	✗	✓	✗	✗
Train	✗	✓	✗	✗
Bike	✗	✗	✓	✗
Boat	✗	✗	✓	✗
Table	✗	✗	✓	✗
Motor	✗	✗	✓	✗
Person	✗	✗	✓	✗
Sofa	✗	✗	✓	✗
TV	✗	✗	✓	✗
Aero	✗	✗	✗	✓
Bird	✗	✗	✗	✓
Cat	✗	✗	✗	✓
Cow	✗	✗	✗	✓
Dog	✗	✗	✗	✓
Horse	✗	✗	✗	✓
Plant	✗	✗	✗	✓
Sheep	✗	✗	✗	✓

3 ISLE Framework

Our framework aims to combine the strengths of different methods by just using their predictions for classes where they are performing the best, while not considering predictions of classes where they perform worse compared to other methods. The prerequisite of our framework is a list of candidate state-of-the-art approaches for image-level semantic segmentation. Figure 2 presents an overview of the ISLE framework. We start with collecting the pseudo labels of our candidate methods. In the next step, we can employ several refinement

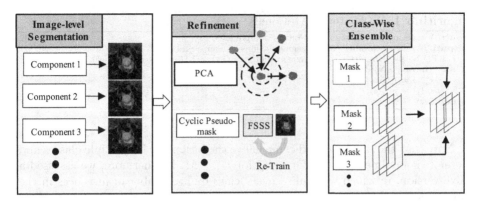

Fig. 2. Overview of the ISLE framework. The first stage is the collection of Image-level semantic segmentation; In the second stage, we can use a number of refinement methods to improve the mask quality; In the third stage, we combine the refinement masks on a class-wise basis to generate the pseudo-labels that reach the best prediction for each class; In the final stage, we are training an FSSS with the pseudo labels.

methods to improve the pseudo-label quality beforehand. In our case, we used AffinityNet [13] and a dense Conditional Random Field (dCRF) [18] for the candidates if the provided pseudo labels did not already undergo refinement methods. Then we can combine the pseudo-labels on a class-wise basis, where we only copy the predictions of classes of the candidate labels to our ensemble if the candidate has a high score in that class. Finally, we use the generated pseudo labels to train an FSSS network. Our proposed version uses the four state-of-the-art methods introduced in the previous section, and for all of them except CLIMS, we also refine their baseline with AffinityNet. AffinityNet uses a random walk, in combination with pixel affinities. Furthermore, as a widespread practice, we use dCRF to the AffinityNet predictions to improve their quality. The refinement of the pseudo labels is not limited to AffinityNet, any combination of additional refinement methods can be employed within our framework.

In the next step, we will evaluate the different candidate pseudo label sets on a class-wise basis and determine which candidate is used for which class for the ensemble. We reshape the pseudo labels ps to the dimensions $ps_i \in \mathbb{R}^{H \times W \times C}$, if they were not already provided in that shape, where i is the specific image, H is the image height, W is the image width and C is the number of classes. We perform the combination by copying for all images the slides $ps_{i,c}^{x} \in \mathbb{R}^{H \times W \times 1}$ of a specific class c by the candidate network x, if x has the high score on c. We do this for every class c in C and then simply concatenate all slides to get a complete prediction, which contains only the best predictions state-of-the-art can muster on a class-wise level:

$$ps_{i,c_1}^{x_1} \times ps_{i,c_2}^{x_2} \times \ldots \times ps_{i,c_N}^{x_M} = ps_i^*,$$

Where N is the number of classes in the used dataset, M the number of candidate methods and ps_i^* is the ensemble prediction of image i.

Algorithm 1. ISLE Step 1 (Optional)

Input: N training-pseudo-segmentations of components: ps
Output: N refined training-pseudo-segmentations of components: ps^*
1: Let F() be a combination of refinement methods (F() = {AffinityNet(), Cycle(),..}.
2: **for** n in range(N) **do**
3:     $ps_n^*(i) = F(ps_n(i))$
4:     $ps_n(i) = ps_n^*(i)$
5: **end for**

Note that the same method can achieve the best score in multiple classes and therefore sometimes $x_i = x_j$ for $i \neq j$ for $i, j \in M$. Furthermore, we assessed a naive version, in which we ranked every class by its number of instances in the training set and then used the complete CAM of candidate x from the whole image if x has the high score on the highest ranked class x present on the image. The naive ISLE performed worse than our final version.

We excluded the *background* class from our ensemble since the background is the inverse of all classes combined. Note that we can perform this class selection method since we already assign the correct class labels to each prediction instead of using a classification network for the assignment, as conventional for image level based semantic segmentation methods. Therefore, it is necessary to train a fully supervised semantic segmentation network with those pseudo-labels. Nevertheless, the FSSS training guarantees that collecting multiple pseudo-label sets is a one-time effort per dataset. Figure 2 illustrates an overview of the process. Further details can be seen in the Pseudocodes 1, 2, 3.

Algorithm 2. ISLE Step 2

Input: N (refined) training-pseudo-segmentations of components: ps
Output: List of best scoring methods for each class: best
1: Let C be the number of classes in the dataset.
2: Let $mIoU_c()$ be the evaluation algorithm on class c.
3: Let Img be the list of all images.
4:
5: **for** c in range(C) **do**
6:     $top_c = 0$
7:     **for** n in range(N) **do**
8:         **for** i in Img **do**
9:             $score{+} = mIoU_c(ps_n(i))$
10:         **end for**
11:         $score = score/\#images$
12:         **if** $score > top_c$ **then**
13:             $top_c = score$
14:             $best(c) = n$
15:         **end if**
16:     **end for**
17: **end for**

Algorithm 3. ISLE Step 3

Input: N refined training-pseudo-segmentations of components: ps^* and list of best scoring methods for each class: $best$

Output: Semantic Segmentation network trained on weakly-supervised predictions: SSN

1: Let ae be the final ensemble.
2: Let Img be the list of all images.
3: Define $ae = 0$ for all classes and all images in the dataset.
4:
5: **for** c in range(C) **do**
6:     $n = best(c)$
7:     **for** i in Img **do**
8:         $ae_c(i) = ps_{n,c}(i)$
9:     **end for**
10: **end for**
11:
12: 4.Step:
13:
14: **for** Epochs x **do**
15:     **for** i in Img **do**
16:         $pred = SSN(i)$
17:     **end for**
18:     $Backpropagation(SSN)$
19: **end for**

---

4   Experiments

First, we will discuss our experimental setup. We completed the experiments on a CentOS 7.9 Operating System executing on an Intel Core i7-8700 CPU with 16GB RAM and 2 Nvidia GeForce GTX 1080 Ti GPUs. The CLIMS pseudo-labels were used as provided by the official GitHub, and we performed Affini-tyNet with a ResNet50 backbone and dCRF on the pseudo-labels provided on the DRS and PMM GitHub. All DeepLabV3+ results were generated using a ResNet50 backbone. The mean Intersection-over-Union (mIoU) ratio is the evaluation metric for all experiments. We used the PASCAL VOC2012 semantic segmentation benchmark for evaluating our framework. It comprises twenty-one classes, including a background class, and most images include multiple objects. Following the conventional experimentation protocol for semantic segmentation, we use the $10,528$ augmented images and image-level labels, for training. Our model is evaluated on the validation set with $1,464$ images and the test set of $1,456$ images to ensure a constant comparison with the state-of-the-art.

For all experiments, the mean Intersection-over-Union (mIoU) ratio is used as the evaluation metric.

4.1   Semantic Segmentation Performance on VOC2012

Next, we compare our ensemble with its components consisting of recent works using image-level supervision Table 2. We trained all pseudo-labels with the same DeepLabV3+ model for comparability using a ResNet50 backbone. We notice that the ensemble outperforms its component by a margin of at least 2%, although the individual components do not show this amount of variance between them. ISLE-2 is the ensemble of just PuzzleCAM and CLIMS, and ISLE

Table 2. Comparison of ISLE mIoU scores with state-of-the-art techniques on the VOC2012 val and test datasets. All methods were trained with DeepLabV3+ with a ResNet50 backbone for comparability. Adding more or different methods to the ensemble is possible, as those work orthogonal to the ISLE.

Method	Val	Test
PuzzleCAM	62.4	62.9
PMM	64.0	64.1
DRS	64.5	64.5
CLIMS	65.0	65.4
ISLE-2 (Ours)	66.6	67.1
ISLE (Ours)	**67.4**	**67.8**

Table 3. Semantic segmentation mIoU performance on the first 11 classes of the VOC2012 **training dataset** for the final pseudo-labels.

Method	bkg	aero	bike	bird	boat	bottle	bus	car	cat	chair	cow
PuzzleCAM	88.6	<u>79.2</u>	43.7	<u>89.0</u>	61.8	72.1	83.3	76.0	<u>92.0</u>	29.5	<u>86.0</u>
CLIMS	89.8	71.2	<u>45.4</u>	81.7	<u>70.2</u>	67.6	84.0	75.7	90.0	20.3	84.2
PMM	89.5	76.8	43.9	88.1	65.8	76.0	<u>84.2</u>	<u>78.0</u>	91.2	30.6	84.3
DRS	<u>90.1</u>	78.9	45.3	85.8	68.4	<u>80.8</u>	83.8	77.4	90.6	<u>31.5</u>	84.0
ISLE-2 (Ours)	90.5	**79.6**	**45.4**	**89.0**	70.0	72.1	84.0	76.1	**92.2**	30.9	**86.1**
ISLE (Ours)	**91.0**	**79.6**	**45.4**	**89.0**	69.7	**81.2**	**84.2**	**78.0**	**92.2**	**31.6**	**86.1**

is the ensemble of all four methods. DRS is the best performing of its component, and the ISLE reaches a 2% higher mIoU score.

Here, we present a more comprehensive analysis by providing a class-wise mIoU breakdown for all classes in the VOC2012 training dataset and a discussion. On the one hand, we see in Table 3 and Table 4 that the difference in the average mIoU score between our four component methods the relatively small, with the lowest scoring PuzzleCAM reaching 69.7% and the highest scoring DRS at 71.3%. On the other hand, the ensemble of all four methods reaches 74.1%, and the ensemble of just PuzzleCAM and CLIMS 73.6% achieves a significant gain compared to its components. Although, we also notice that the gain from adding more image-level segmentation pseudo-labels to the ensemble shrinks over time and needs to be considered when choosing the component for ISLE, as the training set mIoU between ISLE and ISLE-2 differs by less than 1%, while ISLE uses the double amount of components.

Let us take a closer look at the performance of the individual components on a class-wise basis. PMM reaches the best score only in two classes and an average 0.77% improvement in those classes. Although only reaching the highest average score in three classes, DRS provides an average 6.04% improvement in those three classes. CLIMS is the best in seven classes and achieves an average improvement

Table 4. Semantic segmentation mIoU performance on the remaining 10 classes of the VOC2012 **training dataset** for the final pseudo-labels.

Method	table	dog	horse	motor	person	plant	sheep	sofa	train	tv	mIoU
PuzzleCAM	44.0	<u>91.6</u>	<u>83.1</u>	<u>80.1</u>	42.8	<u>68.9</u>	<u>92.6</u>	53.4	64.8	42.6	69.7
CLIMS	<u>57.8</u>	86.9	80.9	80.8	<u>72.7</u>	48.4	90.3	<u>56.5</u>	68.1	<u>58.4</u>	70.5
PMM	48.5	89.3	82.0	79.0	61.4	66.5	89.9	54.4	66.4	38.6	70.7
DRS	41.2	88.7	80.0	79.8	65.4	62.6	89.9	55.0	<u>77.0</u>	41.3	<u>71.3</u>
ISLE-2	**52.5**	**92.0**	**86.0**	**80.9**	71.8	68.5	**92.7**	56.2	68.1	54.1	73.3
ISLE	51.1	91.9	85.9	80.8	72.3	68.5	**92.7**	**56.9**	**77.1**	52.8	**74.2**

of 6.04% as well. Whereas PuzzleCAM is the lowest average scoring method but reaches high scores in eight classes but improves them only by 2.62% on average. Therefore, we conclude that CLIMS and PuzzleCAM contribute the most and PMM the least to the ensemble. Hence, we also evaluated the combination of only CLIMS and PuzzleCAM to see how much improvement we gain while combining the minimum amount of pseudo-label sets. We called this version ISLE-2. We notice that most high scores translated to the ensemble, with only minor losses in some classes, most probably due to overlap with other classes.

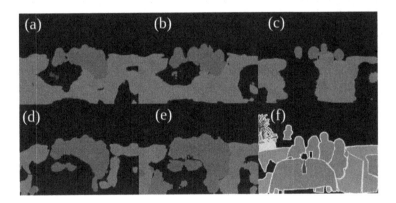

Fig. 3. Pseudo labels from (a) DRS, (b) PMM, (c) PuzzleCAM, (d) CLIMS, (e) ISLE (Ours), (f) Ground truth.

Figure 3 presents one example of our experimental results. (a) shows the pseudo labels of DRS, (b) of PMM, (c) of PuzzleCAM, (d) of CLIMS, (e) of our ISLE, and (f) the Ground truth. We observe that DRS does not recognize the table in the image but over-detects the couch. PMM has a few pixels detected as table but also detects fewer person pixels. PuzzleCAM struggles even more with couch over-prediction and person under-prediction. The best result of the not combined images stems from CLIMs, which only correct couch predictions and the best person detection. Finally, our ISLE expands person detection but also includes some over-predictions, for example in the bottom left. Furthermore, ISLE has the best table detection and successfully expands couch detections.

4.2 Complexity Analysis

In this section, we will provide a complexity analysis of our code. This will help to estimate the additional complexity that is connected with adding more components.

Step 1

Let $\{Comp_1, Comp_2, ..., Comp_N\}$ be the list of Components. Each component takes as input a specific image i from the list of all images I and gives as output class activation maps $CAM_n^{i,c}$ for all classes c in the dataset.

$$Comp_n(i) = \sum_{c=0}^{C} CAM_n^{i,c}, 1 \leq n \leq N$$

As the components are not further defined by the framework, we can only summarize their complexity as follows:

$$O(Step1) = \sum_{n=0}^{N} O(Comp_n^{training}(i)) \times O(Comp_n^{inference}(i)) \times epochs_n \times 2 \times I$$

Step 2

Let $\{Ref_1, Ref_2, ..., Ref_M\}$ be the list of all applied refinements. We assume that all refinements are applied to all components for ease of notation. Then Step. 2 is defined as:

$$\widetilde{CAM_n^i} = Ref_1(CAM_n^i) \otimes Ref_2(CAM_n^i) \otimes ... \otimes Ref_M(CAM_n^i),$$

for any n with $1 \leq n \leq N$ Again, we need to define the complexity of each refinement method as $O(Ref_m())$ as the refinements are not further defined by the framework:

$$O(Step2) = \sum_{m=0}^{M} O(Ref_m^{training}(i)) \times O(Ref_m^{inference}(i)) \times epochs_n \times 2 \times I \times N$$

Step 3

The merging of pseudo-labels is done after a class-wise evaluation for each $\widetilde{CAM_n^i}$ to determine which Component after refinement has the high score for each class c with $1 \leq c \leq C$:

$$AE(i) = \sum_{c=1}^{C} AE^c(i) = \sum_{c=1}^{C} best(\widetilde{CAM_n^{c,i}}),$$

for all i in I The refinement step and Class-Wise Ensemble are just linearly dependent on the number of Components:

$$O(Step3) = O(eval) + O(merger) = I \times N \times C + I \times C$$

Step 4

The training of the DeepLabV3+ model is not different from any other WSSS pipeline:

$$O(Step.4) = O(\texttt{DeepLabV3+}^{training} \times epochs \times images)$$

Nonetheless, for the final deployment of ISLE, only the forward pass of DeepLabV3+ is necessary, independent of the number of components and refinements used:

$$O(Deployment) = O(\texttt{DeepLabV3+}^{inference} \times images)$$

5   Conclusion

In this paper, we have proposed our ISLE framework, which combines the pseudo-labels of several image-level segmentation techniques on a class-wise basis to leverage the strong points of its different components. The combined pseudo labels reach at least 2% higher mIoU scores than its components. Most of those gains stem from bigger variances within particular classes, as we observed that different approaches have different strengths and weaknesses. The ISLE framework combines any number of pseudo-labels to boost the quality of the pseudo-labels for final training. We showed that the predictions generated by the model trained with the pseudo labels of ISLE achieve state-of-the-art performance on the VOC2012 dataset showing its effectiveness. Our framework is open-source to ensure reproducible research and accessibility. The source code is accessible at https://github.com/ErikOstrowski/ISLE.

Acknowledgments. This work is part of the Moore4Medical project funded by the ECSEL Joint Undertaking under grant number H2020-ECSEL-2019-IA-876190. This work was also supported in parts by the NYUAD's Research Enhancement Fund (REF) Award on "eDLAuto: An Automated Framework for Energy-Efficient Embedded Deep Learning in Autonomous Systems", and by the NYUAD Center for Artificial Intelligence and Robotics (CAIR), funded by Tamkeen under the NYUAD Research Institute Award CG010.

References

1. Ren, J., Gaber, H., Al Jabar, S.S.: Applying deep learning to autonomous vehicles: a survey. In: 2021 4th International Conference on Artificial Intelligence and Big Data (ICAIBD), pp. 247–252. IEEE (2021)

2. Feng, D., et al.: Deep multi-modal object detection and semantic segmentation for autonomous driving: datasets, methods, and challenges. IEEE Trans. Intell. Transp. Syst. **22**(3), 1341–1360 (2020)
3. Diakogiannis, F.I., Waldner, F., Caccetta, P., Wu, C.: ResUNet-a: a deep learning framework for semantic segmentation of remotely sensed data. ISPRS J. Photogramm. Remote. Sens. **162**, 94–114 (2020)
4. Meenpal, T., Balakrishnan, A., Verma, A.: Facial mask detection using semantic segmentation. In: 2019 4th International Conference on Computing, Communications and Security (ICCCS), pp. 1–5. IEEE (2019)
5. Khan, K., Mauro, M., Leonardi, R.: Multi-class semantic segmentation of faces. In: 2015 IEEE International Conference on Image Processing (ICIP), pp. 827–831. IEEE (2015)
6. Milioto, A., Lottes, P., Stachniss, C.: Real-time semantic segmentation of crop and weed for precision agriculture robots leveraging background knowledge in CNNs. In: 2018 IEEE International Conference on Robotics and Automation (ICRA), pp. 2229–2235. IEEE (2018)
7. Barth, R., IJsselmuiden, J., Hemming, J., Van Henten, E.J.: Data synthesis methods for semantic segmentation in agriculture: a capsicum annuum dataset. Comput. Electr. Agric. **144**, 284–296 (2018)
8. Rehman, A., Naz, S., Razzak, M.I., Akram, F., Imran, M.: A deep learning-based framework for automatic brain tumors classification using transfer learning. Circ. Syst. Signal Process. **39**(2), 757–775 (2020)
9. Zhao, Z., Voros, S., Weng, Y., Chang, F., Li, R.: Tracking-by-detection of surgical instruments in minimally invasive surgery via the convolutional neural network deep learning-based method. Comput. Assist. Surg. **22**(sup1), 26–35 (2017)
10. Cordts, M., et al.: The cityscapes dataset for semantic urban scene understanding. In: Proceedings of the IEEE Conference on Computer Vision and Pattern Recognition, pp. 3213–3223 (2016)
11. Zhou, B., Khosla, A., Lapedriza, A., Oliva, A., Torralba, A.: Learning deep features for discriminative localization. In: Proceedings of the IEEE Conference on Computer Vision and Pattern Recognition, pp. 2921–2929 (2016)
12. Everingham, M., Van Gool, L., Williams, C.K., Winn, J., Zisserman, A.: The pascal visual object classes (VOC) challenge. Int. J. Comput. Vision **88**(2), 303–338 (2010)
13. Ahn, J., Kwak, S.: Learning pixel-level semantic affinity with image-level supervision for weakly supervised semantic segmentation. In: Proceedings of the IEEE Conference on Computer Vision and Pattern Recognition, pp. 4981–4990 (2018)
14. Jo, S., Yu, I.-J.: Puzzle-CAM: improved localization via matching partial and full features. In: 2021 IEEE International Conference on Image Processing (ICIP), pp. 639–643. IEEE (2021)
15. Xie, J., Hou, X., Ye, K., Shen, L.: CLIMS: cross language image matching for weakly supervised semantic segmentation. In: Proceedings of the IEEE/CVF Conference on Computer Vision and Pattern Recognition, pp. 4483–4492 (2022)
16. Li, Y., Kuang, Z., Liu, L., Chen, Y., Zhang, W.: Pseudo-mask matters in weakly-supervised semantic segmentation. In: Proceedings of the IEEE/CVF International Conference on Computer Vision, pp. 6964–6973 (2021)
17. Kim, B., Han, S., Kim, J.: Discriminative region suppression for weakly-supervised semantic segmentation. In: Proceedings of the AAAI Conference on Artificial Intelligence, vol. 35, pp. 1754–1761 (2021)
18. Yuan, Z. H., et al.: Deep-dense conditional random fields for object co-segmentation. In: IJCAI, vol. 1, p. 2 (2017)

Particulate Mapping Centerline Extraction (PMCE), a Novel Centerline Extraction Algorithm Based on Patterns in the Spatial Distribution of Aggregates

Jerry Zhou[1]([⊠]), Jack Zhou[1], Jie Xu[1], Bruce Gaynes[2], Parisa Maribod[1], and Mengren Wu[3]

[1] University of Illinois at Chicago, Chicago, IL 60607, USA
jzhou3379@gmail.com, jkzhou2005@gmail.com
[2] Loyola University Chicago, Chicago, IL 60660, USA
[3] Christian Brothers University, Memphis, TN 38104, USA

Abstract. The Particulate Mapping Centerline Extraction (PMCE) algorithm indirectly segments vessels and calculates their radii by mapping the locations of aggregates and finding patterns among their spatial distributions, something that is novel in the current literature. By utilizing aggregate detection, the PMCE method identifies erythrocyte aggregates and maps them into coordinate distributions that can be used for analysis. Experiments using microfluidic captures of artificial vessels were conducted to simulate blood flow and validate its accuracy. Results show close agreement between predicted and actual vessel radii. PMCE offers potential applications in studying clinical interpretations of microvascular hemorheological abnormality and coagulopathy.

Keywords: Centerline Extraction · Aggregate Distributions · Radii Estimation

1 Introduction

The bulbar conjunctiva is a densely vascularized tissue covering the sclera of the eye. It is one of a limited number of locations in the human body where red blood cell movement within the microcirculation can be directly and non-invasively visualized [1]. Viewing the microcirculation of the human eye involves a technique termed capillaroscopy, an efficient non-invasive method for obtaining videography of conjunctival blood flow. Capillaroscopy has evolved into an accepted method of describing the intravascular milieu from both hemorheological and microangiopathic perspectives. Disorders such as stroke and various forms of coagulopathy such as those related to COVID-19 are strongly correlated with abnormal hemorheological metrics [2–4] that may be observed by conjunctival capillaroscopy. Conjunctival capillaroscopy is based on the phenomena of color subtraction which exploits the hemoglobin absorption spectrum to demonstrate erythrocytes as dark objects against a bright background of light reflected by the sclera. With appropriate optics, one may resolve single erythrocytes which typically are seen as aggregates under various physical influences of pressure and shear as well as disease conditions. Erythrocyte aggregates seen on capillaroscopy often are of variable construct, and depending on the quality of the videography may be blob or daub-like.

Historically, in-vivo assessment of erythrocyte passage within the microvascular lumen has been conducted by iterations of a space-time analysis in which erythrocyte location is transformed on a coordinate system and then interpreted by evaluation of instantaneous velocity of a single erythrocyte temporally. The resultant output can be represented visually by a series of sloped lines indicating factors such as overall velocity, tube hematocrit, and flux [5]. While metrics such as erythrocyte velocity and flux provide important hemorheological measures of cardiovascular hemodynamics, the space-time analytic approach negates assessment of an important corollary to erythrocyte velocity, namely erythrocytic aggregate metrics and assessment of flow field homogeneity. From a hemorheological perspective, prior studies have suggested that assessment of erythrocyte velocity without consideration of flow field composition characterized by shear-induced viscosity, erythrocyte deformability, and flow field homogeneity has uncertain clinical value [6–8]. Homogeneity of the microvascular flow field is an important feature of the microvascular milieu and is thought to improve tissue oxygenation as well as reduce the likelihood of endothelial injury [8]. Accordingly, a sluggish, homogenous low flow may be better tolerated than a heterogenous high flow, even when total blood flow is lower [5]. Identification of "sluggish" flow is a product of erythrocyte aggregation and shear, the latter being a modifying factor in microvascular viscosity. The most common capillary red blood cell tracking method is based on spatiotemporal image (STI) analysis [5, 9]. Although current space-time analysis modalities provide metrics for velocity and identify flux and cell packing [5] from a signal processing perspective, space-time analysis does not fully describe the interaction and correspondence of signal features temporally.

An alternative analytic approach that optimizes the assessment of erythrocyte aggregation via color subtraction and benefits identification of homogeneity in the fluid space would be desirable, allowing for the identification of erythrocyte aggregates as signals applicable to data streaming and pattern recognition. Programs such as space-time analysis and cross-correlation can provide an essential measure of erythrocyte velocity. However, they do not adequately address the dynamic nature of erythrocyte aggregation and disaggregation in real-time conditions [10]. Moreover, modern techniques for the assessment of hemorheology in the conjunctival microvasculature rely on manual or semi-automated methods [11–14] and necessitate considerable user input, and are thus not applicable for high throughput analytics of large vessel networks. In contrast, fully automated vessel segmentation and blood flow detection allow for rapid and objective measurements of conjunctival hemorheological properties in large arteriolar and venular networks and which is compatible with broader AI interfaces is desirable. In this work, we utilize areas of particulates, as calculated from a robust daub detection algorithm, to describe erythrocyte aggregation and characterize flow regions and the vessel's boundary, centerline, radius, and diameter. Our method utilizes a contrast-limited adaptive histogram equalization (CLAHE) and an erosion operation combined with linear regression as a novel approach to daub detection, a process we have termed Particulate Mapping Centerline Extraction (PMCE).

2 Comparison to Existing Methods

The PMCE algorithm was inspired by the work done by Tetteh et al. [17], in which not using a form of vessel segmentation prior to centerline extraction and radius estimation was identified by their paper as being novel yet lacking within the current literature. In this sense, our approach to an old problem is novel, but the methods used in our approach are not. It is the new application of old and revised techniques to solve an old problem that makes the PMCE method novel. Due to our focus on two dimensional videos, we will only discuss existing methods for centerline extraction in this domain. To the best of our knowledge, this is the first method that utilizes aggregate detection and its distribution for centerline extraction and radii estimation purposes in the context of Computational Ophthalmology. In essence, we indirectly segment the vessel by mapping out the distributions of aggregate flow, while others directly segment the vessel by detecting its boundaries and not the particulates that flow within it.

Sang et al. [18] utilized multiscale Gabor even filters to offer flexible frequency bands and effective centerline enhancement. The Gabor filters were employed to detect centerlines in various vessel sizes and orientations. Its ability to tune to specific frequencies allowed for noise suppression and accurate centerline extraction in poor contrast and noisy backgrounds. The method also involved multiscale filtering, local maxima extraction, and hysteresis thresholding for segmentation of vessel boundaries.

Sofka et al. [19] aimed to improve the detection of low-contrast and narrow blood vessels in retinal images while eliminating false detections of non-vascular structures. They proposed a new vessel extraction technique that is based on a likelihood ratio test. The core of the technique includes a new matched-filter response derived in scale-space to handle vessels of varying widths. Additionally, they introduced a vessel confidence measure, computed vessel boundary measures, and associated confidences at potential vessel boundaries in each pixel among others. These responses formed a 6-dimensional measurement vector that was subsequently mapped to a likelihood ratio through histogram-based methods that estimated conditional probability density functions (pdfs) and their "vesselness" score.

Machine learning models for vessel segmentation and skeletonization are also popular. To accurately segment blood vessels in retinal images, Wang et al. [20] proposed using a convolutional neural network (CNN) as a trainable hierarchical feature extractor and a Random Forest (RF) as a classifier. Preprocessing was done by extracting the green channel of the RGB retinal image, followed by a histogram equalization and Gaussian filtering to enhance vessel-background contrast. The CNN was used to learn complex features from raw pixels and the RF predicted whether each pixel belonged to a blood vessel or not by using the learned hierarchical features from the CNN. This proved to be an effective and efficient approach for segmentation, as it achieved high accuracy for blood vessels that had varying widths, bends, and clustering.

3 Data Collection

3.1 Experimental Setup

The experimental setup employed a commercially available linear microfluidic chip (thin XXS LCS0109, IDEX Health & Science, Germany), featuring a square channel measuring 50 μm by 50 μm in cross-sectional area. To simulate blood flow, the microfluidic channel was connected to a syringe pump (Nexus 3000, CHEMYX, United States) via a tube, allowing for the loading of the blood sample (Fig. 1). The experimental setup involved mounting the device on the stage of an inverted microscope system (Nikon Eclipse Ti-S, Nikon Instruments Inc., Japan). The flow dynamics of the sample were observed and recorded using a high-speed camera (Phantom Miro M310, Vision Research Inc., United States). The recorded videos were subsequently analyzed to investigate the microfluidic flow within the 50 × 50 μm channels. To explore different flow conditions, three distinct infusion rates were employed: 0.045 μl/min, 0.06 μl/min, and 0.075 μl/min. These settings were applied to observe the flow under various scenarios, including blood flow both with and without the addition of dextran. To obtain a high-quality image sequence, the capturing parameters were carefully configured. The resolution was set to 1280 × 720, ensuring a clear and detailed image capture. Additionally, the frame rate was set to 60 frames per second (fps), allowing for smooth and fluid motion depiction in the recorded videos.

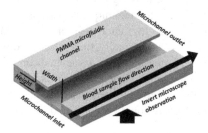

Fig. 1. A three-dimensional representation of the experimental setup

3.2 Sample Preparation

For this experiment, porcine whole blood obtained from Innovative Research (United States) was anticoagulated using a heparin solution. To simulate blood flow scenarios with and without erythrocyte aggregation, two separate groups of samples were prepared. In the erythrocyte aggregation group, a dextran-PBS solution was created by combining dextran with 1× phosphate buffer solution (PBS 1×, Corning, United States). This solution served to induce erythrocyte aggregation within the blood samples. The dextran used was Dx 500 molecular weight (31392 Sigma-Aldrich, United States). To prepare the dextran solution, it was diluted with PBS to obtain a final concentration of 2.5% [3]. Subsequently, the whole blood samples were mixed with the dextran solution. The mixture consisted of 6.25% blood and 93.75% dextran-PBS solution. This proportion ensured the desired concentration for simulating blood flow with erythrocyte aggrega-tion. To compare the effect of erythrocyte aggregation on blood flow, a group without erythrocyte aggregation was prepared for comparison. In this group, whole blood was diluted with $1\times$ PBS solution at the same dilution ratio as the group with dextran. The dilution ratio used for both groups was 6.25% blood and 93.75% PBS solution. The hematocrit in two group samples was considered equivalent, as the dilution ratio was equal in both experimental settings.

4   Methodology

In the PMCE algorithm, we employ two primary methods, beginning with aggregate detection. This algorithm draws inspiration from Koh Zhen's work [16], which aimed to automate the counting of microscopic cells. We made modifications and improvements to cater to our needs. Initially, each input video frame was extracted and stored with a label that corresponded to its chronological position. Erythrocytes, appearing as light gray spots with bright centers, posed a challenge in distinguishing them from the similarly colored phosphate buffer solution in each frame (Fig. 2).

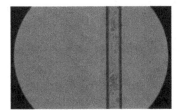

Fig. 2. A frame in a 50 × 50 μm microscope capture

To address this, we initially applied a bitwise not operation to darken erythrocyte centers, aiding distinguishability through pixel value inversion. However, this didn't fully separate them from the buffer solution, leaving indistinct smudges in certain areas. To address this issue, we employed contrast limited adaptive histogram equalization (CLAHE) and an erosion operation to redistribute pixel intensities and shrink erythrocyte boundaries, enhancing local contrasts. We further improved clarity by convoluting the resulting image with a sharpening 3 × 3 kernel, giving extra weight to the center pixel to emphasize the erythrocytes' relatively circular area which enabled differentiation between the foreground (erythrocytes) and background (PBS Solution). Through trial and error, this combination of image processing techniques delivered the best qualitative results despite much noise (Fig. 3).

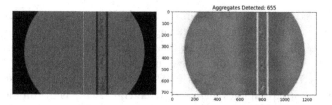

Fig. 3. The original frame (left) with aggregates shaded in (right)

Each extracted frame underwent this treatment, with the contour boundaries calculated via the Teh-Chin Chain approximation algorithm [15]. These boundaries were stored as coordinates in a three-dimensional NumPy array, something that can be understood as a blank canvas onto which all contour areas were filled in the RGB color space for both visualization and subsequent centerline extraction purposes (Fig. 4).

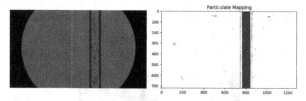

Fig. 4. A sample of the original vessel (left) and all the aggregates overlaid together (right)

Though the artificial vessels lacked cell-free layers, the microscope's shadow created an illusion of their presence near the flow boundaries, making the vessels appear larger than they are in the process. Since aggregate contours were distinguished based on pixel intensity contrasts with the background, the interior shadow boundary (ISB), external shadow boundary (ESB), and noise were also segmented due to their similar contrast with the background. This resulted in three areas of interest: noise, aggregate area of occupation (AAO), and shadow. These areas were distributed as shown in Fig. 5 due to our experimental setup.

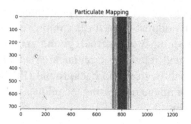

Fig. 5. The ESB (Green), ISB (Pink), Noise (yellow), and AAO (Blue). The shadow regions are comprised of the ISB and ESB (Color figure online)

To denoise, we reapplied the Teh-Chin chain approximation algorithm with a custom threshold on the minimum pixel intensity to the array that contained the previously segmented aggregate areas to isolate the boundaries of the shadow and AAO. Despite intending on removing the ISB and ESB, the pixel intensities of the aggregate contours and shadow were found to be too similar. Removing shadow regions also led to some removal of the AAO. The lower threshold was set through a series of trial-and-error attempts, optimizing noise removal from a qualitative perspective (Fig. 6).

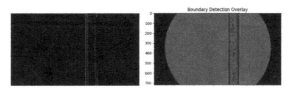

Fig. 6. Results after The-Chin chain approximation (left) and the overlay of the detected boundaries on the vessel (right)

To distinguish the AAO from the ISB, we utilized the rectangular geometry of the vessels and the unique distribution of the regions to collect the point density for each contour point along the x-coordinates. Peaks in point density indicated the likely boundary location. This comes from the assumption that the AAO had higher pixel intensities than those of the ISB due to the concentration of aggregates in flow (Fig. 7).

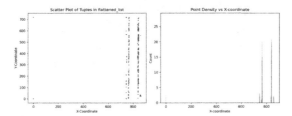

Fig. 7. The coordinate distribution of the detected AAO boundaries (left) and the corresponding point density (right)

Since the vessel boundaries correspond with those of the AAO, the midline between them can be found via midpoints along the vessel's entirety. The linear distance between it and the outer boundaries corresponds to the vessel's radii (Fig. 8).

Fig. 8. The leftmost AAO boundary (blue), Vessel Centerline (red), and rightmost AAO boundary (green) (Color figure online)

5 Accuracy of Method

For testing purposes, we created 24 different artificial vessels, half with dextran, half without, all with 50-μm diameters and variable flow rates (Table 1). To determine the accuracy of the predicted vessel radius, the ground truth radius was determined via a manual drawing on the 1st frame of the stationary microscope capture (Fig. 9).

Fig. 9. The user drawn diameter of the vessel (red, representing the vessel's ground truth radius). Seeing where the darkened inner boundary transitioned into the lighter gray of the background dictated the line's drawing. (Color figure online)

By establishing the pixel-to-micrometer ratio, comparisons could be made between the predicted length and the actual length for accuracy validation. Although we recognize that this may have introduced human error, distinguishing the ISB from the AAO from a visual standpoint was manageable and very discernible. Due to the unknown counts of erythrocytes in flow at different frames, we could not perform quantitative validation of the aggregate detection algorithm (ADA). However, radii and centerline accuracy can be thought of as a form of validation since accurate aggregate detection was vital for computing precise radii and centerlines post-denoising. All code and supporting data can be found at our public GitHub repo: https://github.com/PoohBear2/Particulate-Mapping-Centerline-Extraction.

From experimentation, a pattern emerges in the percent error between samples with and without dextran. On average, samples with dextran had a percent error of 5.02 while their counterparts had an average of 8.51. This trend also extends to the accuracy of estimated radii locations, determined through visual estimation of the graphed boundaries. Compared to dextran samples, the graphed boundaries for samples without dextran showed, at times, significant deviations from what was expected, something that can be explained by the more variable shapes of the aggregates in video.

Table 1. Results from testing 24 separate samples

Video Number	Predicted Radius (px)	Actual Radius (px)	% error	Dextran
1	40.0	38.0	5.263	YES
2	39.5	38.0	3.947	YES
3	38.0	37.5	1.333	YES
4	38.0	36.0	5.556	YES
5	39.0	36.0	8.333	YES
6	39.0	38.0	2.632	YES
7	40.0	38.5	3.896	YES
8	40.0	38.0	5.263	YES
9	38.0	36.0	5.556	YES
10	38.0	36.0	5.556	YES
11	38.5	37.0	4.054	YES
12	37.0	34.0	8.824	YES
13	37.0	35.0	5.714	NO
14	38.0	33.0	15.152	NO
15	38.5	36.0	6.944	NO
16	39.0	34.0	14.706	NO
17	38.0	33.0	15.152	NO
18	38.0	33.5	13.433	NO
19	40.0	37.5	6.667	NO
20	42.0	40.0	5.000	NO
21	38.0	36.5	4.110	NO
22	37.5	36.0	4.167	NO
23	37.5	35.5	5.634	NO
24	38.0	36.0	5.556	NO

6   Limitations and Suggestions for Future Development

The PMCE method consists of two sub methods: one for aggregate detection and another for centerline extraction in this order. We will begin this section by discussing the limitations and areas of improvement for the aggregate detection algorithm, followed by those for the centerline extraction algorithm. It is important to note that the accuracy of the latter algorithm is dependent on that of the former, and so, any changes that affect the aggregate detection algorithm's performance may result in potential modifications to the centerline extraction method, but not vice versa.

6.1 Aggregate Detection

The current aggregate detection algorithm (ADA) operates based on the underlying assumption that the erythrocytes will appear as dark smudges while the background, in comparison, will remain relatively light in coloration. This means that, in the process of capturing vessels on video, the lighting of the environment, combined with the variable resolution of different frames, will heavily dictate the ability for the PMCE algorithm to function correctly and identify erythrocytes accurately (Fig. 10). Furthermore, the only distinguishing factor that separates a potential erythrocyte from the background is its pixel intensity, something that increases the likelihood and abundance of false positives in the form of noise. Thus, we foresee that enhancing the current ADA's ability to distinguish the foreground, consisting of erythrocytes, from a background that has very little contrast in coloration will not only advance the accuracy in the number of identifiable aggregates, but also allow for better subsequent estimations of the vessels' boundaries and underlying statistics. The challenge of this task comes from the need to do this without a form of background subtraction, as doing so would compromise the uniqueness of our approach via the segmentation of vessel boundaries.

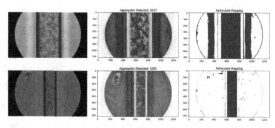

Fig. 10. Under different lighting conditions and levels of resolution, the number of detected aggregates and noise can vary significantly.

One may consider morphology to be an additional distinguishing criterion, but due to the tendency for erythrocytes to form clumps during flow, it is very easy for the variable shape of aggregates to be confused for irrelevant particles or vice versa under the current classification technique that is based on relative contrasts in pixel intensity. For this reason, traditional forms of thresholding may no longer be optimal, and the implementation of a convolutional neural network (CNN) may be necessary for the extraction of meaningful features through supervised training. For most cases, however, the current ADA provides the general framework for understanding the spatial distribution via coordinate mapping of erythrocytes in tubular flow, something that can also have applications in the understanding other statistics like flow rates and shear of different vessels in a vasculature like the bulbar conjunctiva.

6.2 Centerline Extraction

The two fundamental flaws in the current centerline extraction method are its assumption that the vessel in question is relatively straight and singular in number. This poses a compatibility problem with the previous aggregate detection algorithm, which can identify erythrocytes in vessels that are curved, overlapping, and multiple in number, provided that the given resolution and contrast between the background and foreground is high enough (Fig. 11). This is important because we envision the PMCE method to ultimately function for in-vivo vasculatures in the eye, particularly for the bulbar conjunctiva, which are oftentimes highly non-linear, clustered within tight spaces, and poorly separated from each other with little distinguishability.

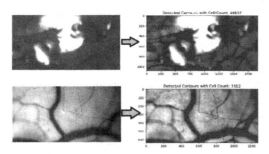

Fig. 11. Provided that the video capture is of good resolution, the ADA is capable of detecting aggregates in curved and bunched vasculatures.

Lee et al. [21] proposed a novel solution that uses the moving least-squares method, combined with a minimum spanning tree, region growth, and iterative refinement, to construct non-intersecting curves that represent the curved centerline of disordered distributions of 2-D points. However, their method does not address bifurcation points, an area of development that will need to be addressed before applications to complex, intersecting vasculatures can be made.

7   Concluding Statements

In conclusion, we have presented the Particulate Mapping Centerline Extraction (PMCE) algorithm, a novel approach for vessel centerline extraction and radii estimation based on the spatial distribution of aggregates in our lab created artificial vessels. PMCE demonstrates promising accuracy in vessel radius estimation and has many areas of improvement that are open for further investigation. While there are limitations, such as the dependence on lighting conditions and vessel shape, PMCE offers a valuable and new approach at assessing microvascular morphology.

References

1. Gaynes, B., Teng, P., Wanek, J., Shahidi, M.: Feasibility of conjunctival hemodynamic measurements in rabbits: reproducibility, validity, and response to acute hypotension. Microcirculation **19**(6), 521–529 (2012)
2. Wagner, C., Steffen, P., Svetina, S.: Aggregation of red blood cells: from rouleaux to clot formation. C. R. Phys. **14**(6), 459–469 (2013)

3. Renoux, C., et al.: Impact of COVID-19 on red blood cell rheology. Br. J. Haematol. **192**(4), e108–e111 (2021)
4. Neumann, F., et al.: Increased plasma viscosity and erythrocyte aggregation: indicators of an unfavourable clinical outcome in patients with unstable angina pectoris. Heart **66**(6), 425–430 (1991)
5. Ellis, C.G., et al.: Application of image analysis for evaluation of red blood cell dynamics in capillaries. Microvasc. Res. **44**(2), 214–225 (1992)
6. Kaliviotis, E., et al.: Quantifying local characteristics of velocity, aggregation and hematocrit of human erythrocytes in a microchannel flow. Clin. Hemorheol. Microcirc. **63**(2), 123–148 (2016)
7. Passos, A., et al.: The effect of deformability on the microscale flow behavior of red blood cell suspensions. Phys. Fluids **31**(9), 091903 (2019)
8. De Backer, D., et al.: How to evaluate the microcirculation: report of a round table conference. Crit. Care **11**(5), 1–9 (2007)
9. Koutsiaris, A.G., et al.: Blood velocity pulse quantification in the human conjunctival pre-capillary arterioles. Microvasc. Res. **80**(2), 202–208 (2010)
10. Yuan, J., Mills, K.: A cross-correlation-based method for spatial–temporal traffic analysis. Perform. Eval. **61**(2–3), 163–180 (2005)
11. Shahidi, M., Wanek, J., Gaynes, B., Wu, T.: Quantitative assessment of conjunctival microvascular circulation of the human eye. Microvasc. Res. **79**(2), 109–113 (2010)
12. Koutsiaris, A.G., et al.: Volume flow and wall shear stress quantification in the human conjunctival capillaries and post-capillary venules in vivo. Biorheology **44**(5), 375–386 (2007)
13. Jiang, D.H., et al.: Functional slit lamp biomicroscopy for imaging bulbar conjunctival microvasculature in contact lens wearers. Microvasc. Res. **92**, 62–71 (2014)
14. Cheung, A.T., Perez, R.V., Chen, P.C.: Improvements in diabetic microangiopathy after successful simultaneous pancreas-kidney transplantation: a computer-assisted intravital microscopy study on the conjunctival microcirculation1, 2. Transplantation **68**(7), 927–932 (1999)
15. Teh, C.-H., Chin, R.T.: On the detection of dominant points on digital curve. IEEE Trans. Pattern Anal. Mach. Intell. **11**, 859–872 (1989). https://doi.org/10.1109/34.31447
16. Blob Detection, designing a cell-counting microscope. https://blogs.ntu.edu.sg/ps9888-2021-g18/2021/07/23/blob-detection/. Accessed 15 May 2023
17. Tetteh, G., et al.: DeepVesselNet: vessel segmentation, centerline prediction, and bifurcation detection in 3-D angiographic volumes. Front. Neurosci. **14**, 1285 (2020). https://doi.org/10.3389/fnins.2020.592352
18. Sang, N., Tang, Q., Liu, X., Weng, W.: Multiscale centerline extraction of angiogram vessels using Gabor filters. In: Zhang, J., He, J.-H., Fu, Y. (eds.) CIS 2004. LNCS, vol. 3314, pp. 570–575. Springer, Heidelberg (2004). https://doi.org/10.1007/978-3-540-30497-5_89
19. Sofka, M., Stewart, C.V.: Retinal vessel centerline extraction using multiscale matched filters, confidence and edge measures. IEEE Trans. Med. Imaging **25**(12), 1531–1546 (2006). https://doi.org/10.1109/TMI.2006.884190
20. Wang, S., Yin, Y., Cao, G., Wei, B., Zheng, Y., Yang, G.: Hierarchical retinal blood vessel segmentation based on feature and ensemble learning. Neurocomputing **149**(Part B), 708–717 (2015). ISSN 0925-2312
21. Lee, I.-K.: Curve reconstruction from unorganized points. Comput. Aided Geom. Des. **17**(2), 161–177 (2000). https://doi.org/10.1016/S0167-8396(99)00044-8

Evaluating Segmentation Approaches on Digitized Herbarium Specimens

Kenzo Milleville[1,2]([✉]) [iD], Krishna Kumar Thirukokaranam Chandrasekar[1] [iD], Nico Van de Weghe[2] [iD], and Steven Verstockt[1] [iD]

[1] IDLab, Ghent University, Gent, Belgium
kenzo.milleville@ugent.be
[2] CartoGIS, Ghent University, Gent, Belgium

Abstract. Herbarium specimens form a physical database of plant bio-diversity. They are frequently used to study species diversity in different geographic regions or their evolution over time. These specimens have been digitized in bulk and made accessible to the public over the past few decades. These digitization efforts open up new research opportunities for automated processing and analysis. However, few publicly available labeled datasets for herbarium specimens exist. This work introduces a novel instance segmentation dataset of 250 digitized herbarium specimens from a diverse selection of herbaria. We experimented with several segmentation approaches on this dataset and discuss their strengths and limitations. For binary plant segmentation, U-Net and UNet++ achieved IoUs of 0.950 and 0.951, respectively. Popular instance segmentation models could accurately detect common herbaria objects with mask APs between 78.3 and 84.1 but typically struggled with the plant class. Only Mask2Former showed promising results on the plant class, achieving a mask AP of 77.0. Because most herbarium sheets contain a single specimen, the problem was also reformulated as a panoptic segmentation task, treating the plant class as a semantic class. In this context, a combination of YOLOv8 and UNet++ outperformed the Mask2Former model, achieving a higher IoU for the plant class and a higher mask AP for the non-plant objects. The dataset and code are available at: https://github.com/kymillev/herbarium-segmentation.

Keywords: Herbarium specimens · Plant segmentation · Deep learning · Instance segmentation

1 Introduction

Herbarium specimens record plant occurrences collected from all corners of the world, forming the foundation of systematic botany. They have been collected over several centuries and are carefully archived and preserved. Each specimen, typically a dried plant, is attached to a herbarium sheet. These sheets also contain essential information such as the plant's scientific name, collection date, geographical origin, and other relevant details. The herbarium sheets thus form

G. Bebis et al. (Eds.): ISVC 2023, LNCS 14362, pp. 65–78, 2023.
https://doi.org/10.1007/978-3-031-47966-3_6

a physical database of plant biodiversity and are used to study species diversity and their evolution over time. Furthermore, herbaria offer a unique opportunity to study past ecological conditions and the effects of climatic and other changes on plant populations. Following a report by the Index Herbatorium from 2021, there are close to 400 million herbarium specimens spread over 182 countries [22].

In the last few decades, many institutions have begun digitizing their archives and making their specimens accessible on various online repositories like GBIF[1] and iDigBio[2]. This digitization effort has led to a dramatic increase in accessibility and research focused on herbarium specimens. The digitization process involves taking a photograph or making a scan of the specimen followed by (manual) data entry for the specimen details (location, date, taxonomy, collector, etc.) [23]. This digitization is time-consuming, considering many collections contain thousands of herbarium sheets. Usually, a ruler and color card are added during digitization to provide color and size references, that are useful for later analysis.

Most herbarium sheets contain little or no metadata about the size and shape of the specimens. Therefore, performing large-scale studies on the morphological features of these specimens typically requires a tremendous manual effort. Several semi-automated tools exist, but most still require manual annotation or corrections, which limits the scope of such studies [5,24]. Luckily, computer vision and deep learning methods can be used to automatically analyze digitized herbarium specimens. The resulting metadata can then be used by researchers and botanists to delve deeper into plant biodiversity studies.

This work evaluates a number of segmentation methods to analyze digitized herbarium specimens. Popular binary, instance, and panoptic segmentation models were trained and evaluated. These models can segment the specimen(s) and common objects (rulers, color cards, notes, etc.) on each herbarium sheet. The strengths and limitations of each approach and model are discussed. Furthermore, we provide a novel instance segmentation dataset of 250 fully labeled herbarium sheets on which our models were trained and evaluated. This dataset was labeled semi-automatically, expanding upon our previous work [15].

The remainder of the paper is organized as follows: Sect. 2 gives an overview of related work regarding different segmentation methods and the processing of digitized specimens. Section 3 details our semi-automatic labeling method and dataset. Next, Sect. 4 describes the different approaches used to segment the herbarium sheets. Our results and findings are discussed in Sect. 5, and the paper concludes in Sect. 6.

2   Related Work

In recent years, deep learning-based object detection and segmentation models have become the most popular state-of-the-art methods. Object detection mod-

---

[1] https://www.gbif.org/.

[2] https://www.idigbio.org/.

els predict a bounding box for each recognized object. Such approaches work well for clearly defined objects and are easy to label. However, plant specimens can have a complex, non-convex shape, which makes these bounding boxes inaccurate with regard to the actual shape. Therefore, image segmentation techniques are preferred. These are categorized into three tasks: semantic, instance, and panoptic segmentation [11]. Semantic segmentation aims to classify each pixel in the image to a certain class, such as "plant" or "background". Instance segmentation not only categorizes each pixel but distinguishes between individual instances of each class. Panoptic segmentation combines these two types, segmenting both "stuff" (semantic) and "things" (instance) within the same framework.

Different segmentation models have been developed over the years to tackle these tasks. For semantic segmentation, U-Net [20] has been widely used, especially in the biomedical field. DeepLabV3+ [2] is another notable model used for semantic segmentation tasks. For object detection, YOLO [19] models are popular and performant. YOLOv8 [10] is one of the newer YOLO architectures, that is also capable of instance segmentation. Detectron2 [28] is another popular framework for instance and panoptic segmentation. It includes implementations of several popular models, such as Mask R-CNN [7]. More recently, vision transformers, which typically contain both convolutional and transformer layers, are among the state-of-the-art for segmentation tasks. Mask2Former [3] and OneFormer [9] are notable examples, which achieve outstanding accuracy and combine the three segmentation tasks into a single unified model. However, these newer architectures typically require more computational resources.

Semantic segmentation methods are frequently used to separate the specimen(s) from the background and tend to be very accurate. In [26], the authors published a dataset of 400 digitized fern specimens. They used a color thresholding method with manual corrections to extract the specimens from the background. Their retrained U-Net model achieved an F_1 score of 0.95. Similarly, [8] retrained DeeplabV3 and FRRN-A [18] models on a custom dataset of 395 herbarium specimens, achieving mIoU (mean intersection over union) scores of 0.981 and 0.992, respectively. Similar approaches are also applied to other types of specimens. In [27], the Mothra toolkit was developed to segment moth specimens, labels, and rulers, which were used to measure phenotypic characteristics. They then applied this method to over 180,000 specimens to perform large-scale studies.

The detection of leaves or other objects is typically performed via object detection or instance segmentation models. In [1], a modified YoloV3 model was used to detect leaves, buds, flowers, and fruits. After data augmentation, they achieved an F_1 score of 0.938, compared to 0.899 without augmentation. Deep Leaf [24] is an instance segmentation model, based on Mask R-CNN, that segmented leaves and common objects from herbarium specimens. It achieved a mIoU of 0.905 for the leaf segmentation on a dataset of 4000 images. Furthermore, the length of the recognized rulers was used to accurately estimate leaf morphological traits.

3   Dataset

This section details the dataset creation and the semi-automatic labeling method. The labeling was done in two steps, namely, the semi-automatic labeling of the plant specimen(s) followed by manual annotation of common herbaria objects.

3.1   Semi-automatic Labeling

We started with a random sample of 1500 images from the LifeCLEF 2020 Plant Identification Challenge [6] and included the 250 specimens from [4]. These images were resized such that their longest side measured 1024 pixels. We used this dataset to fine-tune our semi-automatic labeling approach for the plants.

First, the images were transformed into the LAB color space, which groups similar colors closer together than the traditional RGB color space. Next, k-means clustering was used with a k value of 3, to reduce the number of colors in the image. This facilitated the extraction of the foreground regions (plants and objects) from the background sheet. Then, the foreground regions were split via a connected components analysis.

We noticed that most non-specimen objects were rectangular and close to the image borders. Therefore, these were filtered based on their relative size, shape, and overlap with the page borders. For each foreground object, we calculated the overlap with the page border (outer 10% of the image) and the ratio of its area compared to the area of its bounding box. If these exceeded a predefined threshold, the object was filtered out. These thresholds were determined qualitatively and the full algorithm details are made available with our code. After filtering, each remaining specimen's mask was saved independently. Figure 1 shows the result after extracting the foreground objects and after filtering the non-specimen objects.

When the image contains multiple clearly separated specimens as in Fig. 1, it is trivial to separate the resulting masks and label each specimen independently. However, when multiple specimens overlap, separating them correctly becomes extremely difficult. Similarly, when a piece of the specimen is detached (e.g., a leaf or branch), it is difficult to determine whether this piece is part of the same specimen. Furthermore, many specimens are attached to the page with small pieces of tape. This tape is often not included in the foreground mask, resulting in disconnected specimens. Luckily, most of these issues were solved by dilating the masks first, then filtering, followed by an intersection with the original mask. The tape is sometimes (partly) included in the specimen mask, which is currently one of the main limitations of the semi-automatic labeling method.

After this process, the specimen masks were manually validated. Using an interactive script, we overlaid the masks on the original image and used keyboard inputs to quickly label them as correct or incorrect. The plant specimens were correctly extracted from 506 of the 1750 images (28.9%). The algorithm mainly failed due to the large variety of specimens, background colors, and objects in the dataset. For instance, some specimens had a larger surface area than

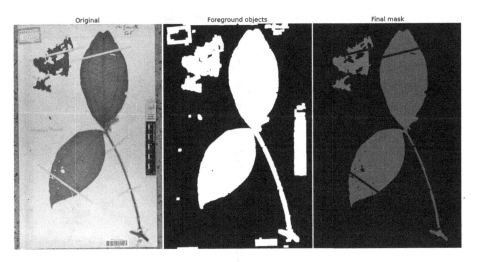

Fig. 1. From left to right: The original herbarium image. Result after segmenting and dilating the foreground objects. Final result after filtering the non-specimen objects (each color denotes a separate specimen). (Color figure online)

the background, which incorrectly labeled their color as background. The most common failure occurred when parts of another object were contained within the specimen mask. This frequently occurred when they were positioned close to one another or overlapping.

We selected a sample of 250 images from the manually validated images and labeled seven common object classes (ruler, color card, note, barcode, stamp, attachment, and other) with their bounding polygons via the LabelMe annotation tool [25]. The class "note" details any attached note or textual information on the page. "Attachment" was used to label additional items such as envelopes, or attached fruit. The class "other" denotes rare objects, such as photographs. We noticed that many color cards contained a ruler, therefore this ruler strip was also labeled separately as a ruler. This way, there is no need for an additional class indicating the presence of both. Finally, these annotations were converted to the COCO [14] format and merged with the specimen masks, to construct a complete instance segmentation dataset. Figure 2 visualizes two fully labeled herbarium sheets from the training set.

From the 250 labeled images, 30 were randomly selected as part of the validation set used throughout this work. Table 1 lists the number of labeled objects for each class and the percentage of images on which they occur. Due to the low number of "other" objects (8 occurrences in 3 images), these were deliberately not included in the validation set. The other classes are relatively balanced, with "note" being the most prominent class. Surprisingly, some labeled images did not contain a ruler, while others had multiple.

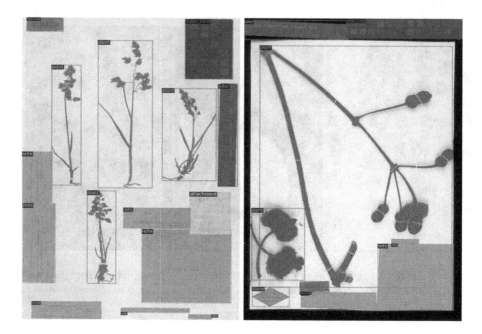

Fig. 2. Two herbarium sheets from the training set with their labels visualized. Different instances of the same class are visualized with the same color to improve clarity. Best viewed in color and with zoom.

Table 1. Number of different labeled objects in the dataset and the percentage of images on which they occur.

Class	Train (%)	Validation (%)
Note	551 (99.5)	83 (100)
Barcode	231 (95.9)	34 (96.7)
Stamp	221 (80.5)	30 (80.0)
Ruler	216 (92.3)	29 (86.7)
Color card	145 (59.5)	21 (60.0)
Attachment	125 (56.8)	19 (63.3)
Other	8 (1.4)	0 (0)

4   Herbarium Specimen Segmentation

This section details the different segmentation approaches used to analyze the herbarium sheets. First, binary specimen segmentation models are discussed. Next, several instance segmentation models are compared. Finally, a comparison is made between combining both types of models and using a single panoptic segmentation model to segment both specimens and objects.

4.1   Binary Plant Segmentation

Three semantic segmentation models were trained to extract the plants from the background. These include U-Net, UNet++ [29] (an improved version of U-Net), and DeeplabV3+. Each model was trained with the same encoder, namely EfficientNet-B0 [21], starting from weights pretrained on Imagenet. The herbarium images and masks were resized to (608,800) and each model was trained for a maximum of 200 epochs. We used Dice loss to train the models and saved the model with the lowest validation loss. During training, the images were augmented with random color jittering, rotations, and reflections. Table 2 lists the intersection over union (IoU) and F_1 scores for each model on the validation set. The results show a large difference between the U-Net and DeeplabV3+ models. Even though the Unet++ architecture is more complex and was shown to outperform U-Net for biomedical image segmentation, we found little difference for the plant segmentation.

Table 2. Binary plant segmentation results.

Model	IoU	F1
UNet++	**0.951**	**0.975**
U-Net	0.950	0.974
DeeplabV3+	0.915	0.954

4.2   Instance Segmentation

To detect both the plants and the other objects, we evaluated multiple instance segmentation models. These include YOLOv8l-seg (large), Mask R-CNN with FPN head, and Mask2Former (Swin-T backbone). For Mask R-CNN, we used the implementation from Detectron2 and also from Pytorch, both with a Resnet50 encoder. For YOLOv8 and Detectron2, their default training augmentations were used. For the Mask R-CNN and Mask2Former, we used custom data augmentations. Each model was trained for 200 epochs and the model with the lowest validation loss was saved.

To train the YOLOv8 model, the instance masks had to be converted to the YOLO format, namely a single polygon annotation per instance. This was done using their supplied conversion script. However, many plant masks contain holes and have complex shapes, which makes the resulting polygon representations inaccurate.

The resulting average precision (AP) scores for both the bounding boxes and masks are presented in Table 3, as well as the mask AP for the plant class and the average mask AP of all other classes (object AP). These scores were calculated using the official COCO evaluation code[3]. For the non-plant objects, all models

---

[3] https://cocodataset.org/#detection-eval.

72   K. Milleville et al.

Table 3. Results of the instance segmentation models.

Model	Box AP	Box AP50	Mask AP	Mask AP50	Plant AP	Object AP
Detectron2	76.7	95.7	68.4	85.4	9.0	78.3
Mask R-CNN	78.2	94.6	76.7	92.7	31.9	**84.1**
YOLOv8	**87.0**	**98.5**	78.5	**96.1**	48.1	83.5
Mask2Former	80.7	93.2	**78.9**	91.0	**77.0**	79.2

performed relatively well, with mask AP scores ranging from 78.3 to 84.1. For
the plant class, the Detectron2 and Mask R-CNN models scored poorly and their
predictions often contained only a part of the entire plant. Mask R-CNN scored
slightly better, potentially due to the custom data augmentation. The YOLOv8
model often predicted masks that were much bigger than the actual plant, which
also led to poor performance. The Mask2Former model scored well on both
plants and objects, making it a solid all-around choice. Figure 3 visualizes the
predictions with a minimum confidence score of 0.5 for each model on a sample
image from the validation set.

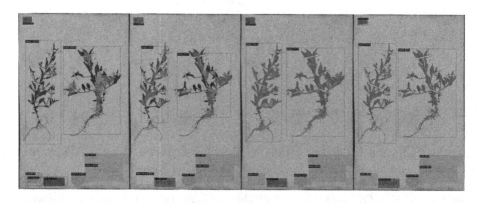

Fig. 3. Predictions from each model on a sheet from the validation set. From left to
right: Detectron2, Mask R-CNN, YOLOv8, and Mask2Former. Different instances of
the same class are visualized with the same color to improve clarity. Best viewed in
color and with zoom.

4.3 Panoptic Segmentation

Because most herbarium sheets only contain a single specimen, the problem
can be reformulated as a panoptic segmentation task. The specimen(s) can be
considered as a single "stuff" class (semantic segmentation) and the other objects
as "things" (instance segmentation). So every pixel denoting a specimen will be
labeled the same value, regardless of the number of specimens on the sheet. This

way, predictions for the specimens will not be incorrectly split into multiple instances.

We have tested two approaches: a combined output of the previous UNet++ for the plant class paired with a retrained YOLOv8 for the objects and a single Mask2Former model, retrained on the panoptic labels. The same train and validation splits as before were used. Each model was trained for a maximum of 200 epochs. Table 4 shows the resulting mask AP scores for the objects and IoU scores for the plant class.

Table 4. Results of the panoptic segmentation approaches. Mask AP scores were calculated for the non-plant classes only.

Model	Mask AP	Mask AP50	Plant IoU
YOLOv8 + UNet++	**83.7**	**98.3**	**0.951**
Mask2Former	81.6	95.7	0.899

The results show that the combined approach outperforms the Mask2Former model on both the objects and plant classes. Interestingly, the panoptic Mask2Former model performed slightly better on the objects than the previous instance segmentation model (mask AP of 81.6 vs 79.2). The combined approach achieved a mask AP of 83.7 and IoU for the plant class of 0.951, which are both better than the single Mask2Former model. Especially for the plant class, the difference in performance is clear. The Mask2Former model often struggled with segmenting smaller parts of the plants and objects. An example of this problem is shown in Fig. 4, where predictions for both approaches are visualized (instance predictions were thresholded with a minimum score of 0.5).

5 Discussion

Our results for binary plant segmentation are in line with [8,15,26], which also achieved IoU and F_1 scores upwards of 0.95. We can conclude that the U-Net architecture can quickly and accurately segment plants from the background. However, instance segmentation proved a much more difficult task. Only the Mask2Former model achieved a good segmentation of the plants, while the other models struggled. We suspect this is partly due to the Mask R-CNN architecture, which often smooths larger objects, removing the finer details [13]. The predictions from the YOLOv8 model were better, but still inaccurate, which was partly due to incorrect polygon labels.

For the non-plant objects, all models achieved a good performance, with mask APs ranging from 78.3 to 84.1. We suspect these results can be further improved by labeling additional data and using additional augmentation methods. Regarding processing time, the YOLOv8 model was the clear winner, which is an important consideration when processing large herbarium collections. The

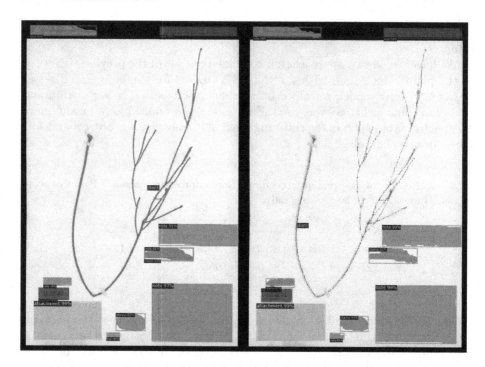

Fig. 4. Panoptic predictions on a sheet from the validation set for the combined app-roach (YOLOv8 and Unet++) on the left and for Mask2Former on the right. Best viewed in color and with zoom.

ruler class was generally the hardest to segment correctly, likely due to the many variations in the dataset. After post-processing, the extracted rulers can be used in combination with the plant masks to estimate the size and morphological traits of the specimens. Other objects can prove useful too, for instance, the notes can be cropped from multiple sheets and stacked into a single image. This reduces processing time for OCR tools and can often improve OCR results [16]. These results could then be used to improve or validate the manual data entry process during digitization.

By treating the segmentation as a panoptic segmentation task, we can leverage the performance and accuracy of the YOLOv8 and UNet++ models by combining their outputs. Such an approach achieves superior results compared to instance segmentation and is applicable when the herbaria sheets contain a single specimen or when semantic segmentation suffices for the plant class. We showed that this model combination outperformed a single panoptic Mask2Former model. Further tuning of the Mask2Former model can likely reduce this difference in accuracy. There are both benefits and drawbacks to using multiple models. The main drawback is that each model needs to be trained individually and then run separately for inference, which can increase processing time. Luckily, both UNet++ and YOLOv8 are quite performant and not memory-intensive. The benefit of using multiple models is that these can be trained on separate datasets. It is generally much easier to combine all the available binary plant segmentation datasets and retrain a plant segmentation model than it is to add object labels to these datasets, which are required to train a single panoptic model. This is also true for the instance segmentation model, although the used datasets would need to be normalized to contain the same object classes.

Because the binary segmentation models were trained on specimens labeled using the semi-automatic technique, this might bias the trained models and provide optimistic results. Therefore, we performed an additional qualitative evaluation of unlabeled specimens from the LifeCLEF dataset. We noticed that the segmentation results are generally comparable to the labeled dataset, but noticed some common segmentation errors. Plants were frequently not segmented entirely or split into multiple parts. Other times the predicted masks were larger than the plant. Three examples of predictions on the unlabeled dataset containing such errors are shown in Fig. 5. These errors also occurred on the labeled dataset, but typically to a lesser extent.

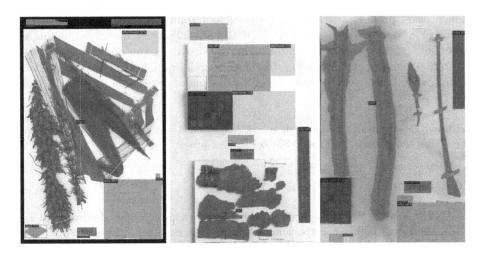

Fig. 5. Results of panoptic segmentation on the unlabeled dataset highlighting some common segmentation errors.

Regarding data labeling, the Segment Anything [12] model (SAM) or similar tools could be used to speed up the annotation of herbarium sheets. Our initial tests with SAM showed mixed results. Often, plants were split into multiple parts. This could however prove useful to annotate the specimens in a more detailed way, separating the leaves, branches, fruits, etc. [24] already showed promising results in calculating morphological features from leaves and we suspect such an approach can be generalized to additional parts of the specimens.

The main limiting factor for a more generic image processing approach is the lack of labeled image data [17]. It is a tedious and often difficult task to fully annotate herbarium sheets due to the diversity in species, objects, and quality. While this work introduced a novel instance segmentation dataset and promising results, additional research and labeled data are needed to further improve and evaluate the automated processing of herbarium sheets.

6 Conclusion

This work presented a novel instance segmentation dataset of herbarium specimens and evaluated different segmentation approaches. A semi-automatic labeling technique was used to label the dataset of 250 digitized herbarium specimens with plant masks. Next, polygon annotations for seven common herbarium objects were manually added. Different binary plant segmentation models were tested, with UNet++ achieving the highest IoU of 0.951. Four popular instance segmentation models were evaluated. YOLOv8l-seg and Mask R-CNN performed best on the object classes, achieving mask APs of 83.5 and 84.1, but they performed poorly on the plants. Mask2Former achieved the best overall results, with a mask AP of 78.9. The segmentation task was also reformulated as a panoptic segmentation problem, with the plant class as a semantic class. A combination of YOLOv8 and UNet++ outperformed the Mask2Former model, achieving a higher IoU for the plant class and a higher mask AP for the non-plant objects. While these results are promising, further research and labeled data are needed to improve and evaluate the automated processing of herbarium specimens on a larger scale.

Acknowledgements. The research activities described in this paper were funded by Ghent University, Imec, and the DiSSCo Flanders project.

References

1. Abdelaziz, B.: Walid: a deep learning-based approach for detecting plant organs from digitized herbarium specimen images. Eco. Inform. **69**, 101590 (2022). https://doi.org/10.1016/j.ecoinf.2022.101590. https://www.sciencedirect.com/science/article/pii/S1574954122000395
2. Chen, L.-C., Zhu, Y., Papandreou, G., Schroff, F., Adam, H.: Encoder-decoder with atrous separable convolution for semantic image segmentation. In: Ferrari, V., Hebert, M., Sminchisescu, C., Weiss, Y. (eds.) ECCV 2018. LNCS, vol. 11211, pp. 833–851. Springer, Cham (2018). https://doi.org/10.1007/978-3-030-01234-2_49
3. Cheng, B., Misra, I., Schwing, A.G., Kirillov, A., Girdhar, R.: Masked-attention mask transformer for universal image segmentation. In: Proceedings of the IEEE/CVF Conference on Computer Vision and Pattern Recognition (CVPR), pp. 1290–1299 (2022)
4. Dillen, M., et al.: A benchmark dataset of herbarium specimen images with label data. Biodiversity Data J. (7) (2019)
5. Gaikwad, J., Triki, A., Bouaziz, B.: Measuring morphological functional leaf traits from digitized herbarium specimens using Traitex software. Biodiversity Inf. Sci. Standards **3**, e37091 (2019). https://doi.org/10.3897/biss.3.37091

6. Goëau, H., Bonnet, P., Joly, A.: Overview of lifeCLEF plant identification task 2020. In: CLEF 2020-Conference and Labs of the Evaluation Forum, vol. 2696 (2020)

7. He, K., Gkioxari, G., Dollár, P., Girshick, R.: Mask R-CNN. In: Proceedings of the IEEE International Conference on Computer Vision, pp. 2961–2969 (2017)

8. Hussein, B.R., Malik, O.A., Ong, W.-H., Slik, J.W.F.: Semantic segmentation of herbarium specimens using deep learning techniques. In: Alfred, R., Lim, Y., Haviluddin, H., On, C.K. (eds.) Computational Science and Technology. LNEE, vol. 603, pp. 321–330. Springer, Singapore (2020). https://doi.org/10.1007/978-981-15-0058-9_31

9. Jain, J., Li, J., Chiu, M.T., Hassani, A., Orlov, N., Shi, H.: OneFormer: one transformer to rule universal image segmentation. In: Proceedings of the IEEE/CVF Conference on Computer Vision and Pattern Recognition, pp. 2989–2998 (2023)

10. Jocher, G., Chaurasia, A., Qiu, J.: YOLO by Ultralytics (2023). https://github.com/ultralytics/ultralytics

11. Kirillov, A., He, K., Girshick, R., Rother, C., Dollár, P.: Panoptic segmentation. In: Proceedings of the IEEE/CVF Conference on Computer Vision and Pattern Recognition, pp. 9404–9413 (2019)

12. Kirillov, A., et al.: Segment anything. arXiv preprint arXiv:2304.02643 (2023)

13. Kirillov, A., Wu, Y., He, K., Girshick, R.: PointRend: image segmentation as rendering. In: Proceedings of the IEEE/CVF Conference on Computer Vision and Pattern Recognition, pp. 9799–9808 (2020)

14. Lin, T.-Y., et al.: Microsoft COCO: common objects in context. In: Fleet, D., Pajdla, T., Schiele, B., Tuytelaars, T. (eds.) ECCV 2014. LNCS, vol. 8693, pp. 740–755. Springer, Cham (2014). https://doi.org/10.1007/978-3-319-10602-1_48

15. Milleville, K., Thirukokaranam Chandrasekar, K.K., Verstockt, S.: Automatic extraction of specimens from multi-specimen herbaria. ACM J. Comput. Cultural Heritage 16(1), 1–15 (2023)

16. Owen, D., et al.: Towards a scientific workflow featuring natural language processing for the digitisation of natural history collections. Res. Ideas Outcomes 6, e55789 (2020). https://doi.org/10.3897/rio.6.e55789

17. Pearson, K.D., et al.: Machine learning using digitized herbarium specimens to advance phenological research. BioScience 70(7), 610–620 (2020). https://doi.org/10.1093/biosci/biaa044

18. Pohlen, T., Hermans, A., Mathias, M., Leibe, B.: Full-resolution residual networks for semantic segmentation in street scenes. In: Proceedings of the IEEE Conference on Computer Vision and Pattern Recognition, pp. 4151–4160 (2017)

19. Redmon, J., Divvala, S., Girshick, R., Farhadi, A.: You only look once: unified, real-time object detection. In: Proceedings of the IEEE Conference on Computer Vision and Pattern Recognition, pp. 779–788 (2016)

20. Ronneberger, O., Fischer, P., Brox, T.: U-net: convolutional networks for biomedical image segmentation. In: Navab, N., Hornegger, J., Wells, W.M., Frangi, A.F. (eds.) MICCAI 2015. LNCS, vol. 9351, pp. 234–241. Springer, Cham (2015). https://doi.org/10.1007/978-3-319-24574-4_28

21. Tan, M., Le, Q.: EfficientNet: rethinking model scaling for convolutional neural networks. In: Chaudhuri, K., Salakhutdinov, R. (eds.) Proceedings of the 36th International Conference on Machine Learning. Proceedings of Machine Learning Research, vol. 97, pp. 6105–6114. PMLR (2019). https://proceedings.mlr.press/v97/tan19a.html

22. Thiers, B.M.: The world's herbaria 2021: a summary report based on data from index herbariorum (2022). https://sweetgum.nybg.org/science/wp-content/uploads/2022/02/The_Worlds_Herbaria_Jan_2022.pdf
23. Thiers, B.M., Tulig, M.C., Watson, K.A.: Digitization of the New York botanical garden herbarium. Brittonia **68**, 324–333 (2016)
24. Triki, A., Bouaziz, B., Gaikwad, J., Mahdi, W.: Deep leaf: mask R-CNN based leaf detection and segmentation from digitized herbarium specimen images. Pattern Recogn. Lett. **150**, 76–83 (2021)
25. Wada, K.: Labelme: Image Polygonal Annotation with Python. https://github.com/wkentaro/labelme
26. White, A.E., Dikow, R.B., Baugh, M., Jenkins, A., Frandsen, P.B.: Generating segmentation masks of herbarium specimens and a data set for training segmentation models using deep learning. Appl. Plant Sci. **8**(6), e11352 (2020)
27. Wilson, R.J., et al.: Applying computer vision to digitised natural history collections for climate change research: temperature-size responses in British butterflies. Methods Ecol. Evol. **14**(2), 372–384 (2023)
28. Wu, Y., Kirillov, A., Massa, F., Lo, W.Y., Girshick, R.: Detectron2 (2019). https://github.com/facebookresearch/detectron2
29. Zhou, Z., Rahman Siddiquee, M.M., Tajbakhsh, N., Liang, J.: UNet++: a nested U-Net architecture for medical image segmentation. In: Stoyanov, D., et al. (eds.) DLMIA/ML-CDS -2018. LNCS, vol. 11045, pp. 3–11. Springer, Cham (2018). https://doi.org/10.1007/978-3-030-00889-5_1

Semantic Scene Filtering for Event Cameras in Long-Term Outdoor Monitoring Scenarios

Tobias Bolten[1]($\boxtimes$) , Regina Pohle-Fröhlich[1], and Klaus D. Tönnies[2]

[1] Institute for Pattern Recognition, Hochschule Niederrhein,
Reinarzstr. 49, 47805 Krefeld, Germany
{tobias.bolten,regina.pohle}@hs-niederrhein.de
[2] Department of Simulation and Graphics, University of Magdeburg,
Universitätsplatz 2, 39106 Magdeburg, Germany
klaus@isg.cs.uni-magdeburg.de

Abstract. Event cameras are biologically inspired devices. They are fundamentally different from conventional frame-based sensors in that they directly transmit an (x, y, t) output stream of asynchronously and independently detected changes in brightness. For the development of monitoring systems, scenario-based long-term experiments are much more representative than day-to-day experiments. However, unconstrained "real-world" factors pose processing challenges.

To perform a semantic scene filtering on the output stream of an event camera in such an outdoor monitoring scenario, this paper describes a multi-stage processing chain. The goal is to identify and store only those segments that contain events that were triggered by a specific set of objects of interest. The main idea of the proposed processing pipeline is to pre-process the data stream using different filters to identify Patches-Of-Interest (PoIs). These PoIs, natively represented as space-time event clouds, are further processed by PointNet++, a 3D-based semantic segmentation network. An evaluation was performed on about 89 h of real-world outdoor sensor data, achieving a semantic filtering with a false negative rate of $\approx$3.8% and a true positive rate of $\approx$96.2%.

Keywords: Event Camera · Semantic Filtering · Semantic Segmentation · Long-Term Monitoring

1 Introduction

As a result of neuromorphic engineering, event cameras such as Dynamic Vision Sensors (DVS) are sensors with a fundamental difference in the basic output paradigm compared to classical CCD or CMOS image sensors. The pixels of a DVS operate independently and asynchronously and are activated by local changes in brightness above a defined threshold [6].

This work was supported by the European Regional Development Fund under grant number EFRE-0801082 as part of the project "plsm" (https://plsm-project.com/).

G. Bebis et al. (Eds.): ISVC 2023, LNCS 14362, pp. 79–92, 2023.
https://doi.org/10.1007/978-3-031-47966-3_7

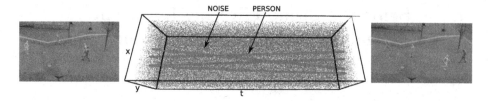

Fig. 1. DVS space-time event cloud output example for scene with moving people (polarity information discarded and false-color applied for highlighting).

The result is a sparse, multi-dimensional output stream of triggered pixels at a variable data rate, rather than traditional 2D frames captured at a fixed rate. Each of these pixel activations in this stream is called an "event" and contains (a) the local (x, y) coordinates within the sensor array for the activated pixel, (b) an activation timestamp for that event, and (c) a polarity indicator describing the direction of the triggering brightness change. An example of such an output stream is shown in Fig. 1.

Dynamic Vision Sensors are well suited for use in monitoring scenarios due to their characteristics such as high dynamic range, high temporal resolution, low power consumption and low signal redundancy [6]. In this paper, we address the task of semantic scene filtering within a DVS-based long-term monitoring in the context of a real outdoor scenario to identify temporal segments of further interest. The main challenges that need to be addressed include sensor noise, small-sized objects of interest, environmental influences that originate from the outdoor context, and limited computational capacity within the application scenario itself. A multi-stage processing chain is presented to address these issues.

The rest of this paper is organized as follows. Section 2 provides an overview of the measurement scenario and summarizes related work. The proposed multi-stage processing pipeline is described in Sect. 3. Practical results are presented and evaluated in Sect. 4. Finally, conclusions are drawn in Sect. 5.

2   Measurement Scenario and Goal

The proposed semantic filtering pipeline aims at identifying temporal segments containing triggered DVS events caused by a limited set of object classes. Sensor noise as well as environmental influences should be ignored and filtered out by this processing. The identified temporal segments will be stored for further, more detailed offline analysis, e.g. to extract movements and behavior of the detected objects of interest within the monitored area.

As part of this work, a DVS-based monitoring system was installed in an urban public space that served as a Living-Lab. The data collected during this monitoring was used to develop and evaluate the proposed pipeline. The sensor mounting was realized on a pole at a height of ≈6 m with an angle of inclination of about 25° to the ground (an exemplary sensor FoV is given in Fig. 3c). As the measurement system is completely self-sufficient using buffered solar energy it has limited power and computing resources.

2.1   Related Work

Ideally, an output event should be triggered only when there is an actual brightness change in the scene. However, the output of currently available sensors contains a significant amount of noise [8,11]. A major form of noise in Dynamic Vision Sensors are so-called background activity events. These are DVS events triggered by pixels that are not caused by a brightness change in the scene.

DVS event stream filters are one way to deal with them (see [8] for a comprehensive overview). Simple spatio-temporal filters, such as neighborhood and time filters (like [9,11]) or deep-learning based denoising approaches [2] are described in the literature.

However, for outdoor measurements, as described in [4], in addition to background noise, artifacts from environmental influences can be expected in the sensor signal. The work in [4] has also shown that, while these simple spatio-temporal filters achieve a significant reduction in background noise, larger amounts of environmental noise remain in the signal. These environmental artifacts are triggered, for example, by rain or flying insects, global brightness changes due to clouds or shadows, and object motion due to wind, and must be accounted for in the processing pipeline.

As a result, simple processing that relies solely on event filtering, with a subsequent decision based only on the number of events, will be prone to false positives in an outdoor scenario. A higher level semantic analysis of the event stream is necessary. Adapting object detection approaches (like [5,10,13]) or applying semantic segmentation (like [1,3]) to the event stream are two possible strategies to solve this problem.

Due to the privacy requirements of the monitored persons, a technical solution without classical video/image acquisition is desired. DVS-based monitoring allows analysis without processing gray or color values within the software logic, as the detection of changes is already handled in the sensor hardware. Classical CCTV surveillance systems and their processing are therefore not considered in this work. However, to the best of the authors' knowledge, there is currently no prior work that applies and evaluates such semantic DVS stream analysis in the context of a real-world outdoor measurement scenario to derive semantic scene filtering.

3   Processing Pipeline

A multi-stage semantic filtering pipeline is described, where the object recognition part is triggered only by a defined set of classes by means of segmentation. To reduce the subsequent computational load, the event stream is spatiotemporally pre-filtered to identify potential sliding time windows as well as patches of interest within these windows. This is followed by semantic segmentation of the selected space-time event cloud patches (see also Fig. 4a). Based on this segmentation, a decision is made whether to save the current data. The complete process, outlined in Fig. 2, is described in detail in the following subsections.

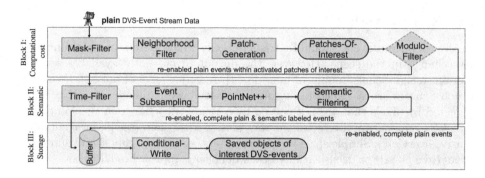

Fig. 2. Structure of proposed conditional writing pipeline.

All processing stages have in common that the continuous event stream is processed in non-overlapping sliding time windows of 60 ms duration.

3.1   Block I: Patches-of-Interest (PoI)

The basic idea of this step is a classical divide and conquer approach. The goal is to pre-process the input stream with simple and fast operators. Thus, only patches of interest need to be processed by subsequent steps with significantly higher computational requirements. It is assumed and intended that regions containing mainly environmental noise and artifacts may pass these steps, but will be rejected later. The processing starts with the removal of all events outside the monitored area (mask-filter of fixed areas, e.g. public sidewalks). This is followed by restrictive filtering of sensor noise.

Compared to the patching performed in [15], where small 6×6 px 2D-frame patches are built and processed together by a transformer network, we divide the sensor plane into patches that contain enough spatial resolution to be processed meaningfully and independently using just the (x, y, t) information of each patch itself. For the identification of active areas, we divide the (x, y) sensor plane into equal-sized patches. The usable resolution[1] of 768×512 px of the DVS is divided into 16 fields, each with the size of 192×128 px. The choice of this patch size depends directly on the requirements of the next processing step and is described and justified in the next subsection.

To mark a patch as active or inactive for further processing, we rely on spatio-temporal filtering and thresholding. Following the analysis of spatio-temporal event filters in [4] and the runtime requirements for real-time event stream filtering as in our use case, we decided to apply the *Neighborhood-Filter* logic mentioned in their work to reduce the noise artifacts contained.

---

[1] The used CeleX-IV DVS [7] offers a total resolution of 768×640 px, but due to technical limitations of the sensor hardware, the upper 128 pixel lines were deactivated for recording.

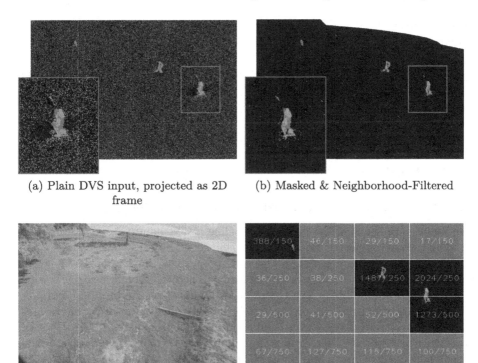

(a) Plain DVS input, projected as 2D frame

(b) Masked & Neighborhood-Filtered

(c) Grayscale image of empty scene given for clarification

(d) PoI extraction by thresholding

Fig. 3. Step-by-step visualization of Patch-of-Interest (PoI) generation. (Active PoIs are selected by applying an event threshold depending on the row of the patch, shown as (#triggeredEvents/#threshold) after filtering in Fig. 3d. Discarded patches are grayed out.)

For each event, a filter decision is evaluated based on a minimum number of other events in the 8-connected neighborhood. This filter was chosen because the above-mentioned analysis showed that this filter, in addition to a deep learning based approach, achieves a very restrictive filtering result while still maintaining enough true object events for subsequent identification of active areas. These steps are illustrated in Figs. 3a and 3b.

Due to the basic properties of a DVS, a separation of static background and moving parts is already done at the sensor-level. Therefore, the accumulated number of filtered events within these patches can be used as a simple measure of changes within the scene (ignoring their semantic origin). Finally, to flag a patch as an active *Patch-Of-Interest* (PoI), a threshold is applied to the filtered event count. To account for different perspective distances and the corresponding differences in the number of triggered events, different thresholds are used for each row of patches. These thresholds were empirically optimized and selected

during the performed long-term monitoring. This thresholding procedure is illustrated in Fig. 3d.

Only active flagged patches will be processed further. Sometimes the filtered
event counts in many or even all patches may exceed the threshold for a long
period of time (e.g. due to heavy rain) and be marked as active. This would
lead to very high runtime requirements in the later processing. Therefore, it
is possible to skip the downstream processing for a limited number of sliding
windows (shown as Modulo-Filter in Fig. 2). Skipped time windows are stored
directly in the write-buffer, and their final processing is based on the result of
adjacent, fully processed segments.

3.2   Block II: Semantic Analysis Utilizing PointNet++

The main component of the proposed pipeline is a semantic segmentation step
for the previously selected PoIs into a specific set of object classes.

We suggest using the work of [3] for this step, as they have published an evaluation of different neural network approaches to achieve semantic segmentation
in DVS long-term monitoring scenarios based on 3D space-time event cloud processing. In addition, the authors have published detailed network configurations
as well as pre-trained network weights from their experiments. The 3D-based
processing proved to be faster and of equal or higher quality than a counterpart
based on frame conversion and the application of classical 2D CNN segmentation
networks. Further details are given in Sect. 4.

However, the number of input events forming the space-time event clouds
must be limited for this processing. Figure 4a visualizes such an input cloud,
which is directly generated from the (x, y) and t coordinates of the DVS event
stream without any further processing. Using the CeleX-IV DVS, the average
number of events for an unprocessed and complete sliding time window in our
scenario is approximately 60k events (see Fig. 4b), as measured by the data
further evaluated in Sect. 4. The number of events is too large in terms of computation and runtime for the intended segmentation. Therefore, the previously
created Patches-of-Interest are further processed separately.

For each active PoI from the previous computation block, the performed
neighborhood filtering is reset, and the plain event stream is restored within
these patches. It is necessary because the previous filtering is rather restrictive
and may remove events belonging to the desired object structures. To adapt the
work of [3], we follow their described DVS preprocessing methodology to meet
the requirements of the pre-trained PointNet++ [14]. The first step is to apply
a less restrictive time filter to suppress some included background activity noise.
It removes events that were not supported by other events at the same spatial
position within the last 10 ms. It results in an average event count per PoI that
approximately matches the expected input size of 4096 events for the provided
network configurations (see Fig. 4c). The Patches-of-Interest are then randomly
sampled to exactly match this input size.

After applying PointNet++ for semantic segmentation to the pre-processed
(x, y, t) event cloud, each event has a class label associated with it. Figures 4a

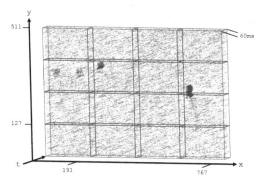

(a) 3D (x, y, t) Space-time event cloud; PoI borders and semantic segmentation visualized

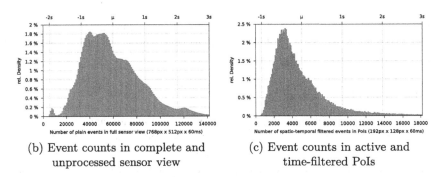

(b) Event counts in complete and unprocessed sensor view

(c) Event counts in active and time-filtered PoIs

Fig. 4. Space-time event cloud visualization and event count considerations.

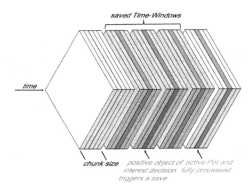

Fig. 5. Visualization of conditional buffer write logic (sliding time windows marked in green indicate a positive filtering decision that results in writing the gray chunks). (Color figure online)

Table 1. Runtimes for CPU-intensive computation parts at different input event counts in kilo events [kE] (averaged over 150 sliding time windows of 60 ms, computed on an Intel(R) Core(TM) i7-8700 CPU @ 3.20 GHz).

Processing step	Mean runtime for one 60 ms time window		
	50kE	170kE	420kE
Mask-Filter	1.026 ms	1.415 ms	3.230 ms
	±0.25	±0.45	±1.00
Neighborhood-Filter	6.494 ms	13.638 ms	42.946 ms
	±1.54	±1.96	±5.31
Time-Filter	0.379 ms	21.740 ms	46.167 ms
	±0.11	±4.42	±7.46

and 6 show sample results of this semantic segmentation. The final write decision is made in the next processing block based on the number of events belonging to a specific set of object classes of interest.

3.3   Block III: Conditional Write

The complete and incoming sliding windows may or may not have labels within their patches due to the ability to skip semantic segmentation. They are stored in a temporal first-in-first-out buffer capable of holding a fixed number of time windows. The size of this buffer depends on a defined number of *chunks*. Each chunk contains at least one time window in which a PointNet++ based semantic segmentation must have taken place, regardless of any skipping.

The binary decision to write a complete sliding window of temporal data to disk is based on the number of events labeled as objects of interest within the fully processed and semantically segmented PoIs of each chunk. Events predicted as background or environmental noise are discarded. A patch-based minimum thresholding is applied to the remaining events. It is equivalent to the thresholding approach described above for determining active PoIs earlier in the pipeline, except that the thresholding is applied *only* to the events labeled as objects of further interest.

To ensure the continuity of the saved sliding window chunks, not only the chunk that contains the positive object count threshold is saved, but also the chunk immediately before and after it. This procedure is visualized in Fig. 5.

4   Practical Application and Results

Based on the use of the semantic segmentation network of [3], including its pretrained weights and thus also its underlying training dataset of [4], we inherit the class categorization of PERSON, DOG, BICYCLE, and SPORTSBALL as objects of interest for our experiments. The classes BACKGROUND NOISE, BIRD, INSECT, RAIN, TREE, and SHADOW are considered as unwanted environmental artifacts.

Table 2. Patch-of-Interest (PoI) generation statistics for the entire sensor stream

Date	Rain in $1/m^2$	Time windows w/o any active PoI per day	Mean number of active PoIs per time-window
Thu, July 02	6.4	71.34%	1.95
Fri, July 03	0.0	38.30%	5.97
Sat, July 04	0.9	42.63%	2.12
Sun, July 05	0.1	43.34%	4.09
Mon, July 06	1.7	44.31%	4.49
Tue, July 07	1.2	44.23%	4.66
Wed, July 08	7.3	92.63%	0.61
Thu, July 09	0.0	47.13%	3.16
Fri, July 10	1.0	40.15%	5.85
Sat, July 11	0.0	9.53%	6.83
All		46.93%	4.57

4.1 Runtimes

As mentioned in Sect. 2, the used on-site system is completely solar powered. The semantic segmentation of the events within the selected PoIs by the PointNet++ network has the highest computational requirements in the entire processing chain. An advantage of this network architecture is that each point is processed by *shared* Multi-Layer Perceptrons (MLPs). This results in relatively small networks, which is very advantageous in the application scenario. As a result, we were able to use an NVIDIA Jetson TX2 module on site as an energy-efficient edge AI computing device instead of a power-hungry traditional GPU.

Using this resource-limited module results in an average runtime of 159 ms (±7.14 ms, measured over 10k individual executions, each with a batch size of one for live processing) for the PointNet++ inference. In a worst-case scenario with all 16 PoIs permanently activated, this enables a possible complete processing every ≈2.54 s. However, a real-world analysis of activated PoIs (see Table 2) shows that this scenario is very unlikely to occur. In the analyzed period of 10 days about ≈47% of the sliding time windows contained no activated PoI at all. In the remaining time, on average, less than a third of the PoIs were active. This shows that PointNet++ processing could generally be achieved at a higher frequency.

The test period evaluated included different days of the week, usage scenarios, and weather conditions with widely varying rates of activated PoIs. E.g., compare Wednesday, July 8th with Saturday, July 11th. On that Wednesday, there was no significant activity except for some very short and heavy rain showers. It resulted in a high percentage of data that can be discarded in the first processing step. On the other hand, on the aforementioned Saturday, a high level of activity

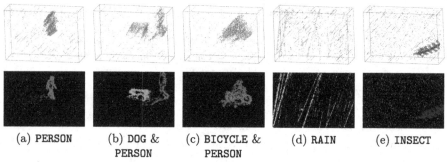

(a) PERSON   (b) DOG &   (c) BICYCLE &   (d) RAIN   (e) INSECT
                    PERSON   PERSON

(top row: 3D space-time event cloud; bottom row: 2D false-color frame projection)

Fig. 6. Example segmentation results (best viewed in color).

combined with environmental influences such as moving shadows resulted in many PoIs that had to be processed later.

Apart from semantic segmentation, the event stream filters consume most of the runtime. These operations are implemented with an $O(\text{eventCount})$ complexity and are each executed by individual threads. Therefore, the real-time requirement is satisfied if each step is processed in less than the length of a sliding time window. Table 1 shows the average runtimes per filter used in relation to typical total input event counts under different environmental conditions. The practical tests indicate that each of these filters is capable of running fast enough to process the event stream in real time, since the continuous event stream is processed in sliding windows of 60 ms.

4.2   Quality

Semantic Segmentation

According to the work of [3], whose shared PointNet++ pre-trained weights are also the basis for the semantic segmentation within our presented pipeline, very satisfying results are achieved. Their performed evaluation reports an F1-score of ≈ 0.93 for the separation of the semantic classes of the DVS-OUTLAB dataset [4]. For a qualitative evaluation of the results, examples of PoI segmentations are shown in Fig. 6. However, the goal of the proposed pipeline is not just the semantic segmentation of event streams processed as space-time event clouds formed over short sliding time windows, but the analysis of continuous recordings at the scene level. In order to further assess the capability of PointNet++ to separate the previously described objects of interest from environmental influences, we extended their evaluation by taking into account the learned features.

The basic assumption is that good features should be discriminative. This means that features of the same object category should be close together, while features of different object categories should be far apart. For this purpose, we consider the feature vectors generated by PointNet++ before the last fully connected layer, which generates the final probability distribution vector. For

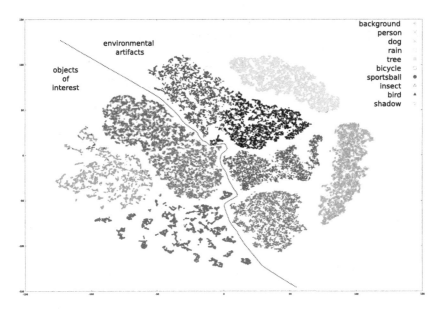

Fig. 7. Two-dimensional t-SNE [12] visualization of the PointNet++'s feature space used for segmentation.

the selected network configuration, this is a 128-dimensional feature vector per input point.

We computed these vectors for 5000 randomly selected input points per class and applied t-SNE [12] to project the features onto a 2D plane. Figure 7 shows the visualization of this latent feature space, which indicates that the desired class groups can be easily separated by the chosen network structure and weights.

Scene Filtering

To evaluate the quality of the filtering achieved, we focus on the two types of errors (a) *false negatives* (wanted but not recorded) and (b) *false positives* (recorded but not wanted). To determine these errors, we examined the complete, unprocessed recordings of one DVS over 10 days, as shown in Table 3. This results in a total of 88.95 h of recording. The results are compared with manual annotations made by a human observer. This comparison was made as follows for keeping annotation costs in an acceptable range.

A 2D frame representation of the DVS stream was exported for every 32nd sliding time-window of the unprocessed event stream by projecting the events onto the xy plane. It results in one frame every $32 \cdot 60 \,\mathrm{ms} = 1.92 \,\mathrm{s}$. Considering the size of the observed area, this temporal sub-sampling is acceptable because desired objects such as people would still be visible while crossing the area due to their expected speed. This sampling procedure results in a total of $\approx 166.7 \,\mathrm{k}$ exported frames which were manually checked for objects of interest.

Table 3. Filtering quality results of the proposed pipeline (TP/TN $\hat{=}$ true positive, true negative; FP/FN $\hat{=}$ false positive, false negative).

Date	activity annotated by human	TP Rate "sensitivity"	TN Rate "specificity"	FP Rate "false alarm"	FN Rate "missed"	F1 Score
Thu, July 02	11.27%	0.994	0.993	0.007	0.006	0.969
Fri, July 03	18.20%	0.962	0.988	0.012	0.038	0.954
Sat, July 04	32.16%	0.971	0.985	0.015	0.029	0.970
Sun, July 05	23.30%	0.952	0.981	0.019	0.048	0.944
Mon, July 06	10.21%	0.977	0.974	0.026	0.023	0.886
Tue, July 07	10.37%	0.946	0.986	0.014	0.054	0.916
Wed, July 08	1.50%	0.848	0.994	0.006	0.152	0.761
Thu, July 09	13.37%	0.979	0.985	0.015	0.021	0.945
Fri, July 10	4.63%	0.937	0.990	0.010	0.063	0.873
Sat, July 11	28.55%	0.957	0.976	0.024	0.043	0.948
All	15.13%	0.962	0.985	0.015	0.038	0.941

False negatives: In this process, 969 detections were marked by the human observers that were not saved by the proposed processing pipeline. This results in a false negative rate of ≈4%. However, almost all (724 out of 969, ≈75%) of these missing detections occurred in the top row of recorded patches, where recorded content was far away from the sensor. The resulting small object sizes, mentioned as one of the main challenges for processing, make it difficult even for human observers to distinguish between objects and noise. Therefore, these cases are also likely to be very difficult for other automated processing approaches.

False positives: The execution of the proposed processing chain on the plain recordings resulted in the storage of about ≈14.06 h of the total input data. These saved time windows were compared to the manually annotated frames from the previous step. The modulo 32 step of these exported and manually annotated frames corresponds to the modulo skip setting during automatic processing. In this way, the resulting chunks were compared to each other. This resulted in 2090 chunks stored by the automated processing that were not marked as active by the human reference, resulting in a false positive rate of ≈1.45%.

Due to the good results of the applied semantic segmentation, the presented pipeline overcomes the aforementioned artifacts caused by environmental influences. In the presented numerical results, this is shown by the inclusion of rain.

However, on rainy days fewer people use the outdoor area (e.g. Wednesday, July 08 with only 1.5% annotated activity time) and the processing becomes more complicated. On particularly rainy days, the false negative rate increases and objects are missed. However, the false alarm rate and the specificity remain at an acceptable level. This shows that good robustness to rain is achieved.

However, desired objects may be (partially) occluded by rain in the sensor's field of view, resulting in lower detection sensitivity.

In general, the evaluation shows that the presented processing pipeline is able to identify relevant time segments in the context of a long-term observation and to store them for later, more detailed evaluation.

5   Summary and Conclusion

We presented a processing chain capable of semantically filtering temporal segments containing only movements caused by a specific set of objects of interest within a DVS long-term outdoor monitoring. While the evaluation is application specific, the proposed processing pipeline can be generalized to other use cases since the classes for objects of interest and "unwanted" events can be easily changed. The use of DVS in real-world setups is still very rare. A comparison with other approaches or on other labeled datasets was not possible due to unavailability. This is also due to the novelty of the sensor technology. However, the proposed pipeline and application can be used as a positive reference for other researchers.

The processing first identifies potentially relevant Patches-of-Interest through filtering and thresholding. The main part uses 3D semantic segmentation to identify the parts of the sensor signal that contain only events caused by objects of interest. An evaluation showed a high capability of semantic filtering. On a large test dataset, an overall F1 result of ≈ 0.94 was achieved for the separation of continuous long-term recordings at the scene level, taking into account limited computational resources.

A possible further extension of the pipeline is a post-processing of the obtained segmentation, e.g. by deriving motion and velocity parameters of segmented objects over time. This information could be integrated into the pipeline to improve the discrimination between objects of interest and noise. Another interesting point that will be addressed in future work is the performed selection of *fixed* sized patches. These areas are used to determine the Patches-of-Interest for further processing by the pipeline, and are formed to meet the input event count requirements for semantic processing. An adaptive selection of PoI sizes may improve the described processing.

References

1. Alonso, I., Murillo, A.C.: EV-SegNet: semantic segmentation for event-based cameras. In: 2019 IEEE/CVF Conference on Computer Vision and Pattern Recognition Workshops (CVPRW), pp. 1624–1633 (2019). https://doi.org/10.1109/CVPRW.2019.00205
2. Baldwin, R.W., Almatrafi, M., Asari, V., Hirakawa, K.: Event probability mask (EPM) and event denoising convolutional neural network (EDnCNN) for neuromorphic cameras. In: Proceedings of the IEEE/CVF Conference on Computer Vision and Pattern Recognition (CVPR) (2020). https://doi.org/10.1109/CVPR42600.2020.00177

3. Bolten, T., Lentzen, F., Pohle-Fröhlich, R., Tönnies, K.: Evaluation of deep learning based 3D-point-cloud processing techniques for semantic segmentation of neuromorphic vision sensor event-streams. In: Proceedings of the 17th International Joint Conference on Computer Vision, Imaging and Computer Graphics Theory and Applications - Volume 4: VISAPP, pp. 168–179. INSTICC, SciTePress (2022). https://doi.org/10.5220/0010864700003124

4. Bolten, T., Pohle-Fröhlich, R., Tönnies, K.D.: DVS-OUTLAB: a neuromorphic event-based long time monitoring dataset for real-world outdoor scenarios. In: Proceedings of the IEEE/CVF Conference on Computer Vision and Pattern Recognition (CVPR) Workshops, pp. 1348–1357 (2021). https://doi.org/10.1109/CVPRW53098.2021.00149

5. Chen, G., et al.: Multi-cue event information fusion for pedestrian detection with neuromorphic vision sensors. Front. Neurorobot. **13**, 10 (2019). https://doi.org/10.3389/fnbot.2019.00010

6. Gallego, G., et al.: Event-based vision: a survey. IEEE Trans. Pattern Anal. Mach. Intell. **44**(1), 154–180 (2022). https://doi.org/10.1109/TPAMI.2020.3008413

7. Guo, M., Huang, J., Chen, S.: Live demonstration: a 768 × 640 pixels 200Meps dynamic vision sensor. In: 2017 IEEE International Symposium on Circuits and Systems (ISCAS), p. 1 (2017). https://doi.org/10.1109/ISCAS.2017.8050397

8. Guo, S., Delbruck, T.: Low cost and latency event camera background activity denoising. IEEE Trans. Pattern Anal. Mach. Intell. (2022). https://doi.org/10.1109/TPAMI.2022.3152999

9. Guo, S., Wang, L., Chen, X., Zhang, L., Kang, Z., Xu, W.: SeqXFilter: a memory-efficient denoising filter for dynamic vision sensors (2020). https://doi.org/10.48550/arXiv.2006.01687

10. Jiang, Z., et al.: Mixed frame-/event-driven fast pedestrian detection. In: 2019 International Conference on Robotics and Automation (ICRA), pp. 8332–8338 (2019). https://doi.org/10.1109/ICRA.2019.8793924

11. Khodamoradi, A., Kastner, R.: O(N)-space spatiotemporal filter for reducing noise in neuromorphic vision sensors. IEEE Trans. Emerg. Top. Comput. 15–23 (2018). https://doi.org/10.1109/TETC.2017.2788865

12. Van der Maaten, L., Hinton, G.: Visualizing data using t-SNE. J. Mach. Learn. Res. **9**(11) (2008)

13. Perot, E., De Tournemire, P., Nitti, D., Masci, J., Sironi, A.: Learning to detect objects with a 1 megapixel event camera. In: Advances in Neural Information Processing Systems, vol. 33, pp. 16639–16652 (2020). https://doi.org/10.48550/arXiv.2009.13436

14. Qi, C.R., Yi, L., Su, H., Guibas, L.J.: PointNet++: deep hierarchical feature learning on point sets in a metric space. In: Proceedings of the 31st International Conference on Neural Information Processing Systems, NIPS 2017, pp. 5105–5114. Curran Associates Inc., Red Hook (2017). https://doi.org/10.48550/arXiv.1706.02413

15. Sabater, A., Montesano, L., Murillo, A.C.: Event transformer. a sparse-aware solution for efficient event data processing. In: Proceedings of the IEEE/CVF Conference on Computer Vision and Pattern Recognition, pp. 2677–2686 (2022). https://doi.org/10.1109/CVPRW56347.2022.00301

SODAWideNet - Salient Object Detection with an Attention Augmented Wide Encoder Decoder Network Without ImageNet Pre-training

Rohit Venkata Sai Dulam[(✉)] and Chandra Kambhamettu

Video/Image Modeling and Synthesis (VIMS) Lab, University of Delaware, Newark,
DE 19716, USA
{rdulam,chandrak}@udel.edu

Abstract. Developing a new Salient Object Detection (SOD) model involves selecting an ImageNet pre-trained backbone and creating novel feature refinement modules to use backbone features. However, adding new components to a pre-trained backbone needs retraining the whole network on the ImageNet dataset, which requires significant time. Hence, we explore developing a neural network from scratch directly trained on SOD without ImageNet pre-training. Such a formulation offers full autonomy to design task-specific components. To that end, we propose SODAWideNet, an encoder-decoder-style network for Salient Object Detection. We deviate from the commonly practiced paradigm of narrow and deep convolutional models to a wide and shallow architecture, resulting in a parameter-efficient deep neural network. To achieve a shallower network, we increase the receptive field from the beginning of the network using a combination of dilated convolutions and self-attention. Therefore, we propose Multi Receptive Field Feature Aggregation Module (MRFFAM) that efficiently obtains discriminative features from farther regions at higher resolutions using dilated convolutions. Next, we propose Multi-Scale Attention (MSA), which creates a feature pyramid and efficiently computes attention across multiple resolutions to extract global features from larger feature maps. Finally, we propose two variants, SODAWideNet-S (3.03M) and SODAWideNet (9.03M), that achieve competitive performance against state-of-the-art models on five datasets. We provide the code and pre-computed saliency maps here.

Keywords: Salient Object Detection · CNN · Self-Attention

1 Introduction

2D Salient Object Detection (SOD) is a dense prediction task to identify objects of interest in images that attract humans' immediate attention. Earlier works on SOD used hand-crafted priors, while recently, the focus has shifted to learning-based approaches using Convolutional Neural Networks (CNN) [5,16,25] and Transformers [14,27,31].

G. Bebis et al. (Eds.): ISVC 2023, LNCS 14362, pp. 93–105, 2023.
https://doi.org/10.1007/978-3-031-47966-3_8

SOD has vastly benefitted from multi-scale features extracted by pre-trained backbones [6,15,20], so most current works [5,8,13,14,17,23–25,29,31] build on top of them. Nevertheless, they have some drawbacks. Firstly, pre-trained backbones designed for image classification are trained on the ImageNet dataset. [7] suggests that models trained on the ImageNet dataset utilize local information like textures and contrast information to classify objects. Since SOD requires a sound understanding of local and global features, ImageNet pre-training might be sub-optimal. Additionally, designing a deep learning model for Image Classification and developing new feature refinement modules to fine-tune a downstream task like SOD takes significant time and effort. Also, architecturally, the most famous pre-trained convolutional backbone for SOD, ResNet-50, uses a stack of small convolution kernels with identical receptive fields at each layer. Hence, attaining a global receptive field requires significant downsampling of the input, causing a dilution of essential features and an increase in parameters. Owing to these shortcomings, we propose a deep learning model for SOD that does not use ImageNet pre-training and performs comparatively against other state-of-the-art methods at a fraction of the parameters.

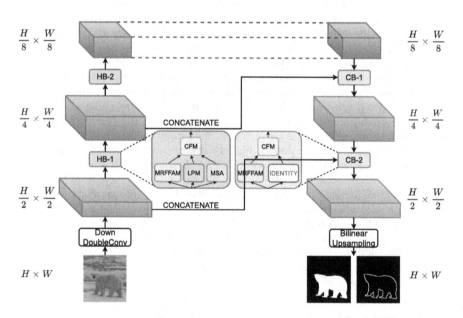

Fig. 1. SODAWideNet. Each of the hybrid blocks (HB) consists of three parallel streams, namely MRFFAM, LPM, and MSA. Features extracted by these individual modules are input to the CFM, which becomes the output of the hybrid block. In the convolution block (CB), features are refined by the MRFFAM before upsampling. [Best viewed in color] (Color figure online)

Inspired by vision transformers' ability to attain a global receptive field at every layer, we propose a novel encoder-decoder-style neural network called

SODAWideNet, which uses large convolutional kernels and self-attention for Salient Object Detection. Furthermore, to expand the receptive field at every layer of our network, we propose Multi-Receptive Field Feature Aggregation Module (MRFFAM), a fully convolutional module made of dilated convolutions to encode long-range dependencies. To increase the receptive field further, we employ self-attention in our model. Although very powerful, calculating attention is computationally intensive, especially for high-resolution feature maps. To remedy this shortcoming, we propose Multi-Scale Attention (MSA), which creates a feature pyramid using average pooling and then computes attention across scales. Local information, including contrast and texture, is also necessary to identify an object. Hence, we propose a Local Processing Module (LPM) to extract features from a local area using 3 × 3 convolutions. Finally, we use contour information as an auxiliary learning task to generate better saliency predictions. This use of contour detection changes the problem into multi-task learning, which helps our model learn more discriminative features beneficial to both SOD and contour detection. We briefly summarize our contributions below -

1. We propose **SODAWideNet** and **SODAWideNet-S**, two deep learning models that use large convolutional kernels and attention at every layer to extract long-range features without significant downsampling of the input.
2. To efficiently extract and combine features from multiple receptive fields using dilated convolutions from larger resolutions, we propose Multi Receptive Field Feature Aggregation Module (MRFFAM).
3. To compute self-attention on high-resolution inputs efficiently, we propose Multi-Scale Attention (MSA).

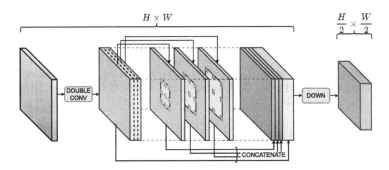

Fig. 2. Multi Receptive Field Feature Aggregation Module (MRFFAM) [Best viewed in color]

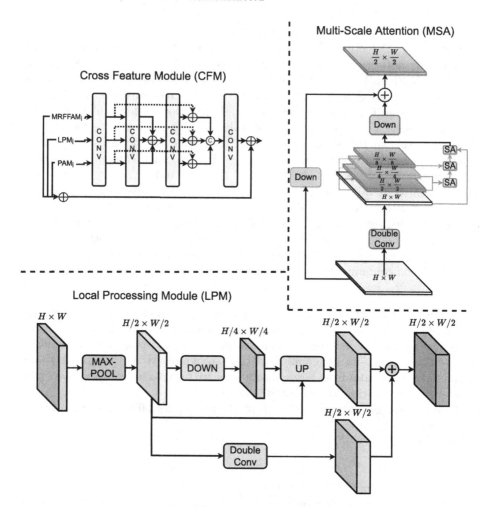

Fig. 3. Cross Feature Module (CFM), Multi-Scale Attention (MSA), and Local Processing Module (LPM). In MSA, ⟶ indicates the feature map used to compute the keys and values, and⟶ indicates the feature map to compute the queries. [Best viewed in color] (Color figure online)

2   Related Works

The first works in SOD used non-learning-based techniques whose performance was limited. Then came deep learning-based approaches based on fully convolutional neural networks that gave promising results.

Liu *et al.* [13] (PiCANet-R) proposes a pixel-wise contextual attention module to selectively attend to informative context locations for each pixel from the features from the Resnet-50 backbone [6]. Qin *et al.* [17] (BASNet) uses a pretrained ResNet34 [6] deep learning model and a boundary refinement module to generate saliency predictions. Wei *et al.* [24] (F3-Net) use a cross-feature module (CFM) and cascaded feedback decoder (CFD) to generate saliency predictions using a pre-trained ResNet-50 model [6]. Liu and Zhang *et al.* [14] (VST) propose a transformer-based SOD model using a T2T-ViT [30] pre-trained transformer. Yang *et al.* [29] use a progressive self-guided loss function that simulates a morphological closing operation on the model predictions to progressively create auxiliary training supervisions to guide the training process incrementally. They use the ResNet-50 model [6] as a pre-trained backbone. Zhang *et al.* [31] (Generative Transformer) propose a vision transformer following an energy-based prior for salient object detection. Ke *et al.* [8] (RCSB) uses contour information and a pre-trained ResNet-50 model [6] to generate crisp boundaries for saliency prediction. Cheng *et al.* [5] (CSF-Net) add cross stage fusion (CSF) to a Res2Net50 [4] pre-trained on the ImageNet dataset [1] to produce saliency predictions. Wu and Liu *et al.* [25] (EDNet) use an extreme downsampling technique to obtain high-level features essential for accurate saliency prediction. First, they pre-train their backbone on the ImageNet dataset [1] before fine-tuning it for SOD. Xie *et al.* [27] (PGNet) generates saliency predictions by combining features from a pre-trained Resnet18 backbone [6] and a Swin-B 224 transformer [15] encoder to produce saliency predictions. Zhuge and Fan *et al.* [32] use a Swin-B-22k [15] encoder to extract semantic features refined by novel feature aggregation modules. Lee *et al.* [9] uses an EfficientNet [21] backbone to produce saliency predictions. Different from all the above methods, we do not use any pre-training.

3 Method

Our model SODAWideNet, is shown in Fig. 1 builds upon the famous U-Net [18] deep learning architecture. In this section, we briefly introduce the U-Net architecture and list some of its components. We then go into details of individual pieces of the SODAWideNet model, namely MRFFAM, LPM, MSA, Hybrid, and Convolutional blocks. Finally, we describe the loss function used to train the proposed model.

3.1 Overview of U-Net

U-Net is an encoder-decoder-style model that consists of a series of downsampling and upsampling layers. Below, we describe the downsampling block -

$$ConvB(x, d) = ReLU(BN(F_{3\times3, d}(x)))$$

$$Double\_Conv(x) = ConvB(ConvB(x, 1), 1)$$

$$Down(x) = Double\_Conv(max\_pool(x))$$

Similarly, the upsampling block can be described as shown below -

$$Up(x, y) = Double\_Conv(cat(Upsampling(x), y))$$

where $F_{3\times3,d}$, BN, ReLU, max_pool, cat, and Upsampling imply a 3×3 convolution with dilation rate 'd', Batch Normalization, Rectified Linear Unit, Maxpooling, concatenation operation, and bilinear upsampling by a factor of two, respectively.

3.2 Multi-receptive Field Feature Aggregation Module (MRFFAM)

Multi-Receptive Field Feature Aggregation module extracts and aggregates semantic information from multiple receptive fields. Similar to transformers which attain a global receptive field through self-attention, these convolution kernels obtain information from larger contexts. As shown in Fig. 2, at each layer, the input to MRFFAM is divided in the channel dimension and is input to various dilated convolutions with different dilation rates. Like *Double_Conv*, we use two dilated convolutions in series for each dilation rate. Dilation rates used at each layer are shown in Table 1, obtained through thorough experimentation.

Table 1. Configuration of MRFFAMs used at each block of SODAWideNet.

Input Resolution	Layer	Dilation Rates	Output Resolution
$192 \times 192 \times 64$	HB1	6, 10, 14, 18, 22	$96 \times 96 \times 128$
$96 \times 96 \times 128$	HB2	6, 10, 14, 18	$48 \times 48 \times 128$
$48 \times 48 \times 64$	CB2	6, 10, 14, 18	$48 \times 48 \times 64$
$96 \times 96 \times 64$	CB3	6, 10, 14, 18, 22	$96 \times 96 \times 64$

Distinction From ASPP Module. The primary difference between MRFFAM and ASPP is the location of these modules. ASPP extracts long-range features from the output of a pre-trained backbone, whereas MRFFAM is employed at each layer of our network, making it an essential component of the backbone. Secondly, dilated convolutions in MRFFAM work on a subset of the input, unlike ASPP, where every convolution operation processes the entire feature maps. Finally, our formulation provides scope for future works to explore different dilation rates for various input resolutions.

3.3 Local Processing Module

Local features like texture and contrast are essential to differentiate between foreground and background. Instead of solely relying on a single scale to extract local features, we use two different scales, as seen in Fig. 3. Context from multiple scales enables the network to obtain richer local features. The successive max-pooling layers help obtain the most discriminative features from a smaller neighborhood which are further refined by the network.

3.4   Multi Scale Attention (MSA)

Self-attention is one of the most significant contributors to the success of vision transformers. This is because self-attention enables a global receptive field and introduces input dependency in the network. Unlike convolutional weights, which are frozen during inference, the dot product between queries and keys instills reliance on the input, forcing the network to extract semantically rich features. Although very powerful, calculating attention is computationally expensive. Hence, we create a feature pyramid and compute attention across multiple resolutions. To construct the feature pyramid, we reduce the spatial resolution of the input using average pooling and refine them using *Double_Conv*. Once created, we compute attention among the top two resolutions in the stack and continue the process until we reach the lowest resolution in the feature map stack. Finally, we calculate attention between the lowest resolution and the input of the feature map stack. The lowest resolution in each of the pyramids is $R^{H/16 \times W/16}$ where $H \times W$ is the spatial resolution of the input image. Figure 3 illustrates the MSA module. The keys and values are computed from higher resolution feature map, whereas the queries are computed from smaller resolution. Hence, the output's spatial resolution is the same as the query's.

Differences From Spatial Reduction Attention (SRA). SRA uses strided convolutions to reduce the spatial resolution of feature maps before computing attention. However, strided convolutions can only summarize features effectively with large amounts of training data. Additionally, SRA reduces the resolution once and calculates attention between the queries and the downsampled keys. In contrast, we adopt a hierarchical approach to reducing the spatial resolution to compute attention, thus retaining essential features.

3.5   Cross Feature Module (CFM)

Features from the MRFFAM, LPM, and MSA entail varying semantic contexts. We modify the CFM layer in [24] to effectively combine them. The architecture is illustrated in Fig. 3. The output at each layer of our model is the output of the CFM block. As seen from the architecture, each input passes through a series of *Conv* layers which is similar to *ConvB* but uses GroupNorm [26].

3.6   Hybrid and Convolution Blocks

Although our model is an encoder-decoder-style network, the encoder is heavier than the decoder. Furthermore, each encoder layer is a hybrid block since it contains convolutional and attention modules. $MRFFAM_i$, LPM_i, and MSA_i are the outputs of the previously proposed models. The output of a hybrid block is -

$$HB_i = CFM_i(MRFFAM_i, LPM_i, MSA_i)$$

Similarly, each decoding block is called a convolution block due to only using the MRFFAM, which is a fully convolutional module. The only other operation in this block is the identity operation which indicates using the input X_i to the convolutional block as is.

$$CB_i = CFM_i(MRFFAM_i, X_i)$$

3.7   Loss Function

Fig. 4. Given the image and its groundtruth in images one and two, α in Eq. 1 determines the weight for individual pixels, shown in three. Red indicates a more significant weight, whereas blue indicates a lower weight. (Color figure online)

We modify the loss function proposed by [24] which is a custom Weighted Binary Cross-Entropy loss (BCE) and IoU loss. The authors calculate a parameter $\alpha_{i,j}$ to assign weights for each pixel (i, j). It is the difference between the average values of all pixels in a window centered at a particular pixel and the center pixel's value. Instead, we use the maximum value in the window. Figure 4 shows the weights assigned to each pixel. The third image shows each pixel's $\alpha_{i,j}$ value. Intuitively, the pixels of the salient object and its surroundings should have a higher weight, which we obtain through our formulation of $\alpha_{i,j}$. Equation 1 shows the calculation of α.

$$\alpha_{ij} = max(A_{ij}) \tag{1}$$

where A_{ij} represents the area surrounding pixel (i, j). Hence, the final loss function is defined as -

$$L_{Salient} = L_{wBCE} + L_{wiou} + L_{wL1} + L_{SSIM} \tag{2}$$

where L_{wiou} is the weighted IOU loss used in [24], L_{wL1} is the L1-loss, and L_{SSIM} is the SSIM loss. 'w' indicates that the loss value is calculated per pixel and then multiplied with that pixel's $\alpha_{i,j}$. Similarly, we use a weighted combination of BCE, Dice Loss [2], and SSIM loss for contour generation.

$$L_{Contour} = 0.001 \cdot L_{bce} + L_{dice} + L_{SSIM} \tag{3}$$

4 Results and Ablation Experiments

Table 2. Comparison of our method with 15 other methods in terms of max F-measure F_{max}, MAE, and E_m measures. The greater the value in all measures except MAE, the better performance. * indicates models trained from scratch on SOD instead of ImageNet pre-trained weights.

Method	Params. (M)	DUTS-TE [22]			DUT-OMRON [28]			HKU-IS [10]			ECSSD [19]			PASCAL-S [11]		
		F_{max}	MAE	E_m	F_{max}	MAE	E_m	F_{max}	MAE	E_m	F_{max}	MAE	E_m	F_{max}	MAE	E_m
Models with Pre-trained Backbone																
PiCANet-R$_{CVPR'18}$ [13]	47.22	0.860	0.051	0.862	0.803	0.065	0.841	0.918	0.043	0.936	0.935	0.046	0.913	0.868	0.078	0.837
BASNet$_{CVPR'19}$ [17]	87.06	0.860	0.048	0.884	0.805	0.056	0.869	0.928	0.032	0.946	0.942	0.037	0.921	0.860	0.079	0.850
F3-Net$_{AAAI'20}$ [24]	26.5	0.891	0.035	0.902	0.813	0.053	0.870	0.937	0.028	0.953	0.945	0.033	0.927	0.882	0.064	0.863
PoolNet+$_{TPAMI'21}$ [12]	-	0.889	0.037	0.896	0.805	0.054	0.868	0.936	0.030	0.953	0.949	0.035	0.925	0.892	0.067	0.859
VST$_{ICCV'21}$ [14]	44.48	0.890	0.037	0.892	0.825	0.058	0.861	0.942	0.029	0.953	0.951	0.033	0.918	0.890	0.062	0.846
PSG$_{TIP'21}$ [29]	25.55	0.886	0.036	0.908	0.811	0.052	0.870	0.938	0.027	0.958	0.949	0.031	0.928	0.886	0.063	0.863
EnergyTransf$_{NeurIPS'21}$ [31]	118.96	0.910	0.029	0.918	0.839	0.050	0.886	0.947	0.023	0.961	0.959	0.023	0.933	0.900	0.055	0.869
RCSB$_{WACV'22}$ [8]	27.90	0.889	0.035	0.903	0.810	0.045	0.856	0.938	0.027	0.954	0.944	0.033	0.923	0.886	0.061	0.850
CSF-R2Net$_{TPAMI'22}$ [5]	36.53	0.890	0.037	0.897	0.815	0.055	0.861	0.935	0.030	0.952	0.950	0.033	0.928	0.886	0.069	0.855
EDNet$_{TIP'22}$ [25]	42.85	0.895	0.035	0.908	0.828	0.048	0.876	0.941	0.026	0.956	0.951	0.032	0.929	0.891	0.065	0.867
PGNet$_{CVPR'22}$ [27]	72.70	0.917	0.027	0.922	0.835	0.045	0.887	0.948	0.024	0.961	0.960	0.027	0.932	0.904	0.056	0.878
ICON-S$_{TPAMI'22}$ [32]	92.40	0.920	0.025	0.930	0.855	0.042	0.897	0.951	0.022	0.965	0.961	0.023	0.932	0.906	0.051	0.875
TRACER1$_{AAAI'22}$ [9]	9.96	0.888	0.033	0.913	0.822	0.046	0.879	0.935	0.027	0.957	0.948	0.031	0.926	0.891	0.059	0.870
TRACER7$_{AAAI'22}$ [9]	66.27	0.927	0.022	0.934	0.834	0.042	0.878	0.951	0.020	0.964	0.959	0.026	0.927	0.911	0.049	0.880
Models without Pre-trained Backbone																
U^2-Net$_{PR'20}$ [16]	44.02	0.873	0.045	0.886	0.823	0.054	0.871	0.935	0.031	0.948	0.951	0.033	0.924	0.868	0.078	0.845
SODAWideNet-S (Ours)	**3.03**	**0.872**	**0.044**	**0.890**	**0.825**	**0.054**	**0.875**	**0.934**	**0.031**	**0.949**	**0.941**	**0.039**	**0.918**	**0.868**	**0.083**	**0.849**
SODAWideNet (Ours)	**9.03**	**0.883**	**0.039**	**0.895**	**0.834**	**0.050**	**0.887**	**0.938**	**0.028**	**0.952**	**0.949**	**0.037**	**0.924**	**0.871**	**0.079**	**0.850**
U-Net	10.28	0.742	0.075	0.834	0.666	0.100	0.773	0.858	0.057	0.910	0.867	0.076	0.883	0.786	0.111	0.819
PGNet*	72.70	0.823	0.060	0.851	0.779	0.068	0.837	0.909	0.042	0.934	0.916	0.054	0.907	0.839	0.094	0.824
ICON-S*	92.40	0.733	0.080	0.818	0.704	0.082	0.811	0.837	0.071	0.894	0.859	0.085	0.874	0.764	0.129	0.796
TRACER-1*	9.96	0.711	0.092	0.801	0.704	0.087	0.800	0.833	0.069	0.890	0.853	0.080	0.875	0.764	0.128	0.793

4.1 Datasets and Implementation Details

We train our model on the DUTS [22] dataset, containing 10,553 images for training. We augment the data using horizontal and vertical flipping to obtain a training dataset of 31,659 images. We use five datasets to evaluate the proposed model. They are DUTS-Test [22] consisting of 5019 images, DUT-OMRON [28] which consists of 5168 images, HKU-IS [10] which consists of 4447 images, ECSSD [19] which consists of 1000 images and PASCAL-S [11] dataset consisting of 850 images. SODAWideNet is trained for 41 epochs on DUTS [22] with an initial learning rate of 0.001, and multiplied by 0.1 after 30 epochs. Two Nvidia RTX 3090 GPUs have been used to train our model with a batch size of six. Images are resized to 384×384 for training and 416×416 for testing. We use Adam optimizer with its default parameters to update the weights. The evaluation metrics used for comparing the proposed models with prior works are the Mean Absolute Error(MAE), maximum F-measure, and the E-measure [3].

Fig. 5. Visual comparison of 15 state-of-the-art methods.

4.2 Quantitative and Visual Comparison

Table 2 shows the quantitative comparison against 15 state-of-the-art models for SOD. Additionally, we train PGNet, ICON, and TRACER-1 from scratch without ImageNet pre-trained weights and report their results. The proposed models perform competitively against other state-of-the-art methods. Moreover, SODAWideNet outperforms all other models that do not use a pre-trained backbone. Interestingly, the smaller SODAWideNet-S with only 3.03M, outperforms the larger U^2-Net on most metrics. On the other hand, models relying on features from ImageNet pre-trained backbones suffer catastrophically without pre-trained weights. For example, the performance gap between using a pre-trained backbone and training from scratch ranges from 10% for PGNet to 18.87% for ICON on the DUTS dataset. On the other datasets, this performance gap tends to reduce to 13%. Finally, U-Net outperforms ICON and TRACER-1 on most metrics, clearly showing the challenges of training from scratch and the robustness of encoder-decoder-style models for dense prediction tasks.

Figure 5 shows some representative examples of our model predictions compared to other SOTA models. The first two images are the input and the ground truth respectively. The images from the third to last column follow the same order as in Table 2 from SODAWideNet to PiCANet-R. SODAWideNet performs well on smaller objects in a challenging environment (rows 1 and 2), segmenting large objects (rows 3). Additionally, the SODAWideNet-S performs comparatively well against other state-of-the-art models.

4.3 Influence of MSA, MRFFAM, and LPM

Table 3 illustrates the influence of each component in our model architecture where ✓ indicates the presence of a module and × means a component is not present. The table below shows that contour supervision as an auxiliary task significantly improves model performance. Furthermore, this additional supervision also enables adding more complexity to the proposed model. MSA is the next component to affect the model performance profoundly. Without MSA, the F_{max} score drops by 1.2%, showing the significance of using attention from the initial layers. Furthermore, removing MRFFAM in the hybrid and conv block also had a substantial impact (1.0% and 0.5%, respectively), indicating the effectiveness of long-range convolutional features. * indicates the removal of MRFFAM in the conv block. Finally, the model also suffers significantly (-0.6%) with the absence of LPM, showing the importance of local features.

Table 3. Influence of individual components in SODAWideNet.

Contours	MSA	MRFFAM	LPM	F_{max}	MAE
✗	✓	✓	✓	0.868	0.045
✓	✗	✓	✓	0.871	0.044
✓	✓	✗	✓	0.873	0.043
✓	✓	✓	✗	0.877	0.042
✓	✓	✗*	✓	0.878	0.041
✓	✓	✓	✓	**0.883**	**0.039**

5 Conclusion

We propose a novel encoder-decoder model for Salient Object Detection using dilated convolutions and self-attention without ImageNet pre-training. Inspired by Vision transformers, we use large convolution kernels at every layer to obtain semantic information from farther regions. This strategy contrasts modern convolutional backbones like ResNet-50, which use small convolution kernels with a deep network. Furthermore, to induce self-attention into our network through Multi-Scale Attention (MSA) that computes attention at higher resolutions. Finally, the competitive results with a parameter-efficient model reveal a promising direction toward designing robust vision models without expensive ImageNet pre-training.

References

1. Deng, J., Dong, W., Socher, R., Li, L.J., Li, K., Fei-Fei, L.: Imagenet: a large-scale hierarchical image database. In: 2009 IEEE Conference on Computer Vision and Pattern Recognition, pp. 248–255. IEEE (2009)
2. Deng, R., Shen, C., Liu, S., Wang, H., Liu, X.: Learning to predict crisp boundaries. In: Proceedings of the European Conference on Computer Vision (ECCV), pp. 562–578 (2018)
3. Fan, D.P., Gong, C., Cao, Y., Ren, B., Cheng, M.M., Borji, A.: Enhanced-alignment measure for binary foreground map evaluation. arXiv preprint arXiv:1805.10421 (2018)
4. Gao, S.H., Cheng, M.M., Zhao, K., Zhang, X.Y., Yang, M.H., Torr, P.: Res2net: a new multi-scale backbone architecture. IEEE TPAMI (2020). https://doi.org/10.1109/TPAMI.2019.2938758
5. Gao, S.-H., Tan, Y.-Q., Cheng, M.-M., Lu, C., Chen, Y., Yan, S.: Highly efficient salient object detection with 100k parameters. In: Vedaldi, A., Bischof, H., Brox, T., Frahm, J.-M. (eds.) ECCV 2020. LNCS, vol. 12351, pp. 702–721. Springer, Cham (2020). https://doi.org/10.1007/978-3-030-58539-6_42
6. He, K., Zhang, X., Ren, S., Sun, J.: Deep residual learning for image recognition. In: Proceedings of the IEEE Conference on Computer Vision and Pattern Recognition, pp. 770–778 (2016)

7. Hermann, K., Chen, T., Kornblith, S.: The origins and prevalence of texture bias in convolutional neural networks. Adv. Neural. Inf. Process. Syst. **33**, 19000–19015 (2020)
8. Ke, Y.Y., Tsubono, T.: Recursive contour-saliency blending network for accurate salient object detection. In: Proceedings of the IEEE/CVF Winter Conference on Applications of Computer Vision (WACV), pp. 2940–2950 (2022)
9. Lee, M.S., Shin, W., Han, S.W.: Tracer: extreme attention guided salient object tracing network (student abstract). In: Proceedings of the AAAI Conference on Artificial Intelligence, vol. 36, pp. 12993–12994 (2022)
10. Li, G., Yu, Y.: Visual saliency based on multiscale deep features. In: IEEE Conference on Computer Vision and Pattern Recognition (CVPR), pp. 5455–5463 (2015)
11. Li, Y., Hou, X., Koch, C., Rehg, J.M., Yuille, A.L.: The secrets of salient object segmentation. In: Proceedings of the IEEE Conference on Computer Vision and Pattern Recognition, pp. 280–287 (2014)
12. Liu, J.J., Hou, Q., Liu, Z.A., Cheng, M.M.: Poolnet+: exploring the potential of pooling for salient object detection. IEEE TPAMI **45**(1), 887–904 (2023). https://doi.org/10.1109/TPAMI.2021.3140168
13. Liu, N., Han, J., Yang, M.H.: Picanet: learning pixel-wise contextual attention for saliency detection. In: Proceedings of the IEEE Conference on Computer Vision and Pattern Recognition, pp. 3089–3098 (2018)
14. Liu, N., Zhang, N., Wan, K., Shao, L., Han, J.: Visual saliency transformer. In: Proceedings of the IEEE/CVF International Conference on Computer Vision (ICCV), pp. 4722–4732 (2021)
15. Liu, Z., et al.: Swin transformer: hierarchical vision transformer using shifted windows. In: Proceedings of the IEEE/CVF International Conference on Computer Vision, pp. 10012–10022 (2021)
16. Qin, X., Zhang, Z., Huang, C., Dehghan, M., Zaiane, O., Jagersand, M.: U2-net: going deeper with nested u-structure for salient object detection, vol. 106, p. 107404 (2020)
17. Qin, X., Zhang, Z., Huang, C., Gao, C., Dehghan, M., Jagersand, M.: Basnet: boundary-aware salient object detection. In: Proceedings of the IEEE/CVF Conference on Computer Vision and Pattern Recognition, pp. 7479–7489 (2019)
18. Ronneberger, O., Fischer, P., Brox, T.: U-Net: convolutional networks for biomedical image segmentation. In: Navab, N., Hornegger, J., Wells, W.M., Frangi, A.F. (eds.) MICCAI 2015. LNCS, vol. 9351, pp. 234–241. Springer, Cham (2015). https://doi.org/10.1007/978-3-319-24574-4_28
19. Shi, J., Yan, Q., Xu, L., Jia, J.: Hierarchical image saliency detection on extended CSSD. IEEE Trans. Pattern Anal. Mach. Intell. **38**(4), 717–729 (2015)
20. Simonyan, K., Zisserman, A.: Very deep convolutional networks for large-scale image recognition. arXiv preprint arXiv:1409.1556 (2014)
21. Tan, M., Le, Q.: Efficientnet: rethinking model scaling for convolutional neural networks. In: International Conference on Machine Learning, pp. 6105–6114. PMLR (2019)
22. Wang, L., et al.: Learning to detect salient objects with image-level supervision. In: CVPR (2017)
23. Wang, W., et al.: Pyramid vision transformer: a versatile backbone for dense prediction without convolutions. In: Proceedings of the IEEE/CVF International Conference on Computer Vision, pp. 568–578 (2021)
24. Wei, J., Wang, S., Huang, Q.: F^{3}net: fusion, feedback and focus for salient object detection. In: Proceedings of the AAAI Conference on Artificial Intelligence, vol. 34, pp. 12321–12328 (2020)

25. Wu, Y.H., Liu, Y., Zhang, L., Cheng, M.M., Ren, B.: EDN: salient object detection via extremely-downsampled network. IEEE Trans. Image Process. **31**, 3125–3136 (2022)
26. Wu, Y., He, K.: Group normalization. In: Proceedings of the European Conference on Computer Vision (ECCV), pp. 3–19 (2018)
27. Xie, C., Xia, C., Ma, M., Zhao, Z., Chen, X., Li, J.: Pyramid grafting network for one-stage high resolution saliency detection. In: CVPR (2022)
28. Yang, C., Zhang, L., Lu, H., Ruan, X., Yang, M.H.: Saliency detection via graph-based manifold ranking. In: Proceedings of the IEEE Conference on Computer Vision and Pattern Recognition, pp. 3166–3173 (2013)
29. Yang, S., Lin, W., Lin, G., Jiang, Q., Liu, Z.: Progressive self-guided loss for salient object detection. IEEE Trans. Image Process. **30**, 8426–8438 (2021). https://doi.org/10.1109/TIP.2021.3113794
30. Yuan, L., et al.: Tokens-to-token vit: training vision transformers from scratch on imagenet. In: Proceedings of the IEEE/CVF International Conference on Computer Vision (ICCV), pp. 558–567 (2021)
31. Zhang, J., Xie, J., Barnes, N., Li, P.: Learning generative vision transformer with energy-based latent space for saliency prediction. In: 2021 Conference on Neural Information Processing Systems (2021)
32. Zhuge, M., Fan, D.P., Liu, N., Zhang, D., Xu, D., Shao, L.: Salient object detection via integrity learning. IEEE Trans. Pattern Anal. Mach. Intell. **45**(3), 3738–3752 (2022)

Applications

Foil-Net: Deep Wave Classification for Hydrofoil Surfing

Zachary Mossing, Sean Wu, Kevin Hong, Fabien Scalzo, and Eun Sang Cha[✉]

Pepperdine University, Malibu, CA, USA
{zak.mossing,sean.wu,kevin.hong,fabien.scalzo,eunsang.cha}@pepperdine.edu

Abstract. Hydrofoil surfing is a distinct subclass of surfing, where riders navigate unbroken waves while elevated above the water's surface through the use of a hydrofoil affixed to the underside of the surfboard. Foiling has been popularized due to an increase in riding distance capabilities. In particular, the downwind technique allows riders to surf on open ocean wind swells taking advantage of the hydrofoil's hydrodynamic ability to generate lift. However, the downwind technique in hydrofoil surfing maintains a high barrier to entry for novice users due to the real-time task of visually identifying and transitioning between the frequently changing wind waves. Thus, there arises a need for a user-friendly system capable of prompt identification and assessment of wave quality for foiling. To meet this demand, we propose Foil-Net, a wave classification tool developed for hydrofoil surfing. Foil-Net leverages a combination of an autoencoder [10] and convolutional neural network (CNN) [11] classifier to categorize and index waves based on their suitability for hydrofoil surfing.

Keywords: Hydrofoil Surfing · Wave Classification · Marine Wearables

1 Introduction

Hydrofoil surfing necessitates a heightened attention to wave selection, enabling riders to maneuver on unbroken, dynamic waves. In the context of downwind foiling in open ocean conditions, an additional challenge arises, as riders must identify ride-able wind swells while preserving both momentum and speed. Failure to do so will result in falling, requiring the user to paddle distances in excess of a mile to shore unless a source of propulsion, capable of accelerating the users' hydrofoil, exists.

Propulsion comes in the form of a wave breaking behind the rider pushing the rider forward or the rider utilizing a long paddle to push the water around him to generate speed. However, utilizing these methods to resume the ride is exhausting and detracts from the user's experience. To avoid this, the rider must constantly optimize their heading relative to oncoming wind swell to ensure they are always positioned on the face of a wind wave where optimal propulsion takes

© The Author(s), under exclusive license to Springer Nature Switzerland AG 2023
G. Bebis et al. (Eds.): ISVC 2023, LNCS 14362, pp. 109–120, 2023.
https://doi.org/10.1007/978-3-031-47966-3_9

place. If a rider finds themselves behind the trough of a wave, they will experience an abrupt loss of lift, effectively ending the ride.

Extensive development of deep learning systems for wave identification and classification exists in various applications, such as nearshore safety, offshore operations optimization, and wave energy harnessing [1–5]. This suggests the feasibility of a system tailored for wind wave identification for downwind foiling. By "wind wave", we refer to the the short period waves generated from the wind blowing on the surface of the water. For novice surfers aspiring to engage in downwind foiling, the primary obstacle is the ability to identify high-quality waves in windy, open ocean conditions. The inherent complexity of the ocean's dynamic surface, coupled with the swift and often unpredictable nature of wind swells, makes the manual identification of waves a daunting task, for beginners.

Thus, we present Foil-Net, an open source, low cost classification system, capable of analyzing and interpreting wave images, and producing a consistent wave classification that accounts for key characteristics such as height, speed, period, and direction. Foil-Net provides users with an analysis of wave conditions for wave selection during downwind foiling, offering a seamless user-friendly experience. Foil-Net facilitates a quicker learning curve for novices by reducing empirical trial-and-error and enhancing overall performance in downwind foiling.

Our contributions are as follows:

- *Foil-Net, a deep learning based wave classification system* to enhance user experience in hydrofoil surfing.
- Demonstration of a *low-cost, wearable, camera module* for wave classification.
- An *open-source wave image dataset* with accompanying code to facilitate further research in hydrofoil surfing.

Github Link: https://github.com/zakmoss/Foil-Net-datasetandcode

1.1 Active Wave Classification Models

2 Existing Work

In the field of active wave classification, various methods have been developed over the last few years. An expansive survey on sea waves applies data-driven machine learning models to classify and predict wave parameters, comparing their efficiency with numerical models [8] For example, a coastal wave-tracker was proposed to enhance video quality, extracting wave movement information, and differentiating foreground, background, and mask components. [6]. Despite its focus on near-shore conditions, this hinted at the possibility of classifying waves for hydro foiling (Table 1).

In the field of active wave classification, various methods have been developed over the last few years. An expansive survey on sea waves applies data-driven machine learning models to classify and predict wave parameters, comparing their efficiency with numerical models [8] For example, a coastal wave-tracker

Table 1. Strengths and Weaknesses of Different Approaches for Wave Classification

Comparative Analysis of Wave Classification Models	
Model 1	**Data-driven ML models** [8]
Pros	Superior wave parameter prediction.
Cons	Ignores downwind foiling wave quality.
Model 2	**Coastal wave-tracker** [6]
Pros	Enhances video clarity; extracts vital wave info.
Cons	Focuses mainly on near-shore conditions.
Model 3	**Bathymetry computation** [7]
Pros	Detailed wave breaking categorization.
Cons	Complex and requires costly sensors.
Model 4	**Infrared imagery with DCNN** [4]
Pros	Precisely classifies wave breaking types.
Cons	Misses wind swell wave features for foiling.
Model 5	**Video imagery wave ID** [2]
Pros	Identifies foam from active wave processes.
Cons	Insufficient in downwind swell ID and quality indexing.
Model 6	**Breaking wave analysis** [3]
Pros	Detailed real-time data through various techniques.
Cons	Overemphasizes turbulent processes; misses key foiling features.
Model 7	**Supervised ML framework** [9]
Pros	Accurate wave replication with low computational cost.
Cons	Overlooks wave quality aspects for downwind foiling.
Model 8	**DL for large ocean areas** [1]
Pros	Assesses offshore operational safety.
Cons	Insufficient for downwind foiling assessments.

was proposed to enhance video quality, extracting wave movement information, and differentiating foreground, background, and mask components. [6]. Despite its focus on near-shore conditions, this hinted at the possibility of classifying waves for hydro foiling.

Bathymetry computation-based approaches also exist, which deploy a wave shoaling model, a breaking model, and a wave dissipation model to categorize the various stages of wave breaking [7]. Despite its innovative approach, the model's key limitation is its heightened complexity, attributed to its dependency on these sensors. While these sensors may be advantageous for surf zone depth inversion, they are not cost effective, suggesting the need for low-cost solutions that do not rely on expensive sensors for the quality indexing of sea surface wind-waves.

Other proposed works use infrared imagery and deep convolutional neural networks to classify wave breaking with high accuracy in estimating wave breaking types [4] such as non-breaking, spilling, and plunging waves. These methods suggest that it is possible develop a relevant quality index for foilers in a downwinding context.

A further wave identification model exhibits similarities with previous models by detecting active wave breaking using video imagery data. This model, however, introduces a unique distinction between foam specifically generated from active wave breaking and foam produced by other passive processes [2]. In downwind swell identification, where the wave patterns do not produce foam, the model's accuracy or applicability may be compromised. Moreover, this model falls short in providing a wave quality index that would be useful in the context of downwind foiling.

Yet another model concentrates on understanding the breaking process of ocean waves, its influence on ocean-atmosphere interaction and coastal engineering, and the shortcomings in current numerical methods to accurately model breaking waves. This project deploys remote sensors, video analysis, convolutional neural networks (CNNs), and video classification algorithms to extract real-time, detailed information [3]. However, the project's focus on breaking wave analysis and turbulent processes may not sufficiently capture the specific wave features required for wind swell waves suitable for foiling, which necessitate clean, well-structured waves with consistent height, shape, and direction.

A machine learning framework uses supervised training to predict ocean-wave conditions. Its strength lies in its high accuracy in replicating wave heights and characteristic periods with minimal computational cost compared to physics-based models, making it beneficial for real-time forecasting systems [9]. However, this study does not specifically consider the detailed aspects of wave quality important for downwind foiling and primarily focuses on predicting significant wave heights and periods.

Lastly, a broad approach to wave identification employs a deep learning model to classify large oceanic areas for assessing sea state conditions, primarily for offshore operations safety [1]. However, this broad approach might lack the specific information required for optimizing downwind foiling, highlighting the need for a more targeted and specialized algorithm. Such an algorithm must accurately identify and analyze wave patterns and characteristics crucial for maximizing the performance and efficiency of downwind foiling techniques. Despite the strengths of these active wave classification models, their limitations must be carefully considered when integrating them into wind swell identification systems for downwind foiling (Fig. 1).

3   Methods

3.1   Data Collection and Preprocessing

Our data collection technique involves collecting video footage via a head-mounted wide-angle GoPro Hero9 action camera during a downwind run. The decision to use an off-the-shelf action camera came after several failed attempts

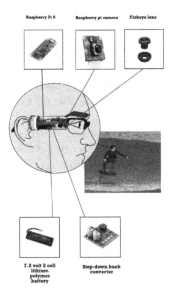

Fig. 1. Data collection module

to build a low-cost data collection module. This module consisted of a screw-top plastic container housing a Raspberry Pi Zero 2 W, and a Raspberry Pi V2 Camera equipped with a 220-degree fish-eye lens powered by a 7.2-volt two-cell lithium polymer battery. This device was capable of capturing visual data from the rider's perspective and transferring it to a deep learning algorithm which minimized the time required for data pre-processing. The container is securely attached to the left temple of the glasses frames using 3D printed thermoplastic polyurethane mounts. A counterweight is mounted on the right temple, and an adjustable headband is connected to both temples.

The Raspberry Pi Zero 2 W executes a script that commands the camera to capture still images at a rate of 40 frames per second. Furthermore, data sets were saved every ten minutes. Unfortunately, lack of reliable waterproofing lead to multiple revisions in repairs. The GoPro Hero9 action camera images were the final images used in our data collection process. Attached to a bite mount and held securely in the rider's mouth, this camera provided a comparable first-person perspective of downwind foil runs.

Using multiple action cameras allowed for the simultaneous participation of multiple riders, effectively doubling our data collection capacity. This approach not only enhanced the diversity of our data set, but also provided valuable insights into different riding styles and wave selections, contributing significantly to the refinement and precision of our wave classification model.

After gathering footage, the next step entailed a transformation of the data. The video data was converted into a sequence of individual images, allowing for examination of specific waves ridden during each foiling run. For compatibility with the autoencoder algorithm, these images were subsequently resized from their original high resolution to a smaller resolution of 224 × 224 pixels. This critical preprocessing step ensured that image data could be efficiently fed into the machine learning model, balancing computational efficiency with the retention of essential features for accurate wave classification. The resulting images maintained the barrel lens distortion effect applied by the wide angle lenses used in the data collection process. To mitigate this effect, picture of a checkerboard pattern was taken with each of the cameras used in data collection. Finally, the images were undistorted using the obtained distortion coefficients. Afterward, each image was assigned a quality index score between 1 and 5.

Objectively indexing a wave's quality from an image alone is nearly impossible as the viewer of the wave image has no insight into how the wave impacted the quality of the ride. Therefore, it was essential that we drew upon the perspectives of the riders who captured our data set as we graded each individual image. In the process of assigning classification values to each wave, several crucial factors were considered. These factors included wave size, longevity, speed gain and its alignment with the desired propulsion direction, each of which constitute fundamental considerations in the assessment of a wave's suitability for catching. If a particular wave is not large enough to provide substantial propulsion, it should be ruled out. Similarly, if the wave is not traveling in the direction of the prevailing winds, the quality grade will be impacted negatively. While catching a wave directed against the wind might at first appear appealing due to the convenience of its immediate availability, catching the wave will ultimately act as a hindrance. The opposing wind would significantly reduce the rider's ability to generate speed and thus, the rider would struggle to generate enough lift to continue the ride. If a wave does not provide propulsion for a distance long enough to significantly reduce the need for pumping to maintain lift, its grade will be lower. While this is all information that would not be apparent to a rider prior to catching the wave, its use in hindsight to consider a wave's potential benefit is invaluable especially for beginners to whom such insight is entirely unavailable.

The dataset, comprising 18,652 wave images under varied conditions, was segmented into training (14,961 images), validation (1,870 images), and testing (1,871 images) subsets for the autoencoder model built using PyTorch. Leveraging the "albumentations" Python library enhanced the training set diversity through augmentation. The autoencoder entails a tri-layer convolutional encoder using ReLU activations, facilitating sparse representation for improved decoder-stage image reconstruction. The ensuing encoded tensors feed into Foil-Net, a convolutional neural network (CNN) incorporating dual convolutional layers each succeeded by ReLU activation and max pooling. The system operates with a CrossEntropyLoss function, ideal for exclusive class classification, and utilizes a Stochastic Gradient Descent optimizer with a 0.01 learning rate (Fig. 2 and 3).

3.2   Foil-Net Algorithm

Foil-Net incorporates an both autoencoder and a CNN classifier to grade wave quality. By leveraging the autoencoder's image compression and feature extraction capabilities, we effectively reduce the size and complexity of the classifier's

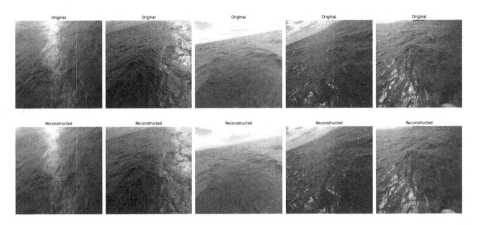

Fig. 2. Example autoencoder reconstructions in the testing set

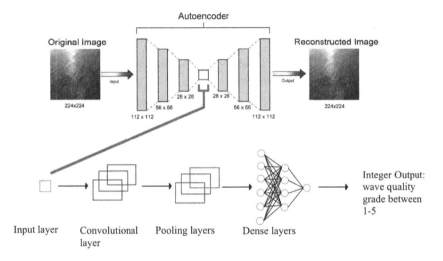

Fig. 3. Foil-Net: The convolutional neural network classifier was benchmarked against different classifiers

input, ensuring superior accuracy and efficiency. We use the extracted image features in the latent space as input for the classifier. Moreover, the autoencoder demonstrates high-quality image reconstructions, highlighting its proficiency in extracting essential features. Each image in the input dataset is labeled with a quality index value, associating latent space information with wave quality. This function significantly enhances the wave quality grading system by providing vital insights into wave characteristics necessary for accurate assessment.

Algorithm 1. Foil-Net

1: $\theta \leftarrow$ Initialize parameters for the autoencoder
2: **repeat**
3: Step 1
4:     $X_{M_1} \leftarrow$ Select random minibatch of M_1 wave images
5:     **Forward pass:**
6:         $h \leftarrow f_{\theta_{\mathrm{enc}}}(X)$ ▷ Wave Encoder
7:         $\hat{X} \leftarrow f_{\theta_{\mathrm{dec}}}(h)$ ▷ Wave Decoder
8:     Calculate loss $L(X, \hat{X})$
9:     $g \leftarrow \nabla_\theta L$ ▷ Gradients of the loss with respect to parameters θ
10:     $\theta \leftarrow$ Update parameters based on g
11: **until** θ Convergence
12: **return** h ▷ Return the encoded representations as input for the convolutional network classifier
13: **repeat**
14: Step 2
15:     $h_{M_2} \leftarrow$ Select random minibatch of M_2 latent embeddings
16:     **Forward pass:**
17:         $\hat{X}_{index} \leftarrow f_{\theta_{\mathrm{cnn}}}(h)$ ▷ Convolutional Network Classifier
18:     Calculate cross-entropy loss $L(X_{index}, \hat{X}_{index})$
19:     $g \leftarrow \nabla_\theta L$ ▷ Gradients of the loss with respect to parameters θ
20:     $\theta \leftarrow$ Update parameters based on g
21: **until** θ Convergence

Moreover, the autoencoder's pre-training capability allows it to learn meaningful features in advance of the classification stage. Consequently, the classifier can focus on refining decision boundaries and class separation within the reduced feature space rather than directly processing the raw, potentially high-dimensional wave images. This leads to expedited training times, improved generalization, and ultimately, elevated classification accuracy (Fig. 4).

4 Results

We chose a CNN classifier over more traditional machine learning models for several reasons. Firstly, our CNN-based classifier can effectively process the feature map generated by the autoencoder. Secondly, it can recognize higher-level features in the earlier layers and then build upon them in the deeper layers to recognize even more complex structures. Thirdly, CNNs can better handle and utilize the information contained in the autoencoder's latent vectors (Tables 2 and 3).

Table 2. Precision scores of different classifiers

Comparison of Classifier Precision Scores						
Classifier Type	Precision Score					
	1	2	3	4	5	Mean
Random Forest	0.72	0.00	0.04	0.84	0.79	0.47
SVM	0.79	0.00	0.00	0.95	0.74	0.49
Logistic Regression	0.66	0.20	0.00	0.69	0.74	0.46
KNN	0.66	**0.09**	0.02	0.79	0.81	0.47
MLP	0.75	**0.09**	0.08	0.83	**0.82**	0.51
Foil-Net	**0.94**	0.08	**0.09**	**1.00**	0.74	**0.57**

Table 3. Accuracy scores of different classifiers

Comparison of Classifier Accuracy Scores	
Classifier Type	Accuracy Score
Random Forest	76%
SVM	76%
Logistic Regression	71%
KNN	75%
MLP	75%
Foil-Net	80%

5   Discussion

5.1   Analysis

A thorough evaluation of several baseline classification models was conducted to establish a performance baseline for our wave quality grading task. We evaluated Random Forest, k-Nearest Neighbors (KNN), Support Vector Machine (SVM) with a radial basis function (RBF) kernel, Logistic Regression, and Multilayer Perceptron (MLP). This comprehensive analysis provided valuable insights into the strengths and weaknesses of each algorithm in handling wave quality grades. Our Random Forest ensemble classifier demonstrated higher performance for grade 5 wave quality, while facing challenges with grades 2 and 3.

Likewise, the SVM classifier with the RBF kernel achieved an accuracy of 0.76. Similarly to the Random Forest, it exhibited adeptness in correctly classifying wave quality grades, particularly for grade 5. On the other hand, Logistic Regression yielded an accuracy of 0.71, once again, with the highest performance observed for grade 5. K-Nearest Neighbors performed with an accuracy of 0.75, facing challenges with grades 2 and 3 in terms of precision and recall.

As for the Multilayer Perceptron (MLP), it achieved an accuracy of 0.75, again showing its highest performance for grade 5 wave quality. Each of the

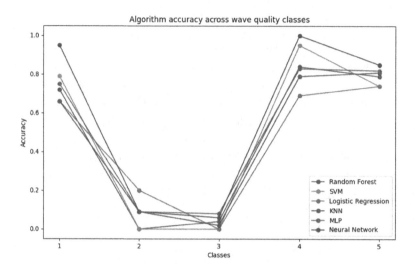

Fig. 4. Classifier wave index accuracy comparison

models' struggle to correctly identify waves of grades 2 and 3 is due to the lack of obvious difference between wave images in this range. While images labeled with a 5 and 4 are infrequent and exhibit dramatic features that differentiate from waves within other classes, images of with labels 2 and 3 maintain a finer distinction between each other and therefore they are easy to confuse. By mitigating the class imbalance and developing strategies to handle the nuanced differences between grades 2 and 3, we can effectively improve the overall performance and reliability of our wave quality grading system.

To mitigate the inaccurate identification of wave images in classes 2 and 3, we altered the dataset by relabeling the autoencoder's encoded tensors. The modified dataset consisted of four quality classes instead of five, with classes 2 and 3 being combined into class 2, and classes 4 and 5 being relabeled as 3 and 4. We did this assuming that the classifier was mistaking waves of class 2 for those of class 3 because the differences between the two were extremely subtle. We also hoped that combining the two classes would partially mitigate class imbalance as waves of classes 2 and 3 are critically underrepresented within our data set. This failed to improve the algorithm's ability to accurately grade images contained in class 2.

Our CNN reached a peak accuracy of .80, consequently marking it as the most accurate model in our experiments. In spite of the modifications made to the input tensors, our CNN encountered difficulties in the accurate classification of images assigned grades 2 and 3 now assigned grade 2. However, the CNN model notably scored higher accuracy than every other model we tested in identifying images in every class as well as scoring the highest average precision score by a six percent over the second most precise model.

5.2   Limitations

Our project faced notable hurdles, including initial waterproofing failure, delaying data collection, and necessitating the use of a GoPro, which introduced a lengthy preprocessing step. Furthermore, all tested classification models had difficulty distinguishing between wave grades 2 and 3 due to a class imbalance; these categories comprised just 12.6 percent of the dataset. While Foil-Net marginally outperformed simpler models by 9 percent, the minimal accuracy difference questions the benefit of its added complexity. A broader dataset is vital to fully address these issues.

5.3   Implications and Applications

Despite these shortcomings, this project significantly advances the field of deep learning and computer visions applications in sports analytics, particularly hydrofoil surfing, demonstrating the practical use of action cameras and machine learning algorithms for wave quality grading. Practical applications could include real-time wave grading systems for foilers and surfers alike, with potential adaptations for other watersports. Overall, the results provide a solid foundation for more advanced and practical applications of deep learning in real-world sports analytics.

6   Conclusion

6.1   Future Work

To enhance the precision of the wave grading system, future work will entail refining the autoencoder and classifier algorithms to better distinguish subtle class differences, supplemented by additional data such as the rider's speed at the moment the image was captured. This would provide a more nuanced differentiation between wave quality classes. To incorporate real-time processing, future work will require the model to be optimized for immediate on-device data processing. This involves further refinement of the autoencoder and classifier for faster yet accurate performance. This would enable the system's integration into a wearable augmented reality device potentially capable of displaying useful information directly to the rider's field of view. Ultimately, these advancements could lead to a more interactive and responsive system for downwind foiling.

This project represents a novel application of machine learning in the niche sport of downwind hydrofoiling, using image data collected from action cameras, processed by a custom autoencoder and classified by a convolutional neural network. The real-time application potential of this technology, particularly with integration into an interactive format for immediate feedback to surfers, presents an exciting avenue for future research. Not only does this study contribute valuable findings to the fields of sports analytics and machine learning, but it also has direct practical implications, serving to enhance the hydrofoil surfing experience.

References

1. Umair, M., et al.: A novel deep learning model for sea state classification using visual-range sea images. Symmetry **14**(7), 1487–1500 (2022). https://doi.org/10.3390/sym14071487
2. Eadi Stringari, C., et al.: Deep neural networks for active wave breaking classification. Sci. Rep. **11**, 3604 (2021). https://doi.org/10.1038/s41598-021-83188-y
3. Reniers, A.J.H.M., et al.: Classification of surf zone hydrodynamics: a systematic review. Ocean Eng. **147**, 589–611 (2017). https://doi.org/10.1016/j.oceaneng.2017.10.006
4. Buscombe, D., Carini, R.J.: A data-driven approach to classifying wave breaking in infrared imagery. Remote Sens. **11**(7), 859 (2019). https://doi.org/10.3390/rs11070859
5. Duong, N.T., et al.: Prediction of breaking wave height by using artificial neural network-based approach. Ocean Model. **182**, 102177 (2023). https://doi.org/10.1016/j.ocemod.2023.102177. ISSN: 1463–5003
6. Kim, J., et al.: Wave-tracking in the surf zone using coastal video imagery with deep neural networks. Atmosphere **11**(3), 304 (2020). https://doi.org/10.3390/atmos11030304
7. Umair, M., Hashmani, M.A., Hasan, M.H.B.: Survey of sea wave parameters classification and prediction using machine learning models, pp. 1–6 (2019). https://doi.org/10.1109/AiDAS47888.2019.8970706
8. Smith, R., et al.: Pre-computation of image features for the classification of dynamic properties in breaking waves. Eur. J. Remote Sens. **56**(1), 2163707 (2023). https://doi.org/10.1080/22797254.2022.2163707
9. James, S.C., Zhang, Y., O'Donncha, F.: A machine learning framework to forecast wave conditions. Coast. Eng. **137**, 1–10 (2018). https://doi.org/10.1016/j.coastaleng.2018.03.004
10. Bank, D., Koenigstein, N., Giryes, R.: Autoencoders. arXiv preprint arXiv:2003.05991 (2020)
11. O'Shea, K., Nash, R.: An introduction to convolutional neural networks. arXiv preprint arXiv:1511.08458 (2015)

Inpainting of Depth Images Using Deep Neural Networks for Real-Time Applications

Roland Fischer[✉], Janis Roßkamp, Thomas Hudcovic, Anton Schlegel, and Gabriel Zachmann

University of Bremen, Bremen, Germany
`r.fischer@uni-bremen.de`

Abstract. Depth sensors enjoy increased popularity throughout many application domains, such as robotics (SLAM) and telepresence. However, independent of technology, the depth images inevitably suffer from defects such as holes (invalid areas) and noise. In recent years, deep learning-based color image inpainting algorithms have become very powerful. Therefore, with this work, we propose to adopt existing deep learning models to reconstruct missing areas in depth images, with the possibility of real-time applications in mind. After empirical tests with various models, we chose two promising ones to build upon: a U-Net architecture with partial convolution layers that conditions the output solely on valid pixels, and a GAN architecture that takes advantage of a patch-based discriminator. For comparison, we took a standard U-Net and LaMa. All models were trained on the publically available NYUV2 dataset, which we augmented with synthetically generated noise/holes.

Our quantitative and qualitative evaluations with two public and an own dataset show that LaMa most often produced the best results, however, is also significantly slower than the others and the only one not being real-time capable. The GAN and partial convolution-based models also produced reasonably good results. Which one was superior varied from case to case but, generally, the former performed better with small-sized holes and the latter with bigger ones. The standard U-Net model that we used as a baseline was the worst and most blurry.

Keywords: Image Inpainting · Depth Completion · Real-Time · Depth Images · Deep Learning · CNN · GAN · LaMa · U-Net · Azure Kinect

1 Introduction

With the growing availability of low-cost depth sensors and RGB-D cameras (e.g., Azure Kinect), their popularity and employment increased throughout various research areas and industries. Typical use cases are SLAM and object detection in computer vision and robotic applications, or real-time capturing of

G. Bebis et al. (Eds.): ISVC 2023, LNCS 14362, pp. 121–135, 2023.
https://doi.org/10.1007/978-3-031-47966-3_10

point cloud avatars for telepresence systems. A long-lasting challenge is, however, handling the inherent sensor noise, as well as artifacts and holes that lead to an incomplete depth image. These issues are inevitable consequences of the time-of-flight principle many depth sensors use. Concretely, multipath inference, caused by repeated reflection of the infrared rays between objects, and signals that are too powerful or too weak lead to ambiguous or invalid depth values. Having accurate and dense depth maps is important for many downstream tasks such as safe motion planning, reliable vision in autonomous vehicles, or industrial inspection. One solution would be to adapt those downstream, domain-specific algorithms and models to work with incomplete input. However, experience shows that specialized algorithms and models that only focus on the specific task of denoising/inpainting the input data are more effective and lead to better overall results. Therefore, preprocessing and enhancing the depth images is an important task. Reconstructing the missing areas in real-time is not trivial, though, as there are strong spatial dependencies between the data points, both locally and globally. Additionally, previous work in the area of hole filling and image inpainting was mostly focused on regular color images and is not necessarily well-suited for direct application on depth images.

With this work, we propose an approach of real-time depth image inpainting using neural networks. Our main contribution is the investigation of the depth image reconstruction quality of two fast U-Net-based network models that were originally designed for color image inpainting, including a comparison with a basic U-Net and a more sophisticated state-of-the-art model. In contrast to many others, the models we use do not need any color images for guidance, which makes them more generally applicable as they can be also employed in use cases where no color information is available. The first model we chose uses partial convolutions, while the second one is based on a GAN architecture. Furthermore, we present a detailed quantitative and qualitative evaluation using two public datasets and a custom one we recorded ourselves.

2 Related Work

Traditionally, missing areas in pictures are reconstructed, or painted-in, using pixel- or patch-based exemplar methods [18], diffusion methods [25], or hybrids of the two [22]. In recent years, however, deep-learning-based methods outclassed traditional methods, especially when restoring larger areas, as they are able to learn and consider the semantics of the image. The most common CNN variants for image inpainting are FCN and U-Net. However, to avoid filling missing areas with noise and then convoluting this information further, some authors proposed non-standard convolutions. For instance, Liu et al. [13] proposed partial convolution layers that dynamically mask out invalid pixels and cope better with irregular holes. Yu et al. [30] introduced gated convolutions that generalize partial convolutions and provide a learnable dynamic feature selection mechanism across all channels and layers. Similarly, Xie et al. [27] suggested using learnable bidirectional attention maps. In order to better and effectively capture long-distance information, Ning et al. [16] proposed adding a multi-scale attention module. Yan et al. [28] introduced shift connection layers that shift features of known areas to serve as guidance for missing areas and Suvorov et al. [23] presented a combination of Fourier convolutions, a high receptive field perceptual loss, and large training masks for inpainting of large areas. Moreover, many approaches for deep-learning-based inpainting employ one of the various GAN architectures, such as the one proposed by Isola et al. [5], as they feature strong data generation capabilities. Other examples include the works by Shen et al. [21], Yeh et al. [29], and Shao et al. [20]. Similarly, diffusion-based networks such as the one by Rombach et al. [17] achieved impressive results in various image synthesis tasks. These models consist of a hierarchy of denoising autoencoders and can model complex, multi-modal distributions, however, inference tends to be very expensive.

Very recently, transformer networks, usually employed for natural language processing, were discovered to be very effective for computer vision and image processing tasks, such as denoising, too [2]. The main benefit is their ability to model long-range dependencies. Interestingly, Makarov and Borisenko [14] used vision transformers for color-guided depth completion and Li et al. [9] proposed a combination of convolutions and transformers for large hole inpainting. Similarly, Yu et al. [31] presented a bidirectional autoregressive transformer model for diverse inpainting, and Deng et al. [3] designed a transformer for inpainting with a focus on efficiency. However, transformers are usually rather slow.

Most research is focused on inpainting color images, and only very few works consider reconstructing depth images. Works that do consider depth images usually are situated in the field of RGB-D reconstruction or lidar-based depth completion and use the color image for guidance. For instance, Ma and Karaman [15] employed a deep regression network to predict depth images based on corresponding color images and sparse depth samples. Fujii et al. [4] used a late fusion GAN to simultaneously reconstruct color and depth images by exploiting the complementary relationship between RGB and depth information. Lee et al. [8] proposed multi-scaled and densely connected locally convolutional layers for depth completion, Tao et al. [24] use a neural network for the prediction of dense depth maps as well as uncertainty estimates, and Jeon et al. [6] performs depth completion based on line features by bridging the conventional and deep learning-based approaches. All these works require color input as well, though. Similarly, Zhang and Funkhouser [33], as well as Satapathy and Sahay [19], rely on color guidance. In contrast, Jin et al. [7] and Li and Wu [11] presented solutions for depth inpainting without color guidance, however, they are only designed to handle smaller holes. Other works that solely work on depth images can be found in the medical domain, i.e., to reconstruct and in-paint CT or MRI scans. Both, Li et al. [10] and Armanious et al. [1], for instance, presented promising solutions using patch-based GANs. For a more comprehensive overview, we refer to the excellent literature review by Zhang et al. [32].

3 Our Approach

To tackle the issue of (real-time) depth image inpainting, and after thoroughly experimenting with the current state of the art in deep color image inpainting, we decided to adopt two promising works that we considered suitable as a foundation. The first model we chose is the one by Liu et al. that introduced partial convolutions [13], and the second one is the GAN model proposed by Isola et al. [5]. As a baseline for comparison, we also took a standard U-Net model and the more sophisticated state-of-the-art model by Suvorov et al. [23], LaMa, which we expected to be significantly slower, though.

3.1 Datasets and Preprocessing Pipeline

For the training and evaluation of our models, we resorted to using two publicly available depth datasets, namely, the SceneNet RGB-D dataset by McCormac et al. and the NYU Depth V2 dataset by Silberman et al. The SceneNet dataset provides 5 million photo-realistic RGB-D images of synthesized indoor scenes. We only use the depth images. These are 16-bit encoded which is similar to real-world input, however, the image resolution is significantly lower than the ones of common depth sensors such as the Azure Kinect. In order to prevent upsampling artifacts from influencing the training, we use this dataset only for evaluation. The NYUV2 dataset was collected by capturing a wide range of indoor locations within a large city using a Kinect V1 RGB-D camera. Additionally, we created our own custom dataset consisting of mostly static and a few dynamic scenes using the Microsoft Azure Kinect RGB-D camera. As this data lacks a ground truth, we use it only for evaluation, too. In the end, we trained our models with a split of 44984 depth images for the training set, 654 for the validation set, and 5704 for the test set (NYUV2). For the evaluation, we used additional 23 scenes with 6900 images (SceneNet) and 23 scenes with 6739 images (custom dataset).

For the training procedure, the images go through a preprocessing pipeline. First, the images get resized to 512^2 and scaled to the range of 0–1 for compatibility purposes with the models. Then, an illumination mask similar to the one of the Azure Kinect is generated and applied to adapt the dataset's images to real-world input conditions. As the dataset used for training doesn't contain any holes, we generate synthetic ones as well as single outlier pixels. The synthetic holes are created by combining multiple random masks with different scales and frequencies that are generated with sci-kit-image. To guarantee a diverse input, the final noise masks are evenly drawn from multiple categories with varying percentages of invalid pixels and sizes of holes. Finally, we apply classical data augmentation techniques such as random flipping (90-degree angles) and homogeneous intensity shifts.

3.2 Network Details

In the following, the network details of our models get briefly described. For more details, we refer to the corresponding original papers.

Partial Convolution: Our first network model is based on the one presented by Liu et al. [13] and, like the original, follows a U-Net architecture with partial convolution layers. Our model features only one input and output channel, respectively, though. We chose an input resolution of 512^2, as it is the closest square number to the resolution of the Azure Kinect images. The kernel sizes for the partial convolutions in the encoder part are 7, 5, 5, 3, 3, 3, 3 and 3, following the presented layer order. The decoder uses filter sizes of 3 for all convolutions. For all convolutions in the network, stride values of 2 are used. The implementation of this network is based on the existing third-party implementation of Ryan Wongsa for the U-Net architecture [26] and loss functions. However, adjustments were made due to the fact that the crucial weight initializations as well as the input normalizations of the VGG-16 network were missing. Moreover, the implementation of the partial convolutional layer from the original authors was used [12], too.

GAN: Our second network model is based on the GAN architecture presented by Isola et al. [5] that uses a U-Net for the generator and a convolutional PatchGAN classifier for the discriminator. The latter penalizes structure at the scale of image patches. The generator part of the GAN is very close to the previous U-Net: The encoder consists of 8 identical blocks instead of 7, which are Conv-BN-LeakyRelu blocks that use the same filter sizes of 64, 128, 256, 512, 512, 512, 512, 512. The decoder consists of seven Upsampling-Concat-BN-Relu blocks. Additional dropouts of 50% are applied to the first three blocks after the normalization process. A final convolution maps the number of output channels. The input dimensions are $512^2 \times 3$, as three depth images are stacked. All convolutions of the network use filters of size 4 with a stride of 2. The discriminator consists of one Conv-LeakyReLu layer followed by 3 Conv-BN-LeakyReLU blocks and a single Conv-ZeroPadding-Sigmoid block. This outputs a 30^2 image patch that can classify a 70^2 portion of the input image.

Convolutional U-Net: As a baseline for comparison of the previous models, we utilize a CNN with a standard U-Net architecture, although models with normal convolutional layers that treat all image pixels the same and even share filter weights are not ideal for image inpainting. The architecture is similar to the one of the partial convolution model but with regular convolutions.

LaMa: To get a more complete picture and to compare the models with more sophisticated networks, we also adopted the LaMa network by Suvorov et al. [23]. It is specifically designed for the inpainting of large areas by using fast Fourier convolutions that provide a large receptive field, as well as an adapted perceptual loss and large training masks. However, as it is more complex, we expect it to be significantly slower and possibly not real-time capable. For details about the architecture, we refer to the original paper, from which we directly adopted it.

3.3 Training Procedure

For convenience, from now on, we abbreviate the models' names with Conv, PConv, GAN, and LaMa. The models were trained for 7 epochs (LaMa: 5) using a batch size of 2 (LaMa: 5), due to the huge memory load. As a loss function, we used, similarly to the partial convolution paper by Liu et al., a combination consisting of two per-pixel accuracy losses, a perceptual loss, two style losses, and a total variation loss. We experimented with different weights but found the ones used in the paper to be the best-performing ones. In the case of the GAN model, the generator loss is a combination of the previous total loss and the original generator loss as described in the paper by Isola et al. The losses for LaMa were directly adopted from the original paper.

4 Results

First, we measured the duration of inference needed for inpainting a 512^2 depth image, using an Intel Core i5-10400F CPU, 16 GB of RAM, and an NVIDIA GeForce RTX 2070. A fast inference is crucial for practical real-time applications, i.e., as a preprocessing step in a longer pipeline. As depth sensors usually capture with 30 Hz, the inference time must stay below 33 ms for real-time use. To replicate a data stream of images, the images were inpainted one after another, instead of as a batch. For the GAN method, we measured a pure inference time of 24.3 ms, for the Conv method 24.93 ms, and for the PConv method 9.37 ms. Including preprocessing, we get 27.69 ms, 26.29 ms, and 34.34 ms, respectively. The PConv model takes the longest for the preprocessing as it needs more steps than the other models, i.e., an extra input mask. However, the time for pure inference is the quickest. Generally, even though there is still potential for optimization, these models are quick enough for real-time application. In contrast, LaMa takes 60.02 ms and, thus, is significantly slower and not quite real-time capable. Out of interest, we also tested a diffusion-based model [17] but, as expected, the inference was extremely slow with 3–4 s for an image with 50 sampling steps (which was, as we found, a "sweet spot" for image legibility and speed). Unfortunately, the inpainting results were still comparatively poor. And although better output quality can be achieved with more sampling steps during inference, doing so only impacts inference time even more, which is why we did not consider latent diffusion-based models further.

To quantitatively evaluate the performance of our models, we calculated and compared the MAE, MSE, PSNR, and SSIM on the test sets of the NYUV2 and SceneNet RGB-D datasets (only depth used). Moreover, we separately computed the metrics for the different hole/mask categories, which bundle images with similar ratios of valid/invalid areas to get more detailed insights. The results on the NYUV2 dataset show that LaMa consistently performs best. Moreover, we see a better performance of the GAN method on the first four mask categories, especially if looking at the MAE and MSE, see Table 1 (left). The performance gradually decreases with each category, though, and after the fourth category, the PConv method overtakes the GAN performance in terms of SSIM and PSNR values. In comparison, the Conv method is (as expected) the worst-performing one. Generally, the PConv method seems to be the most consistent method and better at dealing with bigger holes than the GAN and Conv methods. Overall, the models seem to perform similarly on the SceneNet RGB-D dataset (see Table 1 (right)): For the lower mask categories, the GAN method outperforms the Conv and PConv methods, while the PConv method shows better results on the higher categories, and is the most consistent one. LaMa again performs most often the best. However, in terms of SSIM, here, GAN/PConv perform better.

Table 1. Inpainting results on the NYUV2 (left) and SceneNet RGB-D (depth only) (right) test sets using 6 hole categories (percent of invalid pixels; more/bigger holes to the right). The best value per block is marked in bold. Most often, LaMa performs best. The GAN method performs second best on smaller mask categories while the PConv method performs second best on bigger ones and has the most consistent results.

Model		NYUV2						SceneNet RGB-D					
		.01/.1	.1/.2	.2/.3	.3/.4	.4/.5	.5/.6	.01/.1	.1/.2	.2/.3	.3/.4	.4/.5	.5/.6
MAE	PConv	4.89	5.24	5.10	5.32	5.79	7.61	66.89	81.85	77.27	65.85	63.67	110.62
	Conv	3.53	3.24	3.27	3.52	5.64	13.35	118.68	103.84	101.80	113.30	182.04	438.79
	GAN	1.79	1.77	1.93	2.46	4.48	11.18	66.49	65.07	72.18	89.61	176.30	414.24
	LaMa	**0.06**	**0.18**	**0.31**	**0.42**	**0.64**	**1.00**	**4.28**	**10.52**	**16.09**	**20.75**	**30.77**	**45.54**
MSE	PConv	47.82	54.00	54.21	60.67	77.99	154.54	21732	23122	21622	18157	**16787**	32051
	Conv	62.90	56.49	58.45	69.16	131.46	612.88	73128	66152	66116	78239	133677	669006
	GAN	6.79	7.34	10.93	16.68	67.83	415.20	8414	9023	13010	21732	95940	588678
	LaMa	**0.28**	**0.87**	**1.67**	**2.48**	**4.81**	**12.18**	**5044**	**8187**	**9521**	**10858**	17161	**29519**
PSNR	PConv	35.12	34.81	34.70	34.43	33.27	30.47	38.83	39.08	39.18	38.91	37.85	35.58
	Conv	32.29	32.40	32.13	31.64	28.59	22.40	35.50	35.89	35.77	35.41	32.41	26.33
	GAN	41.42	40.51	38.94	37.01	31.13	23.72	44.37	43.76	42.38	40.34	34.32	26.90
	LaMa	**55.04**	**50.15**	**47.38**	**45.74**	**43.01**	**39.22**	**57.31**	**53.02**	**50.59**	**49.23**	**46.93**	**43.82**
SSIM	PConv	.9799	.9771	.9746	.9701	.9630	.9385	.9881	.9876	.9867	**.9866**	**.9855**	**.9818**
	Conv	.9344	.9230	.9184	.9026	.8819	.8264	.9659	.9606	.9556	.9510	.9388	.8919
	GAN	.9935	.9874	.9815	.9759	.9480	.8814	**.9960**	**.9931**	**.9885**	.9834	.9674	.9166
	LaMa	**.9987**	**.9966**	**.9943**	**.9927**	**.9898**	**.9842**	.9958	.9899	.9855	.9829	.9793	.9755

We also did a qualitative evaluation of the inpainting performance based on a selection of test images from different mask categories. This evaluation is, naturally, subjective but possibly also more relatable. Figure 1 shows the results using the NYUV2 dataset. For all three mask categories, LaMa produces the best results that are very close to the original. The PConv method is also able to create good results without apparent visual artifacts, apart from a slight blur in the last row with a mask of 40%–50% hole-to-image ratio. For the GAN method, the results for the small mask are very close to the ground truth image. However, on

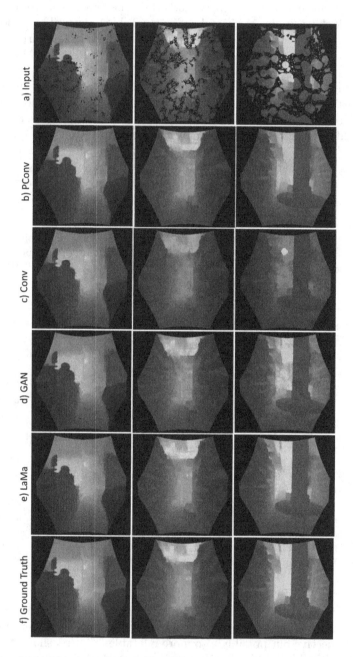

Fig. 1. Visual inpainting results on the NYUV2 test set using various hole categories (columns). LaMa performs best, the PConv method performs second best, the GAN struggles with bigger holes, and the Conv method is the worst.

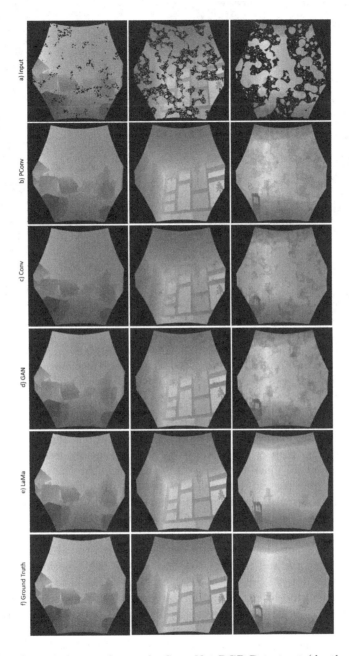

Fig. 2. Visual inpainting results on the SceneNet RGB-D test set (depth only) using various hole categories (columns). All methods apart from LaMa, which performs best, produce distinct artifacts. However, PConv and GAN perform reasonably well in the medium/small categories, and Conv is again the worst-performing method.

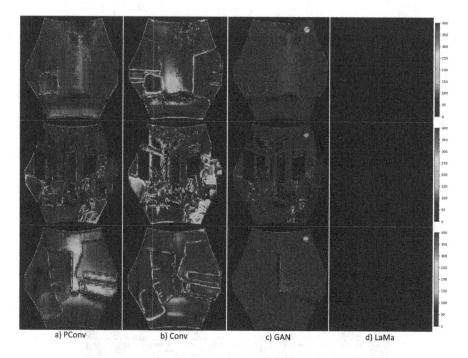

a) PConv   b) Conv   c) GAN   d) LaMa

Fig. 3. Color-coded pixel-wise deltas of originally valid areas after inpainting using our dataset. The holes were reintegrated from the input data. The Conv method alters the original data around holes the most (for smoother transitions), GAN the least, and LaMa not at all.

the medium and big masks, we can see slight deteriorations and then even more artifacts occurring, respectively. The Conv method visibly leads to the worst results throughout all mask categories, as can be seen by the increased blurriness and other (dark, cloudy) artifacts. Generally, we find that the qualitative results are consistent with the quantitative ones. The results using the SceneNet RGB-D dataset in Fig. 2 are similar: LaMa performs better than all the others, especially for the bigger mask categories. The PConv method creates reasonably good results for the small and medium mask categories, the GAN performs well in the small category, and the Conv method is the worst-performing method. However, on this dataset, all methods apart from LaMa have issues with artifacts in the form of too-bright or too-dark areas that get more severe with bigger masks. This could be because of systemic differences between this dataset and the one used for training (NYUV2). For instance, this dataset with synthetically created images generally has sharper edges/objects than the NYUV2 dataset, which also incorporated errors that slightly degrade the images.

To evaluate our models on real-world data, we first investigate the effects of the inpainting methods on the valid areas. Ideally, they should remain unchanged. As can be seen in Fig. 3, which shows the color-coded deltas between

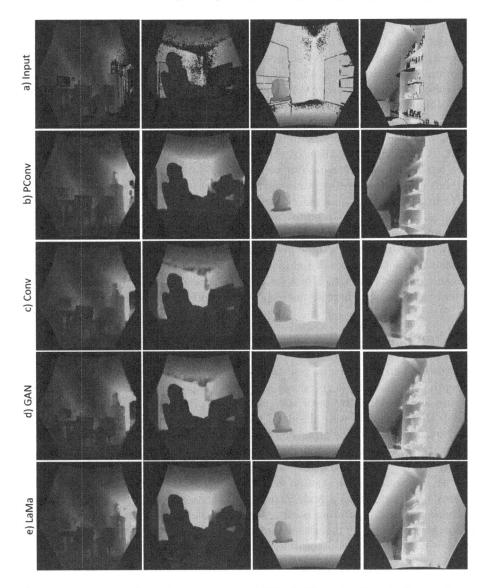

Fig. 4. Inpainting results with our own dataset. The LaMa method most often produces the best visual results. PConv behaves quite similarly, and both struggles with outliers. However, in some cases, the GAN performs the best.

the original and inpainted images, this is mostly not the case. The PConv method leads to relatively small differences, mostly along the edges of objects, corners, or at thin shapes. This could be an effect of the model trying to prevent hard edges and instead favoring slow transitions. The GAN method performs better at far corners and edges and, generally, produces images with more even deltas.

Moreover, it creates the sharpest results with more abrupt object transitions. An odd issue with the GAN method is the distinct artifacts that occur consistently in the upper right corner. We suspect this to be an issue with the value of the introduced weighting factor λ for the loss function, as the authors of the original method suggested that lower values lead to sharper results but, in turn, lead to more artifacts. The Conv method, again, leads to the worst results and produces the biggest deltas throughout the whole image. Interestingly, in contrast to the others, LaMa does not change the originally valid areas at all, which is the best result. For a final comparison of the models, we compare the resulting images after inpainting, again, using our own custom dataset. As visible in Fig. 4, all methods are able to create reasonable predictions for the missing areas, although the Conv method produces more blurry results. Interestingly, PConv and LaMa as well as Conv and GAN tend to have a similar behavior. Generally, LaMa tends to create the most plausible and visually pleasing results, followed by PConv. However, one drawback of these methods seems to be the prediction around outlier pixels. The advantage of LaMa on this real-world dataset is smaller as with the other datasets though. Moreover, in some cases, the GAN method produces better results, hence, there seems to be no method that is categorically superior.

5   Conclusion

We presented an approach for real-time reconstruction of missing or invalid areas in depth images using deep neural networks. In particular, our approach does not use any guidance by color images. We adopted two different U-Net-based models that originally were designed for color-image inpainting, one using partial convolutions, and the other one being a patch-based GAN. For comparison, we took also a basic U-Net and a more sophisticated state-of-the-art model, namely LaMa. The training was done using the public NYU Depth V2 dataset that we augmented with custom holes. Our quantitative and qualitative evaluations with the NYUV2 and SceneNet datasets showed that LaMa, overall, produces the best inpainting results, the GAN method performs especially well on images with smaller hole-to-image ratios, the partial convolution approach achieves consistently good results (images with various hole sizes and ratios), and the regular convolution-based approach fares the worst. Applied to a custom dataset we recorded with an Azure Kinect sensor, we found that the LaMa model, on average, leads to the visually most pleasing inpainting results, although the PConv and GAN methods also achieve reasonably good and coherent results (the latter sometimes even being superior). To conclude, all methods are able to reconstruct holes of any shape, size, or location without any postprocessing procedures, with reasonable to good visual quality. Also, apart from LaMa which is notably slower, they achieve this in a real-time fashion. In the future, we plan to also incorporate RGB data as additional input, if available, to enhance the inpainting results with this extra information. Other network architectures such as transformer models, originally from the natural language processing domain, should be investigated to also take advantage of temporal coherency between subsequent images. Moreover, producing ground truth data for our own dataset (recorded with the Azure Kinect) would be highly beneficial for the training and evaluation of the models. One approach for this challenging task would be to couple the Azure Kinect with another precisely, externally registered depth-sensing device, such as a stereo camera, from which the depth for the missing areas can be produced.

References

1. Armanious, K., Mecky, Y., Gatidis, S., Yang, B.: Adversarial inpainting of medical image modalities. In: IEEE International Conference on Acoustics, Speech and Signal Processing (ICASSP), pp. 3267–3271 (2019)
2. Chen, H., et al.: Pre-trained image processing transformer. In: Proceedings of the IEEE/CVF Conference on Computer Vision and Pattern Recognition, pp. 12299–12310 (2021)
3. Deng, Y., Hui, S., Zhou, S., Meng, D., Wang, J.: T-former: an efficient transformer for image inpainting. In: Proceedings of the 30th ACM International Conference on Multimedia, MM 2022, pp. 6559–6568. Association for Computing Machinery (2022)
4. Fujii, R., Hachiuma, R., Saito, H.: RGB-D image inpainting using generative adversarial network with a late fusion approach. ArXiv: abs/2110.07413 (2020)
5. Isola, P., Zhu, J.Y., Zhou, T., Efros, A.: Image-to-image translation with conditional adversarial networks. In: IEEE Conference on Computer Vision and Pattern Recognition (CVPR), pp. 5967–5976 (2017)
6. Jeon, J., Lim, H., Seo, D.U., Myung, H.: Struct-mdc: mesh-refined unsupervised depth completion leveraging structural regularities from visual slam. IEEE Robot. Autom. Lett. **7**(3), 6391–6398 (2022)
7. Jin, W., Zun, L., Yong, L.: Double-constraint inpainting model of a single-depth image. Sensors **20**(6), 1797 (2020)
8. Lee, S., Yi, E., Lee, J., Kim, J.: Multi-scaled and densely connected locally convolutional layers for depth completion. In: 2022 IEEE/RSJ International Conference on Intelligent Robots and Systems (IROS), pp. 8360–8367 (2022)
9. Li, W., Lin, Z., Kun, Z., Qi, L., Wang, Y., Jia, J.: Mat: mask-aware transformer for large hole image inpainting. In: 2022 IEEE/CVF Conference on Computer Vision and Pattern Recognition (CVPR), pp. 10748–10758 (2022)
10. Li, Z., et al.: Promising generative adversarial network based sinogram inpainting method for ultra-limited-angle computed tomography imaging. Sensors **19**(18), 3941 (2019)
11. Li, Z., Wu, J.: Learning deep CNN denoiser priors for depth image inpainting. Appl. Sci. **9**(6), 1103 (2019)
12. Liu, G.: Pytorch implementation of the partial convolution layer for padding and image inpainting (2018). https://github.com/NVIDIA/partialconv
13. Liu, G., Reda, F.A., Shih, K.J., Wang, T.C., Tao, A., Catanzaro, B.: Image inpainting for irregular holes using partial convolutions. In: European Conference on Computer Vision (2018)
14. Makarov, I., Borisenko, G.: Depth inpainting via vision transformer. In: 2021 IEEE International Symposium on Mixed and Augmented Reality Adjunct (ISMAR-Adjunct), pp. 286–291 (10 2021)

15. Mal, F., Karaman, S.: Sparse-to-dense: depth prediction from sparse depth samples and a single image. In: 2018 IEEE International Conference on Robotics and Automation (ICRA), pp. 1–8 (2018)

16. Ning, W., Li, J., Zhang, L., Du, B.: Musical: multi-scale image contextual attention learning for inpainting. In: Proceedings of the Twenty-Eighth International Joint Conference on Artificial Intelligent, pp. 3748–3754 (2019)

17. Rombach, R., Blattmann, A., Lorenz, D., Esser, P., Ommer, B.: High-resolution image synthesis with latent diffusion models. In: Proceedings of the IEEE/CVF Conference on Computer Vision and Pattern Recognition, pp. 10684–10695 (2022)

18. Ruzic, T., Pizurica, A.: Context-aware patch-based image inpainting using Markov random field modeling. IEEE Trans. Image Process. **24**(1), 444–456 (2015)

19. Satapathy, S., Sahay, R.R.: Robust depth map inpainting using superpixels and non-local gauss-Markov random field prior. Signal Process.: Image Commun. **98**, 116378 (2021)

20. Shao, M., Zhang, W., Zuo, W., Meng, D.: Multi-scale generative adversarial inpainting network based on cross-layer attention transfer mechanism. Knowl.-Based Syst. **196**, 105778 (2020)

21. Shen, L., Hong, R., Zhang, H., Zhang, H., Wang, M.: Single-shot semantic image inpainting with densely connected generative networks. In: Proceedings of the 27th ACM International Conference on Multimedia, MM 2019, pp. 1861–1869 (2019)

22. Starck, J.L., Elad, M., Donoho, D.: Image decomposition via the combination of sparse representations and a variational approach. IEEE Trans. Image Process. **14**(10), 1570–1582 (2005)

23. Suvorov, R., et al.: Resolution-robust large mask inpainting with Fourier convolutions. In: Proceedings of the IEEE/CVF Winter Conference on Applications of Computer Vision (WACV), pp. 2149–2159 (2022)

24. Tao, Y., Popovic, M., Wang, Y., Digumarti, S., Chebrolu, N., Fallon, M.: 3d lidar reconstruction with probabilistic depth completion for robotic navigation. In: 2022 IEEE/RSJ International Conference on Intelligent Robots and Systems (IROS), pp. 5339–5346 (2022)

25. Tschumperle, D., Deriche, R.: Vector-valued image regularization with PDEs: a common framework for different applications. IEEE Trans. Pattern Anal. Machine Intell. **27**(4), 506–517 (2005)

26. Wongsa, R.: Pytorch implementation of the paper: image inpainting for irregular holes using partial convolutions. https://github.com/ryanwongsa/Image-Inpainting (2020)

27. Xie, C., et al.: Image inpainting with learnable bidirectional attention maps. In: 2019 IEEE/CVF International Conference on Computer Vision (ICCV), pp. 8857–8866 (2019)

28. Yan, Z., Li, X., Li, M., Zuo, W., Shan, S.: Shift-net: image inpainting via deep feature rearrangement. In: European Conference on Computer Vision (2018)

29. Yeh, R., Chen, C., Lim, T.Y., Schwing, A., Hasegawa-Johnson, M., Do, M.: Semantic image inpainting with deep generative models. In: 2017 IEEE Conference on Computer Vision and Pattern Recognition (CVPR), pp. 6882–6890 (2017)

30. Yu, J., Lin, Z., Yang, J., Shen, X., Lu, X., Huang, T.: Free-form image inpainting with gated convolution. In: 2019 IEEE/CVF International Conference on Computer Vision (ICCV), pp. 4470–4479 (2019)

31. Yu, Y., et al.: Diverse image inpainting with bidirectional and autoregressive transformers. In Proceedings of the 29th ACM International Conference on Multimedia (2021)

32. Zhang, X., Zhai, D., Li, T., Zhou, Y., Lin, Y.: Image inpainting based on deep learning: a review. Inf. Fusion **90**, 74–94 (2022)
33. Zhang, Y., Funkhouser, T.: Deep depth completion of a single RGB-D image. In: Proceedings of the IEEE Conference on Computer Vision and Pattern Recognition (CVPR) (2018)

Using 2D and 3D Face Representations to Generate Comprehensive Facial Electromyography Intensity Maps

Tim Büchner[1]([envelope]) [ID], Sven Sickert[1] [ID], Roland Graßme[2], Christoph Anders[2] [ID], Orlando Guntinas-Lichius[3] [ID], and Joachim Denzler[1] [ID]

[1] Computer Vision Group, Friedrich Schiller University Jena, 07743 Jena, Germany
{tim.buechner,sven.sickert,joachim.denzler}@uni-jena.de
[2] Division of Motor Research, Pathophysiology and Biomechanics, Clinic for Trauma, Hand and Reconstructive Surgery, Jena University Hospital, 07747 Jena, Germany
{roland.grassme,christoph.anders}@med.uni-jena.de
[3] Department of Otorhinolaryngology, Jena University Hospital, 07747 Jena, Germany
orlando.guntinas@med.uni-jena.de

Abstract. Electromyography (EMG) is a method to measure muscle activity. Physicians also use EMG to study the function of facial muscles through intensity maps (IMs) to support diagnostics and research. However, many existing visualizations neglect anatomical structures and disregard the physical properties of EMG signals. The variance of facial structures between people complicates the generalization of IMs, which is crucial for their correct interpretation. In our work, we overcome these issues by introducing a pipeline to generate anatomically correct IMs for facial muscles. An IM generation algorithm based on a template model incorporates custom surface EMG schemes and combines them with a projection method to highlight the IMs on the patient's face in 2D and 3D. We evaluate the generated and projected IMs based on their correct projection quality for six base emotions on several subjects. These visualizations deepen the understanding of muscle activity areas and indicate that a holistic view of the face could be necessary to understand facial muscle activity. Medical experts can use our approach to study the function of facial muscles and to support diagnostics and therapy.

Keywords: Medical Visualization · EMG Intensity Maps · Projections · Emotion · Mimics · Facial Muscles

Supported by Deutsche Forschungsgemeinschaft (DFG - German Research Foundation) project 427899908 BRIDGING THE GAP: MIMICS AND MUSCLES (DE 735/15-1 and GU 463/12-1).

G. Bebis et al. (Eds.): ISVC 2023, LNCS 14362, pp. 136–147, 2023.
https://doi.org/10.1007/978-3-031-47966-3_11

1   Introduction

Many medical imaging techniques utilize 2D or 3D visualizations to support decision-making during clinical routine and research. To gain insight into the function of the facial muscles, medical experts utilize electromyography (EMG) schemes applied to the face [11,16]. Intensity maps (IMs) are a common way to display the spatial relations among muscles [11,16,19]. Given the complexity of the facial muscles and their 3D movement [7], IMs are a valuable tool for studying the function of facial muscles and support diagnostics and therapy. However, such visualizations often neglect the anatomical locations of surface electrodes, the physical properties of EMG signals, the interaction of individual facial muscles, and the individual's facial structure for highlighting.

We overcome these limitations by introducing a pipeline for anatomically correct facial muscle intensity maps. First, we use a canonical template face model as a base for the complex interwoven network of facial muscles [13,18]. Based on this model, we support two standard EMG schemes and interpolate between surface electrodes incorporating the physical properties of EMG signals [11,16]. Lastly, we project the IMs onto the patient's face in 2D and 3D to indicate muscular activity. Our projection algorithm considers the patients' facial head shape, pose, and expression. As a result, we give physicians a tool to study the facial muscles' functions projected onto the patient's face and support diagnostics and therapy by releasing our work as independent open source libraries[1].

2   Methods

The main limitations of current EMG IM visualizations are the lack of 3D anatomical information in general and the missing relations of individual facial structures, which is crucial for correct interpretation. First, we focus on generating anatomically correct IMs employing a canonical face template model [13]. We demonstrate the process using two standardized EMG schemes [11,16]. However, our method is not limited to these schemes and is extendable to custom mappings to enable specialized research. Projecting the generated IMs onto the patient's face highlights the muscular activity in a 2D image or 3D face model.

2.1   EMG Intensity Map Generation

By definition, muscle activity is the electrical response of the muscle cells under load measured in volts [22]. The acquired time series of the electrical response is called an electromyogram (EMG). Experts visualize the spatial relations using intensity maps (IMs) based on a planar grid structure neglecting anatomical placement and three-dimensionality of the muscles and their movements (see Fig. 1) [16]. However, electrode placement is crucial for interpolation as the EMG

---

[1] www.github.com/cvjena/electromyogram, www.github.com/cvjena/face-projection.

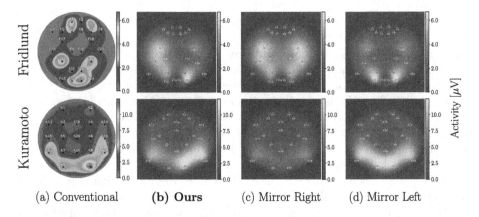

(a) Conventional   **(b) Ours**   (c) Mirror Right   (d) Mirror Left

Fig. 1. Displaying the intensity maps for a smiling expression for two different EMG schemes (Fridlund scheme, upper row; Kuramoto scheme, lower row): The first column shows the conventional approach neglecting anatomical structures, and the second column shows the proposed intensity maps. The third and fourth column shows the lateral mirrored maps focusing on the face's left and right sides.

signal drops off quadratically with distance [22]. Furthermore, a categorical colormap implies that large areas around the electrodes have the same intensity intervals, which conflicts with the EMG's physical properties.

We propose to circumvent these limitations by explicitly considering: anatomical electrode locations, an interpolation comprising correct physical properties, and a continuous colormap [5]. First, we define the anatomical electrode locations based on the facial structure inside the canonical face model [13]. Such an approach offers several advantages: (i) The template model ensures a patient-independent visualization, which is crucial for interpolation. (ii) Semantic facial landmarks ensure proper electrode location definition, and (iii) we can utilize existing models for correct facial landmark detection for the projections [18].

The canonical face model contains 468 facial landmarks [13], which we use to determine the electrode locations in a planar view. We define the electrode locations for two standardized facial EMG schemes, Fridlund [11] and Kuramoto [16], which we compare in our evaluation. Figure 2 displays the anatomical and corresponding locations on the canonical face model. Additionally, the warped view helps to comprehend the spatial connections among the electrodes and the facial landmarks. The blue dots mark the electrode locations, and the green squares depict the hull boundary of the face model.

These electrode locations are crucial for approximating the EMG signal's spatial properties via interpolation in the next step. Points of the outer hull form an interpolation boundary and act as electrodes without muscle activity, having an amplitude of 0 V. We deploy radial basis function (RBF) interpolation to approximate the EMGs' spatial properties inside the canonical face model [9,28]. Specifically, a thin plate spline as a kernel function in the form of $r^2 \cdot \log r$ models the signal drop off [28], with r being the distance of each location to the center

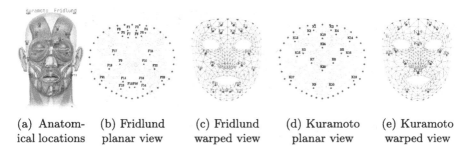

| (a) Anatomical locations | (b) Fridlund planar view | (c) Fridlund warped view | (d) Kuramoto planar view | (e) Kuramoto warped view |

Fig. 2. The anatomical electrode locations of the Fridlund (blue) [11] and Kuramoto (green) [16] schemes are shown in (a). The matching locations (blue) on the canonical face are shown as planar and warped views in (b, c) and (d, e). (Color figure online)

point. As we ensured correct anatomical placement beforehand, the electrode values can be interpolated without weights ensuring a valid spatial behavior approximation of the EMG signal between the electrodes.

Visualizing unilateral muscle activity is highly relevant for some medical diseases, such as unilateral facial palsy [26]. In this case, the muscle activity is not symmetric due to muscle inactivity or hypoactivity on the palsy side, compensatory hyperactivity of the contralateral side, or both combined. We can mitigate interpolation artifacts by laterally mirroring along the midline of the face model and interpolating each side separately. Thus, we enforce a symmetric interpolation of the face sides and remove contralateral artifacts, giving insight into the unilateral muscle activity. In Fig. 1, we visually compare the conventional approach [16] with our proposed method. We show the IMs of a smiling expression and use a sequential colormap (*Imola*) to visualize the continuous data [5]. 2D grid interpolation neglects the anatomical electrode locations and gives the impression of discrete areas of muscle activity, resulting in a distorted visualization. The connection between electrode locations and interpolated values is not apparent and might hinder the interpretation of the IMs. However, both approaches still capture the properties of the EMG schemes, as Fridlund specializes in specific muscles, while Kuramoto is better for muscle activity regions [19].

2.2 Anatomical 2D Face Projection

We have seen in the previous section that interpolating the EMG signal's spatial properties is crucial for the IMs' quality. However, the IMs are still 2D visualizations of the spatial relations between muscle activations without a patient's facial structure. We propose further enhancing the generated IMs' quality by projecting them onto the face while preserving anatomical properties. This step enhances muscle activity visualization, improving the IMs' interpretability.

One of the main advantages of the canonical face model is that we can deploy existing facial landmark detection algorithms [18]. Thus, we can avoid fine-tuning our data and ensure general visualization capabilities. Using the same 468 facial

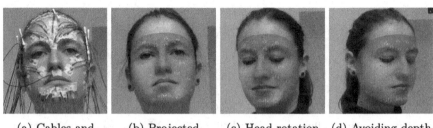

| (a) Cables and electrodes | (b) Projected Fridlund IMs | (c) Head rotation invariant | (d) Avoiding depth clipping |

Fig. 3. We show the projection of the IMs onto the face model. In (a), the face is covered in cables and electrodes while acquiring the EMG signals. The restored facial features with the overlaid muscle activity are shown in (b). Figures (c) and (d) depict head rotation invariance and the prevention of depth clipping.

landmarks allows us to generate a one-to-one mapping between the IMs and the face[2]. However, during the acquisition of the EMG signals, the face is covered in cables and electrodes, as shown in Fig. 3a. Hence, many facial features are obstructed, and existing algorithms cannot detect them. We follow the work of [3] and restore the original facial features, which visually improves the overlaid muscle activity, as shown in Fig. 3b.

As the interpolation approximates the EMG signal's spatial relations over the entire template model, areas without muscle activity also have interpolated values, including the eyes, mouth, and lips; see Fig. 1a. However, we remove these areas for a more natural and intuitive impression of the face and muscle activity by masking them out in the IMs. A consequence of deleting the areas of the eyes and mouth is that the triangulation of the canonical face model is no longer valid. Therefore, a newly calculated triangulation maps the template model to the face [15,24], depicted in Fig. 4. We obtain corresponding pairs $(T_{\text{face}}^{(i)}, T_{\text{IM}}^{(i)})$ for each triangle $T^{(i)}$ in the triangulation to compute the projection.

First, we extract the bounding boxes for each triangle pair, from which we compute the affine homomorphism described by the matrix $M \in \mathbb{R}^{3 \times 3}$. Each pixel in the triangle $T_{IM}^{(i)}$ is then mapped to the corresponding pixel in the triangle $T_{face}^{(i)}$ using M. Bicubic interpolation approximates intermediate pixel values as the projection might contain different scales between the IM and the face. Additionally, the projection algorithm discards pixels outside the triangle to ensure a valid projection without overlap. As face parts might not be visible during head rotation, shown in Fig. 3c, depth clipping artifacts might occur. We circumvent this issue by sorting the triangles from back to front using the estimated depth values of each triangle [18]. Please note the default resolution for IMs is 1024×1024 pixels, while the face images have a resolution of 256×256 pixels. Thus, we obtain a highly detailed projection with electrode locations and the interpolated values blended onto the face, as shown in Fig. 3b.

---

[2] All shown individuals agreed to have their images published in terms with the GDPR.

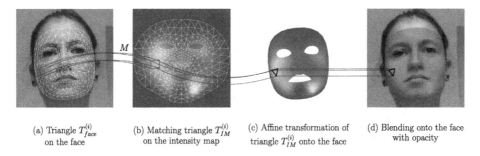

(a) Triangle $T^{(i)}_{face}$ on the face   (b) Matching triangle $T^{(i)}_{IM}$ on the intensity map   (c) Affine transformation of triangle $T^{(i)}_{IM}$ onto the face   (d) Blending onto the face with opacity

Fig. 4. Triangle correspondence between the face and the IM: We compute the affine matrix M between the bounding boxes (red) of $T^{(i)}_{\text{IM}}$ and $T^{(i)}_{\text{face}}$. Each pixel of the IM is transformed to the corresponding pixel in the face using M. (Color figure online)

Since our projection solely depends on facial landmarks, we can project the IMs onto any face [18]. Furthermore, our approach is independent of the facial pose and rotation, as shown in Fig. 3c. This advantage allows our method to be used on static images and videos, opening up the research of dynamic analysis of muscle activity. The combination of interpolation and projection allows us to visualize muscle activity more intuitively for medical professionals and patients.

2.3 Anatomical 3D Face Projection

Leveraging the 3D structure of the face will further enhance the interpretability of muscle activity. Such a step would enable visualization in a virtual reality environment or with holographic displays[3]. To achieve this, we utilize the resulting 2D projection as the basis for the 3D transformation. As this projection already ensures the anatomical correctness of the muscle activity, the 3D representation is also anatomically correct. We present two 3D model generation approaches based on depth sensors and monocular depth estimation models, respectively.

Our first approach operates on depth maps provided by cameras such as the Intel RealSense D435. Given the RGBD data and the intrinsic camera parameters, the computed point cloud describes the 3D face structure. However, replacing the RGB image with the projected 2D intensity map only changes the vertex color of the point cloud. To obtain a mesh representation of the face, we use Poisson surface reconstruction [14]. Reconstructed areas with lower confidence than 0.03 are removed, and only the largest connected component is kept. Lastly, using Laplacian smoothing along the z-axis ensures that the face's surface is smooth and contains no artifacts from the depth sensor [25,27]. We show the resulting mesh from the depth sensor in Fig. 5a.

Our second approach utilizes monocular depth estimation models to obtain a 3D representation of the face. Hence, it does not require a depth sensor and can be retrospectively employed on existing images and videos. Such monocular

---

[3] We support LookingGlass Portrait (Looking Glass Factory Inc., New York, USA) natively in our pipeline.

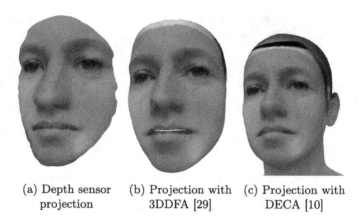

(a) Depth sensor   (b) Projection with   (c) Projection with
    projection   3DDFA [29]   DECA [10]

Fig. 5. We display three different 3D reconstruction variants with projected intensity maps. They include a head scan reconstruction (a), the monocular depth model *3DDFA* (b) [29], and the 3D morphable model *DECA* (c) [10].

models are trained on large data sets of facial images with corresponding 3D scans to approximate the underlying facial structure. Given an RGB image, the 3DDFA model [12,29] estimates the Basel Face Model [20] to obtain a 3D mesh of only the face. The DECA model [10] predicts the FLAME model [21], which includes the head, neck, and upper torso. They are not accurate compared to a 3D scan, and significant deviations occur due to the underlying template model assumptions, as is visible in Fig. 5b and Fig. 5c. However, they are sufficient for visualizing muscle activity on a 3D face.

3   Data Acquisition

Our dataset combines synchronous surface EMG and RGBD data recording for healthy probands. We use an Intel RealSense D435 camera with a 1280×720 pixels resolution and a frame rate of 30 fps. All probands are seated in front of the camera at eye level with a distance of 1.0 meters to ensure the face is visible in the depth sensor's field of view. Our surface EMG measurements follow the work of Mueller et al. [19], merging doubled electrodes for Fridlund and Kuramoto [11,16]. Each proband has 62 surface electrodes attached while mimicking voluntary facial expressions instructed by a video tutorial [23].

Our probands are recorded with and without applied surface electrodes to restore the facial expression using CycleGANs [3]. Otherwise, existing landmark detection methods would fail and result in incorrect projections. The restored facial expressions are used for the projection in all visualizations, as shown in Fig. 3b. The processing of the EMG data follows the guidelines discussed in [11,16,19]. The muscle activity is measured with 4096 samples per second. We normalize each channel's average to zero and remove power line noise with a notch filter at 50 Hz. Furthermore, we apply an FIR band-pass filter in this

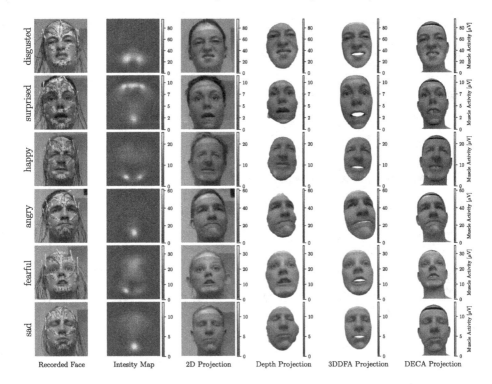

Fig. 6. Muscle activity patterns for the base emotions [6] using Fridlund [11] scheme: We show the original facial expression with the attached surface electrodes, the generated corresponding intensity maps (IMs), and projection onto the restored facial expression [3]. The Fridlund scheme visualizes individual muscle activity during expressions. (Best viewed digitally.)

range because most muscle activity ranges from 10 to 500 Hz [11]. Lastly, we compute the root mean square with a 128 ms sliding window to match video frames and EMG data. Thus, data is synchronous with an error of up to 8 ms.

4 Evaluation

Our evaluation focuses on the visual quality and the possible insights gained from the generated intensity maps of the resulting muscle activity patterns for the six base emotions [6]. We do not assess the muscle activity patterns' correctness regarding the defined facial action coding system [7], as this is not the focus of our work and is still disputed [1,8]. However, our method allows medical professionals to evaluate the correctness of the muscle activity patterns in future research. We measure with the Fridlund [11] and Kuramoto [16] schemes jointly during the recording but evaluate them separately to avoid visual interference. The resulting muscle activity patterns are shown in Fig. 6 and Fig. 7 for six different probands varying in gender and age. Please note that we do not normalize

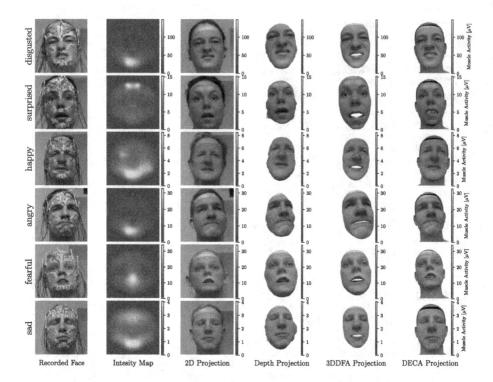

Fig. 7. Muscle activity patterns for the base emotions [6] using Kuramoto [16] scheme: We show the original facial expression with the attached surface electrodes, the generated corresponding intensity maps (IMs), and projection onto the restored facial expression [3]. The Kuramoto scheme visualizes the muscle activity areas during expressions. (Best viewed digitally.)

amplitudes between the emotions as they can contribute to their differentiation, as visible in Fig. 6 for **sad** and **angry**. Furthermore, we refrain from adding the label locations to the visualizations to avoid visual clutter and instead refer to the electrode locations in Fig. 2. For the Fridlund scheme, we observe that mainly single muscles are dominating, as expected [7], but also that other facial areas are involved to a lesser extent. This observation could indicate that the interwoven network of facial muscles is more active during facial expressions than previously thought [1,2,4]. The overall facial activations are even more visible with the Kuramoto scheme, highlighting the importance of a more holistic view of the facial muscles' activity. Combining both schemes' advantages could benefit future work to understand the facial muscles' activity better.

Our 2D IM projection algorithm works for different head shapes, orientations, expressions, and probands, as visible in Fig. 6 and Fig. 7. Comparing the surface electrode locations with the highlighted areas in the face, they largely overlap and thus confirm the correctness of our method. As we remove eye and mouth areas from the IMs, the mouth opening for **surprised** and eye closing for **sad** are not overlaid. Hence, our work allows for an individual analysis of the muscle activity patterns for each proband, not only for a generic face model.

The 3D visualizations differ considerably between the probands and methods, respectively. Only the depth sensor-based approach correctly captures the proband's original head shape, whereas the monocular methods strongly resemble the underlying template model. The projected IMs might lose some information due to underlying model biases during the computation, as visible for **happy** in Fig. 7 where the mouth is *not open* but predicted *open* by the model. However, the monocular methods are still helpful for visualizing muscle activity patterns in 3D space, given that no depth sensor is available.

5 Conclusion

The proposed visualization methodology allows for an individualized analysis of muscle activity patterns by projecting the intensity maps onto the face's surface in 2D and 3D. This is a significant step from a generic face model and can help clinicians and researchers understand the variations in emotional expressions between individuals and patients, including those of different genders and ages. Our method is not limited to a specific head shape, orientation, or expression, as visible in Fig. 6 and Fig. 7.

Evaluation of these maps can provide insights into how multiple muscles and facial areas contribute to a particular emotional expression. Understanding the subtleties of facial muscle activation can be extremely useful for diagnosing patients with facial diseases in biofeedback and facial rehabilitation. For patients recovering from conditions like Bell's palsy or stroke that often affect facial muscles [17,26], these visualizations could help therapists track recovery progress and plan individualized rehabilitation programs. Knowledge gained from understanding the subtle use of facial muscles can be applied in additional fields, like psychophysical experiments in psychology, acting, animation, advertising, etc., to make non-verbal communication appear more authentic and impactful.

Our evaluation results indicate that the muscle activity patterns are not as simple as previously postulated [1,7]. The detailed results and comprehensive visual representations illustrated in this study establish a solid foundation for further investigation in the field. There is still ongoing dispute on facial expressions and muscles, and having such concrete visualizations and analysis could potentially aid in resolving these issues. A more holistic view of the facial muscles' activity seems to be necessary to understand the underlying processes better. The results and visualizations of this research can aid psychologists in studying and interpreting human emotions more accurately, thus enriching the science of understanding human behavior. The novelty of this approach lies not only in the specific techniques used but also in the fresh perspective it offers into the simultaneous mapping of muscle activations with corresponding facial expressions by bridging the gap between mimics and muscles.

References

1. Barrett, L.F., Adolphs, R., Marsella, S., Martinez, A.M., Pollak, S.D.: Emotional expressions reconsidered: challenges to inferring emotion from human facial movements. Psychol. Sci. Public Interest **20**(1), 1–68 (2019). https://doi.org/10.1177/1529100619832930
2. Benitez-Quiroz, C.F., Srinivasan, R., Martinez, A.M.: Facial color is an efficient mechanism to visually transmit emotion. Proc. Natl. Acad. Sci. **115**(14), 3581–3586 (2018). https://doi.org/10.1073/pnas.1716084115
3. Büchner, T., Sickert, S., Volk, G.F., Anders, C., Guntinas-Lichius, O., Denzler, J.: Let's get the FACS straight - reconstructing obstructed facial features. In: International Conference on Computer Vision Theory and Applications (VISAPP), pp. 727–736. SciTePress (2023). https://doi.org/10.5220/0011619900003417
4. Cowen, A., Sauter, D., Tracy, J.L., Keltner, D.: Mapping the Passions: toward a high-dimensional taxonomy of emotional experience and expression. Psychol. Sci. Public Interest **20**(1), 69–90 (2019). https://doi.org/10.1177/1529100619850176
5. Dasgupta, A., Poco, J., Rogowitz, B., Han, K., Bertini, E., Silva, C.T.: The effect of color scales on climate scientists' objective and subjective performance in spatial data analysis tasks. IEEE Trans. Visual Comput. Graph. **26**(3), 1577–1591 (2020). https://doi.org/10.1109/TVCG.2018.2876539
6. Ekman, P.: An argument for basic emotions. Cogn. Emot. **6**(3–4), 169–200 (1992). https://doi.org/10.1080/02699939208411068
7. Ekman, P., Friesen, W.: Facial action coding system: a technique for the measurement of facial movement. Palo Alto: Consult. Psychol. Press (1978). https://doi.org/10.1037/t27734-000
8. Elfenbein, H.A., Ambady, N.: On the universality and cultural specificity of emotion recognition: a meta-analysis. Psychol. Bull. **128**(2), 203–235 (2002). https://doi.org/10.1037/0033-2909.128.2.203
9. Fasshauer, G.E.: Meshfree approximation methods with matlab: (With CD-ROM), Interdisciplinary Mathematical Sciences, vol. 6. World Scientific (2007). https://doi.org/10.1142/6437
10. Feng, Y., Feng, H., Black, M.J., Bolkart, T.: Learning an animatable detailed 3D face model from in-the-wild images. ACM Trans. Graph. **40**(4), 1–13 (2021). https://doi.org/10.1145/3450626.3459936
11. Fridlund, A.J., Cacioppo, J.T.: Guidelines for human electromyographic research. Psychophysiology **23**(5), 567–589 (1986). https://doi.org/10.1111/j.1469-8986.1986.tb00676.x
12. Guo, J., Zhu, X., Yang, Y., Yang, F., Lei, Z., Li, S.Z.: Towards fast, accurate and stable 3d dense face alignment. In: Vedaldi, A., Bischof, H., Brox, T., Frahm, J.-M. (eds.) ECCV 2020. LNCS, vol. 12364, pp. 152–168. Springer, Cham (2020). https://doi.org/10.1007/978-3-030-58529-7_10
13. Kartynnik, Y., Ablavatski, A., Grishchenko, I., Grundmann, M.: Real-time facial surface geometry from monocular video on mobile GPUs. arXiv:1907.06724 (2019)
14. Kazhdan, M., Bolitho, M., Hoppe, H.: Poisson surface reconstruction. The Eurographics Association (2006). https://doi.org/10.2312/SGP/SGP06/061-070
15. Kloeckner, A., et al.: MeshPy (2022). https://doi.org/10.5281/zenodo.7296572
16. Kuramoto, E., Yoshinaga, S., Nakao, H., Nemoto, S., Ishida, Y.: Characteristics of facial muscle activity during voluntary facial expressions: imaging analysis of facial expressions based on myogenic potential data. Neuropsychopharmacol. Rep. **39**(3), 183–193 (2019). https://doi.org/10.1002/npr2.12059

17. Loyo, M., McReynold, M., Mace, J.C., Cameron, M.: Protocol for randomized controlled trial of electric stimulation with high-volt twin peak versus placebo for facial functional recovery from acute Bell's palsy in patients with poor prognostic factors. J. Rehabil. Assist. Technol. Eng. **7**, 2055668320964142 (2020). https://doi.org/10.1177/2055668320964142

18. Lugaresi, C., et al.: MediaPipe: a framework for building perception pipelines (2019). https://doi.org/10.48550/arXiv.1906.08172

19. Mueller, N., Trentzsch, V., Grassme, R., Guntinas-Lichius, O., Volk, G.F., Anders, C.: High-resolution surface electromyographic activities of facial muscles during mimic movements in healthy adults: a prospective observational study. Front. Hum. Neurosci. **16**, 1029415 (2022). https://doi.org/10.3389/fnhum.2022.1029415

20. Paysan, P., Knothe, R., Amberg, B., Romdhani, S., Vetter, T.: A 3D face model for pose and illumination invariant face recognition. In: 2009 Sixth IEEE International Conference on Advanced Video and Signal Based Surveillance, pp. 296–301. IEEE (2009). https://doi.org/10.1109/AVSS.2009.58

21. Ranjan, A., Bolkart, T., Sanyal, S., Black, M.J.: Generating 3D faces using convolutional mesh autoencoders. In: Ferrari, V., Hebert, M., Sminchisescu, C., Weiss, Y. (eds.) ECCV 2018. LNCS, vol. 11207, pp. 725–741. Springer, Cham (2018). https://doi.org/10.1007/978-3-030-01219-9_43

22. Robertson, D.G.E., Caldwell, G.E., Hamill, J., Kamen, G., Whittlesey, S.N.: Research Methods in Biomechanics. Illinois, second edn., Human Kinetics, Champaign (2014)

23. Schaede, R.A., Volk, G.F., Modersohn, L., Barth, J.M., Denzler, J., Guntinas-Lichius, O.: Video instruction for synchronous video recording of mimic movement of patients with facial palsy. Laryngorhinootologie **96**(12), 844–849 (2017). https://doi.org/10.1055/s-0043-101699

24. Shewchuk, J.R.: Triangle: engineering a 2D quality mesh generator and Delaunay triangulator. In: Lin, M.C., Manocha, D. (eds.) WACG 1996. LNCS, vol. 1148, pp. 203–222. Springer, Heidelberg (1996). https://doi.org/10.1007/BFb0014497

25. Taubin, G.: Curve and surface smoothing without shrinkage. In: Proceedings of IEEE International Conference on Computer Vision, pp. 852–857 (1995). https://doi.org/10.1109/ICCV.1995.466848

26. Volk, G.F., Leier, C., Guntinas-lichius, O.: Correlation between electromyography and quantitative ultrasonography of facial muscles in patients with facial palsy. Muscle Nerve **53**(5), 755–761 (2016)

27. Vollmer, J., Mencl, R., Müller, H.: Improved Laplacian smoothing of noisy surface meshes. Comput. Graph. Forum **18**(3), 131–138 (1999). https://doi.org/10.1111/1467-8659.00334

28. Wahba, G.: Spline Models for Observational Data. CBMS-NSF Regional Conference Series in Applied Mathematics, Society for Industrial and Applied Mathematics (1990). https://doi.org/10.1137/1.9781611970128

29. Zhu, X., Liu, X., Lei, Z., Li, S.Z.: Face alignment in full pose range: a 3d total solution. IEEE Trans. Pattern Anal. Mach. Intell. **41**(1), 78–92 (2017)

Real-World Image Deblurring
via Unsupervised Domain Adaptation

Hanzhou Liu[1]([✉]), Binghan Li[1], Mi Lu[1], and Yucheng Wu[2]

[1] Texas A&M University, College Station, TX, USA
hanzhou1996@tamu.edu
[2] Columbia University, New York, NY, USA

Abstract. Most deep learning models for image deblurring are trained on pairs of clean images and their blurry counterparts, where the blurry inputs are artificially generated. However, it is impossible for these synthesized blurry images to cover all the real-world blur. Even in two synthetic datasets, the blur type, illumination, and other important image parameters could be different. Consequently, the performance of most existing deblurring models decreases when applied to real-world images and artificial blurry images from a different synthetic dataset. Very few previous deblurring works consider the gap among blurry images from different domains. Inspired by the current success of unsupervised domain adaptation (UDA) on image classification tasks, we develop, UDA-Deblur, a novel deblurring framework that utilizes domain alignment to attenuate effects of the aforementioned gap. In our work, channel attention modules are adopted to exploit the inter-channel relationship for features; multi-scale feature classifiers are designed to discriminate domain difference. UDA-Deblur is trained adversarially to align the feature distributions of the source domain and the target domain. We provide adequate quantitative and qualitative analysis to show the state-of-the-art performance of UDA-Deblur. Firstly, we evaluate the proposed UDA-Deblur on synthesized datasets related to real-life scenarios, which achieves satisfying deblurring results. We further demonstrate that our approach also outperforms prior models on real-world blurry images. For a persuasive comparison, we carefully design experiments on GoPro, HIDE and ReaBlur datasets. More importantly, this is the first work considering real-world image deblurring from a feature-level domain adaptation perspective.

Keywords: Image deblurring · Unsupervised domain adaptation · Deep learning

1 Introduction

Computer vision technology plays a key role in smart transportation [16,18]. Visual traffic information is crucial for ensuring road safety and security. However, the existence of blur adversely affects information extraction from traffic

G. Bebis et al. (Eds.): ISVC 2023, LNCS 14362, pp. 148–159, 2023.
https://doi.org/10.1007/978-3-031-47966-3_12

images, misleading intelligent driving systems to make incorrect decisions [17,33]. In fact, considering the wide application of vision systems nowadays, blurry images also cause serious issues in other areas. To address these problems, researchers proposed a variety of deblurring algorithms [19]. Traditional image deblurring methods formulate the deblurring task as an inverse filtering problem [32,40], and recover a clean image from a blurry one via a blur kernel [3,12,35]. On the other hand, incorrect kernel estimation introduces undesired artifacts in the cases of abrupt motion discontinuities and occlusion [21].

Thanks to rapid growth of artificial intelligence, numerous convolutional neural networks (CNN) based models succeed in low level computer vision tasks, including image deblurring [1,7,9,26]. More recently, Generated Adversarial Networks (GAN) is gaining popularity in image deblurring [13,14]. However, most of these deblurring models are trained on paired image datasets in an end to end way. In real-world scenarios, e.g., a vehicle speeding up on the road, it is hard to capture a blurry image of its license plate along with a corresponding clean one. Thus, unsupervised image deblurring is a promising research track [40].

One prevalent unsupervised deblurring baseline model is CycleGAN [42]. CycleGAN-based deblurring networks are trained on unpaired datasets, and generate both fake blurry images and fake clean images during the training phase [34,36]. Zhang et al. [39] provided an important new direction, which is to synthesize fake blurry images from real sharp images to form pseudo pairs, and then train a deblurring neural network in a paired manner. These existing approaches ignore the distinguishable gap between generated fake blurry images and original real blurry images.

Inspired by recent success of Unsupervised Domain Adaptation (UDA) on image classification tasks [4,11], we reinvestigate real-world image deblurring from a UDA perspective, which coincides with the idea of [10]. Formally, given a set of source domain samples as pseudo image pairs $\mathcal{S} = \{b_i^s, c_i^s\}_{i=1}^{N_s}$, and target domain samples $\mathcal{T} = \{b_i^t\}_{i=1}^{N_t}$, b^s and c^s represent synthetic blurry images and corresponding clean images respectively, and b^t denotes real blurry images. We are interested in restoring clear images c^t from real blurry images b^t. Different from [10], which learns domain-invariant representations from clean images, our purpose is to extract homogeneous features at multiple depth levels and then map these features to reconstructed images.

In this paper, we propose UDA-Deblur, a novel framework with unsupervised domain adaptation for single image deblurring. To reduce the domain discrepancy between b^s and b^t, we apply multi-scale discrimination to latent features extracted by the encoder. To diminish the impact of the unavoidable domain difference, we employ a weighted-channel mechanism similar to efficient channel attention [31]. MPRNet [37] is selected as the baseline model. We show that our explicit and effective network design attains competitive results both quantitatively and qualitatively.

Our contributions are of three-fold:

– To the best of our knowledge, this the first work considering real-world image deblurring from a feature-level domain adaptation perspective.

- We propose a novel domain alignment approach to improve the performance of image deblurring networks on real-world datasets.
- We provide in-depth studies to show that our design has competitive advantages over the existing image deblurring solutions.

2   Related Work

2.1   Single Image Deblurring

Single image deblurring is a classic while highly ill-posed problem in low-level computer vision. Non-deep learning methods show unsatisfactory performance in complicated yet common cases such as images with heavy motion blur [40]. In this section, we revisit deep learning deblurring methods.

Dominant deblurring methods rely on and only on pairs of clean images and blurry counterparts in the same dataset. Nah et al. [21] successfully removed blur caused by various sources via a multi-scale convolutional neural network. Tao et al. [27] investigated the coarse-to-fine scheme and proposed a scale-recurrent network for the deblurring task. Kupyn et al. [14] presented a powerful generative adversarial network, and obtain excellent restoration results on the GoPro dataset. However, these models fail to achieve the same deblurring performance when tested on a different dataset. According to the qualitative analysis provided by Zhang et al. [39], the deblurring models of Nah et al. [21] and Tao et al. [27] underperform on real-world blurry images. Jalata et al. [10] evaluated the performance of DeblurGAN-v2 [14] on the HIDE test dataset, and noticed that it decreased by 9.95% and 6.32% in terms of PSNR and SSIM respectively. Considering the deblurring performance drops to a great extent on different image datasets, fully supervised image deblurring is still far away from the real-world deblurring.

Unsupervised deblurring frameworks are mainly based on CycleGAN. Lu et al. [19] presented an unsupervised model for domain-specific single image deblurring via disentangled representations. However, aforementioned approaches ignore the difference between the synthetic blur and real-word blur. Remarkably, Zhang et al. [39] proposed a deblurring-by-blurring method. They blurred the sharp images based on a noise map to mimic real-world blur, and then train the deblurring network on pseudo pairs in a supervised manner. Although the noise map is from real-world images, there is still an obvious domain gap between real blurry images and generated blurry images.

2.2   Unsupervised Domain Adaptation

Unsupervised domain adaptation (UDA) addresses domain shift problems [23]. Given a labeled source domain and an unlabeled target domain with a similar but different distribution, the objective is to predict labels on the latter [23]. UDA is popularly employed in the image classification field [6]. Recently published papers demonstrated the satisfied performance of UDA in semantic segmentation [41,43]. Jalata et al. [10] introduced a generalized domain adaptation approach, bijective maximum likelihood [28], to image deblurring tasks. However, their adaptation method works only on high resolution images and assume that images in the target domain and source domain share similar distributions, which lacks convincing explanation. Multiple studies show that distribution discrepancy minimization can also be achieved by training a domain classifier C (the discriminator) and a feature extractor E (the encoder) with an adversarial loss [5,29,30]. In this paper, we leverage feature-level domain adaptation via adversarial training to improve deblurring performance on real data.

3   Methods

Given source domain samples as image pairs $\mathcal{S} = \{b_i^s, c_i^s\}_{i=1}^{N_s}$, and target domain samples $\mathcal{T} = \{b_i^t\}_{i=1}^{N_t}$, b^s and c^s represent synthetic blurry images and corresponding clean images respectively, and b^t denotes real-world blurry images or synthetic blurry images from a different dataset. We clarify that $\mathcal{S}$ and $\mathcal{T}$ are collected from two different datasets while they share similar distributions. We aim to restore clear images from real blurry images b^t, without knowing any ground truth image in the target domain. In the following subsections, we initially introduce the overall architecture of the proposed UDA-Deblur. Following that, we discuss the key part of UDA-Deblur, multi-scale domain classifiers and fast channel attention. Finally, we explore how to optimize the UDA-Deblur (Fig. 1).

3.1   Architecture of the Proposed UDA-Deblur

In this section, we describe the overall architecture of our proposed UDA-Deblur. The baseline model is MPRNet [37], a multi-stage deblurring network simplified as a single encoder-decoder model in our paper. We mainly focus on the encoder E, to which our domain adaptation techniques are applied. The encoder E is to map input blurry images b^s to latent feature space, and the decoder D is to reconstruct clean images c^s from these features. We also use the same encoder E as a feature extractor, to obtain multi-scale features from both b^s and b^t. A fast channel attention layer is attached to each encoder block so that UDA-Deblur pays attention to the features with similar information across two domains. The features extracted at the first, second and third levels are denoted as $\{E^{(1)}, E^{(2)}, E^{(3)}\}$. Importantly, we design a novel domain adaptation technique for image deblurring, i.e., multi-scale domain classifiers. The domain classifier is denoted as C_k for feature discrimination at the k-th level, where $k \in (1, 2, 3)$. Each classifier is a separate patch discriminator that does not share weights with others. The adversarial learning is applied to features at these three depth levels.

Channel Attention. The number of channels increases with the downsampling process forwarding, leading to a critical issue. That is, some channels may contain

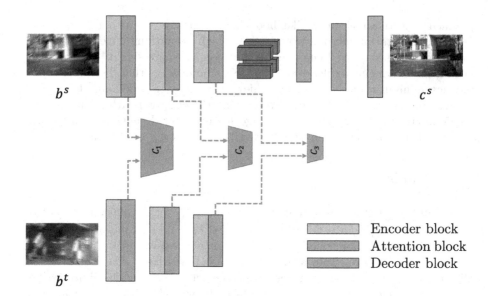

Fig. 1. Proposed architecture for single image deblurring via unsupervised domain adaptation (UDA-Deblur).

the unavoidable domain discrepancy despite adversarial domain alignment. On the other hand, we cannot ignore and drop these channels directly, which may be related to important image information. To solve this issue, we employ a fast channel attention mechanism without reducing feature dimensionality. Our channel attention layer has a similar structure to the ECA-Net [31]. Different from some works applying attention techniques to the decoder part, we make use of attention layers during the encoding phase to work together with multi-scale feature discrimination, so that the domain gap will shrink further.

3.2 Domain Adaptation

In UDA-Deblur, multi-scale feature discrimination increases the overlap between distributions of latent features in two different domains. Out domain alignment strategy is adopted at multiple feature levels.

Multi-scale Feature Discrimination. The encoder E is composed of three downsampling stages. At different depth, the extracted features are fed into a single domain classifier C_k (the discriminator). Adversarial domain alignment loss is adopted at multiple feature levels, and the corresponding objective function is given in this subsection,

$$\min_E \mathcal{L}_{align}(E) = \sum_{k=1}^{n} (\mathbb{E}_{b_t \sim \mathcal{T}(b)}[(C_k(E^{(k)}(b_t)) - 0.5)^2]$$
$$+ \mathbb{E}_{b_s \sim \mathcal{S}(b)}[(C_k(E^{(k)}(b_s)) - 0.5)^2]) \quad (1)$$

$$\min_{C} \mathcal{L}_{align}(C) = \sum_{k=1}^{n} (\mathbb{E}_{b_t \sim \mathcal{T}(b)}[(C_k(E^{(k)}(b_t)) - 1)^2] + \mathbb{E}_{b_s \sim \mathcal{S}(b)}[C_k(E^{(k)}(b_s))^2]), \tag{2}$$

where C_k is the k-th domain classifier used for the training at the k-th depth level. $E^{(k)}$ is the features extracted by the encoder at the k-th level. n is the number of downsampling stages inside the encoder, which equals to 3 in our case. Note that n is also used to average the alignment loss in our codes.

By adversarial training on multi-scale features from two different domains, domain classifiers distinguish source blurry images and target blurry images in feature levels, and the encoder preserves rich domain invariant information. Thereby, the decoder synthesizes high-quality clean images on the target domain.

3.3 Objective

The full objective function is the weighted sum of losses in MPRNet [37] and domain alignment loss discussed in Sect. 3.2,

$$\mathcal{L} = \mathcal{L}_{char} + \alpha \cdot \mathcal{L}_{edge} + \beta \cdot \mathcal{L}_{align}, \tag{3}$$

where α and β are set to 0.05 and 0.01 respectively. α and β control the relative importance of each loss item. $\mathcal{L}_{char}$ is the Charbonnier loss [2],

$$\mathcal{L}_{char} = \sqrt{\|r^s - c^s\|^2 + \epsilon^2}, \tag{4}$$

where r^s is the restored images from blurry images b^s in the source domain and c^s is the ground-truth in the source domain. ϵ is a constant which is set to 10^{-3} in all experiments. $\mathcal{L}_{edge}$ is the edge loss defined as,

$$\mathcal{L}_{edge} = \sqrt{\|\nabla^2 r^s - \nabla^2 c^s\|^2 + \epsilon^2}, \tag{5}$$

where ∇^2 denotes the Laplace operator. Optimizing $\mathcal{L}_{edge}$ enhances the edge quality. $\mathcal{L}_{align}$ is already given in the Sect. 3.2, where the least squares loss function is adopted in the same way as the Least Squares Generative Adversarial Network (LSGAN) [20] due to its stable performance and high-quality image generation. Minimizing $\mathcal{L}_{align}$ helps the encoder E obtain domain-invariant latent space representations.

4 Experiments

We use GoPro [21] as the source dataset, while HIDE [25] and ReaBlur [24] as target datasets. Firstly, we overview the datasets and training details. Then, we compare UDA-Deblur with existing deblurring models both qualitatively and quantitatively. We also conduct ablation studies to demonstrate the effectiveness of UDA-Deblur design.

4.1 Datasets

GoPro. Nah et al. [21] created a large-scale dataset which includes blur caused by various sources. The GoPro dataset contains 2103 image pairs in the training set and 1111 pairs in the test set. The blurry images are synthesized by averaging consecutive frames. The clean images are from the central frame.

HIDE. Shen et al. [25] constructed a motion blurred dataset covering pedestrian and street scenes. The dataset consists of 6397 and 2025 image pairs for training and testing respectively. The way to form image pairs is similar to the GoPro dataset.

RealBlur. Rim et al. [24] built a high-quality dataset for benchmarking real-world image deblurring approaches. The whole dataset includes two subsets, RealBlur-J and RealBlur-R. Each contains 3758 image pairs in the training set, and 980 pairs in the test set.

4.2 Training Details

We implement UDA-Deblur in PyTorch and train the model on two NVIDIA A-100 GPUs with a batch size of 16. For data augmentation, we randomly crop images with the patch size of 128×128. After that, image patches are horizontally and vertically flipped at random. The initial learning rate is set to 1×10^{-4}, which decreases to 1×10^{-6} using the cosine annealing schedule. We train our full model for 400k iterations within 3 days. To compare UDA-Deblur with state-of-the-art networks, we directly harness the officially released models. For a fair study, we retrain the baseline network using the same training strategy and tune it with the patch size of 128×128. At the beginning, we pretrain the encoder-decoder with the patch size of 256×256 for 400k iterations. After that, we further tune the encoder-decoder with the patch size of 128×128 and pretrain domain classifiers for 80k iterations. The last step is to train the whole UDA-Deblur. We select a multiple-stage training strategy.

4.3 Comparison Experiments

In this section, we compare our proposed UDA-Deblur with state-of-the-art methods. Our network is trained on GoPro as the source domain and another dataset as the target domain, i.e., HIDE, ReaBlur-J, and RealBlur-R. We test UDA-Deblur on HIDE, RealBlur-J, and RealBlur-R.

For quantitative analysis, we use standard deblurring metrics PSNR and SSIM for evaluation, though they do not match human perception very well in image deblurring [15]. According to Table 1, our approach shows superior performance to other deblurring methods. For a more persuasive comparison, we provide deblurred images by several state-of-the-art methods, as exemplified in Fig. 2. Compared to the deblurring results by ours, DeblurGAN-v2 [14] and the model proposed by Nah et al. [21] disrupt the quality of images by introducing distortion; SRN [27] performs poorly on image patches with characters.

Fig. 2. Deblurred images on the ReaBlur-J. From left to right, blurred images, blurred patches, ground truth, results of ours, DeblurGAN-v2 [14], Nah et al. [21], and SRN [27]. Higher SSIM values mean better results. Ours preserves fine texture and structural patterns.

Table 1. Performance comparisons with state-of-the-art models on the benchmarks: GoPro → HIDE, GoPro → ReaBlur-R, GoPro → ReaBlur-J.

Methods	HIDE		ReaBlur-R		ReaBlur-J	
	PSNR	SSIM	PSNR	SSIM	PSNR	SSIM
DeblurGAN [13]	24.51	0.871	33.79	0.903	27.97	0.834
SRN [27]	28.36	0.904	-	-	-	-
DeblurGAN-v2 [14]	26.61	0.875	-	-	-	-
DMPHN [38]	29.09	0.918	-	-	-	-
Nah et al. [21]	25.73	0.874	32.51	0.841	27.87	0.827
Hu et al. [8]	-	-	33.67	0.916	26.41	0.803
Pan et al. [22]	-	-	34.01	0.916	27.22	0.790
UDA-Deblur	**30.86**	**0.916**	**36.08**	**0.953**	**28.56**	**0.868**

4.4 Ablation Study

We perform an ablation study to analyze the effectiveness of domain adaptation. The networks are trained on GoPro as the source domain; HIDE, ReaBlur-J and RealBlur-R as the target domain. We keep the training strategy the same.

Quantitative Analysis. Table 2 gives a report of deblurring performance measured by image quality metrics PSNR and SSIM, which proves that multi-scale feature discrimination improves the baseline model quantitatively.

Qualitative Analysis. We notice that PSNR and SSIM values in Table 2 fail to reflect the significant performance improvement, which is visible to naked eyes. In the first row of Fig. 3, our full UDA-Deblur recovers the complicated wood grain perfectly. In the second row of Fig. 3, UDA-Deblur successfully reconstructs the gap between two adjacent bricks without introducing white artifacts.

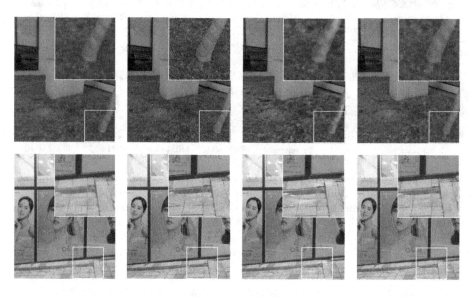

Fig. 3. Component evaluation on the GoPro → ReaBlur-J benchmark. From left to right, blurred images, ground truth, results of the baseline, and ours.

Table 2. Component evaluation on the benchmarks: GoPro → HIDE, GoPro → ReaBlur-R, GoPro → ReaBlur-J. The baseline model is the enhanced MPRNet [37] tuned with the patch size of 128 × 128. UDA-Deblur is our proposed full model.

Methods	HIDE		ReaBlur-R		ReaBlur-J	
	PSNR	SSIM	PSNR	SSIM	PSNR	SSIM
Baseline	30.41	0.908	35.95	0.951	28.29	0.861
UDA-Deblur	**30.86**	**0.916**	**36.08**	**0.953**	**28.56**	**0.868**

5   Conclusion and Limitation

In this paper, we proposed a novel deblurring model, termed as UDA-Deblur. Firstly, we employed fast channel attention so that the network pays more attention to deblurring relevant information. Secondly, we designed multi-scale domain classifiers in order to differentiate the source domain and the target domain. Also, a multi-stage training strategy was adopted to overcome the instability of GAN-style models. Finally, we reported quantitative and visual results to demonstrate the promising performance of ours compared to other state-of-the-art methods. Importantly, our work provides a new perspective to solve the real-world image deblurring problems.

There are possible limitations of the proposed deblurring method. Firstly, the training on GoPro to RealBlur is unstable due to the significant differences between the source and the target. Secondly, the feature-level domain adaptation doesn't perform expected improvement compared to the most recent transformer models In our future work, we will try more baseline models and training strategies to stablize the training phase; we will also combine feature-level domain adaptation with other levels to boost the deblurring performance.

References

1. Chakrabarti, A.: A neural approach to blind motion deblurring. In: Leibe, B., Matas, J., Sebe, N., Welling, M. (eds.) ECCV 2016 Part III. LNCS, vol. 9907, pp. 221–235. Springer, Cham (2016). https://doi.org/10.1007/978-3-319-46487-9_14
2. Charbonnier, P., Blanc-Feraud, L., Aubert, G., Barlaud, M.: Two deterministic half-quadratic regularization algorithms for computed imaging. In: Proceedings of 1st International Conference on Image Processing, vol. 2, pp. 168–172. IEEE (1994)
3. Cho, T.S., Paris, S., Horn, B.K., Freeman, W.T.: Blur kernel estimation using the radon transform. In: CVPR 2011, pp. 241–248. IEEE (2011)
4. Ganin, Y., Lempitsky, V.: Unsupervised domain adaptation by backpropagation. In: International Conference on Machine Learning, pp. 1180–1189. PMLR (2015)
5. Ganin, Y., et al.: Domain-adversarial training of neural networks. J. Mach. Learn. Res. **17**(1), 2096–2030 (2016)
6. Ghifary, M., Kleijn, W.B., Zhang, M., Balduzzi, D., Li, W.: Deep reconstruction-classification networks for unsupervised domain adaptation. In: Leibe, B., Matas, J., Sebe, N., Welling, M. (eds.) ECCV 2016 part IV. LNCS, vol. 9908, pp. 597–613. Springer, Cham (2016). https://doi.org/10.1007/978-3-319-46493-0_36
7. Hradis, M., Kotera, J., Zemcik, P., VSroubek, F.: Convolutional neural networks for direct text deblurring. In: Proceedings of BMVC, vol. 10 (2015)
8. Hu, Z., Cho, S., Wang, J., Yang, M.H.: Deblurring low-light images with light streaks. In: Proceedings of the IEEE Conference on Computer Vision and Pattern Recognition, pp. 3382–3389 (2014)
9. Hua, Y., Liu, Y., Li, B., Lu, M.: Dilated fully convolutional neural network for depth estimation from a single image. In: 2019 International Conference on Computational Science and Computational Intelligence (CSCI), pp. 612–616. IEEE (2019)

10. Jalata, I., Chappa, N.V.S.R., Truong, T.D., Helton, P., Rainwater, C., Luu, K.: Eqadap: equipollent domain adaptation approach to image deblurring. IEEE Access **10**, 93203–93211 (2022)
11. Kang, G., Jiang, L., Yang, Y., Hauptmann, A.G.: Contrastive adaptation network for unsupervised domain adaptation. In: Proceedings of the IEEE/CVF Conference on Computer Vision and Pattern Recognition, pp. 4893–4902 (2019)
12. Krishnan, D., Tay, T., Fergus, R.: Blind deconvolution using a normalized sparsity measure. In: CVPR 2011, pp. 233–240. IEEE (2011)
13. Kupyn, O., Budzan, V., Mykhailych, M., Mishkin, D., Matas, J.: DeblurGAN: blind motion deblurring using conditional adversarial networks. In: Proceedings of the IEEE Conference on Computer Vision and Pattern Recognition, pp. 8183–8192 (2018)
14. Kupyn, O., Martyniuk, T., Wu, J., Wang, Z.: Deblurgan-v2: deblurring (orders-of-magnitude) faster and better. In: Proceedings of the IEEE/CVF International Conference on Computer Vision, pp. 8878–8887 (2019)
15. Lai, W.S., Huang, J.B., Hu, Z., Ahuja, N., Yang, M.H.: A comparative study for single image blind deblurring. In: Proceedings of the IEEE Conference on Computer Vision and Pattern Recognition, pp. 1701–1709 (2016)
16. Li, B., Hua, Y., Lu, M.: Advanced multiple linear regression based dark channel prior applied on dehazing image and generating synthetic haze. arXiv preprint arXiv:2103.07065 (2021)
17. Li, B., Zhang, W., Lu, M.: Multiple linear regression haze-removal model based on dark channel prior. In: 2018 International Conference on Computational Science and Computational Intelligence (CSCI), pp. 307–312. IEEE (2018)
18. Liu, H., Lu, M.: A crosswalk stripe detection model based on gradient similarity tags. In: 2022 7th International Conference on Image, Vision and Computing (ICIVC), pp. 114–122. IEEE (2022)
19. Lu, B., Chen, J., Chellappa, R.: Unsupervised domain-specific deblurring via disentangled representations. In: Proceedings of the IEEE/CVF Conference on Computer Vision and Pattern Recognition, pp. 10225–10234 (2019)
20. Mao, X., Li, Q., Xie, H., Lau, R.Y., Wang, Z., Paul Smolley, S.: Least squares generative adversarial networks. In: Proceedings of the IEEE International Conference on Computer Vision, pp. 2794–2802 (2017)
21. Nah, S., Hyun Kim, T., Mu Lee, K.: Deep multi-scale convolutional neural network for dynamic scene deblurring. In: Proceedings of the IEEE Conference on Computer Vision and Pattern Recognition, pp. 3883–3891 (2017)
22. Pan, J., Sun, D., Pfister, H., Yang, M.H.: Blind image deblurring using dark channel prior. In: Proceedings of the IEEE Conference on Computer Vision and Pattern Recognition, pp. 1628–1636 (2016)
23. Pinheiro, P.O.: Unsupervised domain adaptation with similarity learning. In: Proceedings of the IEEE Conference on Computer Vision and Pattern Recognition, pp. 8004–8013 (2018)
24. Rim, J., Lee, H., Won, J., Cho, S.: Real-world blur dataset for learning and benchmarking deblurring algorithms. In: Vedaldi, A., Bischof, H., Brox, T., Frahm, J.-M. (eds.) ECCV 2020 XXV. LNCS, vol. 12370, pp. 184–201. Springer, Cham (2020). https://doi.org/10.1007/978-3-030-58595-2_12
25. Shen, Z., et al.: Human-aware motion deblurring. In: Proceedings of the IEEE/CVF International Conference on Computer Vision, pp. 5572–5581 (2019)
26. Sun, D., Yang, X., Liu, M.Y., Kautz, J.: PWC-NET: CNNs for optical flow using pyramid, warping, and cost volume. In: Proceedings of the IEEE Conference on Computer Vision and Pattern Recognition, pp. 8934–8943 (2018)

27. Tao, X., Gao, H., Shen, X., Wang, J., Jia, J.: Scale-recurrent network for deep image deblurring. In: Proceedings of the IEEE Conference on Computer Vision and Pattern Recognition, pp. 8174–8182 (2018)
28. Truong, T.D., Duong, C.N., Le, N., Phung, S.L., Rainwater, C., Luu, K.: Bimal: bijective maximum likelihood approach to domain adaptation in semantic scene segmentation. In: Proceedings of the IEEE/CVF International Conference on Computer Vision, pp. 8548–8557 (2021)
29. Tzeng, E., Hoffman, J., Darrell, T., Saenko, K.: Simultaneous deep transfer across domains and tasks. In: Proceedings of the IEEE International Conference on Computer Vision, pp. 4068–4076 (2015)
30. Tzeng, E., Hoffman, J., Saenko, K., Darrell, T.: Adversarial discriminative domain adaptation. In: Proceedings of the IEEE Conference on Computer Vision and Pattern Recognition, pp. 7167–7176 (2017)
31. Wang, Q., Wu, B., Zhu, P., Li, P., Zuo, W., Hu, Q.: ECA-Net: efficient channel attention for deep convolutional neural networks. In: Proceedings of the IEEE/CVF Conference on Computer Vision and Pattern Recognition, pp. 11534–11542 (2020)
32. Wang, R., Tao, D.: Recent progress in image deblurring. arXiv preprint arXiv:1409.6838 (2014)
33. Wei, B., Zhang, L., Wang, K., Kong, Q., Wang, Z.: Dynamic scene deblurring and image de-raining based on generative adversarial networks and transfer learning for internet of vehicle. EURASIP J. Adv. Signal Process. **2021**(1), 1–19 (2021)
34. Wen, Y., et al.: Structure-aware motion deblurring using multi-adversarial optimized cyclegan. IEEE Trans. Image Process. **30**, 6142–6155 (2021)
35. Yan, Y., Ren, W., Guo, Y., Wang, R., Cao, X.: Image deblurring via extreme channels prior. In: Proceedings of the IEEE Conference on Computer Vision and Pattern Recognition, pp. 4003–4011 (2017)
36. Yuan, Q., Li, J., Zhang, L., Wu, Z., Liu, G.: Blind motion deblurring with cycle generative adversarial networks. Vis. Comput. **36**, 1591–1601 (2020)
37. Zamir, S.W., et al.: Multi-stage progressive image restoration. In: Proceedings of the IEEE/CVF Conference on Computer Vision and Pattern Recognition, pp. 14821–14831 (2021)
38. Zhang, H., Dai, Y., Li, H., Koniusz, P.: Deep stacked hierarchical multi-patch network for image deblurring. In: Proceedings of the IEEE/CVF Conference on Computer Vision and Pattern Recognition, pp. 5978–5986 (2019)
39. Zhang, K., et al.: Deblurring by realistic blurring. In: Proceedings of the IEEE/CVF Conference on Computer Vision and Pattern Recognition, pp. 2737–2746 (2020)
40. Zhang, K., et al.: Deep image deblurring: a survey. Int. J. Comput. Vis. **130**(9), 2103–2130 (2022)
41. Zhang, Q., Zhang, J., Liu, W., Tao, D.: Category anchor-guided unsupervised domain adaptation for semantic segmentation. In: Advances in Neural Information Processing Systems, vol. 32 (2019)
42. Zhu, J.Y., Park, T., Isola, P., Efros, A.A.: Unpaired image-to-image translation using cycle-consistent adversarial networks. In: Proceedings of the IEEE International Conference on Computer Vision, pp. 2223–2232 (2017)
43. Zou, Y., Yu, Z., Kumar, B., Wang, J.: Unsupervised domain adaptation for semantic segmentation via class-balanced self-training. In: Proceedings of the European Conference on Computer Vision (ECCV), pp. 289–305 (2018)

Object Detection and Recognition

Reliable Matching by Combining Optimal Color and Intensity Information Based on Relationships Between Target and Surrounding Objects

Rina Tagami[✉], Hiroki Kobayashi, Shuichi Akizuki,
and Manabu Hashimoto[✉]

Chukyo University, Nagoya, Japan
{tagami,mana}@isl.sist.chukyo-u.ac.jp

Abstract. Due to the revitalization of the semiconductor industry and efforts to reduce labor and unmanned operations in the retail and food manufacturing industries, objects to be recognized in image processing technology are becoming increasingly colorful and diversified in design. In this paper, we optimize the combination of color and intensity information of a small number of pixels used for matching based on the interrelationship between the target object and surrounding objects. We propose a fast and reliable matching method using these few pixels. Pixels with a low pixel pattern frequency are selected from color and grayscale images of the target object, and pixels that are highly discriminative from surrounding objects are carefully selected from these pixels. The use of color and intensity information makes the method highly versatile for object design. The use of a small number of pixels that are not shared by surrounding objects enables high discriminability and fast matching. Experiments using real images have confirmed that when 68 pixels are used for matching, the processing time is 18 msec and the recognition success rate is 99.7%.

Keywords: Object detection · Template matching · Genetic algorithms

1 Introduction

The demand for image processing technology has become even higher due to the increase in semiconductor production and the trend toward labor-saving and unmanned operations in the retail and food manufacturing industries. Objects are becoming more and more diverse in terms of color and design, and the recognition of these objects is becoming more and more difficult. When considering reliable matching in object recognition, it would be appropriate to use intensity information for the object in Fig. 1(a) because of its black or gray design, and to use color information for the object in (b) because of its green or red color. In particular, in the case of object (c), since the design consists of black and pink colors, the recognition accuracy is expected to be the highest when both intensity and color information are used. However, most conventional image processing techniques convert color images into grayscale images before processing them, resulting in lower recognition accuracy for objects composed of colored objects. Although there are pattern matching methods that use information from color images, it is extremely difficult to achieve both high speed and reliability in matching. A possible solution is object recognition using deep learning, but there are strong limitations in the hardware and memory of computers at production sites. In the case of food package recognition, there are many types of objects to be recognized, and preparing a huge amount of training data is not considered to be cost-effective.

Therefore, we consider using Template Matching (TM), which is often used in object recognition. It is often used in production because it does not require a large amount of training data and has a certain degree of robustness. The advantage of TM is that it is not limited by the frequency of the image, which can reduce the recognition accuracy of Keypoint Matching. Here, we consider a fast and reliable TM that uses both color and intensity information to optimize the combination of pixels used for matching. By selecting a small number of pixels from the target object that are effective and unambiguous for matching, carefully selecting pixels that are highly discriminative from surrounding objects from these pixels, and optimizing the combination of color and intensity, a fast and reliable matching can be achieved. This research enables stable matching even when the design of the target and surrounding objects is colorful or achromatic, thus contributing to automated recognition of objects with a wide range of color variations.

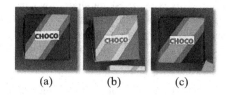

(a)   (b)   (c)

Fig. 1. Example of food packages. (a) is achromatic, (b) is chromatic colors, and (c) is object with design that includes both achromatic and chromatic colors.

2   Related Works and Their Problems

Various methods of object detection have been proposed, but in a production line, where computational resources are limited, methods that are understandable to the user, fast, and reliable are preferred. For this reason, Keypoint Matching (KPM) [1] and TM [2], which are both simple and practical, are often used on production lines. TM, in particular, is a relatively simple algorithm with low memory requirements, and FPGA (Field Programmable Gate Array) can be used to speed up similarity calculations [3].

SIFT [4] is a well-known method for KPM. It is a rotation-invariant feature, but it is very costly in terms of generating Difference of Gaussian (DoG) images and calculating gradient information. AKAZE [5] is an improved method, but it detects feature points for each input image, which is fast but requires a certain amount of processing time. Various methods with higher speed and accuracy have been proposed for TM. There are methods [6] that use only the edge pixels of an object, methods [7] that detect edges that change little in each frame over time, and flexible matching methods [8] that use a segmented set of edges. However, they can only be used when the image frequency is high and edge information is sufficiently extractable.

Other methods include Best-Buddies-Similarity (BBS) [9,10], that counts the number of best buddies by splitting the target and search images into small patches for each RGB value and calculating similarities between the two patch images, and Deformable Diversity Similarity (DDIS) [11], that improves the similarity calculation of BBS [9] and reduces the computational cost, thus enabling faster processing. Occlusion Aware Template Matching (OATM) [12] achieves high speed by searching neighborhoods between vectors sampled from images. We consider that the number of similarity calculations to be a bottleneck for these methods [9–12], making it difficult to achieve a practical level of speed.

There are also methods [13,14] that reduce the search area and methods [15,16] that reduce the number of pixels used for matching in order to achieve high speed. Fast Affine Template Matching (FAsT-Match) [13] is fast because it focuses only on pixels with similar neighboring values, while Co-occurrence Probability Template Matching (CPTM) [15] achieves both high speed and high reliability by using only pixels with low pixel value co-occurrence. Color Co-occurrence of Multiple Pixels in Template Matching (CoPTM) [16], which extends CPTM [15] to color information, focuses on the co-occurrence of hue values and achieves high speed in color images. Co-occurrence based Template Matching (CoTM) [17], which uses co-occurrence histograms of quantized RGB values for similarity calculation, enables matching that is robust to deformations. However, it is not very versatile, because it is limited by the target object images: FAsT-Match [13] is not reliable for high-frequency images, FAsT-Match [13] and CPTM [15] are unreliable for color images, and CoPTM [16] and CoTM [17] are unreliable for grayscale images.

Recently, feature matching [18–21] to apply "Transformer" has also been proposed, in which global information in one image and potential matches are utilized on the basis of an analysis of the relationship between two images. And, recent methods [22] on deep learning for matching often focus on learning better features and descriptors from images using Convolutional Neural Networks (CNNs). When an object is different in color from the surrounding objects, it can be recognized as shown in Fig. 2(a), but when the objects are similar, it is misrecognized as shown in Fig. 2(b). This is because learning is performed using only information from grayscale images.

In this paper, we use TM, which is often used in pattern matching and object recognition. We consider optimizing the combination of pixel color and intensity information used for matching to achieve fast and reliable object recognition. By selecting a small number of unambiguous pixels from a target object image and carefully selecting pixels that have little in common with surrounding objects, a combination of pixels with high discriminability between the target object and surrounding objects can be selected to reduce the misrecognition of similar objects. This method is fast and reliable because it optimizes pixels depending on the design and colors of the target object and surrounding objects, and it calculates similarity using a small number of pixels to maximize the discriminative performance. This method can contribute to the automation of object recognition for objects with rich variations in color and intensity.

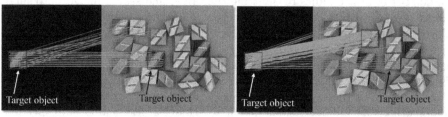

(a) Example of correct recognition   (b) Example of misrecognition

Fig. 2. Successes and failures in recognition by related method (LoFTR) [19]. (a) is result of correct recognition, (b) is result of misrecognition. Proposed method makes these two cases recognizable.

3   Proposed Method

In this paper, we consider the selection of a small number of pixels combined with color and intensity information in order to solve the problems described in Sect. 2. We consider that an optimal combination of color and intensity information can be versatile for object package design, and that matching only a small number of pixels allows for fast processing.

The first step in the process is to select pixels from the color image that are effective for matching as color information and pixels from the grayscale image that are effective for matching as intensity information. Next, pixels that do not share the same surrounding objects with the selected pixels are carefully selected using a Genetic Algorithm (GA). The pixel with the best discrimination performance against surrounding objects is used for the final matching.

3.1   Selection of Effective Pixels for Matching in Object Image

The proposed method uses the co-occurrence of two pixels in the target image (starting pixel P and ending pixel Q) as an indicator of pixel distinctiveness. First, pixel pairs are applied to all locations in the image in a raster scan, and the values p and q of P and Q, respectively, are used as indexes to vote for the number of occurrences in a 2-dimensional matrix. After all pixel pairs have been voted on, a co-occurrence histogram is completed. Pixel pairs (displacement vectors d) can have several patterns of pixel distances, but in this case we used the patterns $d = 1, 2, 4, 8, 16$ in the horizontal and vertical directions. The more of this pattern there are, the more the spatial frequency of the image can be represented.

The specific process of the method is shown in Fig. 3. First, from the grayscale image of the target object, frequencies of the occurrence of intensity values per pixel pair are calculated, and from the color image, frequencies of the occurrence of hue values (Hue values of HSV, quantized to 256 levels) per pixel pair are calculated. From each generated co-occurrence histogram, the pixel pairs with the lowest occurrence frequency are selected.

In other words, the pixel pair occurrence frequency F_r is defined by Eqs. (1), (2), and (3), where P and Q are pixel pairs, p and q are pixel pair values, $v_P = (x_P, y_P)$ and $v_Q = (x_Q, y_Q)$, respectively, the displacement vector of Q relative to P is $d = (k, l)$, $\mathcal{P}$ is the position vector in the entire target object image, and $f(\cdot)$ is a value for some coordinate. Pixels with a high frequency of occurrence are patterns that often appear in the image, and by not selecting them, it is possible to carefully select only those pixels that are effective for matching. These pixels are disambiguated, and a certain reduction in mismatches can be expected. In addition, the selected pixels are a mixture of pixels that are valid as color information and pixels that are valid as intensity information, as shown in the left side of Fig. 3, leading to improved versatility in the design and colors of the object.

$$F_r(p, q) = \sum_{v_P, v_Q \,\in\mathcal{P}} \delta(v_P, v_Q, p, q) \tag{1}$$

$$\delta = \begin{cases} 1 \ if \quad \{f(v_P) = p\} \wedge \{f(v_Q) = q\} \\ 0 \ otherwise \end{cases} \tag{2}$$

$$where, \quad v_Q = v_P + d \tag{3}$$

3.2 Pixel Selection Based on Interrelationships with Surrounding Objects

In the proposed method, the discriminative performance with surrounding objects is considered. Pixels that are not common to both the target object and the surrounding objects are selected, and should not be mismatched with the surrounding objects. The first step of the process is to evaluate the selected pixels using a set of assumed images prepared in advance, as shown in the upper right corner of Fig. 4. The group of assumed images consists of two types: the group of images for the target objects, and the group of images for the surrounding objects. Then, similarities between selected pixels and the two image groups are calculated. If pixels are selected in the process of 3.1 as pixels with

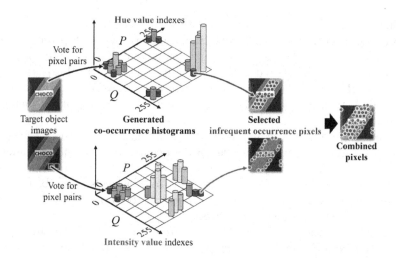

Vote for pixel pairs

Hue value indexes

P

Q

Target object images

Generated co-occurrence histograms

Selected infrequent occurrence pixels

Combined pixels

P

Q

Vote for pixel pairs

Intensity value indexes

Fig. 3. Process for selecting unambiguous pixels from target object images.

infrequent intensity values, the similarities are calculated on the basis of their intensity value. If pixels are selected as pixels with infrequent hue values, the similarities are calculated on the basis of hue value. Using the calculated similarities, histograms are generated with similarity C_i on the horizontal axis and the frequency of similarity C_i on the vertical axis (bottom center of Fig. 4), and three evaluation indices D, S, and p_{max} calculated from these histograms are used to evaluate the discrimination performance of the selected pixels by Eq. (4).

The larger the evaluation value F, the higher the discrimination performance, meaning that the values of D and p_{max} should be large and the value of S should be small. w_1, w_2, and w_3 are weighing factors, and ϵ is a supplementary factor. The reselection of pixels in the GA and the evaluation of discrimination performance are repeated so that the evaluation value F becomes larger. This automatically determines the optimal combination of color and intensity information depending on the target object and surrounding objects.

$$F = w_1 \frac{1}{S + \epsilon} + w_2 D + w_3 p_{max} \qquad (4)$$

Next, the evaluation indices are described in detail. The first evaluation index is the difference between the mean values of the histograms of the target and surrounding object images, defined as the degree of class segregation D. The larger the class segregation D is, the further apart the histogram distributions of the two image groups are, and thus better discriminability can be expected from the thresholding process.

The second index is the overlap between the histograms of the two image groups, defined as the overlap area S. The smaller this area is, the smaller the risk of mismatching with surrounding objects.

The third evaluation index p_{max} is the value with the highest similarity among the target images of assuming. This value can suppress the stagnation of the evaluation value F when the histogram distribution of the surrounding object images has a higher similarity.

The pixel with the largest evaluation value F can be judged to be superior. The proposed method evaluates the discriminability of pixels using the above idea, and finally determines pixels with a certain level of goodness from a practical standpoint as an approximate solution.

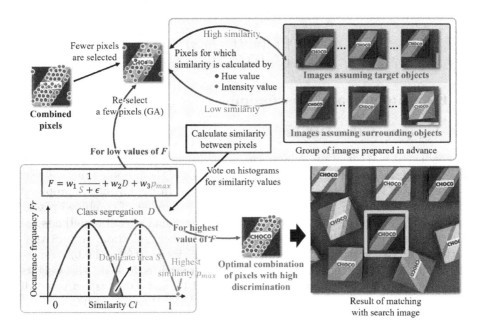

Fig. 4. Pixel selection and matching based on interrelationships with surrounding objects.

3.3 Matching

The object detection is performed by calculating the similarity with the search image using the pixels selected by the process in Sect. 3.2. The similarity is calculated while raster-scanning the search image, and the best match position is the one with the highest similarity. SSD (Sum of Squared Differences) is used to calculate the similarity, and SSDA (Sequential Similarity Detection Algorithm) is used to speed up the calculation.

In the process flow, selected pixels $f(n)$ are stored as either intensity values or hue values in a 1D array $f_G(n)$ or $f_H(n)$. The i-coordinate and j-coordinate of the selected pixel are also stored in a 1D array as $f_i(n)$ and $f_j(n)$. The sum of the squares of the difference between the pixels of the target image and the search image when they are shifted by (δ_x, δ_y) pixels and superimposed on each other is calculated using Eqs. (5) and (6). In this case, the value of the search image is $g(i, j)$, and it switches between intensity value and hue value depending on the information $f_R(n)$ of the object image. The information $f_R(n)$ is given to the target object image as 0 if the pixel has an intensity value and 1 if the pixel has a hue value. In this case, the number of selected pixels is M.

$$S_{SSD} = \sum_{n=0}^{M-1} (g(f_i(n) + \delta_x, f_j(n) + \delta_y) - f(n))^2 \tag{5}$$

$$f(n) = \begin{cases} f_G(n) \; if & f_R(n) = 0 \\ f_H(n) \; if & f_R(n) = 1 \end{cases} \tag{6}$$

4 Experiments and Discussion

4.1 Implementation Details

We conducted a verification experiment after discussing the pixels selected by the proposed method. The recognition performance of the proposed method was compared with that of the state-of-the-art methods. In the GA of the proposed method, the number of genes in each individual is number of combined pixels. The population size is 2500. The crossover, mutation and selection methods are uniform crossover, bit-flip mutation and roulette wheel selection, respectively. Furthermore, the crossover and mutation probabilities are 0.98 and 0.02, respectively. The number of max generations for the search is 50,000. The weights w_1, w_2, and w_3 of the evaluated value are 0.49, 0.49, and 0.02, respectively. All experiments are conducted on 64 GB RAM and AMD Ryzen 5 5600X.

4.2 Result of Pixels Selected by Proposed Method

Table 1 shows the pixels selected by the proposed method. The upper row in the cells shows the pixels selected from objects A to E, and the lower row shows the color and intensity ratio of the selected pixels. The horizontal axis is the images of the surrounding objects used, showing the location of target objects A to E. We used 300 images of such surrounding objects and selected the best combination of pixels using GA. In the case of object D, the color tones of the surrounding objects and the object are particularly similar, so the color information was not effective for matching, resulting in a high percentage of combinations of intensity information. In the case of object E, many pixels were selected from the red band pattern. This is because the red band pattern does not exist in the surrounding objects. In conclusion, the proposed method is able to optimize pixels on the basis of the interrelationship between the target and surrounding objects.

Table 1. Relation between target and surrounding objects and selected pixels.

4.3 Relationship Between Optimal Combination of Pixels and Number of Successful Recognitions

As a verification experiment, we confirmed the relationship between the recognition success rate of the optimal combination of pixels obtained by the proposed method and pixels that are not optimal (pixels optimized by fixing the ratio of the combination). Table 2 shows the result. The pink cells show the ratio of color and intensity in the selected pixels. The blue cell shows the number of successful recognitions, and in the case of 600, the recognition success rate is 100%. The number of pixels used in this case was fixed at 68. The recognition success rate (99.6%/ number of successful recognitions, 598) was the highest for the pixel with the best color/intensity combination (in red), which means that the pixels obtained by the proposed method were optimal.

Table 2. Relationship between ratio of color and intensity information of selected pixels and number of successful recognitions.

Color : Intensity	0:10	1:9	1.5:8.5	3:7	4:6	5:5	6:4	7:3	8:2	9:1	10:0
Recognition success rate	299	505	598	511	473	493	292	246	571	570	425

4.4 Performance Comparisons

Figure 5(a) shows the recognition success rate for each number of selected pixels for the proposed method and the comparison methods [5,9,15,16,19,23,24]. The results shown in the Fig. 5 are using the target image of D in Table 1 and surrounding object images of the middle row. The horizontal axis N is the number

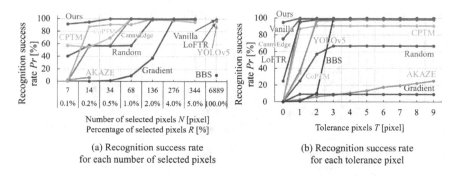

(a) Recognition success rate
for each number of selected pixels

(b) Recognition success rate
for each tolerance pixel

Fig. 5. Matching performance comparisons.

of selected pixels in 83×83 pixels, which is the size of the target image, and the bottom row shows the ratio of the number of selected pixels in the target image, R. The vertical axis P_r is the recognition success rate (GT$\pm$2 pixels) when 600 search images were used. Even when the proposed method used only 34 pixels for matching, the recognition success rate was 99.7%. This indicates that the proposed method is capable of stable matching even with a small number of pixels, independent of the color and intensity of the target object and its surroundings. Figure 5(b) shows the recognition success rates of the proposed method and the comparison methods for each tolerance pixel. Tolerance pixels are the number of pixels that can be considered as successfully recognized no matter how many pixels are off from GT. Compared with LoFTR, which is a state-of-the-art feature assignment method, the proposed method had a higher recognition success rate even when the number of tolerance pixels was small. This indicates that the proposed method is able to match with high positional accuracy. Figure 6 shows the processing time t of the proposed method and the comparison methods for each selected pixels N. (i) is the processing time for CPTM, CannyEdge, Gradient and (ii) is that for CoPTM, Random. Processing time of proposed method was the shortest compared with the other methods. The proposed method shows that fast and reliable matching is possible even with a small number of pixels. Figure 7 shows the matching results and a similarity heatmap. The redder the color in the heat map, the higher the similarity. It can be seen that the proposed method had low similarity in the surrounding area and high similarity only in the area where the object was located. BBS, the state-of-the-art for TM, has a similar heatmap, but the matching process took about 300 s, so the proposed method was more versatile.

5   Results on Real Data and Limitations

To analyze the limitations of the proposed method, we experimented with the OTB dataset [25]. Figure 8(a)–(d) shows examples of successful recognition and (e)–(h) shows examples of failed recognition. First, we found that the performance degraded when the background was complex or when the shielding was

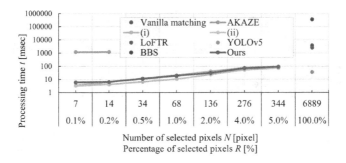

Fig. 6. Processing time comparisons.

large, and also when the deformation of the target was large. Finally, many of these failure cases are not addressed by the proposed method and are left for future research.

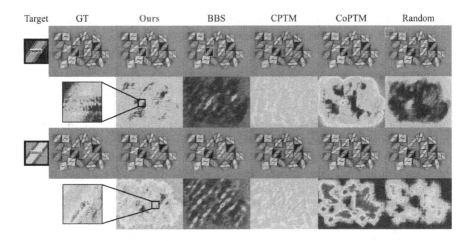

Fig. 7. Matching results and similarity heatmaps.

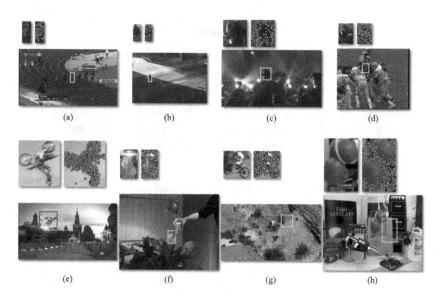

Fig. 8. Recognition success and failure. Upper left: Target image, Upper right: Selected pixels. Bottom: recognition result. The green line is the output result, and the red line is GT. (Color figure online)

6 Conclusion

We proposed a fast and reliable matching method that optimizes the combination of color and intensity of selected pixels. Experimental results showed that the optimal combination of pixels changed depending on the color and intensity of the target object and its surroundings. The optimal pixels had the highest recognition success rate compared with other combinations of pixels, and the average processing time was 18 msec when the number of selected pixels was 68. The method can contribute to the automation of recognition for objects with a wide range of colors because it reduces the misrecognition of peripheral objects and enables reliable matching.

Acknowledgements. This work was partially supported by JSPS KAKENHI, Grant-in-Aid for Scientific Research(C), Grant Number 21K03984.

References

1. Rublee, E., et al.: ORB: an efficient alternative to SIFT or SURF. In: 2011 International Conference on Computer Vision, pp. 2564–2571. IEEE (2011)
2. Cheng, J., et al.: QATM: quality-aware template matching for deep learning. In: Proceedings of the IEEE/CVF Conference on Computer Vision and Pattern Recognition, pp. 11553–11562 (2019)
3. Chen, Z., et al.: Eye-to-hand robotic visual tracking based on template matching on FPGAs. IEEE Access **7**, 88870–88880 (2019)

4. Lowe, D.G.: Object recognition from local scale-invariant features. In: Proceedings of the Seventh IEEE International Conference on Computer Vision, vol. 2, pp. 1150–1157 (1999)
5. Alcantara, P.F., et al.: Fast explicit diffusion for accelerated features in nonlinear scale spaces. IEEE Trans. Patt. Anal. Mach. Intell **34**(7), 1281–1298 (2011)
6. Dubuisson, M.P., et al.: A modified Hausdorff distance for object matching. In: Proceedings of 12th International Conference on Pattern Recognition, vol. 1, pp. 566–568 (1994)
7. Xiao, J., et al.: Scale-invariant contour segment context in object detection. Image Vis. Comput. **32**(12), 1055–1066 (2014)
8. Yu, Q., et al.: Local part chamfer matching for shape-based object detection. Pattern Recogn. **65**, 82–96 (2017)
9. Dekel, et al.: Best-buddies similarity for robust template matching. In: Proceedings of the IEEE Conference on Computer Vision and Pattern Recognition, pp. 2021–2029 (2015)
10. Oron, S., et al.: Best-buddies similarity—robust template matching using mutual nearest neighbors. IEEE Trans. Pattern Anal. Mach. Intell. **40**(8), 1799–1813 (2017)
11. Talmi, I., et al.: Template matching with deformable diversity similarity. In: Proceedings of the IEEE Conference on Computer Vision and Pattern Recognition, pp. 175–183 (2017)
12. Korman, S., et al.: OATM: occlusion aware template matching by consensus set maximization. In: Proceedings of the IEEE Conference on Computer Vision and Pattern Recognition, pp. 2675–2683 (2018)
13. Korman, S., et al.: Fast-match: fast affine template matching. In: Proceedings of the IEEE Conference on Computer Vision and Pattern Recognition, pp. 2331–2338 (2013)
14. Lai, J., et al.: Fast and robust template matching with majority neighbour similarity and annulus projection transformation. Pattern Recogn. **98**, 107029 (2020)
15. Hashimoto, M., et al.: Extraction of unique pixels based on co-occurrence probability for high-speed template matching. In: ISOT2010, pp. 1–6 (2010)
16. Tagami, R., et al.: Template matching using a small number of pixels selected by distinctiveness of quantized hue values. In: IWAIT2022, vol. 12177, pp. 662–667 (2022)
17. Kat, R., et al.: Matching pixels using co-occurrence statistics. In: Proceedings of the IEEE Conference on Computer Vision and Pattern Recognition, pp. 1751–1759 (2018)
18. Sarlin, P.E., et al.: Superglue: learning feature matching with graph neural networks. In: Proceedings of the IEEE/CVF Conference on Computer Vision and Pattern Recognition, pp. 4938–4947 (2020)
19. Sun, J., et al.: LoFTR: detector-free local feature matching with transformers. In: Proceedings of the IEEE/CVF Conference on Computer Vision and Pattern Recognition, pp. 8922–8931 (2021)
20. Bökman, G., Kahl, F.: A case for using rotation invariant features in state of the art feature matchers. In: Proceedings of the IEEE/CVF Conference on Computer Vision and Pattern Recognition, pp. 5110–5119 (2022)
21. Lindenberger, P., et al.: LightGlue: local feature matching at light speed, arXiv preprint arXiv:2306.13643 (2023)
22. DeTone, D., et al.: Superpoint: self-supervised interest point detection and description. In: Proceedings of the IEEE Conference on Computer Vision and Pattern Recognition Workshops, pp. 224–236 (2018)

23. Canny, J.: A computational approach to edge detection. IEEE Trans. Pattern Anal. Mach. Intell. **6**, 679–698 (1986)
24. Jocher, G., et al.: YOLOv5, Code repository (2020)
25. Wu, Y., Lim, J., Yang, M.H.: Online object tracking: a benchmark. In: Proceedings of the IEEE Conference on Computer Vision and Pattern Recognition, pp. 2411–2418 (2013

Regularized Meta-Training with Embedding Mixup for Improved Few-Shot Learning

Reece Walsh$^{(\boxtimes)}$ and Mohamed Shehata

University of British Columbia, Vancouver, Canada
`rkwalsh@alumni.ubc.ca`

Abstract. Few-shot learning has enabled techniques to grasp new, unseen tasks from a small set of labelled samples using previously taught knowledge. Although subfields in few-shot learning, such as metric learning, have demonstrated relative success, generalization towards unseen tasks continues to prove difficult, especially in an out-of-domain setting. To address this issue, we propose Embedding Mixup for Meta-Training (EMMeT), a novel regularization technique that creates new tasks through embedding shuffling and averaging for training metric-based backbones. In an experimental setting, our findings across in-domain and out-of-domain datasets indicate that application of EMMeT promotes generalization and increases few-shot accuracy across a range of backbone models.

Keywords: few-shot learning · image classification · regularization · out-of-domain

1 Introduction

Metric learning, specifically in the context of few-shot learning, has received increasing attention in recent years as it offers the potential for generalization in the face of limited amounts of data. Previously proposed metric backbones [1,9,17] have enabled the development of successful few-shot learning approaches, however, these models can exhibit degraded accuracy due to overfitting, especially when tested on out-of-domain datasets. Although more performant and generalizable few-shot learning techniques are consistently being investigated, regularization, in a few-shot setting, is largely neglected.

In this work, we show that overfitting exhibited by a metric backbone can be effectively mitigated through batch-based and embedding-based augmentation. Similar to regularization in supervised learning, we also show that increased generalization and significant accuracy improvements are possible through augmentations applied during training and finetuning. Unlike previous meta-regularization approaches, we focus on regularization within a single episodic batch alone; no extra data or dataset-specific considerations are necessary for our approach.

© The Author(s), under exclusive license to Springer Nature Switzerland AG 2023
G. Bebis et al. (Eds.): ISVC 2023, LNCS 14362, pp. 177–187, 2023.
https://doi.org/10.1007/978-3-031-47966-3_14

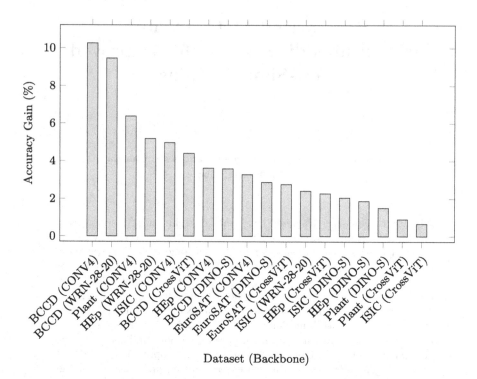

Fig. 1. Accuracy gains respective to each dataset and backbone after application of EMMeT. For each bar on the bar char, we note the difference between the original backbone, without EMMeT applied, versus the EMMeT-applied backbone for a specific dataset. All accuracy gains noted are representative of EMMeT training and finetuning.

In prior work, Metric-learning approaches have been widely used in the context of few-shot learning [1,9,14]. These approaches typically involve learning a distance metric between data points, such as Euclidean distance [17], which can be used to measure the similarity between labelled points (the support set) and unknown points (the query set). This metric is subsequently used to classify the query set based on similarity to classes within the support set in a given episodic batch. Although new metric-learning-based approaches have made strides towards better generalization, accuracy degradation remains a significant issue when testing on unseen classes, particularly in out-of-domain settings.

In a similarly related area, progress in meta-regularization, a field involving regularization of few-shot learning approaches, has largely fallen into two categories: sample augmentation-based regularization and episodic construction-based regularization. Sample augmentation-based approaches involve generating additional training data by applying a variety of image-based transformations to samples within an episodic batch [10]. Episodic construction-based approaches, on the other hand, involve augmented construction of episodic training data batches [12]. Although both of these approaches do succeed in regularizing a network, scalability, efficiency, and application effectiveness vary depending on the dataset and model. Testing on out-of-domain classes, in particular, is largely neglected in previously proposed approaches.

To this end, we present Embedding Mixup for Meta-Training (EMMeT), a meta-regularization technique for metric backbones. In our proposed process, we show that efficient and scalable operations are capable of effectively regularizing a metric-learner. The main contributions of this works are as follows: (1) We propose a novel meta-regularization technique for metric backbones, which can be applied to any existing metric-learning approach. (2) We propose a novel fine-tuning process that takes advantage of the regularization provided by EMMeT for improved in-domain and out-of-domain accuracy by up to 10.26% (illustrated in Fig. 1).

2 Proposed Approach

We propose **E**mbedding **M**ixup for **M**eta-**T**raining (EMMeT), a novel regularization technique that creates new episodic batches through an embedding shuffling and averaging regime (illustrated in Fig. 2). Given an image-based episodic batch, EMMeT is applied in three, consecutive stages: a class shuffling stage, a sample shuffling stage, and an embedding averaging stage. Application of these stages requires no external data and produces a regularized episodic batch for use in meta-training a metric-based backbone. Additionally, we further enhance out-of-domain performance through application of EMMeT in a novel finetuning process. To this end, EMMeT is applied to the support set within an episodic batch for iterative adjustment of the metric backbone model. For the following sections, we explore EMMeT in more detail.

2.1 Episodic Class-Based Shuffling

Shuffling operations act as the basis for EMMeT's regularization process. Episodic batches, defined by Vinyals *et al.* [18], are the primary target for EMMeT during both training and out-of-domain finetuning. An episodic batch is primarily composed of two hierarchical components: n-classes (pertaining to a specific domain) and k-samples for each class.

For EMMeT's first stage, we consider the n-classes available as the first dimension of an episodic batch. We define A as a set composed of n classes, indexed from 0 to $n-1$, and k-samples for each respective class, indexed from 0 to $k-1$. For all class indices in A, we apply the Fisher-Yates shuffle [7] to create a shuffled set of class indices. The shuffled indices are then used to extract each class respective to a shuffled index and store them in a new copy of A, defined as $\hat{A}$. After extraction is complete, $\hat{A}$ represents a new permutation of the A's class dimension.

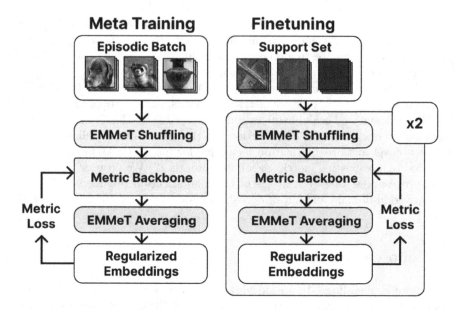

Fig. 2. Our proposed approach for EMMeT. During meta-training and finetuning we shuffle classes and samples within an episodic batch and average the resulting embeddings.

2.2 Episodic Sample-Based Shuffling

EMMeT's second stage consists of an operation similar to its first. Rather than shuffling classes, though, samples within each class, respectively, are shuffled instead. We specifically target the samples within $\hat{A}$ (generated in the previous stage) for shuffling operations.

In an effort to prevent the mixing of different classes, each of the k samples for n classes is considered as a separate shuffling operation. To this end, we apply the Fisher-Yates shuffle to n sets of indices from 0 to k. Each of the shuffled sets of indices is used to respectively shuffle the samples within one class. After all the samples are shuffled, we define the fully shuffled episodic batch as $\hat{A}_s$.

2.3 Embedding Averaging

The final stage of EMMeT involves three steps. First, the shuffled samples within $\hat{A}_s$ are embedded using a given metric backbone, producing an episodic batch of embeddings defined as $\hat{A}_e$. Second, a copy of $\hat{A}_e$ is created and shuffled class-wise and embedding-wise, creating $\hat{B}_e$. Third, the shuffled embeddings within $\hat{A}_e$ and $\hat{B}_e$ are averaged together on an embedding-wise basis, producing $\hat{C}_e$, a regularized episodic batch. We define our full, proposed process for shuffling and averaging in code within Listing 1.

We observe that averaging shuffled embeddings serves as an important part of the regularization provided by EMMeT. Through averaging, we produce new

```
# Shuffle Shots
b,c,h,w = data.shape
shuffled = data.reshape(WAYS,(SHOTS+QUERY),c,h,w)[:,:SHOTS]
shuffled_embeddings = torch.randperm(SHOTS)
shuffled = shuffled[:, shuffled_embeddings]

if shuffled_data.shape[1] < (SHOTS + QUERY):
    # Repeat dimension to fill episodic batch
    repeat_axis = (SHOTS + QUERY) // SHOTS
    shuffled = shuffled.repeat(1, repeat_axis, 1, 1, 1)

# Shuffle Ways
shuffled_ways = torch.randperm(WAYS)
shuffled = shuffled[shuffled_ways].reshape(b,c,h,w)

embeddings = model(shuffled)

# Averaging
a = embeddings.reshape(WAYS, (SHOTS + QUERY), -1)
b = a[torch.randperm(WAYS), :, :]
b = b[:, torch.randperm(SHOTS + QUERY), :]
emmet_embeddings = ((a + b)/2).reshape(WAYS * (SHOTS + QUERY), -1)
```

Listing 1: A PyTorch-style example of employing EMMeT using a given n-way k-shot batch and a metric-backbone model.

embeddings that exist as a midpoint between two classes. As such, embeddings not normally represented within a typical distribution are present in the EMMeT-regularized batch. Since each of the embeddings within a class are usually averaged with embeddings of a differing class, relative relationships between the new EMMeT embeddings are, ideally, preserved within each averaged class. We find that application of embedding averaging reduces class-specific overfitting and increases the robustness of a given metric backbone's latent space, increasing performance on in-domain and out-of-domain tasks.

2.4 Meta-Training

As described by Snell et al. [17], meta-training a given metric backbone serves as a key step in preparing a model for few-shot learning. We find that application of EMMeT during meta-training effectively regularizes the model and enhances generalization. To this end, we apply EMMeT through the aforementioned three stages consecutively to all episodic batches during training. Additionally, we find that a shorter meta-training session increases in-domain and out-of-domain performance while using EMMeT. As such, our approach utilizes a 100 epoch long training session (with each epoch consisting on 100 episodic batches) when meta-training with EMMeT.

2.5 Finetuning

As a further extension to our proposed approach, we find that EMMeT can be effectively applied to support set data during meta-testing. To this end, we fine-tune a given metric backbone with an EMMeT-augmented support set in order to provide, effectively, a mini meta-training session. As discussed in Sect. 2.3, EMMeT offers a degree of regularization that can prevent a metric backbone from overfitting to the small amount of data present in a support set, thereby improving performance on the accompanying query set. In particular, we take an approach similar to Hu *et al.*'s proposed work [9]. To this end, our proposed finetuning process is run on every episodic batch, wherein each episode's support set is used to finetune a given metric backbone. We find, through hyperparameter testing, that 2 iterations worth of finetuning results in an optimal accuracy for all tested metric backbones (as demonstrated in Fig. 3). We also observe that EMMeT-based finetuning results in a significant accuracy increase across all in-domain and out-of-domain datasets tested.

Table 1. Out-of-domain 5-Way 5-Shot and 5-Way 20-Shot Results for ISIC, EuroSAT, and Plant Disease.

Method (Backbone)	Out-of-Domain					
	ISIC		EuroSAT		Plant Disease	
	5w5s	5w20s	5w5s	5w20s	5w5s	5w20s
ProtoNet (RN10)	39.57	49.50	73.29	82.27	79.72	88.15
RelationNet (RN10)	39.41	41.77	61.31	74.43	68.99	80.45
MetaOptNet (RN10)	36.28	49.32	64.44	79.19	68.41	82.89
Finetune (RN10)	48.11	59.31	79.08	87.64	89.25	95.51
CHEF (RN10)	41.26	54.31	74.15	83.31	86.87	94.78
STARTUP (RN10)	47.22	58.63	82.29	89.26	93.02	97.51
DeepCluster2 (RN50)	40.73	49.91	88.39	92.02	93.63	96.63
P>M>F (DINO-S)	50.12	65.78	85.98	91.32	92.96	98.12
EMMeT (CONV4)	44.55	56.33	76.57	86.48	86.10	93.79
EMMeT (WRN-28-10)	45.88	57.49	79.55	89.97	86.74	96.85
EMMeT (CrossViT)	38.77	46.98	75.32	86.51	85.55	95.34
EMMeT (DINO-S)	**51.94**	**65.85**	**88.60**	**93.54**	**94.17**	**98.24**

3 Experiments

In this section, we present few-shot learning classification results on mini-imagenet [13], EuroSAT [8], ISIC2018 [4], Plant Disease [15], HEp-2 [11], and BCCD WBC [16]. We also ablate several properties and hyperparameters of EMMeT. Using precedent set by Vinyals *et al.* [18], all reported episodic classification results are obtained from an average over 600 episodic batches.

Table 2. In-domain and Out-of-domain 5-Way 1-Shot and 5-Way 5-Shot Results for mini-imagenet (MIN) and 5-way 5-shot results for BCCD WBC (BCCD) and HEp-2 (HEp) with EMMeT. BCCD WBC and HEp-2 results for previous approaches are sourced our prior work [19].

Method (Backbone)	In-Domain		Out-of-Domain	
	MIN		BCCD	HEp
	5w1s	5w5s	5w5s	5w5s
Reptile (CONV4)	49.97	65.62	50.91	51.76
AmdimNet (Amdim)	76.82	89.75	48.35	54.32
EPNet+SSL (WRN28-10)	79.2	88.66	47.39	55.12
SimpleCNAPS (ResNet-18)	79.9	90.11	47.06	53.15
ProtoNet (CONV4)	49.42	68.20	46.89	50.7
S2M2R (WRN28-10)	64.93	82.81	44.15	54.41
PT+MAP (WRN28-10)	82.9	88.02	42.94	54.73
MAML (CONV4)	48.7	64.62	42.81	45.21
LaplacianShot (WRN28-10)	75.57	82.27	34.75	44.69
P>M>F (DINO-S)	93.10	98.00	-	-
EMMeT (CONV4)	50.05	69.48	67.68	58.87
EMMeT (WRN-28-10)	68.38	77.11	**67.77**	67.11
EMMeT (CrossViT)	**95.48**	**99.56**	57.77	48.41
EMMeT (DINO-S)	93.72	98.40	64.83	**68.18**

3.1   Datasets

Under the episodic testing framework detailed by Vinyals *et al.*, we test on one in-domain dataset and five out-of-domain datasets: mini-imagenet [13] (in-domain), derived from ImageNet-1k [5] with 20 testing classes. EuroSAT [8] (out-of-domain), European satellite imagery with 10 testing classes. ISIC2018 [4] (out-of-domain), skin lesion imagery dataset with 7 classes. Plant Disease [15] (out-of-domain), plant imagery with 38 classes. HEp-2 [11] (out-of-domain), microscopic imagery of human epithelial cells with 6 classes. BCCD WBC [16] (out-of-domain), microscopic images of white blood cells with 5 classes.

3.2   Implementation Details

Taking into account past work [6,9,17], we use four previously proposed backbones for our work: (1) CONV4 [18], (2) DINO ViT-S [2], (3) WRN-28-10 [14,20], and (4) CrossViT [3].

3.3   Results

We compare four, EMMeT-enabled metric backbones against other state-of-the-art few-shot learning approaches across several few-shot learning classification

Table 3. EMMeT Ablation Studies using a CONV4 backbone in a 5-way 5-shot settings. A CONV4 backbone is trained with Snell *et al.*'s proposed training process [17] on the mini-imagenet training set with EMMeT augmented meta-training. Default settings are highlighted in gray and significant results are bolded.

(a) Finetuning Iterations: During finetuning, 20 iterations worth is found to be an optimal values across all tested in-domain and out-of-domain datasets.

Iters.	MIN	ISIC	HEp	BCCD
0	68.42	39.57	55.25	57.42
1	69.11	40.98	55.99	62.03
2	69.31	**44.55**	**58.87**	**67.68**
5	69.15	41.89	56.32	63.44
10	**69.48**	42.96	57.12	65.96
15	69.39	43.01	57.98	67.53
20	69.36	43.72	57.22	67.59
50	68.1	44.35	58.71	67.53

(b) EMMeT Stage Contribution: Each stage within EMMeT contributes a meaningful amount of regularization during meta-training and finetuning. Applying them together results in the highest accuracy.

Regularization	MIN	ISIC	HEp	BCCD
No Reg	68.42	39.57	55.25	57.42
Class Shuffle	69.34	43.97	58.23	67.19
Sample Shuffle	69.34	43.99	58.27	67.21
Class+Sample	69.36	43.99	58.29	67.22
Averaging	69.26	42.64	58.04	66.88
EMMeT	**69.48**	**44.55**	**58.87**	**67.68**

(c) Finetuning Learning Rate Search Space: A search space consisting of 20 learning rates (ranging from 1e-3 to 1e-6) is found to be an optimal value for finetuning a metric backbone across different datasets.

Points	MIN	ISIC	HEp	BCCD
5	65.88	44.01	58.28	67.35
10	68.53	**44.64**	58.68	67.63
20	**69.48**	44.55	**58.87**	**67.68**
50	66.54	44.36	58.53	67.57

datasets. We report results using metric backbones that have EMMeT meta-training and EMMeT finetuning applied.

As established in Tables 1 and 2 as well as illustrated in Fig. 1, EMMeT is capable of significantly increasing the accuracy of metric backbones for both small (i.e. CONV4) and large (i.e. DINO-S or CrossViT) model sizes, across several different datasets. EMMeT-enabled CONV4, WRN-28-10, CrossViT, and DINO-S are shown to outperform strong baselines, such as P>M>F [9] and ProtoNet [17], by up to 6.83%.

In particular, we specifically underscore the results achieved by EMMeT-enabled metric backbones in out-of-domain settings. Comparing an EMMeT-enabled CONV4 to ProtoNet (RN10), we note an average increase of 2.87% across all out-of-domain datasets. These results verify the regularization capabilities of EMMeT in a meta-training and finetuning capacity.

Additionally, we ablate several properties of EMMeT in Table 3 and Fig. 3. All ablations are conducted using an EMMeT meta-trained backbones in a 5-way 5-shot setting. We specifically examine the finetuning iteration count, regularization stage effects, and finetuning learning rate search space. We find that optimal values for both the iteration count and learning rate hyperparameter search space are consistent across all datasets tested. Additionally, we observe that each stage within EMMeT contributes to regularization and accuracy, overall.

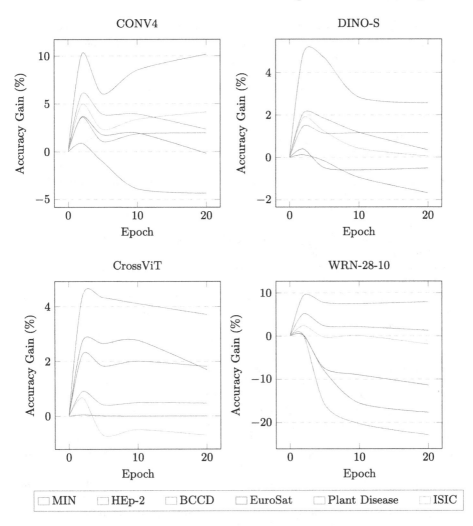

Fig. 3. EMMeT ablations studies for finetuning duration across all tested datasets and metric backbone models. We examine how accuracy is affected relative to the number of finetuning iterations performed.

4   Conclusion

In this work, we propose EMMeT, a novel meta-regularization technique that creates new episodic batches through a shuffling and averaging scheme. The experiments performed in this work demonstrate the effectiveness of our approach towards regularizing a given metric backbone model. Additionally, be leveraging a novel finetuning process, we also show that our approach can significantly improve accuracy in out-of-domain settings. Our results show that EMMeT-enabled metric backbones are capable of performing up to 6.83% better than their counterparts on in-domain and out-of-domain datasets. Finally, we achieve state-of-the-art results with our proposed technique on mini-imagenet, ISIC, EuroSAT, Plant Disease, BCCD WBC, and HEp-2.

References

1. Bateni, P., Goyal, R., Masrani, V., Wood, F., Sigal, L.: Improved few-shot visual classification. In: Proceedings of the IEEE/CVF Conference on Computer Vision and Pattern Recognition (CVPR) (2020)
2. Caron, M., et al.: Emerging properties in self-supervised vision transformers. In: Proceedings of the IEEE/CVF International Conference on Computer Vision (ICCV), pp. 9650–9660 (2021)
3. Chen, C.F.R., Fan, Q., Panda, R.: CrossViT: cross-attention multi-scale vision transformer for image classification. In: Proceedings of the IEEE/CVF International Conference on Computer Vision (ICCV), pp. 357–366 (2021)
4. Codella, N., et al.: Skin lesion analysis toward melanoma detection 2018: a challenge hosted by the international skin imaging collaboration (isic). arXiv preprint arXiv:1902.03368 (2019)
5. Deng, J., Dong, W., Socher, R., Li, L.J., Li, K., Fei-Fei, L.: ImageNet: a large-scale hierarchical image database. In: 2009 IEEE Conference on Computer Vision and Pattern Recognition, pp. 248–255. IEEE (2009)
6. Finn, C., Abbeel, P., Levine, S.: Model-agnostic meta-learning for fast adaptation of deep networks. In: Precup, D., Teh, Y.W. (eds.) Proceedings of the 34th International Conference on Machine Learning. Proceedings of Machine Learning Research, vol. 70, pp. 1126–1135. PMLR (2017). https://proceedings.mlr.press/v70/finn17a.html
7. Fisher, R.A., Yates, F.: Statistical Tables for Biological, Agricultural and Medical Research. Hafner Publishing Company (1953)
8. Helber, P., Bischke, B., Dengel, A., Borth, D.: Eurosat: a novel dataset and deep learning benchmark for land use and land cover classification. IEEE J. Sel. Top. Appl. Earth Observ. Remote Sens. (2019)
9. Hu, S.X., Li, D., Stühmer, J., Kim, M., Hospedales, T.M.: Pushing the limits of simple pipelines for few-shot learning: external data and fine-tuning make a difference. In: Proceedings of the IEEE/CVF Conference on Computer Vision and Pattern Recognition, pp. 9068–9077 (2022)
10. Ni, R., Goldblum, M., Sharaf, A., Kong, K., Goldstein, T.: Data augmentation for meta-learning. In: International Conference on Machine Learning, pp. 8152–8161. PMLR (2021)
11. Qi, X., Zhao, G., Chen, J., Pietikäinen, M.: Exploring illumination robust descriptors for human epithelial type 2 cell classification. Pattern Recogn. **60**, 420–429 (2016)
12. Rajendran, J., Irpan, A., Jang, E.: Meta-learning requires meta-augmentation. Adv. Neural. Inf. Process. Syst. **33**, 5705–5715 (2020)
13. Ravi, S., Larochelle, H.: Optimization as a model for few-shot learning. In: International Conference on Learning Representations (2017). https://openreview.net/forum?id=rJY0-Kcll
14. Rodríguez, P., Laradji, I., Drouin, A., Lacoste, A.: Embedding propagation: smoother manifold for few-shot classification. In: Vedaldi, A., Bischof, H., Brox, T., Frahm, J.-M. (eds.) ECCV 2020. LNCS, vol. 12371, pp. 121–138. Springer, Cham (2020). https://doi.org/10.1007/978-3-030-58574-7_8

15. Saroj Raj Sharma: Plant Disease. https://www.kaggle.com/datasets/saroz014/plant-disease
16. shenggan: BCCD Dataset (2022). https://github.com/Shenggan/BCCD_Dataset. original-date: 2017-12-07T11:54:25Z
17. Snell, J., Swersky, K., Zemel, R.: Prototypical networks for few-shot learning. In: Advances in Neural Information Processing Systems, vol. 30 (2017)
18. Vinyals, O., et al: Matching networks for one shot learning. In: Advances in Neural Information Processing Systems, vol. 29 (2016)
19. Walsh, R., Abdelpakey, M.H., Shehata, M.S., Mohamed, M.M.: Automated human cell classification in sparse datasets using few-shot learning. Sci. Rep. **12**(1), 1–11 (2022)
20. Zagoruyko, S., Komodakis, N.: Wide residual networks. In: British Machine Vision Conference 2016. British Machine Vision Association (2016)

Visual Foreign Object Detection
for Wireless Charging of Electric Vehicles

Bijan Shahbaz Nejad$^{(\boxtimes)}$, Peter Roch, Marcus Handte, and Pedro José Marrón

University of Duisburg-Essen, Essen, Germany
bijan.shahbaz-nejad@uni-due.de

Abstract. Wireless charging of electric vehicles can be achieved by
installing a transmitter coil into the ground and a receiver coil at the
underbody of a vehicle. In order to charge efficiently, accurate alignment of the charging components must be accomplished, which can be
achieved with a camera-based positioning system. Due to an air gap
between both charging components, foreign objects can interfere with
the charging process and pose potential hazards to the environment.
Various foreign object detection systems have been developed with the
motivation to increase the safety of wireless charging. In this paper, we
propose an object-type independent foreign object detection technique
which utilizes the existing camera of an embedded positioning system.
To evaluate our approach, we conduct two experiments by analyzing
images from a dataset of a wireless charging surface and from a publicly
available dataset depicting foreign objects in an airport environment.
Our technique outperforms two background subtraction algorithms and
reaches accuracy scores that are comparable to the accuracy achieved
by a state-of-the-art neural network (~97%). While acknowledging the
superior accuracy results of the neural network, we observe that our approach requires significantly less resources, which makes it more suitable
for embedded devices. The dataset of the first experiment is published
alongside this paper and consists of 3652 labeled images recorded by a
positioning camera of an operating wireless charging station in an outdoor environment.

Keywords: Computer Vision · Electric Vehicles · Wireless Charging ·
Foreign Object Detection · Machine Learning

1 Introduction

Deteriorating air quality due to air pollution is a serious problem in many cities
and can lead to an array of health problems [11,32]. Various studies such as
from Soret et al. [43] or Li et al. [22] have shown that electric vehicles have
the potential to reduce air pollution in cities. In addition to electric cars that
are charged by cable, there are several upcoming approaches realizing wireless
charging of electric vehicles [10]. Wireless power transfer in the context of stationary wireless charging requires a transmitter coil embedded into the ground
and a receiver coil attached to the underbody of the vehicle [35].

© The Author(s), under exclusive license to Springer Nature Switzerland AG 2023
G. Bebis et al. (Eds.): ISVC 2023, LNCS 14362, pp. 188–201, 2023.
https://doi.org/10.1007/978-3-031-47966-3_15

Efficient wireless charging requires an accurate alignment of the charging components in a given tolerance range [12]. Considering the fact that the charging components are not within the driver's field of vision, reaching a minimal deviation of the coils is a challenging activity. Accordingly, Birrel et al. [5] found in studies that only 5% of the vehicles achieved an accurate position that allowed efficient wireless charging. There are several techniques to reduce misalignment of charging components, such as mechanical [18], RFID [27], or wireless sensor-based methods [33]. Furthermore, there are camera-based positioning systems that rely on a camera integrated into the vehicle [20] or statically attached to the charging station [40].

To make wireless charging suitable for everyday use, it is essential to consider various safety aspects. Particularly, neither living beings nor objects should be exposed to any harm in the context of wireless charging. The presence of foreign objects during the charging process, such as metal objects, can pose potential threats, such as high magnetic field exposure or fire [17]. In order to avoid hazardous situations, several foreign object detection methods exist.

Motivated by the goal to increase the safety of wireless charging stations, we present a supplementary approach that augments existing foreign object detection techniques. Since charging stations come with a camera-based positioning system as depicted in Fig. 1, we utilize a given positioning camera to automatically analyze the state of the charging surface. In order to not expand the hardware of the existing positioning system, we propose a resource-friendly approach which can operate on an embedded device. Alongside this paper, we provide a dataset that contains images and labels of various foreign objects on a charging surface recorded by a positioning camera. In order to evaluate our approach, we conduct two experiments. We first analyze images of the provided dataset and then of a dataset which depicts foreign objects in a different context. To summarize the main contributions of our paper, we present:

- An object-type independent foreign object detection method, which can reach high accuracy and robustness while being suitable for embedded devices
- A dataset containing labeled images recorded at an operating wireless charging station

2   Related Work

Foreign objects potentially impose significant safety hazards in wireless charging. Accordingly, several approaches exist to detect foreign objects. According to Zhang et al. [49] there are system parameters, field-based, and wave-based foreign object detection methods in inductive power transfer systems, whereas Cheng et al. [9] refer to the latter two in the context of wireless charging of electric vehicles. In the context of system parameter detection methods, various system parameters such as temperature [19] or power loss [21] may indicate the presence of a foreign object. Furthermore, field-based detection methods observe

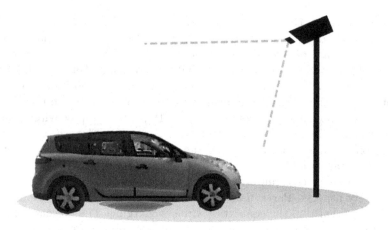

Fig. 1. Illustration of a camera-based positioning system for stationary wireless charging

field-based characteristics such as capacitance [15] or inductance [16] variations to detect foreign objects. Wave-based methods utilize sensors such as radars [37], thermal- [42] or hyperspectral cameras [44] as well as sensor combinations including video cameras [4,13]. Depending on the hardware, wave-based methods can provide high precision, however they can also be costly [9,49].

Cameras are less expensive than many other sensor types and can be used for various tasks such as image classification [28] and object detection [52] using computer vision algorithms. Positioning systems can include a single camera that observes the transmitting coil as well as the surrounding area [40]. Charging stations incorporating the aforementioned type of positioning system could cost-effectively increase their safety by utilizing the existing positioning camera for foreign object detection instead of integrating additional sensors. Hence, computer vision algorithms could detect various foreign objects before a vehicle approaches the transmitting coil by employing the positioning system's camera. Furthermore, existing systems based on e.g. system parameters or field-based foreign object detection methods could be supplemented with information from the mentioned approach.

Indoor. Indoor applications often provide suitable conditions to detect foreign objects. For example, regions of interest will be constantly illuminated and protected from external influences. The approach presented by Lu et al. [29] detects and classifies falling objects in liquids inside transfusion bottles as foreign objects. For detection the approach employs background subtraction and an adapted mean-shift tracker. Furthermore, Al-Sarayreh et al. [1] utilize a neural network on footage recorded in a hypersprectral imaging system setup to detect contamination by foreign objects on meat products. Moreover, X-Ray images of lungs may contain foreign objects due to buttons of worn gowns. Based on the round shape of the buttons, Xue et al. [47] try to detect circular objects by utilizing Circle Hough transform [2] and Viola-Jones algorithm [45].

Outdoor. Outdoor application setups are often exposed to unknown events and circumstances caused by weather and changing illumination conditions. To increase safety and reduce the risk of accidents, various outdoor scenarios demand the detection of foreign objects. In the context of airports, it is crucial to detect and remove various types of objects from runways. Qunyu et al. [38] detect foreign objects on runways by preprocessing an image, subtracting background, postprocessing, and connected component labeling of the foreign object regions. A preliminary experiment demonstrated that all foreign objects were detected on an image. However, several state-of-the-art systems of that context utilize neural networks for foreign object detection, which are trained beforehand to detect known objects. Systems that utilize neural networks are for example, the system proposed in [36] which utilizes Microsoft Azure Custom Vision [30], the approach from [34] using YOLOv4 [6] as well as [23,31] applying YOLOv3 [39] or SSD [26]. Energy infrastructure is another application field that demands a high level of safety utilizing neural networks for foreign object detection. Using for example FODN4PS proposed by Xu et al. [46], intrusions of foreign bodies in power substations are detected in order to be able to prevent potential failures of power supplies. Furthermore, there is RCNN4SPTL [48] for the inspection of power transmission lines, which can detect entangled foreign objects like balloons or kites.

Analysis. All of the aforementioned approaches that operate in an indoor environment provide a suitable solution for the application scenarios in which they are designed and tested. However, wireless charging stations often operate in an outdoor environment with challenging conditions. Typically weather and light conditions vary and the set of potentially occurring foreign objects can not be completely defined. Thus, the foreign object detection system must be robust to environmental conditions and unspecified foreign objects. Based on the unknown appearance of foreign objects, we conclude that shape-based techniques such as Circle Hough Transform [2] would limit the system. In contrast, background subtraction techniques as used by [38] provide a higher flexibility with respect to the potential object shape. However, generated masks contain much noise if the environmental conditions vary, which can produce false positives.

Many modern systems utilize neural networks that can be an effective tool for the detection of foreign objects in various contexts. Foreign object detection using neural networks performs effectively, especially when the set of potentially occurring object classes is completely explored. Although neural networks provide highly accurate results, they require extensive resources, to utilize them. In order to save costs, our positioning system runs on an embedded system with limited resources. Consequently, the model would require to be executed using additional hardware. Accordingly, we conclude that the system should be accurate, robust and resource-friendly at the same time.

3 Approach

Detection of foreign objects can be facilitated by knowing the potentially occurring object types and their possible states. This enables to apply various approaches like neural networks that can be trained with object-specific data. Since several wireless charging stations operate in an outdoor environment, we can not specify the set of potential foreign objects. Thus, we present a procedure that enables object type-independent foreign object detection without considering any depicted object features.

3.1 Training Stage

In general, the charging surface will not be replaced and will be regularly maintained. We assume that the charging surface will not change significantly, and its appearance will be affected mainly by environmental conditions. Hence, our approach is based on features extracted from the charging surface that we obtain during a training stage to fit a model for anomaly detection. Anomaly detection is a helpful tool assisting to identify significant deviations in given data [8]. Therefore, our approach bases on anomaly detection by classifying charging surface regions as normal and diverging occurrences as anomalies.

We define F as the set of all training frames. Each frame $f \in F$ having a size of $w_f \times h_f$ will be preprocessed by transforming it into grayscale format and increasing the contrast. This amplifies the gradient between the charging surface and foreign objects, which supports to distinguish foreign objects that have a similar color or texture as the charging surface. In the first step of feature extraction, the granularity parameter $\gamma \in \mathbb{N}$, where $\gamma \leq \min(w_f, h_f)$ needs to be defined. During training stage, each frame f will be divided into a set of patches P having a width w_p and height h_p:

$$w_p = \frac{w_f}{\gamma} \qquad h_p = \frac{h_f}{\gamma} \tag{1}$$

Higher values of γ enable the algorithm to detect the contour of foreign objects more precisely. In contrast, lower values of γ decrease the processing time. Hence, γ has an impact on granularity of the shape of detected objects,

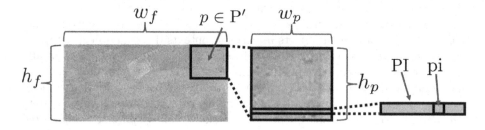

Fig. 2. Illustration of the analyzed image components and their dimensions

while affecting the performance. Each patch p that collides with a bounding box of a foreign object is removed from the set P, resulting in the subset $P' \subseteq P$. All patches $p \in P'$ are composed of multiple rows r and columns c with a size of w_p and h_p, respectively, which can be defined as an array PI containing pixels $pi \in PI$. Figure 2 gives an overview of the described components. As defined in Eq. 2, we determine the arithmetic mean $\overline{PI}$ and the variance σ^2, resulting in $n = (w_p + h_p) * |P'|$ tuples of $(\overline{PI}, \sigma^2)$.

$$\overline{PI} = \frac{1}{|PI|} \sum_{i=1}^{|PI|} pi_i \qquad \sigma^2 = \frac{1}{|PI|} \sum_{i=1}^{|PI|} (pi_i - \overline{PI})^2 \tag{2}$$

According to Liu et al. [25], Isolation Forests [24] provide low-linear time complexity, robustness as well as small memory requirement and outperform other approaches including Local Outlier Factor [7], Random Forests [41] and ORCA [3]. Thus, all extracted feature tuples $(\overline{PI}, \sigma^2)$ are then used to fit a model $\mathcal{M}$ for anomaly detection using an Isolation Forest:

$$\mathcal{M} = \text{fit}\left(\left\{(\overline{PI}, \sigma^2)_1, \ldots, (\overline{PI}, \sigma^2)_n\right\}\right) \tag{3}$$

3.2   Detection Stage

After training stage, gathered information can then be used to identify foreign objects on target frames. Based on granularity parameter γ, a target frame $f \in F$ will be divided into patches $p \in P$. For each pixel array PI given by the rows r and columns c of an individual patch p, arithmetic mean $\overline{PI}$ and variance σ^2 will be calculated to obtain tuples of $(\overline{PI}, \sigma^2)$. All $(w_p + h_p)$ tuples of $(\overline{PI}, \sigma^2)$ will then be classified by the trained model $\mathcal{M}$. This results in a set C_p containing all classifications for a patch p. Classification returns a Boolean value $b \in \mathbb{B} := \{\text{True}, \text{False}\}$, whereas False indicates the absence and True the presence of a foreign object in the region of a given row r or column c.

In order to reduce the risk of misclassifying a specific region of the charging surface, a patch-based majority vote will be conducted, considering the results of the rows and columns. Based on the set of all True classifications C_{True}, Eq. 4 defines the function $FO_p(C_{\text{True}})$ that determines if a patch p contains a foreign object. Thus, a patch p is classified as a foreign object if more than the half of the classifications result in True.

$$FO_p(C_{\text{True}}) = \begin{cases} \text{True}, & \text{if } \dfrac{|C_{\text{True}}|}{w_p + h_p} > 0.5 \\ \text{False}, & \text{otherwise} \end{cases} \tag{4}$$

Based on the information gathered by classifying all patches, a binary mask can be generated. Consequently, the binary mask indicates the presence as well as the location of foreign objects, whereas the precision of the object contour is modulated by granularity γ. Figure 3a depicts an example image from the proposed dataset, which shows sunglasses on the charging surface. Utilizing our approach with $\gamma = 20$, a binary detection mask will be generated as illustrated in Fig. 3b.

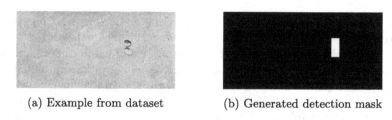

(a) Example from dataset   (b) Generated detection mask

Fig. 3. Demonstration of the proposed approach generating a binary mask to detect foreign objects.

4   Dataset

To the best of our knowledge there is no dataset publicly available that provides images of foreign objects in the context of wireless charging of electric vehicles. Aiming to expand contributions in this field of research, we present the **F**oreign **O**bjects in **W**ireless **C**harging (FOWC) dataset containing images recorded at an operating wireless charging station. The charging station was constructed as part of the TALAKO project [14] and is frequently accessed by vehicles that are equipped with a wireless charging interface. A transmitter coil was integrated into the ground and embedded into a robust concrete casing. The positioning system utilizes a wide angle camera which is installed at a height of approximately 2 m and focuses the positioning area including the charging point.

The operation of the charging station was temporarily interrupted to be able to capture the images using the positioning camera. Figure 4a illustrates an example frame from the positioning camera's perspective. Foreign object detection is limited to the area of the transmitting coil. Hence, the dataset focuses on the region of interest (ROI). We crop the surrounding environment and perform a homography transformation of the ROI to obtain a bird's eye view perspective as shown in Fig. 4b.

There are three different categories of images in the dataset. The first category includes images that do not contain any foreign objects, such as depicted in Fig. 4b. The second category includes images that contain a single foreign object from a set of predefined object types, namely can, coin, glasses, hairpin, key, ring and wrench. The objects are systematically placed at seven predefined positions as illustrated with blue crosses in Fig. 5a. Figure 5b shows an example image from the third category, that contains an extension of the predefined object types and places them at random locations and quantities. The dataset is split into a test set and a training set containing 1035 and 2617 images, respectively. For all 7 object types there are 15 images for each of the 7 positions that were illustrated in Fig. 5a. In addition, there are 200 images in the random object category such as 100 images without objects. The training set is a mixture of all the categories containing the rest of the recorded images. All foreign objects depicted in the dataset were manually labeled in the Darknet format as used by YOLO [39]. The images and labels are publicly available at https://www.nes.uni-due.de/research/data/.

(a) Camera perspective   (b) Region of interest

Fig. 4. Example image from the dataset showing the state before and after transformation.

(a) Single object   (b) Random objects

Fig. 5. Examples of images illustrating the possible amounts foreign objects and their distribution among the image.

5   Evaluation

The foreign object detection system should be accurate, robust and resource-friendly at the same time. If the state of the charging surface will be analyzed inaccurately, false alarms could be triggered, which can affect ongoing operation. Thus, attractiveness might suffer if wireless charging services are mistakenly not available to the users. Accordingly, the state of the charging surface should be reproduced accurately. Thus, we first conduct two experiments to examine accuracy and robustness, and then we analyze performance.

5.1   Experimental Setup

In the first experiment, we train our approach with the training images of the presented dataset. The presented dataset depicts big objects like a wrench as well as small objects like a coin. Unknown environmental conditions or foreign object types might reduce the accuracy of the detection. Thus, we create multiple training subsets of our training dataset to explore the robustness of our approach while analyzing of the full test dataset, which contains 1035 images. The subsets consist of a sample of 10, 50 and 100 randomly selected images, whereas the full set contains 2617 images.

To reconstruct the shape of big objects and simultaneously to be able to detect small objects, we set the granularity parameter $\gamma = 20$ to split the image into small patches. For each analyzed image, our approach generates a binary mask, which semantically depicts the regions of foreign objects and regions of the charging surface in contrast. In order to be able to compare the resulting binary mask to binary masks based on ground truth data, we expand the detected foreign object regions to the shape of a corresponding rectangular bounding box. For analyzing to what extent the detection reflects the ground truth, we compute an accuracy score. Thus, we compare the set of correctly classified pixels $\text{PI}_{\text{correct}}$ to the amount of all pixels of each frame, resulting in:

$$\text{Accuracy} = \frac{|\text{PI}_{\text{correct}}|}{\text{width} * \text{height}} \tag{5}$$

In the second experiment, we repeat the same steps as in the first experiment, but analyze images recorded in a different context and also with unknown objects. The FOD-A dataset [31] depicts more than 30 object categories in the context of airports. In contrast to the first experiment, the objects of the FOD-A dataset are located on various backgrounds having several weather and illumination conditions. As with the first dataset, we create in addition to the full dataset training subsets of 10, 50 and 100 random images, but also a subset of 1035 test images for comparable conditions.

Existing applications typically utilize background subtraction [29,38] or neural networks [34,36]. Accordingly, we repeat both experiments with other techniques to compare our approach. As a baseline, we use YOLOv4 [6] with a default configuration, which is a state-of-the-art neural network used for object detection. Additionally, we use two background subtraction approaches [50,51], which we call in the following KNN and MOG2, respectively.

Isolation Forests are an ensemble of estimating trees. Liu et al. [25] use a default value of 100 trees and further show that a lower number can be sufficient. Hence, we compose the Isolation Forest with 100 and 10 trees for each dataset condition.

In addition to the accuracy evaluation, we also analyze the time and the resources required to execute the studied techniques. For comparison, we examine the average image processing time in seconds with each algorithm using a powerful computer and embedded device. The algorithms are executed on a Dell G7 with an Intel Core i7-9750H CPU and on a Raspberry Pi 3 B+, respectively.

5.2   Results

We summarize the achieved accuracy scores by calculating the 95% confidence intervals and the arithmetic mean for each condition in percent. Figure 6 presents an overview of the first two experiments. The figure groups the accuracy of the utilized technique by the analyzed dataset.

In the first experiment, all approaches reach comparable results. The accuracy lays in an interval between around 95% and 98%, whereas YOLOv4 and our approach have a slightly higher accuracy than the background subtraction algorithms. Summarized for the subset conditions, MOG2 background subtraction reaches scores between 76% and 80% in the second experiment. Moreover, MOG2 scores an improvement of 5% in the full dataset condition, reaching an

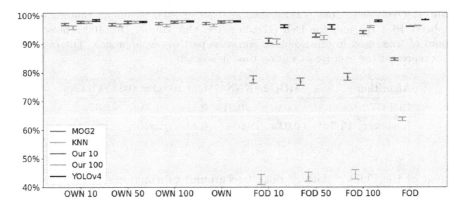

Fig. 6. Illustration showing the accuracy results of both experiments for all dataset conditions. The horizontal whiskers depict the lower and the upper boundary of the 95% confidence intervals. The circle between both whiskers represents the average accuracy. OWN and FOD-A represent the full datasets, whereas OWN and FOD-A with post-fix 10, 50 or 100 represent the subset conditions. In the legend, Our 10 and Our 100 represent the amount of trees used in the Isolation Forest as part of our approach.

accuracy score of around 85%. When using the random subsets of the FOD-A dataset, KNN background subtraction reaches significantly less accurate results, which lie in a range between around 41% and 46%. In contrast to MOG2 background subtraction, KNN improves its score by around 20% in the full training dataset reaching a score of approximately 64%. Furthermore, our proposed approach improves accuracy gradually up to around 95% on average starting from 91% for the subset of 10 images. Finally, YOLOv4 scores in an interval around 96% to 97% in all observed conditions.

Table 1 summarizes the results of the performance analysis in seconds. All of the approaches increase time to analyze an image significantly, when executed on the Raspberry Pi. We observe that YOLOv4 runs for around 2.67 s to analyze a given frame, when using the powerful computer. In contrast, when running YOLOv4 on the Raspberry Pi it requires more than 285 s per image on average. Furthermore, our approach with an ensemble of 100 trees processes an image in around 0.35 s on the Dell G7 and nearly 2.7 s on the Raspberry Pi. Independently of the hardware, when reducing the number of trees to 10, our approach processes a given frame in more than three times faster. In terms of speed, both background subtraction techniques outperform YOLOv4 and the proposed approach with an average execution time which is less than 0.01 s on the powerful computer and around 0.03 on the embedded device.

5.3 Discussion

Both background subtraction techniques provide accurate results in the dataset depicting the wireless charging environment. However, in the more challenging

Table 1. Overview of the performance analysis of each technique running on the Raspberry Pi 3 B+ and the Dell G7 computer. Our 10 and Our 100 represent the amount of trees used in the Isolation Forest as part of our approach. The presented values represent the average execution time in seconds.

Algorithm	MOG2	KNN	Our 10	Our 100	YOLOv4
Dell G7	<0.01 s	<0.01 s	0.11 s	0.35 s	2.67 s
Raspberry Pi 3 B+	0.03 s	0.03 s	0.88 s	2.69 s	285.74 s

context of the FOD-A dataset both background subtraction methods decrease accuracy significantly. While acknowledging the superior accuracy results of YOLOv4, we observe that our approach provides comparable scores, when analyzing images of the wireless charging surface and nearly similar in the FOD-A condition. In most cases, our approach is slightly more accurate with an ensemble of 100 trees than with 10 trees.

Furthermore, we discover that the sample of training images affects the resulting accuracy of the proposed approach. In the results based on the training with the subset of 10 images from the FOD-A dataset, we observe that our approach scores accuracy which is lower than 80% in around 14% of the test cases. Correspondingly, when increasing the subset to 100 images or to the full dataset, the proportion of the images with low accuracy decreases to 7% and 2%, respectively.

Moreover, there is a continuous video stream in the application scenario of wireless charging. In addition to creating a suitable dataset, considering the presence of foreign objects over time can help to increase robustness by filtering false-positives. Accordingly, detections over a reasonable period of time can probably indicate the presence of a foreign object.

Summarized, background subtraction techniques KNN and MOG2 are dramatically faster, but also significantly less accurate and robust to unseen conditions than the other techniques. However, our approach is slightly less accurate than YOLOv4, but up to 24 times faster on a powerful machine and more than 300 times on an embedded device. We observe that fewer trees lead to similar accuracy results but accelerate image analysis, which makes it suitable for embedded devices.

6   Conclusion

Wireless charging stations should not endanger persons or objects of the environment. To avoid hazardous situations, there are various systems that detect foreign objects which may potentially pose a risk. Motivated by the goal to increase the safety of wireless charging stations, we propose an approach to augment existing foreign object detection mechanisms. As there are charging stations with a camera-based positioning system, our approach utilizes the existing positioning camera to automatically analyze the state of the charging surface. We aim to provide an approach which can run on an embedded device, to not extend the hardware of the existing positioning system. Thus, the system should be resource-friendly, while providing accurate results and robustness to unseen conditions.

In advance of utilizing the proposed technique, a training stage is required. During training, target frames depicting the charging surface will be divided into patches based on a granularity parameter. In order to fit an Isolation Forest for anomaly detection, features will be extracted from all rows and columns of patches not containing a foreign object. After training stage, a target image can be analyzed by dividing it into patches according to the defined granularity parameter. Then, all features of the rows and columns of each patch will be analyzed with the fitted Isolation Forest to detect anomalies. Finally, a majority vote is used to determine whether a foreign object exists in a certain patch by checking if more than half of the rows and columns contain a foreign object.

To evaluate our approach, we conduct two experiments by analyzing images from a dataset of a wireless charging surface and from a publicly available dataset depicting foreign objects in a different scenario. Across both contexts, our technique outperforms two background subtraction algorithms and reaches accuracy scores that are comparable to the accuracy achieved by a state-of-the-art neural network. Moreover, we observe that our approach requires significantly less resources than the neural network, which makes it suitable for embedded devices.

Acknowledgment. This research is funded by the Bundesministerium für Wirtschaft und Energie as part of the TALAKO project [14] (grant number 01MZ19002A).

References

1. Al-Sarayreh, M., Reis, M.M., Yan, W.Q., Klette, R.: A sequential CNN approach for foreign object detection in hyperspectral images. In: CAIP (2019)
2. Atherton, T., Kerbyson, D.: Size invariant circle detection. IMAVIS **17**, 795–803 (1999)
3. Bay, S.D., Schwabacher, M.: Mining distance-based outliers in near linear time with randomization and a simple pruning rule. In: KDD (2003)
4. Bell, D., Leabman, M.A.: Systems and methods of object detection using one or more sensors in wireless power charging systems (Nov 19 2019), US Patent 10,483,768
5. Birrell, S.A., Wilson, D., Yang, C.P., Dhadyalla, G., Jennings, P.: How driver behaviour and parking alignment affects inductive charging systems for electric vehicles. TR_C, **58**, 721–731 (2015)
6. Bochkovskiy, A., Wang, C., Liao, H.M.: Yolov4: optimal speed and accuracy of object detection. CoRR (2020)
7. Breunig, M.M., Kriegel, H.P., Ng, R.T., Sander, J.: LOF: identifying density-based local outliers. In: MOD (2000)
8. Chandola, V., Banerjee, A., Kumar, V.: Anomaly detection: a survey. ACM Comput. Surv. **41**, 1–58 (2009)
9. Cheng, B., Lu, J., Zhang, Y., Pan, G., Chabaan, R., Mi, C.C.: A metal object detection system with multilayer detection coil layouts for electric vehicle wireless charging. Energies **13**, 2960 (2020)

10. Colombo, C.G., Miraftabzadeh, S.M., Saldarini, A., Longo, M., Brenna, M., Yaici, W.: Literature review on wireless charging technologies: future trend for electric vehicle? In: SMART (2022)
11. Fu, F., Purvis-Roberts, K.L., Williams, B.: Impact of the COVID-19 pandemic lockdown on air pollution in 20 major cities around the world. Atmosphere **11**, 1189 (2020)
12. Gao, Y., Ginart, A., Farley, K.B., Tse, Z.T.H.: Misalignment effect on efficiency of wireless power transfer for electric vehicles. In: APEC (2016)
13. Hoffman, P.F., Boyer, R.J., Henderson, R.A.: Foreign object detection system and method suitable for source resonator of wireless energy transfer system (Apr 5 2016), US Patent 9,304,042
14. IAM, Universität Duisburg-Essen: Taxiladekonzept für Elektrotaxis im öffentlichen Raum. talako.uni-due.de (2022). Accessed 14 Jan 14
15. Jeong, S.Y., Kwak, H.G., Jang, G.C., Rim, C.T.: Living object detection system based on comb pattern capacitive sensor for wireless EV chargers. In: SPEC (2016)
16. Jeong, S.Y., Kwak, H.G., Jang, G.C., Choi, S.Y., Rim, C.T.: Dual-purpose nonoverlapping coil sets as metal object and vehicle position detections for wireless stationary EV chargers. TPEL **33**, 7387–7397 (2018)
17. Jiang, H., Brazis, P., Tabaddor, M., Bablo, J.: Safety considerations of wireless charger for electric vehicles - a review paper. In: ISPCE (2012)
18. Karakitsios, I., et al.: An integrated approach for dynamic charging of electric vehicles by wireless power transfer-lessons learned from real-life implementation. SAE Int. J. Altern. Powertrains **6**, 15–24 (2017)
19. Karanth, A., Dorairaj, H.H.K., Kumar, R.B.R.: Foreign object detection in inductive coupled wireless power transfer environment using thermal sensors (Jun 27 2013), US Patent App. 13/808,786
20. Kobeissi, A.H., Bellotti, F., Berta, R., De Gloria, A.: IoT grid alignment assistant system for dynamic wireless charging of electric vehicles. In: IOTSMS (2018)
21. Kuyvenhoven, N., Dean, C., Melton, J., Schwannecke, J., Umenei, A.: Development of a foreign object detection and analysis method for wireless power systems. In: ISPCE (2011)
22. Li, N., et al.: Potential impacts of electric vehicles on air quality in Taiwan. STOTEN **566**, 919–928 (2016)
23. Li, P., Li, H.: Research on FOD detection for airport runway based on yolov3. In: CCC (2020)
24. Liu, F.T., Ting, K.M., Zhou, Z.H.: Isolation forest. In: ICDM (2008)
25. Liu, F.T., Ting, K.M., Zhou, Z.H.: Isolation-based anomaly detection. TKDD **6**, 1–39 (2012)
26. Liu, W., et al.: SSD: single shot multibox detector. In: Leibe, B., Matas, J., Sebe, N., Welling, M. (eds.) ECCV 2016. LNCS, vol. 9905, pp. 21–37. Springer, Cham (2016). https://doi.org/10.1007/978-3-319-46448-0_2
27. Loewel, T., Lange, C., Noack, F.: Identification and positioning system for inductive charging systems. In: EDPC (2013)
28. Lu, D., Weng, Q.: A survey of image classification methods and techniques for improving classification performance. IJRS **28**, 823–870 (2007)
29. Lu, J., nan Wang, Y., Zhang, J., wen Zhou, B.: On-line detection of foreign substances in glass bottles filled with transfusion solution through computer vision. In: ICIA (2008)
30. Microsoft: What is custom vision? (2023). https://learn.microsoft.com/en-us/azure/cognitive-services/custom-vision-service/overview. Accessed 07 Feb 2023

31. Munyer, T., Huang, P.C., Huang, C., Zhong, X.: FOD-a: a dataset for foreign object debris in airports. CoRR (2021)
32. Nazar, W., Niedoszytko, M.: Air pollution in Poland: a 2022 narrative review with focus on respiratory diseases. IJERPH **19**, 895 (2022)
33. Ni, W., et al.: Radio alignment for inductive charging of electric vehicles. TII **11**, 427–440 (2015)
34. Noroozi, M., Shah, A.: Towards optimal foreign object debris detection in an airport environment. Expert Syst. Appl. **213**, 118829 (2023)
35. Panchal, C., Stegen, S., Lu, J.: Review of static and dynamic wireless electric vehicle charging system. JESTECH **21**, 922–937 (2018)
36. Parker, A., Gonzalez, F., Trotter, P.: Live detection of foreign object debris on runways detection using drones and AI. In: AERO (2022)
37. Poguntke, T., Schumann, P., Ochs, K.: Radar-based living object protection for inductive charging of electric vehicles using two-dimensional signal processing. Wirel. Power Transfer **4**, 88–97 (2017)
38. Qunyu, X., Huansheng, N., Weishi, C.: Video-based foreign object debris detection. In: IST (2009)
39. Redmon, J., Farhadi, A.: Yolov3: an incremental improvement. CoRR (2018)
40. Shahbaz Nejad, B., Roch, P., Handte, M., Marrón, P.J.: A driver guidance system to support the stationary wireless charging of electric vehicles. In: Bebis, G., et al. (eds.) ISVC 2020. LNCS, vol. 12510, pp. 319–331. Springer, Cham (2020). https://doi.org/10.1007/978-3-030-64559-5_25
41. Shi, T., Horvath, S.: Unsupervised learning with random forest predictors. JCGS **15**, 118–138 (2006)
42. Sonnenberg, T., Stevens, A., Dayerizadeh, A., Lukic, S.: Combined foreign object detection and live object protection in wireless power transfer systems via real-time thermal camera analysis. In: APEC (2019)
43. Soret, A., Guevara, M., Baldasano, J.: The potential impacts of electric vehicles on air quality in the urban areas of Barcelona and Madrid (Spain). Atmos. Environ. **99**, 51–63 (2014)
44. Tian, Y., et al.: Metal object detection for electric vehicle inductive power transfer systems based on hyperspectral imaging. Measurement **168**, 108493 (2021)
45. Viola, P., Jones, M.: Rapid object detection using a boosted cascade of simple features. In: CVPR (2001)
46. Xu, L., Song, Y., Zhang, W., An, Y., Wang, Y., Ning, H.: An efficient foreign objects detection network for power substation. IMAVIS **109**, 104159 (2021)
47. Xue, Z., et al.: Foreign object detection in chest x-rays. In: BIBM (2015)
48. Zhang, W., et al.: RCNN-based foreign object detection for securing power transmission lines (RCNN4SPTL). Procedia Comput. Sci. **147**, 331–337 (2019)
49. Zhang, Y., Yan, Z., Zhu, J., Li, S., Mi, C.: A review of foreign object detection (FOD) for inductive power transfer systems. ETransportation **1**, 100002 (2019)
50. Zivkovic, Z.: Improved adaptive gaussian mixture model for background subtraction. In: ICPR (2004)
51. Zivkovic, Z., van der Heijden, F.: Efficient adaptive density estimation per image pixel for the task of background subtraction. Pattern Recogn. Lett. **27**, 773–780 (2006)
52. Zou, Z., Shi, Z., Guo, Y., Ye, J.: Object detection in 20 years: a survey. CoRR (2019)

Deep Representation Learning for License Plate Recognition in Low Quality Video Images

Kemeng Zhao⓪, Liangrui Peng$^{(\boxtimes)}$⓪, Ning Ding⓪, Gang Yao⓪, Pei Tang⓪, and Shengjin Wang⓪

Beijing National Research Center for Information Science and Technology, Department of Electronic Engineering, Tsinghua University, Beijing, China
penglr@tsinghua.edu.cn

Abstract. License plate recognition is an important technology in many application scenarios such as traffic monitoring and vehicle management. Due to variations of viewpoint, illumination, motion-blur, and degradation in imaging process, it is still a challenging problem to detect and recognize license plates in low quality video images. In this paper, we focus on efficient deep representation learning for license plate recognition, detection and tracking. For license plate recognition, we mainly investigate the configuration of different network structures, and propose to use a network structure with a Convolutional Neural Network (CNN) backbone, an Long Short-Term Memory (LSTM) encoder and a Transformer decoder. For license plate detection, a Transformer encoder-decoder based method is adopted. For license plate tracking, a multi-object tracking method is incorporated by using Kalman filtering and temporal matching to associate detected license plates in video frames. Experiments are carried out on the public large-scale video-based license plate dataset (LSV-LP) to validate the proposed methods.

Keywords: License plate recognition · Object detection and tracking · Deep learning

1 Introduction

License plate recognition is an important technology in a wide range of applications including traffic monitoring, traffic law enforcement, vehicle management and parking management. In recent years, there are increasing needs to detect and recognize license plates in video images captured in uncontrolled scenarios [14], such as a video footage captured by a police car dash camera. Compared to high resolution frontal views of license plates captured at the entrance of a parking lot, the quality of video images in uncontrolled scenarios is relatively low. The variations of viewpoint, illumination, motion-blur, and degradation in imaging process bring more challenges for license plate detection and recognition.

Existing license plate detection and recognition methods can be generally divided into two categories, traditional methods and deep learning based methods. Traditional license plate detection and recognition methods are mainly

G. Bebis et al. (Eds.): ISVC 2023, LNCS 14362, pp. 202–214, 2023.
https://doi.org/10.1007/978-3-031-47966-3_16

based on hand crafted features [13], which are relatively sensitive to image quality and noise. With the advent of deep learning, various deep neural network based methods have been proposed for license plate detection and recognition [12,13]. Recently Transformer [18] based encoder-decoder models with self-attention mechanism have shown promising performance on natural language processing, computer vision and other machine learning tasks. In this paper, we focus on deep representation learning for license plate detection, recognition and tracking, and explore a solution by using self-attention mechanism based encoder-decoder models.

For license plate recognition, the main problem is how to find efficient and robust representations in sequence modeling for low quality license plate images. We mainly investigate the configuration of different network structures of encoder-decoder framework, and propose to use a network structure with a CNN backbone using ResNet-29 [6], an LSTM encoder and a Transformer decoder. We further explore the utilization of image rectification module for image preprocessing, and use synthetic samples to pre-train the recognition model.

For license plate detection, we incorporate the TESTR [22] method, which is a Transformer based encoder-decoder model originally designed for scene text spotting. We fine-tune the available pre-trained TESTR model on a license plate dataset.

For license plate tracking, we adopt the ByteTrack method [23], which is a multi-object tracking method using Kalman filtering and temporal matching to associate detected text boxes in video frames. A license plate recognition prototype system is finally implemented by integrating the modules of recognition, detection and tracking for license plates. Experiments are conducted on a public large-scale video-based Chinese license plate dataset (LSV-LP) [19].

The main contributions of this paper are summarized as follows:

1. A license plate recognition method with a CNN backbone, an LSTM encoder and a Transformer [18] decoder is proposed. The effect of using image rectification and pre-training with synthetic samples is further explored.
2. The TESTR method [22] based on Transformer encoder-decoder framework is adopted for license plate detection, and the ByteTrack method [23] is utilized for license plate tracking. A license plate recognition prototype system is further implemented by integrating the modules of recognition, detection and tracking for license plates.
3. Experimental results on the public video-based Chinese license plate dataset (LSV-LP) have validated the proposed methods.

2   Related Work

2.1   License Plate Recognition

License plate recognition methods can be roughly categorized into character segmentation based methods and segmentation free methods. Many deep learning based license plate recognition networks choose light-weight CNN structures [9], e.g. LPRNet [24]. The combination of CNN and Recurrent Neural Network (RNN) is also used for license plate recognition. Tian et al. [17] propose a method using CNN and Gated Recurrent Unit (GRU) network.

The encoder-decoder structure is a typical neural network architecture and has shown promising performance for sequence modeling tasks. Recently, Transformer [18] based on self-attention mechanism has outperformed RNN based encoder-decoder method [3] on various machine learning tasks including scene text recognition [15]. In this paper, different configurations of encoder and decoder using RNN or Transformer are compared, and a method is proposed by using a ResNet backbone, an RNN encoder and a Transformer decoder.

In addition, image preprocessing and model pre-training methods are useful in license plate recognition stage. Dong et al. [7] utilize a temporally and spatially based sampling network to rectify the deformation of the license plate region before recognition. Bjorklun et al. [4] use a large amount of synthesized images to train their model. In our recognition model, two kinds of image rectification methods are compared, and model pre-training with synthetic samples is also used.

2.2 License Plate Detection and Tracking

Deep learning based license plate detection methods usually adopt object detection algorithms, which can be broadly classified into two categories, i.e. single-stage methods [8,10] and two-stage methods [11]. Recently, Transformer encoder-decoder based methods have achieved improved performance on object detection tasks [5]. TExt Spotting Transformers (TESTR) is a generic end-to-end scene text spotting framework adopting Transformer encoder-decoder structure [22]. In this paper, the TESTR method [22] is adopted for multi-oriented license plate detection.

It is feasible to use temporal information to enhance the detection or recognition performance. Zweng et al. [25] propose to use redundant information in image sequences to improve the performance of license plate recognition. Multiple Frames License Plate Recognition Network (MFLPR-Net) [19] uses decoupled attention network [20] for license plate recognition and a U-shaped CNN for detection. Furthermore, MFLPR-Net incorporates optical flow network to propagate information between adjacent frames. As for deep learning based object tracking, one of the multi-object tracking methods is ByteTrack [23]. This method uses low-score detection frames additionally to differentiate the tracked object from the background, which can effectively improve tracking accuracy. In this paper, the ByteTrack method [23] is adopted for license plate tracking.

3 Method

3.1 System Framework

Figure 1 shows the overall framework of our license plate recognition system, which contains detection, recognition and tracking modules. The recognition model consists of a CNN backbone, an LSTM encoder and a Transformer decoder. The system first detects license plates in the consecutive video frames and then obtains license plate numbers through the recognition module. In addition, the tracking module utilizes Kalman filtering and temporal matching to track license plates.

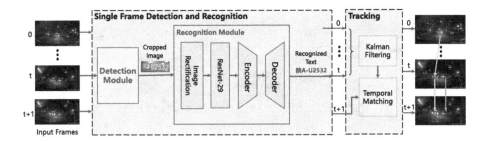

Fig. 1. The framework of the proposed license plate recognition system.

3.2   Encoder-Decoder Recognition Models

In encoder-decoder model, the encoder is responsible for converting the input sequence into a fixed-length vector representation, and the decoder is designed to decode the vector representation into the target sequence. There are two main categories of encoder-decoder based frameworks, i.e. RNN-based model and Transformer-based model. RNN can model contextual information by introducing feedback loops in the network structure, while Transformer uses self-attention mechanism for sequence modeling. It is interesting to find a better encoder-decoder network structure by combining the merits of these two categories of encoder-decoder based frameworks.

Therefore, we attempt to compare encoders and decoders by using different combinations of RNN and Transformer [16]. RNN encoder or decoder adopts a 2-layers bidirectional LSTM network with 216 hidden units in each layer. Dropout with probability 0.3 is introduced on the inputs of each RNN layer. Transformer encoder or decoder consists of 2 layers with 4 heads.

Different feature extraction networks based on variants of ResNet are compared, including ResNet-18, ResNet-29 [6], ResNet-34 and ResNet-50. For the purpose of feature extraction, the final average pooling layer and linear layer of these networks have been removed.

3.3   Image Rectification

We utilize two image rectification methods for image processing. The first method is a pixel-level image rectification module based on CNN [21]. The network is able to predict offsets and modulation scalars for pixels of input images, followed by a modulated bilinear interpolation sampler to generate rectified images. The structure of this network is shown in Fig. 2. It consists of five basic convolutional blocks and a global convolutional block, each of which is appended with a batch normalization layer as well as a Leaky ReLU as the activation function. The second method is affine transformation, which can convert the detected license plate region of a quadrilateral into a rectangle.

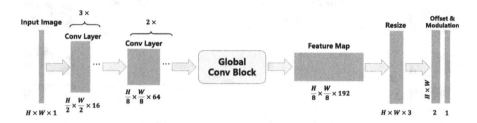

Fig. 2. The main structure of image rectification module.

3.4 Data Synthesis and Data Augmentation

Training a deep learning model usually requires large scale training samples. It is helpful to use synthetic samples to pre-train the license plate recognition model. By using an open-source tool [1], a large-scale synthetic dataset has been built and utilized. The synthetic license plate images have a blue background with white numbers on them, following the most common style of license plates in China. To simulate low-quality license plate images, random distortions, rotations, hue variations and noises are also added. The synthetic dataset consists of 400,000 images. The size of a synthetic image is 32×120 pixels. Figure 3 shows some examples of the synthetic license plate images.

Fig. 3. Examples of synthetic license plate images. The total number of synthetic images is 400,000.

The pretrained model is further fine-tuned on a real license plate dataset. During the fine-tuning process, data augmentation techniques are also used, including image translation, rotation and other conventional image transforms.

3.5   License Plate Detection and Tracking

To detect multi-oriented license plates, the TESTR [22] method is adopted. The TESTR model includes a backbone network, an encoder and two decoders including a location decoder and a character decoder. The two decoders are used for joint text-box control point regression and character recognition. An input image is first converted into feature maps by using a backbone network and positional encoding. Then coarse detection boxes are generated from the feature maps by using the encoder that employs DETR [5] with multi-scale self-attention mechanism. These boxes are further encoded and added to the learnable control point query embeddings to guide the acquisition of control points. The control point queries are then fed into the location decoder, and feed-forward networks to obtain the predicted coordinates. Both the location decoder and character decoder incorporate the multi-scale cross-attention mechanism.

For license plate detection, we employ the pre-trained TESTR model [22], and fine-tune the model on a license plate dataset.

For the implementation of license plate detection and recognition of single frame in video images, we compare two schemes in the subsequent experiments. One is to use the fine-tuned TESTR model directly for end-to-end license plate detection and recognition. The other is to use TESTR detection results only, and use our recognition method to get the final recognition results. Our experimental results have shown that the latter scheme can achieve better results.

For license plate tracking, we implement the multi-object tracking algorithm by using the ByteTrack method [23]. It can exploit the similarity between tracklets and detection boxes among video frames to recover true objects and filter out the detection boxes in the background.

4   Experiments

4.1   Dataset and Evaluation Metrics

Our experiments are conducted on a large-scale video license plate dataset (LSV-LP) [19]. The dataset is divided into three subsets, move2static, static2move and move2move, according to whether the photographer and the captured vehicles are stationary or moving. In the move2static subset, most of the images are captured from hand-held cell phone shots of cars on the side of the road or in a parking lot. In the static2move subset, the vehicles are moving against the background. In the move2move subset, the video images are usually captured by dash cameras.

Our models are implemented by using the PyTorch deep learning framework. We integrate the detection and tracking models by employing the MMTracking [2] toolkit, which provides a variety of advanced object detection and tracking algorithms. All our training and testing tasks are carried out on a server with four Nvidia Tesla V100 GPUs. License plate images are cropped from the video frames according to labels for the training and testing of recognition models. In the training stage, all three subsets of the dataset are used. For the training process, batch size is set to 16, and the number of training epochs is set to 20.

For the recognition model, we choose two common performance evaluation metrics, Accuracy (AR) for whole license plate and Character Recognition Rate (CRR). AR stands for the ratio of the number of correctly recognized license plates to the total number of license plates. By using edit distance, CRR is calculated as

$$CRR = (N_t - D_e - S_e - I_e)/N_t \tag{1}$$

where D_e, S_e and I_e represent the total number of deletion, substitution and insertion errors, respectively, and N_t refers to the total number of characters.

For detection, the performance evaluation metrics are Precision, Recall and F_1 score [19] using an Intersection-over-Union (IoU) threshold of 0.5, which are calculated as

$$Precision = TP/(TP + FP) \tag{2}$$

$$Recall = TP/(TP + FN) \tag{3}$$

$$F_1 = 2/(1/Precision + 1/Recall) \tag{4}$$

where TP stands for the number of true positive predictions. FP stands for the number of false positive predictions. FN denotes false negative, which is the number of missing targets.

As for tracking, we use the Multi-Object Tracking Accuracy (MOTA) metric to measure the overall accuracy in terms of missing targets, false detection, and changes in object IDs. MOTA is calculated as

$$MOTA = 1 - \sum_t (FN_t + FP_t + IDSW_t)/\sum_t GT_t \tag{5}$$

where t denotes the index of a video frame, IDSW refers to how many times the ID of the same object is switched (ID Switch), and GT is the number of objects in ground-truth.

All the performance evaluation metrics mentioned above are presented as percentages (%) in the subsequent tables of experimental results.

4.2　Experiments on License Plate Recognition

The Effect of Different Network Structures. Table 1 compares the recognition performance of recognition models with different encoders and decoders. In this experiment, ResNet-34 is chosen as the feature extraction network for all models. The results show that the RNN encoder-Transformer decoder model performs best on all subsets of the LSV-LP dataset.

Table 1. Comparisons of encoder-decoder models with different structures.

Model	static2move		move2static		move2move		average	
	CRR	AR	CRR	AR	CRR	AR	CRR	AR
RNN-RNN	80.67	25.90	69.53	13.76	83.38	52.93	79.75	36.67
RNN-Transformer	**92.84**	**68.49**	**85.98**	**56.61**	**91.74**	**71.92**	**90.93**	**67.46**
Transformer-RNN	91.28	60.57	82.98	45.70	89.56	66.06	88.77	60.29
Transformer-Transformer	92.35	67.12	85.44	52.37	91.70	69.98	90.64	65.55

We further conduct experiments with the RNN encoder-Transformer decoder model to investigate the effect of using different feature extraction networks. Table 2 shows that ResNet-29 [6] has achieved the best performance.

Table 2. Comparisons of different feature extraction networks.

Model	static2move		move2static		move2move		average	
	CRR	AR	CRR	AR	CRR	AR	CRR	AR
ResNet-18	93.08	68.64	88.27	63.87	91.50	71.14	91.33	68.88
ResNet-29	**93.15**	**70.56**	**89.40**	**65.73**	**92.23**	**72.11**	**91.94**	**70.34**
ResNet-34	92.84	68.49	85.98	56.61	91.74	71.29	90.93	67.46
ResNet-50	89.43	53.97	70.58	21.15	86.22	55.77	84.06	48.28

The experiments in subsequent sections are conducted by using the ResNet-29 backbone and the RNN encoder-Transformer decoder network, denoted as "Ours (RRT)" in Table 3 and Table 4.

The Effect of Image Rectification. Experiments are carried out to further analyze the effect of two image rectification methods, i.e. the pixel-level image rectification module introduced in Sect. 3.3 and affine transformation. The experimental results in Table 3 show that the affine transformation performs better than pixel-level image rectification module. This is partly because license plates are rigid objects.

Table 3. Comparisons of different image rectification methods.

Model	static2move		move2static		move2move		average	
	CRR	AR	CRR	AR	CRR	AR	CRR	AR
Ours (RRT)	93.15	70.56	89.40	65.73	92.23	72.11	91.94	70.34
+ Pixel-level Rectification Module	93.63	71.73	89.00	64.97	**92.33**	72.47	91.93	70.52
+ Affine Transformation	**93.70**	**73.97**	**90.38**	**72.05**	92.29	**73.14**	**92.34**	**73.18**

The Effect of Synthetic Samples. The effect of pre-training on synthetic samples is tested and the results are shown in Table 4. Adding pre-training with synthetic samples alone can improve the recognition accuracy. But it seems that adding pixel-level image rectification weakens the effect of pre-training on synthetic samples. One possible reason might be that the adopted tool for synthesizing samples has limited ability to generate various types of license plate images.

Table 4. The results of using synthetic data for pre-training.

Model	static2move		move2static		move2move		average	
	CRR	AR	CRR	AR	CRR	AR	CRR	AR
Ours (RRT)	93.15	70.56	89.40	65.73	92.23	72.11	91.94	70.34
+ Synthetic Data Pre-training	93.54	71.81	89.33	64.74	**92.51**	**72.93**	92.19	70.93
+ Pixel-level Image Rectification Module + Synthetic Data Pre-training	92.69	68.14	89.04	64.71	92.40	71.87	91.81	69.27
+ Affine Transformation + Synthetic Data Pre-training	**93.57**	**72.58**	**90.57**	**71.91**	92.34	72.83	**92.28**	**72.47**

Comparisons with SOTA Methods. The comparisons of our recognition method with other State-Of-The-Art (SOTA) methods are shown in Table 5. The performance of our recognition method (RRT with affine transformation) is competitive with better results on the move2static subset.

We also compare TESTR's recognition performance with our recognition model while using the TESTR detection results only. The recognition results are compared with ground truth texts for true positive detection results with an IoU threshold of 0.5. Two schemes are compared. The first one uses the fine-tuned TESTR model as an end-to-end license plate detection and recognition model directly. The second one uses TESTR detection results only, and adopts our recognition method (RRT with affine transformation) to get the final recognition results. Table 6 shows that the second scheme can achieve better results.

Figure 4 exhibits several examples of low-quality video license plate images and corresponding recognition results. The recognition results show that the proposed method is effective on most uncontrolled scenarios.

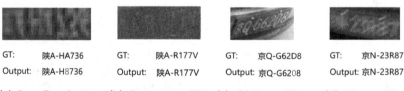

GT: 陕A-HA736   GT: 陕A-R177V   GT: 京Q-G62D8   GT: 京N-23R87

Output: 陕A-H8736   Output: 陕A-R177V   Output: 京Q-G6208   Output: 京N-23R87

(a) Low Resolution (b) Improper Illu- (c) Oblique View- (d) Motion-blur
                        mination   point

Fig. 4. Examples of recognition results.

Table 5. Comparisons with SOTA methods on the LSV-LP test set.

Model	static2move	move2static	move2move	average
LPRNet [19,24]	71.85	44.51	59.38	60.03
MFLPR-Net [19]	**78.57**	69.23	**74.31**	**74.49**
Ours	73.97	**72.05**	73.14	73.18

Table 6. Comparison of the TESTR recognition model with our model.

Recognition Model	static2move		move2static		move2move		average	
	CRR	AR	CRR	AR	CRR	AR	CRR	AR
TESTR	84.05	48.60	89.47	61.96	81.97	54.60	83.83	53.27
Ours	**94.67**	**76.62**	**89.70**	**63.44**	**94.39**	**76.56**	**93.89**	**74.88**

4.3 Experiments on License Plate Detection and Tracking

Table 7 shows the performance indexes of Precision, Recall, F_1 score and MOTA of our detection and tracking model on the LSV-LP test set. The pretrained TESTR model is fine-tuned with different training epochs on the LSV-LP training set. The results show that the model fine-tuned with 6 epochs is the best. Figure 5 visualizes the attention weights of multi-scale deformable self-attention mechanism in the encoder and decoder of the detection model, which indicates that the detection model performs well under challenging illumination and motion blurring situations.

Table 7. Detection and tracking performance on the LSV-LP test set with models at different fine-tuning epochs on the LSV-LP training set.

Epochs	static2move				move2static				move2move				average			
	P	R	F_1	MOTA	P	R	F_1	MOTA	P	R	F_1	MOTA	P	R	F_1	MOTA
2	50.67	58.73	54.40	−3.71	80.23	57.72	67.14	40.90	65.93	57.88	61.64	24.77	62.14	58.11	60.06	18.97
4	61.87	38.12	47.17	10.14	80.52	66.39	72.78	47.64	74.87	43.16	54.76	26.39	72.34	46.04	56.27	25.39
6	55.82	59.90	57.79	6.49	79.05	80.29	79.67	55.16	66.79	59.49	62.93	26.55	65.46	63.61	64.52	25.77
8	52.60	60.79	56.40	−0.02	77.11	81.94	79.45	53.92	63.58	59.88	61.67	22.01	62.41	64.39	63.38	21.25

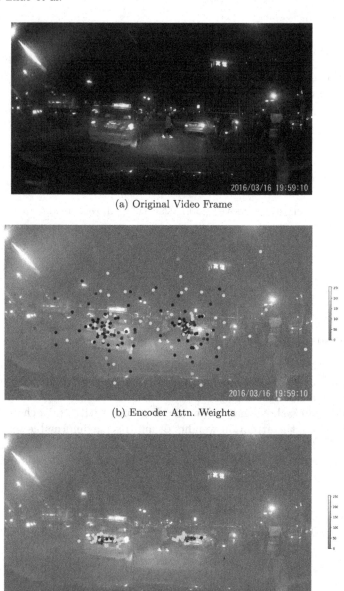

(a) Original Video Frame

(b) Encoder Attn. Weights

(c) Decoder Attn. Weights

Fig. 5. Visualization of self-attention mechanism in detection module. The query point is represented by a red cross symbol, while the green rectangle in Fig. (c) shows the prediction bounding box. The color of sampling points indicates their corresponding attention weights (Color figure online).

5   Conclusion

In this paper, a license plate recognition method is proposed by using a ResNet backbone, an RNN encoder and a Transformer decoder. We also investigate the effect of using image rectification for image pre-processing and using synthetic samples for pre-training the recognition model. By incorporating the TESTR [22] based license plate detection module and the ByteTrack [23] based license plate tracking module, a license plate recognition prototype system is implemented. Experimental results on the LSV-LP [19] dataset have demonstrated the effectiveness of the proposed method. For future work, it is possible to design more powerful end-to-end detection and recognition networks for license plate images acquired in an open environment.

References

1. Synthetic Chinese license plate. https://github.com/CV-deeplearning/gen-Chinese-plate. Accessed 20 July 2023
2. MMTracking: OpenMMLab video perception toolbox and benchmark (2020). https://github.com/open-mmlab/mmtracking
3. Bahdanau, D., Chorowski, J., Serdyuk, D., et al.: End-to-end attention-based large vocabulary speech recognition. In: ICASSP, pp. 4945–4949 (2016)
4. Björklund, T., Fiandrotti, A., Annarumma, M., Francini, G., Magli, E.: Automatic license plate recognition with convolutional neural networks trained on synthetic data. In: 19th International Workshop on Multimedia Signal Processing (MMSP), pp. 1–6 (2017)
5. Carion, N., Massa, F., Synnaeve, G., Usunier, N., Kirillov, A., Zagoruyko, S.: End-to-end object detection with transformers. In: Vedaldi, A., Bischof, H., Brox, T., Frahm, J.-M. (eds.) ECCV 2020. LNCS, vol. 12346, pp. 213–229. Springer, Cham (2020). https://doi.org/10.1007/978-3-030-58452-8_13
6. Cheng, Z., Bai, F., Xu, Y., et al.: Focusing attention: Towards accurate text recognition in natural images. In: ICCV, pp. 5086–5094 (2017)
7. Dong, M., He, D., Luo, C., Liu, D., Zeng, W.: A CNN-based approach for automatic license plate recognition in the wild. In: BMVC (2017)
8. Liu, W., et al.: SSD: single shot multibox detector. In: Leibe, B., Matas, J., Sebe, N., Welling, M. (eds.) ECCV 2016. LNCS, vol. 9905, pp. 21–37. Springer, Cham (2016). https://doi.org/10.1007/978-3-319-46448-0_2
9. Pham, T.A.: Effective deep neural networks for license plate detection and recognition. Vis. Comput. **39**(3), 927–941 (2023)
10. Redmon, J., Divvala, S., Girshick, R., Farhadi, A.: You only look once: unified, real-time object detection. In: CVPR, pp. 779–788 (2016)
11. Ren, S., He, K., Girshick, R., Sun, J.: Faster R-CNN: towards real-time object detection with region proposal networks. NIPS 28 (2015)
12. Schirrmacher, F., Lorch, B., Maier, A., Riess, C.: Benchmarking probabilistic deep learning methods for license plate recognition. IEEE Trans. Intell. Transp. Syst. **24**, 9203–9216 (2023)
13. Shashirangana, J., Padmasiri, H., Meedeniya, D., Perera, C.: Automated license plate recognition: a survey on methods and techniques. IEEE Access **9**, 11203–11225 (2021)

14. Silva, S.M., Jung, C.R.: License plate detection and recognition in unconstrained scenarios. In: Ferrari, V., Hebert, M., Sminchisescu, C., Weiss, Y. (eds.) ECCV 2018. LNCS, vol. 11216, pp. 593–609. Springer, Cham (2018). https://doi.org/10.1007/978-3-030-01258-8_36

15. Tan, Y.L., Kong, A.W.K., Kim, J.J.: Pure transformer with integrated experts for scene text recognition. In: Avidan, S., Brostow, G., Cissé, M., Farinella, G.M., Hassner, T. (eds.) ECCV 2022. LNCS, vol. 13688, pp. 481–497. Springer, Cham (2022). https://doi.org/10.1007/978-3-031-19815-1_28

16. Tang, P., Peng, L., Yan, R., et al.: Domain adaptation via mutual information maximization for handwriting recognition. In: ICASSP, pp. 2300–2304 (2022)

17. Tian, X., Wang, L., Zhang, R.: License plate recognition based on CNN. In: International Conference on Computer Research and Development (ICCRD), pp. 244–249 (2022)

18. Vaswani, A., Shazeer, N., Parmar, N., et al.: Attention is all you need. In: NIPS, pp. 5998–6008 (2017)

19. Wang, Q., Lu, X., Zhang, C., Yuan, Y., Li, X.: LSV-LP: large-scale video-based license plate detection and recognition. PAMI 45(1), 752–767 (2023)

20. Wang, T., Zhu, Y., Jin, L., et al.: Decoupled attention network for text recognition. In: AAAI, pp. 12216–12224 (2020)

21. Xiao, S., Peng, L., Yan, R., Wang, S.: Deep network with pixel-level rectification and robust training for handwriting recognition. In: ICDAR, pp. 9–16 (2019)

22. Zhang, X., Su, Y., Tripathi, S., Tu, Z.: Text spotting Transformers. In: CVPR, pp. 9509–9518 (2022)

23. Zhang, Y., Sun, P., Jiang, Y., et al.: ByteTrack: multi-object tracking by associating every detection box. In: Avidan, S., Brostow, G., Cissé, M., Farinella, G.M., Hassner, T. (eds.) ECCV 2022. LNCS, vol. 13682, pp. 1–21. Springer, Cham (2022). https://doi.org/10.1007/978-3-031-20047-2_1

24. Zherzdev, S., Gruzdev, A.: LPRNet: license plate recognition via deep neural networks. arXiv preprint arXiv:1806.10447 (2018)

25. Zweng, A., Kampel, M.: High performance implementation of license plate recognition in image sequences. In: Bebis, G., Boyle, R., Parvin, B., Koracin, D., Kuno, Y., Wang, J., Pajarola, R., Lindstrom, P., Hinkenjann, A., Encarnação, M.L., Silva, C.T., Coming, D. (eds.) ISVC 2009. LNCS, vol. 5876, pp. 598–607. Springer, Heidelberg (2009). https://doi.org/10.1007/978-3-642-10520-3_57

Optimizing PnP-Algorithms for Limited Point Correspondences Using Spatial Constraints

Peter Roch[✉], Bijan Shahbaz Nejad, Marcus Handte, and Pedro José Marrón

University of Duisburg-Essen, Essen, Germany
peter.roch@uni-due.de

Abstract. Pose Estimation is an important component of many real-world computer vision systems. Most existing pose estimation algorithms need a large number of point correspondences to accurately determine the pose of an object. Since the number of point correspondences depends on the object's appearance, lighting and other external conditions, detecting many points may not be feasible. In many real-world applications, movement of objects is limited due to gravity. Hence, detecting objects with only three degrees of freedom is usually sufficient. This allows us to improve the accuracy of pose estimation by changing the underlying equation of the perspective-n-point problem to allow only three variables instead of six. By using the improved equations, our algorithm is more robust against detection errors with limited point correspondences. In this paper, we specify two scenarios where such constraints apply. The first one is about parking a vehicle on a specific spot, while the second scenario describes a camera observing objects from a birds-eye view. In both scenarios, objects can only move in the ground plane and rotate around the vertical axis. Experiments with synthetic data and real-world photographs have shown that our algorithm outperforms state-of-the-art pose estimation algorithms. Depending on the scenario, our algorithm usually achieves 50% better accuracy, while being equally fast.

Keywords: Computer Vision · Pose Estimation · Perspective-n-Point

1 Introduction

Estimating the orientation of an object in 3d space is an important research topic. In 1841, Grunert [13] presented a mathematical approach to calculate the position of a point based on the orientation of three known points. In 1981, Fischler and Bolles [7] introduced the term perspective-n-point problem (PnP) describing the problem to find the position of the center of perspective using angles of control points. This problem can be translated to camera pose estimation [30], which is useful for different applications in robotics [25,48], augmented and virtual reality (AR & VR) [20,31,51] or autonomous driving [5,14,24].

Many algorithms [17,22,26,47,49] already exist for the general case, where it is necessary to detect the pose of the camera in relation to the object with no further constraints. However, many real-world applications have fixed camera perspectives and limited possible object poses. For example, the KITTI dataset [11]

G. Bebis et al. (Eds.): ISVC 2023, LNCS 14362, pp. 215–229, 2023.
https://doi.org/10.1007/978-3-031-47966-3_17

was collected by mounting cameras on top of a driving car. Since cameras are fixed to the car and objects of interest, e.g. other cars, cyclists or pedestrians, are moving on the ground plane, pose estimation requires only three degrees of freedom.

Similar constraints also apply to fixed cameras observing objects in the environment. The KITTI dataset [11] is used to train and evaluate egomotion algorithms, which are useful for self-driving applications. In contrast, external vehicle positioning scenarios [6, 21, 41] use a camera fixed in the environment to observe a positioning area, e.g. a parking lot. Industrial applications [15] can benefit from a camera observing objects underneath and computing their pose for robotic manipulation. To increase accuracy in these scenarios, some algorithms reduce the result space by taking gravity into account [8, 46].

Most algorithms need many points to achieve high accuracy. If enough points are detected, a RANSAC approach can be used to reject outliers. However, detecting many points may not be feasible, since the number of detectable points depends on the observed object, illumination conditions or the environment. In such cases, it is not possible to reject outliers, since not enough point correspondences are available. To improve robustness of pose estimation algorithms in constrained scenarios, we propose a mathematical definition of the perspective-n-point problem respecting physical constraints in the real world, which is solved by using an iterative optimization strategy to find the pose of the camera in relation to the object. Hence, our algorithm is more accurate in scenarios where only few keypoints are available and can tolerate higher inaccuracies in the detected keypoints.

While the algorithm is only applicable if the camera is aligned with the coordinate system, slight deviations of the physical camera setup can be countered by transforming the image. As long as the camera position is fixed and the ground is flat, the transformation can be calibrated beforehand and the pose can be computed as if the camera was aligned.

To evaluate our algorithm, we compare it to existing six degrees of freedom PnP algorithms in experiments using synthetic data as well as data extracted from photographs. Annotated images were taken from published datasets showing side-view images of cars [41] and images of household objects from above [29]. Our main contribution is an alternative solution to the perspective-n-point problem making use of physical constraints. These limit the solution, so that our method is applicable in scenarios with only few detectable keypoints. Further, our solution is more robust against inaccurately detected keypoints. Experiments have shown that the translation error usually can be reduced by up to 50%.

2   Related Work

In this paper, we propose a new solution to the perspective-n-point problem. Fischler and Bolles [7] described the term perspective-n-point problem (PnP) as the challenge to find the location of a point called "center of projection" (P_{cp}) in relation to a set of n control points. They also describe mathematical implications of different values for n. In the case of $n = 1$ and $n = 2$, the location of P_{cp} cannot be determined. The P3P-Problem can be reduced to an equation system with at most 8 possible solutions, where each positive solution has a geometrically isomorphic negative solution. Both $n = 4$ and $n = 5$ yield up to 2 possible solutions, while $n \geq 6$ produces a unique solution.

These mathematical considerations have resulted in a number of different implementations of P3P [9,23,38,40], P4P [1,12,52] and PnP [3,36] algorithms, which are useful in different scenarios and account for different kinds of errors. In general, PnP algorithms can further be classified into iterative, non-iterative and deep learning methods.

Iterative PnP algorithms define an objective function based on 2d-3d point correspondences, which is then minimized to find an optimal set of parameters that can be transformed into the final projection matrix. Possible optimization techniques include the Levenberg-Marquardt [27,32], Gauss-Newton [2,28] and Nelder-Mead [34] algorithms. Other iterative PnP algorithms [10,44] reformulate the minimization function to improve accuracy or runtime complexity of the algorithm.

Since iterative PnP algorithms only approximate the solution, they can find local minima of the objective function, which results in less accurate results. Non-iterative PnP algorithms avoid this by computing the optimal solution in a direct way. The EPnP algorithm [26] was developed to have a low computational cost of $O(n)$ and low sensitivity to noise. Another efficient PnP algorithm is IPPE [4], which requires 3d points to be coplanar. Hesch and Roumeliotis [17] have implemented a direct-least-squares method which is not dependent on the number of points. Hence, their method is more scalable than other methods. The SQPnP algorithm [47] casts the problem as a quadratically constrained quadratic program, which is robust to noise and computationally fast. In addition to algorithms solving the PnP problem by using mathematical equations, deep learning approaches [37,53] use neural networks to estimate the pose of objects. While they are able to achieve accurate results, they need more hardware resources to achieve comparable performance. For example, DiffPoseNet [37] was trained using four Nvidia P6000 GPUs. In contrast, mathematical approaches do not need to be trained and can usually run on less expensive CPUs.

Common to general PnP algorithms is the approach to detect six degrees of freedom (6-DoF) in a static scenario. However, many scenarios impose constraints on the environment, which can be used to improve the resulting pose. Some authors try to estimate the position of the camera while moving, which can be applied to cars [16,43] or robots [19,35]. This has the advantage, that much fewer points are necessary to determine the camera pose. Instead of estimating the pose in a single image, these approaches track points in multiple images. Since movement properties of the camera are known, the pose of the camera can be estimated. Hence, these approaches are useful in scenarios, where the camera is mounted on a moving object which needs to locate itself. However, these approaches fail in scenarios where a camera is fixed in the environment.

Other approaches without movement constraints [8,46] make use of additional knowledge, such as a known gravity direction, to increase accuracy. This can be applied to e.g. augmented reality applications using an inertial measurement unit (IMU) to obtain the gravity direction. While this leads to very accurate results, these algorithms require a large amount of correspondences.

If many point correspondences are available, a RANSAC approach can be used to reject outliers and improve accuracy. However, this is only possible if enough points are available. If only few points are available as described in our scenario, no points can be rejected, since all points are necessary to compute the pose of the object. Therefore, we propose a new 3-DoF PnP algorithm, which can estimate poses of objects with only few point correspondences. Compared to 6-DoF algorithms, our approach is more accurate in the described scenarios, since the result space is reduced. Compared to 3-DoF algorithms, our approach needs less information to obtain useful results. No motion is required, and the pose can be estimated with limited point correspondences.

3   Problem Description

The general case of the perspective-n-point problem is to find the pose of an object using n 2d-3d point correspondences. This can be understood as the inverse operation of projecting points from 3d space coordinates into 2d screen coordinates, which is defined as follows: Let K be the camera matrix containing the focal length f_x, f_y and the principal point (c_x, c_y). Let R and t be the rotation matrix and the translation vector, respectively. These variables are defined in Eq. 1:

$$K = \begin{pmatrix} f_x & 0 & c_x \\ 0 & f_y & c_y \\ 0 & 0 & 1 \end{pmatrix} \qquad R = \begin{pmatrix} r_{11} & r_{12} & r_{13} \\ r_{21} & r_{22} & r_{23} \\ r_{31} & r_{32} & r_{33} \end{pmatrix} \qquad t = \begin{pmatrix} t_1 \\ t_2 \\ t_3 \end{pmatrix} \tag{1}$$

The projection from a local 3d point with coordinates (X, Y, Z) to a 2d camera point with coordinates (x', y') can be computed as shown in Eq. 2:

$$\begin{pmatrix} x' \\ y' \end{pmatrix} = \begin{pmatrix} u/w \\ v/w \end{pmatrix} \qquad \begin{pmatrix} u \\ v \\ w \end{pmatrix} = \begin{pmatrix} f_x & 0 & c_x \\ 0 & f_y & c_y \\ 0 & 0 & 1 \end{pmatrix} \begin{pmatrix} r_{11} & r_{12} & r_{13} & t_1 \\ r_{21} & r_{22} & r_{23} & t_2 \\ r_{31} & r_{32} & r_{33} & t_3 \end{pmatrix} \begin{pmatrix} X \\ Y \\ Z \\ 1 \end{pmatrix} \tag{2}$$

This can be understood as a two-step process. The first operation $(X'\ Y'\ Z')^T = (R|t)(X\ Y\ Z\ 1)^T$ projects the point in the object's local coordinate system into the 3d camera frame, while $(u\ v\ w)^T = K(X'\ Y'\ Z')^T$ projects the 3d point into the 2d camera coordinate system. Based on Eq. 2, we can derive Eq. 3:

$$\begin{aligned} \frac{x' - c_x}{f_x} &= \frac{r_{11} * X + r_{12} * Y + r_{13} * Z + t_1}{r_{31} * X + r_{32} * Y + r_{33} * Z + t_3} \\ \frac{y' - c_y}{f_y} &= \frac{r_{21} * X + r_{22} * Y + r_{23} * Z + t_2}{r_{31} * X + r_{32} * Y + r_{33} * Z + t_3} \end{aligned} \tag{3}$$

Since keypoint detection in the camera image, measurement of the object coordinates and calibration of the camera parameters may be inaccurate, Eq. 3 can be converted to a minimization problem. If a minimum value of Eq. 4 is found, the resulting projection matrix is considered optimal.

$$
\min \sum_{k=1}^{n} \left| \frac{x'_k - c_x}{f_x} - \frac{r_{11}X_k + r_{12}Y_k + r_{13}Z_k + t_1}{r_{31}X_k + r_{32}Y_k + r_{33}Z_k + t_3} \right| + \left| \frac{y'_k - c_y}{f_y} - \frac{r_{21}X_k + r_{22}Y_k + r_{23}Z_k + t_2}{r_{31}X_k + r_{32}Y_k + r_{33}Z_k + t_3} \right| \tag{4}
$$

4   Implementation

To describe our implementation, we first describe real-world constraints, which apply in many typical pose estimation scenarios. Afterward, we describe the implementation, leveraging the aforementioned constraints to improve robustness against noise with limited point correspondences.

4.1   Real-World Constraints

In many real-world applications, objects can only move on a 2-dimensional plane due to gravity. Rotation is only possible around the vertical axis. For example, when the camera is observing a parking spot [6,21,41], it can be aligned to the ground plane. Observed cars can move in the camera's field of view on the x/z-plane (the ground plane) and rotate around the y-axis, but can neither fly nor rotate around any other axis. A similar scenario is a camera mounted above a table, conveyor belt or similar [15]. In this case, items can only move in the x/y-plane and rotate around the z-axis. Both scenarios are illustrated in Fig. 1.

Even if the camera is slightly misaligned, movement constraints still apply. As long as the camera setup is fixed and its orientation is calibrated, the camera-view can be transformed so that objects appear as if the camera was aligned to the coordinate system. This transformation can be applied to the keypoints or the complete image, depending on the applied keypoint detection algorithm. If the keypoint detection algorithm is able to detect keypoints in the original image, the detected keypoints can be transformed. Otherwise, the image can be transformed before keypoints are detected.

4.2   The Proposed Solution

The aforementioned constraints imply that we can simplify the general equations. For reference, rotation matrices for rotation around the camera's y- and z-axes are shown in Eq. 5:

$$
R_y = \begin{pmatrix} \cos\theta & 0 & \sin\theta \\ 0 & 1 & 0 \\ -\sin\theta & 0 & \cos\theta \end{pmatrix} \qquad R_z = \begin{pmatrix} \cos\theta & -\sin\theta & 0 \\ \sin\theta & \cos\theta & 0 \\ 0 & 0 & 1 \end{pmatrix} \tag{5}
$$

 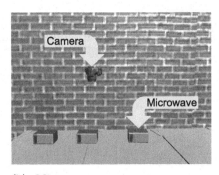

(a) A car in a parking spot. The camera is aligned with the ground, observing the car from the side.

(b) Microwave ovens on an assembly line. The ovens move from left to right and are observed by the camera mounted above.

Fig. 1. Illustrations of both scenarios. The observed object can only move in one plane. Since the camera is aligned with the world coordinate system, only three degrees of freedom are possible.

Hence, we can simplify Eq. 3 to Eq. 6 for rotation around the y-axis with movement in the x-z-plane. A similar equation can be constructed for rotation around the z-axis with movement in the x-y-plane, but is omitted for brevity.

$$
\begin{aligned}
\frac{x' - c_x}{f_x} &= \frac{\cos\theta * X + \sin\theta * Z + t_1}{-\sin\theta * X + \cos\theta * Z + t_3} \\
\frac{y' - c_y}{f_y} &= \frac{Y + t_2}{-\sin\theta * X + \cos\theta * Z + t_3}
\end{aligned}
\tag{6}
$$

The resulting minimization function can be solved by a standard optimization solver. In this case, we use the Nelder-Mead simplex method [34], since it is more precise than other optimization algorithms in low-dimensional spaces, i.e. scenarios with less than 5 variables [39]. Since only three variables need to be computed, this approach needs fewer point correspondences and can tolerate more noise in the detected keypoints than other PnP algorithms.

5 Evaluation

We compare our algorithm to SQPnP [47] and EPnP [26], which are used in various recent projects [48,50]. Additionally, we compare our algorithm to an iterative Levenberg-Marquardt [27,32] optimization based pose estimation algorithm in a standard configuration using 6 degrees of freedom and our improved configuration using 3 degrees of freedom. We extend the comparison by using SQPnP, EPnP and Levenberg-Marquardt with a projected result. After computing the pose by the respective algorithm, the result is projected to the ground plane to reduce it to three degrees of freedom. The resulting algorithms are called

SQPnP', EPnP' and Levenberg-Marquardt' in the following evaluation. This is done to compare the described Nelder-Mead solver, which uses only three degrees of freedom in its computation, to solvers derived from six degrees of freedom, which project the result to the ground afterwards.

To evaluate our approach, we split our evaluation in three parts. First, we use generated data to test our algorithm and compare it to existing solutions. Second, we also use photographs taken in the described scenarios to demonstrate the applicability of our algorithm to real-life applications. Third, we measure the execution time of each tested algorithm.

5.1 Evaluation Metrics

We are applying each algorithm in different scenarios. Hence, it is important to define a metric independent of the scenario. We use the proportion of the length of the error vector compared to the length of the result vector for algorithm comparison, as was done by Lepetit et al. [26]. Computation of rotation error e_r and translation error e_t is also shown in Eq. 7:

$$e_r = \frac{|Q_{\text{gt}} - Q_{\text{e}}|}{|Q_{\text{e}}|} \qquad e_t = \frac{|t_{\text{gt}} - t_{\text{e}}|}{|t_{\text{e}}|} \qquad (7)$$

Q_{gt} and Q_{e} denote the quaternions corresponding to the ground truth and estimated rotation matrices, respectively. Similarly, t_{gt} and t_{e} denote the ground truth and estimated translation vector.

5.2 Evaluation Using Synthetic Data

To generate data to compare our algorithm with existing solutions, we first generate keypoints in 3d space which represent an object at a random location. The keypoints are then projected onto the image plane of a virtual camera. Finally, we apply Gaussian noise to each image coordinate, simulating inaccurate detection of the keypoints. To show robustness of each algorithm, we increase the standard deviation of the Gaussian noise in the test data. Since each algorithm is expected to be precise with no or very low noise, it is important to compare precision with high noise levels.

To achieve comparable results, we use test scenarios similar to EPnP [26] and SQPnP [47]. Additionally, we generate test data simulating a car detection scenario, as well as objects on a table viewed from above. The described configurations are defined as EPnP_σ, SQPnP_σ, Car_σ and Table_σ, where σ is the standard deviation of the Gaussian noise.

Each configuration is run 1000 times to compute the average accuracy for each solver. Figure 2 shows the error of each algorithm in the different tests. To increase visibility in the lower range of the results, we have cut the range of each figure. Hence, comparatively inaccurate results were left out. Figure 2a, 2c, 2e, and 2g show the translation error. As can be seen, the Nelder-Mead algorithm outperforms the other algorithms. In all tests, the algorithm shows less error than the compared 6-DoF algorithms. Especially in the EPnP scenario, the error of the presented 3-DoF algorithm only increases slightly, while errors of the other algorithms increase significantly with higher noise levels. Figure 2e shows that the error of the Nelder-Mead solver increases from 1% to 4%, while other algorithms show errors of more than 10%. Similar observations can be made in the other tests, where the error is always below 5%. This test displays that our algorithm can be used to accurately determine the translation of objects in the presented scenarios.

Figure 2b, 2d, 2f, and 2h show the rotation error of each algorithm. Here, the Nelder-Mead algorithm performs slightly less accurate than EPnP and SQPnP in the EPnP 2f and Table 2d configurations. Nevertheless, the Nelder-Mead solver is the most accurate in the SQPnP configuration, which can be seen in Fig. 2h.

5.3 Evaluation Using Photographs

To evaluate the usefulness of the proposed algorithm using images, datasets with known objects are needed. Many existing datasets [33, 45] are useful to track the camera in some environment, but do not contain annotations of objects in this environment. Hence, these datasets cannot be used in our scenario. Instead, we use two published datasets showing images of objects with known pose in relation to the camera as well as known size.

To evaluate the first scenario, we use a Car Pose Estimation Dataset [41]. This dataset features 250 pictures of a car with known ground truth pose. Since we are interested in matches of 2d image points and 3d object points, we can extract the required information from the image before computing the pose of the car. Four 2d image points, two on each wheel, are detected using ORB [42], while 3d object points are known based on the size of the car.

The second scenario is evaluated using images from the HOPE [29] dataset. This dataset features 28 toy grocery items in different poses. While most objects are not depicted exactly from above, the images can be transformed so that the resulting image is showing the object as if it were recorded from above. Not all images of the dataset are suitable for the described transformation. Hence, we filter out non-suitable images. For the remaining 147 images, ORB [42] is used to detect corners of the top layer of the object. Real-world dimensions are read from the 3d object model.

Table 1 shows the comparison of each PnP Solver in both scenarios. Columns *avg* show the average error and columns σ show the standard deviation. As can be seen, the Nelder-Mead based PnP Solver has the lowest error in most cases. Only in the car scenario, the rotation is detected slightly less accurate than by EPnP. However, EPnP has the highest translation error in the table scenario, where the Nelder-Mead algorithm is the most accurate in both translation and rotation errors. The 3-DoF implementation of the Levenberg-Marquardt algorithm is less accurate than the Nelder-Mead implementation using the same equation. This suggests that the choice of the optimization algorithm is equally important to an accurate solver as the optimized equation.

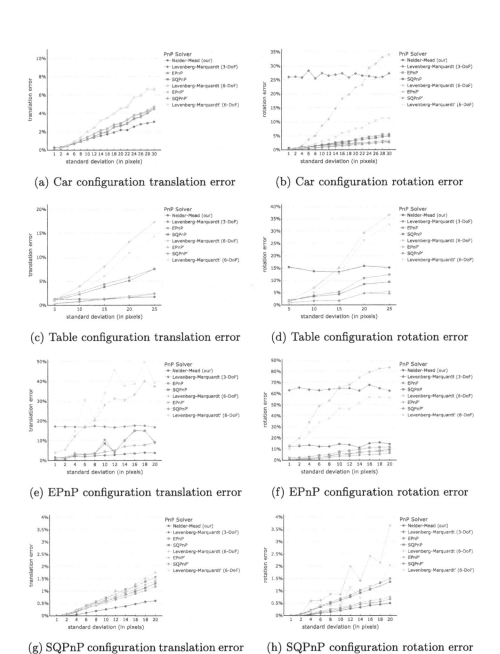

(a) Car configuration translation error

(b) Car configuration rotation error

(c) Table configuration translation error

(d) Table configuration rotation error

(e) EPnP configuration translation error

(f) EPnP configuration rotation error

(g) SQPnP configuration translation error

(h) SQPnP configuration rotation error

Fig. 2. Errors in each configuration

Table 1. Errors of tested algorithms

PnP Solver	Car Test				Table Test			
	Translation		Rotation		Translation		Rotation	
	avg	σ	avg	σ	avg	σ	avg	σ
Nelder-Mead (our)	4%	4%	12%	6%	2%	4%	10%	25%
Levenberg-Marquardt (3-DoF)	15%	7%	15%	5%	19%	7%	45%	56%
EPnP	7%	9%	11%	10%	103%	299%	38%	40%
SQPnP	16%	11%	24%	9%	34%	126%	30%	39%
Levenberg-Marquardt (6-DoF)	14%	10%	23%	8%	30%	164%	26%	31%
EPnP'	7%	9%	11%	10%	5%	7%	15%	41%
SQPnP'	16%	11%	24%	9%	4%	5%	8%	25%
Levenberg-Marquardt' (6-DoF)	14%	10%	23%	8%	3%	4%	7%	26%

The results are also visualized in Fig. 3. In each case, the box marks the first and third quartile. The median is also marked inside the box. Additionally, whiskers extend the box by 1.5 times the interquartile range. The mean is marked as a dashed line. As can be seen, the blue box representing our solution is smaller and lower than the boxes of the 6-DoF solvers.

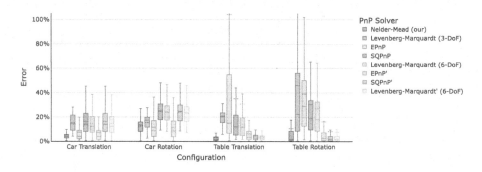

Fig. 3. Boxplots of errors in the Car and Table tests

5.4 Time

In addition to the accuracy, we compare the execution time of each algorithm in different configurations. The results are shown in Fig. 4. Figure 3a shows the time in milliseconds for each algorithm with an increasing number of point correspondences. Figure 3b shows a comparison of execution time in relation to increasing error rates of the detected points. As illustrated in Fig. 3a, for less than 10 points, the Nelder-Mead based solver is equally fast as EPnP and SQPnP, while

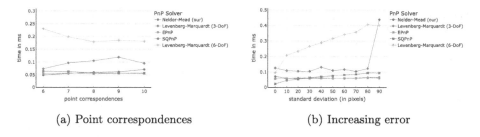

(a) Point correspondences

(b) Increasing error

Fig. 4. Execution time of each algorithm in different configurations

the Levenberg-Marquardt based solver is substantially slower. When comparing increasing error rates (see Fig. 3b), our algorithm performs equally fast as EPnP and SQPnP. Additionally, the time does not increase depending on the gaussian error.

6   Conclusion

In this paper, we presented a new approach to solve the perspective-n-point problem based on an adaptation of the underlying mathematical expression. While this adaptation itself is quite simple, it is noteworthy that our approach outperforms state-of-the-art PnP algorithms in scenarios with limited point correspondences. If many keypoints are available, most algorithms are optimized to determine outliers and compute the pose based on accurate point correspondences. However, these algorithms fail to compute an accurate pose if only few keypoints are detected.

Most objects in real life scenarios can only move on the ground plane and rotate around the vertical axis. This constraint allows us to reduce the variables in the mathematical expression describing the problem, since part of the solution is already known. To solve the resulting equation, we use a simplex based optimization method. Both the redefinition and the optimization method are kept as simple as possible. While other algorithms may be optimized to reduce errors introduced by outliers and inaccurate keypoints, typical approaches like RANSAC are not effective if only few, i.e. less than 10, points are available. In contrast, our algorithm does not attempt to determine and reject any outliers in the input data and computes the result based on all available point correspondences. As a result, our algorithm requires fewer keypoints to be detected and is much more robust to noise in the described scenarios.

Different experiments have shown that our solution results in better accuracy when compared to existing six degrees of freedom pose estimation algorithms. Experiments used both synthetic randomized data and data obtained from photographs in published datasets. The main benefit of the proposed algorithm is its ability to handle very few matches of image and world coordinates, while allowing high error rates in the detection step. This makes our approach more robust in cases where objects cannot be detected accurately.

Acknowledgments. This research is funded by the Bundesministerium für Wirtschaft und Energie as part of the TALAKO project ("Taxiladekonzept für Elektrotaxis im öffentlichen Raum" tr. "Taxi Charging Concept for Public Spaces") [18] (grant number 01MZ19002A).

References

1. Bujnak, M., Kukelova, Z., Pajdla, T.: A general solution to the P4P problem for camera with unknown focal length. In: CVPR (2008). https://doi.org/10.1109/CVPR.2008.4587793
2. Burke, J.V., Ferris, M.C.: A gauss–newton method for convex composite optimization. Math. Program. **71**, 179–194 (1995). https://doi.org/10.1007/BF01585997
3. Chen, J., Zhang, L., Liu, Y., Xu, C.: Survey on 6D pose estimation of rigid object. In: CCC (2020). https://doi.org/10.23919/CCC50068.2020.9189304
4. Collins, T., Bartoli, A.: Infinitesimal plane-based pose estimation. Int. J. Comput. Vis. **109**(3), 252–286 (2014). https://doi.org/10.1007/s11263-014-0725-5
5. Dhall, A., Dai, D., Van Gool, L.: Real-time 3D traffic cone detection for autonomous driving. In: IV (2019). https://doi.org/10.1109/IVS.2019.8814089
6. Einsiedler, J., Becker, D., Radusch, I.: External visual positioning system for enclosed carparks. In: WPNC (2014). https://doi.org/10.1109/WPNC.2014.6843287
7. Fischler, M.A., Bolles, R.C.: Random sample consensus: a paradigm for model fitting with applications to image analysis and automated cartography. Commun. ACM **24**, 381–395 (1981). https://doi.org/10.1145/358669.358692
8. Fragoso, V., DeGol, J., Hua, G.: gDLS*: generalized pose-and-scale estimation given scale and gravity priors. In: CVPR (2020). https://doi.org/10.1109/CVPR42600.2020.00228
9. Gao, X.S., Hou, X.R., Tang, J., Cheng, H.F.: Complete solution classification for the perspective-three-point problem. In: TPAMI (2003)
10. Garro, V., Crosilla, F., Fusiello, A.: Solving the PnP problem with anisotropic orthogonal procrustes analysis. In: 3DIMPVT (2012). https://doi.org/10.1109/3DIMPVT.2012.40
11. Geiger, A., Lenz, P., Stiller, C., Urtasun, R.: Vision meets robotics: the KITTI dataset. Int. J. Robot. Res. **32**, 1231–1237 (2013). https://doi.org/10.1177/0278364913491297
12. Grafarend, E.W., Shan, J.: Closed-form solution of P4P or the three-dimensional resection problem in terms of Möbius barycentric coordinates. J. Geodesy **71**, 217–231 (1997). https://doi.org/10.1007/s001900050089
13. Grunert, J.A.: Das Pothenot'sche Problem, in erweiterter Gestalt; nebst Bemerkungen über seine Anwendung in der Geodäsie. Archiv der Mathematik und Physik (1841)
14. Gu, R., Wang, G., Hwang, J.N.: Efficient multi-person hierarchical 3D pose estimation for autonomous driving. In: MIPR (2019). https://doi.org/10.1109/MIPR.2019.00036
15. Hagelskjær, F., Savarimuthu, T.R., Krüger, N., Buch, A.G.: Using spatial constraints for fast set-up of precise pose estimation in an industrial setting. In: CASE (2019). https://doi.org/10.1109/COASE.2019.8842876
16. Hajder, L., Barath, D.: Least-squares optimal relative planar motion for vehicle-mounted cameras. In: ICRA (2020). https://doi.org/10.1109/ICRA40945.2020.9196755

17. Hesch, J.A., Roumeliotis, S.I.: A direct least-squares (DLS) method for PnP. In: ICCV (2011). https://doi.org/10.1109/ICCV.2011.6126266
18. IAM, Universität Duisburg-Essen: Taxiladekonzept für Elektrotaxis im öffentlichen Raum. talako.uni-due.de (2022). Accessed 14 Jan 2022
19. Jiao, Y., et al.: Robust localization for planar moving robot in changing environment: a perspective on density of correspondence and depth. In: ICRA (2021). https://doi.org/10.1109/ICRA48506.2021.9561539
20. Kim, I.S., Jung, T.W., Jung, K.D.: Augmented reality service based on object pose prediction using PnP algorithm. IJACT **9**, 295–301 (2021)
21. Kim, S.T., Fan, M., Jung, S.W., Ko, S.J.: External vehicle positioning system using multiple fish-eye surveillance cameras for indoor parking lots. IEEE Syst. J. **15**, 5107–5118 (2021). https://doi.org/10.1109/JSYST.2020.3019296
22. Kneip, L., Li, H., Seo, Y.: UPnP: an optimal $O(n)$ solution to the absolute pose problem with universal applicability. In: Fleet, D., Pajdla, T., Schiele, B., Tuytelaars, T. (eds.) ECCV 2014. LNCS, vol. 8689, pp. 127–142. Springer, Cham (2014). https://doi.org/10.1007/978-3-319-10590-1_9
23. Kneip, L., Scaramuzza, D., Siegwart, R.: A novel parametrization of the perspective-three-point problem for a direct computation of absolute camera position and orientation. In: CVPR (2011). https://doi.org/10.1109/CVPR.2011.5995464
24. Lee, S., Moon, Y.K.: Camera pose estimation using voxel-based features for autonomous vehicle localization tracking. In: ITC-CSCC (2022). https://doi.org/10.1109/ITC-CSCC55581.2022.9895071
25. Lee, T.E., et al.: Camera-to-robot pose estimation from a single image. In: ICRA (2020). https://doi.org/10.1109/ICRA40945.2020.9196596
26. Lepetit, V., Moreno-Noguer, F., Fua, P.: EPnP: an accurate o(n) solution to the PnP problem. IJCV **81**, 155–166 (2009). https://doi.org/10.1007/s11263-008-0152-6
27. Levenberg, K.: A method for the solution of certain non-linear problems in least squares. Q. Appl. Math. **2**, 164–168 (1944)
28. Li, C., Wang, X.: On convergence of the gauss-newton method for convex composite optimization. Math. Program. **91**, 349–356 (2002)
29. Lin, Y., Tremblay, J., Tyree, S., Vela, P.A., Birchfield, S.: Multi-view fusion for multi-level robotic scene understanding. In: IROS (2021). https://doi.org/10.1109/IROS51168.2021.9635994
30. Lu, X.X.: A review of solutions for perspective-n-point problem in camera pose estimation. In: Journal of Physics: Conference Series (2018). https://doi.org/10.1088/1742-6596/1087/5/052009
31. Marchand, E., Uchiyama, H., Spindler, F.: Pose estimation for augmented reality: a hands-on survey. TVCG **22**, 2633–2651 (2016). https://doi.org/10.1109/TVCG.2015.2513408
32. Marquardt, D.W.: An algorithm for least-squares estimation of nonlinear parameters. J. Soc. Ind. Appl. Math. **11**, 431–441 (1963)
33. Martull, S., Peris, M., Fukui, K.: Realistic CG stereo image dataset with ground truth disparity maps. Technical report of IEICE, PRMU (2012)
34. Nelder, J.A., Mead, R.: A simplex method for function minimization. Comput. J. **7**, 308–313 (1965). https://doi.org/10.1093/comjnl/7.4.308
35. Ortín, D., Montiel, J.M.M.: Indoor robot motion based on monocular images. Robotica **19**, 331–342 (2001). https://doi.org/10.1017/S0263574700003143

36. Pan, S., Wang, X.: A survey on perspective-n-point problem. In: CCC (2021). https://doi.org/10.23919/CCC52363.2021.9549863

37. Parameshwara, C.M., Hari, G., Fermüller, C., Sanket, N.J., Aloimonos, Y.: Diff-PoseNet: direct differentiable camera pose estimation. In: CVPR (2022). https://doi.org/10.1109/CVPR52688.2022.00672

38. Persson, M., Nordberg, K.: Lambda twist: an accurate fast robust perspective three point (P3P) solver. In: Ferrari, V., Hebert, M., Sminchisescu, C., Weiss, Y. (eds.) ECCV 2018. LNCS, vol. 11208, pp. 334–349. Springer, Cham (2018). https://doi.org/10.1007/978-3-030-01225-0_20

39. Pošík, P., Huyer, W.: Restarted local search algorithms for continuous black box optimization. Evol. Comput. **20**, 575–607 (2012). https://doi.org/10.1162/EVCO_a_00087

40. Qingxuan, J., Ping, Z., Hanxu, S.: The study of positioning with high-precision by single camera based on p3p algorithm. In: ICII (2006). https://doi.org/10.1109/INDIN.2006.275618

41. Roch, P., Shahbaz Nejad, B., Handte, M., Marrón, P.J.: Car pose estimation through wheel detection. In: Bebis, G., et al. (eds.) ISVC 2021. LNCS, vol. 13017, pp. 265–277. Springer, Cham (2021). https://doi.org/10.1007/978-3-030-90439-5_21

42. Rublee, E., Rabaud, V., Konolige, K., Bradski, G.: Orb: An efficient alternative to sift or surf. In: ICCV (2011). https://doi.org/10.1109/ICCV.2011.6126544

43. Scaramuzza, D.: 1-point-RANSAC structure from motion for vehicle-mounted cameras by exploiting non-holonomic constraints. IJCV **95**, 74–85 (2011). https://doi.org/10.1007/s11263-011-0441-3

44. Schweighofer, G., Pinz, A.: Globally optimal O(n) solution to the PnP problem for general camera models. In: BMVC (2008)

45. Sturm, J., Engelhard, N., Endres, F., Burgard, W., Cremers, D.: A benchmark for the evaluation of RGB-D SLAM systems. In: IROS (2012). https://doi.org/10.1109/IROS.2012.6385773

46. Sweeney, C., Flynn, J., Nuernberger, B., Turk, M., Höllerer, T.: Efficient computation of absolute pose for gravity-aware augmented reality. In: ISMAR (2015). https://doi.org/10.1109/ISMAR.2015.20

47. Terzakis, G., Lourakis, M.: A consistently fast and globally optimal solution to the perspective-n-point problem. In: Vedaldi, A., Bischof, H., Brox, T., Frahm, J.-M. (eds.) ECCV 2020. LNCS, vol. 12346, pp. 478–494. Springer, Cham (2020). https://doi.org/10.1007/978-3-030-58452-8_28

48. Tremblay, J., To, T., Sundaralingam, B., Xiang, Y., Fox, D., Birchfield, S.: Deep object pose estimation for semantic robotic grasping of household objects. CoRR (2018). https://doi.org/10.48550/arXiv.1809.10790

49. Urban, S., Leitloff, J., Hinz, S.: MLPnP - a real-time maximum likelihood solution to the perspective-n-point problem. ISPRS (2016). https://doi.org/10.5194/isprs-annals-iii-3-131-2016

50. Velichkovsky, B.M., Kotov, A., Arinkin, N., Zaidelman, L., Zinina, A., Kivva, K.: From social gaze to indirect speech constructions: how to induce the impression that your companion robot is a conscious creature. Appl. Sci. **11**, 10255 (2021). https://doi.org/10.3390/app112110255

51. Wang, Z., Yang, X.: V-head: face detection and alignment for facial augmented reality applications. In: Amsaleg, L., Guðmundsson, G.Þ, Gurrin, C., Jónsson, B.Þ, Satoh, S. (eds.) MMM 2017. LNCS, vol. 10133, pp. 450–454. Springer, Cham (2017). https://doi.org/10.1007/978-3-319-51814-5_40

52. Zhang, B., Zhang, Q., Wang, Y., Tian, Z.: The method of solving the non-coplanar perspective-four-point (P4P) problem. In: CCC (2014). https://doi.org/10.1109/ChiCC.2014.6896771

53. Zhou, G., Wang, H., Chen, J., Huang, D.: PR-GCN: a deep graph convolutional network with point refinement for 6D pose estimation. In: ICCV (2021). https://doi.org/10.1109/ICCV48922.2021.00279

Deep Learning

Unsupervised Deep-Learning Approach for Underwater Image Enhancement

Alejandro Rico Espinosa(✉), Declan McIntosh, and Alexandra Branzan Albu

University of Victoria, Victoria, BC, Canada
{arico,declanmcintosh,aalbu}@uvic.ca

Abstract. Underwater images often contain color casting and blurriness which reduce the quality. State-of-the-art shows different deep-learning models to handle these degradations. However, they required ground truth to train, which is impossible to acquire when studying underwater images. We present an unsupervised deep-learning approach for underwater image enhancement based on the mathematical model of a hazy image. This allows us to train networks without the need for a reference image. We use three networks to estimate the transmission map, the atmospheric light, and the enhanced image and propose a compound loss function to train our approach accurately. We achieve state-of-the-art results in the structural similarity index (SSIM) while performing optimally nearly real-time inference speeds.

Keywords: Underwater · Unsupervised · Enhancement

1 Introduction

Underwater images constantly suffer from physical degradation, such as occlusion and color cast, due to environmental conditions. Factors like scattering due to suspended particles result in disturbing the image conditions by introducing homogeneous noise [11]. Also, due to the wavelength transmission in the water, the red channel is highly attenuated by the absorption effect, causing the colors displayed in the image not to be accurate [5]. These disturbances often cause species identification and marine life behavior studying to be more difficult for scientists [13,25,26]. Also, accuracy on object identification and classification in different applications such as autonomous underwater vehicles (AUV) explorations, are decreased [3]. Therefore, an enhancement of these images is valuable in the field.

Different approaches have been studied in the field [28,29]. Methods could primarily be separated into traditional computer vision approaches and deep learning approaches [2,9,19]. Each of these groups might have benefits and limitations. Traditional computer vision approaches can be highly efficient, but they are usually not generalized and require a level of expertise to apply them [6,9]. On the other side, deep learning is generally slow but has an excellent performance in improving image quality [14]. Moreover, these are limited to the training data, and the current approaches require ground truth to train.

G. Bebis et al. (Eds.): ISVC 2023, LNCS 14362, pp. 233–244, 2023.
https://doi.org/10.1007/978-3-031-47966-3_18

Plenty of datasets do not contain ground truths since it is not possible to obtain real underwater images free of disturbances. Then, the proposed deep-learning approaches have been trained using synthetic datasets [4,14,21,24,28]. These are normally created by purely intuitive human perspectives of how objects should look [21]. Sometimes their contrast is over-exaggerated, contains plenty of artifacts, and displays the wrong colors, as possibly noticed in the examples of Fig. 1. Also, the other approach to generate training data is to emulate water disturbances on normal images [20]. However, these are not the real conditions of the environment, which can reduce model performance on real applications [15].

Fig. 1. Examples of underwater images and the ground truths generated for those images in which models are trained.

To avoid dealing with this lack of information, we propose an unsupervised deep learning approach based on the mathematical image formation model to enhance underwater images. Our approach reaches state-of-the-art results in the structural similarity index and is performed optimally. We primarily concentrate our attention on formulating a methodology to improve the images, rather than designing a new CNN architecture. Specifically, our main contributions could be listed as:

- To the best of our knowledge, this is one of the first unsupervised deep-learning approaches proposed for underwater image enhancement.
- Introduction of two novel loss functions to regulate contrast and the transmission map.
- An efficient approach capable of real-time data processing once trained.
- A methodology that learns and generalizes the necessary transformations for enhancing underwater images in various water types and disturbances.

2   Related Works

Different terrestrial prior-based computer vision approaches have been used on underwater image enhancement showing better performances than other techniques [31]. Recently, Fayaz et al. [7] presented an efficient underwater image restoration using the well-known dark channel prior with some variations. They proposed to use arithmetic Mode operation as a new global atmospheric light estimator. They show better results than other methods with evaluation on non-reference metrics such as underwater color image qualitative evaluation (UCIQE) and underwater image quality metric (UIQM).

Also, multiple deep-learning approaches have been suggested for underwater image quality improvement. For instance, Ma et al. [24] suggest the use of a dual network to handle the color cast and blurry details in underwater images. They use the discrete wavelength transform (DWT) to extract the different frequency subbands and use them as inputs for their networks. One of the models targets color recovery by employing the feature representations from multiple color spaces. The other architecture is designed to enhance the image details by using high-frequency sub-bands. Their model was trained under a synthetic dataset due to the lack of ground truths for underwater images.

In contrast, Li et al. [18] proposed to use three networks and the mathematical model of a terrestrial haze image as an enhancement unsupervised method. Two of the models avoid downsampling to retain image details, while the third one is based on the latent Gaussian distribution that global atmospheric light has on terrestrial images. It is possible to assume this distribution for A since the atmospheric is global and independent from the image content. They achieve state-of-the-art results and beat other unsupervised deep-learning approaches in the SSIM and PSNR. However, this method is proposed to only train in a single image. This means it is designed to enhance in a non-general way, which is not efficient for real-time applications or large amounts of processing data (like a video).

3 Proposed Approach

We describe an unsupervised approach capable of improving underwater images and operating efficiently based on the mathematical formulation of hazy images.

3.1 RGB Channels

In underwater images, all pixels tend to distribute near a specific plane in the RGB space [23]. Liu et al. proposed a linear transformation into the UV space based on a universal observation that projecting the pixels will not lead to a severe color shift.

Instead of reducing the dimensionality of color space, we propose to split images into three single channels (RGB) and treat them independently. This will help us to estimate the appropriate distribution of pixels across each dimension. This will allow the network to create a haze-free representation of the image channel-wise while being able to do a color shifting.

3.2   Image Haze Mathematical Equation

Equation 1 presents the general underwater optical image formation model, where I_c is the corrupted image, J_c is the haze-free enhanced image, T_c is the transmission map and A_c is the global atmospheric light.

$$I_c(x) = J_c(x) * T_C(x) + A_c * (1 - T_c(x)), c\epsilon(R, G, B) \qquad (1)$$

Inspired by [18], our approach is based on the previous mathematical model. We use three networks to individually estimate the transmission map, the ambient light, and the enhanced image. Figure 2 illustrates this idea. Then, we could construct a predicted hazed image using the model outputs in Eq. 1 and compare it directly to our input.

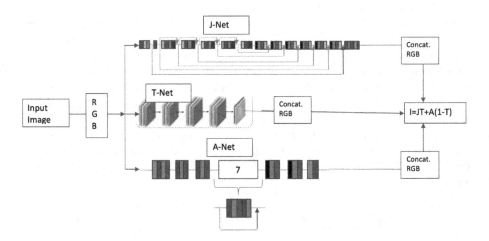

Fig. 2. Approach schematic using DWT branch of [6] as J net, Res-Net with 7 residual blocks as A-Net and [18] light network as T-Net.

3.3   Networks

In order to maximize our possible output through this approach, we use the light model described by [6] as our J network. Their key components, like channel and attention blocks, plus the use of the Discrete Wavelength Transform, make it ideal to recover color and enhance shapes on underwater images. Also, the network showed to be efficient by being able to process in real-time, being practical for diverse applications.

On the other hand, it is possible to assume in A network that the atmospheric light is global and independent from the image content [18]. Hence, we decided to use a ResNet with 7 residual blocks and a global skip connection, commonly used to enhance the image from blurring and integrate the residual image knowledge on aerial and underwater images [6,16,17]. Due to the nature of this architecture, we can estimate the light conditions in a general way for different types of underwater images. Therefore, this network would help retain the common pattern allowing training in multiple images at once instead of individually doing it. Using this network increases computational complexity compared with the lither model of [18]. However, this will only be determinant during the training process since inference enhanced image will, after all, only require the J network.

For the T network, we use the structure defined by [18,22], which is a non-degenerative light architecture since it avoids down-sampling. Then, it is designed to retain the details and perform optimally.

3.4 Loss Function

Since our approach is purely based on the mathematical formulation of an underwater hazy image, the loss function plays a key role in the output results generated by the model.

Mean Square Error (MSE) Loss. Let I_h be the input image, I_{hp} be the hazed image obtained through Eq. 1 with the J, T, and A networks outputs. The MSE loss is defined by Eq. 2 where n is the total number of pixels in the image.

$$MSE = \frac{1}{n} * \sum_{i=1}^{n}(I_h(i) - I_{hp}(i))^2 \tag{2}$$

Variational Inference Atmospheric Error (VAE) and Blur Losses. As proposed in the work of [18], these losses make the A model learn the latent Gaussian distribution of the atmospheric light. The blur loss compares the disentangled atmospheric light $(F * A(x))$ and the original output prediction of the A network $(A(x))$. Equation 3 presents the formulation of this loss, where F is a mean (average) filter of 5 by 5, MSE is the Mean Squared Error and $*$ denotes convolution operation. On the other side, the variational inference (VAE) aims to minimize the difference between the latent code and the predicted one [18]. Equation 4 shows how this loss is defined, where μ is the mean of the input and σ is the variance.

$$Blur = mse(A(x) * F, A(x)) \tag{3}$$

$$VAE = \frac{1}{2} \sum ((\mu)^2 + (\sigma)^2 - 1 - exp(\sigma)^2) \tag{4}$$

CAP Loss. This loss is based on [33] observations and formulated by [18] which states that the deep of a clean image is positively correlated to the difference between the brightness and the saturation.

$$CAP = ||V(J(x)) - S(J(x))||_p \tag{5}$$

LOG Loss. We propose an additional loss to control the transmission map estimation. We want to minimize the distance L1 between the second-order derivative of the transmission map (T) and the Laplacian of Gaussian of the recovered image. This avoids blurriness and preserves the edges in the recovered image (J). It is valid since the medium of transmission describes the portion of the light that is not scattered and reaches the camera [12].

$$LOG = \sum \sqrt{(LoG(T(x)) - LoG(J(x)))^2} \tag{6}$$

In Eq. 6, LoG defines the convolution of the image with the Laplacian of Gaussians filter [0 1 0; 1 −4 1; 0 1 0].

LC Loss. Finally, we defined a loss to control the brightness and enhance the contrast on the output image. The contrast could be defined as the difference between the pixel with maximum intensity and the pixel with minimum intensity 7. Although, this does not guarantee that the image will enhance its contrast uniformly. Then, we decide to compare the contrast of the global image with the contrast of random patches as defined by Eq. 9, where $G_C(x)$ is the global contrast of the image, $Np_C(x)$ is the contrast of the n-th patch and n is the number of patches. We used 10 patches with size 7×7.

$$Contrast(x) = max(x) - min(x) \tag{7}$$

$$LC = \sqrt{(G_C(x) - \frac{1}{n}\sum_{i=1}^{n} Np_C)^2} \tag{8}$$

Total Loss. Note that all the losses depend only on the input image or on the predicted output images. Therefore, there is no actual need to have a ground truth to train using this approach. The total loss can be computed as:

$$TotalLoss = a*MSE + b*VAE + c*CAP + d*Blur + e*LOG + f*LC \tag{9}$$

where a = 1.5, b = 0.7, c = 0.7, d = 0.01, e = 0.3, and f = 0.7 are constants determined through hyperparameter tuning.

4   Results and Discussion

We present state-of-the-art results in the UIEBD [21] while training without ground truth and operating efficiently in nearly real-time.

4.1   Dataset

We use a combination of two different datasets OceanDark [28] and UIEBD [21] (including the additional 60 challenging images), to train our model. Note that we decide to use only real-world data in our training since we want a model to be able to work in real-time applications, and we do not have limitations for ground truth. OceanDark dataset presents low-light underwater images while the UIEBD includes degradation related to color cast and blurriness. Then, a combination of both makes our models to improve in generalization and reduce the probability of bias. Additionally, UIEBD contains 890 real underwater images with their corresponding ground truths, being one of the most common underwater datasets to evaluate model performances. Therefore, working with it allows us to directly compare our approach with multiple deep-learning models. However, the obtained ground truths are based on human subjective ratings after comparing 12 different underwater enhanced images created by various classical enhancement pipelines [21].

4.2   Ablation

Table 1. Ablation study performed on the UIEDB [21] test set

	SSIM	PSNR
YOLY	0.70538	14.8915
Processing R,G,B channels individual	0.69834	14.5108
Adding LOG loss	0.8313	18.3508
Adding LC loss	0.8334	18.4501

Figure 3 and Table 1 present the qualitative and quantitative analysis of the main components introduced in our approach. It can be observed that channel splitting led to a decrease in SSIM and PSNR scores. However, the visual comparison shows that edges and objects are sharpened compared to the YOLY approach. Additionally, the LOG function reduced noise and blurriness in the image, although it added some overbrightness. Finally, the use of the LC loss resulted in a more natural-looking version.

Fig. 3. Visual ablation experiments for the proposed training methodology.

4.3   Training

We trained our model on a GPU NVIDIA GeForce RTX 3060 with 12 GB of memory and used a batch size of 1. We use the same augmentation described by [6], but instead of cropping the patches, we re-scale the images to 256 × 256. We train using the Adam optimizer for 300 epochs reducing the learning rate by half every 100 epochs.

4.4   Quantitative Results

We evaluate the performance of our proposed approach in the UIEBD dataset [21], which contains real-world underwater images. We use standard splits, evaluating the performance of the approach on 190 images for direct comparison [6,10]. Ground truths were only used to compute the structural similarity index (SSIM) and the peak signal-to-noise ratio (PSNR). Table 2 presents a comparison with multiple methods in these two metrics of performance.

Table 2. Quantitative results on the UIEDB [21] test set. We show state-of-the-art results in SSIM.

Method	PSNR↑	SSIM↑	Inference Time↓ (s)	Type
IBLA [27]	14.3856	0.4299	38.71	Classic
Fusion [2]	21.1849	0.8222	6.58	Classic
GLCHE [9]	21.027	0.8487	0.05	Mix
DWG [8]	19.6727	0.8614	0.4487	Deep
Water-Net [21]	19.3134	0.8303	0.61	Deep
Ucolor [19]	20.63	0.77	2.75	Deep
SCNet [10]	22.08	0.8625	0.4495	Deep
Deep WaveNet [14]	21.57	0.8	1.16	Deep
DDC [6]	20.8694	0.8703	0.025	Deep
Ours	18.4501	0.8334	0.0996	Deep-Unsupervised

Compared to other methods, our approach achieves better SSIM scores of 0.8313 and an inference time of 0.0996 s, faster than the traditional computer vision approaches in the field. Also, quantitative results show improvements in the images near the deep learning methods training in a supervised way, showing that our approach is comparable with the current state of the art. Notably our method still has deficiencies that could be improved since we reached low state-of-the art results on the PSNR. However, different authors have shown that small differences are not significant since PSNR is not as good of a tool in underwater image quality enhancement [6,21,30,32].

4.5 Qualitative Results

The UIEDB dataset was built for subjective visual improvement of images not accurate reconstruction of the underlying hazy and discolored objects, based on the feedback of a set of human judges. For that reason often other methods supervised methods [10,19,21] generate these same kinds of images improved but towards a specific subjective goal, often including exaggerated contrast and vibrance of color. Our method however is built directly from the hazy image formulation and therefore does not seek to create images with extremely high contrast and color vibrance but rather more subtle improvements as seen in Fig. 4. From the zoomed regions of the image, the quantitative performance of the method becomes clear, with our dehazing and sharpening part of the coral as well as improving the contrast and lighting vibrance slightly. These somewhat more measured improvements still increase the scores on the target dataset as we do improve both the contrast and the color vibrance. However, our method is based on the hazy image model and not the subjective goals of the dataset ground truths. Then, our model's image enhancements look more subdued. This subdued improvement is generally a welcome feature for fields such as underwater biological applications where large shifts in color vibrance or over-zealous sharpening can lead to incorrect species identification.

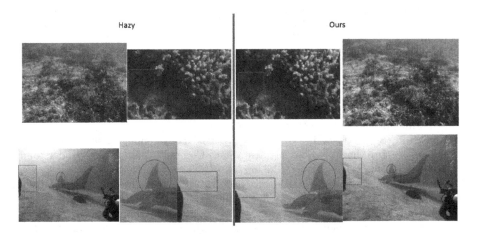

Fig. 4. Qualitative results with scaled samples showing improvement in light and shadows, colors, and edges

5 Conclusion

We presented an efficient unsupervised approach for underwater image enhancement which achieves state-of-the-art results with a score of 0.8313 in the SSIM index. Our approach is primarily based on the mathematical definition of a haze image, training independent networks to estimate the atmospheric light, the transmission map, and the enhanced image. We defined two new loss functions to control the image contrast and ensure the transmission map preserves the details. Our approach showed fast processing since the architectures used were light. Finally, we run our approach in different types of water showing that our suggested method could generalize well in the enhancement task.

Future approaches should involve comparing the performance in various ways, as some configurations of our method achieved higher human perception enhancement but lower structural similarity index scores. Moreover, it is crucial to explore the same methodology to estimate individual components in other mathematical models when needed. For instance, other formulations such as the one proposed by Akkaynak et al. [1] take into account the wavelength-dependent attenuation in underwater images, making it suitable for color improvement. Integrating this approach could potentially enhance our presented results since our current approach focuses on improving contrast, sharpness, and blurriness in underwater images.

References

1. Akkaynak, D., Treibitz, T.: A revised underwater image formation model. In: Proceedings of the IEEE Conference on Computer Vision and Pattern Recognition (CVPR) (2018)
2. Ancuti, C., Ancuti, C.O., Haber, T., Bekaert, P.: Enhancing underwater images and videos by fusion. In: IEEE Conference on Computer Vision and Pattern Recognition, pp. 81–88. IEEE (2012)
3. Bazeille, S., Quidu, I., Jaulin, L.: Color-based underwater object recognition using water light attenuation. Intell. Serv. Robot. **5**, 109–118 (2012). https://doi.org/10.1007/s11370-012-0105-3
4. Berman, D., Levy, D., Avidan, S., Treibitz, T.: Underwater single image color restoration using haze-lines and a new quantitative dataset. IEEE Trans. Pattern Anal. Mach. Intell. **43**, 2822–2837 (2020)
5. Emberton, S., Chittka, L., Cavallaro, A.: Underwater image and video dehazing with pure haze region segmentation. Comput. Vis. Image Understand. **168**, 145–156 (2018). https://doi.org/10.1016/j.cviu.2017.08.003. https://www.sciencedirect.com/science/article/pii/S1077314217301418. Special Issue on Vision and Computational Photography and Graphics
6. Espinosa, A.R., McIntosh, D., Albu, A.B.: An efficient approach for underwater image improvement: deblurring, dehazing, and color correction. In: 2023 IEEE/CVF Winter Conference on Applications of Computer Vision Workshops (WACVW), pp. 206–215 (2023). https://doi.org/10.1109/WACVW58289.2023.00026

7. Fayaz, S., Parah, S.A., Qureshi, G.J.: Efficient underwater image restoration utilizing modified dark channel prior. Multimedia Tools Appl. **82**(10), 14731–14753 (2023). https://doi.org/10.1007/s11042-022-13828-6

8. Fu, M., Liu, H., Yu, Y., Chen, J., Wang, K.: DW-GAN: a discrete wavelet transform GAN for nonhomogeneous dehazing. In: 2021 IEEE/CVF Conference on Computer Vision and Pattern Recognition Workshops (CVPRW), pp. 203–212 (2021). https://doi.org/10.1109/CVPRW53098.2021.00029

9. Fu, X., Cao, X.: Underwater image enhancement with global-local networks and compressed-histogram equalization. Sig. Process. Image Commun. **86**, 115892 (2020). https://doi.org/10.1016/j.image.2020.115892. https://www.sciencedirect.com/science/article/pii/S0923596520300965

10. Fu, Z., Lin, X., Wang, W., Huang, Y., Ding, X.: Underwater image enhancement via learning water type desensitized representations (2021). https://doi.org/10.48550/ARXIV.2102.00676. https://arxiv.org/abs/2102.00676

11. Fu, Z., Lin, X., Wang, W., Huang, Y., Ding, X.: Underwater image enhancement via learning water type desensitized representations. In: ICASSP 2022–2022 IEEE International Conference on Acoustics, Speech and Signal Processing (ICASSP), pp. 2764–2768 (2022). https://doi.org/10.1109/ICASSP43922.2022.9747758

12. He, K., Sun, J., Tang, X.: Single image haze removal using dark channel prior. In: 2009 IEEE Conference on Computer Vision and Pattern Recognition, pp. 1956–1963 (2009). https://doi.org/10.1109/CVPR.2009.5206515

13. Heesemann, M., Insua, T.L., Scherwath, M., Juniper, K.S., Moran, K.: Ocean networks Canada: from geohazards research laboratories to smart ocean systems. Oceanography **27**(2), 151–153 (2014)

14. Islam, M.J., Xia, Y., Sattar, J.: Fast underwater image enhancement for improved visual perception. IEEE Robot. Autom. Lett. (RA-L) **5**(2), 3227–3234 (2020)

15. James, S., Harbron, C., Branson, J., Sundler, M.: Synthetic data use: exploring use cases to optimise data utility. Discov. Artif. Intell. **1**(1), 1–13 (2021). https://doi.org/10.1007/s44163-021-00016-y

16. Johnson, J., Alahi, A., Fei-Fei, L.: Perceptual losses for real-time style transfer and super-resolution. In: Leibe, B., Matas, J., Sebe, N., Welling, M. (eds.) ECCV 2016. LNCS, vol. 9906, pp. 694–711. Springer, Cham (2016). https://doi.org/10.1007/978-3-319-46475-6_43

17. Kupyn, O., Budzan, V., Mykhailych, M., Mishkin, D., Matas, J.: Deblurgan: Blind motion deblurring using conditional adversarial networks. In: 2018 IEEE/CVF Conference on Computer Vision and Pattern Recognition, pp. 8183–8192 (2018). https://doi.org/10.1109/CVPR.2018.00854

18. Li, B., Gou, Y., Gu, S., Liu, J.Z., Zhou, J.T., Peng, X.: You only look yourself: unsupervised and untrained single image dehazing neural network. Int. J. Comput. Vision **129**(5), 1754–1767 (2021). https://doi.org/10.1007/s11263-021-01431-5

19. Li, C., Anwar, S., Hou, J., Cong, R., Guo, C., Ren, W.: Underwater image enhancement via medium transmission-guided multi-color space embedding. IEEE Trans. Image Process. **30**, 4985–5000 (2021)

20. Li, C., Anwar, S., Porikli, F.: Underwater scene prior inspired deep underwater image and video enhancement. Pattern Recogn. **98**, 107038 (2020). https://doi.org/10.1016/j.patcog.2019.107038. https://www.sciencedirect.com/science/article/pii/S0031320319303401

21. Li, C., et al.: An underwater image enhancement benchmark dataset and beyond. IEEE Trans. Image Process. **29**, 4376–4389 (2020). https://doi.org/10.1109/TIP.2019.2955241

22. Li, R., Pan, J., Li, Z., Tang, J.: Single image dehazing via conditional generative adversarial network. In: 2018 IEEE/CVF Conference on Computer Vision and Pattern Recognition, pp. 8202–8211 (2018). https://doi.org/10.1109/CVPR.2018. 00856

23. Liu, Y., Rong, S., Cao, X., Li, T., He, B.: Underwater image dehazing using the color space dimensionality reduction prior. In: 2020 IEEE International Conference on Image Processing (ICIP), pp. 1013–1017 (2020). https://doi.org/10.1109/ ICIP40778.2020.9190901

24. Ma, Z., Oh, C.: A wavelet-based dual-stream network for underwater image enhancement. In: ICASSP 2022–2022 IEEE International Conference on Acoustics, Speech and Signal Processing (ICASSP), pp. 2769–2773 (2022). https://doi. org/10.1109/ICASSP43922.2022.9747781

25. Mallet, D., Pelletier, D.: Underwater video techniques for observing coastal marine biodiversity: a review of sixty years of publications (1952–2012). Fish. Res. **154**, 44–62 (2014)

26. McIntosh, D.G., Porto Marques, T., Branzan Albu, A., Rountree, R., De Leo Cabrera, F.: Movement tracks for the automatic detection of fish behavior in videos. In: NeurIPS 2020 Workshop on Tackling Climate Change with Machine Learning (2020). https://www.climatechange.ai/papers/neurips2020/36

27. Peng, Y.T., Cosman, P.: Underwater image restoration based on image blurriness and light absorption. IEEE Trans. Image Process. **26**, 1579–1594 (2017). https:// doi.org/10.1109/TIP.2017.2663846

28. Marques, T.P., Albu, A.B.: L2UWE: a framework for the efficient enhancement of low-light underwater images using local contrast and multi-scale fusion. In: Proceedings of the IEEE/CVF Conference on Computer Vision and Pattern Recognition Workshops, pp. 538–539 (2020)

29. Porto Marques, T., Branzan Albu, A., Hoeberechts, M.: A contrast-guided approach for the enhancement of low-lighting underwater images. J. Imaging **5**(10), 79 (2019)

30. Sara, U., Akter, M., Uddin, M.S.: Image quality assessment through FSIM, SSIM, MSE and PSNR-a comparative study. J. Comput. Commun. **7**(3), 8–18 (2019)

31. Sathya, R., Bharathi, M., Dhivyasri, G.: Underwater image enhancement by dark channel prior. In: 2015 2nd International Conference on Electronics and Communication Systems (ICECS), pp. 1119–1123 (2015). https://doi.org/10.1109/ECS. 2015.7124757

32. Setiadi, D.R.I.M.: PSNR vs SSIM: imperceptibility quality assessment for image steganography. Multimedia Tools Appl. **80**(6), 8423–8444 (2021)

33. Zhu, Q., Mai, J., Shao, L.: A fast single image haze removal algorithm using color attenuation prior. IEEE Trans. Image Process. **24**(11), 3522–3533 (2015). https:// doi.org/10.1109/TIP.2015.2446191

LaneNet++: Uncertainty-Aware Lane Detection for Autonomous Vehicle

Meghana Basavaraj[1], Upendra Suddamalla[1(✉)], and Shenxin Xu[2]

[1] Moovita Pte Ltd., Singapore, Singapore
upendra@moovita.com
[2] National University of Singapore, Singapore, Singapore

Abstract. Deep learning (DL) algorithms have gained significant popularity in the field of Autonomous Driving (AD), particularly for ensuring safe navigation. However, these algorithms often exhibit overconfidence in their predictions, leading to higher probabilities assigned to their outputs. In this paper, we present a novel approach to estimate uncertainty in lane detection, drawing inspiration from Multi-task Consistency principles. Our method builds upon the LaneNet architecture, which utilizes a dual head network to address the lane detection problem. By incorporating uncertainty estimation through the analysis of inconsistencies between the two heads, we effectively reduce false positives and the detection of unusual road markings. We evaluate our approach using the widely accessible TuSimpleLanes [17] and VIL-100 [20] datasets. Our experimental results demonstrate a significant reduction of 2.99% in false positives, highlighting the effectiveness of our method in enhancing real-time and trustworthy lane detection.

Keywords: Uncertainty Estimation · Dual Task Consistency · Lane Detection

1 Introduction

Autonomous vehicles (AVs) rely on a multitude of sensors, such as Lidar, Radar, and Cameras, to perceive their surroundings and make informed decisions in real-time. To achieve this, Deep learning (DL) algorithms have been increasingly used in perception and decision-making tasks by leveraging complex architectures, abundant data, and high-performance computing capabilities. However, DL algorithms often exhibit overconfidence or under-confidence in their output estimates [8], potentially leading to unsafe manoeuvres and undermining their reliability.

To ensure the reliability of software components in automotive industry, regulatory bodies have developed standards such as MISRA and ISO26262. These standards are conceived keeping human drivers in mind. Recently, as AI is increasingly used in autonomous automotive vehicles, the regulatory bodies are

---

M. Basavaraj and U. Suddamalla—These authors contributed equally to this work

© The Author(s), under exclusive license to Springer Nature Switzerland AG 2023
G. Bebis et al. (Eds.): ISVC 2023, LNCS 14362, pp. 245–258, 2023.
https://doi.org/10.1007/978-3-031-47966-3_19

Fig. 1. Examples of challenging lane conditions for AV: road cracks, patches, shadows, tunnels and faded lanes. Images are taken from TuSimpleLanes and VIL-100.

working on defining the safety standards for evaluation of AI for autonomous products [18]. These are inspired from the guidelines for AI systems in highly regulated aviation industry [4]. These standards emphasise the need for safety evaluations and the provision of uncertainty information by DL algorithms.

Uncertainty estimation by neural networks provides a measure of certainty of the algorithm on the outputs predicted. The uncertainty may be caused due to the model (epistemic) or the data (aleatoric). Several approaches, such as Bayesian networks, ensemble networks and Monte Carlo (MC) Dropout [7], are explored to characterise these uncertainties.

This paper focuses on uncertainty estimation for lane segmentation, a crucial task for autonomous vehicles that involves identifying driving zone boundaries and managing lane changes. Figure 1 showcases various driving situations, such as occlusions, adverse weather conditions and poor lane markings, where uncertainty estimation in lane detection is helpful in identifying ambiguous situations and enabling the system to adapt for safer navigation. Lane detection typically employs camera-based algorithms that utilize structural and gradient characteristics [16] or convolutional neural networks [1]. We utilize the publicly available LaneNet [12] architecture, which adopts a dual head design for binary mask segmentation and instance segmentation. Moreover, we explore the use of the LaneNet's dual task architecture to estimate uncertainty based on the inconsistency between the two tasks. The efficacy of the proposed method is gauged through a comparative analysis of performance metrics against both the reference LaneNet and the proposed method (LaneNet++) which incorporates uncertainty measure. This evaluation encompasses essential metrics including true positives (TP), false positives (FP), and the F1 score. The key contributions of this paper are: 1. Investigating multi-task inconsistency as a measure of uncertainty for neural networks and proposing an add-on post-processing step to the LaneNet architecture. 2. Exploring calibration of uncertainty threshold for a given DL model based on F1 score.

The paper is organised as follows: Sect. 2 discusses uncertainty estimation for DL and revisits the design details of the LaneNet architecture. Section 3 introduces the proposed method for uncertainty estimation. Section 4 presents experimental details and results. We discuss our observations and future direction in Sect. 5, followed by the conclusion.

2 Uncertainty in DL and LaneNet

2.1 Uncertainty in DL

In the realm of deep learning algorithms, uncertainty can be broadly categorized as either model-specific (epistemic) or data-specific (aleatoric). Model uncertainty arises from factors such as inadequate model architectures, training procedure errors, sub-optimal hyper parameters, or encountering unseen test data [7]. On the other hand, data uncertainty originates from noise in the data source (sensor), data loss, or errors in labeling the training data. Model uncertainty can be theoretically reduced by enhancing the model architecture, learning process, and dataset. However, data uncertainty remains challenging to mitigate [9].

Various approaches are studied in literature for assessing DL uncertainty. In Bayesian networks [2,5], model parameters are explicitly modeled as random variables and the model uncertainty is formalised as a probability distribution over the model parameters. For a single forward pass the parameters are sampled from this distribution. Therefore, the prediction is stochastic and each prediction is based on different model weights. These methods necessitate modifications to the network architecture and retraining to acquire a probabilistic distribution over the network parameters. On the other hand, Ensemble methods [10,19], Monte Carlo Dropout [5,6] and test time data augmentation approaches [15] require multiple inferences of the same input data and assess the output consistency to estimate uncertainty. While for ensemble methods a variety among the single models is crucial, dropout method create dynamic models from the same network by random selection of nodes. Whereas, single pass methods [14] incorporate internal or external operations to estimate uncertainty and are more suitable for real-time applications. External methods, which can be applied to existing networks, include using an additional neural network for uncertainty estimation, measuring the gradient slope of a trained model, or predicting probabilities using softmax on logits.

Furthermore, [11] propose an approach for uncertainty quantification by measuring mean and variance of output from multi-decoders of a network. They leverage this approach during training to enhance the model's consistency in medical image analysis.

2.2 LaneNet

The LaneNet [12] model architecture consists of a backbone network for feature extraction, a dual output instance segmentation module and a lane fitting module. The dual head architecture predicts both instance masks and binary segmentation masks simultaneously. Instance masks distinguish individual lane instances with representative feature embedding, while binary segmentation masks classify pixels as lane or non-lane. These masks are further post processed to derive lane markings.

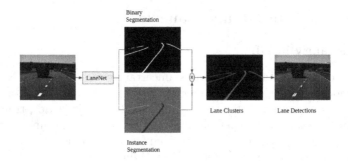

Fig. 2. LaneNet Overview. Dual output based lane detection.

LaneNet is originally evaluated on the TuSimple dataset, which contains a large number of challenging lane detection scenarios. The binary segmentation network is trained with the standard weighted cross-entropy loss function [13], to handle the class imbalance. Whereas, the instance embedding branch is trained using a clustering loss function [3] to produce embeddings for each lane pixel. This encourages the embeddings of pixels belonging to the same lane to be close together while maximizing the distance between embeddings of pixels from different lanes, resulting in distinct clusters for each lane. Experimental results demonstrate that LaneNet achieves accurate and robust lane detection performance.

Figure 2 gives system overview of the LaneNet implementation. Given an input image, LaneNet outputs a one channel lane binary segmentation map and a N-channel instance mask containing pixel embeddings. Next, clustering is performed to output a collection of pixels per lane followed by polynomial fit for each lane.

3   Proposed Method

This section presents LaneNet++, an improved version of LaneNet that incorporates an uncertainty estimation technique utilizing dual task segmentation outputs. Our proposed method aims to quantify the inconsistency between two outputs that estimate lanes for a given input image, thereby determining the uncertainty in lane detection. The architecture of LaneNet++ is depicted in Fig. 3. The fundamental concept is to leverage the dual outputs of the network to assess the confidence level of the detected lanes. This is accomplished by generating an uncertainty mask from the lane segmentation outputs and subsequently quantifying the uncertainty for each lane, as discussed in Sect. 3.1 and Sect. 3.2, respectively. We provide the pseudo code for the LaneNet++ method in Algorithm 1.

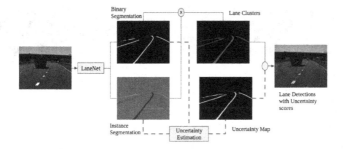

Fig. 3. LaneNet++ Overview. An improved version of LaneNet that incorporates an uncertainty estimation technique utilizing dual task segmentation outputs.

3.1 Uncertainty Map Estimation Using Dual Segmentation Outputs

Despite having different objectives and loss functions, binary and instance segmentation outputs of LaneNet share activated pixel locations that correspond to lane pixels. To combine these outputs, we calculate mask representations for the binary output p^{bin} and instance output p^{inst}. From the 4 channel instance segmentation data, mask representation of instance output p^{inst} is generated by performing sum of absolute values of 4 features at a pixel and then applying a threshold. By applying a *logical OR* operation as per Eq. 1, we merge these masks to create a pixel map P^{map} that identifies all potential lane pixels within the image.

$$P_i^{map} = p_i^{bin}|p_i^{inst} \tag{1}$$

Further, to determine the probability of a pixel being a lane point $\hat{p}_i$, we assess the agreement between the two outputs by assigning equal weight to each output, as depicted in Eq. 2. Subsequently, we generate an uncertainty map U_{map} for the input image by estimating the uncertainty at each pixel using the entropy Eq. 3, where C represents number of classes.

$$\hat{p}_i = \frac{1}{2}\left(p_i^{bin} + p_i^{inst}\right) \qquad (2) \qquad\qquad u_i = -\sum_{i=1}^{C}\hat{p}_i log\hat{p}_i \tag{3}$$

A sample pixel map with uncertainty pixels is illustrated in Fig. 4. The pixels in gray color indicate the lane pixels with higher uncertainty and pixels in white indicate low/no uncertainty. In further visualization of results in this paper, we use red pixels to indicate uncertain lane pixels.

3.2 Quantification of Uncertainty

Following the estimation of the uncertainty map and the clustering of lanes using LaneNet post-processing, our next step involves quantifying the uncertainty associated with each lane cluster. To facilitate quantification at the lane

Fig. 4. From Left: Input, Binary Segmentation, Instance Segmentation, Pixel Map highlighting the uncertain lane pixels in gray (Color figure online)

level, we normalize the uncertainty map utilizing Eq. 4 to generate q_i. By considering the lane pixel locations obtained from the clustered output, along with the normalized uncertainty value q_i for a pixel on the respective lane marking, we calculate the uncertainty of a lane cluster u_j^l according to Eq. 5. The value of u_j^l is between 0 to 1.0 and indicates the ratio of uncertain pixels to total pixels in a lane.

$$q_i = \begin{cases} 1, & \text{if } u_i \geq 0.1 \\ 0, & \text{otherwise} \end{cases} \quad (4) \qquad u_j^l = \frac{1}{N} \sum_{i=1}^{N} q_i \quad (5)$$

Algorithm 1. Uncertainty Estimation for Lane Detection using Binary and Instance segmentation in LaneNet

---

for Every input image **do**

    Predict binary and instance segmentation outputs using a DL model

    p^{bin} - Create mask of pixels activated in binary segmentation output

    p^{inst} - Create mask of pixels activated in instance segmentation output

    P^{map} - Combine p^{bin} and p^{inst} to compute all potential lane pixels as per eq 1

    Estimate U^{map} - Calculate uncertainty at each pixel using p^{bin} and p^{inst} as per eq 3

    Perform **Clustering** using instance segmentation and P^{map} to estimate lane pixel clusters

    for Every lane cluster **do**

        Calculate **Lane image coords** - X,Y values of clustered pixels

        Calculate **Uncertainty score** per lane u_j^l as per eq 5

    end for

end for

3.3 Calibration of Uncertainty Quantification

The method presented above aims to quantify the model uncertainty, which refers to the inconsistency observed in the dual outputs of the model when processing a given image. To effectively utilize the quantified uncertainty value in real-world applications, it is crucial to calibrate and characterize the uncertainty quantification specifically for a given model and estimate an optimal uncertainty threshold. It should be noted that this optimal threshold value is specific to the particular DL model being used.

This can be achieved by employing a post-hoc method that evaluates on a dedicated validation dataset that is distinct from the training set. One approach is by leveraging the well-known F1 score as shown in Eq. 6. By systematically varying the uncertainty threshold and evaluating the corresponding F1 scores, it is possible to identify the threshold that maximizes the model's performance in terms of both true positives and false positives/negatives. We execute the proposed method across a range of uncertainty threshold value configurations and measure the F1 score for each configuration. Ultimately, we select the threshold value that yields the maximum F1 score as the optimal uncertainty threshold value for the given DL model. Further details of optimal uncertainty threshold value for our model are discussed in the subsequent section.

$$F1 = \frac{2TP}{2TP + FP + FN} \tag{6}$$

4   Experiment Setup and Results

Datasets Description. For our experiments we use publicly available TuSimple and VIL100 datasets.

The TuSimple dataset serves as a crucial and well-established benchmark for lane detection. It contains real-world driving scenes captured from highway scenarios, making it highly relevant for evaluating lane detection algorithms in practical driving conditions. The dataset provides a comprehensive test and train split, with the training set containing around 10,000 frames and the test set comprising approximately 2,782 frames. The TuSimple dataset's ground truth comprises annotations of discernible lane markings, encompassing both prominently occluded lanes and distantly situated lanes within multi-lane road scenarios. However, inconsistencies arise in annotations involving road cracks and faint markings as shown in Fig. 5.

The VIL-100 Dataset is a large annotated dataset designed for video instance lane detection. It comprises 100 videos, each containing 100 frames with 0–6 lanes per frame, resulting in a total of 10,000 frames. The dataset covers diverse scenarios such as normal, crowded, curved road, damaged road, shadows, road markings, dazzle light, haze, night, and crossroad.

Leveraging the TuSimple dataset for training and evaluation, we explore how uncertainty estimation can reduce false positives and improve lane detection performance under uncertain conditions, while evaluating our method's generalization and uncertainty estimation on the VIL-100 dataset to demonstrate adaptability and robustness across diverse and unseen road scenes.

Network and Training Details. Our implementation of LaneNet is based on LaneNet's publicly available code. We use VGG backbone for feature extraction module. Our LaneNet is trained with an embedding dimension of 4, with $\delta_v = 0.5$

Fig. 5. Examples of GT inconsistency on the TuSimple dataset. first and third columns: input image, second and fourth columns: GT marked in blue lines (Color figure online)

and $\delta_d = 3$. The images are rescaled to 512×256 and the network is trained using SGD with a batch size of 8 and a learning rate 1e−4 until convergence. We use GTX 1080Ti GPU for our experiments.

In our LaneNet implementation, to extract lane coordinates from binary mask and instance embedding outputs of the network for a given image, we calculate P^{map} as described in Eq. 1. Using P^{map} and predicted instance embedding, we use DBSCAN for clustering operation and estimating lane clusters. We calculate pixel locations of clustered pixels as lane coordinates. Note that in our implementation of LaneNet, we don't use H-NET based transformation matrix and 3rd order polynomial for lane fitting. We report the results of our implementation on TuSimple test set in Table 1, which are at par with the original paper [12]. While LaneNet showcases impressive performance when dealing with clearly visible lane markings, its efficacy becomes less consistent when confronted with certain scenarios. Notably, challenges arise in situations involving substantial occlusions caused by other vehicles and disparities in annotations. For instance, a significant portion of false positives within the ego lane can be attributed to factors like road cracks and variations in road gradient, where the annotations themselves exhibit inconsistencies. Figure 5 depicts sample inconsistencies in the annotation of TuSimple dataset.

Analysis of Results on TuSimple dataset. Incorporating the proposed enhancements of LaneNet++, we conducted evaluations on the TuSimple dataset. To establish the optimal threshold for uncertainty, we performed calibration, as detailed in Sect. 3.3, utilizing the TuSimple test data. Subsequently,

Table 1. Quantitative results of LaneNet as per the reference paper, our implementation (Our Baseline) and Baseline with different uncertainty score thres on TuSimple dataset

	Acc	FPR	FNR	TP	FP	FN	F1
LaneNet [12]	0.964	0.078	0.0244				
Our Baseline (B)	0.952	0.075	0.0434	9359	882	415	0.935
B (u_score thr 0.8)	0.951	0.072	0.0439	9348	833	421	0.937
B (u_score thr 0.5)	0.949	0.059	0.0464	9283	676	447	0.943
B (u_score thr 0.3)	0.945	0.044	0.0551	9058	486	538	0.946
B (u_score thr 0.1)	0.891	0.024	0.1343	8089	252	1315	0.912

we proceeded to assess lane detection performance across a range of uncertainty threshold values (0.1, 0.3, 0.5, 0.8), calculating corresponding F1 scores, true positives (TP), false positives (FP), and false negatives (FN). During the performance assessment, the uncertainty threshold was employed to filter out lanes with uncertainty estimates exceeding the predefined threshold.

For the evaluation, prediction lanes that exhibited an overlap with ground truth lanes of 85% or more were classified as true positives (TP). The performance outcomes are presented in Table 1. Our analysis indicates that a threshold of 0.3 yields the highest F1 score on the TuSimple evaluation dataset. This suggests that lanes with uncertainty surpassing 30% were deemed ambiguous. Notably, we observed a significant reduction of 2.99% in false positives (FP), albeit accompanied by a marginal decrease of 1.17% in true positives (TP).

While the decrease in false positives (FP) was expected, we delve deeper into the underlying causes for the decline in true positives (TP). Among the 301 missed lanes, only 5 lanes pertain to the ego lane, encompassing instances such as road cracks, faded markings, and variations in road gradient. These instances are shown in Fig. 6. The remaining miss-detection arise from distantly positioned markings or instances of significant occlusions by vehicles. As previously discussed, the model exhibits reduced confidence in these scenarios due to compromised visibility. Through the incorporation of uncertainty assessment introduced by LaneNet++, these uncertain detections are effectively filtered out. This validation reinforces the notion that the proposed method eliminates low-confidence model outputs, ultimately ensuring heightened reliability.

Figure 7 presents visual results obtained using LaneNet++ on the TuSimple dataset. The uncertain regions are highlighted in red on calculated p^{map}. Lanes with uncertainty greater than 0.5 are highlighted in red, uncertainty ranging from 0.5 to 0.3 are marked in blue, and uncertainty below 0.3 is depicted in green. In Row 1 and 2, examples illustrates uncertain lane detection due to road cracks present on the road surface. Rows 3 and 4 showcase instances of shadow regions on the road causing ambiguity in lane detection. Row 5 demonstrates uncertainty arising from faded lane markings. Row 6 exhibits the uncertainty caused by occlusions resulting from vehicles on the road. These visual examples

Images   Baseline (B)   B + u_score thres 0.3

Fig. 6. Missed TP lanes after using uncertainty score. Yellow: Matched GT lanes, Green: Matched Prediction lanes, Blue: Missed GT lanes, Pink: Uncertain predicted lanes. Better viewed in colour (Color figure online)

demonstrate how our uncertainty estimation effectively identifies challenging scenarios and differentiates uncertain lane detections from reliable ones.

Behaviour on Unseen Dataset. We conduct an evaluation of LaneNet++ on the VIL100 dataset to assess the effectiveness of uncertainty estimation in handling unfamiliar or unseen lane markings that may arise in real-world scenarios. Unlike the TuSimple dataset used for training, our model is not trained on the VIL100 dataset, which presents a broader range of challenging driving conditions. Figure 8 showcases visual results obtained by evaluating LaneNet++ on VIL100 dataset. Example in Row 1 demonstrates LaneNet's ability to detect valid lanes accurately when they are visible and correctly represented in the new dataset. In Row 2, uncertain lane detections are observed due to the presence of unfamiliar objects appearing in the road view like hills and bridges, challenging the model's detection capability. Row 3 illustrates ambiguity in lane detection caused by arrow marks present on the roads. Furthermore, Row 4 demonstrates

| Images | Binary Mask | Instance Mask | Uncertain regions | Lanes |

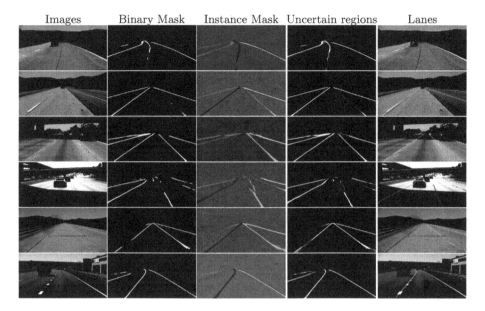

Fig. 7. Examples of uncertainty prediction for lanes on the TuSimple dataset (Color figure online)

uncertainty arising from occlusions caused by vehicles on the road, which poses additional challenges to the lane detection process. Lastly, Row 5 exhibits the uncertainty caused by glare during nighttime conditions, affecting the model's performance. These visual examples emphasize our method's ability in estimation of uncertainty in handling unfamiliar or unseen road scenarios encountered in real-world driving situations.

Failure Cases. In cases where both binary and instance segmentation outputs are inaccurate, the uncertainty estimation based on dual task consistency may fail. Figure 9 provides some examples of failure. This includes scenarios such as varying road color, occluded lanes and false lane marking. These failures stem from consistent false predictions in the dual lane segmentation, which can be addressed by improving the model's accuracy and robustness. These may be due to limited variations or errors the annotation of the dataset. By addressing these limitations may improve uncertainty estimation in lane detection.

5   Discussion and Future Directions

Binary and Instance segmentation serve different purposes in lane detection, making them useful for identifying inconsistencies in ambiguous road scenes. Binary segmentation classifies pixels as lane or non-lane, but may fail in complex situations with faint or occluded lane markings, leading to uncertainty. On the other hand, instance segmentation groups pixels belonging to individual lanes, providing valuable information about lane continuity and accurately

Images	Binary Mask	Instance Mask	Uncertain regions	Lanes

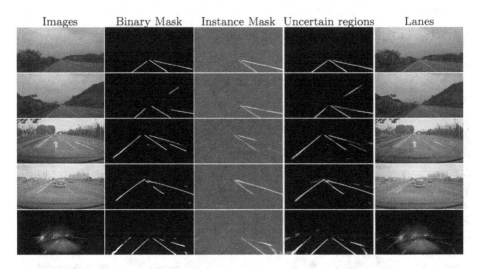

Fig. 8. Examples of uncertainty prediction for lanes on the VIL100 dataset (Color figure online)

detecting lanes even in challenging scenarios. The complementary nature of both techniques enhances uncertainty estimation and improves lane detection performance in challenging road conditions.

Incorporating Dual Task Consistency as an Additional Loss: One potential direction is to leverage Dual task consistency as an additional loss during the training of LaneNet or similar lane detection models. By encouraging consistency between binary and instance segmentation outputs, the model can learn to generate more reliable and accurate lane predictions in challenging road scenarios.

Uncertain Region Elimination instead of Complete Rejection: Instead of completely rejecting a lane detection based on estimated uncertainty, one can use the per-pixel uncertainty information to eliminate uncertain regions within a lane while preserving the more confident regions.

By exploring these future directions, uncertainty estimation based on Dual task consistency can pave the way for more reliable and robust lane detection, contributing to safer and more efficient autonomous driving experiences.

Images   Binary Mask   Instance Mask   Uncertain regions   Lanes

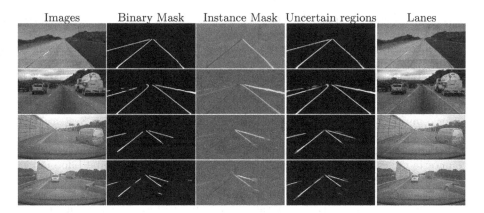

Fig. 9. Failure cases of uncertain estimated in lanes on both TuSimple and VIL100 datasets (Color figure online)

6 Conclusion

Uncertainty measurement in Deep Learning is an essential requirement to enhance their reliability, especially in safety-critical applications. This paper introduces an uncertainty estimation and quantification algorithm that effectively assess the consistency between two sub-tasks within a lane detection algorithm. Additionally, we delve into the calibration process, which determines an optimal uncertainty threshold for a given model. Empirical evaluations demonstrate the efficacy of our proposed method in mitigating confident false positive detections, particularly when the model encounters ambiguous input scenarios. Notably, this approach operates in real-time and seamlessly integrates with single-pass deep learning algorithms. Overall, the proposed method enhances the LaneNet architecture to create a robust and trustworthy lane detection system for safe navigation of autonomous vehicles.

References

1. Baek, S., Kim, M., Suddamalla, U., et al.: Real-time lane detection based on deep learning. J. Electr. Eng. Technol. **17**, 655–664 (2022)
2. Blundell, C., Cornebise, J., Kavukcuoglu, K., Wierstra, D.: Weight uncertainty in neural networks. in Proceedings of the 32nd International Conference on International Conference on Machine Learning, vol. 37, pp. 1613–1622 (2015)
3. Brabandere, B.D., Neven, D., Gool, L.V.: Semantic instance segmentation with a discriminative loss function. ArXiv abs/1708.02551 (2017)
4. Report - concepts of design assurance for neural networks (CoDANN). https://www.easa.europa.eu/en/document-library/general-publications/concepts-design-assurance-neural-networks-codann
5. Gal, Y., Ghahramani, Z.: Dropout as a Bayesian approximation: representing model uncertainty in deep learning. In: International Conference on Machine Learning, pp. 1050–1059 (2016)

6. Gal, Y., Hron, J., Kendall, A.: Concrete dropout. In: Advances in Neural Information Processing Systems, pp. 3581–3590 (2017)
7. Gawlikowski, J., et al.: A survey of uncertainty in deep neural networks (2022)
8. Guo, C., Pleiss, G., Sun, Y., Weinberger, K.Q.: On calibration of modern neural networks. In: International Conference on Machine Learning, pp. 1321–1330. PMLR (2017)
9. Kendall, A., Gal, Y.: What uncertainties do we need in Bayesian deep learning for computer vision? In: Advances in Neural Information Processing Systems, pp. 5574–5584 (2017)
10. Lakshminarayanan, B., Pritzel, A., Blundell, C.: Simple and scalable predictive uncertainty estimation using deep ensembles. In: Advances in Neural Information Processing Systems, pp. 6402–6413 (2017)
11. Li, Y., Luo, L., Lin, H., Chen, H., Heng, P.-A.: Dual-consistency semi-supervised learning with uncertainty quantification for COVID-19 lesion segmentation from CT images. In: de Bruijne, M., et al. (eds.) MICCAI 2021. LNCS, vol. 12902, pp. 199–209. Springer, Cham (2021). https://doi.org/10.1007/978-3-030-87196-3_19
12. Neven, D., Brabandere, B.D., Georgoulis, S., Proesmans, M., Gool, L.V.: Towards end-to-end lane detection: an instance segmentation approach (2018)
13. Paszke, A., Chaurasia, A., Kim, S., Culurciello, E.: ENet: a deep neural network architecture for real-time semantic segmentation (2016)
14. Raghu, M., et al.: Direct uncertainty prediction for medical second opinions. In: International Conference on Machine Learning, pp. 5281–5290. PMLR (2019)
15. Shorten, C., Khoshgoftaar, T.M.: A survey on image data augmentation for deep learning. J. Big Data **6**(1), 1–48 (2019)
16. Suddamalla, U., Kundu, S., Farkade, S.: A novel algorithm of lane detection addressing varied scenarios of curved and dashed lanemarks. In: International Conference on Image Processing Theory, Tools and Applications, pp. 87–92. IPTA (2015)
17. TuSimple: TuSimple benchmark. https://github.com/TuSimple/tusimple-benchmark. Accessed June 2023
18. UL-4600: Standard for safety for the evaluation of autonomous products, work in progress (2019)
19. Valdenegro-Toro, M.: Deep sub-ensembles for fast uncertainty estimation in image classification. In: Bayesian Deep Learning Workshop at Neural Information Processing Systems (2019)
20. VIL-100: a new dataset and a baseline model for video instance lane detection (ICCV 2021). https://github.com/yujun0-0/MMA-Net. Accessed June 2023

Task-Driven Compression for Collision Encoding Based on Depth Images

Mihir Kulkarni$^{(\boxtimes)}$ ⓘ and Kostas Alexis ⓘ

Norwegian University of Science and Technology (NTNU), O. S. Bragstads Plass 2D,
7034 Trondheim, Norway
`mihir.kulkarni@ntnu.no`

Abstract. This paper contributes a novel learning-based method for aggressive task-driven compression of depth images and their encoding as images tailored to collision prediction for robotic systems. A novel 3D image processing methodology is proposed that accounts for the robot's size in order to appropriately "inflate" the obstacles represented in the depth image and thus obtain the distance that can be traversed by the robot in a collision-free manner along any given ray within the camera frustum. Such depth-and-collision image pairs are used to train a neural network that follows the architecture of Variational Autoencoders to compress-and-transform the information in the original depth image to derive a latent representation that encodes the collision information for the given depth image. We compare our proposed task-driven encoding method with classical task-agnostic methods and demonstrate superior performance for the task of collision image prediction from extremely low-dimensional latent spaces. A set of comparative studies show that the proposed approach is capable of encoding depth image-and-collision image tuples from complex scenes with thin obstacles at long distances better than the classical methods at compression ratios as high as 4050:1.

Keywords: Task-driven compression · Collision prediction · Robotics

1 Introduction

Methods for autonomous collision-free navigation of aerial robots have traditionally relied on motion planning techniques that exploit a dense map representation of the environment [3,24,27,28]. Departing from such methods, the community has recently investigated the potential of deep learning to develop navigation methods that act directly on exteroceptive data such as depth images instead of reconstructed maps in order to plan the aerial vehicle's motions with minimal latency [12,15,16,22]. However, such methods face the challenge that exteroceptive data and especially depth images coming from stereo vision or other sensors are typically of very high dimensionality and the involved neural networks include layers that partially act as lossy information compression stages. This is reflected in the architectures of otherwise successful methods such as the works

This work was supported by the AFOSR Award No. FA8655-21-1-7033.

in [12,16,22] that exploit depth images to evaluate which among a set of candidate robot trajectories would collide or not. In [16] the input depth image involves more than 300, 000 pixels (640×480 resolution) but through stages of a pre-trained MobileNetV3 architecture it gets processed to M feature vectors of size 32 each, where M is the number of candidate trajectories for which this method derives collision scores. Eventually by combining the 640×480 pixels depth image with robot pose information, the method attempts to predict which among M trajectories are safe, thus representing a process of information downsampling and targeted inference. In other words, despite the dimensionality reduction taking place through the neural network it is attempted that the method still ensures collision avoidance. However, it is known that such techniques do not provide 100% success ratio especially in complex and cluttered scenes.

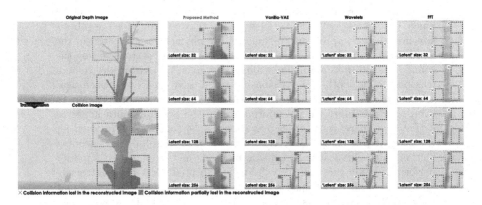

Fig. 1. Aggressive compression/encoding of depth images on aggresively low-dimensional latent spaces using conventional techniques is likely to lead to major loss of collision information. On the contrary, a task-driven compression paradigm is proposed that allows to retain most of the collision information even in exceptionally low latent spaces. This work serves as a modular step that delivers compressed latent spaces that retain collision information and can thus be utilized for further processing by methods that predict the possible collision of candidate trajectories of robots in complex scenes.

Responding to the above, this work contributes the concept of task-driven compression and encoding of depth images as visualized in Fig. 1. Departing from the concept that methods aiming to predict the safety of candidate robot trajectories based on depth images should train collision prediction either a) directly in an end-to-end fashion through depth data [16,22] or through b) an explicit intermediate compression stage of the depth image itself [23], we propose the approach of using the depth image to encode a latent space presenting major dimensionality reduction that reflects not the depth image itself but instead a "collision image". The latter is a remapping of the depth image that has accounted about the robot's size and thus presents reduced overall complexity and greatly reduced presence of narrow/thin features that are hard-to-retain in an aggressive compression step.

To achieve this goal, the method employs a probabilistic encoder-decoder architecture that is trained in a supervised manner such that given a depth image as input, it learns to encode and reconstruct the collision image. To train this collision-predicting network –dubbed Depth image-based Collision Encoder (DCE)– the depth image is first processed such that the collision image is calculated given information for the robot's size. Focusing on aggressive dimensionality reduction, it is demonstrated that the scheme allows to get accurate reconstructions through a latent space that is more than 3 orders of magnitude smaller than the input image. The benefits of the approach are demonstrated through comparisons both with a conventional Variational Autoencoder (VAE) trained to encode the depth image and assessed regarding the extent to which the reconstructed image can serve as basis to derive a correct collision image, as well as traditional compression methods using the Fast Fourier Transform (FFT) and wavelets.

In the remaining paper Sect. 2 presents related work and Sect. 3 details the proposed method involving generation of training data, image augmentation and the training of the neural network. Section 4 compares our proposed method against traditional image compression methods and evaluates the performance of task-driven and task-agnostic compression methods at similar degrees of compression. Finally, conclusions are drawn in Sect. 5.

2   Related Work

This work draws its motivation from the set of deep learning methods that rely on directly processing sensor data (such as depth images) in order to predict if a candidate trajectory of a flying robot shall be in collision or not [12, 15, 16, 22, 23] and accordingly enable safe autonomous navigation. A subset of such methods instead of relying on direct end-to-end learning from exteroceptive data and robot pose information to predict if a certain candidate action/trajectory shall allow collision-free flight, they employ modularization and accordingly an explicit step of compression that pre-processes high-dimensional input image data arriving to a low-dimensional latent space [12, 23].

Technically, the contribution relates to the body of work on image compression. In this large body of work, multiple methods are available including classical schemes that rely on FFT or wavelets [4, 14]. Within the breadth of relevant techniques, of special interest is the utilization deep learning approaches [2, 19] and especially variational autoencoders [5, 9, 26] as means to achieve good reconstruction quality for high compression ratios [30, 31]. Nevertheless, the majority of such methods follow the main paradigm of compression which implies that a uniform metric (e.g., mean squared loss) of over pixel-level reconstruction against the original image is employed. Even for works that exploit additional cues such as semantics [29], conventional compression remains the prime goal. Departing from this paradigm this work reflects the fact that in the line of works of collision prediction [12, 15, 16, 22, 23] it is the information over candidate collisions that matters and not the depth pixels themselves. In other words, it is the question if the robot - with the specific volume that it occupies - can fly along a path within the volume observed and captured by the depth image. This calls for a new concept that hereby is called purposeful task-driven depth image compression/encoding for collision prediction utilizing minimal latent spaces. It is highlighted that the goal to arrive at a latent space that is multiple orders of magnitude smaller than the high dimensional depth images –offered by sensing solutions such as modern stereo vision– is driven from the need of robust performance and generalization in diverse natural environments. As established by seminal works such as ResNet [8], deeper models with more parameters require much more data to train. A low-dimensional compression latent space enables methods that shall then use it for collision prediction [12] to utilize smaller and simpler networks for the task, while they further combine with robot data which are also low-dimensional (e.g., pose states of a quadrotor aerial vehicle over the SE(3) special Euclidean group [13]).

3   Proposed Method

The proposed approach on task-driven compression and particularly depth image-based collision encoding is outlined below. First, the process to generate relevant training data is discussed, followed by the method to derive the collision image associated with each depth image. Subsequently, the depth images-based collision encoder motivated by the architecture of variational autoencoders is presented.

3.1   Dataset Generation

Deep learning techniques for data compression require large amounts of data for training. Moreover, the generalizability of the learned models depends on the quality of the training data and the variety of samples provided for learning. Available depth image datasets primarily focus on specific tasks to be performed using the depth images such as depth completion [21] or autonomous driving [7]. These datasets contain images from scenes that include urban structured indoor settings and open streets respectively with large-sized obstacles that are sparsely distributed in the environment. Consequently, such datasets - that are otherwise common within both research and industry - do not contain images from highly cluttered complex environments that present challenges to aerial robot navigation. For the latter, it is important to note that environments with a) high clutter leading to uncertainty as to the safest flying direction, and b) obstacles with narrow cross section ("thin" obstacles) are particularly hard to fly through. In order to train our neural network models for such cluttered environments containing narrow/thin obstacles, while ensuring generalizability, we rely on two popular robot simulators - namely Gazebo Classic [25] and Isaac Gym [18] to generate diverse simulated depth image data. These simulators provide the necessary interfaces that allow us to rearrange different objects randomly in a simulated environment. Images from Gazebo Classic are collected using the onboard depth camera of a simulated aerial robot in an obstacle-rich environment using the RotorS Simulator [6]. Subsequently, we utilize the Isaac Gym-based Aerial Gym Simulator [11] in order to simulate environments with randomly placed obstacles and collect depth images in a parallelized manner from multiple randomly generated environments simultaneously. $85,000$ depth images are collected in environments consisting of a variety of objects ranging from multi-branched tree-like objects with thin cross-sections to large obstacles with cavities in them. Depth images are collected and aggregated to be processed for computing a robot-specific collision image.

3.2 Collision Image Generation

While the collected depth images provide information about the projected distance to a surface along the central axis of the camera, it is difficult to infer the collision-free regions in the robot's field-of-view. Traditional approaches to compute collision-free regions involve representing the depth image in an intermediate volumetric map-based representation [10,20,24] that can be queried to derive collision-free regions. These representations are limited by their discretization capabilities and often require a large amount of memory to maintain a persistent map [24]. Generation of such representations is also a computationally expensive step [10]. Finally, such reconstructions rely on aggregating multiple depth image readings and thus necessitate consistent pose estimation. At the same time, methods that use depth images to directly predict if a candidate path is collision-free or not [16,22] implicitly have to learn that the depth image itself is not a map of collision-free space but instead this information can be acquired by further correlating the range to a point and the size of the robot. Contrary to the current techniques on that front that typically either a) resort on end-to-end learning of collisions via depth, state and action tuples [16,22] or b) compress the depth image and use this lossy latent space to then learn collision prediction [12,23], we here propose the re-mapped representation of depth images in a new form that directly provides the collision-free distance that can be traversed by a robot along any direction. A collision image is defined as an image representing the collision-free distance (projected along the central axis of the camera) traversable by a robot of known dimensions along the rays corresponding to each pixel in an image. This revised image representation that encodes all necessary collision information can then be utilized directly for robot navigation tasks.

To derive collision images from depth images, we propose a computationally efficient method illustrated in Fig. 2. Motivated by the observation that the most significant change between the depth image and the collision image occurs at the edges of obstacles in the field-of-view of the camera, a rendering-based approach is utilized to appropriately inflate the objects in the camera's field-of-view about their edges. We cannot perform this inflation accurately using traditional 2D computer vision techniques since the modified area around each edge pixel is both dependent on the size of the robot and the distance to the point in 3D space making the computation intractable. We rely on parallelized rendering frameworks to visualize virtual robot-sized meshes around the regions corresponding to the edges of the obstacles in order to inflate them by the size of the robot. Projecting them back onto the camera plane captures the appropriately inflated regions of the environments that represent the regions of collision for the robot. Edge detection is performed on the original depth image $\mathcal{D}$ using OpenCV [1] to obtain the set of pixels corresponding to the edges $\mathcal{E}$ as shown in Fig. 2(a). A fraction of the

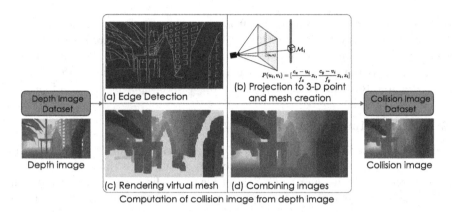

Fig. 2. The acquired dataset is processed for task-driven compression. Edge-detection is performed on the depth images and each edge pixel is projected to it's 3D coordinates to form a pointcloud and a virtual 3D mesh is rendered. The depth image of the virtual mesh is obtained and combined with an offset range image to form a collision image.

edge pixels are randomly selected to render meshes. For each selected edge pixel i with coordinates $(u_i, v_i) \in \mathcal{E}$, the position of the corresponding point $P_i \in \mathbb{R}^3$ is calculated as:

$$P_i = (x_i, y_i, z_i), \tag{1}$$

where

$$x_i = \frac{c_x - u_i}{f_x} z_i, \tag{2}$$

$$y_i = \frac{c_y - v_i}{f_y} z_i, \tag{3}$$

$$z_i = \mathcal{D}(u_i, v_i). \tag{4}$$

A pinhole model of the camera is considered, with f_x and f_y as the focal lengths and c_x and c_y as the optical centers. The shape of the robot is considered to be cubical with edge length $2r$. For each projected point P_i, a robot-sized mesh $\mathcal{M}_i$ is centered at the coordinates (x_i, y_i, z_i) as shown in Fig. 2(b). Meshes created around each point are merged into a single aggregated mesh $\mathcal{M}$. We use NVIDIA Warp [17], a high-performance graphics and simulation package that enables rendering simulated depth cameras in a virtual environment consisting of this aggregated mesh. A parallelized ray-casting operation is performed to project rays into this virtual mesh environment and obtain a depth image $\mathcal{D}_\mathcal{M}$ only containing these virtual meshes (Fig. 2(c)). This depth image only contains the information regarding the distances to the virtual meshes corresponding to the edge pixels in the original depth image $\mathcal{D}$. Since rendering of virtual meshes is a computationally expensive step, it is reserved only for the edge pixels in the image. For pixels lying in the interior regions of the object in the depth image, an offset depth image $\mathcal{D}_{\text{offset}}$ is created with all range values brought closer by the size of the robot r using the following operation:

$$\mathcal{D}_{\text{offset}} = \mathcal{R}^{-1}(\mathcal{R}(\mathcal{D}) - r), \tag{5}$$

where the transformation $\mathcal{R}$ converts the depth image to a range image, i.e., the value in each pixel of the image represents the Euclidean distance to the corresponding point on the object. The inverse function $\mathcal{R}^{-1}$ converts the range image back to a depth image. Finally, an approximate collision image $\mathcal{D}_{\text{coll}}$ is obtained by taking pixel-wise minimum values of the offset depth image $\mathcal{D}_{\text{offset}}$ and rendered image with inflated meshes $\mathcal{D}_{\mathcal{M}}$ as shown in Fig. 2(d). This operation is given by:

$$\mathcal{D}_{\text{coll}} = min(\mathcal{D}_{\mathcal{M}}, \mathcal{D}_{\text{offset}}). \tag{6}$$

We use this to generate a collision image dataset given the depth image dataset with each image in the original dataset being processed in the above manner to produce a collision image. Both the original image and the collision image are aggregated into a common dataset to be used for training the probabilistic encoder-decoder network to derive and encode the collision information from the original depth images.

3.3   Depth Image Compression and Collision Encoding

The interpretation and representation of depth information to derive collision images requires spatial understanding of the environment. We utilize artificial neural networks to perform this task by learning a compressed representation that compresses and encodes the depth image to its associated collision image. The overall architecture is motivated by the success of VAEs but with the important distinction that the involved learning includes training of the depth-to-collision image map transformation. We consider a dataset containing depth images $\mathbf{x} \in \mathbb{D}$, and its derived secondary dataset containing collision images $\mathbf{x}_{coll} \in \mathbb{D}_{coll}$. A surjective function $\mathcal{P} : \mathbb{D} \mapsto \mathbb{D}_{coll}$ maps each element from the depth image dataset to an image in the collision image dataset. This function is imitated in the collision image generation step (Sect. 3.2). Each $\mathbf{x}_{coll} \in \mathbb{D}_{coll}$ can be assumed to be generated by a process using a latent random variable $\mathbf{z}$.

We employ probabilistic encoders and decoders to perform dimensionality reduction of the input depth data and learn a highly compressed latent representation for predicting collision images. A probabilistic decoder $p_\theta(\mathbf{x}_{coll}|\mathbf{z})$, given $\mathbf{z}$ produces a distribution over the possible values of $\mathbf{x}_{coll}$, while a probabilistic encoder $q_\phi(\mathbf{z}|\mathbf{x})$ learns to encode the input image $\mathbf{x}$ to a latent distribution with mean $\boldsymbol{\mu}$ and standard deviation $\boldsymbol{\sigma}$. This distribution is sampled to obtain $\mathbf{z}$ such that $\mathbf{z} \sim \mathcal{N}(\boldsymbol{\mu}, \boldsymbol{\sigma} \cdot \mathbf{I})$. The encoder and decoder networks are jointly trained to produce a highly compressed but well performing latent representation $\mathbf{z}$ given a depth image $\mathbf{x}$ and its $\mathbf{x}_{coll}$. The decoder can be used to derive a collision image that approximates $\mathbf{x}_{coll}$ and accurately predicts the distances for collision-free traversal using the given depth image. Figure 3 shows the structure of the DCE for task-driven compression. To train the DCE the loss function is defined as:

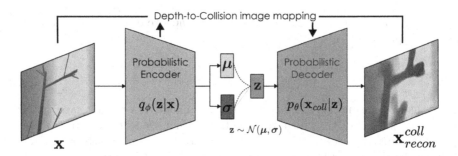

Fig. 3. The proposed neural network with an encoder-decoder architecture inspired by variational autoencoders and tailored to compress and re-map a depth image $\mathbf{x}$ to a latent representation $\mathbf{z}$ that can be used to produce the reconstructed image $\mathbf{x}_{recon}^{coll}$ that approximates the associated collision image $\mathbf{x}_{coll}$.

$$\mathcal{L} = \mathcal{L}_{recon} + \beta_{norm}\mathcal{L}_{KL}, \tag{7}$$

where

$$\mathcal{L}_{recon}(\mathbf{x}_{coll}, \mathbf{x}_{recon}^{coll}) = \mathrm{MSE}(\mathbf{x}_{coll}, \mathbf{x}_{recon}^{coll}), \tag{8}$$

$$\mathcal{L}_{KL}(\boldsymbol{\mu}, \boldsymbol{\sigma}) = -\frac{1}{2}\sum_{j=1}^{J}\left(1 + \log(\sigma_j^2) - \mu_j^2 - \sigma_j^2\right). \tag{9}$$

Here, $\mathcal{L}$ denotes the overall loss term while $\mathcal{L}_{recon}$ and $\mathcal{L}_{KL}$ (scaled by a constant β_{norm} [9]) denote the reconstruction loss and the KL-divergence loss terms respectively in a manner motivated by autoencoder literature [5]. The Mean-Square Error (MSE) loss function is modified to ignore the errors of the pixels from the depth image that are invalid, i.e., the pixels that do not contain accurate depth information owing to the obstacles being too close to the camera in simulated images or also in case of the incorrect depth from stereo shadows for real-world depth images. The encoder is a residual neural network consisting of convolutional layers at each block and uses the ELU activation function. The final layers of the encoder network are fully connected layers that produce the mean and variance describing the latent distribution. The decoder consists of two fully connected layers followed by non-residual de-convolutional layers with ReLU activation functions. The last convolutional layer has a sigmoid activation to have bounded values for the collision image. The network is trained on a dataset consisting of $70,000$ depth and collision image pairs and tested on a dataset containing $15,000$ image pairs. Each image has a dimension of 270×480 pixels and contains the distance to the given obstacle projected along the central axis of the camera. As discussed in the next section, well performing latent spaces as low as 32 variables are achieved which represents more than 3 orders of magnitude compression, while simultaneously delivering and exploiting the described depth-to-collision image transformation.

4   Evaluation and Results

The main premise of the work is that the implicitly learned transformation of depth-to-collision image mapping, not only allows to learn directly the information pertinent to collision prediction, but also allows major compression while retaining the necessary information. To demonstrate this fact, we conduct a comprehensive set of evaluation studies comparing the performance of our proposed approach against traditional task-agnostic compression methods such as using the wavelet transform and the Fast Fourier Transform (FFT). We also compare our task-driven compression method against a conventionally trained task-agnostic VAE (vanilla-VAE) that shares the same neural network architecture as the DCE. We first show that neural network-based compression outperforms traditional compression methods such as FFT and wavelet transform-based compression for very high compression ratios for depth images. Furthermore, the reconstructed collision image obtained from the task-driven DCE accurately represents the calculated collision image as compared to the derived collision information from the image reconstructed from the vanilla-VAE. The performance of the proposed approach is evaluated for a set of different latent dimensions representing varying levels of extreme compression. Latent spaces of 32, 64, 128 and 256 latent dimensions corresponding to compression factors of 4050, 2025, 1012.5 and 506.25 respectively are considered. The proposed learning-based compression and image domain transformation method not only outperform the currently established approaches while achieving large compression ratios but also are capable of encoding spatial information from the depth image to represent collision information. This is made evident from the results where the depth image is accurately (and range- and robot size-dependent) "inflated" to obtain a collision image that occludes the obstacles in the background.

4.1   Comparison of Vanilla-VAE with Traditional Compression Methods

We compare a vanilla-VAE based compression with FFT and wavelet transform-based compression. The task-agnostic vanilla-VAE is trained using $70,000$ images to encode a depth image $\mathbf{x}$ into a latent distribution and also to reconstruct the input depth image $\mathbf{x}_{recon}^{vanilla}$. This is done to first ensure a fair comparison between task-agnostic methods. A separate network is trained on the dataset for each latent space size.

We obtain the image representation in the wavelet domain by decomposing the image with the Daubechies wavelet 'db1'. To obtain the compressed representation in this domain corresponding to a latent space size of n, the largest n magnitudes in the wavelet domain are retained, while all other values are set to 0. The resultant wavelet domain representation is reconstructed using the inverse wavelet transform to obtain $\mathbf{x}_{recon}^{wv}$. Similarly, to compress the image using FFT, the complex numbers in the frequency domain that correspond to the $n/2$ largest magnitudes are retained (with both their real and complex coefficients), while all others are set to 0. A reconstruction $\mathbf{x}_{recon}^{FFT}$ is obtained from this compressed representation by performing an inverse FFT. It must be noted that both these representa-

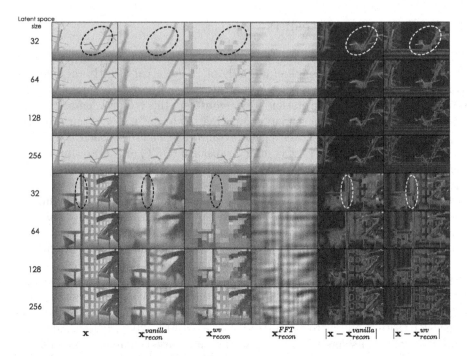

Fig. 4. Comparison between the reconstruction performance on depth images using traditional methods and the vanilla-VAE for different levels of compression. The images compressed and reconstructed using vanilla-VAE ($\mathbf{x}_{recon}^{vanilla}$), wavelet transform ($\mathbf{x}_{recon}^{wv}$) and FFT ($\mathbf{x}_{recon}^{FFT}$) are shown. The errors in the reconstruction are also highlighted.

tions are computationally represented as ordered lists that contain the position-dependent coefficients for the decoder to reconstruct the image. While we retain only the top n coefficients, we do not remove their position information to allow the reconstruction software to work seamlessly. As a result, information retained using this scheme is *more* than just the n dimensional variable that we use in the case of the neural networks. Figure 4 compares the reconstructed images from the compressed representation for different latent space sizes using different compression methods. The vanilla-VAE preserves the features in the depth image for complex scenes for small latent sizes, while the wavelet transform-based compression performs well for larger latent space sizes. The difference between the reconstructed image using the vanilla-VAE and the wavelet transforms and the input image is shown to highlight the regions with a higher reconstruction error. A visual inspection of the reconstructed images from wavelets and frequency domain representations show that these methodologies are unable to encode the information in complex depth images for smaller latent space dimensions. The difference is especially highlighted in images that contain complex and cluttered settings, where the FFT reconstructions generate artificial patterns, while the wavelet reconstructions discretize regions of the image non-uniformly, losing out on the sharper details of the image.

The results are tabulated in Table 1 demonstrating that for high compression ratios corresponding to latent spaces of 32, 64 and 128 dimensions, the vanilla-VAE based depth image compression method produces images with a lower MSE value with the input image. Interestingly, the wavelet transform-based method produces a lower MSE in the case where the information corresponding to the top 256 coefficients is retained. As shown in Fig. 4, the wavelet reconstruction corresponding to this size produces sharper edges in the reconstructed image owing to the capability to encode more information regarding the smaller discretized regions in the image.

Table 1. Comparison of MSE for reconstructed images with vanilla-VAE, FFT and wavelet transform for different compressed latent dimensions.

MSE against input image x				
Latent dims:	32	64	128	256
$\mathbf{x}_{recon}^{vanilla}$	**1249.58**	**827.00**	**543.38**	477.88
$\mathbf{x}_{recon}^{wv}$	1481.36	952.58	612.31	**382.43**
$\mathbf{x}_{recon}^{FFT}$	2223.87	1634.52	1181.93	840.38

4.2   Task-Driven Compression for Collision Representation

While the task-agnostic vanilla-VAE demonstrates good compression capacity of complex depth images to a small latent code, it still faces limitations in producing reconstructions that can be used to derive an accurate collision representation especially in cluttered and complex scenes. As expected, aggressive compression leads to loss of important information. However, compared to the depth image, a collision image would typically contain less complex and more low-frequency information regarding the same scene owing to the "inflation" of the obstacles. Due to this process, pixels corresponding to thin features in a depth image end up being represented by a larger region of pixels showing collision-free distance values. It is noted, transforming the depth image to a collision image requires a spatial understanding of the scene as robot size-inflated regions in the collision image occlude the regions near the edges of obstacles represented in depth images. Nonetheless, once a network is trained to predict this, it also implies reduction in the information that has to be kept during compression.

We compare the performance of the proposed DCE against the task agnostic vanilla-VAE to compare the capability of these networks in retaining collision prediction information in the compressed latent space spanning from the depth image. The DCE is trained to directly reconstruct the collision image, while the vanilla-VAE is trained to reconstruct the input depth image and thus for the purposes of assessing its capacity to retain the information needed for collision prediction, a new collision image is derived (as in Sect. 3) from the images reconstructed from its latent space through the decoder. Essentially, to ensure a fair comparison, we use the mapping $\mathcal{P}(\mathbf{x}_{recon}^{vanilla})$ to obtain the derived collision image from the reconstructed input depth image. Figure 5 presents examples of images reconstructed using both the DCE and vanilla-VAE.

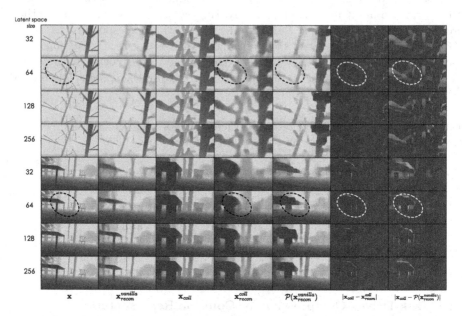

Fig. 5. Comparison between DCE and vanilla-VAE to derive the collision information from the input depth image for different levels of compression. The images compressed and reconstructed using DCE ($\mathbf{x}_{recon}^{coll}$), vanilla-VAE ($\mathbf{x}_{recon}^{vanilla}$) are shown. A collision image $\mathcal{P}(\mathbf{x}_{recon}^{vanilla})$ is derived from $\mathbf{x}_{recon}^{vanilla}$. The derived collision images are compared against the ground-truth collision image $\mathbf{x}_{coll}$ for errors.

The reconstructed collision image $\mathbf{x}_{recon}^{coll}$ and the derived collision image from the vanilla-VAE reconstruction $\mathcal{P}(\mathbf{x}_{recon}^{vanilla})$ are compared against the true collision image. The areas of errors are highlighted in Fig. 5. The collision image derived from the vanilla-VAE reconstruction shows a greater number of regions with erroneous collision information, while the image from the DCE $\mathbf{x}_{recon}^{coll}$ shows both smaller error magnitudes and only small regions of error when compared to the true collision image $\mathbf{x}_{coll}$. Moreover, the reconstructed collision image captures thin features such as branches in the environment and reconstruct the regions of collisions in the same. The results calculating the MSE of the reconstructed collision image and the derived collision image from the depth image reconstruction are presented in Table 2. As presented, the task-driven DCE outperforms the vanilla-VAE by a large margin.

Table 2. Comparison of MSE for reconstructed images with DCE and a transformed collision representation of the image reconstructed using vanilla-VAE.

MSE against Collision Image $\mathbf{x}_{coll}$				
Latent dims:	32	64	128	256
$\mathbf{x}_{recon}^{coll}$	**783.718**	**516.487**	**418.03**	**402.66**
$\mathcal{P}(\mathbf{x}_{recon}^{vanilla})$	4828.50	4339.76	2532.14	2539.89

5 Conclusions and Future Work

This paper presented a learning-based method for task-driven aggressive compression of depth images to a highly compressed latent representation tailored to infer collision-free travel distances for a robot in the environment. A novel method was proposed to generate robot size-specific collision prediction data from given depth images using rendering frameworks. Such depth and collision prediction image tuples are then used to train a neural network performing the task-driven compression of encoding a latent space that captures collision information from depth images. We show that our proposed approach is able to encode depth images by a compression factor over 4000 : 1, while retaining the information necessary to predict collisions from depth images of complex cluttered scenes. Moreover, we show that such purposeful neural network-based compression techniques demonstrate superior performance against traditional methods using FFT and wavelets or even conventional variational autoencoders for image reconstruction from highly compressed latent spaces.

References

1. Bradski, G.: The OpenCV Library. Dr. Dobb's Journal of Software Tools (2000)
2. Cheng, Z., Sun, H., Takeuchi, M., Katto, J.: Deep residual learning for image compression. In: CVPR Workshops (2019)
3. Dang, T., Tranzatto, M., Khattak, S., Mascarich, F., Alexis, K., Hutter, M.: Graph-based subterranean exploration path planning using aerial and legged robots. J. Field Robot. **37**, 1363–1388 (2020)
4. Dhawan, S.: A review of image compression and comparison of its algorithms. Int. J. Electron. Commun. Technol. **2**(1), 22–26 (2011)
5. Doersch, C.: Tutorial on variational autoencoders. arXiv preprint arXiv:1606.05908 (2016)
6. Furrer, F., Burri, M., Achtelik, M., Siegwart, R.: RotorS—a modular Gazebo MAV simulator framework. In: Koubaa, A. (ed.) Robot Operating System (ROS). SCI, vol. 625, pp. 595–625. Springer, Cham (2016). https://doi.org/10.1007/978-3-319-26054-9_23
7. Guizilini, V., Ambrus, R., Pillai, S., Raventos, A., Gaidon, A.: 3D packing for self-supervised monocular depth estimation. In: IEEE Conference on Computer Vision and Pattern Recognition (CVPR) (2020)

8. He, K., Zhang, X., Ren, S., Sun, J.: Deep residual learning for image recognition. In: Proceedings of the IEEE Conference on Computer Vision and Pattern Recognition, pp. 770–778 (2016)
9. Higgins, I., et al.: beta-VAE: learning basic visual concepts with a constrained variational framework. In: International Conference on Learning Representations (2017). https://openreview.net/forum?id=Sy2fzU9gl
10. Hornung, A., Wurm, K.M., Bennewitz, M., Stachniss, C., Burgard, W.: OctoMap: an efficient probabilistic 3D mapping framework based on octrees. Auton. Robots **34**, 189–206 (2013)
11. Kulkarni, M., Forgaard, T.J.L., Alexis, K.: Aerial gym - Isaac gym simulator for aerial robots (2023)
12. Kulkarni, M., Nguyen, H., Alexis, K.: Semantically-enhanced deep collision prediction for autonomous navigation using aerial robots (2023)
13. Lee, T., Sreenath, K., Kumar, V.: Geometric control of cooperating multiple quadrotor UAVs with a suspended payload. In: 52nd IEEE Conference on Decision and Control, pp. 5510–5515. IEEE (2013)
14. Lewis, A.S., Knowles, G.: Image compression using the 2-D wavelet transform. IEEE Trans. Image Process. **1**(2), 244–250 (1992)
15. Loquercio, A.: Agile Autonomy: Learning High-Speed Vision-Based Flight, vol. 153. Springer, Cham (2023). https://doi.org/10.1007/978-3-031-27288-2
16. Loquercio, A., Kaufmann, E., Ranftl, R., Müller, M., Koltun, V., Scaramuzza, D.: Learning high-speed flight in the wild. In: Science Robotics (2021)
17. Macklin, M.: Warp: a high-performance python framework for GPU simulation and graphics (2022). https://github.com/nvidia/warp. nVIDIA GPU Technology Conference (GTC)
18. Makoviychuk, V., et al.: Isaac gym: High performance GPU-based physics simulation for robot learning (2021). https://doi.org/10.48550/ARXIV.2108.10470, https://arxiv.org/abs/2108.10470
19. Mishra, D., Singh, S.K., Singh, R.K.: Deep architectures for image compression: a critical review. Signal Process. **191**, 108346 (2022)
20. Museth, K.: VDB: high-resolution sparse volumes with dynamic topology. ACM Trans. Graph. **32**(3), 1–22 (2013). https://doi.org/10.1145/2487228.2487235
21. Silberman, N., Hoiem, D., Kohli, P., Fergus, R.: Indoor segmentation and support inference from RGBD images. In: Fitzgibbon, A., Lazebnik, S., Perona, P., Sato, Y., Schmid, C. (eds.) ECCV 2012. LNCS, vol. 7576, pp. 746–760. Springer, Heidelberg (2012). https://doi.org/10.1007/978-3-642-33715-4_54
22. Nguyen, H., Fyhn, S.H., De Petris, P., Alexis, K.: Motion primitives-based navigation planning using deep collision prediction. In: 2022 International Conference on Robotics and Automation (ICRA), pp. 9660–9667. IEEE (2022)
23. Niu, C., Newlands, C., Zauner, K.P., Tarapore, D.: An embarrassingly simple approach for visual navigation of forest environments. Front. Robot. AI **10** (2023)
24. Oleynikova, H., Taylor, Z., Fehr, M., Siegwart, R., Nieto, J.: Voxblox: incremental 3D Euclidean signed distance fields for on-board MAV planning. In: IEEE/RSJ International Conference on Intelligent Robots and Systems (IROS) (2017)
25. Organization, O.R.: Gazebo classic simulator. https://classic.gazebosim.org/
26. Pu, Y., et al.: Variational autoencoder for deep learning of images, labels and captions. In: Advances in Neural Information Processing Systems, vol. 29 (2016)
27. Rocha, L., Saska, M., Vivaldini, K.: Overview of UAV trajectory planning for high-speed flight. In: 2023 International Conference on Unmanned Aircraft Systems (ICUAS), pp. 110–117. IEEE (2023)

28. Tordesillas, J., Lopez, B.T., How, J.P.: Faster: fast and safe trajectory planner for flights in unknown environments. In: 2019 IEEE/RSJ International Conference on Intelligent Robots and Systems (IROS), pp. 1934–1940. IEEE (2019)

29. Wang, C., Han, Y., Wang, W.: An end-to-end deep learning image compression framework based on semantic analysis. Appl. Sci. **9**(17), 3580 (2019)

30. Wen, S., Zhou, J., Nakagawa, A., Kazui, K., Tan, Z.: Variational autoencoder based image compression with pyramidal features and context entropy model. In: CVPR Workshops (2019)

31. Zhou, L., Cai, C., Gao, Y., Su, S., Wu, J.: Variational autoencoder for low bit-rate image compression. In: Proceedings of the IEEE Conference on Computer Vision and Pattern Recognition Workshops, pp. 2617–2620 (2018)

Eigenpatches—Adversarial Patches from Principal Components

Jens Bayer[1,2](✉) ⓘ, Stefan Becker[1,2] ⓘ, David Münch[1,2] ⓘ,
and Michael Arens[1,2] ⓘ

[1] Fraunhofer Center for Machine Learning, Gutleuthausstr. 1,
76275 Ettlingen, Germany
[2] Fraunhofer IOSB, Gutleuthausstr. 1, 76275 Ettlingen, Germany
`jens.bayer@iosb.fraunhofer.de`

Abstract. Adversarial patches are still a simple yet powerful white-box attack that can be used to fool object detectors by suppressing possible detections. The patches of these so-called evasion attacks are computational expensive to produce and require full access to the attacked detector. This paper addresses the problem of computationally expensiveness by analyzing 375 generated patches, calculating the principal components of these and shows, that traversing the spanned up subspace of the resulting "eigenpatches" can be used to create patches that can be used to fool the attacked YOLOv7 object detector successfully. Furthermore, the influence regarding the mean average precision of the number of principal components used for the patch recreation and the sampling size for the principal component analysis are investigated. Patches generated this way can either be used as a starting point for further optimization or as an adversarial patch as it is.

Keywords: Adversarial Patch Attack · Object Detection · Principal Component Analysis

1 Introduction

Despite the good performance in image classification, object detection and semantic segmentation, computer vision systems are still prone to adversarial attacks. A prominent white-box attack scenario is an evasion attack against object detectors using adversarial patches, whereas these patches are sometimes also referred to as a form of camouflage [6] or invisibility cloak [26,27]. This is possible since the patches depict specifically calculated patterns, that alter the activations of the attacked object class for an object detector.

As "simple" and straightforward the generation process of such a patch is, as time-consuming and computation intensive it is as well. To speed up the patch calculation and gain a more profound understanding if there are common attributes that can be extracted to harden an object detector, this paper investigates:

G. Bebis et al. (Eds.): ISVC 2023, LNCS 14362, pp. 274–284, 2023.
https://doi.org/10.1007/978-3-031-47966-3_21

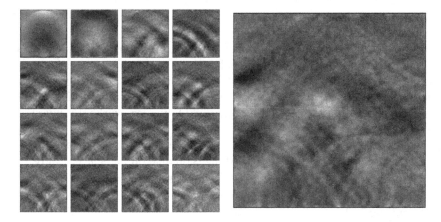

Fig. 1. Left: the first sixteen principal components extracted from the trained patches. Right: the unweighted mean image of these sixteen principal components.

1. If patches that are combinations of principal components generated by a set of precalculated patches can be used to create valid patches?
2. How many principal components are necessary for recreating patches with a sufficiently high impact on the detection score?
3. The influence of set size used to generate the principal components, regarding the quality of the resulting patches.

Towards this end, the well-known YOLOv7 object detector [22] is attacked with various adversarial patches. These patches are trained on a subset of the *INRIA Person* dataset [4] and are analyzed with a principal component analysis (PCA). The extracted principal components are then used to recreate the patches and even create new patches by combining them linearly (e.g., Fig. 1).

To the best of our knowledge, this is the first approach in investigating and creating adversarial patches that attack object detectors by using principal components.

The organization of the paper is as follows: In Sect. 2, the related work regarding the investigation and analysis of adversarial attacks is addressed. A brief introduction of what eigenpatches are and how they can be crafted is given in Sect. 3. Section 4 covers all necessary information to recreate the experimental results. The used object detector, the dataset, and the generation process of the patches that are the base for eigenpatch generation are further explained. The results of the experiments and the used metrics are presented in Sect. 5. Finally, Sect. 6 summarizes the paper and gives a conclusion as well as a brief outlook.

2   Related Work

In the following section, selected works regarding the analysis of adversarial attack patterns and sampling from lower dimensional embeddings are presented.

For a broader overview, we refer to these surveys on adversarial attacks [1,3,13, 23] and the YOLO object detector family [19].

The approach of using dimensionality reduction algorithms like principal component analysis to investigate the patterns generated by adversarial attacks for image classifiers is an active research area. Nonetheless, most investigations are performed solely on image classifiers with attacks that induce high-frequent noise on the whole image [5,8,14,15,21,24,25]. Only a few works [18] investigate adversarial patches.

Tramer et al. explore the space of transferable adversarial examples by proposing methods for estimating the dimensionality of the space of adversarial inputs [21]. By investigating untargeted misclassification attacks, they show that perturbing a data point in such a way, that it crosses a model's decision boundary, is likely to result in similar performance degradation when applied to other models.

Wang et al. present a fast black-box adversarial attack that finds key differences between different classes based on PCA that later can be used to drive a sample to a target class or the nearest other class [24].

Energy Attack [15] is a transfer-based black-box L_∞ adversarial attack that uses PCA to obtain the energy distribution of perturbations, generated by whitebox attacks on a surrogate model. For the attack, patches are sampled from the energy distribution, tiled and applied to the target image.

Dohmatob et al. investigate whether neural networks are vulnerable to blackbox attacks inherently [5]. After analyzing low-dimensional adversarial perturbations, they hypothesize, that adversarial perturbations exist with high probability in low-dimensional sub-spaces that are much smaller than the dimension of the image space.

Theoretical bounds on the vulnerability of classifiers against adversarial attacks are shown by Shafahi et al. using the unit sphere and unit cube [14]. They claim that by using extremely large values for the class density functions, the bounds can be potentially escaped.

Weng et al. perform a singular value decomposition to improve adversarial attacks on convolutional neural networks [25]. They combine the top-1 decomposed singular value-associated features for computing the output logits with the original logits, used to optimize adversarial examples and thus boost the transferability of the attacks.

Recently, Tarchoun et al. examined adversarial patches from an information theory perspective and measured the entropy of random crops of the patches [18]. The results indicate that the mean entropy of adversarial patches is higher than in natural images. Based on these findings, they create a defense mechanism against adversarial patches.

Further research on the relationship between adversarial vulnerability and the number of perturbed dimensions is performed by Godfrey et al. [9]. Their results strengthen the hypothesis that adversarial examples are a result of the locally linear behavior of neural networks with high dimensional input spaces.

3 Eigenpatches

This section covers the generation process of the eigenpatches. The term eigenpatches is derived from eigenfaces (the most prominent example of eigenimages [16]) which are calculated similarly. Eigenimages is the name of the eigenvectors that can be derived from a set of training images. They can be used as a low-dimensional representation of the original training images and recreating these through a linear combination.

Given a set of adversarial patches

$$\mathcal{P} = \{\boldsymbol{P}_i | i = 1, \ldots, n\}, \quad \boldsymbol{P}_i \in [0,1]^{C \times H \times W} \tag{1}$$

where H is the height in pixel, W is the width in pixel and C is the number of channels. A principal component analysis is performed on $\mathcal{P}$. With the top k principal components $\boldsymbol{E}_j, j \in \{1, \ldots, k\}$ and the weights $\lambda_{i,j}$, the set

$$\hat{\mathcal{P}} = \{\hat{\boldsymbol{P}}_i | i = 1, \ldots, n\} \quad \hat{\boldsymbol{P}}_i = \sum_{j=1}^{k} \lambda_{i,j} \boldsymbol{E}_j \tag{2}$$

can be generated that consists of linear combinations of the principal components and is a recreation of $\mathcal{P}$. Figure 1 shows the first sixteen principal components as well as the patch resulting from calculating the mean of the components.

4 Experimental Setup

In the following, all the necessary information to recreate the experimental results is presented. In addition, the full source code and revised ground-truth annotations are also provided[1]. The attacked object detector is YOLOv7 [22] with the official pretrained weights. The used dataset is the *INRIA Person* dataset [4].

4.1 Object Detector

Due to its prominence and good performance, YOLOv7 [22] is selected as the object detector to be attacked. The smallest model of YOLOv7 with an input size of 640×640 pixels and the official pretrained weights are used. The generated patches can therefore be used without specific finetuned weights, and the results can easily be verified.

4.2 Dataset

For the generation of the patches, the positive images of the *INRIA Person* dataset [4] are used. Instead of using the provided ground truth bounding boxes of the dataset, the object detector first generates new ground truth data for each

---

[1] https://github.com/JensBayer/PCAPatches.

Fig. 2. Left: Unpatched input image with bounding boxes, predicted by the attacked object detector. The numbers above the bounding boxes indicate the output probabilities after the non-maximum suppression. Right: Patched input image as it would be used in the evaluation. The image is resized and padded to match the required input size of 640 × 640 px. Then, the tested patch is embedded in the center of each bounding box and resized according to a scaling factor. The bounding boxes are usually not visible, of course.

train image. Then, the newly created bounding boxes are manually reviewed. False positives and bounding boxes of highly obscured target classes (persons) are removed. The resulting ground truth data for both, the train and test split, are available in the source code repository. Since the input size of the used YOLOv7 model is 640 × 640 px, the images are resized and padded to match this size. A resized and patched example image as it would be used in the evaluation is given in Fig. 2.

4.3   Patch Generation

The training procedure of the patches follows the procedure described in [20]: During the generation process of a patch, it is placed inside the bounding boxes of selected target classes in images of a training dataset. To improve the robustness of the patch, different randomized transformations, such as translation, rotation, perspective and also color jitter are applied. The altered image is then propagated through the object detector and the objectness score of the target classes is minimized. In addition, a smoothness loss that punishes high-frequent noise in the patches is also calculated and applied.

All patches are initialized with random values in the range [0, 1] and optimized with the *AdamW* [12] optimizer with an initial learning rate of 0.01. The color jitter changes the brightness, contrast, and saturation of the patch randomly by values in the range of [0.9, 1.1], [0.95, 1.05], and [0.97, 1.03] respectively. For the perspective, the distortion scale parameter is set to 0.5. The resize range

Table 1. Different parameterization for the patch generation. The resize range is the range of the scaling factor, relatively to the bounding box.

Run ID	n	Epochs	LR-Scheduler	Resize range	Rotation
191	175	100	StepLR	[0.75, 1.0]	30
885	100	100	CosineAnnealingLR	[0.75, 1.0]	30
905	50	100	StepLR	[0.75, 1.0]	45
371	25	125	StepLR	[0.5, 0.75]	30
243	25	125	StepLR	[0.5, 0.75]	45

of the patch, the learning rate scheduler, and the number of training epochs are defined by the values in Table 1.

The random translation of the patch is performed in such a way that the resized and transformed patch is placed inside the bounding box.

5 Evaluation

This section covers the used metrics, the results, and a final limitations section that discusses, under which circumstances these results are generalizable and how valid they are. The arrows ($\uparrow$, $\downarrow$) in the following tables indicate whether a higher or lower value in the column is desired.

5.1 Metrics

To quantify the results, the well-known mean average precision object detector metrics mAP@.5 [7] and mAP@.5:.95 [11] are used. While mAP@.5 is the mean average precision for bounding boxes with an intersection over union (IoU) threshold of at least 0.5, the mAP@.5:.95 is the average across ten IoU thresholds and therefore more strict. Both metrics are calculated for the unpatched and the patched images. The higher the difference between the unpatched and patched metric scores, the stronger is the impact of the patches on the detector. For Table 2, the differences (Δ) between the unpatched and patched inputs images is also given.

5.2 Experimental Setup

Similar to the training data, the test split and positive images of the *INRIA Person* dataset are used for the evaluation. New ground truth bounding boxes are generated the same way as described in Subsect. 4.2. To generate reproducible results, the evaluation procedure is as follows: A patch is placed in the center of each bounding box as given in the ground truth information and resized to a relative size of 0.75 times the longer side of the bounding box. Other transformations such as the ones mentioned in Subsect. 4.3 are not applied. An example of a test image is given in Fig. 2. After this, the mAP@.5 and mAP@.5:.95 is calculated according to the provided detector evaluation script.

280 J. Bayer et al.

Table 2. Mean average precision for the unpatched and patched test data. "Gray value" refers to gray values in the range of zero to one with a linear step size. "Count" is the numbers of patches on which the result mean and standard deviation values are calculated. The last two columns are the differences of the mAPs of the patched and unpatched images.

Applied Patches	Count	$mAP@.5\downarrow$	$mAP@.5:.95\downarrow$	$\Delta mAP@.5\uparrow$	$\Delta mAP@.5:.95\uparrow$
No	1	0.73	0.71		
Gray value	11	0.74 ± 0.03	0.71 ± 0.03	-0.01 ± 0.03	0.00 ± 0.02
Trained	375	$\mathbf{0.46\pm0.03}$	$\mathbf{0.35\pm0.03}$	$\mathbf{0.27\pm0.03}$	$\mathbf{0.36\pm0.03}$
PCA(2) recovered	375	0.63 ± 0.03	0.58 ± 0.03	0.10 ± 0.03	0.13 ± 0.03
PCA(4) recovered	375	0.60 ± 0.04	0.54 ± 0.04	0.13 ± 0.04	0.17 ± 0.04
PCA(8) recovered	375	0.58 ± 0.03	0.51 ± 0.03	0.15 ± 0.03	0.20 ± 0.03
PCA(16) recovered	375	0.57 ± 0.03	0.51 ± 0.03	0.16 ± 0.03	0.20 ± 0.03
PCA(32) recovered	375	0.57 ± 0.03	0.51 ± 0.04	0.16 ± 0.03	0.20 ± 0.04
PCA(64) recovered	375	0.57 ± 0.04	0.49 ± 0.04	0.16 ± 0.04	0.22 ± 0.04
PCA(128) recovered	375	0.55 ± 0.05	0.46 ± 0.06	0.18 ± 0.05	0.25 ± 0.06
PCA(256) recovered	375	0.51 ± 0.07	0.41 ± 0.07	0.22 ± 0.07	0.30 ± 0.07

5.3 Results

As shown in Table 2, the trained patches have a significant impact on the object detector. While the mAP of the detector on the test data is about 0.73 (0.71), the mAP drops to 0.46 (0.35) when attacked with the adversarial patches. To verify that this is not a result of covering the persons in the image with the patches, we also checked eleven single-colored gray valued patches. Each of these patches has one particular shade of gray, out of the uniformly distributed range from zero to one. As the second row of Table 2 shows, the gray valued patches do not cover important parts and have almost no impact on the metrics.

As expected, the PCA recovered patches are not as good as the trained ones and the more principal components are used to recreate the patch, the higher the mAP drop is (see Fig. 3). The rising but still small standard deviation suggests that some patches can be recreated better than others, which seems plausible, since the number of patches with the same parameterization as given in Table 1 is unevenly distributed. In addition, the mAP@.5 difference between the patches that use 128 principal components for recreation and the patches that only use eight principal components with about 0.03 is relatively small. Yet, the impact on the mAP@.5:.95 is almost twice as high (0.05).

In comparison to Fig. 3, the curves in Fig. 4 are not that intuitive. Here, the number of patches used to compute the PCA and the resulting mAPs are plotted. Since a PCA with n components requires at least n elements in the input set, the number of principal components is given by $min(n, 64)$. As a result, the number of principal components used for this plot equals either the input set size or 64. As expected, the recreation of all 375 patches with only two components results in a small standard deviation of 0.01 while achieving a mean mAP:.5 of 0.52,

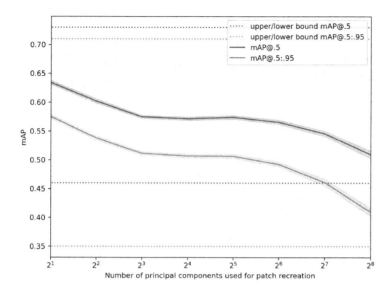

Fig. 3. Visualization of the mAP@.5 and mAP@.5:.95 for varying numbers of principal components used to recover the patches. The mAP@.5 and mAP@.5:95 drop as the number of principal components used to recover the patches increases.

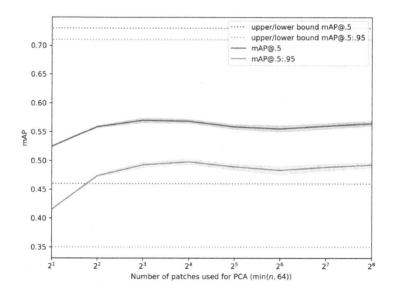

Fig. 4. Visualization of the mAP@.5 and mAP@.5:.95 for different numbers of input patches for the PCA to recreate all 375 patches with $\min(n, 64)$ principal components. The metric scores increase, as the number of input patches rises.

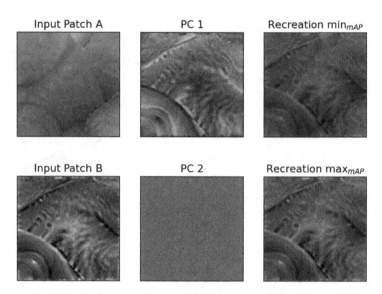

Fig. 5. Left: The input set $\mathcal{P} = \{PatchA, PatchB\}$ for the PCA. Middle: The two computed principal components. Right: Example recreations of the 375 patches with the minimal and maximal achievable mAP by the two principal components.

which differs from the PCA(256) by only a small percentage. A possible reason is that with such a small input set size, the resulting patch recreations do not vary a lot and reassemble, at best, one of the two patches that are given in the input set. A look at the reassembled patches (see Fig. 5) as well as the minimum achieved mAP values (0.41, 0.31) support this statement.

6   Conclusion

This paper investigates the applicability of the principal component analysis for adversarial patches to fool object detectors. The evaluation shows that the recreation and sampling of patches based on the principal components is possible. As expected, those patches are generally not as good as carefully trained ones, yet the subspace spanned by the principal components can be traversed to initialize new patches for further fine-tuning. The evaluation also shows that the more principal components are used, the higher the mAP drop is. Nonetheless, the usage of the first eight principal components results already in a noticeable mAP drop. The influence of the set size used for the PCA is after eight patches also quite stable.

Since these experiments are performed on a comparable small dataset and only a single object detector, future work should check the behavior with larger datasets (e.g., OpenImages [10]) and other object detectors (e.g., EfficientDet [17] or DETR [2]).

Acknowledgements. This work was developed in Fraunhofer Cluster of Excellence "Cognitive Internet Technologies".

References

1. Akhtar, N., Mian, A.: Threat of adversarial attacks on deep learning in computer vision: a survey. IEEE Access **6**, 14410–14430 (2018). https://doi.org/10.1109/ACCESS.2018.2807385
2. Carion, N., Massa, F., Synnaeve, G., Usunier, N., Kirillov, A., Zagoruyko, S.: End-to-end object detection with transformers. In: Vedaldi, A., Bischof, H., Brox, T., Frahm, J.-M. (eds.) ECCV 2020. LNCS, vol. 12346, pp. 213–229. Springer, Cham (2020). https://doi.org/10.1007/978-3-030-58452-8_13
3. Chakraborty, A., Alam, M., Dey, V., Chattopadhyay, A., Mukhopadhyay, D.: A survey on adversarial attacks and defences. CAAI Trans. Intell. Technol. **6**(1), 25–45 (2021). https://doi.org/10.1049/cit2.12028
4. Dalal, N., Triggs, B.: Histograms of oriented gradients for human detection. In: CVPR, vol. 1, pp. 886–893. IEEE (2005). https://doi.org/10.1109/CVPR.2005.177
5. Dohmatob, E., Guo, C., Goibert, M.: Origins of low-dimensional adversarial perturbations. In: Proceedings of The 26th International Conference on Artificial Intelligence and Statistics, vol. 206, pp. 9221–9237. PMLR (2023)
6. Duan, Y., et al.: Learning coated adversarial camouflages for object detectors. In: Proceedings of the Thirty-First International Joint Conference on Artificial Intelligence, pp. 891–897. International Joint Conferences on Artificial Intelligence Organization, California (2022). https://doi.org/10.24963/ijcai.2022/125
7. Everingham, M., et al.: The 2005 PASCAL visual object classes challenge. In: Quiñonero-Candela, J., Dagan, I., Magnini, B., d'Alché-Buc, F. (eds.) MLCW 2005. LNCS (LNAI), vol. 3944, pp. 117–176. Springer, Heidelberg (2006). https://doi.org/10.1007/11736790_8
8. Garcia, W., Chen, P.Y., Clouse, H.S., Jha, S., Butler, K.R.B.: Less is more : dimension reduction finds on-manifold adversarial examples in hard-label attacks. In: First IEEE Conference on Secure and Trustworthy Machine Learning (2023)
9. Godfrey, C., et al.: How many dimensions are required to find an adversarial example? In: 2023 IEEE/CVF Conference on Computer Vision and Pattern Recognition Workshops (CVPRW), pp. 2353–2360. IEEE (2023). https://doi.org/10.1109/CVPRW59228.2023.00232
10. Krasin, I., et al.: OpenImages: a public dataset for large-scale multi-label and multi-class image classification (2017). https://storage.googleapis.com/openimages/web/index.html
11. Lin, T.-Y., et al.: Microsoft COCO: common objects in context. In: Fleet, D., Pajdla, T., Schiele, B., Tuytelaars, T. (eds.) ECCV 2014. LNCS, vol. 8693, pp. 740–755. Springer, Cham (2014). https://doi.org/10.1007/978-3-319-10602-1_48
12. Loshchilov, I., Hutter, F.: Decoupled weight decay regularization. In: 7th International Conference on Learning Representations, ICLR 2019 (2019)
13. Pauling, C., Gimson, M., Qaid, M., Kida, A., Halak, B.: A tutorial on adversarial learning attacks and countermeasures. In: arXiv preprint (2022). https://arxiv.org/abs/2202.10377
14. Shafahi, A., Huang, R., Studer, C., Feizi, S., Goldstein, T.: Are adversarial examples inevitable? In: 7th International Conference on Learning Representations, ICLR 2019 (2019)

15. Shi, R., Yang, B., Jiang, Y., Zhao, C., Ni, B.: Energy attack: on transferring adversarial examples. In: arXiv preprint (2021). https://arxiv.org/abs/2109.04300
16. Sirovich, L., Kirby, M.: Low-dimensional procedure for the characterization of human faces. J. Opt. Soc. Am. A **4**(3), 519 (1987). https://doi.org/10.1364/josaa.4.000519
17. Tan, M., Pang, R., Le, Q.V.: EfficientDet: scalable and efficient object detection. In: CVPR, pp. 10778–10787. IEEE (2020). https://doi.org/10.1109/CVPR42600.2020.01079
18. Tarchoun, B., Khalifa, A.B., Mahjoub, M.A., Abu-ghazaleh, N.: Jedi : entropy-based localization and removal of adversarial patches. In: CVPR, pp. 4087–4095 (2023)
19. Terven, J., Cordova-Esparza, D.: A comprehensive review of YOLO: from YOLOv1 to YOLOv8 and beyond. In: arXiv preprint, pp. 1–27 (2023). https://arxiv.org/abs/2304.00501
20. Thys, S., Ranst, W.V., Goedeme, T.: Fooling automated surveillance cameras: adversarial patches to attack person detection. In: CVPR Workshops 2019-June, pp. 49–55 (2019). https://doi.org/10.1109/CVPRW.2019.00012
21. Tramèr, F., Papernot, N., Goodfellow, I., Boneh, D., McDaniel, P.: The space of transferable adversarial examples. In: arXiv preprint, pp. 1–15 (2017). https://arxiv.org/abs/1704.03453
22. Wang, C.Y., Bochkovskiy, A., Liao, H.Y.M.: YOLOv7: trainable bag-of-freebies sets new state-of-the-art for real-time object detectors. In: 2023 IEEE/CVF Conference on Computer Vision and Pattern Recognition (CVPR), pp. 7464–7475. IEEE (2023). https://doi.org/10.1109/CVPR52729.2023.00721
23. Wang, S., Veldhuis, R., Strisciuglio, N.: The robustness of computer vision models against common corruptions: a survey. arXiv preprint, pp. 1–23 (2023). https://arxiv.org/abs/2305.06024
24. Wang, Z.M., Gu, M.T., Hou, J.H.: Sample based fast adversarial attack method. Neural Process. Lett. **50**(3), 2731–2744 (2019). https://doi.org/10.1007/s11063-019-10058-0
25. Weng, J., Luo, Z., Lin, D., Li, S., Zhong, Z.: Boosting adversarial transferability via fusing logits of top-1 decomposed feature. arXiv preprint (2023). https://arxiv.org/abs/2305.01361
26. Wu, Z., Lim, S.-N., Davis, L.S., Goldstein, T.: Making an invisibility cloak: real world adversarial attacks on object detectors. In: Vedaldi, A., Bischof, H., Brox, T., Frahm, J.-M. (eds.) ECCV 2020. LNCS, vol. 12349, pp. 1–17. Springer, Cham (2020). https://doi.org/10.1007/978-3-030-58548-8_1
27. Zhu, X., Hu, Z., Huang, S., Li, J., Hu, X.: Infrared invisible clothing: hiding from infrared detectors at multiple angles in real world. In: CVPR, pp. 13307–13316. IEEE (2022). https://doi.org/10.1109/CVPR52688.2022.01296

Edge-Guided Image Inpainting
with Transformer

Huining Liang[ID] and Chandra Kambhamettu[✉][ID]

VIMS Lab, University of Delaware, Newark, DE 19716, USA
{huining,chandrak}@udel.edu

Abstract. Image inpainting aims to complete missing regions by extracting the features of the image through the information of the known region. Traditional image inpainting approaches like patch-based and diffusion-based methods are robust for simple images, but fail to reconstruct photo-realistic results when the image contains a lot of texture and objects or the object covers a large region in the images. In recent years, transformer-based models are proven to be capable of achieving promising results in numerous image processing tasks. Transformer-based models can better cope with image long-range dependencies which are important for image inpainting. In this paper, we propose a transformer-based generative adversarial network for edge-guided image inpainting. We present the two-step image inpainting approach that first generates edge information and then completes the image. Our experiments demonstrate that the proposed network is able to regenerate the missing regions in images smoothly and realistically and produce visually appealing results against the state-of-the-art image inpainting approaches.

Keywords: Image inpainting · Transformer · Generative adversarial network

1 Introduction

Image inpainting is the process of filling missing regions in the image by extracting the features of the image through the information of the known region. Image inpainting is an important step in image editing and it can be used in many image processing tasks such as unwanted object removal and image restoration. Traditional approaches like patch-based [3, 6, 7] and diffusion-based [13, 14, 21] methods are proposed for image inpainting tasks but their output quality heavily relies on the existing regions of the input image. Unable to generate features that do not appear in the input images, these methods are suitable for background repairing and robust for simple images, but fail to reconstruct photo-realistic results when the image contains a lot of texture and objects or the object covers a large region in the images.

More recently, deep-learning-based methods [19, 24, 27] have shown remarkable improvement for the image inpainting task. These approaches use learned

G. Bebis et al. (Eds.): ISVC 2023, LNCS 14362, pp. 285–296, 2023.
https://doi.org/10.1007/978-3-031-47966-3_22

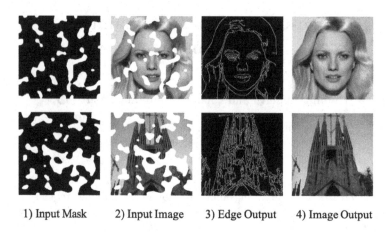

1) Input Mask   2) Input Image   3) Edge Output   4) Image Output

Fig. 1. Examples of the inputs and outputs of our proposed network. Images from left to right: (1) Input masks of missing regions. (2) Input images with missing regions. (3) Generated edge maps from the network in the first step. (4) Final outputs from the reconstruction network in the second step.

data distribution to recover the missing pixels and they are capable of reproducing coherent structures in the regeneration of the missing regions, which is very difficult when using traditional techniques. While the regeneration of the missing regions has reasonable structures, it still suffers from artifacts and blurry outputs, since these methods struggle to reconstruct object information accurately.

To improve this, we adopt a two-step framework to generate fine details in the missing regions. In the first step, we extract the edge structure from the input image. Since there are missing regions in the input image, the extracted edge information is also incomplete. Inspired by the work of Nazeri et al. [18], we take the assumption that edge recovery would be an easier task than color image completion. Following the coarse-to-fine idea, we first train the edge generation network to regenerate edges in the missing areas. With the completed edge structure, we then train an image completion network in the second step. The network combines edge information in the missing regions with color and texture information of the known regions in the image to generate the missing pixels.

Aiming for a more accurate and photo-realistic reconstruction of the image, we propose a transformer-based generative adversarial network for both steps of our edge-guided image inpainting framework. Inspired by its success in the NLP field, the transformer has been adapted for various vision tasks and achieved promising results. Transformer-based models can better cope with image long-range dependencies which are important for image inpainting.

We evaluated our model quantitatively and qualitatively on the CelebA-HQ dataset [12] and the European Cities dataset [1]. Our experiments demonstrate that the proposed network is able to regenerate the missing regions in images smoothly and realistically and produce visually appealing results against the state-of-the-art image inpainting approaches.

2   Related Work

2.1   Image Inpainting

Deep learning methods for image inpainting often take an encoder-decoder architecture, where the input image with missing regions is mapped into a low-dimensional feature space by the encoder and then the upsampling and reconstruction is done by the decoder. Due to the information bottleneck in the channel-wise fully connected layer, the recovered regions in the output often suffer from visual artifacts and blurriness. To address this problem, [10] uses a series of dilated convolution layers instead of the channel-wise fully connected layer. They also reduce the number of downsampling layers in the encoder, which is compensated by setting varying dilation factors. But their method takes much longer training time, since large dilation factors can create extremely sparse filters. Partial convolution is proposed by Liu et al. [16], which normalizes convolution weights and improves the recovery quality of irregularly shaped missing regions. In [19], Pathak et al. train a GAN-based model and show that their proposed context encoders can be used for semantic inpainting tasks.

Additional information like semantic segmentation mask and edge structure is shown to be helpful for image inpainting. [2] proposes learning a Sketch Tensor space to restore structure information for inpainting man-made scenes. An end-to-end image inpainting network with two auxiliary branches for semantic segmentation and edge textures is developed by [29]. Yu et al. propose contextual attention [28] for generative image inpainting. They take a two-step approach that first generates a coarse estimate of the missing region and then uses a refinement network to sharpen the result. Their refinement network takes an attention mechanism and searches for the collection of background patches that shows the highest similarity to the coarse estimate. Their method has the weakness of the possibly inaccurate coarse estimation and is unsuitable for missing regions of arbitrary shapes. Our proposed method follows an edge-guided two-step approach which has a better accuracy of the generated estimation in the first step and also has the capability to handle the missing regions of arbitrary shapes.

2.2   Transformer

Transformer is first proposed for Natural Language Processing (NLP) tasks and its strength lies in learning the long-range interactions of sequential data with its Self-Attention and Feed Forward Neural Network. Inspired by the impressive performance of the transformer in NLP field, many works have been done trying to apply the transformer to various Computer Vision(CV) tasks in recent years. In [5], Vision Transformer (ViT) model has been proposed for image recognition at scale. Strudel et al. introduce Segmenter [22] showing the good capacity of the transformer model for semantic segmentation. With better expressivity, recent transformer-based frameworks [4,15,17] also achieved promising results with image inpainting. In this paper, the transformer is used as the substitution of dilated convolutional layers in the GAN-based CNN models for both edge generation and image completion, and our proposed transformer-based generative adversarial network shows satisfying performance compared with CNN-based methods.

3   Methodology

We propose a two-step image inpainting framework that consists of two neural network modules: an edge generator and an image reconstruction network. Examples of the expected input and output images from our proposed network are shown in Fig. 1. Both step one and step two networks are transformer-based GAN architecture. Thus, the entire image inpainting network would have one pair of generator G1 and discriminator D1 for step one (edge generation) and another pair of G2 and D2 for step two (image reconstruction). Figure 2 shows the overview of the architecture of our proposed network.

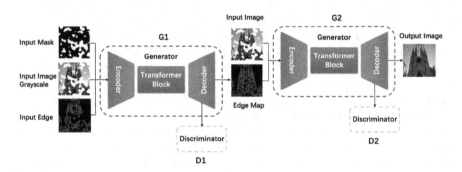

Fig. 2. Overview of the proposed network structure. The entire framework contains two steps: (1) Step one is an edge generator network. It takes the mask of missing regions, the incomplete grayscale image, and the incomplete edge as input and generates a predicted complete edge map. (2) Step two is the image reconstruction network. It takes the step-one output and the color image with missing regions as input and returns the final output image. Both steps follow a transformer-based GAN structure.

3.1   Edge Estimation

In this step, we generate the estimated full edge maps from the input image with missing regions. The edge generator is aimed to output a prediction of the edge image that is as similar as possible to the ground truth edge image extracted from the complete input image. The generated full edge maps would be used to guide the generation of the features in the next step and help to improve the sharpness of the image completion.

We first take the complete color image $\mathbf{I}$ and the binary mask for the missing regions $\mathbf{M}$ in which 1 means the missing regions. Then we make the grayscale image $\mathbf{I}'$ from the complete color image $\mathbf{I}$ and extract the ground truth edge map $\mathbf{I}_e$ from $\mathbf{I}$ using a standard Canny edge detector. We apply the mask $\mathbf{M}$ to $\mathbf{I}'$ and $\mathbf{I}_e$:

$$\mathbf{I}'_{masked} = \mathbf{I}' \odot (1 - \mathbf{M}) \tag{1}$$

$$\mathbf{I}_{e\,masked} = \mathbf{I}_e \odot (1 - \mathbf{M}) \tag{2}$$

where $\odot$ is the Hadamard product operator.

The edge generator takes the incomplete grayscale image $\mathbf{I}'_{masked}$, the incomplete edge map $\mathbf{I}_{e\,masked}$ and the mask $\mathbf{M}$ as input and generates the edge map $\tilde{\mathbf{I}}_e$ for the whole image including the masked regions. This edge estimation process can be formulated as follows:

$$\tilde{\mathbf{I}}_e = G1(\mathbf{I}'_{masked}, \mathbf{I}_{e\,masked}, \mathbf{M}) \tag{3}$$

The discriminator D1 takes the generated edge estimation $\tilde{\mathbf{I}}_e$ and the ground truth edge map $\mathbf{I}_e$ and the grayscale image $\mathbf{I}'$ as the input and determines if the edge map is real.

3.2 Image Reconstruction

In the second step, we use the image completion network to reconstruct the missing regions in the input image with the guidance of the edge structure information. The incomplete input image is obtained by applying the mask $\mathbf{M}$ to the original color image:

$$\mathbf{I}_{masked} = \mathbf{I} \odot (1 - \mathbf{M}) \tag{4}$$

The edge structure information is provided by the edge map $\mathbf{I}_e^*$ which consists of the estimated edge from the previous step in the masked regions and the ground truth edge in the other regions. $\mathbf{I}_e^*$ is defined as

$$\mathbf{I}_e^* = \tilde{\mathbf{I}}_e \odot \mathbf{M} + \mathbf{I}_e \odot (1 - \mathbf{M}) \tag{5}$$

The image completion network takes the incomplete input image $\mathbf{I}_{masked}$ and the edge map $\mathbf{I}_e^*$ as input and generates missing pixels in the masked regions to output the completed image $\tilde{\mathbf{I}}$. Then the discriminator D2 is used to predict whether the output image is real or fake. The image reconstruction process can be formulated as

$$\tilde{\mathbf{I}} = G2(\mathbf{I}_{masked}, \mathbf{I}_e^*) \tag{6}$$

3.3   Loss Function

For the edge estimation network, the loss function consists of a feature loss L_f adapted from [25] and an adversarial loss L_{adv1}.

The feature loss L_f is used to match the activation maps in the discriminator D1 and helps to make the generator G1 output edge estimation that has the similar features to the real edge map. The feature loss L_f is defined as

$$L_f = E \left[\sum_i^L \frac{1}{N_i} \left\| D1^i(\mathbf{I}_e) - D1^i(\tilde{\mathbf{I}}_e) \right\| \right] \tag{7}$$

where $D1^i$ is the activation map for the ith layer of D1.

The adversarial loss is defined as

$$L_{adv1} = E_{(\mathbf{I}_e, \mathbf{I}')} \left[log D1(\mathbf{I}_e, \mathbf{I}') \right] + E_{\mathbf{I}'} log \left[1 - D1(\tilde{\mathbf{I}}_e, \mathbf{I}') \right] \tag{8}$$

Therefore, the total loss of the edge estimation step is the weighted sum of the feature loss L_f and the adversarial loss L_{adv1}:

$$L_{step1} = \lambda_f L_f + \lambda_{adv1} L_{adv1} \tag{9}$$

For the image reconstruction network, our loss function combines a style loss L_s [20], a perceptual loss L_p [11], a reconstruction loss L_{rec} and an adversarial loss L_{adv2}.

The style loss L_s is the squared Frobenius norm of the Gram matrix and it measures the differences between covariances of the activation maps obtained from the pre-trained VGG network. The style loss can help to eliminate the checkerboard artifact and thus improve the quality of the output image. The style loss L_s is defined as

$$L_s = E \left[\left\| G2^\phi(\tilde{\mathbf{I}}) - G2^\phi(\mathbf{I}_{masked}) \right\| \right] \tag{10}$$

where ϕ denotes the Gram matrix of the activation maps.

The perceptual loss L_p has the similar idea to the feature loss in the first step. It compares the activation map of the ground truth image $\mathbf{I}$ and the output completed image $\tilde{\mathbf{I}}$ under a pre-trained VGG-19 network. The perceptual loss L_p is defined as

$$L_p = E \left[\sum_i \frac{1}{N_i} \left\| \phi^i(\mathbf{I}) - \phi^i(\tilde{\mathbf{I}}) \right\| \right] \tag{11}$$

where ϕ^i denotes the activation map of the ith layer of the pre-trained VGG.

The reconstruction loss L_{rec} is the difference between the generated pixels and the corresponding original ones. It directly judges the inpainting quality at the image level. The reconstruction loss L_{rec} is defined as

$$L_{rec} = \left\| \mathbf{I} - \tilde{\mathbf{I}} \right\| \tag{12}$$

The adversarial loss L_{adv2} is used to help the generator G2 utilize the critics received from the discriminator D2 and try to output the completed image similar to the real image making the discriminator D2 unable to tell the difference. The adversarial loss L_{adv2} is defined as

$$L_{adv2} = E_{(\mathbf{I},\mathbf{I}_e^*)}\left[logD2(\mathbf{I},\mathbf{I}_e^*)\right] + E_{\mathbf{I}_e^*}log\left[1 - D2(\tilde{\mathbf{I}},\mathbf{I}_e^*)\right] \qquad (13)$$

Therefore, the total loss of the image reconstruction step is defined as

$$L_{step2} = \lambda_s L_s + \lambda_p L_p + \lambda_{rec}L_{rec} + \lambda_{adv2}L_{adv2} \qquad (14)$$

4 Experiments

We evaluate our proposed model on the CelebA-HQ dataset [12] and the European Cities dataset [1]. We resize the image to 256 × 256 pixels and use Canny edge detector to generate the ground truth image for the edge estimation step. For each data set, we randomly pick 80% of the data as the training set, 10% of the data as the validation set and the rest 10% of the data as the test set. We train our model with Adam optimizer and set the learning rate for the generator 10 times the learning rate for the discriminator. For the mask, we use a mix of regular square masks and irregular masks. As Fig. 3 shows, the regular square masks include the center mask (128 × 128) that takes 25% of the pixels, the 4-scattered mask (64 × 64 × 4) that takes 25% of the pixels, and the 9-scattered mask (44 × 44 × 9) that takes 26.6% of the pixels. On the other hand, the irregular masks consist of randomly distributed shapes and can be divided into six groups according to their masking rates: (0%–10%], (10%–20%], (20%–30%], (30%–40%], (40%–50%], (50%–60%]. We compare our qualitative and quantitative results with state-of-the-art image inpainting approaches EC [18], CTSDG [8], and ICT [23].

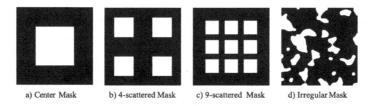

a) Center Mask   b) 4-scattered Mask   c) 9-scattered Mask   d) Irregular Mask

Fig. 3. Regular square masks and irregular masks: (a) Square Center Mask (25%). (b) Square 4-scattered Mask (25%). (c) Square 9-scattered Mask (26.6%). (d) Irregular Mask (0%–60%).

4.1 Qualitative Results

As is shown in Fig. 4 and Fig. 5, our model shows better image inpainting results than other state-of-the-art methods, given less blurriness and better feature details. Transformer blocks provide better long-range dependencies leading to a better recovery of both structure and texture information. Our proposed model not only generates complete semantic contours, but mitigates visual artifacts and creates a more photorealistic output image as well.

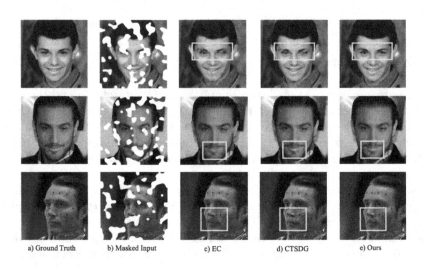

a) Ground Truth   b) Masked Input   c) EC   d) CTSDG   e) Ours

Fig. 4. Qualitative results of EC [18], CTSDG [8], and ours on the CelebA-HQ dataset. Areas with the most difference are marked out with red boxes. (Color figure online)

4.2 Quantitative Results

For the quantitative evaluation, we utilize Frećhet inception distance (FID) [9], structural similarity index measure (SSIM) [26], and peak signal-to-noise ratio (PSNR) metrics to compare the performance of our proposed model against other state-of-the-art image inpainting models on the CelebA-HQ dataset [12] and the European Cities dataset [1]. Our proposed model achieves better results compared with other state-of-the-art methods on both datasets. The results are shown in Table 1 and Table 2.

4.3 Ablation

Edge Information. To show the effect of the guidance from the edge structure information for image inpainting, we compare the image completion results with/without the estimated edge map. The result is shown in Fig. 6. As we can see from the output completed images, there are better painted details and less

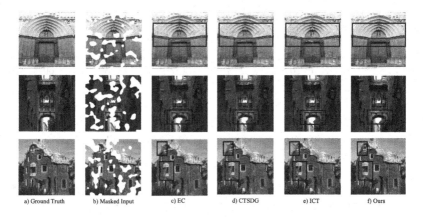

a) Ground Truth   b) Masked Input   c) EC   d) CTSDG   e) ICT   f) Ours

Fig. 5. Qualitative results of EC [18], CTSDG [8], ICT [23], and ours on the European Cities dataset. Areas with the most difference are marked out with red boxes. (Color figure online)

Table 1. Quantitative results with EC, CTSDG, and our model on the CelebA-HQ dataset.

	Mask	0%–10%	10%–20%	20%–30%	30%–40%	40%–50%	50%–60%	Mixed
FID↓	EC	2.83	**3.45**	5.78	16.24	21.77	36.49	13.53
	CTSDG	2.88	3.62	6.13	15.52	20.09	35.31	12.85
	Ours	**2.75**	3.53	**5.77**	**15.35**	**19.98**	**34.79**	**12.73**
SSIM↑	EC	0.954	0.927	0.885	0.841	0.769	0.724	0.862
	CTSDG	0.961	0.932	0.884	0.850	0.782	0.737	0.864
	Ours	**0.968**	**0.935**	**0.890**	**0.863**	**0.795**	**0.750**	**0.879**
PSNR↑	EC	31.85	30.43	26.68	24.49	21.33	19.92	25.18
	CTSDG	32.17	30.79	27.05	24.91	22.87	20.64	25.63
	Ours	**32.84**	**31.10**	**27.15**	**25.07**	**23.19**	**20.71**	**26.02**

blurriness in those generated under the guidance of the edge information, which demonstrates that edge structure information can benefit the performance of image completion.

Transformer Blocks. We experiment on changing the transformer blocks to dilated convolutional layers in either or both of our edge estimation network and image reconstruction network, and evaluate with mixed masks. The result shown in Table 3 demonstrates that our proposed model with the transformer blocks outputs better image inpainting results than a similar network without the transformer blocks.

Table 2. Quantitative results with EC, CTSDG, ICT and our model on the European Cities dataset.

	Mask	0%–10%	10%–20%	20%–30%	30%–40%	40%–50%	50%–60%	Mixed
FID↓	EC	2.85	3.67	6.29	16.37	26.42	35.86	15.21
	CTSDG	2.53	3.18	**5.97**	14.61	23.34	**32.85**	13.92
	ICT	2.80	3.75	6.33	16.16	24.71	36.64	15.09
	Ours	**2.48**	**3.12**	6.04	**14.57**	**23.30**	33.26	**13.75**
SSIM↑	EC	0.913	0.904	0.858	0.807	0.775	0.751	0.823
	CTSDG	**0.915**	0.907	0.861	0.814	0.780	0.766	0.837
	ICT	0.910	0.899	0.855	0.809	0.772	0.757	0.829
	Ours	**0.915**	**0.908**	**0.869**	**0.823**	**0.788**	**0.770**	**0.842**
PSNR↑	EC	26.68	25.93	23.89	22.17	20.04	15.33	23.19
	CTSDG	27.24	26.57	24.18	22.36	20.79	**16.63**	23.98
	ICT	26.83	25.91	23.97	22.19	19.23	16.30	23.23
	Ours	**28.31**	**27.04**	**25.11**	**22.95**	**20.82**	16.61	**24.20**

a) Ground Truth   b) Masked Input   c) Without Edge   d) With Edge

Fig. 6. Image inpainting result with/without edge information on the European Cities dataset.

Table 3. Quantitative results with/without transformer blocks (T-BLK) on the European Cities dataset.

Method	FID↓	SSIM↑	PSNR↑
Only Step 1 with T-BLK	14.69	0.828	23.74
Only Step 2 with T-BLK	14.52	0.831	23.35
Both Steps w./o. T-BLK	15.33	0.822	23.17
Both Steps with T-BLK	**13.75**	**0.842**	**24.20**

5 Conclusions

We propose a transformer-based generative adversarial network for edge-guided image inpainting. Our two-step approach includes an edge estimation network and an image completion network and fills in the missing regions in the image based on the estimated edge structure information. We evaluate our model against other state-of-the-art image inpainting methods and the experiments demonstrate that our model shows a better performance of generating pixels in missing regions and produces visually appealing results for image recovery. For future work, we plan to explore the refinement of our model for better recovery of images with higher resolution.

References

1. Avrithis, Y., Kalantidis, Y., Tolias, G., Spyrou, E.: Retrieving landmark and non-landmark images from community photo collections. In: Proceedings of ACM Multimedia (Full paper) (MM 2010), Firenze, Italy (2010)
2. Cao, C., Fu, Y.: Learning a sketch tensor space for image inpainting of man-made scenes. In: Proceedings of the IEEE/CVF International Conference on Computer Vision, pp. 14509–14518 (2021)
3. Darabi, S., Shechtman, E., Barnes, C., Goldman, D.B., Sen, P.: Image melding: combining inconsistent images using patch-based synthesis. ACM Trans. Graph. (TOG) **31**(4), 1–10 (2012)
4. Dong, Q., Cao, C., Fu, Y.: Incremental transformer structure enhanced image inpainting with masking positional encoding. In: Proceedings of the IEEE/CVF Conference on Computer Vision and Pattern Recognition, pp. 11358–11368 (2022)
5. Dosovitskiy, A., et al.: An image is worth 16×16 words: transformers for image recognition at scale. arXiv preprint arXiv:2010.11929 (2020)
6. Fan, Q., Zhang, L.: A novel patch matching algorithm for exemplar-based image inpainting. Multimed. Tools Appl. **77**(9), 10807–10821 (2018)
7. Guo, Q., Gao, S., Zhang, X., Yin, Y., Zhang, C.: Patch-based image inpainting via two-stage low rank approximation. IEEE Trans. Visual Comput. Graph. **24**(6), 2023–2036 (2018)
8. Guo, X., Yang, H., Huang, D.: Image inpainting via conditional texture and structure dual generation. In: Proceedings of the IEEE/CVF International Conference on Computer Vision, pp. 14134–14143 (2021)
9. Heusel, M., Ramsauer, H., Unterthiner, T., Nessler, B., Hochreiter, S.: GANs trained by a two time-scale update rule converge to a local Nash equilibrium. In: Advances in Neural Information Processing Systems, vol. 30 (2017)
10. Iizuka, S., Simo-Serra, E., Ishikawa, H.: Globally and locally consistent image completion. ACM Trans. Graph. (ToG) **36**(4), 1–14 (2017)
11. Johnson, J., Alahi, A., Fei-Fei, L.: Perceptual losses for real-time style transfer and super-resolution. In: Leibe, B., Matas, J., Sebe, N., Welling, M. (eds.) ECCV 2016. LNCS, vol. 9906, pp. 694–711. Springer, Cham (2016). https://doi.org/10.1007/978-3-319-46475-6_43
12. Lee, C.-H., Liu, Z., Wu, L., Luo, P.: MaskGAN: towards diverse and interactive facial image manipulation. In: IEEE Conference on Computer Vision and Pattern Recognition (CVPR) (2020)
13. Li, H., Luo, W., Huang, J.: Localization of diffusion-based inpainting in digital images. IEEE Trans. Inf. Forensics Secur. **12**(12), 3050–3064 (2017)

296   H. Liang and C. Kambhamettu

14. Li, K., Wei, Y., Yang, Z., Wei, W.: Image inpainting algorithm based on tv model and evolutionary algorithm. Soft. Comput. **20**(3), 885–893 (2016)
15. Li, W., Lin, Z., Zhou, K., Qi, L., Wang, Y., Jia, J.: MAT: mask-aware transformer for large hole image inpainting. In: Proceedings of the IEEE/CVF Conference on Computer Vision and Pattern Recognition, pp. 10758–10768 (2022)
16. Liu, G., Shih, K., Wang, T.-C., Tao, A., Catanzaro, B., et al.: Image in-painting for irregular holes using partial convolutions, 26 September 2019. US Patent App. 16/360,895
17. Liu, H., Wang, Y., Wang, M., Rui, Y.: Delving globally into texture and structure for image inpainting. In: Proceedings of the 30th ACM International Conference on Multimedia, pp. 1270–1278 (2022)
18. Nazeri, K., Ng, E., Joseph, T., Qureshi, F.Z., Ebrahimi, M.: EdgeConnect: generative image inpainting with adversarial edge learning. arXiv preprint arXiv:1901.00212 (2019)
19. Pathak, D., Krahenbuhl, P., Donahue, J., Darrell, T., Efros, A.A.: Context encoders: feature learning by inpainting. In: Proceedings of the IEEE Conference on Computer Vision and Pattern Recognition, pp. 2536–2544 (2016)
20. Sajjadi, M.S.M., Schölkopf, B., Hirsch, M.: EnhanceNet: single image super-resolution through automated texture synthesis. arXiv preprint arXiv:1612.07919 (2016)
21. Sridevi, G., Srinivas Kumar, S.: Image inpainting based on fractional-order nonlinear diffusion for image reconstruction. Circuits Syst. Signal Process. **38**(8), 3802–3817 (2019)
22. Strudel, R., Garcia, R., Laptev, I., Schmid, C.: Segmenter: transformer for semantic segmentation. In: Proceedings of the IEEE/CVF International Conference on Computer Vision, pp. 7262–7272 (2021)
23. Wan, Z., Zhang, J., Chen, D., Liao, J.: High-fidelity pluralistic image completion with transformers. In: Proceedings of the IEEE/CVF International Conference on Computer Vision, pp. 4692–4701 (2021)
24. Wang, H., Jiao, L., Hao, W., Bie, R.: New inpainting algorithm based on simplified context encoders and multi-scale adversarial network. Procedia Comput. Sci. **147**, 254–263 (2019)
25. Wang, T-C., Liu, M.-Y., Zhu, J.-Y., Tao, A., Kautz, J., Catanzaro, B.: High-resolution image synthesis and semantic manipulation with conditional GANs. In: Proceedings of the IEEE Conference on Computer Vision and Pattern Recognition, pp. 8798–8807 (2018)
26. Wang, Z., Bovik, A.C., Sheikh, H.R., Simoncelli, E.P.: Image quality assessment: from error visibility to structural similarity. IEEE Trans. Image Process. **13**(4), 600–612 (2004)
27. Yeh, R.A., Chen, C., Lim, T.Y., Schwing, A.G., Hasegawa-Johnson, M., Do, M.N.: Semantic image inpainting with deep generative models. In: Proceedings of the IEEE Conference on Computer Vision and Pattern Recognition, pp. 5485–5493 (2017)
28. Yu, J., Lin, Z., Yang, J., Shen, X., Lu, X., Huang, T.S.: Generative image inpainting with contextual attention. In: Proceedings of the IEEE Conference on Computer Vision and Pattern Recognition, pp. 5505–5514 (2018)
29. Yu, Y., Du, D., Zhang, L., Luo, T.: Unbiased multi-modality guidance for image inpainting. In: Avidan, S., Brostow, G., Cissé, M., Farinella, G.M., Hassner, T. (eds.) ECCV 2022. LNCS, vol. 13676, pp. 668–684. Springer, Cham (2022). https://doi.org/10.1007/978-3-031-19787-1_38

Posters

Bayesian Fusion Inspired 3D Reconstruction via LiDAR-Stereo Camera Pair

Ickbum Kim$^{(\boxtimes)}$ (ID) and Sandeep Singh (ID)

Advanced Space Concepts Lab (ASCLab), Rensselaer Polytechnic Institute,
Troy, NY 12180, USA
`kimi7@rpi.edu`
`http://www.asclabrpi.com`

Abstract. A Bayesian Inference inspired methodology is presented for 3D reconstruction using LiDAR-Stereo Pair fusion. While low-cost LiDARs provide limited detail, stereo vision algorithms suffer from illumination and parameter tuning challenges. The proposed approach uses a Gaussian Process Regression (GPR) model trained on the sparse LiDAR depth-map and leverages the statistical measures from the predictive model to perform linear correction and confidence region denoising with the dense Stereo depth-map. The methodology is demonstrated on a complex 3D printed object and the results demonstrate efficacy in compensating for the sparsity of LiDAR point clouds and stereo inaccuracies, resulting in denser 3D reconstructions and highly accurate depth maps. The integration of GPR-based fusion showcases the potential for robust scene reconstruction and localization.

Keywords: 3D Reconstruction · Sensor Fusion · Gaussian Process Regression · Stereo Vision

1 Introduction

Creating an accurate digital twin of the surroundings provides a critical solution to analyze the environment for robust localization, anomaly detection, and path planning. With the recent development of low-cost LiDARs, the technology has become more accessible to general users, enabling 3D scanning at a coarse level. However, the data retrieved by the low-cost LiDARs is insufficient to provide a detailed interpretation of the surroundings and can merely estimate a superficial trend. Although there are LiDARs that are able to provide image-quality 3D point clouds, economic viability is a major challenge.

An alternative to LiDAR is stereo vision. Stereo vision is a technique that uses two or more images from slightly different perspectives to perceive depth and create a 3D representation of a scene. Stereo Processing algorithms such as

G. Bebis et al. (Eds.): ISVC 2023, LNCS 14362, pp. 299–310, 2023.
https://doi.org/10.1007/978-3-031-47966-3_23

Semi-Global Matching [5] can produce dense disparity maps that can be post-processed for estimating depth. However, such intensity-based matching algorithms are susceptible to illumination conditions. Therefore, multiple parameters such as focal length and baseline need to be adjusted to achieve optimal accuracy [6] which in most cases, is worse than that induced by time of flight for their LiDAR counterparts.

Over the past few years, many researchers have worked on integrating LiDAR and Stereo depth using deep Convolutional Neural Networks (CNNs) [2,9,15]. CNN-based techniques take stereo images and sparse LiDAR data as input to create denser 3D maps but their performance is highly correlated to the quality of the images and the accuracy of the feature extraction algorithms. Real-time probabilistic methods have shown promise by increasing the computation efficiency and accuracy by using LiDAR data as anchor points [8]. The application of Gaussian processes is demonstrated in [3]. In this work, a multi-sensor data fusion model is constructed by initially making predictions using a high-density dataset. These predictions are then refined with greater accuracy using a low-density dataset, achieved through the introduction of a linkage model. Another noteworthy approach to data fusion utilizing GPs is presented in [14]. This approach involves enhancing hyperparameters by incorporating new data into an existing GP model and employing dependent GPs to individually model each dataset. These dependent GPs facilitate the learning of spatial correlations through covariances. In the context of data fusion with varying modalities, inference-based regression methods offer a promising solution. For bi-sensor fusion, one approach involves treating data from one source as sparse but more accurate. Here, we fit an interpolating function to this data and employ statistical measures from the predictive model to condition denser but less accurate data from the second source. Non-parametric regression techniques, exemplified in [4,7,13], have proven highly effective for sparse datasets. These Bayesian-inference-based methods introduce a stochastic element, yielding a confidence metric for the predictive model. This valuable information facilitates intelligent data fusion, a feature lacking in traditional parametric approaches.

In this paper, we present an approach to explore multi-modality sensor fusion and provide a methodology for up-scaled 3D reconstruction through intelligent data fusion from a LiDAR and stereo camera pair. Our approach is inspired by the Gaussian Process Regression (GPR) method, and we apply the methodology to experimental data to demonstrate its applicability. Unlike the traditional methodology for sensor fusion shown in [3,14], the GP model is trained on the sparse sensor data with higher accuracy to effectively filter higher density data points. The rest of the paper explores fundamental principles and techniques of stereo depth estimation, evaluates the performance of our approach, and examines the challenges and considerations in sensor fusion, including data alignment, loss of data, and denoising.

2 Preliminaries

2.1 Stereo Depth Using Semi-Global Matching

Occlusion and discontinuous scenes are the major challenges for traditional block matching algorithms. These algorithms generally consider small local regions without taking global context into consideration. Therefore, discontinuities in the object boundaries and occlusions that differ in the stereo pair images often lead to incorrect correspondence matching. Semi-Global Matching (SGM) was first introduced in [5] and has undergone further refinements and variations to make notable improvements over the traditional block matching algorithms.

2.2 Gaussian Process Regression

Gaussian Process Regression (GPR) is a non-parametric Bayesian approach for modeling complex relationships in data. It is based on the concept of Gaussian Processes (GPs) and its application in machine learning is introduced in [11]. A GP is a group of random variables, where any finite number of its collection follows a joint Gaussian distribution [11]. Rather than modeling a single deterministic function, GPs provide a way to model a distribution of possible functions that are consistent with the observed data.

A GP is fully defined by the combination of a mean function and a covariance function as [12]:

$$f(x) \sim \mathcal{GP}(\mu(x), k(x, x')), \tag{1}$$

where $\mu(x)$ is the mean function and $k(x, x')$ is the covariance function of the relationship between points x and x', also known as the kernel.

The objective of GPR is to model a function given a set of input and output pairs (x_i, y_i). It makes no assumptions about the fundamental form of the training data, unlike conventional parametric models. Instead, it defines a prior distribution over the function and updates it based on the observed data (x_i, y_i). The joint distribution of the observed data and the predicted values is defined as:

$$\begin{bmatrix} y \\ f_* \end{bmatrix} \sim [\mathcal{N}] \left(0, \begin{bmatrix} K(X, X) & K(X, X_*) \\ K(X_*, X) & K(X_*, X_*) \end{bmatrix} \right), \tag{2}$$

where y is the observed data, f_* is the predicted values at new input locations X_*, and K is the covariance matrix of observed input points. Consequently, a posterior distribution conditioned on the known data points is computed via Baye's rule. The predictive mean at x^* can be evaluated by:

$$\mu(x^*) = k(x^*, X)(K + \sigma^2 I)^{-1} y, \tag{3}$$

where X represents the observed input points, y is the vector of observed outputs, σ^2 is the noise variance, and I is the identity matrix. The predictive variance at x^* indicates the uncertainty in its prediction, and it can be evaluated with the following:

$$\sigma^2(x^*) = k(x^*, x^*) - k(x^*, X)(K + \sigma^2 I)^{-1} k(X, x^*). \tag{4}$$

Since GPs produce a scalable multi-resolution prediction of the trained model, it can be sampled at any desired resolution [14]. The ability to provide flexible sampling and an uncertainty measure allows quantification of prediction confidence and can be used for intelligent fusion of data. In this paper, GPR is used to perform LiDAR-Stereo Fusion.

3   LiDAR-Stereo Fusion

In the following section, the Bayesian approach to LiDAR-Stereo fusion is explored to counteract the existing challenges. An interesting methodology is proposed for depth estimation from stereo vision, data integration, and data denoising leveraging a trained GPR model on sparse LiDAR data.

3.1   Problem Formulation and Overview

In this paper, the LiDAR-Stereo fusion is performed using the Solid State LiDAR Intel Realsense L515 and two Allied Vision 1800 U-500 cameras. The fusion process encounters a common challenge arising from the stochastic nature of the observed data in both sensors. While alignment between the sensors can be achieved with minimal error, maintaining consistent correspondence globally poses a significant challenge. It is evident from Fig. 1, that the depth information observed at a specific pixel in one sensor may be absent in the other. Another obstacle is the absence of a reliable metric to evaluate inaccuracies. Stereo depth estimation techniques, such as Semi-Global Block Matching (SGBM), often generate inaccurate depth estimations due to their local nature. To address this issue and avoid reliance on inaccurate information, a deterministic model coupled with pixel-level uncertainty becomes essential.

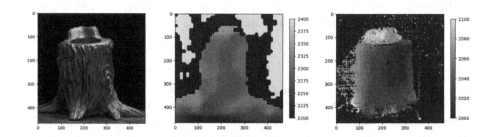

Fig. 1. Aligned RGB, LiDAR, Stereo Depth data.

Figure 2 shows the overview of our approach. The approach can be divided into four major steps:

1. **Stereo Depth Estimation**: Semi-Global Block Matching algorithm is used to estimate depth, providing dense but noisy data.

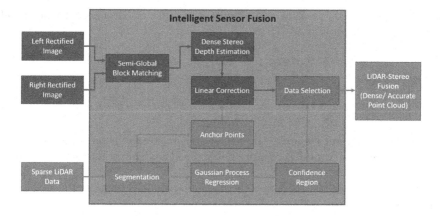

Fig. 2. Schematic of LiDAR-Stereo fusion.

2. **Segmentation of LiDAR data**: Sparse LiDAR data is segmented to minimize inaccurate integration in the object boundaries
3. **GPR on sparse LiDAR data**: GPR model is trained on the sparse LiDAR data to compute a confidence region based on the predicted uncertainties.
4. **Data Selection and Integration**: Using the confidence region calculated from the GPR prediction, inaccurate data are discarded.

The following sections explore these steps in detail, demonstrating how the Bayesian approach offers a viable solution to the aforementioned challenges.

3.2 Stereo Depth Estimation

Two RGB images taken from the stereo setting are rectified using the known intrinsic and extrinsic parameters. Figure 3 shows the rectified images. The RGB images used are 2592X1944 in resolution.

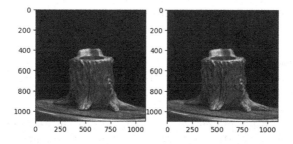

Fig. 3. Rectified Images from Left and Right RGB cameras.

The disparity map is generated using the SGBM algorithm. The Semi-Global Matching algorithm scans along the epipolar lines to determine the disparity where the aggregated cost is at a minimum. The efficient Birchfield-Tomasi pixel dissimilarity function is used [1]:

$$\bar{d}(x_L, x_R, I_L, I_R) = \min_{x_{R-\frac{1}{2}} \leq x \leq x_{R+\frac{1}{2}}} |I_L(x_L) - \hat{I}_R(x)|, \tag{5}$$

$$\bar{d}(x_R, x_L, I_R, I_L) = \min_{x_{L-\frac{1}{2}} \leq x \leq x_{L+\frac{1}{2}}} |\hat{I}_L(x) - I_R(x_R)|, \tag{6}$$

where x_L, x_R are pixel values in the left and right stereo vision cameras, I_L, I_R represent the intensity, and $\hat{I}_L, \hat{I}_R$ are defined as the linearly interpolated intensity functions.

Birchfield and Tomasi [1] define the dissimilarity as the minimum of the two quantities above:

$$d(x_L, x_R) = min[\bar{d}(x_L, x_R, I_L, I_R), \bar{d}(x_R, x_L, I_R, I_L)], \tag{7}$$

where $d(x_L, x_R)$ symbolizes the dissimilarity d between the pixels. In this work, 8 directions scan was used to maximize performance. However, the number of directions can be decreased to avoid memory overload (i.e. single pass, 3-way). Due to noisy disparity output for single pixel-wise cost calculation, blocks with pixel size 7 were matched for accuracy. The penalty parameters determining the smoothness of the disparity are tuned to avoid discontinuities while maintaining the level of complexity to capture details. The depth is calculated using the following equation.

$$Z_{xy} = (B * f)/D_{xy}, \tag{8}$$

where Z_{xy} is the depth at pixel location (x,y), B is the baseline, f is the focal length in pixels and D_{xy} is the disparity at the pixel.

3.3 Segmentation of LiDAR Data

Computation time for training a GPR model increases quadratically with the number of training data. GPR involves computing the covariance matrix between all pairs of training data points, which requires $O(n^2)$ computations, where O is the order of growth and n is the number of input data points. Therefore, dividing the LiDAR data into smaller segments decreases the computation time. In addition, solid state LiDARs tend to have background interference on smaller objects. Therefore, training GPR on the boundaries may lead to wrong predictions coupled with exorbitant uncertainties. The background interference on smaller objects is shown in Fig. 4.

The denoising technique employed in our approach, as elaborated later in Sect. 3.5, relies on the GPR covariance predictions. Consequently, training the model on misleading data can introduce biases into the integration result. To mitigate this, a segmentation process is employed to isolate different objects within the observed data, thereby minimizing background interference and enabling more accurate calculation of confidence regions.

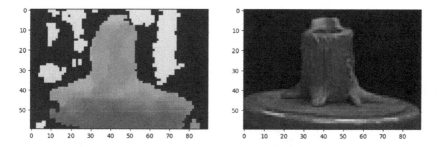

Fig. 4. (Left) LiDAR data with noisy boundary prediction. (Right) Aligned color image of the same resolution. (Color figure online)

Object segmentation involves analyzing the local maxima and minima within the point cloud population density curves of the point cloud in the x, y, and z directions. The highest population densities correspond to the centers of the objects, while the boundaries between multiple objects can be identified by the lowest local points.

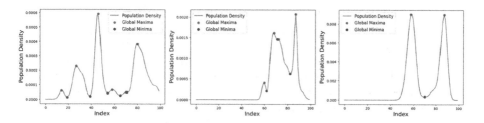

Fig. 5. Population Density Curves in x, y, z

Figure 5 illustrates the population density curve in the x, y, and z directions. The evaluation of population density curves in the x and y directions occurs after the segmentation in the z (distance) direction, enabling a clear distinction between multiple objects at the same distance. In complex scenes where multiple objects are intertwined, multiple iterations are often required to accurately detect the object boundaries. However, rough segmentation is sufficient to minimize the misleading information for the GPR training. Figure 6 shows the original scene on the left, and one of the segmentation results in the z, x, and y directions from left to right.

3.4   GPR on Sparse LiDAR Data

The Rational Quadratic (RQ) kernel from [10] is used to train each segmented sparse LiDAR data. The kernel determines the shape of the covariance bounds after data fitting:

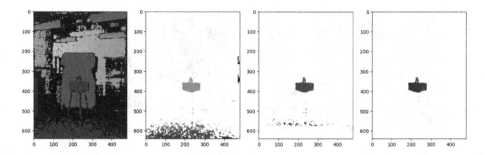

Fig. 6. Segmentation Result of our population density methodology applied to the target object. From left to right, the figures shows the original depth map, *detph*, *x*, and *y* direction segmentation results.

$$k(x_i, x_j) = \left(1 + \frac{d(x_i, x_j)^2}{2\alpha l^2}\right)^{-\alpha}, \tag{9}$$

where $d(x_i, x_j)$ is the Euclidean distance, l is the length-scale parameter and α is the scale mixture parameter. The α parameter controls the smoothness of the trained model, offering the ability to react to the complexity of the data set.

Segmented LiDAR point clouds are used as inputs for training separate GPR models. 99% confidence region, equivalent to approximately $\pm 3\sigma$ covariance bounds, is calculated for individual pixels based on the trained model. Figure 7 depicts the segmented point cloud along with their corresponding GPR predictions. The covariance bounds associated with the predictions tend to be narrower in regions of observed LiDAR point cloud raw data. This information is used to discard outlier depth estimates from the stereo-pair, thereby providing an accurate, up-scaled point cloud. The following section discusses the integration approach in more detail.

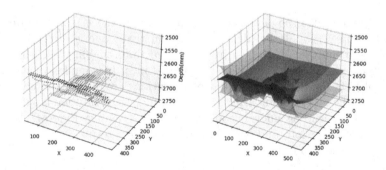

Fig. 7. (Left) Point cloud data. (Right) GPR prediction result including three surfaces: prediction (color varying with depth), upper (blue) and lower (red) covariance bounds with 0.1 transparency. (Color figure online)

3.5 Data Selection and Integration

Integrating the LiDAR data and Stereo depth estimation requires two stages:

Linear Correction. The Intel Realsense L515 model provides depth accuracy ranging from 5 mm to 14 mm within a maximum depth of 9 m. Sparse yet accurate LiDAR points are utilized as reference points for calculating the offset of stereo depth estimation. To interpolate the stereo estimation error on the reference points, the Quickhull algorithm was employed which provided a highly efficient and fast interpolation method and computes the convex hull by recursively partitioning and connecting extreme points.

Confidence Region Denoising. Linearly corrected stereo depth estimation is denoised using the confidence region predicted by the GPR prediction. The upper and lower bounds in respective pixels provide a quantifiable metric to determine the accuracy of the predictions. Any stereo depth estimate that falls outside of this confidence region is considered unreliable and thus discarded. Finally, raw LiDAR points are appended to the selected stereo depth estimates to perform the comprehensive fused dataset.

4 Experimental Results and Discussion

Integration results with different approaches are demonstrated and evaluated in this section. Integration without post processing is provided in Fig. 8.

Fig. 8. Original data integrated without post-processing. From left to right, raw LiDAR data, stereo depth estimation, and integrated results are shown (in [m]).

The original LiDAR data depicted in Fig. 8 exhibits a sparse yet accurate representation of the 3D space. However, the limited quantity of available data restricts our ability to interpret the environment with a high degree of precision. In contrast, the stereo depth estimation output in the middle provides a substantial amount of data points. Despite the abundance of data, the noise level is too high to allow for meaningful interpretation. These discrepancies become evident

Fig. 9. (Left) Linearly corrected stereo depth. (Right) Linearly corrected stereo depth with prediction bounds filtering (in $[m]$).

when examining the integrated result on the right, as the alignment between the LiDAR reference points and the values obtained from stereo depth estimation is compromised.

In Fig. 9, the integration results are presented, demonstrating the impact of applying linear correction alone and combining it with confidence region denoising. The integration outcome when linear correction is applied reveals a more precise alignment of the depth information. Nevertheless, the integration result exhibits a noisy point cloud. In contrast, the synergistic application of both linear correction and confidence region denoising yields an environment reconstruction that not only achieves precise alignment but also effectively reduces prominent noise artifacts. The final integration result is shown in Fig. 10.

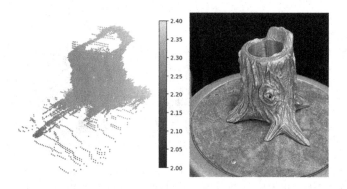

Fig. 10. (Left) Corrected stereo depth estimation integrated with the LiDAR raw data (in $[m]$). (Right)Isometric color view of the object. (Color figure online)

The integration result is assessed in Table 1, providing the corresponding data point counts achieved at each stage and with each approach. To gauge the performance of the methodology, we calculate the Chamfer Distance (CD), which reflects the minimum total distance between the LiDAR data and Stereo depth data. Then it is normalized by dividing by the total number of points. Real world unit (in m) is used to calculate the CD.

Table 1. Performance Evaluation

Data Type (methodology)	Number of Data Points (N)	Upscaled	CD/N
LiDAR only	1813	1x	0
Stereo only	117048	64.6x	0.1716
LiDAR + Stereo (raw)	117703	64.9x	0.1689
Stereo (linear)	117703	64.9x	0.0186
Stereo (linear + denoising)	73312	40.4x	0.0102
LiDAR + Stereo (linear + denoising)	74314	41.0x	0.0099

Given the absence of ground truth and the substantially lower depth error exhibited by LiDAR in comparison to stereo depth estimation, we consider raw LiDAR points as the reference for performance quantification. Table 1 sheds light on key insights concerning the effects of linear correction and confidence region denoising. The raw stereo data exhibits a high deviation, yielding a normalized Chamfer Distance (CD) of 0.1716. However, this deviation primarily arises from baseline calculation errors during camera calibration, which can be readily rectified through linear correction, resulting in a significant decrease to 0.0186. The performance of confidence region denoising is also promising, further reducing the normalized CD to 0.0102. Data fusion between the corrected stereo depth and LiDAR increases the total data points to 74,314 while reducing the normalized CD to 0.0099. This fusion enhances data density by a remarkable 41 times compared to the sparse LiDAR data. Furthermore, linear correction and confidence bounds filtering make substantial improvements to the noisy stereo data, achieving a significant 94.2% reduction from 0.1716 to 0.0099.

5   Conclusion

This paper introduces a novel Bayesian Inference approach to 3D reconstruction, integrating LiDAR and stereo depth estimation. A Gaussian Process Regression fit on accurate sparse data is leveraged to append less accurate dense data intelligently. Through effective error correction in depth estimation and noise reduction techniques, the presented methods significantly enhance the reliability and precision of the reconstruction process. The resulting upscale in the reconstructed 3D environment holds considerable potential, enabling researchers and practitioners to extract valuable insights and make well-informed decisions based on a denser and more accurate representation.

References

1. Birchfield, S., Tomasi, C.: A pixel dissimilarity measure that is insensitive to image sampling. IEEE Trans. Pattern Anal. Mach. Intell. **20**(4), 401–406 (1998)
2. Choe, J., Joo, K., Imtiaz, T., Kweon, I.S.: Volumetric propagation network: stereo-lidar fusion for long-range depth estimation. IEEE Robot. Autom. Lett. **6**(3), 4672–4679 (2021). https://doi.org/10.1109/LRA.2021.3068712
3. Colosimo, B.M., Pacella, M., Senin, N.: Multisensor data fusion via Gaussian process models for dimensional and geometric verification. Precis. Eng. **40**, 199–213 (2015)
4. Deringer, V.L., Bartók, A.P., Bernstein, N., Wilkins, D.M., Ceriotti, M., Csányi, G.: Gaussian process regression for materials and molecules. Chem. Rev. **121**(16), 10073–10141 (2021)
5. Hirschmuller, H.: Accurate and efficient stereo processing by semi-global matching and mutual information. In: 2005 IEEE Computer Society Conference on Computer Vision and Pattern Recognition (CVPR 2005), vol. 2, pp. 807–814 (2005). https://doi.org/10.1109/CVPR.2005.56
6. Kytö, M., Nuutinen, M., Oittinen, P.: Method for measuring stereo camera depth accuracy based on stereoscopic vision. In: Beraldin, J.A., et al. (eds.) Three-Dimensional Imaging, Interaction, and Measurement, vol. 7864, p. 78640I. International Society for Optics and Photonics, SPIE (2011). https://doi.org/10.1117/12.872015
7. Liu, H., Cai, J., Ong, Y.S.: Remarks on multi-output Gaussian process regression. Knowl.-Based Syst. **144**, 102–121 (2018)
8. Maddern, W., Newman, P.: Real-time probabilistic fusion of sparse 3D lidar and dense stereo. In: 2016 IEEE/RSJ International Conference on Intelligent Robots and Systems (IROS), pp. 2181–2188 (2016). https://doi.org/10.1109/IROS.2016.7759342
9. Park, K., Kim, S., Sohn, K.: High-precision depth estimation with the 3D lidar and stereo fusion. In: 2018 IEEE International Conference on Robotics and Automation (ICRA), pp. 2156–2163 (2018). https://doi.org/10.1109/ICRA.2018.8461048
10. Pedregosa, F., et al.: Scikit-learn: machine learning in Python. J. Mach. Learn. Res. **12**, 2825–2830 (2011)
11. Rasmussen, C.E., Williams, C.K., et al.: Gaussian Processes for Machine Learning, vol. 1. Springer, Cham (2006)
12. Singh, S.K., Junkins, J.L.: Stochastic learning and extremal-field map based autonomous guidance of low-thrust spacecraft. Sci. Rep. **12**(1), 17774 (2022)
13. Singh, S.K., Junkins, J.L., Majji, M., Taheri, E.: Rapid accessibility evaluation for ballistic lunar capture via manifolds: a Gaussian process regression application. Astrodynamics **6**(4), 375–397 (2022)
14. Vasudevan, S.: Data fusion with Gaussian processes. Robot. Auton. Syst. **60**(12), 1528–1544 (2012). https://doi.org/10.1016/j.robot.2012.08.006. https://www.sciencedirect.com/science/article/pii/S0921889012001388
15. Wang, T.H., Hu, H.N., Lin, C.H., Tsai, Y.H., Chiu, W.C., Sun, M.: 3D lidar and stereo fusion using stereo matching network with conditional cost volume normalization. In: 2019 IEEE/RSJ International Conference on Intelligent Robots and Systems (IROS), pp. 5895–5902 (2019). https://doi.org/10.1109/IROS40897.2019.8968170

Marimba Mallet Placement Tracker

Daniel Beer and Andrea Salgian$^{(\boxtimes)}$

Department of Computer Science, The College of New Jersey, Ewing, NJ 08628, USA
{beerd1,salgian}@tcnj.edu

Abstract. When playing the marimba, percussionists must always be aware of mallet placement. Striking on top of the rope produces a very dead sound with little resonance, so it should always be avoided. Beginner players often make this mistake, but can learn to avoid it if it is pointed out to them. In this paper we present a system that uses a video recording of a percussionist playing the marimba, and highlights the frames in which they struck above the rope. Since the visual information alone is not enough to accomplish this, the system uses a combination of audio and video processing to detect which of the possible four mallets struck the marimba, and then estimate its position, classifying it as correct or incorrect.

Keywords: marimba · mallet · visual detection · audio processing

1 Introduction

In this paper we present a practice tool that aids marimba percussionists with their mallet positions. Using a video and audio recording of the marimba player, the system will provide feedback that informs them of their improper striking positions. These positions are located above the rope that keeps the bars together.

There is no prior research involving the marimba. The only related research involves drum transcription using recurrent neural networks, where peaks in percussive audio were used to detect mallet strikes [1]. Other works covered multiple percussion instruments [2], but all the research focused on audio recordings [3].

In our case visual processing is required to detect whether the mallet strikes the marimba bar in the correct location. However, the camera position that provides the best view for this purpose, doesn't provide an adequate view for detecting the exact moment of the strike (see Fig. 1). The fact that marimba players use four mallets at a time makes detection even harder, as the top camera view does not provide enough information to detect which mallet struck.

We use audio processing to find the instance that the marimba was struck, as well as the note that was played. Using this information, we can zero in on the bar and the mallet above it, detecting whether the strike occurred in the correct location or not.

The output of our system is a video accompanied by images that highlight the points in time when the percussionist struck in an incorrect spot.

G. Bebis et al. (Eds.): ISVC 2023, LNCS 14362, pp. 311–319, 2023.
https://doi.org/10.1007/978-3-031-47966-3_24

Fig. 1. Top view of a marimba and player with four mallets.

2   Background

2.1   Marimba

Construction and Layout. The marimba is a pitched percussion instrument that is comprised of wooden bars, resonators, and a set of ropes that connect the bars. It is intended to be struck with mallets to produce sound. Figure 2 displays a top view of the marimba that was used for testing. Each bar sounds a different pitch when struck, and this pitch is dependent on the length of the bar. The layout of pitches on a marimba is identical to the layout of a piano, so we will be referring to sharp/flat bars located on the top half of the marimba as the black keys and the natural bars located on the bottom half of the marimba as the white keys. There is one rope that connects the white keys and one rope that connects the black keys. Each rope runs through holes located in the sides of each bar; one hole is positioned towards the top of the bar and the other is positioned towards the bottom of the bar. Each rope bends back around on the right side of the marimba to run through both the top and bottom holes and is connected by two spring hooks on the left side.

Playing the Marimba. Percussionists typically play the marimba with either two or four mallets (one or two in each hand). When using four mallets, we will number the mallets from left to right starting with 1, so the leftmost mallet is known as mallet 1 and the rightmost mallet is known as mallet 4. For our implementation, we asked the players to use blue-headed mallets to create a contrast with the color of the marimba (colorful marimba mallets are not unusual). The color mask used to find the mallets that will be discussed later is also calibrated to single out this shade of blue.

Fig. 2. Standard 4 1/3 octave marimba.

Resonance. Mallet positioning is a topic of interest and concern for many marimba players. With careful striking positions, percussionists can play with varying levels of resonance [4]. When striking the bar in the center, the most resonant sound is produced. This position is considered the best in most scenarios, especially when playing legato sections in music. On the other hand, striking the bar on top of the rope produces the least resonant sound and is almost always advised against. The last striking position is on the edge of the bars—typically the bottom edge of the white keys. This produces a sound that is not quite as resonant as striking in the center, but it is adequate. Striking on the edge is often used when playing chords that involve playing a white and black key with the same hand where the center of the bar cannot be practically reached.

2.2   The Physics of Music

Volume and Pitch. The frequency that a sound wave oscillates at corresponds to the pitch that our ears perceive from it. The amplitude of sound waves corresponds to their intensity/volume [5]. Since frequencies can be any positive number, many of them do not correspond to a perfectly tuned note in Western music. Assuming that a marimba was constructed properly and has not been severely damaged, its bars will always sound frequencies that are extremely close, if not exact, to notes in Western music. Figure 3 displays a handful of these notes and their corresponding frequencies [6]. A marimba strike will generate a sound wave whose amplitude will decay over time.

Harmonic Frequencies. The harmonic series is a natural occurrence and is present whenever sound waves are oscillating. This series involves a multitude of

C_3	130.81
$C^{\#}_3/D^{b}_3$	138.59
D_3	146.83
$D^{\#}_3/E^{b}_3$	155.56
E_3	164.81
F_3	174.61
$F^{\#}_3/G^{b}_3$	185.00
G_3	196.00
$G^{\#}_3/A^{b}_3$	207.65
A_3	220.00
$A^{\#}_3/B^{b}_3$	233.08
B_3	246.94
C_4	261.63

Fig. 3. Table of Frequencies Ranging from C3 to C4

frequencies, known as overtones, resonating at decreasing volumes in response to the initial frequency. Mathematically, the frequencies that are double, triple, quadruple, etc. the initial frequency will sound [5]. Many of these frequencies correspond directly to a Western pitch, but as the multiplier continues, the frequencies stray further and further from an established pitch. The harmonic series of A2 is annotated with the appropriate tuning offsets in Fig. 4.

Fig. 4. The Harmonic Series of A2 110 Hz [7]

3 Methodology

3.1 Audio Processing

We use the MoviePy Python library [8] to extract the audio for analysis. Since percussionists typically play with either two or four mallets, we need to find the mallet(s) that were used to strike a bar each time an audio peak was produced. In order to pinpoint the mallet(s), we need to find the pitches of the peak in the amplitude of the sound wave(s). Given that there can be anywhere from one to four strikes per peak, and outliers can pop up from the initial detection that will be discussed later, we need thresholds to filter out the incorrect pitches and retain the correct pitches.

Detecting Peaks. Percussion instruments are struck, which implies that the sounds they produce are loudest at the attack, and fade away to nothing over time. This is an important contrast to wind instruments, where the volume of a note can peak at any time depending on the player's airflow. As a result, the frame at which the bar is struck is very close to the frame at which the peak occurs. To detect these peaks in the audio, we used the peak_pick from the Librosa Python library [9], to scan the audio and return the frame of each peak. This function requires parameters that refine the range of choices, as well as the number of samples to wait after picking a peak to avoid detecting the same note twice. Figure 5 shows an isolated audio clip in which this function would detect the peak. We use the piptrack function from Librosa to extract the frequencies and magnitudes of these peaks.

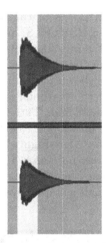

Fig. 5. Sound wave of struck Marimba bar

Tuning Threshold. Since every note in Western music has a matching standardized frequency, we converted every detected strike to its appropriate note. Since the bars of the marimba are constructed to play specific Western notes, we implemented a tuning offset threshold that removes any frequencies that are at least 0.2 fractions of a bin (1.16%) away from the standard frequency of their assigned notes.

Some frequencies that do not match the frequencies of the bars that were struck still passed this filter. These are the overtones of the initial frequency. When striking on the rope, the overtones resonate at a much louder volume, particularly the fourth harmonic (two octaves above the starting note). As stated earlier, not all overtones fit neatly into the equal tempered tuning system, but the second and fourth harmonics are exactly in tune. As a result, the tuning offset threshold cannot dismiss these additional frequencies, but they will be discarded during the visual processing stage as explained below. Acknowledging these frequencies is important. Extracting only the notes that were struck would require additional filtering.

Magnitude Threshold. White noise can permeate an audio file to extensive degrees depending on the quality of the microphone or the surroundings in general. When an audio file contains white noise, the piptrack function returns the frequencies for it as well. Generally, this white noise is quieter than the sound of the marimba, so we use a volume/magnitude threshold to help filter it out. The threshold value is based on the average magnitude for all of the detected pitches and was determined experimentally.

3.2   Visual Bar and Mallet Segmentation

To segment the bars, we use an image of the marimba that doesn't contain mallets. We use a combination of HSV, HLS, and RGB masks to segment the marimba from the background. A canny edge detector and a probabilistic Hough lines transform are used to extract the outlines of the marimba, showed in Fig. 6: the vertical edges of the bars are shown in green, the horizontal line separating the "black" and "white" keys of the marimba is shown in blue, and the outer edges of the marimba are shown in red. These lines are used to extract the bounding boxes of each bar. The position of the rope is also estimated based on the location of the horizontal outer edge. Figure 7 Bars are then associated with their notes, starting with the lowest note on a 4 1/3 octave marimba (A2), and repeatedly multiplying its frequency by $2^{1/12}$ and converting to the appropriate pitch. This will always move us half a step above the previous note.

Fig. 6. Masked marimba image (left), and Hough transform output (right)

Each time a bar is struck, we crop the bar from the image, and use a color mask to segment the mallet Fig. 8. If no mallet is found, the frequency is the result of an overtone that was not eliminated by the thresholds, and is discarded. Otherwise, we measure the distance between the position of the mallet and the rope, to detect whether this was a rope strike or not.

Fig. 7. Segmented bars (keys) and estimated rope position

Fig. 8. Binary image of mallet on cropped marimba bar

After each frame is processed, we concatenate everything into an output video that shows every strike with its corresponding note. Figure 9 shows a frame. At the end of the video, we also show the overall number of strikes and rope strikes.

Fig. 9. Frame from output video showing a rope strike

4   Results

Due to the Covid pandemic, we had limited access to a marimba. We tested our system on three video recordings: two videos where the percussionist struck notes mostly one at a time in isolation at a slow pace, mixing in rope strikes at random, and one where the percussionist played the piece, "A Cricket Sang and Set the Sun" by Blake Tyson, which requires fast playing with precision, and striking multiple notes at a time.

Results are shown in Table 1. Our system missed all but one strike, and had two false positive strike detections. The rope strikes were correctly detected 100% of the time.

Table 1. Detection results

Video	Total Strikes	Detected Strikes	False Positives	Rope Strikes	Detected Rope Strikes	False Positives
random	12	12	0	5	5	0
random2	10	9	0	4	4	0
cricket	68	68	2	3	3	0
Total	90	89 (98.8%)	2	12	12 (100%)	0

5   Conclusion and Future Work

In this paper we presented an application that uses a video recording with audio of a percussionist playing the marimba with one to four mallets, to generate a video and images highlighting where the player struck bars over the rope. The utilization of audio processing allowed us to determine which mallet struck the marimba. Visual detection algorithms allowed us to isolate the marimba and mallet, and to compare the mallet's position to the rope's position. With this program, percussionists can enhance their practice sessions by having a camera watch over and pinpoint any mistakes that they might not have noticed.

Unfortunately we were not able to test the application on too many videos. A few more videos would allow for better parameter adjustment, and would further demonstrate performance.

Further additions can make this application more accurate and versatile. By incorporating the sheet music that a percussionist is playing when practicing the marimba, we can cross-reference with the score to ensure that the musician played the correct note, and alert them when an incorrect note was played. The current version of the application only catches rope strikes, not generally incorrect notes.

Other pitched percussion instruments, such as the vibraphone, xylophone, and glockenspiel, are structured very similarly to the marimba, with the only differences being in colors and sizes. Minor modifications to our approach could accommodate these instruments.

References

1. Vogl, R., Dorfer, M., Knees, P.: Drum transcription from polyphonic music with recurrent neural networks. In: 2017 IEEE International Conference on Acoustics, Speech and Signal Processing (ICASSP), New Orleans, LA, pp. 201–205 (2017)
2. Tian, M., Srinivasamurthy A., Sandler, M., Serra, X.: A study of instrument-wise onset detection in Beijing Opera percussion ensembles. In: 2014 IEEE International Conference on Acoustics, Speech and Signal Processing (ICASSP), Florence, pp. 2159–2163 (2014)
3. Manoj Kumar, P.A., Sebastian, J., Murthy, H.A.: Musical onset detection on carnatic percussion instruments. In: 2015 Twenty First National Conference on Communications (NCC), Mumbai, pp. 1–6 (2015)
4. Kastner, K.: The emergence and evolution of a generalized marimba technique. DMA thesis, University of Illinois at Urbana-Champaign (1989)
5. Johnston, I.: Measured Tones: The Interplay of Physics and Music, 3rd edn. CRC Press, Boca Raton (2009)
6. Physics of Music Notes. Frequencies of Musical Notes, A4 = 440 Hz. pages.mtu.edu/ suits/notefreqs.html. Accessed 14 June 2023
7. Oberton. The Harmonic Series. https://www.oberton.org/en/overtone-singing/harmonic-series/. Accessed 14 June 2023
8. User Guide - MoviePy 1.0.2 Documentation. zulko.github.io/moviepy/. Accessed 14 June 2023
9. librosa - librosa 0.10.0 documentation. https://librosa.org/doc/latest/index.html. Accessed 14 June 2023

DINO-CXR: A Self Supervised Method Based on Vision Transformer for Chest X-Ray Classification

Mohammadreza Shakouri[(✉)], Fatemeh Iranmanesh, and Mahdi Eftekhari

Department of Computer Engineering, Shahid Bahonar University of Kerman, Kerman, Iran
{mohammadrezashakouri,firanmanesh}@eng.uk.ac.ir, m.eftekhari@uk.ac.ir

Abstract. The limited availability of labeled chest X-ray datasets is a significant bottleneck in the development of medical imaging methods. Self-supervised learning (SSL) can mitigate this problem by training models on unlabeled data. Furthermore, self-supervised pretraining has yielded promising results in visual recognition of natural images but has not been given much consideration in medical image analysis. In this work, we propose a self-supervised method, DINO-CXR, which is a novel adaptation of a self-supervised method, DINO, based on a vision transformer for chest X-ray classification. A comparative analysis is performed to show the effectiveness of the proposed method for both pneumonia and COVID-19 detection. Through a quantitative analysis, it is also shown that the proposed method outperforms state-of-the-art methods in terms of accuracy and achieves comparable results in terms of AUC and F-1 score while requiring significantly less labeled data.

Keywords: Deep Learning · Self-supervised Learning · Chest X-ray Classification

1 Introduction

The use of medical image classification has grown significantly in the last decade [14]. Despite a recent slowdown [13], medical imaging remains a vital diagnostic tool, particularly in the detection of pneumonia and COVID-19. Pneumonia is the leading cause of death in children under the age of five worldwide [20]. Additionally, the outbreak of the novel COVID-19 in late 2019 rapidly evolved into a global pandemic, affecting millions of people worldwide. Chest X-rays are one of the most common ways to diagnose pneumonia and COVID-19. They can show lung abnormalities that are consistent with pneumonia or COVID-19.

Chest X-ray (CXR) classification is a more challenging task than natural image classification in that, 1) the identification of diseases in chest X-rays may be contingent on the presence of abnormalities in a small number of pixels, 2) chest X-rays are different from natural images in terms of their data attributes:

G. Bebis et al. (Eds.): ISVC 2023, LNCS 14362, pp. 320–331, 2023.
https://doi.org/10.1007/978-3-031-47966-3_25

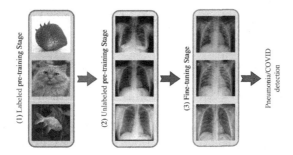

Fig. 1. The pre-training strategy for self-supervised models.

X-rays are larger, grayscale, and have similar spatial structures across images, 3) the number of unlabeled chest X-ray images is significantly less than the number of unlabeled natural images.

Acquiring knowledge from a small amount of labeled data is a significant challenge in machine learning, especially in medical image analysis, where the annotation of medical images is a labor-intensive and costly process that requires the involvement of specialists. In recent years, self-supervised learning, particularly contrastive learning [10], has emerged as a promising new approach for addressing the challenges of limited labeled data in various domains by creating pre-trained models from unlabeled data for subsequent fine-tuning on labeled data. Contrastive learning frameworks such as DINO [2] maximize agreement between positive image pairs using a contrastive loss function, while differing in their data augmentation and sampling strategies.

There are two widely used methods for pretraining models to learn from a limited amount of labeled data. The first method is *supervised pretraining*, which involves training the model on a large labeled dataset (e.g., ImageNet). The second method is *self-supervised pretraining*, which involves using contrastive learning on unlabeled data [4].

Transformers [24] have recently emerged as a viable alternative to convolutional neural networks (CNNs) for visual recognition tasks. The success of transformers has inspired many following works that apply them to various computer vision tasks [7,28].

This paper presents DINO-CXR, an innovative adaptation of a self-supervised technique, DINO, based on ViTAEv2 [26] vision transformer as the backbone for CXR classification. ViTAEv2 is a promising new vision transformer architecture that takes advantage of inductive biases such as *locality* and *scale-invariance*, which we demonstrate that are useful for CXR classification. This goes beyond current state-of-the-art techniques that rely on CNN or ViT [6] as a backbone. We also modify DINO to make it less computationally expensive with better performance for CXR classification.

Self-supervised learning is used as a pre-training strategy for CXR classification. In this regard, first, a model is pre-trained using supervised learning on a labeled dataset of natural images (Fig. 1). Next, self-supervised pre-training is employed on a large dataset of unlabeled CXR images. Finally, the model is fine-tuned on a small dataset of labeled CXR images.

Various experiments are conducted to show the effectiveness of DINO-CXR for CXR classification. An extensive comparison is performed between self-supervised approaches with different networks and frameworks, and it is demonstrated that DINO-CXR outperforms other methods in terms of accuracy, AUC, and F-1 score. DINO-CXR also outperforms state-of-the-art self-supervised methods for pneumonia and COVID detection in terms of accuracy. In addition, DINO-CXR achieves comparable results for CVOID-19 detection in terms of precision and F-1 score while using significantly less labeled data.

In summary, this paper presents the following contributions:

- We propose a self-supervised method by adapting DINO based on a vision transformer, ViTAEv2, for chest X-ray classification.
- We modify DINO to make it less computationally expensive while achieving better results for CXR classification.
- To the best of our knowledge, this work is the first work to compare self-supervised pre-training approaches with different networks and frameworks for CXR classification.
- The proposed method is shown to outperform state-of-the-art self-supervised methods in terms of accuracy for pneumonia and COVID-19 detection. It is also shown to achieve comparable results for COVID-19 detection in terms of precision and F-1 score while using significantly less (6%) of labeled data.

2   Related Work

In recent years, there has been a significant advancement in the use of deep learning techniques to detect pneumonia and COVID-19 using medical imaging data, particularly chest X-rays. These approaches can be broadly classified into supervised and self-supervised learning methods.

2.1   Supervised CXR Classification

Supervised learning techniques have been broadly utilized for pneumonia and COVID-19 detection by utilizing big annotated datasets to train deep-learning models. In recent years, many studies have investigated the use of deep neural networks for CXR classification tasks [1,25]. Kermany et al. [15] use transfer learning, which trains a neural network with a fraction of the data of conventional approaches. In the context of COVID-19 detection, Wang et al. [25] used a supervised learning approach to train a deep learning model for COVID-19 detection using chest X-ray images.

2.2   Self-supervised CXR Classification

Self-supervised learning, particularly contrastive learning, has gained significant attention in recent years for its ability to learn useful representations from unlabeled data. In the context of pneumonia and COVID-19 detection, leveraging

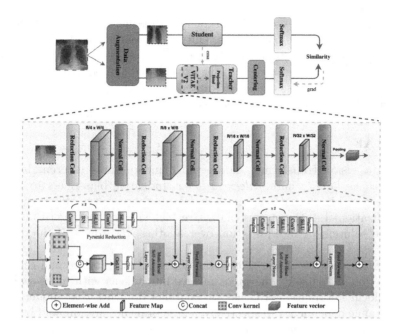

Fig. 2. The architecture of DINO-CXR

self-supervised learning can be advantageous due to the scarcity of labeled medical images. Recent studies have demonstrated the potential of self-supervised learning for CXR classification [8,11]. Han et al. [11] proposed a pneumonia detection method based on radiomic features and contrastive learning that uses self-supervised learning to extract features from chest X-rays.In 2020, Gazda et al. [8] proposed a self-supervised deep convolutional neural network for chest X-ray classification, including pneumonia and COVID-19 detection.

3 Proposed Method

In this section, we present our proposed method, DINO-CXR, for chest X-ray classification. DINO-CXR is a novel adaptation of DINO based on a vision transformer, ViTAEv2, for chest X-ray classification.

3.1 DINO

DINO (self-**di**stillation with **no** labels) is a knowledge distillation-based contrastive self-supervised learning algorithm that maximizes the similarity of representations generated from augmented views of the same input image. This similarity is measured with a cross-entropy loss.

Two augmented images are fed to student and teacher networks with the same architecture but different parameters. Output vectors are normalized by softmax with temperature parameters. Teacher is a momentum network, meaning that its parameters are updated with the exponential moving average of student parameters. DINO avoids collapse by centering and sharpening the momentum of teacher outputs. This balances their effects and prevents collapse.

3.2   ViTAE

ViTAE is a vision transformer model which incorporates inherent inductive biases, such as *locality* and *scale-invariance*. Inductive bias refers to a set of assumptions or biases that help machine learning models to achieve the power of generalization. In other terms, inductive bias enables the algorithm to prioritize one solution or interpretation over another, regardless of the observed data [19].

ViTAE employs two basic cells: reduction cell (RC) and normal cell (NC). The reduction cell embeds the input images into tokens with multi-scale context and local information. RC has two parallel branches that model locality and long-range dependency, respectively. These branches are followed by a feedforward neural network for feature transformation. One of the branches includes a Pyramid Reduction module to extract multi-scale context and a Multi-Head Self-Attention module to model long-range dependencies, and the other contains a Parallel Convolutional Module to embed local context into the tokens. The normal cell is utilized to enhance the modeling of both local and long-range dependencies within the tokens. Technically, NC has a similar structure to the reduction cell but does not include the Pyramid Reduction module.

ViTAEv2 [27], a new version of ViTAE, used another inductive bias, such as local window attention introduced in [17], in the RC and NC modules. As a result, the model achieves a better balance between memory usage, speed, and performance.

3.3   DINO-CXR

Vision transformers have demonstrated considerable promise in various computer vision tasks due to their robust ability to model long-range dependencies using the self-attention mechanism. Long-range dependency refers to the ability to identify patterns that are spread out over the entire image. This is important for pneumonia/COVID-19 detection, as the disease can often manifest as a combination of different abnormalities in the lungs.

On the other hand, current methods lack inductive biases such as *locality* and *scale-invariance*, and requires large-scale training datasets and longer training schedules to achieve optimal performance.

Locality in images refers to the spatial relationships between nearby pixels or regions. In the context of chest X-rays, these structures can help identify patterns and features that are indicative of pneumonia, such as the shape and texture of the lungs, the presence of consolidations, or the appearance of ground-glass opacities. By capturing these local structures, a model can be trained to differentiate between healthy and pneumonia-affected lungs.

Moreover, *scale invariance* refers to the ability of a model to recognize patterns and structures at different scales or sizes within an image. In the field of chest X-rays, scale invariance is important because the size and shape of the lungs, as well as the appearance of pathological features, can vary significantly between patients due to factors such as age, body size, and the severity of the condition.

One of the key innovations of DINO is the use of multi-cropping, which involves training the model on multiple crops of the same image. However, multi-cropping also has a high computational cost. This is because the model needs to be trained on a large number of crops, which can significantly increase the training time and memory usage. To address this issue, we replace multi-cropping with our own data augmentation strategy (Sect. 3.4), which uses a fixed size for the teacher and student network inputs. By doing so, our adapted DINO requires less computation and it is demonstrated that the adapted DINO has better performance than the original DINO.

With all that said, DINO-CXR is built based on ViTAEv2 which is able to model long-range dependency as well as local structures and deal with scale variance. Thus, DINO-CXR is capable of effectively capturing these properties, making it more likely to achieve high performance in detecting pneumonia/COVID-19.

Figure 2 shows the architecture of DINO-CXR. The model feeds two randomly transformed versions of an input image to the student and teacher networks, respectively. The student and teacher networks have the same architecture, but they have different sets of parameters. A stop-gradient operator was applied to the teacher to propagate gradients only through the student. The teacher parameters are updated using an exponential moving average of the student parameters. For instance, we depicted the inside of the teacher block, which includes ViTAEv2 as an encoder and projection head.

3.4   Augmentation Strategy

In this work, some data augmentation inspired by the study of image augmentations for Siamese networks was investigated [22]. Random resized cropping is employed to construct crops with a random aspect ratio of $3/4$–$4/3$ and scale parameter of 0.3–0.9; We utilize color distortion that is composed of color jittering and color dropping. Finally, Gaussian blurring is applied to the image with a probability of 50%. The standard deviation of the Gaussian kernel is randomly sampled from the range [0.1, 2.0], and the kernel size is set to be 10% of the image height or width.

4   Experiments Setup

In this section, our experiments setup including setups used for pre-training and fine-tuning are described. All experiments were conducted on Google Colab

Table 1. Datasets used in this study

Task	Dataset	Samples	Negative	Positive
Pretext	ChestX-ray14-v3	13,000	-	-
Target	Cell	5,323	1,349	3,883
	COVIDGR	852	426	426

Pro, which provides access to a powerful GPU. The specific GPU used was an NVIDIA A100 with 40 GB of RAM.

4.1 Datasets

In this study, three CXR datasets are utilized (Table 1). Initially, for pre-training, ChestX-ray14-v3[1] is used, which contains 13,000 X-rays images of three classes - Normal, Pneumonia, and Covid-19. Although labels are available, the unlabelled dataset is employed for all self-supervised pre-training experiments.

For the first downstream task, the Cell dataset [15] is utilized, which comprises 5,323 chest X-ray images from children. All chest X-ray labels were generated by two expert physicians and validated by a third physician.

For the second downstream task, the COVIDGR dataset [23] is used which contains 426 positive (Covid-19) and 426 negative (Non-Covid-19) chest x-rays. It is important to note that 76 of the 426 COVID-19 patients diagnosed positive by PCR had normal chest X-rays, which makes the task of classifying COVID-19 cases more challenging.

4.2 Pretraining Protocol

DINO-CXR is pre-trained with an effective batch size of 64. We use Adam optimizer [18] over 100 epochs with a learning rate of 0.000125 and fixed the weight decay value from $1e-7$ to $1e-6$. The learning rate and weight decay are decayed with a cosine schedule. A summary of all the setups utilized in this study is presented in Table 2.

4.3 Fine-Tuning Protocol

We evaluate the learned representations on the Cell and COVIDGR datasets using the standard linear evaluation protocol for all experiments. This protocol involves training a linear classifier on top of the frozen representation without updating the network parameters [16]. We employ batch size of 512 for all SSL approaches with CNN and ViT backbones and batch size of 256 for ViTAEv2, SGD optimizer with a momentum parameter of 0.9 over 50 epochs. We resize images to 256×256 for preprocessing and took a single center crop of 224×224.

---

[1] https://www.kaggle.com/datasets/haipham1202/chestx-ray14-v3.

Table 2. All pre-training setups that are used in this study.

Framework	Model	Learning rate	Optimizer	Weight decay
SimSiam [5]	ResNet-50 [12]	0.025	SGD	1e−4
	ViT-S/16 [6]	0.025	SGD	1e−4
	ViTAEv2	0.0125	SGD	1e−4
SimCLR [3]	ResNet-50	0.15	LARS	1e−5
	ViT-S/16	0.15	LARS	1e−5
	ViTAEv2	0.075	LARS	1e−5
BYOL [9]	ResNet-50	0.1	LARS	1e−5
	ViT-S/16	0.1	LARS	1e−5
	ViTAEv2	0.05	LARS	1e−5
Adapted DINO	ResNet-50	0.00025	Adam	1e−6 to 1e−5
	ViT-S/16	0.00025	Adam	1e−6 to 1e−5
	ViTAEv2	0.000125	Adam	1e−7 to 1e−6

A comprehensive search over the hyperparameter space is performed. We select the learning rate and weight decay after a grid search of the learning rate space {1e−2, 1e−3, 1e−4} and the weight decay space {1e−3, 1e−4, 1e−5}. Additionally, the learning rate is linearly ramped up during the first 10 epochs to prevent the model from overfitting.

5   Experiments and Results

In this section, we present results for the ablation study to show the effectiveness of DINO-CXR. Then we present results for pneumonia and COVID-19 detection.

5.1   Ablation Study

In this section, we first evaluate our adapted DINO compared to original DINO for chest X-ray classification. And then compare DINO-CXR with different combinations of networks and frameworks.

Table 3 illustrates the results of comparing our adapted DINO vs. original DINO. ResNet-50, the most common backbone, is used for this comparison. Adapted DINO outperforms the original DINO in terms of accuracy, AUC, and F1-score while requiring significantly less computational resources.

Next we compare DINO-CXR with different combinations of networks and frameworks, including our adapted DINO. To fairly compare the networks, we picked networks that have approximately the same number of parameters.

Table 4 presents the results for this comparison. DINO-CXR outperforms other methods in terms of accuracy, AUC, and F-1 score. Adapted DINO outperforms BYOL, SimCLR, and SimSaim by large margins, regardless of whether we use CNN or vision transformer as the backbone.

Table 3. Comparing our adapted DINO with original DINO

Network	Framework	ACC	AUC	F1-score	GPU RAM
ResNet-50	Adapted DINO	**94.0685**	**0.9405**	**0.9466**	**25.9** GB
	DINO	93.7343	0.9381	0.9432	39 GB

5.2 Pneumonia Detection

Next, we evaluate the performance of DINO-CXR for pneumonia detection. Cell dataset is used as the target dataset to compare DINO-CXR with state-of-the-art self-supervised methods for pneumonia detection. Table 5 shows the results. DINO-CXR outperforms other methods in terms of accuracy and achieves com-

Table 4. Ablation study results on the Cell dataset. The performance of models was measured by accuracy (%), area under the curve (AUC), and F1-score.

Method	Network	Framework	Params (Million)	ACC	AUC	F1-score
DINO-CXR	ViTAEv2	Adapted DINO	19.35	**95.66**	**0.9553**	**0.9613**
	ResNet-50	Adapted DINO	23.5	94.10	0.9405	0.9466
	ViT-S/16	Adapted DINO	22.05	94.10	0.9437	0.9453
	ViTAEv2	SimSiam	19.35	83.01	0.8181	0.8587
	ViTAEv2	SimCLR	19.35	93.31	0.9322	0.9402
	ViTAEv2	BYOL	19.35	93.32	0.9179	0.9321
	ResNet-50	SimSiam	23.5	91.65	0.9160	0.9248
	ResNet-50	SimCLR	23.5	93.40	0.9329	0.9410
	ResNet-50	BYOL	23.5	91.65	0.9264	0.9130
	ViT-S/16	SimSiam	22.05	73.77	0.7064	0.8054
	ViT-S/16	SimCLR	22.05	89.56	0.8880	0.9106
	ViT-S/16	BYOL	22.05	92.24	0.9179	0.9321

Table 5. Comparing DINO-CXR with SOTA **SSL** methods. The numbers for other methods are obtained from [8,21].

Dataset	Method	ACC	AUC
	Gazda et. al [8]	91.5	**97.7**
Cell dataset	Kermany et. al [15]	92.8	96.8
	DINO-CXR	**95.65**	95.53
	Gazda et .al[8]	78.4	87.1
COVIDGR dataset	COVID-SDNet[23]	76.18±2.70	-
	DINO-CXR	**76.47±3.53**	75.78±4.22

parable results in terms of AUC. We did not compare F-1 score as that score was not reported in other works.

5.3 COVID-19 Detection

Finally, we evaluate DINO-CXR for COVID-19 detection compared to *supervised* and *self-supervised* methods. The COVDIGR dataset is used for this purpose. The dataset is split into 80% training, 10% testing, and 10% validation sets. The performance of DINO-CXR is assessed using the average and standard deviation values of the 5 different executions performed on the 5-fold cross-validation.

Table 6. Comparative analysis of the proposed method with **supervised** deep learning based methods on the COVIDGR dataset. The numbers for other methods are obtained from [21].

Method	ACC	Non-COVID-19		COVID-19		
		F1-Score	Precision	F1-Score	Precision	Recall
COVIDNet-CXR [25]	67.82±6.11	73.31±3.79	3.36±6.15	56.94±5.05	81.65±6.02	46.82±17.59
COVID-CAPS [1]	65.34±3.26	65.15±5.02	65.62±3.98	64.87±4.42	66.07±4.49	64.93±9.71
COVID-SDNet [23]	76.18±2.70	76.94±2.82	74.74±3.89	75.71±3.35	78.67±4.70	72.59±6.77
Panetta et. al [21]	75.11±1.76	75.86±2.11	74.75±3.61	74.02±3.15	76.41±7.38	72.65±6.83
DINO-CXR	**76.47±3.53**	78.03±1.96	73.49±5.5	72.86±7.13	79.93±1.94	66.93±11.72

As one can see in Table 6 and Table 5, DINO-CXR outperforms other methods in terms of accuracy and achieves comparable results in other metrics while using significantly less labeled data. For instance, compared to COVIDNet-CXR [25], we use roughly 6% (725 vs. 13,975) of the labeled data for fine-tuning.

6 Conclusion

The combination of self-supervised pre-training and supervised fine-tuning has shown success in image recognition, particularly in scenarios where labeled samples are scarce. However, this approach has not been widely investigated in medical image analysis.

In this paper, we proposed DINO-CXR which is a novel adaptation of DINO based on a vision transformer for chest X-ray classification. Through extensive experiments, we showed the effectiveness of DINO-CXR and also demonstrated that DINO-CXR outperforms other methods for pneumonia and COVID-19 detection in terms of accuracy and achieves comparable results in terms of precision and F-1 score while requiring significantly less labeled data.

To the best of our knowledge, this is the first study to investigate the impact of different backbones on self-supervised pre-training approaches, and also show the benefit of inductive bias and its effectiveness on chest X-ray classification. We anticipate that this paper will contribute to the widespread adoption of self-supervised approaches in medical image analysis.

References

1. Afshar, P., Heidarian, S., Naderkhani, F., Oikonomou, A., Plataniotis, K.N., Mohammadi, A.: Covid-caps: a capsule network-based framework for identification of COVID-19 cases from x-ray images. Pattern Recogn. Lett. **138**, 638–643 (2020)
2. Caron, M., et al.: Emerging properties in self-supervised vision transformers. In: Proceedings of the IEEE/CVF International Conference on Computer Vision, pp. 9650–9660 (2021)
3. Chen, T., Kornblith, S., Norouzi, M., Hinton, G.: A simple framework for contrastive learning of visual representations. In: International Conference on Machine Learning, pp. 1597–1607. PMLR (2020)
4. Chen, T., Kornblith, S., Swersky, K., Norouzi, M., Hinton, G.E.: Big self-supervised models are strong semi-supervised learners. Adv. Neural. Inf. Process. Syst. **33**, 22243–22255 (2020)
5. Chen, X., He, K.: Exploring simple siamese representation learning. In: Proceedings of the IEEE/CVF Conference on Computer Vision and Pattern Recognition, pp. 15750–15758 (2021)
6. Dosovitskiy, A., et al.: An image is worth 16 × 16 words: transformers for image recognition at scale. arXiv preprint arXiv:2010.11929 (2020)
7. Dosovitskiy, A., et al.: An image is worth 16×16 words: transformers for image recognition at scale. arXiv preprint arXiv:2010.11929 (2020)
8. Gazda, M., Plavka, J., Gazda, J., Drotar, P.: Self-supervised deep convolutional neural network for chest x-ray classification. IEEE Access **9**, 151972–151982 (2021)
9. Grill, J.B., et al.: Bootstrap your own latent-a new approach to self-supervised learning. Adv. Neural. Inf. Process. Syst. **33**, 21271–21284 (2020)
10. Hadsell, R., Chopra, S., LeCun, Y.: Dimensionality reduction by learning an invariant mapping. In: 2006 IEEE Computer Society Conference on Computer Vision and Pattern Recognition (CVPR 2006), vol. 2, pp. 1735–1742. IEEE (2006)
11. Han, Y., Chen, C., Tewfik, A., Ding, Y., Peng, Y.: Pneumonia detection on chest x-ray using radiomic features and contrastive learning. In: 2021 IEEE 18th International Symposium on Biomedical Imaging (ISBI), pp. 247–251. IEEE (2021)
12. He, K., Zhang, X., Ren, S., Sun, J.: Deep residual learning for image recognition. In: Proceedings of the IEEE Conference on Computer Vision and Pattern Recognition, pp. 770–778 (2016)
13. Hong, A.S., Levin, D., Parker, L., Rao, V.M., Ross-Degnan, D., Wharam, J.F.: Trends in diagnostic imaging utilization among medicare and commercially insured adults from 2003 through 2016. Radiology **294**(2), 342–350 (2020)
14. Huang, H., et al.: Unet 3+: a full-scale connected unet for medical image segmentation. In: ICASSP 2020–2020 IEEE International Conference on Acoustics, Speech and Signal Processing (ICASSP), pp. 1055–1059. IEEE (2020)
15. Kermany, D.S., et al.: Identifying medical diagnoses and treatable diseases by image-based deep learning. Cell **172**(5), 1122–1131 (2018)
16. Kolesnikov, A., Zhai, X., Beyer, L.: Revisiting self-supervised visual representation learning. In: Proceedings of the IEEE/CVF Conference on Computer Vision and Pattern Recognition, pp. 1920–1929 (2019)
17. Liu, Z., et al.: Swin transformer: hierarchical vision transformer using shifted windows. In: Proceedings of the IEEE/CVF International Conference on Computer Vision, pp. 10012–10022 (2021)
18. Loshchilov, I., Hutter, F.: Fixing weight decay regularization in adam (2018)

19. Mitchell, T.M.: The need for biases in learning generalizations. Citeseer (1980)
20. Owayed, A.F., Campbell, D.M., Wang, E.E.: Underlying causes of recurrent pneumonia in children. Arch. Pediatr. Adolesc. Med. **154**(2), 190–194 (2000)
21. Panetta, K., Sanghavi, F., Agaian, S., Madan, N.: Automated detection of COVID-19 cases on radiographs using shape-dependent Fibonacci-p patterns. IEEE J. Biomed. Health Inform. **25**(6), 1852–1863 (2021)
22. Van der Sluijs, R., Bhaskhar, N., Rubin, D., Langlotz, C., Chaudhari, A.: Exploring image augmentations for siamese representation learning with chest x-rays. arXiv preprint arXiv:2301.12636 (2023)
23. Tabik, S., et al.: COVIDGR dataset and COVID-SDNet methodology for predicting COVID-19 based on chest x-ray images. IEEE J. Biomed. Health Inform. **24**(12), 3595–3605 (2020)
24. Vaswani, A., et al.: Attention is all you need. In: Advances in Neural Information Processing Systems, vol. 30 (2017)
25. Wang, L., Lin, Z.Q., Wong, A.: COVID-Net: a tailored deep convolutional neural network design for detection of COVID-19 cases from chest x-ray images. Sci. Rep. **10**(1), 19549 (2020)
26. Xu, Y., Zhang, Q., Zhang, J., Tao, D.: Vitae: Vision transformer advanced by exploring intrinsic inductive bias. Adv. Neural. Inf. Process. Syst. **34**, 28522–28535 (2021)
27. Zhang, Q., Xu, Y., Zhang, J., Tao, D.: ViTAEv2: vision transformer advanced by exploring inductive bias for image recognition and beyond. Int. J. Comput. Vis. **131**, 1–22 (2023)
28. Zheng, S., et al.: Rethinking semantic segmentation from a sequence-to-sequence perspective with transformers. In: Proceedings of the IEEE/CVF Conference on Computer Vision and Pattern Recognition, pp. 6881–6890 (2021)

Social Bias and Image Tagging: Evaluation of Progress in State-of-the-Art Models

Ethan Shafer[✉][iD], Jesse Wood, Sheyla Street, Enoch Crow, and Calvin Lu

United States Military Academy, West Point, NY 10996, USA
{ethan.shafer,jesse.wood,sheyla.street,enoch.crow,
calvin.lu}@westpoint.edu

Abstract. Image tagging algorithms, which assign a descriptive term to identify objects in pictures, are often used to organize and increase accessibility to images for users. Several commercial image tagging services are available, such as Amazon Rekognition, Clarifai, Imagga, Google Cloud Vision, Imagga, and Microsoft Azure. The aim of our study was to evaluate the progress of the applications in addressing the social bias issues found among them over several findings in the past decade. By applying the image tagging applications to a set of standardized images from the United States Military Academy, we found that the image taggers often avoid categories of potentially useful tags and a statistically significant difference between the number of tags in several categories (i.e. masculine, feminine, clothing, etc.) applied across gender and racial groups.

Keywords: image annotation · social implications of technology · ethics · machine learning · computer vision · feature detection

1 Introduction

Image tagging aims to assign a descriptive word or phrase to an image to identify the subject(s) for users. The process has been widely associated with image subject identification and facial attribute classification. Although image tagging algorithms (ITAs) help organize images and make them more accessible to users, the lack of high-quality training data, obscure taxonomy definitions, and inaccurate results lead to social bias in the results of the algorithms [5]. Nevertheless, computer vision has become entrenched in everyday functions, such as search engines, law enforcement surveillance, hiring systems, housing entry systems, and more. [7] Therefore, the existence of social bias in the output of computer vision applications has strong potential for reinforcing wide-spread racial and gender discrimination.

In fact, many commercially available image tagging services have been shown to produce results that reinforce racial, ethnic, and gender bias. For example, Google's Cloud Vision labeled a darker skin hand holding a thermometer as holding a "gun" in comparison to a lighter skin hand holding the same thermometer

G. Bebis et al. (Eds.): ISVC 2023, LNCS 14362, pp. 332–344, 2023.
https://doi.org/10.1007/978-3-031-47966-3_26

as holding an "electronic device". In 2015, Google's image recognition tool output the tag "gorillas" for images of two Black males. Additionally, the American Civil Liberties Union (ACLU)'s evaluation of Amazon's Rekognition algorithm demonstrated the misidentification and mugshot image matching of twenty-eight Congress members, disproportionately made up of people of color [10].

Although ITAs sort people in categories to create organization, the ancillary consequences of the categorization include reinforcing existing bias and widening gaps created by inequity. Bias may arise from definitions, specifically when defining the default as white and or male [2]. Supervised machine learning algorithms also require training data to identify trends from the past to calculate the likelihood of a future outcome [7]. Thus, patterns contributing to social bias in historical data may propagate to the results of ITAs. For instance, the over-representation and under-representation of groups may reduce the accuracy of the results of ITAs for a minority population. Further, the training data may represent the social bias of the individuals involved in providing, collecting, and/or using the data. For instance, while images of men are associated with tags "boss" and "aggressiveness", images of white women are most associated with "beauty, fragility, and delicacy" [4]. Further, black men and women are not shown as actors regarding "kindness" but instead as subjects, receiving this act from white people [4]. Thus, reliance on past data to inform future decisions may enforce the status quo including existing inequities.

2 Related Works

With the rapid growth of deep learning-based models, layers of information are processed through hierarchical stages consisting of a single layer of nonlinear feature transformation. With a nonlinear architecture, hierarchical models use layers to build off each other and eventually convert observed data to representations [6]. This conversion leads to the discovery of high-level data from low-level origins.

Supervised models use labeled data during training and predict the probability of an independent variable based on the values of the dependent variables and the parameters identified during the training process [9]. Linear Regression, Logistic Regression, Support Vector Machines, K Nearest Neighbors, Decision Trees, and, most recently, Convolutional Neural Networks (CNNs) are supervised models that have been used for image tagging [7,10]. Of the approaches, CNNs have proven to be the most promising and continue to be the basis for state-of-the-art image tagging techniques [7,8].

2.1 Evaluation of Social Bias in Image Tagging Results

Several studies have identified social bias in the output of applications that rely on computer vision. In 2013, a within platform approach found that the Google AdSense model was more likely to provide ads related to arrest for searches on names commonly given to Black children. When describing images of women, models tend to use physical attractiveness tags but less often for images of Black individuals compared to other social groups. For instance, a 2018 "Gender Shades" study used a within platform approach to evaluate bias in models and found that classification algorithms from IBM, Amazon, Facebook, Microsoft, and Kairos all performed worst on darker-skinned females, in comparison to darker-skinned males, lighter skinned females, and lighter skinned males, with accuracy differences between lighter-skinned males and darker-skinned females ranging from 20.8% to 34.4% [3].

In a study most closely related to ours, Kyriakou et al. also examined the output of several image tagging APIs on images from the Chicago Face Database, noting that Microsoft's Computer Vision rarely used feminine tags, while Clarifai demonstrated a lower likelihood of using gender tags appropriately for Black people in comparison to other races [8].

Following the 2019 study, Barlas, Kyriakou, Kleanthous, and Otterbacher went further into examining proprietary APIs by conducting a 2021 study in which they examined potential for reinforcing dehumanization. For six ITAs (Amazon's Rekognition, Clarifai, Google Cloud Vision, Imagga Auto-tagging, Microsoft Computer Vision, IBM Watson Visual Recognition), more images of women lacked recognition of humanness than men, with higher proportions of Black people (specifically Black women) failing to receive a humanness tag [2]. They defined dehumanization as a failure to tag individuals with a humanness tag or explicitly tagging a human with "no person" [2]. Stemming from a person not possessing the quality that an algorithm uses as a standard for detection of a human, dehumanization occurs and implies standards for humanness that are often centered around white men [2].

Additionally, a 2020 study by Fernanda Carrera used a within platform approach to explore how race and gender were determining factors for search engine results of tags related to the contexts of aggressiveness, kindness, beauty, and ugliness. While men represented more than 60% of the search results for aggressive action, women only represented 18.61% [4]. In the context of beauty, men made up less than one percentage of the results, with Black women making up 10% of the results, and white women making up most of the results. In the context of aggressiveness, Black men were specifically affiliated with violence in photos, white women appeared as victims, and Black women were depicted as agents of aggressiveness in image banks. Therefore, Carrera found these image banks and respective tags to reinforce paternalistic racism and gender roles [4].

Since it has been over a decade since the original work identified the problem, we re-evaluate social bias among the tags generated by commercially available models (Amazon's Rekognition, Google's Cloud Vision, Imagga Auto-tagging, Clarifai, and Microsoft's Azure Cognitive Services) using a highly standardized set of images of cadets at the United States Military Academy. Our study examines potential social bias demonstrated in ITAs on a naturally occurring set of images that, unlike the datasets often used in other studies, has not been curated. In doing so, our study helps inform how the continued commercial use of ITAs may influence society.

3   Design of Experiments

To evaluate the potential social bias in the results of the commercial imaging tagging platforms, we generated tags for a set of 4,259 cadet photos taken at the United States Military Academy from 2001 to 2003, 2010, and 2011. The photos were sampled randomly from the database and only included photos that were larger than 250 pixels in height. The photos are taken at the beginning of enrollment at the Academy for identification purposes in the student information system. The number of images by gender and race is shown in Table 1. An example photo is show in Fig. 1. The figure has been redacted for privacy.

Fig. 1. Sample male photo

Each photo was sent to five publicly available image tagging models: Amazon's Rekognition, Clarifai, Google Cloud Vision, Imaggi, and Microsoft's Azure Cognitive Services (IBM Watson was not available during the time of our experiment). We used each provider's default image tagging service and parameters. The results of the requests included a list of tags and the associated confidence levels for the tags. Any tag with a confidence level less than 0.50 was removed from further consideration. In order to standardize the output across image taggers and allow comparison to previous results, we mapped the tags to a common set of thematic categories in the same manner as Kyriakou, Barlas, Kleanthous, and Otterbacher [8]. A full list of the tags presented by each model is available upon request.

Table 1. Number of Images by Gender and Race

	Race					
Gender	*Asian*	*Black*	*Hispanic/ Latino*	*Others*	*White*	***Totals***
Female	41	53	52	45	472	663
Male	197	201	264	228	2979	3869
Totals	238	254	316	273	3451	4532

We aim to address two research questions in our study:

1. For each ITA, is there a significant difference among social groups (gender and race) for the number of tags assigned in a given category?
2. How do the results of the state-of-the-art ITA compare to one another?

For the two research questions, we adopt a similar evaluation method as Kyriakaou, et. al [8]. We first examined the number of unique tags and the frequency of tags per category each application assigned to the set of images. As we further evaluated potential differences among social groups within each category of tags, we applied Analysis of Variance (ANOVA) and a regression analysis where the independent variable was the number of tags related to a given category assigned to the image and the dependent variables were gender, race, and the interaction between gender and race.

Regarding the comparison between image taggers, we represent the output of each algorithm on each image as a vector with 16 dimensions (one for each category in the previously mentioned schematic). The values within the vector represent the number of tags related to the corresponding concept for an image and were normalized using the total number of tags. The cosine distance between the representations from each pair of image taggers was then used to quantify the similarity between platforms.

4 Experimental Results

4.1 Evaluation of Image Tagger Results by Category

An initial analysis was performed on the type of tags each image tagger produced on the set of cadet images. The mean number of tags assigned by category for each application are shown in Table 2. A few observations from the super-categories are highlighted below. The categories nonbinary, race, and inflammatory have been stripped from the tables because they contained no results. The lack, and inconclusive categories were similarly removed for having very few results.

Demographics Tags. Amazon, Clarifai, Google, and Microsoft all had labels for both feminine and masculine images. The accuracy of the labels is discussed further in Sect. 4.3. Imagga failed to label any images with a feminine tag. There was a distinct lack of Race tags from any of the models. This suggests that rather than address the issue of labelling images with racial features, the models are being trained to avoid those labels. The age labels were scattered, with most models applying tags ranging from baby to adult. Google mostly avoided demographic data tags, except for terms like "moustache" and "caesar cut" which have masculine or feminine connotations but do not directly assign a demographic group.

Table 2. Mean Tags per Category for each Tagger

	Example Tags	Amazon	Clarifai	Google	Imagga	Microsoft
Demographics		4.08	5.56	0.82	1.74	2.36
Feminine	woman, lady, girl	0.25	0.30	0.02	-	0.0
Masculine	man, boy, male	1.82	1.98	0.80	0.96	1.39
Age	adult, child	2.01	3.28	-	0.78	0.94
Concrete		16.15	13.16	15.96	1.70	15.97
Action	smile, laughing	0.62	3.61	0.87	-	0.62
Body / Person	face, head, person	5.91	2.35	5.49	0.02	8.53
Hair	hair, beard, mustache	2.89	1.32	4.13	0.12	1.64
Clothing	accessory, uniform	3.03	3.54	3.20	0.09	2.22
Photo-meta	mug shot, portrait	3.05	1.48	0.95	1.46	2.35
Colors	blond, camouflage	0.65	0.84	1.00	0.00	0.61
Size & Shape	pattern, symmetry	0.00	0.01	0.32	-	-
Abstract		4.35	8.63	4.77	0.64	2.62
Judgement	strange, handsome	-	0.28	0.00	0.02	-
Traits	security, innocent	-	2.49	0.62	0.00	0.02
Emotion	happy, pride	0.68	1.20	1.44	-	0.20
Occupation	military, police	3.67	4.66	2.71	0.62	2.41
Other		0.77	10.05	1.97	0.45	1.05
Ambiguous	crop, official	0.10	5.48	0.90	0.00	0.11
Misc	ammunition, art	0.67	4.47	0.25	0.45	0.94

Concrete Tags. Taggers are generally expressive in this supercategory. Even Imagga, which is the least expressive, has the most tags in the Concrete category. Across all taggers, clothing had the largest number of unique tags within this supercategory. This is surprising given that the photos all have similar uniforms and poses with no other clothing visible.

Abstract Tags. The image taggers generally avoid the Judgment and Traits categories, with the exception of a Clarifai. Imagga and, to some extent, Microsoft avoid Emotion tags while the others do not.

4.2 Significance of Gender and Race on Image Tagger Results

An ANOVA and regression analysis was conducted for each category of tags to determine the impact of gender and race on the number of tags assigned to an image in the respective category by each tagger. The statistical significance of the effect of gender and race on the quantity of tags per category can be found in Table 3 and Table 4, respectively. As shown, both gender and race had a significant effect on the number of tags across the majority of the tag categories. However, the manner in which gender and race impact the number of tags for a given category may be inconsistent among the ITAs. As a matter of convenience, we focus the presentation of results on those categories we determined to be most pertinent to social bias.

E. Shafer et al.

Table 3. ANOVA - Effect of Gender on each Category of Tags, F(1, 4522)

	Amazon	Clarifai	Google	Imagga	Microsoft
Feminine	<0.001***	<0.001***	<0.001***	-	<0.001***
Masculine	<0.001***	<0.001***	<0.001***	<0.001***	<0.001***
Age	<0.01**	<0.001***	<0.001***	<0.001***	<0.001***
Action	<0.001***	<0.001***	0.58	-	<0.001***
Body / Person	<0.001***	0.17	0.7	0.25	<0.001***
Hair	0.21	<0.001***	<0.001***	<0.001***	<0.001***
Clothing	<0.001***	<0.001***	<0.001***	<0.05*	0.39
Photo-meta	<0.001***	<0.001***	<0.001***	<0.001***	<0.001***
Colors	<0.001***	<0.001***	<0.01**	<0.05*	<0.001***
Size & Shape	<0.001***	<0.01**	<0.001***	-	-
Judgement	-	<0.001***	<0.001***	<0.05*	-
Traits	-	<0.001***	<0.001***	<0.05*	<0.001***
Emotion	<0.001***	<0.001***	<0.001***	-	<0.001***
Occupation	0.49	<0.001***	<0.001***	<0.001***	<0.001***
Ambiguous	<0.001***	<0.001***	0.51	0.56	<0.001***
Misc.	<0.001***	<0.001***	0.12	<0.001***	0.58

Table 4. ANOVA - Effect of Race on each Category of Tags, F(4, 4522)

	Amazon	Clarifai	Google	Imagga	Microsoft
Feminine	<0.001***	<0.001***	<0.05*	-	<0.05*
Masculine	<0.001***	<0.001***	<0.001***	<0.001***	<0.001***
Age	0.27	<0.001***	<0.001***	<0.001***	<0.001***
Action	<0.001***	<0.001***	0.36	-	<<0.01**
Body / Person	<0.001***	<0.001***	<0.001***	0.19	<0.001***
Hair	<0.001***	<0.001***	<0.001***	<0.001***	<0.001***
Clothing	<0.001***	<0.01**	<0.001***	0.12	<0.001***
Photo-meta	<0.001***	<0.001***	<0.001***	<0.001***	<0.01**
Colors	<0.001***	<0.01**	<0.001***	0.98	<0.001***
Size & Shape	0.17	<0.01**	<0.001***	-	-
Judgement	-	<0.001***	0.92	<0.001***	-
Traits	-	<0.001***	<0.01**	<0.01**	0.33
Emotion	<0.001***	<0.001***	<0.01**	-	<0.01**
Occupation	<0.001***	<0.001***	<0.001***	<0.001***	<0.001***
Ambiguous	<0.001***	<0.001***	<0.001***	0.21	<0.001***
Misc.	<0.001***	0.14	<0.001***	<0.001***	0.23

A summary of the regression models for predicting the number of feminine tags for an image can be found in Table 5. Note that Imagga did not assign feminine tags to any images in our data. Reassuringly, all of the remaining applications assign more feminine tags for females than males. However, the interaction between gender and race has potentially negative effects on the number of fem-

Table 5. Summary of regression analysis for the Feminine category.

	Amazon	Clarifai	Google	Microsoft
(Intercept)	2.22	0.95	0.12	0.2
Male	−2.18	−0.55	−0.12	−0.2
Black	−1.63	−0.65	−0.12	−0.12
Hispanic	−0.18	−0.32	0.03	0.09
White	−0.67	−0.13	−0.01	0.03
Other	−0.38	0.14	−0.01	0.07
Male:Black	1.6	0.43	0.12	0.12
Male:Hispanic	0.16	0.17	−0.03	−0.09
Male:White	0.65	−0.06	0.01	−0.03
Male:Other	0.37	−0.27	0.01	−0.07

Table 6. Summary of regression analysis for the Masculine category.

	Amazon	Clarifai	Google	Imagga	Microsoft
(Intercept)	0.39	1.68	0.05	0.54	0.14
Male	1.6	0.56	0.7	0.57	1.38
Black	1.21	0.39	0.18	−0.31	−0.01
Hispanic	0.18	−0.16	−0.05	0.06	−0.01
White	0.48	0.19	0.09	−0.16	0.1
Other	0.23	0.56	−0.03	−0.07	−0.06
Male:Black	−1.2	−0.97	-	-	−0.38
Male:Hispanic	−0.19	−0.08	-	-	0.12
Male:White	−0.49	−0.45	-	-	−0.01
Male:Other	−0.25	−0.66	-	-	0.14

inine tags for an image. For instance, Amazon Rekognition, Clarifai, Google Cloud Vision, and Microsoft Azure assigned the fewest feminine tags per image for Black women compared to any other racial group of women. Additionally, Clarifai assigned more feminine tags per image for Asian men than any other racial group of men (Table 6).

Gender and race had a varied effect on the number of tags related to hair for each of the ITAs (see Table 7). For example, Amazon Rekognition identified more hair tags for the White population, while Clarifai favored the Black population (particularly Black men) and Google Cloud Vision favored the Black population but more distinctly Black women. Microsoft Azure gave marginally more hair tags to White men and Asian women. As with several other categories, Imagga largely avoids tags related to hair.

Gender was a main effect on the number of clothing tags identified by Amazon Rekognition, Clarifai, and Google Cloud Vision. Amazon Rekognition and Clarifai both assigned more clothing tags to females than males, while Google Cloud Vision assigned more clothing tags to males. Race also had a significant impact on the number of clothing tags for Amazon Rekognition, Clarifai, and

Table 7. Summary of regression analysis for the Hair category.

	Amazon	Clarifai	Google	Microsoft
(Intercept)	1.63	0.95	0.63	0.24
Male	-	−0.05	3.24	1.34
Black	0.25	0.20	1.63	−0.04
Hispanic	0.71	−0.09	−0.04	−0.05
White	1.48	−0.18	1.29	−0.01
Other	0.70	−0.20	0.57	−0.02
Male:Black	−1.24	1.98	−0.83	0.03
Male:Hispanic	−0.46	0.59	0.31	0.26
Male:White	−0.97	0.60	−0.53	0.32
Male:Other	−0.39	0.75	−0.08	0.28

Table 8. Summary of regression analysis for the Clothing category.

	Amazon	Clarifai	Google	Microsoft
(Intercept)	6.95	3.88	2.83	2.49
Male	−3.77	−0.16	0.28	-
Black	0.03	0.14	−0.47	−0.64
Hispanic	1.22	0.53	−0.54	−0.18
White	0.01	0.48	−0.53	−0.20
Other	0.12	0.32	−0.85	−0.35

Microsoft Azure. Amazon Rekognition and Clarifai both identified more clothing tags for Hispanic subjects; Microsoft Azure identified the most for the Asian population. Additionally, the interaction of gender and race had an effect on the number of clothing tags for Google Cloud Vision, with a preference for men in the Other racial category and Asian women. Once again, Imagga avoided the category of tags. A summary of the regression analysis for the clothing category is in Table 8.

4.3   Gender Inference

As shown in Tables 9 and 10, all ITAs in our study performed better at identifying images of males than those of females. In fact, the performance varied widely when comparing male inference to female inference for 4 of the 5 applications (Amazon Rekognition being the exception).

4.4   Comparison of Image Taggers

As mentioned in Sect. 3, the cosine similarity of each algorithm was generated. The results are listed in Table 11. Amazon and Google are relatively similar to Microsoft, while Amazon and Google are less similar to each other. This has slight implications that Microsoft's model may be, in some ways, an intersection

Table 9. Gender Summary

	Neutral	Female	Male
Amazon	165	374	3990
Clarifai	1277	21	3231
Google	1138	64	3327
Imagga	1027	0	3502
Microsoft	416	141	3972

Table 10. Gender Performance

	Female			Male		
	Prec.	Recall	F_1	Prec.	Recall	F_1
Amazon	0.98	0.56	0.71	0.95	0.98	0.96
Clarifai	1.0	0.03	0.06	0.93	0.78	0.85
Google	1.0	0.1	0.18	0.98	0.84	0.91
Imagga	0.0	0.0	0.0	0.94	0.85	0.89
Microsoft	1.0	0.21	0.35	0.96	0.99	0.98

Table 11. Cosine Similarity of Taggers (mean/median)

	Clarifai	Google	Imagga	Microsoft
Amazon	0.56/0.57	0.77/0.79	0.46/0.47	0.84/0.86
Clarifai	-	0.54/0.54	0.38/0.38	0.48/0.47
Google	-	-	0.19/0.17	0.80/0.83
Imagga	-	-	-	0.30/0.29

of Google and Amazon's model. Imagga is the most dissimilar to all models (with an average cosine similarity of 0.32), largely due to the great disparity between Google and Imagga.

5 Discussion

As mentioned above, it appears that certain categories of labels have largely been avoided such as inflammatory or race. Avoiding these categories can be useful. For example, it may not be beneficial for image taggers to assign inflammatory labels to images. However, some categories may be useful in limited contexts. For instance, there is utility to assigning the correct nonbinary or race-based tags to images for the purpose of addressing specific medical or societal issues. By avoiding or limiting the range of labels available, companies are reducing their exposure to possible social or legal issues. However, this also reduces the utility of the algorithms.

From a social perspective, the gender tags are particularly indicative that the models are not actually learning the facial features that differentiate between the two groups. The images in the dataset are visually very similar, but the models fail to recognize the distinctions between the two genders. This suggests that there is either too little information for the model to make the decision, or that the models are learning proxies for gender instead of gender characteristics. Our suspicion is that the models are learning proxies for gender such as makeup, hair styling, clothing choice, or other factors. Since these elements are largely uniform in this dataset, the model fails to apply the appropriate label.

In comparison to Kyriakou, [8] we found a similar trend in regard to the taggers performance on gender inference. For our dataset, male gender inference improved compared to the previous study (F1 of .92 vs .56). However, female gender inference performance was slightly degraded in our study (F1 of .26 vs .32). Still, the ITAs are more capable of identifying males than females in both studies. In fact, a greater disparity between male and female inference performance was demonstrated in our study. While factors such as uniform and grooming standards among the subjects of our study may have contributed to the difference, the results suggest insufficient progress in gender inference among the ITAs. The performance in both studies highlights the point above that the models have not learned to detect female facial traits when other indicators are not present. This also reflects the work of Barlas [1] in that context (or lack of context) can influence a tagger's behavior.

6   Limitations

Default parameters were utilized for the ITAs instead of more refined parameters for facial recognition. Most of the organizations offer models that are fine-tuned for facial recognition. This limitation could manifest itself in improved accuracy or lower bias for tagging. However, we believe the default parameters are justified for the experiment as the default parameters should work best across a wide variety of applications.

The dataset used in this experiment is predominantly white males. While the photos are consistent, some of the gender:race subgroups have relatively few samples (namely, the minority female groups all have $n < 60$). This may limit the range of tags that females received due to the fewer number of samples.

7   Future Work

This project is looking to continue down multiple avenues. One avenue seeks to quantify the social implications of the identified biases. While this work confirmed that differences in tagging still occur, other work could prove the significance and effect that these differences have in social contexts. Given that some of the first social bias papers in computer vision were over a decade ago, it is long past due for this work to be completed.

Another avenue takes a more adversarial approach. Given the cosine similarity of the models, it is likely that the underlying datasets are similar or that the models have learned similar features from the datasets. The first step would be to demonstrate that adversarial methods could influence these ITAs, and the second step would be to identify if an adversarial attack against one of the ITAs could be applied successfully against a similar ITA.

8   Conclusions

Given the relatively uniform dataset and the wide variety of results, it is evident that there is still social bias present in modern ITAs. Moreover, based on our findings, it appears as though most companies have chosen to avoid the issues by removing controversial tags as an output. Without being able to analyze the models directly, one might assume that the companies are hiding the bias in their models, rather than correcting it. More work should be done to eliminate the social biases in the data that these models are built on.

Specifically, the community should continue to analyze the effect of social bias in ITAs and how that bias can be eliminated in the underlying dataset. With increasing use of computer vision and machine learning algorithms in the public sector–such as courtrooms and police precincts–it is essential that the bias be analyzed and corrected prior to being implemented. While these biases are still present, the use of ITAs should be carefully considered against the context of their application.

Disclaimer

The views expressed in this article are those of the authors and do not reflect the official policy or position of the Department of the Army, Department of Defense, or the U.S. Government.

This study was managed under an approved IRB protocol at the United States Military Academy as study #CA-2023-41.

References

1. Barlas, P., Kyriakou, K., Guest, O., Kleanthous, S., Otterbacher, J.: To "See" is to stereotype: image tagging algorithms, gender recognition, and the accuracy-fairness trade-off. In: Proceedings of the ACM on Human-Computer Interaction, vol. 4. no. CSCW3, pp. 232:1–232:31 (2021). https://doi.org/10.1145/3432931
2. Barlas, P., Kyriakou, K., Kleanthous, S., Otterbacher, J.: Person, human, neither: the dehumanization potential of automated image tagging. In: Proceedings of the 2021 AAAI/ACM Conference on AI, Ethics, and Society, pp. 357–367. AIES 2021, Association for Computing Machinery, New York, NY, USA (2021). https://doi.org/10.1145/3461702.3462567
3. Buolamwini, J., Gebru, T.: Gender shades: intersectional accuracy disparities in commercial gender classification. In: Proceedings of the 1st Conference on Fairness, Accountability and Transparency, pp. 77–91. PMLR (2018). https://proceedings.mlr.press/v81/buolamwini18a.html iSSN: 2640-3498
4. Carrera, F.: Race and gender of aesthetics and affections: algorithmization of racism and sexism in contemporary digital image databases. MATRIZes 14(2), 217–240 (2020). https://doi.org/10.11606/issn.1982-8160.v14i2p217-240. https://www.revistas.usp.br/matrizes/article/view/167187
5. Castelnovo, A., Crupi, R., Greco, G., Regoli, D., Penco, I.G., Cosentini, A.C.: A clarification of the nuances in the fairness metrics landscape. Sci. Rep. 12(1), 4209 (2022). https://doi.org/10.1038/s41598-022-07939-1. https://www.nature.com/articles/s41598-022-07939-1. number: 1 Publisher: Nature Publishing Group
6. Cireşan, D., Meier, U., Schmidhuber, J.: Multi-column deep neural networks for image classification (2012). https://doi.org/10.48550/arXiv.1202.2745 , http://arxiv.org/abs/1202.2745, arXiv:1202.2745 [cs]

7. Fu, J., Rui, Y.: Advances in deep learning approaches for image tagging. APSIPA Trans. Signal and Inf. Process. **6**, e11 (2017). https://doi.org/10.1017/ATSIP.2017.12

8. Kyriakou, K., Barlas, P., Kleanthous, S., Otterbacher, J.: Fairness in proprietary image tagging algorithms: a cross-platform audit on people images. In: Proceedings of the International AAAI Conference on Web and Social Media, vol. 13, pp. 313–322 (2019). https://ojs.aaai.org/index.php/ICWSM/article/view/3232

9. Schwemmer, C., Knight, C., Bello-Pardo, E.D., Oklobdzija, S., Schoonvelde, M., Lockhart, J.W.: Diagnosing gender bias in image recognition systems. Socius **6**, 2378023120967171 (2020). https://doi.org/10.1177/2378023120967171, https://doi.org/10.1177/2378023120967171. publisher: SAGE Publications

10. Villaespesa, E., Crider, S.: Computer vision tagging the metropolitan museum of art's collection: a comparison of three systems. J. Comput. Cultural Heritage **14**(3), 28:1–28:17 (2021). https://doi.org/10.1145/3446621

L-TReiD: Logic Tensor Transformer for Re-identification

Russo Alessandro[✉][iD], Manigrasso Francesco[iD], Lamberti Fabrizio[iD],
and Morra Lia[iD]

Politecnico di Torino, 10129 Torino, TO, Italy
{alessandro.russo,francesco.manigrasso,
fabrizio.lamberti,lia.morra}@polito.it

Abstract. This article proposes a Neuro-Symbolic (NeSy) machine learning approach to Object Re-identification. NeSy is an emerging branch of artificial intelligence which combines symbolic reasoning and logic-based knowledge representation with the learning capabilities of neural networks. Since object re-identification involves assigning the identity of the same object across different images and different conditions, such a task could benefit greatly from leveraging the logic capabilities of a NeSy framework to inject prior knowledge about invariant properties of the objects. To test this assertion, we combined the Logic Tensor Networks (LTNs) NeSy framework with a state-of-the-art Transformer-based Re-Identification and Damage Detection Network (TransRe3ID). The LTN incorporates prior knowledge about the properties that two instances of the same object have in common. Experimental results on the Bent&Broken Bicycle re-identification dataset demonstrate the potential of LTNs to improve re-identification systems and provide novel opportunities to identify pitfalls during training.

Keywords: Neuro-Symbolic learning · Logic Tensor Networks · Object Re-Identification · Transformers

1 Introduction

In recent years, the novel field of Neuro-Symbolic Machine Learning (NeSy) has emerged at the intersection of symbolic artificial intelligence and neural networks [7,8,10]. NeSy combines the strengths of both symbolic reasoning and deep learning to address complex problems by combining the expressive power of logic-based knowledge representation with the learning capabilities of neural networks. While NeSy techniques have been applied in a variety of visual tasks including scene graph extraction [3,4,12], object detection [17], zero-shot image classification and recognition [19,25] and visual query answering [18,20,23], to the best of our knowledge ours is the first attempt to exploit them in the context of Object Re-Identification (ReID).

Current re-identification methods simply perform implicit pattern matching while not making use of more readily available information about similar objects like color and object type labels. The proposed approach could prove beneficial in this sense by using logical rules that encode prior knowledge about properties that are invariant across different images of the same object instance. Specifically, we focus on improving the baseline performance of the transformer-based re-identification and damage detection network (TransRe3ID) [21] by incorporating Logic Tensor Networks (LTNs) [1].

To evaluate our approach, we conduct experiments with the synthetic Bent & Broken bicycle Damage Detection and Re-Identification dataset [21]. In this benchmark, the goal is to re-identify the same object (in this case, a bicycle) in the presence of damages and missing parts, and hence the network must distinguish between large inter-object deformations (e.g., induced by an incident) and subtle intra-object differences (e.g., due the difference texture of the bike frame). In addition, the dataset includes challenges commonly associated to ReID such as changes in viewpoint, and the presence of dirt.

The remainder of this paper is organized as follows. Section 2 provides a brief background on the Logic Tensor Networks framework and an analysis of recent related work in the field of object ReID, with a particular focus on the use of transformers in this area. Section 3 outlines the methodology with the definition of the FOL rules, their integration into the TransRe3ID network, and the loss formulation. Section 4 presents the experimental setup, including the dataset and evaluation metrics. Section 5 discusses the results and analyzes the impact of integrating LTNs on the performance of the ReID system. It also examines the extent to which the proposed logical rules were satisfied during training to explain the properties of the resulting network. Finally, Sect. 6 concludes the paper and highlights possible directions for future research in this area.

2   Background

2.1   Object Re-identification

Object ReID is the task of identifying the same object in multiple images, regardless of its position, illumination, or context. The use of transformers has rapidly increased in recent years, with applications ranging from person ReID [16,24,27] to vehicle ReID [14,15,26]. One of the best representatives of these works is TransReID proposed by [9], which presents a ViT backbone followed by two separate ReID branches, one based on global attention and one that enforces local attention by using a separate module that extracts random local parts of the image. This work was extended by [21] to perform simultaneous damage detection and object ReID, resulting in the TransReI3D architecture trained on the Bent&Broken Bicycle ReID dataset.

2.2   Logic Tensor Networks

Logic Tensor Networks (LTNs), originally proposed by d'Avila Garcez and Serafini [1,2,6], have been used in a variety of different tasks, from object recognition

[4,17,22] to reinforcement learning [2] and sentiment analysis [11], demonstrating their flexibility as a NeSy framework. They combine deep neural networks with a first-order logical knowledge representation. In short, LTNs use a fuzzy logical language, called real-world logic, as the underlying formalism, which consists of a First-Order Logic language (FOL) whose signature includes constants, function, and predicate symbols. Since there is no complete certainty in real-world problems and formulas may be partially true, fuzzy semantics is used as an approximation to real logic, using the concept of *grounding* to define how symbols are concretely interpreted by tensors in the real field.

Given a vector space R^n and a set of predicates $\mathcal{P}$, a grounding $\mathcal{G}$ has the following properties:

$$\mathcal{G}(P) \in \mathbb{R}^{n \star k} \to [0,1], \forall p \in \mathcal{P}$$

As such, predicate symbols are interpreted as functions mapping real vectors to the $[0,1]$ interval, which can be interpreted as the truth level of the predicate. A typical example is the unary predicate *is-a*, which determines the existence of a certain object or property associated with it. Consider the following use case as an example: if $b = \mathcal{G}(x)$ is the grounding for the image of a bicycle, then $\mathcal{G}(Bike)(b) \simeq 1$. A logical condition expressed in FOL allows to define its properties, e.g. $\forall x(\text{Bike}(x) \to \text{hasWheels}(x))$. Thus, the truth value of a logical condition can be calculated by a neural network by first computing the grounding of the unary symbols contained in the logical clause and then combining them through fuzzy logical operators and quantifiers.

Fuzzy logic formulas can be associated with fuzzy logic operators such as conjunctions ($\wedge$), disjunctions ($\vee$), and implications ($\implies$), including logical quantifiers ($\forall$ and $\exists$). Several real-valued differentiable implementations are available in the fuzzy logic domain [13]. The implementation here used follows the one in [1], which is based on the Lukasiewicz formulation [5]:

$$\begin{aligned} \mathcal{G}(-\phi) &= 1 - \mathcal{G}(\phi) \\ \mathcal{G}(\sigma \vee \psi) &= \min(1, \mathcal{G}(\phi) + \mathcal{G}(\psi)) \end{aligned} \tag{1}$$

The combination of connectors, predicates and quantifiers defines axioms, for which examples can be found in Sect. 3.2.

The set of closed formulas such as axioms and logical labels is called a knowledge base $\mathcal{K}$, which stands in combination with the grounding on our examples. In practice, such a grounding is only partially defined for optimization purposes, since our set $\mathcal{K}$ is qualitatively a finite and limited set of examples.

Best Satisfiability Problem. Given a grounding $\hat{\mathcal{G}}_\theta$, where θ is the set of parameters of all predicates, the learning problem in LTNs is formulated as a best satisfiability problem, where the goal is to determine the values of Θ^* that maximize the truth values of the conjunction of all closed formulas $\phi \in \mathcal{K}$:

$$\Theta^* = \text{argmax}_\Theta \, \hat{\mathcal{G}}_\theta \left(\bigwedge_{\phi \in \mathcal{K}} \phi \right) - \lambda \|\Theta\|_2^2 \tag{2}$$

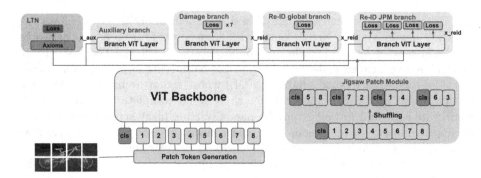

Fig. 1. Architecture of the proposed L-TransReI3D. The original architecture of TransReI3D [21] consists of a ViT backbone that feeds into 3 output branches: (1) the Damage Branch to classify the presence of damage and missing parts; (2) the global ReID branch for the ReID of objects in the global image; and (3) the ReID JPM branch for the local ReID of objects in subsets of image patches as an additional self-supervised task. The architecture has been further extended with an Auxiliary branch, which performs the classification of bike attributes. With the exception of the Damage branch, each branch also feeds into the LTN axioms for the LTN loss calculation.

where $\lambda \|\Theta\|_2^2$ is a regularization term. In real world cases, fully satisfying a grounded theory is highly unlikely given the possibility of exceptions to each rule. Thus, we opt to instead find the grounding that obtains the highest satisfaction while taking into account such exceptions. Examples of these exceptions are common in the visual domain, from occasional deviations from the norm, to features that may not be always visible. For example, a bicycle (normally) has both wheels, but a damaged bicycle or a bicycle under repair may have one or both wheels missing or simply obscured.

3   Methodology

3.1   Overall Architecture

Following the work of [21], we use the TrainsReI3D architecture as backbone, which was already demonstrated on the selected benchmark for damaged object ReID (more information about the dataset can be found in Sect. 4.1). This architecture performs multi-task damage detection and ReID by using a ViT backbone and having three output branches: one for classifying the presence of damage and missing parts, one that performs object ReID on the whole image and the last one, called Jigsaw Patch Branch, that performs object ReID based on local features. This last branch works by using the Jigsaw Patch Module (JPM), which takes as input the patch tokens and randomly reshuffles them into four separate subsets of equal size, each containing a copy of the original [cls] patch token. For more details on the underlying transformer network, the reader can refer to the works of [9,21]. Here we have also added a separate output branch for predicting additional attributes of each bike instance, with a separate classification head for each attribute (multi-attribute, multi-class classification).

Figure 1 shows a representation of the complete architecture.

3.2 Logic Tensor Network Definition

Our LTN-based NeSy approach defines predicates on the images, that are in turn grounded by the output [cls] token features of the ReID and auxiliary branches to obtain subsymbolic representations of IDs (x_{reid}) and bike attributes(x_{attr}), respectively. The core of the LTN is the definition of the knowledge base K, which combines known facts (in the present case, labeled instances) with logical constraints. The Bent&Broken Bicycle dataset, as defined in Sect. 4.1, defines each unique bicycle ID based on the unique combination of instance attributes, and at the same time, contains damaged and undamaged versions of the same bicycle ID. The LTN was used to inject into the learning process prior knowledge that directly derives from the rules underlying the dataset labeling structure. Specifically, we make three basic observations from which we define our knowledge base rules: (1) "Images with the same auxiliary attributes must have the same ID"; (2) "Images of the same object, but with different damage types, must have the same ID"; (3) "Images with the same ID must be associated with feature vectors that are close in the embedding space". In the rest of this section, we define in detail the variables and predicates that form the FOL, and the axioms encoding prior knowledge.

Predicates. The proposed LTN is based on three predicates:

- **IDp**(x_{reid}, ID) is a trainable ID predicate classifier, where x_{reid} is an input image and ID is a term denoting a ID variable. The predicate should return the probability that an image x_{reid} belongs to ID. The predicate is grounded by a classification layer followed by a softmax function, where x_{reid} is grounded by the output [cls] token feature extracted from the ReID branch;
- **AUXp**(x_{aux}, AUX_i) is a trainable predicate classifier for bike attributes, where x_{aux} is the image and AUX_i is the corresponding attribute label (more information in Sect. 4.1). Each $AUXp$ returns the probability that an image x_{aux} belongs to the label of the bike attributes AUX_i. Each predicate is grounded by a classification layer followed by a softmax function, where x_{aux} is grounded by the output [cls] feature extracted from the auxiliary branch;
- **SameInstance**(x_{reid_i}, x_{reid_j}) is a non-trainable predicate indicating whether two images x_{reid_i} and x_{reid_j} contain bikes belonging to the same ID; the predicate is grounded by the cosine similarity between the two input features followed by a sigmoid function, whereas x_{reid_i} and x_{reid_j} are grounded by the output class token features of each image extracted from the ReID branch.

Fuzzy Operators. Here are defined the fuzzy logic operators introduced in the LTN formalism and used in the axioms:

- **Diagonal Quantification** $\mathrm{Diag}(x,\ldots,l)$ quantifies over tuples combining the i-th instance of each of the variables in the argument of Diag [1]. For example, for a dataset with samples x and target label y, $\forall\mathrm{Diag}(x,y)$ quantifies over each (sample, label) pair.
- **Equivalence Connection** $Pred_1 \Leftrightarrow Pred_2$ corresponds to the equivalence logic operator, which states that the two predicates should have the same truth value.
- **Guarded Quantification** $Quantifier(Condition\ Variables\ :\ Condition\ Mask\{Maskedpredicates\})$ applies a mask to select terms to be included in the quantification based on a selected condition variables. For example, given a binary predicate P applied to variables x and y, the axiom $\forall[x,y], x,y\ :\ x == y\{P(x,y)\}$ computes only any combination of x and y for which the condition $x == y$ is satisfied.

Axioms.

The following rules enforce the three observations defined above in dual pairs of positive-negative axioms:

- **Rule #1: Images with the same auxiliary attributes must be assigned to the same ID.** After selecting only pairs of images that (do not) have the same ID (guarded condition), the rules enforce the constraint that the auxiliary attributes of images x_{aux_i} and x_{aux_j} are the same if and only if the two corresponding images x_{reid_i} and x_{reid_j} have the same IDs (and vice versa). The constraint is applied for each auxiliary attribute:

$$\forall\mathrm{Diag}(x_{reid_i}, ID_i, x_{aux_i}, AUX_{k_i}) \left(\forall\mathrm{Diag}(x_{reid_j}, ID_j, x_{aux_j}, AUX_{k_j})\right.$$

$$\mathbf{ID_i, ID_j : ID_i == ID_j}\left\{\left((\mathrm{AUXp}(x_{aux_i}, AUX_{k_i}) \Leftrightarrow \mathrm{AUXp}(x_{aux_j}, AUX_{k_j}))\right) \Leftrightarrow \right. \tag{3}$$

$$\left.\left.\left(\mathrm{IDp}(x_{reid_i}, ID_i) \Leftrightarrow \mathrm{IDp}(x_{reid_j}, ID_j))\right)\right\}\right)$$

$$\forall\mathrm{Diag}(x_{reid_i}, ID_i, x_{aux_i}, AUX_{k_i}) \left(\forall\mathrm{Diag}(x_{reid_j}, ID_j, x_{aux_j}, AUX_{k_j})\right.$$

$$\mathbf{ID_i, ID_j : ID_i! = ID_j}\left\{\neg\left((\mathrm{AUXp}(x_{aux_i}, AUX_{k_i}) \Leftrightarrow \mathrm{AUXp}(x_{aux_j}, AUX_{k_j}))\right) \Leftrightarrow \right. \tag{4}$$

$$\left.\left.\neg\left(\mathrm{IDp}(x_{reid_i}, ID_i) \Leftrightarrow \mathrm{IDp}(x_{reid_j}, ID_j))\right)\right\}\right)$$

- **Rule #2: Images with different damage types, but with the same ID label, must be assigned to the same ID.** After selecting only pairs of images that (do not) have the same ID (guarded condition), we ask the network to ensure that two images, one with an undamaged instance $x_{reid_{und_i}}$ and one with a damaged instance $x_{reid_{dmg_j}}$, (do not) have the same IDs; this is computed for each type of damage and each missing part

$$\forall \text{Diag}(x_{reid_{dmg_i}}, ID_i) \left(\forall \text{Diag}(x_{reid_{und_j}}, ID_j) \right.$$
$$\left. \mathbf{ID_i}, \mathbf{ID_j} : \mathbf{ID_i} == \mathbf{ID_j} \left\{ \text{IDp}(x_{reid_{dmg_i}}, ID_i) \Leftrightarrow \text{IDp}(x_{reid_{und_j}}, ID_j) \right\} \right) \tag{5}$$

$$\forall \text{Diag}(x_{reid_{dmg_i}}, ID_i) \left(\forall \text{Diag}(x_{reid_{und_j}}, ID_j) \right.$$
$$\left. \mathbf{ID_i}, \mathbf{ID_j} : \mathbf{ID_i}! = \mathbf{ID_j} \left\{ \neg \left(\text{IDp}(x_{reid_{dmg_i}}, ID_i) \Leftrightarrow \text{IDp}(x_{reid_{und_j}}, ID_j) \right) \right\} \right) \tag{6}$$

– **Rule #3: Images with the same ID labels must be grounded by feature vectors that are close in the embedding space.** After selecting only pairs of images that (do not) have the same ID (guarded condition), we ask the network to ensure that two images (do not) have close output features from the ReID branch

$$\forall \text{Diag}(x_{reid_i}, ID_i) \left(\forall \text{Diag}(x_{reid_j}, ID_j) \right.$$
$$\left. \mathbf{ID_i}, \mathbf{ID_j} : \mathbf{ID_i} == \mathbf{ID_j} \left\{ \text{SameInstance}(x_{reid_i}, x_{reid_j}) \right\} \right) \tag{7}$$

$$\forall \text{Diag}(x_{reid_i}, ID_i) \left(\forall \text{Diag}(x_{reid_j}, ID_j) \right.$$
$$\left. \mathbf{ID_i}, \mathbf{ID_j} : \mathbf{ID_i}! = \mathbf{ID_j} \left\{ \neg \text{SameInstance}(x_{reid_i}, x_{reid_j}) \right\} \right) \tag{8}$$

We also add another set of axioms for the classification of the k-th bike attribute:

$$\forall \text{Diag}(x_{aux}, AUX_k) \ \text{AUXp}(x_{aux}, AUX_k) \tag{9}$$

In addition to the axioms above, we also analyze an additional axiom which computes the ID classification as follows:

$$\forall \text{Diag}(x_{reid}, ID) \ \text{IDp}(x_{reid}, ID) \tag{10}$$

This axiom is not included in the total satisfiability computation (that is, the LTN loss) since the ID classification is already trained through the global ReID branch.

Each axiom is computed five times, once for the output of the global ReID branch and once for each of the four local outputs of the JPM branch.

3.3 Loss Computation

For the loss calculation, after computing $TotSat$ as the final satisfiability of the Knowledge Base, we add the obtained LTN loss as $\mathcal{L}_{LTN} = 1 - TotSat$ to the original loss of TransReI3D $\mathcal{L}_{TReI3D}$, which has the following form:

$$\mathcal{L}_{final} = \mathcal{L}_{TReI3D} + \mathcal{L}_{LTN} \tag{11}$$

with $\mathcal{L}_{TReI3D}$ having the following structure from [21]:

$$\mathcal{L}_{TReI3D} = \alpha \mathcal{L}_{ID}\left(f_g\right) + \beta \mathcal{L}_T\left(f_g\right) + \gamma \mathcal{L}_{\mathcal{D}}\left(f_d\right)$$
$$+ \frac{1}{k} \sum_{j=1}^{k} \left(\mathcal{L}_{ID}\left(f_l^j\right) + \mathcal{L}_T\left(f_l^j\right) \right) \tag{12}$$

where $\mathcal{L}_T$ and $\mathcal{L}_{ID}$ are the triplet loss and the ID cross-entropy loss, $\mathcal{L}_D$ is the damage detection loss, k $(= 4)$ is the number of classification outputs of the JPM branch, and f_g, f_l, and f_d are the output [cls] features of the global branch, the jigsaw branch, and of the damage detection branch, respectively. To compute $\mathcal{L}_T$, triplets with hard negative and positive mining are sampled online from each batch.

At inference time, the logical rules are not used, as they are only used to support model training by integrating a semantic component to the loss.

4 Experimental Settings

4.1 Dataset

We used the Bent&Broken bicycle dataset [21] with the same split for training and validation as in the original paper. The dataset contains synthetically generated bicycle images both before and after undergoing damage to simultaneously solve the Damage Detection and ReID tasks, and includes challenges such as missing parts, changes in viewpoint, and dirt. The dataset also contains additional attributes for each image, such as the model, type of bicycle, color and texture of the frame, and presence of stickers. The dataset contains a total of 39,200 images of 2,800 unique IDs, each defined by a unique combination of additional information. There are two types of damage, namely frame bending and frame breaking, which are not mutually exclusive, and up to five parts can be missing from each bicycle, including the two wheels, hand brake, pedals and seat. There are 20 base models, which are divided into 6 types of bicycles. For the frame, there are six texture patterns in different styles, with both the base and pattern colors selected from a pool of 50 colors each. A bike can contain a top and/or bottom sticker, both selected from a pool of 11 stickers. We performed two sets of experiments: one in which only the bike type and model are predicted, and one in which all attributes are used. Based on preliminary experiments, bike type and model appeared potentially easier to classify, also taking into account that random data augmentation may occasionally disturb the detection of color, texture and stickers.

4.2 Hyperparamenters

Experiments were performed on a NVIDIA TITAN XP with 12 GB of VRAM. L-TransReI3D was trained for 20 epochs with batch size equal to 16, learning rate 1e−2, weight decay 1e−4, and OneCycle scheduler with a warm-up period of 5 epochs. The experiments were run 3 times with and without the LTN component. The metrics used were mean average precision (mAP) and Recall@K with K=1, 5, 10.

Each trainable predicate consists of a FC layer with an input size of 768, equal to the embedding size, and an output size that depends on the predicted information (i.e., ID, bike model, bike type, etc.). The total satisfiability of the knowledge base $TotSat$ was calculated in the following order: first, for each dual rule pair defined in Sect. 3.2, the axioms calculated on the global ReID branch output and the local ReID JPM branch outputs are aggregated, obtaining their respective rule satisfiability; then all rule satisfiabilities are aggregated to obtain the total final satisfiability.

For the aggregation, as suggested by [1], we approximate the universal ∀ quantifier with the generalized mean w.r.t. error aggregator:

$$A_{pME} = 1 - \left(\frac{1}{n} \sum_{i=1}^{n} (1 - a_i)^{p_\forall} \right)^{\frac{1}{p_\forall}} \tag{13}$$

with the parameter $p_\forall$ defining the stringency in computing the satisfiability of logical constraints. This parameter was scheduled starting at $p_\forall = 2$ and then increasing to $p_\forall = 4$ at the halfway point, after the 10th epoch, since higher p values at the beginning of training might prevent the network from converging, as previously reported by [1]. It should be noted that, while the A_{pME} is also used to aggregate all axioms (see Eq. 2), the scheduling of $p_\forall$ was only applied to the ∀ quantifiers.

5 Results

The results comparison of L-TReI3D with the original TransReI3D architecture are shown in Table 1. Two versions of the LTN were compared, using a sub-

Fig. 2. Retrieval results (Top-5 images) for the network (ID and similarity scores). The correct ID is retrieved despite the presence of missing parts (ID 15), bent (ID 15), or broken (ID 19) frame.

Table 1. Performance comparison of L-TransReI3D with the original TransReI3D on the validation set. Mean average accuracy (mAP) and R@K with K = 1,5,10 are given along with standard deviation over 3 replicates. L-TReID (subset) represents the configuration using only a subset of the additional features, while L-TReID (all) uses all of them.

Network	mAP	R@1	R@5	R@10
TransReI3D	85.3 ± 0.2	79.8 ± 0.7	91.9 ± 1.1	96.3 ± 0.5
L-TReI3D (subset)	**85.7 ± 0.1**	79.8 ± 0.5	**93 ± 0.3**	96.2 ± 0.4
L-TReI3D (all)	85.0	79.1	93.1	96.3

set (mAP = 85.7) or all (mAP = 85.0) the attributes, and both achieve similar performance to the original network (mAP = 85.3). Figure 2 shows some query examples with the corresponding similarity values.

Information about the learning behavior of the network can also be extracted from the satisfiability of the logical rules. For this purpose, Fig. 3 shows, for each rule presented in Sect. 3.2, the satisfiability of their respective dual axiom pairs; results were reported on the experiment in which all attributes were used during training.

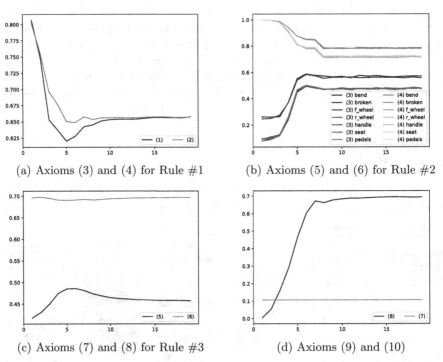

(a) Axioms (3) and (4) for Rule #1   (b) Axioms (5) and (6) for Rule #2

(c) Axioms (7) and (8) for Rule #3   (d) Axioms (9) and (10)

Fig. 3. Satisfiability for the proposed axioms over 20 epochs. Axioms (5) and (6) are depicted separately for each individual type of predicted damage and missing part. Axioms (9) and (10) (bottom right) are also shown together because of the similarity of their logical rules.

As shown in Figure 3a, for Rule #1, axioms (3) and (4) start with a satisfiability of 0.82 and then drop to 0.66 each: this, together with the satisfiability of (8) and (9) and the classification accuracies obtained on the additional bike attributes (which are lower than 20%), suggests that the network has difficulty classifying the bike attributes and correlating them with the corresponding IDs. This could also indicate that the selected bike attributes are not as relevant to the network during ID classification as the training progresses.

In Fig. 3b, for Rule #2, axioms (5) and (6) - shown separately for each individual type of predicted damage and missing part - provide another interesting clue: while the performance of the positive axiom (5) slowly decreases as training progresses, the performance of negative axiom (6), on the contrary, increases. This suggests that, as training progresses, the network finds it more difficult to associate damaged and undamaged instances of the same bike to the same IDs. In addition, axioms related to bent and broken damage show stronger behavior than those related to missing parts, suggesting that the former have a stronger influence on the classification. An explanation for this last result could likely be derived from the fact that most of the auxiliary attributes that define an ID in the Bent&Broken Bicycle dataset (see Sect. 4.1), such as bicycle type, model, sticker, and frame color and texture, are associated with the frame and not with the missing parts, making the changes to the frame caused by the two types of damage more influential on the ReID task than the removal of any of the other parts.

In Fig. 3c, for Rule #3, axioms (7) and (8) provide some information about the behavior of the network when it relates features of frames with similar and different IDs: the positive axiom (7) indicates that the network is relatively good at associating features of bikes belonging to the same IDs from the beginning, while the negative axiom (8) shows that it has difficulty separating features of bikes with different IDs.

Finally, in Fig. 3d, Axiom (9) shows that the network has difficulty classifying bike attributes, which may suggest that such fine-grained characteristics may be too difficult to learn using only an LTN-based loss. Second, Axiom (10) shows that the network only partially learns to classify IDs correctly, suggesting that the effectiveness of the training process largely depends on the triplet loss, rather than the cross entropy used for ID classification.

6   Conclusions

This research investigated the application of NeSy machine learning to object ReID by combining the LTN framework with the TransRe3ID network baseline. Experimental results show the feasibility of applying this framework on a complex computer vision task such as instance-level image retrieval. On the other hand, we observed limited performance improvements, probably due to the fact that the network was able to recover from the Bent&Broken dataset from those already implicit in the original ID labels. Classifying the auxiliary attributes has also proven to be a difficult task for the network. On the other hand, the integration of NeSy machine learning techniques provides a novel method for analyzing the training behavior of the network, which could potentially pave the way for more effective explicability of object ReID architectures. Future research may explore NeSy techniques that differ from LTNs, evolve the proposed logical constraints by providing additional or entirely new rules, or, as mentioned earlier, attempt to optimize and extend the classification task for bike attributes. Finally, the proposed technique should be further investigated in the small data regime.

Acknowledgements. This study was carried out within the FAIR - Future Artificial Intelligence Research and received funding from the European Union Next-GenerationEU (PIANO NAZIONALE DI RIPRESA E RESILIENZA (PNRR) - MISSIONE 4 COMPONENTE 2, INVESTIMENTO 1.3 - D.D. 1555 11/10/2022, PE00000013). This manuscript reflects only the authors' views and opinions, neither the European Union nor the European Commission can be considered responsible for them.

References

1. Badreddine, S., Garcez, A.D., Serafini, L., Spranger, M.: Logic tensor networks. Artif. Intell. **303**, 103649 (2022)
2. Badreddine, S., Spranger, M.: Injecting prior knowledge for transfer learning into reinforcement learning algorithms using logic tensor networks. arXiv preprint arXiv:1906.06576 (2019)
3. Chen, B., Marussy, K., Pilarski, S., Semeráth, O., Varro, D.: Consistent scene graph generation by constraint optimization. In: Proceedings of the 37th IEEE/ACM International Conference on Automated Software Engineering, pp. 1–13 (2022)
4. Donadello, I., Serafini, L.: Compensating supervision incompleteness with prior knowledge in semantic image interpretation. In: 2019 International Joint Conference on Neural Networks (IJCNN), pp. 1–8. IEEE (2019)
5. Dutta, S., Basu, S., Chakraborty, M.K.: Many-valued logics, fuzzy logics and graded consequence: a comparative appraisal. In: Lodaya, K. (ed.) ICLA 2013. LNCS, vol. 7750, pp. 197–209. Springer, Heidelberg (2013). https://doi.org/10.1007/978-3-642-36039-8_18
6. Garcez, A.d., Gori, M., Lamb, L.C., Serafini, L., Spranger, M., Tran, S.N.: Neural-symbolic computing: an effective methodology for principled integration of machine learning and reasoning. arXiv preprint arXiv:1905.06088 (2019)
7. Garcez, A.D., Lamb, L.C.: Neurosymbolic AI: the 3rd wave. In: Artificial Intelligence Review, pp. 1–20 (2023)
8. Gibaut, W., et al.: Neurosymbolic AI and its taxonomy: a survey. arXiv e-prints pp. arXiv-2305 (2023)
9. He, S., Luo, H., Wang, P., Wang, F., Li, H., Jiang, W.: TransReID: transformer-based object re-identification. In: Proceedings of the IEEE/CVF International Conference on Computer Vision, pp. 15013–15022 (2021)
10. Hitzler, P.: Neuro-symbolic artificial intelligence: the state of the art (2022)
11. Huang, H., Zhang, B., Jing, L., Fu, X., Chen, X., Shi, J.: Logic tensor network with massive learned knowledge for aspect-based sentiment analysis. Knowl.-Based Syst. **257**, 109943 (2022)

12. Khan, M.J., Breslin, J.G., Curry, E.: Expressive scene graph generation using commonsense knowledge infusion for visual understanding and reasoning. In: Groth, P., et al. (eds.) ESWC 2022. Lecture Notes in Computer Science, vol. 13261, pp. 93–112. Springer, Cham (2022). https://doi.org/10.1007/978-3-031-06981-9_6

13. van Krieken, E., Acar, E., van Harmelen, F.: Analyzing differentiable fuzzy logic operators. Artif. Intell. **302**, 103602 (2022)

14. Lian, J., Wang, D., Zhu, S., Wu, Y., Li, C.: Transformer-based attention network for vehicle re-identification. Electronics **11**(7), 1016 (2022)

15. Lu, Z., Lin, R., Hu, H.: MART: mask-aware reasoning transformer for vehicle re-identification. IEEE Trans. Intell. Transp. Syst. **24**, 1994–2009 (2022)

16. Ma, H., Li, X., Yuan, X., Zhao, C.: Denseformer: a dense transformer framework for person re-identification. IET Comput. Vision **17**, 527–536 (2022)

17. Manigrasso, F., Miro, F.D., Morra, L., Lamberti, F.: Faster-LTN: a neuro-symbolic, end-to-end object detection architecture. In: Farkaš, I., Masulli, P., Otte, S., Wermter, S. (eds.) ICANN 2021. LNCS, vol. 12892, pp. 40–52. Springer, Cham (2021). https://doi.org/10.1007/978-3-030-86340-1_4

18. Mao, J., Gan, C., Kohli, P., Tenenbaum, J.B., Wu, J.: The neuro-symbolic concept learner: interpreting scenes, words, and sentences from natural supervision. In: International Conference on Learning Representations. International Conference on Learning Representations, ICLR (2019)

19. Martone, S., Manigrasso, F., Lamberti, F., Morra, L.: Prototypical logic tensor networks (proto-LTN) for zero shot learning. In: 2022 26th International Conference on Pattern Recognition (ICPR), pp. 4427–4433. IEEE (2022)

20. Park, J., Bu, S.J., Cho, S.B.: A neuro-symbolic AI system for visual question answering in pedestrian video sequences. In: Bringas, P.G., et al. (eds.) HAIS 2022. LNCS, vol. 13469, pp. 443–454. Springer, Cham (2022). https://doi.org/10.1007/978-3-031-15471-3_38

21. Piano, L., Pratticò, F.G., Russo, A.S., Lanari, L., Morra, L., Lamberti, F.: Bent & broken bicycles: leveraging synthetic data for damaged object re-identification. In: Proceedings of the IEEE/CVF Winter Conference on Applications of Computer Vision, pp. 4881–4891 (2023)

22. Serafini, L., Donadello, I., Garcez, A.D.: Learning and reasoning in logic tensor networks: theory and application to semantic image interpretation. In: Proceedings of the Symposium on Applied Computing, pp. 125–130 (2017)

23. Silver, T., Athalye, A., Tenenbaum, J.B., Lozano-Pérez, T., Kaelbling, L.P.: Learning neuro-symbolic skills for bilevel planning. In: Conference on Robot Learning, pp. 701–714. PMLR (2023)

24. Wang, H., Shen, J., Liu, Y., Gao, Y., Gavves, E.: NFormer: robust person re-identification with neighbor transformer. In: Proceedings of the IEEE/CVF Conference on Computer Vision and Pattern Recognition, pp. 7297–7307 (2022)

25. Wu, T., et al.: ZeroC: a neuro-symbolic model for zero-shot concept recognition and acquisition at inference time. In: Advances in Neural Information Processing Systems, vol. 35, pp. 9828–9840 (2022)

26. Yu, Z., Pei, J., Zhu, M., Zhang, J., Li, J.: Multi-attribute adaptive aggregation transformer for vehicle re-identification. Inf. Process. Manage. **59**(2), 102868 (2022)

27. Zhu, K., et al.: Aaformer: auto-aligned transformer for person re-identification. IEEE Trans. Neural Netw. Learn. Syst. (2023)

Retinal Disease Diagnosis with a Hybrid ResNet50-LSTM Deep Learning

Stewart Muchuchuti[ID] and Serestina Viriri[✉][ID]

School of Mathematics, Statistics and Computer Science, University of
KwaZulu-Natal, Durban, South Africa
221116649@stu.ukzn.ac.za, viriris@ukzn.ac.za

Abstract. Timely diagnosis is paramount in ocular medicine to prevent irreversible vision impairment. Despite the promise of deep learning in automated diagnosis, many existing models are tailored for a singular disease, potentially overlooking coexistent pathologies. This research introduces a hybrid ResNet50-LSTM model, designed for the concurrent detection of multiple ocular conditions. The model achieved a 100% diagnostic accuracy on this dataset, outperforming several contemporary models. Central to the approach used in this research was the combination of two neural network architectures. The Convolutional Neural Network (CNN) adeptly extracts spatial features from retinal images. In tandem, the Long-Short Term Memory (LSTM) Recurrent Neural Network interprets these features sequentially, enhancing diagnostic precision. Given its robust performance and versatility, the model presents itself as a promising diagnostic tool, meriting consideration for clinical application.

Keywords: Ocular Disease Diagnosis · ResNet50 · LSTM · Deep Learning

1 Introduction

The timely diagnosis of ocular diseases stands as a pivotal cornerstone in the realm of effective treatment and safeguarding against vision loss. Remarkably, the advent of automated diagnosis through deep learning models has heralded promising prospects in the augmentation of disease detection's expediency and precision. However, most existing deep learning models for ocular disease diagnosis are designed to detect a single disease, which limits their usefulness in real-life clinical practice and there are few studies that have explored the development of models that can simultaneously diagnose multiple ocular diseases [5]. Undetected ocular diseases that occur simultaneously with others may result in preventable blindness if left undiagnosed. By developing a multi-disease deep learning model that can simultaneously detect multiple ocular diseases, we can provide clinicians with a more complete and more accurate picture of a patient's ocular health, which can improve their ability to provide effective treatment and prevent vision

G. Bebis et al. (Eds.): ISVC 2023, LNCS 14362, pp. 358–369, 2023.
https://doi.org/10.1007/978-3-031-47966-3_28

loss. In this study, a multi-disease deep learning model is proposed for accurate automated diagnosis of ocular diseases using the ODIR dataset. The model is specifically designed to classify images containing one or more ocular diseases present in the image, enabling simultaneous diagnosis of multiple conditions. The researchers employed a fusion of convolutional neural networks (CNNs) and recurrent neural networks (RNNs) to effectively model the spatial and temporal dependencies between the ocular diseases observed in the images. The proposed approach exhibits several potential advantages over existing models in the field. It has the capability to enhance the accuracy of disease diagnosis while also reducing the time and cost associated with manual diagnosis. The researchers conducted comprehensive experiments to demonstrate the effectiveness of their approach, presenting empirical evidence of its performance compared to other state-of-the-art deep learning models typically used for ocular disease diagnosis. This research makes the following contributions to the automatic retinal disease detection body of knowledge:

- A novel approach for multilevel, multiclass retinal image classification using a combined ResNet50-LSTM model was developed in this work.
- By achieving high accuracy rates in the classification of retinal images, this research significantly enhances the ability to diagnose ocular diseases potentially leading to better patient management and improved health outcomes.
- This study provides a robust comparative analysis against other models, highlighting the superiority of the proposed ResNet50-LSTM model. It thus offers a valuable contribution to the ongoing discourse on deep learning models' efficacy in retinal image classification.

2 Related Work

There is a plethora of literature with numerous studies dedicated to detecting retinal diseases through the examination of retinal structures using fundus or OCT images, facilitated by advances in Deep Learning (DL) and retinal photography technology [11]. Research on retinal abnormality detection primarily focuses on segmentation and classification, with the help of purpose-built databases. Multiple models have been proposed for detecting specific retinal diseases, such as Diabetic Retinopathy (DR), Age-Related Macular Degeneration (AMD), and Glaucoma. To this end, disease-specific databases have been utilized, such as MESSIDOR for DR detection, AREDS for AMD, and SCES for Glaucoma detection. These publicly available databases are annotated for binary or three-class classification, with each image assigned mutually exclusive labels.

Ting et al. developed a deep learning system for diabetic retinopathy and related eye diseases using retinal images from multiethnic populations with diabetes. They utilized a CNN architecture to extract features from the retinal images and used transfer learning techniques to fine-tune the pre-trained model for their specific task. Their model achieved high accuracy and outperformed human ophthalmologists in some respects. Similarly, Burlina et al. [1] compared the performance of deep learning models and human experts for grading age-related macular degeneration (AMD). They used a CNN architecture to extract universal deep features from retinal images and transfer learning techniques to adapt the pre-trained model to their task. Their study showed that deep learning models achieved comparable performance to human experts and had the potential to assist ophthalmologists in clinical practice. A multimodal deep learning model for the automated classification of retinal diseases was developed [12]. The model utilized a combination of color fundus photography and optical coherence tomography images to improve the accuracy of disease classification. To its detriment, the model's performance was only evaluated on a small dataset of 220 images, which may limit the generalizability of the model. Tavakoli et al. in [7] developed a multi-task deep learning model for the automated diagnosis of diabetic retinopathy, retinal vein occlusion, and age related macular degeneration (AMD). The model utilized a combination of CNN and RNN architectures to extract features from retinal images and achieved high accuracy. The model's performance was only evaluated on a small dataset of 51 patients, thereby rendering generalizability claims doubtful. A fully convolutional network model for the segmentation of retinal layers and fluid in optical coherence tomography images was proposed in [13]. This model together with the hybrid CNN and RNN networks proposed by Roy et al. in [6] and by Fu et al. in [3], although they achieved high accuracy levels, they suffered from the small dataset sizes throwing generalizability claims in jeopardy.

In [11], authors developed Attention-Guided 3D-CNN Framework for Glaucoma Detection and Structural-Functional Association Using Volumetric Images. The framework employed an attention mechanism alongside a deep convolutional neural network, exhibiting superior performance, outperforming state-of-the-art methods. However, the model solely focused on glaucoma and neglected other ocular diseases. Most existing models are limited to detecting single diseases, hindering real-world clinical practicality, where patients may present with multiple ocular conditions simultaneously. A pressing need exists to expand diagnostic models to address the concurrent detection of various ocular diseases for enhanced clinical utility. It is possible for each eye to have distinct abnormalities, indicating different classes of retinal disease. In some studies like [6], authors made attempts to simultaneously detect more than one ocular disease, but they suffered generalizability limitations owing to the small size of their datasets. There is a need for multi-disease classification models that can simultaneously detect multiple ocular diseases in a single image, validated on large enough databases to provide generalizability comfort. Most models utilized preprocessing techniques, such as data augmentation and normalization to improve the accuracy and reliability of automated diagnosis. Transfer learning techniques, such as fine-tuning and feature extraction, have also been used to transfer knowledge from pre-trained models to new tasks. Evaluation metrics are crucial for assessing the performance of deep learning models for ocular disease diagnosis. Metrics such as accuracy, precision, recall, and F1-score were mostly in the models described in this section to measure the effectiveness of these models

[2,8]. These metrics provide a quantitative measure of the model's performance, allowing for comparison between different models and datasets. It is important to carefully consider the appropriate metric for a specific application to avoid bias and ensure an accurate evaluation of the model's performance. In this study, a multi-disease deep learning model is proposed for the automated diagnosis of ocular diseases, leveraging the ODIR dataset. The model's hybrid architecture integrates convolutional and recurrent neural networks, facilitating the concurrent detection of multiple ocular diseases within retinal images.

3   Methods and Techniques

In this study, a deep learning model that combines CNNs and RNNs, to detect multiple ocular diseases simultaneously. Specifically, a pre-trained ResNet-50 architecture as the CNN component of the model to extract key features from the retinal images. The extracted features were then fed into a bi-directional LSTM network to encode the temporal sequence of the extracted features and classify the image into one or more ocular diseases. The proposed model was trained and evaluated on the ODIR dataset, and its performance was compared to other state-of-the-art models for ocular disease diagnosis. This paper outlines the detailed methodology used for developing and evaluating the deep learning model, encompassing data collection, preprocessing techniques, model architecture, training procedure, evaluation metrics, and ethical considerations. Figure 1 is a depiction of examples of images from the ODIR database.

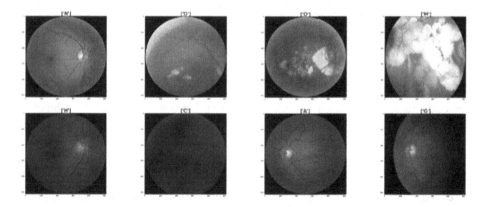

Fig. 1. Examples of images from top left: ['N']: Normal, ['D']: Diabetic Retinopathy, ['O']: Other diseases, ['M']: Myopia, ['H']: Hypertensive retinopathy, ['C']: Cataract, ['A']: AMD, ['G']: Glaucoma.

3.1   Image Preprocessing

The images were resized to $224 \times 224 \times 3$ pixels for uniformity. This is because ResNet-50 was originally trained on the ImageNet dataset, which consists of images that are resized to 224×224 pixels. Data augmentation techniques were applied to increase the size and diversity of the dataset. Apart from increasing the number of images, preprocessing techniques improve model robustness [9]. The data was preprocessed for use with a combination of CNNs and RNNs by extracting key features from the images using a pre-trained ResNet-50 architecture and then encoding them using a bi-directional LSTM network.

3.2   Model Architecture

The proposed deep learning model is designed to detect multiple ocular diseases simultaneously, using a combination of convolutional neural networks (CNNs) and recurrent neural networks (RNNs), shown in Fig. 2. For the CNN component of the model, the pre-trained ResNet-50 architecture is used to extract key features from the retinal images. ResNet-50 is a popular deep learning architecture that has been shown to perform well on image classification tasks [4]. Recent studies have shown that combining ResNet with other deep learning techniques can further improve the accuracy and efficiency of automated diagnosis models for ocular diseases [14]. The proposed deep learning model for automated diagnosis of ocular diseases including diabetes, glaucoma, cataract, AMD, hypertension, myopia, is designed to simultaneously analyze both left and right eye images. The pre-trained ResNet-50 architecture is used as the CNN component of the model to extract key features from the retinal images. ResNet-50 is a 50-layer deep convolutional neural network that has been shown to perform well on image classification tasks. The ResNet-50 model is applied separately to the left and right eye images to extract features from each eye image.

Convolutional Operations. The primary operation of the ResNet50 involves convolutions with the input images to extract low-level features. If I denotes the input image and K denotes the kernel of a convolutional layer, then the convolution operation can be represented as:

$$FI = I * K \tag{1}$$

Here, the symbol '*' denotes the convolution operation. This operation is applied iteratively throughout the layers of the ResNet50 network, allowing the network to progressively extract more complex features from the retinal images.

Feature Maps. The output of each convolutional operation is a feature map. If you have an image I with a set of filters W in the first layer, the produced feature maps F can be calculated as:

$$F = ReLU(I * W + b) \tag{2}$$

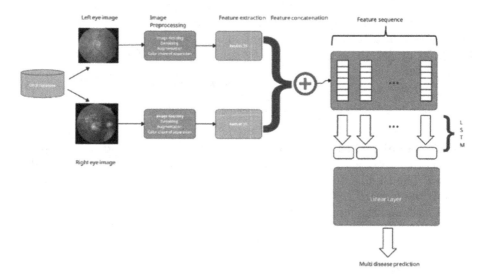

Fig. 2. Hybrid CNN-LSTM Model Architecture

where, b is the bias, and ReLU denotes the rectified linear unit activation function. The feature maps represent various features of the input image, such as edges or textures.

Residual Blocks. The ResNet50 model contains several residual blocks. These blocks help to capture even the minute details that would otherwise be lost in a regular, non-residual deep network. The operation of a residual block can be represented as:

$$Y = F(X, W) + X \tag{3}$$

where, Y is the output of the block, X is the input, and F is the transformation function (generally a stack of convolutions, ReLU activation, and batch normalization). W denotes the weights of these transformation functions.

Bottleneck Blocks. The ResNet50 model uses bottleneck blocks, where a 1×1 convolution reduces the dimensionality before a 3×3 convolution, then another 1×1 convolution restores the dimensionality. This design helps manage the computational resources and reduces the number of parameters, which is beneficial for processing high-resolution retinal images. If we consider input X and transformations $F1$, $F2$, and $F3$ as different layers of the bottleneck block, this operation can be represented as:

$$Y = F3(F2(F1(X))) + X \tag{4}$$

Feature Concatenation. The extracted features from each eye are then concatenated to form a single feature vector which is passed through a bi-directional

LSTM network for final classification. Assuming F_left and F_right are the feature vectors extracted from the left and right eyes respectively using the ResNet50 model, these features can be concatenated to form a single feature vector F_total thus:

$$F\_total = [F\_left, F\_right] \tag{5}$$

The square brackets represent a concatenation operation.

Bi-directional LSTM Network. The LSTM is used to encode the temporal sequence of the extracted features and classify the image into one or more ocular diseases. The Bi-directional LSTM processes the input sequence in both directions. If the forward LSTM is denoted $LSTM\_fwd$ and the backward LSTM as $LSTM\_bwd$, and the input sequence as:

$$X = [x1, x2, ..., xn], \tag{6}$$

the forward and backward pass of the LSTM network can be represented as follows:

$$h\_fwd = LSTM\_fwd(X) \tag{7}$$

$$h\_bwd = LSTM\_bwd(reverse(X)) \tag{8}$$

Here, h_fwd and h_bwd represent the hidden states of the forward and backward LSTM respectively. The final output at each time step i is a concatenation of the forward and backward hidden states:

$$h\_i = [h\_fwd\_i, h\_bwd\_i] \tag{9}$$

The bi-directionality of the LSTM allows it to capture dependencies from both past (left context) and future (right context) elements in the sequence.

Classification. The LSTM's final hidden state is typically used to classify the input sequence. If 'SoftMax' is the activation function used in the output layer, and 'W' and 'b' represent the weight matrix and bias vector of this layer, the probability of the sequence belonging to class 'c' is given by:

$$P(c|X) = softmax(W * h\_n + b) \tag{10}$$

where h_n represents the final hidden state of the LSTM. This corresponds to the probability of the retinal image being classified into a particular disease category. The 'c' with the highest probability would be chosen as the final diagnosis by the system.

The proposed model represents an innovative approach to the automated diagnosis of ocular diseases, combining the strengths of ResNet-50 and LSTM networks to achieve state-of-the-art performance. The ResNet50 network is particularly adept at detecting low-level features such as edges and textures as well as more complex structures with its deeper layers [10]. This network is robust to the vanishing gradient problem using residual connections. This makes it effective in extracting robust features from retinal images. On the other hand, the LSTM can capture long-term dependencies in sequence data which traditional RNNs struggle with due to the vanishing gradient problem [4]. This is particularly important when dealing with multilevel retinal images which have sequential dependencies. The LSTM, following the ResNet-50 in the proposed model, can make use of these dependencies to better classify the retinal images.

3.3 Model Training

The feature maps extracted from the CNN are fed into the LSTM to obtain a final feature vector. To enable multi-label classification of fundus images, the final feature vector is optimized using a combination of the SoftMax activation function and categorical cross-entropy loss function. This allows the model to output a probability distribution for each label, indicating the likelihood of the input image being associated with that label. An Adam optimizer with a learning rate of 1e−5 was used to adjust the weights during training. The model was trained for 30 epochs, with early stopping implemented to prevent overfitting. The LSTM is fully connected to a final layer with 8 nodes (one for each disease class), each of which provides a probability that the patient's condition falls into that class.

3.4 Performance Evaluation

The models' performance was evaluated using various metrics, including accuracy, sensitivity, specificity and loss values. These metrics offer a comprehensive view of the model's performance across multiple aspects, allowing us to make accurate comparisons with other state-of-the-art models. The original annotations of the retinal images are compared with the predicted annotations to determine the performance metrics - accuracy, specificity and sensitivity of the models. The accuracy metric measures the proportion of correctly classified samples out of the total number of samples. The sensitivity estimates the ability to correctly identify positive instances. A model's specificity is its ability to correctly identify negative instances. Four types of statistical values, true positive *(TP)*, true negative *(TN)*, false positive *(FP)* and false negative *(FN)* are used to compute the performance measures as follows:

$$Accuracy = \frac{TP + TN}{TP + FP + TN + FN} \tag{11}$$

$$Sensitivity = \frac{TP}{TP + FN} \tag{12}$$

$$Specificity = \frac{TN}{TN + FP} \tag{13}$$

The models were also evaluated using their training and validation loss values. The loss value indicates how well the model is minimizing its prediction error during training. A lower loss value is an indication of better model performance and is therefore more desirable.

4   Results and Discussion

In this study, the applicability of a combined ResNet50-LSTM model for the classification of retinal images in a multiclass, multilevel setting was explored. Since this is a hybrid model, essentially three models were trained. The first was the model for the left eye images, then one for the right eye images and finally the LSTM model. The three models were trained and evaluated using dedicated training sets and validation sets, respectively, across 30 epochs with early stopping to avoid overfitting.

4.1   Left and Right Models

Both models performed well in terms of accuracy and loss. The left eye model (model 1) achieved a higher final training accuracy of 98.86% compared to 97.66% for the right eye model (model 2). Model 1 also has a superior final validation accuracy of 96% compared to model 2 with 90%. Table 1 shows a summary of the performances of the two models.

Table 1. Left-eye and Right-eye image model performances

Metric	Left Eye Image model	Right Eye Image model
Final Training Accuracy	98.96%	97.66%
Final Validation Accuracy	96.00%	90%
Final Training Loss	0.0402	0.0752
Final Validation Loss	0.1337	0.3120

4.2   LSTM Model

Our hybrid model achieved remarkable results with regard to accuracy, reaching 100% on the validation set by the end of the training process as depicted in Fig. 3. This perfect score suggests that our model was able to classify all retinal image types and stages correctly, thereby confirming the model's high proficiency in handling the complex, multilevel classification task. Figures 3, 4 show the variation of training and validation accuracy with epochs and sensitivity with epochs respectively. Concurrently, both recall and specificity reached perfect scores of 1.0000, demonstrating the model's ability to identify all positive classes and differentiate between distinct retinal conditions. Figure 4 demonstrates that very high sensitivities are achieved with just a few epochs. These outcomes point to the model's robustness and accuracy in handling complex medical imaging datasets and highlight the potential of our ResNet50-LSTM model for clinical applications in ophthalmology. In terms of the loss metric, a consistent decrease in the loss values was observed for both the training and validation sets across

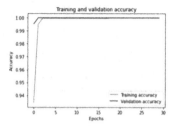

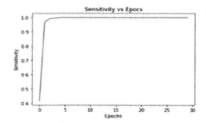

Fig. 3. Training and validation accuracy

Fig. 4. Training and validation sensitivity

the epochs. This indicates that the hybrid model was learning and improving its predictions over time, culminating in a final training loss of 2.602e−04 and a validation loss of 0.0013 at the 30th epoch. These outcomes point to the model's high proficiency in handling the task at hand. However, they may also indicate the possibility of overfitting, a condition where the model learns the detail and noise in the training data to the extent that it negatively impacts the performance on new, unseen data. Table 2, shows that the hybrid model outperforms state-of-the-art models in the literature.

Table 2. Performance comparison of different models

Model	Accuracy	Specificity	Sensitivity
DenseNet 121	95%	94%	96%
EfficientNetB4	96%	95%	97%
ResNet101	96%	95%	97%
MDCF	97%	96%	98%
ResNet-LSTM	**100%**	**100%**	**100%**

5 Conclusion

This study proposed the hybridization of the ResNet50 and LSTM models for the classification of multiclass, multilabel retinal diseases. The combined model is remarkably efficacious in the classification of retinal images, particularly those necessitating a multilevel, multiclass approach. The performance of the hybrid model, evidenced by an accuracy of 100%, a precision of 100%, and a recall of 100%, significantly outperforms those of its predecessors used for analogous tasks. This may be attributable in part to the incorporation of the LSTM following the ResNet50 model, which adeptly captured temporal dependencies intrinsic to the sequences of retinal images, thereby likely enhancing the overall model performance. However, despite these phenomenal results, it is prudent to acknowledge certain constraints inherent to this model. The opaqueness of deep learning models, an issue of interpretability, remains a significant challenge that warrants more intensive investigation.

Acknowledgements. International Development Research Centre (IDRC) and the Swedish International Development Cooperation Agency (SIDA) under the Artificial Intelligence for Development (AI4D) Africa Scholarship program with the Africa Center for Technology Studies (ACTS) for the funding provided.

References

1. Burlina, P., Pacheco, K., Joshi, N., Freund, D., Kong, J., Bressler, N.: Comparing humans and deep learning performance for grading AMD: a study in using universal deep features and transfer learning for automated AMD analysis. Comput. Biol. Med. **109**, 79–86 (2019)
2. Esteva, A., et al.: Dermatologist-level classification of skin cancer with deep neural networks. Nature **542**(7639), 115–118 (2017)
3. Fu, H., et al.: GANet: a deep learning framework for glaucoma diagnosis with gated attention mechanism. IEEE J. Biomed. Health Inf. **25**(4), 1184–1194 (2021)
4. He, K., Zhang, X., Ren, S., Sun, J.: Deep residual learning for image recognition. In: Proceedings of the IEEE Conference on Computer Vision and Pattern Recognition, pp. 770–778 (2016)
5. Neha, K., Gour, D.: Automatic detection of diabetic retinopathy stages using deep convolutional neural network. In: 2019 IEEE International Conference on Electrical, Computer and Communication Technologies (ICECCT), pp. 1–5. IEEE (2019)
6. Saha, S., Srinivasan, S., Krishnan, S.M.: Ocular disease identification using deep learning. Expert Syst. Appl. **157**, 113456 (2020)
7. Tavakoli, M., Rabbani, H.: Multi-task deep learning for the automated diagnosis of diabetic retinopathy, retinal vein occlusion and age-related macular degeneration. In: Computer Methods in Biomechanics and Biomedical Engineering: Imaging & Visualization, vol. 7, no. 2, pp. 177–186 (2019)
8. Ting, D.S.W., Cheung, C.Y.L.: Development and validation of a deep learning system for diabetic retinopathy and related eye diseases using retinal images from multiethnic populations with diabetes. In: JAMA, vol. 322, no. 17, pp. 1661–1670 (2019)
9. Wang, W., Wang, P.: Multi-scale densely connected convolutional features for retinal disease classification. IEEE Access **9**, 81756–81766 (2021)
10. Zhang, L., Shen, C.: Deep learning for automated diabetic retinopathy diagnosis using a multi-scale residual network with attention mechanism. Pattern Recogn. **107**, 107477 (2020)
11. George, Y., Antony, B.J., Ishikawa, H., Wollstein, G., Schuman, J.S., Garnavi, R.: Attention-guided 3D-CNN framework for glaucoma detection and structural-functional association using volumetric images. IEEE J. Biomed. Health Inf. **24**(12), 3421–3430 (2020). https://doi.org/10.1109/JBHI.2020.3001019

12. Zhang, H., et al.: Automatic segmentation and visualization of choroid in oct with knowledge infused deep learning. IEEE J. Biomed. Health Inf. **24**(12), 3408–3420 (2020). https://doi.org/10.1109/jbhi.2020.3023144
13. Azimi, B., Rashno, A., Fadaei, S.: Fully convolutional networks for fluid segmentation in retina images. In: 2020 International Conference on Machine Vision and Image Processing (MVIP), pp. 1–7 (2020). https://doi.org/10.1109/MVIP49855.2020.9116914
14. Zedan, M.J., Zulkifley, M.A., Ibrahim, A.A., Moubark, A.M., Kamari, N.A.M., Abdani, S.R.: Automated glaucoma screening and diagnosis based on retinal fundus images using deep learning approaches: a comprehensive review. Diagnostics **13**(13), 2180 (2023)

Pothole Segmentation and Area Estimation with Deep Neural Networks and Unmanned Aerial Vehicles

Ethan Welborn$^{(\boxtimes)}$ and Sotirios Diamantas

Department of Computer Science and Electrical Engineering, Tarleton State University, The Texas A&M University System, Stephenville, TX 76402, USA
{ewelborn,diamantas}@tarleton.edu

Abstract. In this research, we explore the problems of pothole detection, segmentation, and area estimation using deep neural networks and unmanned aerial vehicles (drones). We start by compiling two datasets, one that contains ground-level and aerial images of potholes, and another that only contains ground-level images, and we train a total of six deep neural network models for pothole detection; we do this to determine whether aerial images are necessary for training UAV-based object detection models. We then determine which pothole detection model is the most accurate and we also determine which combinations of camera angle and UAV altitude are best for detecting potholes. Furthermore, we take the strongest pothole segmentation model and apply it to area estimation using a combination of homography, the intrinsic and extrinsic parameters of the UAV camera, and novel methods. Our method for pothole area estimation using YOLOv8 has an average area estimation error of 9.71%.

Keywords: Pothole detection · Segmentation · Area estimation · Unmanned aerial vehicles

1 Introduction

Computer vision applications encompass a large number of areas from space to industry and transportation, many of which include detection, segmentation, and area estimation methods. Of particular interest are the applications related to transportation in view of the advent of autonomous vehicles. Detection of potholes is crucial not only for vehicles but for drivers as well. More specifically, pothole-free roads not only contribute to safe driving conditions but also to faster and less costly trips. A significant number of car repairs is caused by poor condition of roads. In 2021 alone, potholes cost American drivers a staggering $26.5 billion with an average cost of $600 per repair [1].

The recommended approach to avoid driving a vehicle into a pothole is to detect it as early as possible or to have properly maintained roads in a timely manner. Detecting and classifying potholes based on their area is not an easy

G. Bebis et al. (Eds.): ISVC 2023, LNCS 14362, pp. 370–384, 2023.
https://doi.org/10.1007/978-3-031-47966-3_29

task as it requires a continuous effort to monitor roads and highways and a dedicated group of people to detect potholes. In this research we try to tackle the problem of pothole detection using an Unmanned Aerial Vehicle (UAV) with the view to detect potholes quickly and accurately. UAVs are ideal for pothole detection as they can cover large areas in a small period of time but also because they can continiously scan for potholes even in remote or rural areas rarely used by vehicles. In our proposed research, not only do we detect potholes but also we infer their area so as to classify them based on their size. The algorithms developed for this research are based on Deep Neural Networks (DNNs) where various models have been trained and tested in varying conditions. The results show that our proposed method is promising yet effective in detecting, segmenting, and estimating pothole areas from a UAV.

Our main contributions are as follows:

1. We assembled a dataset for pothole segmentation using a mixture of online images and images taken with our own UAV.
2. We trained and evaluated six UAV-based pothole detection and segmentation models.
3. We answered key questions regarding UAV object detection: which combination of angle and altitude are best for UAV object detection, and if aerial images are required to train an effective UAV object detection model.
4. We designed a novel algorithm for estimating pothole area and compared it to the SOTA.

This research is a continuation of the author's thesis research [20].

2   Background Work

There are generally three categories of automated pothole detection systems: systems which use (1) cameras, (2) LiDAR or other depth measurement sensors, and (3) vibration sensors.

Pothole detection has been studied extensively in recent years by several researchers. YOLO has been used in numerous studies as the primary framework for neural network training and testing. In a recent study, [18], the authors perform real-time pothole detection using YOLOv3 and YOLOv4 using mainly images from a cellphone in the car's windshield. In a similar comparison study [3], the authors have tested YOLOv1 to YOLOv5 on a raspberry pi computer with an accuracy of pothole detection of 90% for Tiny-YOLOv4. YOLOv3 was examined and tested for real-time pothole detection along with GPS information in [22]. YOLOv5 was tested for real-time pothole detection in a study by [4]. Detection of potholes using a smartphone in real-time and using deep neural networks has been the study of [19]. Speed bumps and pothole detection using a ZED camera are presented in [16].

Pothole detection can be achieved with LiDAR sensors as well. LiDAR technology is suited for such type of applications as range measurements on the surface of roads can reveal anomalies on asphalt. In [13], the authors present a model with two sensors, a 2D LiDAR and a camera. In [17], the authors present a model with a LiDAR and a GPS interfaced to a Raspberry Pi. Detection of potholes with a UAV LiDAR and photogrammetry is presented in [9]. Optical flow methods for segmentation appear in [7] as well as background subtraction methods in [6].

An alternative to cameras and depth measurement sensors is the use of vibration sensors. This technology was used several years ago, however, recent advances have revided the interest of vibration sensors. In [5,8,23], the authors have used vibration sensors for the detection of anomalies as well as potholes. More recently, in [21], the authors have used vibration sensors from a smartphone to detect potholes.

3   Methods

3.1   Datasets

Two datasets were compiled for this work. The first dataset, which will be referred to as the "mixed" dataset, contains 260 images of potholes, 212 were taken from ground-level while the other 48 were taken from the air. The second "ground-level" dataset contains 264 images of potholes all captured from ground-level: this dataset is used as a control to test how effective aerial images are for UAV-based object detection models. To achieve this, the differences between the two datasets were minimized.

3.2   Architectures

Three deep neural network architectures were selected, Mask R-CNN [11], YOLOv8 [12], and YOLOX [10], to evaluate for pothole detection. These three architectures were used, in combination with two datasets, to train six unique deep learning models. All three architectures have open source Python implementations which were used for our work. All of the code used to obtain our results will be available on GitHub[1].

Two of the three architectures that were used, YOLOv8 and YOLOX, have several sub-architectures available which provide trade-offs of greater accuracy versus faster inference. The goal was to create a balanced comparison between YOLOv8 and YOLOX while still pushing for high accuracy results. For YOLOv8, the yolov8m-seg model provided by Ultralytics[2] was used as the base for our two YOLOv8 models. The larger model, yolov8l-seg, was also trained, but there was no significant increase in accuracy. For YOLOX, the YOLOX-m model from the MegEngine implementation[3] was used. Again, the larger model, YOLOX-l, was trained as well, but there was no significant increase in accuracy. Both models are

---

[1] https://github.com/TSUrobotics/UAVpotholes.
[2] https://github.com/ultralytics/ultralytics.
[3] https://github.com/MegEngine/YOLOX.

comparable in size, with yolov8m-seg containing 27.3 million parameters versus YOLOX-m containing 25.3 million parameters.

For Mask R-CNN, the implementation provided by Matterport[4] with ResNet101 as the backbone was used. The network was pretrained on Microsoft's Common Objects in Context (COCO) dataset [15].

3.3   Training and Evaluation Criteria

The deep learning models were evaluated against two metrics: accuracy and speed. Our ideal model will have both high recall - very few potholes missed - and high precision - very few false positives. High recall is more important than high precision, because human operators that are supervising our model can easily spot and remove a small number of false positives, while it is much more difficult for human operators to spot false negatives, as they would be forced to watch the UAV videos from beginning to end to determine if any potholes were missed - which defeats the purpose of this work. Our ideal model will be fast enough to detect potholes in a reasonable amount of time using consumer grade hardware. Aside from these two metrics, our ideal model will also support instance segmentation, so that the shapes of detected potholes are recorded: this will allow further analysis of the potholes, including area estimation, which will be introduced later in this work.

Data augmentation was used for all six deep learning models to diversify the training dataset. For YOLOv8, the default data augmentation settings are used, which include Mosaic (from YOLOv4), mirroring the image left-to-right, translating the image and adjusting the hue, saturation, and value of the image. For YOLOX, the data augmentation settings used for PASCAL VOC are retained for this work, which are very similar to YOLOv8 with the addition of MixUp. For Mask R-CNN, there were no default settings provided, so we tried mirroring the image left-to-right and up-and-down, rotating the image, scaling the image, manipulating the brightness of the image, and blurring the image - the exact numbers will be available on GitHub.

All six models were trained until their loss plateaued - the YOLOv8 models trained for 200 epochs, the YOLOX models trained for 300 epochs, and the Mask R-CNN models trained for 130 epochs: The first 100 epochs were spent training the head of the network while the last 30 epochs were used to train both the head and the last few stages of the ResNet backbone.

4   Results

4.1   Hardware

For this work, a server containing an AMD Ryzen Threadripper PRO 3975WX 32-Core CPU along with two NVIDIA GeForce RTX 3090 graphics cards was utilized to train all six deep learning models. The DJI Mavic 2 Zoom drone was used to capture aerial images and videos for this work.

---

[4] https://github.com/matterport/Mask_RCNN.

4.2 Evaluation Criteria

The deep learning models are evaluated for general accuracy using Mean Average Precision (MAP), but the models are also evaluated for accuracy on a specific sequence of videos taken with our UAV. The MAP indicates how well the model is performing over the validation subset of either the mixed or ground-level dataset. Meanwhile, the model's performance on the UAV videos indicates how it will perform in a real-world, aerial scenario. Thus, we located a group of potholes and captured videos of them as the UAV passed over (see Fig. 1). The UAV was flown eight times with varying combinations of height (5 m and 10 m above-ground-level) and camera angle (15°, 30°, 45°, 90°). The six deep learning models are evaluated on all eight combinations of height and angle to determine if they can detect potholes from aerial images in a real-world scenario, and, if so, which combinations of height and angle are most effective for detecting potholes. Demonstration videos are available on our YouTube channel[5].

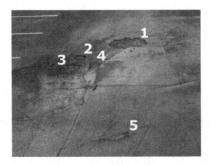

Fig. 1. The cluster of potholes that was used for evaluating detection accuracy of the models. Pothole no. 1 was detected by all six deep learning models in almost all eight videos. Pothole no. 5 was rarely detected.

To evaluate a deep learning model's accuracy on a UAV video, every detection in the video is marked as either a true positive or a false positive, and then the recall and the number of false positives of the model/video combination are reported. To utilize the time dimension in the aerial videos, the following heuristic is used for evaluating the models: if a bounding box remains on the video for a minimum of eight frames in any sequence of ten frames, then it is counted as a detection and marked as either a false or true positive. The idea is that real potholes should be detected continuously while they are in frame, while false positives should only be detected in small bursts as the lighting and perspective are changing during the UAV's flight; thus, the heuristic should be able to remove these false positives while retaining the true positives. In addition, bounding boxes will only be counted as a detection if they contain exactly one

---

[5] https://www.youtube.com/@robotperception6035.

pothole, they will be counted as false positives otherwise. For this work, the detections were marked manually by the researchers for all permutations of deep learning models and UAV flight videos.

4.3   Mixed Dataset Models

Starting the evaluation of the mixed dataset models, it is seen, from Table 1, that YOLOX had the best overall performance with an average pothole detection rate of 60% on the UAV videos, with YOLOv8 in second place at 55%, and Mask R-CNN trailing behind at 38%; these standings closely match the model's MAP (Mean Average Precision), with YOLOX having the highest MAP and Mask R-CNN having the lowest.

Table 1. Percentage of potholes detected from the three deep learning models trained on the mixed dataset, a.k.a. recall

Video	Mask R-CNN	YOLOX	YOLOv8
15° 5 m	0.20	0.60	0.60
15° 10 m	0.20	0.20	0.20
30° 5 m	0.40	0.60	0.60
30° 10 m	0.20	0.60	0.40
45° 5 m	0.60	0.80	0.80
45° 10 m	0.40	0.80	0.60
90° 5 m	0.60	0.40	0.60
90° 10 m	0.40	0.80	0.60
MAP_{50}	0.431	0.703	0.643
Inference Speed	215 ms	5.3 ms	3.6 ms

YOLOX saw no difference overall between the 5 m and 10 m videos, however, both Mask R-CNN and YOLOv8 performed better with the 5 m videos, with Mask R-CNN having an average pothole detection rate of 45% on the 5 m videos compared to 30% on the 10 m videos, and YOLOv8 having 65% on the 5 m videos and 45% on the 10 m videos. This suggests that the instance segmentation models have a higher likelihood of detecting potholes the closer the UAV is to the surface.

All of the models performed worse on the 15–30° angle videos compared to the 45–90° angle videos. Mask R-CNN had an average pothole detection rate of only 25% at 15–30° angles compared to 50% at 45–90° angles, YOLOX had 50% at 15–30° angles and 70% at 45–90° angles, and YOLOv8 had 45% at 15–30° angles and 65% at 45–90° angles. This suggests that all three models perform better when they are viewing the potholes from a birds-eye-view instead of from the side.

The models perform best at the 45–90° angle 5 m videos: Mask R-CNN jumps up from an average pothole detection rate of 38% to 60%, YOLOX maintains its 60% average, and YOLOv8 jumps from 55% to 70%. Referring to Table 2, false positives for all of the models drop as well: Mask R-CNN goes from an average of 1.88 false positives down to 1.5, and both YOLOX and YOLOv8 drop to 0 false positives. It is important to note, however, that this bracket only contains two videos, which is not a very large sample size: further experiments should be conducted to confirm these results.

Table 2. False positives from the three deep learning models trained on the mixed dataset

Video	Mask R-CNN	YOLOX	YOLOv8
15° 5 m	1	4	3
15° 10 m	3	4	2
30° 5 m	1	0	1
30° 10 m	2	2	2
45° 5 m	2	0	0
45° 10 m	2	1	0
90° 5 m	2	0	0
90° 10 m	5	1	0

Lastly, the speed difference between Mask R-CNN and the other two models should be addressed, as YOLOX and YOLOv8 are 40 times and 60 times faster than Mask R-CNN respectively, which is a large margin, and only justifiable if Mask R-CNN had a noticeable lead in accuracy over YOLOX and YOLOv8.

4.4 Ground-Level Dataset Models

Starting the evaluation of the ground-level dataset models, it is seen, from Table 3, the devastating effect that removing the aerial images from the training set had on these three models. Despite the datasets being equal in size, and similar training time being given to these models, there is a large gap in accuracy between these models and the models from Table 1. Mask R-CNN on the ground-level dataset had the best average pothole detection rate of a mere 0.28%, YOLOv8 came in second place at 0.20%, and YOLOX in last place at 0.18%. Special attention should be paid to the MAP of all three models: they are still relatively close to the models from Table 1 - in fact, Mask R-CNN and YOLOv8 have improved their MAP. This indicates that the models in Table 3 were not poorly trained, rather, that they were not sufficiently prepared for the UAV videos. This suggests that the inclusion of aerial images in the training dataset is necessary for UAV-based pothole detection - this is likely to be true for any UAV-based object detection model.

Table 3. Percentage of potholes detected from the three deep learning models trained on the ground-level dataset, a.k.a. recall

Video	Mask R-CNN	YOLOX	YOLOv8
15° 5 m	0.20	0.20	0.20
15° 10 m	0.20	0.00	0.20
30° 5 m	0.40	0.20	0.20
30° 10 m	0.20	0.20	0.20
45° 5 m	0.20	0.20	0.20
45° 10 m	0.20	0.20	0.20
90° 5 m	0.60	0.20	0.20
90° 10 m	0.20	0.20	0.20
MAP_{50}	0.635	0.633	0.691
Inference Speed	215 ms	5.3 ms	3.6 ms

It is clear that the results from Table 3 and Table 4 (the false positives) cannot be utilized for further analysis. It is possible that the three models from Table 3 are performing slightly better on the 45–90° angle 5 m videos, but this is difficult to quantify when the models struggle detecting the most pronounced pothole in the video, let alone the smaller ones. The only clear conclusion that can be drawn is that these models are substantially weaker on the UAV videos compared to the mixed dataset models from Table 1, and this is due to the lack of aerial images in the training dataset.

Table 4. False positives from the three deep learning models trained on the ground-level dataset

Video	Mask R-CNN	YOLOX	YOLOv8
15° 5 m	2	1	3
15° 10 m	2	2	1
30° 5 m	2	1	1
30° 10 m	3	1	1
45° 5 m	2	0	0
45° 10 m	1	0	0
90° 5 m	1	0	0
90° 10 m	2	0	0

Evaluating the results from the mixed dataset models and the ground-level dataset models, it can be determined that YOLOX trained on the mixed dataset is the most accurate pothole detection model, as it has the highest pothole detection rate on the UAV videos at 60%. In second place, and also the most accurate pothole segmentation model, is YOLOv8 trained on the mixed dataset, with a pothole detection rate on the UAV videos of 55%.

5   Area Estimation

5.1   Proposed Algorithm

Following the results from the previous experiments, the strongest pothole segmentation model, YOLOv8 trained on the mixed dataset, was applied to the problem of pothole area estimation. To determine the area of a pothole, the following algorithm is applied:

1. Use the intrinsic and extrinsic parameters of the camera to find the birds-eye-view homography transformation, as well as the pixel-to-meter ratio on the resulting birds-eye-view image
2. Segment foreground pixels (that belong to the pothole) from background pixels
3. Estimate the shape of the pothole (from the foreground pixels) as a polygon
4. Warp the points of the polygon onto the birds-eye-view image and find their pixel positions
5. Calculate the pixel area of the polygon on the birds-eye-view image and convert it to meters using the ratio from step 1

To estimate the homography, the methods outlined in [2] are followed. The first step is to find the intrinsic matrix of the camera, which requires the focal length f in millimeters, the sensor width s in millimeters, and the width w and height h of the video in pixels. In addition, the altitude a of the UAV in meters, the angle θ of the camera in degrees, and the horizontal field-of-view β of the camera in degrees are required for later calculations. All of these values are known in the experiment and require no estimation.

$$K = \begin{bmatrix} \frac{f \cdot w}{s} & 0 & \frac{w}{2} \\ 0 & \frac{f \cdot w}{s} & \frac{h}{2} \\ 0 & 0 & 1 \end{bmatrix} \tag{1}$$

For these experiments, the UAV camera had 0 degrees of roll, so removing the roll was unnecessary, however, the tilt of the camera was adjusted to 90 degrees so that the birds-eye-view of the road could be obtained. In addition, image translation and rotation are unnecessary, as we only need the relative distances between points transformed to the birds-eye-view image. As a result, we not need anything beyond Eq. 5 from [2] to generate our homography matrix. Lastly, it is assumed that the UAV will not be adjusting its altitude, or camera tilt or roll or focal length - thus, the homography matrix H only needs to be calculated once. The effect of the transformation can be seen in Fig. 2.

$$H = K \cdot R_{tilt} \cdot K^{-1} \cdot R_{roll} \tag{2}$$

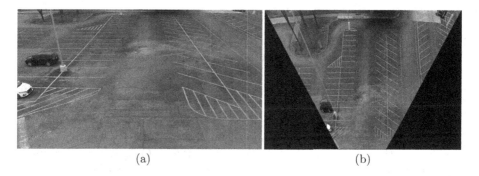

(a)   (b)

Fig. 2. (a) Image captured by the DJI Mavic 2 Zoom drone at an altitude of 10 m and a camera angle of 30°. (b) The same image converted to a birds-eye-view using the calculated homography matrix.

The pixel-to-meter ratio is estimated using a combination of geometry, the birds-eye-view image, and the intrinsic and extrinsic parameters of the UAV camera. It is assumed that the road is a flat plane with no sloping and no hills or valleys. First, the distance in meters from the UAV to the point on the road in the center of the image p_1 is determined using the following equation:

$$d = \frac{a}{sin(\theta)} \tag{3}$$

A second point from the image p_2 lying on the same plane as p_1 is taken by rotating horizontally ϕ degrees in camera-space. The value of ϕ is not important, so long as it is large enough to sufficiently distinguish p_2 from p_1 and small enough so that p_2 is still within the bounds of the image. For our experiments, we used $\phi = 5°$. The following equation is used to determine the distance in meters between p_1 and p_2:

$$g = \frac{d}{sin(90° - \phi)} \cdot sin(\phi) \tag{4}$$

The image width w and height h are used along with the field-of-view β to determine the position of p_1 and p_2 in pixels.

$$p_1 = [\frac{w}{2}, \frac{h}{2}] \tag{5}$$

$$p_2 = [\frac{w}{2} + \frac{w \cdot \phi}{\beta}, \frac{h}{2}] \tag{6}$$

The points are then warped to the birds-eye-view image with the homography matrix H using the following function:

$$warp(p) = [\frac{H_{11}p_0 + H_{12}p_1 + H_{13}}{H_{31}p_0 + H_{32}p_1 + H_{33}}, \frac{H_{21}p_0 + H_{22}p_1 + H_{23}}{H_{31}p_0 + H_{32}p_1 + H_{33}}] \tag{7}$$

$$\hat{p_1} = warp(p_1) \quad \hat{p_2} = warp(p_2) \qquad (8)$$

The Euclidean distance in pixels between the two points on the warped image can then be used in conjunction with the known distance in meters g to determine the pixel-to-meter ratio.

$$\frac{g}{\|\hat{p_1} - \hat{p_2}\|} \qquad (9)$$

YOLOv8 trained on the mixed dataset was used for detecting potholes and segmenting them from the background of the video. The resulting mask of the pothole was then passed to OpenCV's `findContours()` function to estimate the segmented region as a polygon. The area of the polygon transformed to the birds-eye-view image is estimated using OpenCV's `contourArea()` function - the area is returned in pixels. Finally, the pothole area is determined by converting the area in pixels to meters using the pixel-to-meter ratio from step 1 of the algorithm. Visual aids for the area estimation algorithm are found in Fig. 3.

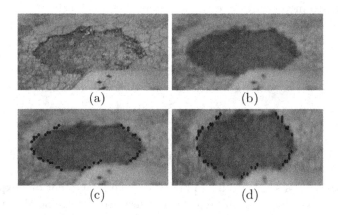

(a)   (b)

(c)   (d)

Fig. 3. (a) Pothole captured by the DJI Mavic 2 Zoom drone at an altitude of 10 m and a camera angle of 30° - cropped from a larger video. (b) The pothole has been segmented from the background using YOLOv8. (c) OpenCV has estimated the points of the polygon that make up the pothole (d) The polygon points are warped to the birds-eye-view image so that the pothole area may be estimated.

5.2   Evaluation

The proposed area estimation algorithm is efficient and quick: Step one of the algorithm only needs to be executed once at the beginning of the video, as the pixel-to-meter ratio should not be changing from frame-to-frame, so any overhead that might come from step one may be overlooked. YOLOv8's instance segmentation step is already used for pothole detection and would remain in-place regardless if pothole area was being estimated or not. The remaining steps - estimating the polygon of the pothole, warping the polygon, and estimating the

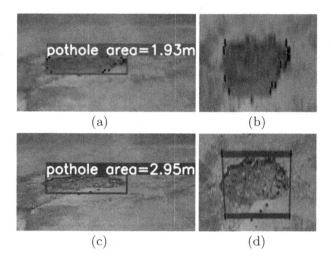

(a)   (b)

(c)   (d)

Fig. 4. (**a**) Pothole detected at an altitude of 5 m and a camera angle of 15°, with the area estimated using our method. (**b**) Image (a) converted to a birds-eye-view. (**c**) The same pothole with the area estimated using Kharel and Ahmed's method. (**d**) Image (c) converted to a birds-eye-view.

area of the warped polygon - are quick. On our system, processing a 4k video, area estimation costs 1.1 ms per frame. With YOLOv8 instance segmentation taking 13.9 ms per frame, and video reading and writing taking up 66 milliseconds per frame, the time spent on area estimation is negligible.

The proposed area estimation algorithm was evaluated against Kharel and Ahmed's method [14], which was to take the corners of the bounding box of each pothole, warp them to the birds-eye-view image, and then estimate the area of the resulting polygon. For this evaluation, both models used YOLOv8 for pothole detection and our novel method for pixel-to-meter ratio estimation. Figure 4 shows a sample of this evaluation.

To evaluate the accuracy of the algorithm, all eight UAV videos were processed using the area estimation script, and then samples of the big pothole (No. 1 from Fig. 1) were taken from each video. Samples were taken for every frame that the pothole was detected and completely in-frame. The median of the samples for each video was then reported in Table 5 for the area estimation, along with the relative error when compared to the ground-truth, where relative error is defined as:

$$\frac{|estimate - truth|}{truth} \cdot 100$$

From Table 5, it is clear that the proposed algorithm for area estimation performed adequately, with the largest error only being 20.57% from the real size of the pothole, and the average error being 9.71%. The largest source of error is likely from YOLOv8 producing inaccurate masks of the potholes. If a stronger pothole segmentation model were used, the error would be lower. Another source of error would be inaccuracy in the UAV camera calibration - an incorrect focal length or sensor width could throw off the area estimation.

Table 5. Percentage of potholes detected from the three deep learning models trained on the ground-level dataset

Video	Our Area in m^2	Our Error	[14] Area in m^2	[14] Error
15° 5 m	1.71	2.29%	2.84	62.00%
15° 10 m	1.6	8.57%	2.64	50.86%
30° 5 m	1.49	14.86%	2.36	34.57%
30° 10 m	1.39	20.57%	2.13	21.71%
45° 5 m	1.47	16.00%	2.24	28.00%
45° 10 m	1.91	9.14%	2.79	59.43%
90° 5 m	1.83	4.57%	2.72	55.43%
90° 10 m	1.72	1.71%	2.49	42.29%
Ground-truth	1.75	–	–	–

[14] overestimated the size of the potholes, with the largest error being 62.00% and the average error being 44.29%. This is not surprising, as the bounding box of an object can only ever give the upper-bound of the object's area.

6   Conclusions and Future Work

Six unique, deep learning models were trained for pothole detection to determine which model was best-fit for detecting potholes using a UAV. Through our experiments, it was determined that YOLOX trained on the mixed dataset - the dataset containing both ground-level and aerial images of potholes - was the best pothole detection model. It was also determined that YOLOv8 trained on the mixed dataset was the best pothole segmentation model, providing both the bounding box and the mask of the pothole. The experiments proved that Mask R-CNN is insufficient for pothole detection and pothole segmentation and can easily be replaced by YOLOX or YOLOv8 respectively. Furthermore, the models were evaluated with different combinations of angles and altitudes to determine which combinations are well suited for pothole detection from the air. It was determined from the experiments that the best angles are between 45° to 90° and the best altitude for detection is 5 m. The strongest pothole segmentation model from our experiments, YOLOv8 trained on the mixed dataset, was then applied to UAV-based pothole area estimation with satisfactory results: an average area estimation error of 9.71%.

There are multiple directions for future work. Training with a larger dataset, especially with more aerial images, could increase the accuracy of the detection, segmentation, and area estimation models. Optical flow could be used as an additional technique for detection, segmentation, and to estimate the depth of the pothole. Finding the homography transformation for the birds-eye-view without knowing the parameters of the camera would improve the usability of the model. Thermal cameras could be used to aid the detection and segmentation of potholes at night. Lastly, evaluating more instance segmentation architectures to replace YOLOv8 with a stronger architecture would improve the accuracy and speed of the entire model.

References

1. AAA: https://newsroom.aaa.com/2022/03/aaa-potholes-pack-a-punch-as-drivers-pay-26-5-billion-in-related-vehicle-repairs/ (2023)
2. Abbas, S.A., Zisserman, A.: A geometric approach to obtain a bird's eye view from an image. In: 2019 IEEE/CVF International Conference on Computer Vision Workshop (ICCVW), pp. 4095–4104 (2019). https://doi.org/10.1109/ICCVW.2019.00504
3. Asad, M.H., Khaliq, S., Yousaf, M.H., Ullah, M.O., Ahmad, A.: Pothole detection using deep learning: a real-time and AI-on-the-edge perspective. Adv. Civil Eng. **2022**, 1–13 (2022)
4. SB, B.K., Guhan, S., Kishore, M., Santhosh, R.: Real-time pothole detection using YOLOv5 algorithm: a feasible approach for intelligent transportation systems. In: 2023 Second International Conference on Electronics and Renewable Systems (ICEARS), pp. 1678–1683 (2023)
5. De Zoysa, K., Keppitiyagama, C., Seneviratne, G.P., Shihan, W.: A public transport system based sensor network for road surface condition monitoring. In: Proceedings of the 2007 Workshop on Networked Systems for Developing Regions, pp. 1–6 (2007)
6. Diamantas, S., Alexis, K.: Modeling pixel intensities with log-normal distributions for background subtraction. In: IEEE International Conference on Imaging Systems and Techniques, Beijing, China, pp. 1–6 (2017)
7. Diamantas, S., Alexis, K.: Optical flow based background subtraction with a moving camera: application to autonomous driving. In: Bebis, G., et al. (eds.) ISVC 2020. LNCS, vol. 12510, pp. 398–409. Springer, Cham (2020). https://doi.org/10.1007/978-3-030-64559-5_31
8. Eriksson, J., Girod, L., Hull, B., Newton, R., Madden, S., Balakrishnan, H.: The pothole patrol: using a mobile sensor network for road surface monitoring. In: Proceedings of the 6th International Conference on Mobile Systems, Applications, and Services, pp. 29–39 (2008)
9. Eriksson, L.H..S.: An Investigation of detecting potholes with UAV LiDAR and UAV Photogrammetry. Ph.D. thesis, University of Gavle (2021)
10. Ge, Z., Liu, S., Wang, F., Li, Z., Sun, J.: Yolox: Exceeding yolo series in 2021 (2021)
11. He, K., Gkioxari, G., Dollar, P., Girshick, R.: Mask R-CNN. In: 2017 IEEE International Conference on Computer Vision (ICCV), pp. 2980–2988 (2017). https://doi.org/10.1109/ICCV.2017.322
12. Jocher, G., Chaurasia, A., Qiu, J.: YOLO by Ultralytics (2023). https://github.com/ultralytics/ultralytics

13. Kang, B.H., Choi, S.i.: Pothole detection system using 2d lidar and camera. In: 2017 Ninth International Conference on Ubiquitous and Future Networks (ICUFN), pp. 744–746 (2017)
14. Kharel, S., Ahmed, K.R.: Potholes detection using deep learning and area estimation using image processing. In: Intelligent Systems with Applications (2021)
15. Lin, T., et al.: Microsoft COCO: common objects in context. CoRR **abs/1405.0312** (2014). http://arxiv.org/abs/1405.0312
16. Peralta-Lopez, J.E., et al.: Speed bump and pothole detection using deep neural network with images captured through zed camera. Appl. Sci. **8349**, 1–17 (2023)
17. Prasad, V., Kumari, S.: Pothole detection using lidar. Adv. Automob. Eng. **10**, 1–3 (2021)
18. Shaghouri, A.A., Alkhatib, R., Berjaoui, S.: Real-time pothole detection using deep learning, pp. 1–10 (2021). https://arxiv.org/abs/2107.06356
19. Silvister, S., et al.: Deep learning approach to detect potholes in real-time using smartphone. In: 2019 IEEE Pune Section International Conference (PuneCon), pp. 1–4 (2019)
20. Welborn, E.A.: Detecting Potholes Using Deep Neural Networks with Unmanned Aerial Vehicles. Ph.D. thesis, Tarleton State University (2023)
21. Wu, C., et al.: An automated machine-learning approach for road pothole detection using smartphone sensor data. Sensors **20**, 1–23 (2020)
22. Yik, Y.K., Alias, N.E., Yusof, Y., Isaak, S.: A real-time pothole detection based on deep learning approach. J. Phys.: Conf. Ser., 1–7 (2021)
23. Yu, B.X., Yu, X.: Vibration-based system for pavement condition evaluation. In: Applications of Advanced Technology in Transportation, pp. 183–189 (2006)

Generation Method of Robot Assembly Motion Considering Physicality Gap Between Humans and Robots

Takahiro Suzuki[(✉)] and Manabu Hashimoto[(✉)]

Chukyo University, 101-2 Yagoto-honmachi Showa-ku, Nagoya, Aichi, Japan
{suzuki,mana}@isl.sist.chukkyo-u.ac.jp

Abstract. In this study, we propose a method for simplifying the assigning of robot motion parameters as this task is very time consuming. Parts used in a factory have different shapes and sizes but are categorized under the same name. With the proposed method, the robot's grasping point for one part is determined using a human's optimal grasping point for another part as a cue. The novelty of our method is that we consider the physicality gap between humans and robots as well as the functions of industrial parts. An example of this gap is the difference between a human and robot's hand shape. A function refers to the role of each component of an industrial part. Grasping points are determined from the grasping function of a target part using features related to the physicality gap. In an experiment using connecting rods, the average success rate of robot motions with the method was 82.8%.

Keywords: Robot motion generation · Physicality gap · Parts function · Assembly task

1 Introduction

A factory assembly line involves various tasks such as inserting connecting rods and links into shafts, connectors into holes, or tightening bolts with screws. There have been increasing efforts to automate these tasks using robots. To automate the tasks, an operator needs to assign certain parameters to the robot, for example, the point grasped by the robot and the point of assembly with other parts. However, it is very time consuming to assign these parameters for each part. In this research, we propose a method for simplifying the task of assigning robot motion parameters.

There have been studies on automatically determining grasping points. Domae et al. [1] convolved a robot hand template with a depth image. Araki et al. [2] proposed a Convolutional Neural Network (CNN)-based method as an improvement to Domae et al.'s method. Zhang et al.'s method [3] is based on topological knowledge. Song et al. [4] proposed a model for determining the 6DoF pose of an object, enabling grasping in various environments. Chen et al. [5] and Kevin et al. [6] dealt with prior experiences of successful grasping.

G. Bebis et al. (Eds.): ISVC 2023, LNCS 14362, pp. 385–396, 2023.
https://doi.org/10.1007/978-3-031-47966-3_30

Two grasping points are determined by these methods. The first is a point that not only can be grasped but should also be grasped by a robot in order to insert a part into another part. The second is a point that can be grasped but should not be grasped by a robot. Even if a robot grasps this point, it cannot insert the part into a shaft. For instance, grasping the threaded parts of bolts and inserting the bolts into a hole or grasping the hole of a connecting rod and inserting the rod into a shaft are contrary to functional use. Therefore, these methods cannot determine the point that should be grasped for the next action.

A method has been proposed that uses machine learning to determine grasping points on the basis of a robot's motion after grasping. Turpin et al. and Qin et al. [7,8] proposed methods that automatically determine key points related to grasping and insertion points. Ardon et al. and Liang et al. [9,10] proposed methods that generate robot motion parameters that can be used to perform the same task even when different parts are used by referring to motions taught to the robot by a human. However, it is necessary to annotate labels for a huge amount of training data and difficult to reflect human-specific knowledge in assembly. That is, these methods are difficult to implement on an assembly line where the parts change frequently. Suzuki et al. proposed a method [11] for transferring robot motion parameters from a source part to a target part. However, because the method is based on geometric deformation, the parameters after transferring are not optimal.

Parts used in a factory often have different shapes and sizes but are categorized under the same name. In our study, such groups of parts are defined as categories. Our proposed method simplifies the task of assigning robot motion parameters. Using a human's optimal grasping point G_{SRC} for part A (hereinafter referred to as a source part) as a cue, the grasping point G_{TGT} of part B (hereinafter referred to as a target part) is determined (Fig. 1).

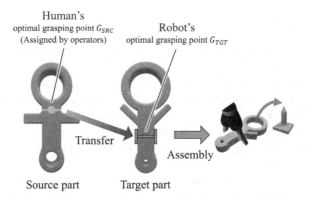

Fig. 1. Outline of proposed method for generating robot motion parameters. Using human's optimal grasping point G_{SRC} for source part as cue, grasping point G_{TGT} of target part is determined. The assigning of robot motion parameters is simplified by our method.

G_{SRC} is the optimal grasping point for a human assembling an object. This point is determined by a human in advance considering motion after grasping, so it is important to use it as a cue. G_{SRC} is the optimal grasping point for a human and G_{TGT} is the optimal grasping point for a robot, but they are not necessarily in the same position. It is difficult to determine G_{TGT} from G_{SRC} without some contrivance. We focus on the physicality gap between humans and robots. An example of the gap is the hand. A human has two arms and five fingers, but a robot often has one arm with two fingers or a suction hand. We determine G_{TGT} from G_{SRC} considering this physicality gap. In addition, we use the commonality between source and target parts. We focus on the functions shared by different parts in the same category as this commonality.

The main contributions of this paper are as follows. (1) Grasping points are determined assuming the motion of a robot after grasping a part in an assembly task. (2) The assigning of robot motion parameters is simplified by our method. (3) We determine grasping points on the basis of the physicality gap between humans and robots.

2 Problem Formulation

In this section, we discuss the robot motion parameters to be determined for target part and how the determination is formulated.

2.1 Definition

Given the point cloud of source part P_{SRC}, target part P_{SRC}, and a human's optimal grasping point G_{SRC} for P_{SRC}, the goal is to determine the optimal robot motion parameters for a target part G_{TGT} using G_{SRC} as a cue.

2.2 Assumption

The following are assumed in this research.

(1) The part is stably placed. (2) The sensor's viewpoint is above the part. (3) The position and orientation of the parts to be assembled are known. (4) The source and target parts are in the same category and perform the same task. (5) The robot has two fingers. (6) The operator assigns a person's optimal grasping point G_{SRC} to the source part.

2.3 Robot Motion Parameters Required in Assembly Tasks

There are two robot motion parameters required for the robot to perform assembly. These parameters are shown in Fig. 2.

The first parameter is the grasping point of a part. When assembling an object, a human or robot needs to grasp parts. This parameter is the point to be grasped at that time. A grasping point consists of x, y, and z in 3D space and grasping angles α, β, and γ.

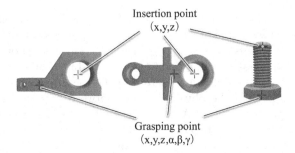

Fig. 2. Robot motion parameters required in assembly tasks. If these parameters are input to robot, object can be assembled.

The second parameter is the point at which a part is inserted, i.e., where the part will be connected to other parts. For example, in the task of inserting a connecting rod into a shaft, the center of gravity of the hole is the insertion point. This point consists of x, y, and z in 3D space.

3   Method

In this section, we discuss our proposed method for determining robot motion parameters.

3.1   Parts Function

Prior studies [12–15] have focused on recognizing the affordances of objects. In addition, Suzuki's method [16] defines the functions of industrial parts to carry out assembly tasks. A function refers to the role of each component of an industrial part. Similar to the previous methods, our study uses functions as cues for determining the optimal parameters for robot motion.

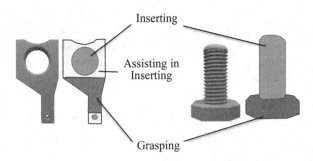

Fig. 3. Functions of industrial parts. Functions consist of grasping (blue region), inserting (red region), and assisting in inserting (yellow region). (Color figure online)

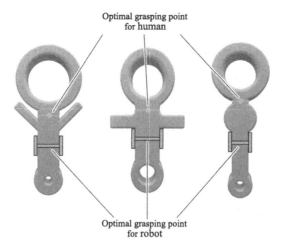

Fig. 4. Physicality gap due to differences in hand geometry. Optimal grasping point of part differs between human (blue) and robot (pink). (Color figure online)

Figure 3 shows an example of the parts used during assembly. Suzuki's method [16] defines three functions of industrial parts.

The first function is "grasping" as shown by the blue region in Fig. 3. This refers to the role of being grasped by a human or robot.

The second function is "inserting" as shown by the red region. This refers to the role of being assembled with another part.

The third function is "assisting in inserting" as shown by the yellow region. For the connecting rod, there is a region with a hole shape in which to insert something. Therefore, this region has the role of assisting in inserting something into the hole.

3.2   Physicality Gap Between Humans and Robots

As mentioned, there are physicality gaps between humans and robots. For example, a human can work dexterously with both arms and five fingers. However, robots often only have one arm with two fingers or a suction hand. Due to the structure of the robot hand, robots are limited in their tasks compared with a human. Robots with two arms and five fingers have been developed, but they are expensive and lack precision. Due to this physicality gap, the optimal grasping point of a part differs between a human and a robot. Since differences in hand geometry are thought to affect the optimal gripping point of a part, this study considers differences in hand geometry as a physicality gap and focuses on it.

An example of the optimal grasping point and angle for a human is shown in blue in Fig. 4, and that for a robot is in pink. In the task of inserting a connecting rod into a shaft, a human typically grasps it close to the hole so that it is easy to insert. However, if the region around the grasping point has a complex geometry, it is not the optimal grasping point for a robot. This is because the contact area between the part and the robot hand is small and cannot be grasped stably. Thus, the optimal grasping point differs between a human and a robot. To determine the optimal robot motion parameters, the physicality gap must be taken into account.

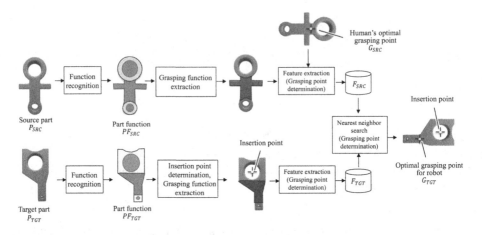

Fig. 5. Flow of proposed method.

3.3   Determining Robot Motion Parameters

The flow of the proposed method is shown in Fig. 5. The method inputs the point cloud of source part P_{SRC}, target part P_{SRC}, and a human's optimal grasping point G_{SRC} of P_{SRC} and outputs grasping point P_{TGT} of the target point.

Function Recognition. In function recognition, the functions of source part PF_{SRC} and target part PF_{TGT} are recognized from P_{SRC}, P_{TGT}. First, depth images are generated from P_{SRC}, P_{TGT}. Next, the images are input to a deep learning model [17] that is segmented by function. Finally, P_{SRC}, P_{TGT} are assigned a function using images segmented by function.

Determining Insertion Point. The insertion point is uniquely determined independent of the operator (human or robot), such as always being inside a hole in the case of a connecting rod or at the tip of a threaded part in the case of a bolt. Therefore, the point is determined directly from P_{SRC}, not from the transition between source and target part.

To determine the insertion point, the insertion function in PF_{SRC}, PF_{TGT} is identified. If a part has a hole with an insertion function, the function is determined by a label after determining the assisting in inserting function. The center of gravity of the insertion function is determined to be the insertion point.

Determing Grasping Point. In the determination of robot motion parameters, optimal grasping point G_{TGT} for the target part is determined on the basis of PF_{SRC}, PF_{TGT}, G_{SRC}. To determine GG_{TGT} from G_{SRC}, the commonality between them must be used. In this study, we use the proximity of distances in the feature space as this commonality. First, the feature F_{SRC} is extracted from G_{SRC}. Next, the point cloud of the grasping function of PF_{TGT} is downsampled. In addition, the feature F_{TGT} is extracted for each grasping direction (x, y, z) at each point. Finally, the point that extracts the feature F_{TGT} most similar to F_{SRC} is searched for. The resulting point and direction are the grasping point G_{TGT}.

The features that can be extracted from a grasping point are classified into two types.

The first type is a feature that depends on the physicality gap between a human and robot (type A), for example, graspability.

Because a human has five fingers, grasping is easier (i.e., graspability is high for a human) if the side of the part has a complex shape, as shown in Fig. 4. However, a robot is more capable of grasping a part if the sides are straight (i.e., graspability is high for the robot). Thus, a grasping point can have a graspability score that is different between humans and robots. Therefore, when extracting type-A features, the extraction methods of F_{SRC} and F_{TGT} must be different.

The second type of feature (type B) does not depend on the physicality gap. For example, there is a relative distance between the insertion point and grasping point, and between the center of gravity of the part and the grasping point. These features do not depend on hand geometry, so human knowledge can be directly reflected in the robot. Therefore, when extracting type B features, the extraction methods for F_{SRC} and F_{TGT} must be the same.

In our study, the following two type-A features are used. (1) The first feature is the grasping confidence F^C (graspability). (2) The second feature is the adhesion between the hand and part F^a. In addition, the relative distance between the insertion point and the grasping point is used as a type B feature (F^l).

The method used to extract F_{TGT}^C was proposed by Domae et al. [1]. This method determines points with a high grasp confidence. In this method, contact and collision region templates are first created on the basis of the pose of the robot hand. Next, the depth image is convolved with these templates. Finally, it is convolved with a Gaussian filter to calculate F^C. The output F^C score ranges from 0.0 to 1.0. The higher the F^C, the easier it is for the robot to grasp. Because G_{SRC} is the optimal grasp point for a human, F_{SRC}^C is 1.0.

F_{TGT}^a is calculated by the following formula. The output F_{TGT}^a score ranges from 0.0 to 1.0. If F_{TGT}^a is high, the part and the hand are adhered together. Because we assume that the hand of the human and the part are perfectly adhered to each other, F_{SRC}^a is 1.0. Details on the variables used in formula 1(a) are shown in Fig. 6(a).

$$F_{TGT}^a = min\{cos^{-1}(\boldsymbol{h}_l, \boldsymbol{p}_l), cos^{-1}(\boldsymbol{h}_r, \boldsymbol{p}_r)\} \tag{1}$$

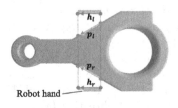

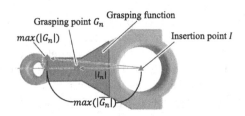

(a) Adhesion between hand and part

(b) Relative distance
between the insertion point and
grasping point

Fig. 6. Variables used in formula 1 and 2

F_{SRC}^l, F_{TGT}^l are calculated by the following formula 2. Details on the variables used in formula 1(b) are shown in Fig. 6(b).

$$F^l = \frac{|l_n|}{max(\bar{G}_n)} \qquad (2)$$

Finally, the F_{TGT} most similar to F_{SRC} is extracted and G_{TGT} is determined (i.e., nearest neighbor search).

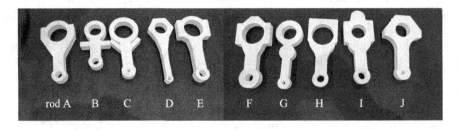

Fig. 7. Parts used in experiment.

4   Experiment

4.1   Setup

The experimental setup is as follows. Noetic was used as the robot operating system (ROS), the robot was an UR5e, and the robot hand was a Robotiq 2F-85. In the experiment, connecting rods were inserted into a shaft. The connecting rods (Fig. 7) were printed using a 3D printer. They were 15 to 20 cm long, 7 to 10 cm wide, and 4 or 6 cm in hole diameter. The hole diameter of the shaft into which the parts were inserted was 3.5 or 5.5 cm, with a clearance of 0.5 cm between the hole and shaft.

The motion procedure of the robot is as follows. First, the robot moved over to the part and approached the grasping point determined by the proposed method. Next, the part was grasped and moved so that the insertion point was over the shaft. Finally, the part was inserted into the shaft.

We created pairs of a connecting rod to which a human assigned a grasping point as the source part and a connecting rod as the target part from ten parts. We operated the robot for ten trials for each pair of connecting rods and evaluated whether the robot was able to insert the connecting rod into the shaft. An operator assigned the grasping point for five types of connecting rods (source parts).

To confirm the effectiveness of the functions used in the proposed method, a method without the functions were used as comparison method A. Comparison method A determines the grasping point on the basis of Domae's method [1] and the insertion point by hole detection. To confirm the necessity of a human assigning G_{SRC}, we chose another method as comparison method B, in which the grasping point is determined by Domae's method [1] on the basis of the grasping function and the insertion point by hole detection.

Table 1. Number of successful tasks.

		Target part ID									
		A	B	C	D	E	F	G	H	I	J
Source part ID	A	-	6	7	8	8	9	8	8	c| 9	10
	B	9	-	8	8	8	8	8	8	8	8
	C	7	9	-	6	9	9	9	9	6	7
	D	10	9	9	-	8	8	8	7	7	9
	E	9	8	8	10	-	9	9	8	8	9
Average (**Ours**)		8.8	8.0	8.0	8.0	8.3	8.6	8.4	8.0	7.6	8.6
Comparison method A		6	5	1	6	6	5	4	7	3	4
Comparison method B		5	4	6	5	5	5	6	6	9	4

4.2 Experimental Results

The results from the experiment with the connecting rods are listed in Table 1. The grasping and insertion points determined by the proposed method are indicated in Fig. 8. The rows in this table show the IDs of the source parts, and the columns are the IDs of the target parts. For example, with the source part as part A and the target part as part B, the grasping point of part B was determined and successfully assembled six times. The IDs correspond to those in Fig. 7. When the connecting rods were the same in a pair, the proposed method was not needed. The third line from the bottom shows the average number of successful tasks with the proposed method, and the second line from the bottom and the bottom

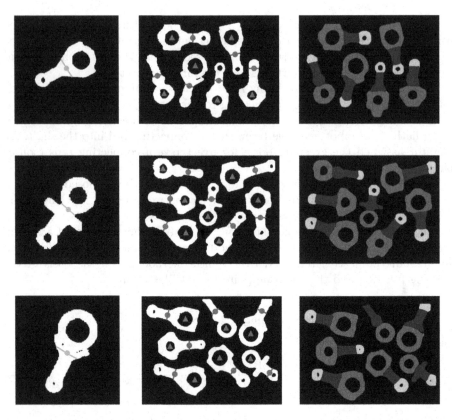

Fig. 8. Result of determining robot motion parameters. Proposed method correctly determined grasping and insertion points. (left) Source part. Blue is human's optimal grasping point. (center) Grasping and insertion points determined by proposed method using human's optimal grasping point as cue. (right) Result of function recognition. Blue region is grasping function. Red and green regions are for assisting in insertion function. (Color figure online)

line show the average number of successful tasks with comparison methods A and B.

The average success rate of robot motions with the proposed method was 82.2%. The grasping and insertion points determined by the proposed method are indicated in Fig. 8. This figure confirms that the proposed method determined the correct grasping and insertion points. In comparison method A, the robot grasped around the insertion function or grasped the part at an angle. In comparison method B, the robot grasped a point away from the insertion point or grasped the part at an angle. This confirms the need for assigning G_{SRC} by human, part function, and F^a.

The grasping points determined by the proposed method are shown in green in Fig. 9. The points determined by the proposed method could be grasped by a robot that has two fingers. The points determined without features F^C and F^A

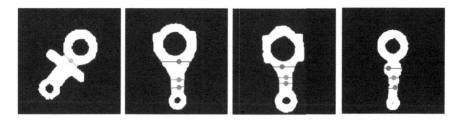

Fig. 9. Results confirm necessity of each feature used in proposed method. (blue) Source part and human's optimal grasping point. (green) Results of determining grasping points using all features used in proposed method. Grasping points for successful assembly were determined. (pink) Results of determining grasping points without using F^c and F^a. Robot cannot grasp part correctly because sides of part are not straight. (orange) Results of determining grasping point without using F^l. In this case, robot grasped point that was far from where human taught point. (Color figure online)

are shown in pink in Fig. 9. In this case, the robot cannot grasp the part correctly because the sides of the part are not straight. The grasping points determined without F^l are shown in blue in Fig. 9. In this case, the robot grasped a point that was far from where the human taught the point. This confirms the necessity of the features used in the proposed method.

There was a failure due to an error in the rotation angle determined by the proposed method and because the parts moved when the robot grasped them, causing the insertion point to shift. This is an issue with downsampling and the resolution of the rotation angle determined by the proposed method. However, if the resolution is too small, the processing time will be long. Therefore, the hyper-parameters should be determined while considering the processing time and success rate of the robot motion.

5   Conclusion

We proposed a method for simplifying the task of assigning robot motion parameters. The grasping point of a target part is determined using the optimal grasping point of a human for a source part as a cue. We clarified the physicality gap between humans and robots, and a robot's grasping point was determined using this gap as a cue. In addition, the functions of industrial parts are utilized. In an experiment using connecting rods, the average success rate of robot motions with the proposed method was 82.2%. We aim to increase the number of feature types and to consider physicality gaps other than robot hands in future work.

Acknowledgement. This paper is based on results obtained from a project, JPNP20006, commissioned by the New Energy and Industrial Technology Development Organization (NEDO).

References

1. Domae, Y., Okuda, H., Taguchi, Y., Sumi, K., Hirai, T.: Fast graspability evaluation on single depth maps for bin picking with general gripper. In: Proceedings of the IEEE Conference on ICRA, HongKong, pp. 1997–2004 (2014)
2. Araki, R., et al.: Grasping detection using deep convolutional neural network with graspability. J. Rob. Soc. Japan **36**(8), 559–566 (2018)
3. Zhang, X., Koyama, K., Domae, Y., Wan, W., Harada, K.: A topological solution of entanglement for complex-shaped parts in robotic bin-picking. In: Proceedings of the IEEE Conference on CASE, pp. 461–467 (2021)
4. Song, S., Zeng, A., Lee, J., Funkhouser, T.: Grasping in the wild: learning 6dof closed-loop grasping from low-cost demonstrations. IEEE Rob. Autom. Lett. **5**(3), 4978–4985 (2020)
5. Chen, X., Ghadirzadeh, A., Bhorkman, M., Jensfelt, P.: Adversarial feature training for generalizable robotic visuomotor control. In: Proceedings of the IEEE Conference on ICRA, pp. 1142–1148 (2020)
6. Kevin, Z., Andy, Z., Johnny, L., Shuran, S.: Form2Fit: learning shape priors for generalizable assembly from disassembly. In: Proceedings of the IEEE Conference on ICRA, pp. 9404–9410 (2020)
7. Turpin, D., Wang, L., Tshogkas, S., Dickinson, S., Garg, A.: GIFT: generalizable interaction-aware functional tool affordances without labels. In Robotics: Science and Systems (2021). https://arxiv.org/abs/2106.14973
8. Qin, Z., Fang, K., Zhu, Y., Fei-Fei, L., Savarese, S.: KETO:learning keypoint representations for tool manipulation. In: Proceedings of the IEEE Conference on ICRA, pp. 7278–7285 (2020)
9. Ardon, P., Pairet, E., Petillot, Y., Petrick, P.A.R., Ramamoorthy, S., Lohan, S.K.: Self-assessment of grasp affordance transfer. In: Proceedings of the IEEE/RSJ Conference on IROS, pp. 9385–9392 (2020)
10. Liang, J., Boularias, A.: Learning category-level manipulation tasks from point clouds with dynamic graph CNNs. In: Proceedings of the IEEE Conference on ICRA, UK, pp. 1807–1813 (2023)
11. Suzuki, T., Hashimoto, M.: A method for transferring robot motion parameters using functional attributes of parts. Lect. Notes Comput. Sci. **13018**, 154–165 (2021)
12. Chu, F.-J., Xu, R., Vela, P.A.: Learning affordance segmentation for real-world robotic manipulation via synthetic images. IEEE Rob. Autom. Lett. **4**(2), 1140–1447 (2019)
13. Chu, F.-J., Xu, R., Vela, P.A.: Toward affordance detection and ranking on novel objects for real-world robotic manipulation. IEEE Rob. Autom. Lett. **4**(4), 4070–4077 (2019)
14. Minh, C., Gilani, S., Islam, S., Suter, D.: Learning affordance segmentation: an investigative study. In: Proceedings of the DICTA, pp. 2870–2877 (2020)
15. Luo, H., Zhai, W., Zhang, J., Cao, Y., Tao, D.: Learning visual affordance grounding from demonstration videos (2021). https://arxiv.org/pdf/2108.05675v1.pdf
16. Suzuki, T., Hashimoto, M.: Estimation of robot motion parameters based on functional consistency for randomly stacked parts. In: Proceedings of the VISAPP, Portugal, pp. 519–528 (2023)
17. He, K., Gkioxari, G., Dollar, P., Girshick, R.: Mask R-RCNN. In: Proceedings of the IEEE Conference on ICCV, Italy, pp. 2961–2969 (2017)

A Self-supervised Pose Estimation Approach for Construction Machines

Ala'a Alshubbak[1,2($\boxtimes$)] and Daniel Görges[1]

[1] Institute of Electromobility, University of Kaiserslautern-Landau,
Kaiserslautern, Germany
{al-shubbak,goerges}@eit.uni-kl.de
[2] German Jordanian University, Amman, Jordan

Abstract. Pose estimation is a computer vision task used to estimate a skeleton of dynamic systems to predict future movements. Most of the research in this direction is based on a supervised learning approach which requires a massive amount of labeled datasets. In this paper, a self-supervised three-stage model based on a contrastive learning approach is introduced for estimating a skeleton of dynamic construction machines; such as excavators without using any labeled images for the first stage. The whole model structure is divided into three stages: the pre-train stage using the SimCLR contrastive approach, and two fine-tuning stages for the transfer learning and the downstream task. The model can leverage the features and learn from a huge unlabeled dataset called ACID to two small datasets generated from NVIDIA Isaac and MATLAB Simscape simulators as well as transfer the knowledge to a smaller dataset with a ratio of 3.5% from the original ACID dataset. The results show that the proposed approach can improve the accuracy of pose estimation for heavy construction machines in real images by 11% and 13% in comparison to the normal self-supervised approach with two backbones ResNet-50 and HRNet-W32, respectively.

Keywords: Self-Supervised Learning · Pose Estimation · Heavy Construction Machines · Deep Neural Network · ResNet · HRNet · Downstream Tasks · Topdown Heatmap · Simulation

1 Introduction

Pose estimation is a computer vision task that is used to estimate a skeleton of dynamic systems to predict future movements [6,23]. Most of the research in this direction is based on a supervised learning which requires a massive amount of labeled data [7,20]. To the best of the authors' knowledge, there is no benchmark data for pose estimation for construction machines produced yet. The only benchmark dataset in this field is the ACID dataset [25], which consists of 10K images of 10 different classes of heavy construction vehicles, such as excavators, backhoes, and trucks. All of these are only labeled in the form of

G. Bebis et al. (Eds.): ISVC 2023, LNCS 14362, pp. 397–408, 2023.
https://doi.org/10.1007/978-3-031-47966-3_31

bounding boxes. This labeled format is only suitable to work with downstream tasks such as object detection and segmentation, which makes the task of pose estimation for such objects a challenging topic. In this paper, a self-supervised contrastive learning model is designed to estimate a skeleton of dynamic heavy machines without using any labeled images, as the model depends on data augmentation to learn the visual representations that distinguish objects from one another in different images. The model leverages the concept that images produced from the same source have similar visual representations and features, while the ones produced from different sources will have a variant representation. The model is trained on a huge dataset and then fine-tuned on smaller ones. By reusing the structure of the SimCLR model [5], the proposed model can detect the keypoints of heavy machines and produce a skeleton in different situations and positions. The model outperforms the supervised approach on two simulated datasets from MATLAB Simscape Multibody [17] and NVIDIA Omnivers environments by 1.7% and 0.8% AP, respectively. In addition, it is fine-tuned over a small amount of the dataset and gives an increase of 11% and 13% AP for two different backbone models.

The contributions of this work are:

- Automatically generate a synthetic dataset with annotation using simulators for pose estimation tasks. This data represents mainly one object class of excavator.
- Design and implement a self-supervised deep neural model based on the Sim-CLR model to generate a skeleton for a heavy construction machine 'excavator' using a smaller amount of annotated dataset.
- Minimize the domain shift between the simulated situation and the real situation using a small dataset from a real environment, which improves the model's performance on real-world data.

This paper is divided into five sections: Sect. 2 introduces the previous works, while Sect. 3 contains the problem statement and the model architecture proposed to solve such a problem. Section 4 explains the experiment setup and the datasets. The results and discussion in Sect. 5 provide a detailed explanation of the performance of the proposed approach. Lastly, a conclusion and future direction are given in Sect. 6.

2   Related Work

2.1   Pose Estimation in Heavy Construction Machines

The interest in safety when using heavy construction machines has grown rapidly in recent years, alongside the development of artificial intelligence models and deep learning. The advancements aim to enhance accuracy and reliability in detecting objects and predicting motion for both humans and machines. Researchers primarily focus on human safety by detecting, tracking, and predicting human motion. However, there is less emphasis on detecting and tracking the motion of construction machines themselves [13,16,21]. One research study discussed a method called the Monocular Vision Marker System [27], which uses a monocular camera to detect markers on an excavator's manipulator parts. This system consists of two phases: camera calibration and pose estimation using the CALTag marker-based approach. The model achieved an error of fewer than 8.5° in orientation and less than 22 mm in position. Within the fewer attempts which have been made to develop pose estimation models for heavy machines using deep neural networks, two main methods were mentioned in the literature. The first method detects the essential keypoints that form the motions in the machines [14,15], while the second method detects the machine parts and then extracts a skeleton [24].

One study [14] designed a pose estimation model using supervised learning with a deep neural network based on a Stacked Hourglass Network (HG) and a Cascaded Pyramid Network (CPN). The model achieves good results in terms of normalized errors, correct keypoints, and area under the curve with six keypoints. Another study [15] built a framework using a Gated Recurrent Unit (GRU) to predict the pose estimation for excavators and dump trucks, achieving an average accuracy of 90.22% of correct keypoints (PCK). The whole dataset used within such a deep neural network consists of 53484 annotated frames.

Table 1. Definition of machine keypoints in literature and this work.

6 Keypoints	Definition
1	"Body_end"
2	"Cab_boom"
3	"Boom_arm"
4	"Arm_bucket"
5	"Left_bucket_end"
6	"Right_bucket_end"

4 Keypoints	Definition
1	"Chassis"
2	"Boom"
3	"Stick"
4	"Bucket"

In contrast, another research [24] proposal used traditional machine learning methods to estimate the skeleton of excavators by detecting their parts. This approach involved multiple stages, including multiple detectors, a cluster model, and an orientation estimator. Although this method suffered from missing some data or keypoints, it achieved reasonable accuracies for detecting the stick, boom, and chassis parts of the excavator. Most efforts in designing machine pose estimation models rely on a large dataset of annotated images, either synthetic or real, and training deep neural networks using a supervised learning approach.

2.2   The State-of-Art: Self-supervised Learning Approach

Self-Supervised Learning (SSL) is one of the emerging technologies in machine learning that eliminates the human interaction in labeling the data and uses unlabeled data directly in initializing a basic neural network by either creating pseudo labels or using positive or negative image pairs to learn representations [1]. Then the model is fine-tuned on a downstream task using a small labeled dataset. The general diagram in Fig. 1 shows the general stages in self-supervised learning approach [8]. Self-supervised learning is classified into two types: the contrastive and non-contrastive approaches (auxiliary pretext tasks) [22]. The first approach is state-of-the-art and achieves higher performance in SSL, such as SimCLR [5], SwAV [3] and recently DINO [19]. In general, the SimCLR framework consists of a data augmentation module, a base encoder, a projection head, and the contrastive loss function. The model produces a huge number of negative and positive samples, then the base encoder and head are trained to maximize the similarity between the augmented image. If those images are close to the original image (positive sample), then the contrastive loss produced will be low. Otherwise, the constructive loss increases.

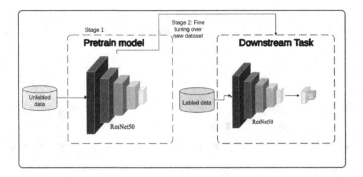

Fig. 1. General diagram of a self-supervised model trained over unlabeled data.

Downstream Task The most popular downstream tasks mentioned in almost all self-supervised approaches are either object detection, segmentation, or classification. Most self-supervised approaches are tested for such downstream tasks.

Researchers are highly interested in pose estimation models due to their ability to predict motion and ensure object safety, particularly for humans [11]. Numerous research studies have focused on detecting and creating skeletons for various subjects, including the entire human body [26], facial gestures [12], and hand movements [10]. Additionally, some research has explored skeleton generation for specific animals [2] and insects [20]. Human pose estimation approaches can be categorized into two main types [11]: the top-down approach and the bottom-up approach. In the top-down approach, the model estimates the pose of individual objects in a single stage by leveraging object detection models to identify keypoints for each object independently. On the other hand, the bottom-up approach involves two stages: detecting keypoints for all objects in the scene using heatmaps and grouping the keypoints through associative embedding [18] or graph neural network techniques [9]. The top-down approach has advantages over the bottom-up in terms of performance and accuracy, but it requires high computational cost, particularly in crowded and multi-object scenarios.

3   Proposed Method

The research on pose estimation for heavy and construction machines is limited, with most of the previous efforts focusing on supervised approaches that require a large labeled dataset. This paper aims to introduce a new method for pose estimation by utilizing state-of-the-art self-supervised learning and automatically generated simulator datasets to learn the main representation of objects in images and their features. The acquired knowledge can then be transferred to a real-time system using a small annotated dataset with only four main keypoints instead of the six keypoints mentioned in previous literature [14]. Two points are removed as the model focuses on detecting the keypoints of the manipulator. Moreover, one keypoint for the bucket will be enough for the study of the movement of such machines as the geometry of the object will be considered.

The proposed model consists of four main steps:

1. Generate synthetic images using simulators
2. Annotate those images automatically using a script based on the 4-keypoints definition in Table 1.
3. Pre-train the deep neural network model based on the self-supervised approach with an unlabelled ACID dataset.
4. Downstream task:
   - Knowledge transfer and feature extraction stage using a synthetically annotated dataset.
   - Fine-tuning stage with a small annotated dataset from real images.

Figure 2 presents the general framework of the proposed approach. The latter two stages can be considered as high-level downstream tasks. The overall approach takes advantage of simulation environments such as Simscape Multibody and NVIDIA Isaac to generate and label data automatically. The usage of two different datasets from different simulators is necessary for higher variance.

In this research, a new direction of pose estimation and skeleton detection is presented by leveraging the strength of both the self-supervised learning approach and the dynamic simulation. The model learns the main features within the images using self-supervised learning without a need for annotation and then fine-tunes and downstreams using an annotated dataset generated automatically from the simulator. This approach reduces the human effort in labeling the dataset as well as increases the accuracy of common keypoint detectors which are based on the supervised learning paradigm. The proposed model is based on a top-down pose estimation approach which is easy to implement and can be developed using simulations.

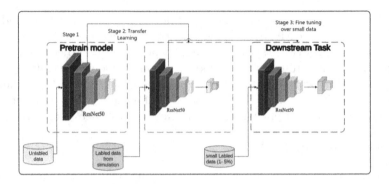

Fig. 2. Diagram of the approach with three-stage self-supervised paradigm.

4   Experimental Setup

4.1   Datasets and Implementation

As mentioned in the previous section, the proposed model consists of three main
stages of knowledge transfer. Different types of datasets are used at each stage.
At the pre-train self-supervised stage, the ACID dataset [25] of 2850 unannotated
images was used to train the SimCLR approach.

On the other hand, the last two stages of downstream tasks require an annotated dataset with the basic keypoints of construction machines. To avoid the
tedious and time-consuming task of annotating the ACID dataset, two additional
simulated datasets have been generated and annotated automatically using the
NVIDIA Isaac (500 images) and MATLAB Simscape Multibody (300 images)
simulators, which are 17.5% and 10.5% of the original ACID dataset, respectively.
Those datasets are used later in the feature extraction stage for the pose estimator model based on both backbones of ResNet-50 and HRNet-W32. Around
3.5% of the whole ACID dataset has been manually annotated with the basic
four keypoints mentioned in the right column of Table 1. This dataset is used in
the last stage to fine-tune the model on a downstream task of pose estimation
and map the features between simulated and real situations. As mentioned in the
related work section, another dataset [14] for real excavators consisting of 6405
images with six keypoints has been used in feature extraction to test its effect
on the performance of the model. Figure 3 shows samples from part of the ACID
dataset that has been annotated manually in the pose estimation. All training
was done with an NVIDIA Tesla V100 with 64GB memory. The self-supervised
models for both backbones are trained with a batch size of 256.

Fig. 3. Image samples from ACID manually annotated for pose estimation.

4.2   Evaluation Metrics

The effectiveness of the proposed approach has been evaluated using the two main metrics Average Precision (AP) and Average Recall (AR) with different Object Keypoint Similarity (OKS) thresholds: OKS = 0.50:0.05:0.95, OKS = 0.50, OKS = 0.75, and different object sizes M (medium) and L (large). The OKS is measured using

$$\text{OKS} = \sum_i [\exp(-d_i^2/2\, s^2 k_i^2)\delta(v_i > 0)]/\sum_i [\delta(v_i > 0)] \tag{1}$$

where d_i is the Euclidean distance between the ground truth and predicted keypoint, s is the object segment area, k is the per-keypoint constant that controls fall-off, and v_i is the visibility flag that can be 0, 1, or 2 for not labeled, labeled but not visible, and visible and labeled, respectively. The OKS is within 0 and 1, where 1 represents perfect predictions while 0 represents poor ones.

5   Results and Discussion

5.1   Main Results

In this subsection, two scenarios of the self-supervised feature extraction approach are presented. The first scenario involves employing a SimCLR model trained on a standard ImageNet dataset using a traditional constructive learning approach. In this case, the model is directly utilized for pose estimation downstream tasks using the small annotated ACID dataset. Table 2 shows the result of such a scenario in comparison to the supervised learning approach for models based on ResNet-50 and HRNet-w32 backbones.

On the other hand, the second scenario uses the proposed approach with three stages of self-supervised feature extraction, transfer learning, and fine-tuning to get more accurate pose estimation results for construction machines. Table 3 shows the results of this proposed self-supervised three-stages-fine-tuning approach. The performance for both scenarios is given in terms of Average Precision (AP), Average Recall (AR), and number of epochs to reach the optimal weights.

Table 2. The first scenario: supervised learning versus normal self-supervised learning approach for learning features for a pose estimation downstream task. There is no intermediate stage in this approach.

Model	Datasets	Status	AP	AP^{50}	AP^{75}	AP^M	AP^L	AR	AR^{50}	AR^{75}	AR^M	AR^L	Epochs
ResNet-50	$ACID_p$	Sup	**0.4455**	**1.0**	**0.3307**	−1.0	**0.4455**	**0.4867**	**1.0**	**0.4667**	−1.0	**0.4867**	120
	ImageNet	Self-Sup	0.37962	0.80528	0.17327	−1.0	0.37962	0.42	0.86667	0.2	−1.0	0.42	590
HRNet-W32	$ACID_p$	Sup	**0.4228**	**1.0**	**0.3187**	−1.0	**0.4228**	**0.520**	**1.0**	**0.5333**	−1.0	**0.520**	120
	ImageNet	Self-Sup	0.3832	0.7958	0.2911	−1.0	0.3832	0.4200	0.8667	0.3333	−1.0	0.4200	450

Table 3. The second scenario: results of fine tuning ResNet-50 on small ACID dataset (3.5% of whole ACID dataset) from different transfer learning models used one of three main pose estimation datasets. The initial self-supervised feature extraction was trained over the whole ACID dataset.

Model	Data	Status	AP	AP^{50}	AP^{75}	AP^M	AP^L	AR	AR^{50}	AR^{75}	AR^M	AR^L	Epochs
ResNet-50	6 keys	Self-Sup	**0.4913**	0.9261	**0.3964**	−1.0	**0.4913**	**0.5400**	0.9333	**0.5333**	−1.0	**0.5400**	_100_
	Nvidia	Self-Sup	0.405	0.861	0.352	−1.0	0.405	0.440	0.867	0.467	−1.0	0.440	560
	Matlab	Self-Sup	0.4562	1.0	0.3030	−1.0	0.4562	0.5133	1.0	0.4000	−1.0	0.5133	440
HRNet-W32	6 keys	Self-Sup	**0.5145**	**1.0**	**0.3634**	−1.0	**0.5145**	**0.5667**	**1.0**	**0.4667**	−1.0	**0.5667**	_330_
	Nvidia	Self-Sup	0.2858	0.61174	0.10396	−1.0	0.2858	0.32667	0.32667	0.13333	−1.0	0.32667	510
	Matlab	Self-Sup	0.1477	0.4738	0.0901	−1.0	0.1477	0.26	0.6667	0.20	−1.0	0.260	480

The self-supervised stage is trained over the ACID whole dataset. Then the learning of downstream task is transferred using three different datasets (two simulated datasets from NVIDIA Issac and MATLAB as well as one real dataset with 6 keypoints) and finally fine-tuned on the small annotated ACID dataset with only 4 keypoints. In addition, the results of the middle stage with a simulated dataset from NVIDIA Isaac and MATLAB Simscape Multibody are mentioned in Table 4. The self-supervised approach is compared to the supervised approach in terms of Average Precision (AP), Average Recall (AR), and optimal epoch for models based on both ResNet-50 and HRNet-W32 backbones. For a comprehensive presentation of the data, we provide images samples trained using conventional supervision and our novel self-supervised model, applied to authentic images of the excavator. The visual representations of both approaches are displayed in Fig. 4, additional results from simulations are given in Fig. 5.

Table 4. Results of pose estimation model training with both supervised and self-supervised approaches on the two simulated datasets with different backbones. Feature extraction in self-supervised stage was trained over whole ACID dataset.

Status	Model	AP	AR	Epochs	Model	AP	AR	Epochs
Dataset: NVIDIA simulated dataset								
Supervised	ResNet-50	0.817	0.863	150	HRNet-w32	0.814	0.871	380
Self-sup		**0.834**	**0.888**	200		**0.940**	**0.961**	600
Dataset: MATLAB simulated dataset								
Supervised	ResNet-50	0.688	0.696	120	HRNet-w32	**0.690**	0.696	90
Self-sup		**0.696**	**0.699**	130		0.684	**0.7**	550

(a) Self-supervised model based on ResNet-50

(b) Self-supervised model based on HRNet-W32

Fig. 4. Samples results of the self-supervised model originally pretrained with ImageNet, and the proposed approach. Red circle shows a new keypoint detection, while the blue box shows a correction in the detection. (Color figure online)

5.2   Discussion

The proposed model of a self-supervised approach trained over three stages boosts up the performance of the pose estimation task by 11% and 13% in comparison to the SimCLR self-supervised baseline for the backbones of ResNet and HR-Net, respectively. In addition, it reduces the number of epochs needed during the training for both encoder models which are the basic deep neural structure in the most recent pose estimation models. It is noticeable that this model outperforms the supervised approach for pose estimation for small data by 4.6% and 9.2% for the mentioned backbones, respectively, after transfer learning on a 6 keypoints real dataset.

The results in Tables 3 and 4 show that the accuracy from training the proposed three-stage model with such simulation datasets of NVIDIA Issac and MATLAB is not as higher as expected. One of the reasons behind that is that the downstream task depends on having some annotated dataset. In this proposed approach, usage of the top-down pose estimation as a downstream task requires

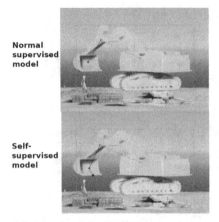
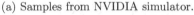

Normal
supervised
model

Self-
supervised
model

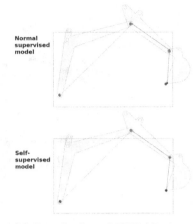

Normal
supervised
model

Self-
supervised
model

(a) Samples from NVIDIA simulator.

(b) Samples from MATLAB simulator.

Fig. 5. Samples from supervised and self-supervised models trained on datasets from NVIDIA Isaac and Simscape Multibody using the ResNet-50 backbone.

Fig. 6. Samples of automatic bounding box computation in green labeling using the minimum bounding box of the six keypoints of excavator pose. (Color figure online)

accurately labeled data, especially in terms of bounding boxes. Since both the Matlab and six-keypoints datasets do not have any boxes over the desired object, an approximate method called Minimum bounding box [4] is used to create such boxes without using human label effort. This method is not so accurate due to multiple reasons: first, we try to use few points to create such boxes, second, those points are the main keypoints that can not present the exact bounding of the excavator in some cases, e.g. when the picture of the machine is taken from the back view. Figure 6 shows such cases. Thus an accurate automatic labeling of the data from the simulation is of high importance to enhance the accuracy of such a top-down pose estimator which will be addressed in future work.

6   Conclusion and Future Work

In this paper, a new pose estimation approach is proposed inherited from both the self-supervised SimCLR model and dynamic simulation. The self-supervised model is used to teach the pose estimator the basic features that help in detecting the keypoints of construction machines, while the dynamic simulators are used to generate a synthetic dataset with annotations to enhance the downstream tasks. Implementing such a synthetic dataset within a self-supervised approach is an emerging area of research, which has been addressed within this work.

With around 3.5% annotated data of real images from the overall ACID dataset, the proposed model was sufficient to detect the main keypoints of construction machines. It increases the accuracy of pose estimation for construction machines for both backbones ResNet-50 and HRNet-W32 by 11% and 13%, respectively compared to pre-train the model using the ImageNet dataset in one stage. Moreover, the pretraining using a self-supervised approach over the ACID dataset and fine-tuning with multiple stages over a smaller dataset helps the model to reach the optimal weights faster with less number of epochs. This approach is boosting the usage of real-time dynamic simulators in improved computer vision models in the agriculture and construction fields that have many limitations in gathering and labeling huge amounts of datasets.

In future work, we plan to investigate and design a pose estimation mode using the recent state-of-the-art SSL Dino v2 model. Using domain adaptation approaches can be tested and integrated with our model to enhance the pose estimation for other types of construction machines as well as autonomous driving machines. In addition, we will integrate our deep neural model into a more complex approach for motion prediction to ensure safety in construction fields.

References

1. Albelwi, S.: Survey on self-supervised learning: auxiliary pretext tasks and contrastive learning methods in imaging. Entropy **24**(4), 551 (2022)
2. Cao, J., Tang, H., Fang, H.S., Shen, X., Lu, C., Tai, Y.W.: Cross-domain adaptation for animal pose estimation. In: IEEE/CVF International Conference on Computer Vision, pp. 9498–9507 (2019)
3. Caron, M., Misra, I., Mairal, J., Goyal, P., Bojanowski, P., Joulin, A.: Unsupervised learning of visual features by contrasting cluster assignments. Adv. Neural. Inf. Process. Syst. **33**, 9912–9924 (2020)
4. Chan, C., Tan, S.: Determination of the minimum bounding box of an arbitrary solid: an iterative approach. Comput. Struct. **79**(15), 1433–1449 (2001)
5. Chen, T., Kornblith, S., Norouzi, M., Hinton, G.: A simple framework for contrastive learning of visual representations. In: International Conference on Machine Learning, pp. 1597–1607 (2020)
6. Dang, Q., Yin, J., Wang, B., Zheng, W.: Deep learning based 2D human pose estimation: a survey. Tsinghua Sci. Technol. **24**(6), 663–676 (2019)
7. Graving, J.M., et al.: Deepposekit, a software toolkit for fast and robust animal pose estimation using deep learning. Elife **8**, e47994 (2019)
8. Jaiswal, A., Babu, A.R., Zadeh, M.Z., Banerjee, D., Makedon, F.: A survey on contrastive self-supervised learning. Technologies **9**(1), 2 (2020)
9. Jin, S., et al.: Differentiable hierarchical graph grouping for multi-person pose estimation. In: 16th European Conference on Computer Vision, pp. 718–734 (2020)
10. Jin, S., et al.: Whole-body human pose estimation in the wild. In: Vedaldi, A., Bischof, H., Brox, T., Frahm, J.-M. (eds.) ECCV 2020. LNCS, vol. 12354, pp. 196–214. Springer, Cham (2020). https://doi.org/10.1007/978-3-030-58545-7_12

11. Lan, G., Wu, Y., Hu, F., Hao, Q.: Vision-based human pose estimation via deep learning: a survey. IEEE Trans. Hum. Mach. Syst. (2022)
12. Lin, C., et al.: Structure-coherent deep feature learning for robust face alignment. IEEE Trans. Image Process. **30**, 5313–5326 (2021)
13. Lin, Z.H., Chen, A.Y., Hsieh, S.H.: Temporal image analytics for abnormal construction activity identification. Autom. Constr. **124**, 103572 (2021)
14. Luo, H., Wang, M., Wong, P.K.Y., Cheng, J.C.: Full body pose estimation of construction equipment using computer vision and deep learning techniques. Autom. Constr. **110**, 103016 (2020)
15. Luo, H., Wang, M., Wong, P.K.Y., Tang, J., Cheng, J.C.: Construction machine pose prediction considering historical motions and activity attributes using gated recurrent unit (GRU). Autom. Constr. **121**, 103444 (2021)
16. Luo, H., Liu, J., Fang, W., Love, P.E., Yu, Q., Lu, Z.: Real-time smart video surveillance to manage safety: a case study of a transport mega-project. Adv. Eng. Inform. **45**, 101100 (2020)
17. Miller, S.: Excavator design with simscape (2023). https://github.com/simscape/Excavator-Simscape/releases/tag/23.1.51.5
18. Newell, A., Huang, Z., Deng, J.: Associative embedding: end-to-end learning for joint detection and grouping. Adv. Neural Inf. Process. Syst. **30** (2017)
19. Oquab, M., et al.: Dinov2: learning robust visual features without supervision (2023)
20. Pereira, T.D., et al.: Fast animal pose estimation using deep neural networks. Nat. Methods **16**(1), 117–125 (2019)
21. Pham, H.T., Rafieizonooz, M., Han, S., Lee, D.E.: Current status and future directions of deep learning applications for safety management in construction. Sustainability **13**(24), 13579 (2021)
22. Rani, V., Nabi, S.T., Kumar, M., Mittal, A., Kumar, K.: Self-supervised learning: a succinct review. Arch. Comput. Methods Eng. **30**(4), 2761–2775 (2023)
23. Sarafianos, N., Boteanu, B., Ionescu, B., Kakadiaris, I.A.: 3D human pose estimation: a review of the literature and analysis of covariates. Comput. Vis. Image Underst. **152**, 1–20 (2016)
24. Soltani, M.M., Zhu, Z., Hammad, A.: Skeleton estimation of excavator by detecting its parts. Autom. Constr. **82**, 1–15 (2017)
25. Xiao, B., Kang, S.C.: Development of an image data set of construction machines for deep learning object detection. J. Comput. Civ. Eng. **35**(2), 05020005 (2021)
26. Zhang, F., Zhu, X., Dai, H., Ye, M., Zhu, C.: Distribution-aware coordinate representation for human pose estimation. In: IEEE/CVF Conference on Computer Vision and Pattern Recognition, pp. 7093–7102 (2020)
27. Zhao, J., Hu, Y., Tian, M.: Pose estimation of excavator manipulator based on monocular vision marker system. Sensors **21**(13), 4478 (2021)

Image Quality Improvement of Surveillance Camera Image by Learning Noise Removal Method Using Noise2Noise

Tomio Goto$^{(\boxtimes)}$ ⓘ and Akira Kuchida ⓘ

Nagoya Institute of Technology, Nagoya 4668555, Aichi, Japan
t.goto@nitech.ac.jp

Abstract. It is known that images captured by cameras, including surveillance cameras, are degraded by noise due to the shooting environment. Noisy images cannot identify a person's face or a car license plate number, making it difficult to identify the culprit, which is the purpose of surveillance cameras. Therefore, it is necessary to perform image denoising. In the field of noise reduction, learning methods are currently in the spotlight. However, it is usually difficult to obtain the noiseless images necessary for learning, and there is a problem that they are not practical. In this paper, we investigate an effective noise elimination technique not only for synthetic noise but also for real noise by using a learning method that introduces a technique that does not require clean images. We will also consider improvements to DRUNet [1], which has been shown to be effective as a noise reduction model, in order to make it much lighter and more practical.

Keywords: Noise Removable Method · Denoising Method · Surveillance Camera

1 Introduction

Research on image denoising has been active for the past several decades, and various models have been proposed, including the Nonlocal Self-Similarity (NSS) model [2–5], the sparse model [5–7], the gradient model [8–10], and the Markov Random Field (MRF) model [11–13]. Among these models, the NSS model is often used in state-of-the-art methods such as BM3D [3], LSSC [5], NCSR [7], and WNNM [14]. However, these methods have two major drawbacks. The first is problem that the denoising process is very time-consuming because it involves a complex optimization problem. In other words, the previous methods cannot achieve high performance without sacrificing computational efficiency. Second, the models of the previous methods are non-convex and contain multiple manually selected parameters, which means that the parameters must be changed depending on the image in order to output the best results. In order to solve these drawbacks, models using learning methods have been developed.

Noise reduction using learning methods is a field that has attracted much attention in recent years, and various models have been proposed, including CNN models such as

G. Bebis et al. (Eds.): ISVC 2023, LNCS 14362, pp. 409–419, 2023.
https://doi.org/10.1007/978-3-031-47966-3_32

DnCNN [15] and Transformer models such as SwinIR [16]. In this paper, we focus on DRUNet [1], which has shown good results in CNN models, and propose a new model based on this network model with fewer parameters and comparable performance to DRUNet by modifying it.

In addition, the target noise for noise reduction is generally synthetic noise such as Gaussian noise and Poisson noise, and there are few research reports showing the results of noise reduction when the noise actually generated by the camera is removed. The synthetic noise and the real noise are strictly different, and applying an AI model trained with the synthetic noise to the real noise does not always give good results, and in many cases, the AI model does not show sufficient performance. In many cases, even if real noise images are studied, only open datasets such as Smartphone Image Denoising Dataset (SIDD) [17] or Darmstadt Noise Dataset (DND) [18] are used. However, there are many images that actually contain more noise, have lower contrast, and are more blurred than those in these open datasets. Therefore, training AI models using these real noise-added images may not perform well for images taken by surveillance cameras and so on. In other words, it is necessary to train AI models on a dataset of images taken by your own devices, not on a publicly available dataset. However, there is a problem that a clean and noise-free image must be acquired in the dataset creation process. Normally, when building an AI model for image restoration, it is necessary to create a dataset that consists of a pair of an image to be restored (in this case, a noisy image) and an ideal output image (in this case, a clean image without noise). However, in general, there is a requirement that these pairs of images be taken under the same shooting conditions against the same background. In low-exposure environments, preparing clean images without noise is a very difficult requirement in terms of both money and time, and it is often impossible to create a data set. In other words, training AI models using actual images under these conditions incurs a large cost, is not feasible, and does not lead to widespread use of the technology. In recent years, a learning method that can train AI models without requiring clean, noise-free images has been proposed. In this paper, we consider a learning method that aims to solve this problem by using Noise2Noise [19], one of the leading methods in this field, and to contribute to the popularization of the technique. Noise2Noise is a learning method that does not require clean images, but pairs images with the same background that contain noise under the condition that the mean of the noise distribution is 0, and thus can obtain results similar to those of ordinary learning. However, in the proposed paper, the experiments were conducted on synthetic noise, and no validation of Noise2Noise on actually captured images was conducted. In this study, we show that Noise2Noise is effective for actually captured images. Noise2Noise also has a weakness that its performance deteriorates drastically when the number of training images is small compared to normal training. In this study, we will investigate a method to reduce the influence of this weakness by pre-training with open datasets such as SIDD, and to show good results even when the number of training images is small.

2 Network Overview

Our proposed network structure is shown in Fig. 1. This network is based on the DRUNet. The DRUNet imitates the structure of U-Net, which consists of four scales, and adopts the residual block, which is the basis of ResNet. The network consists of four types of convolutional layers (Conv), residual blocks (Residual Blocks), stride convolutional layers (SConv), and reverse convolutional layers (TConv). ConvNeXt block was proposed by Liu et al. [20] in 2022. With Transformer models dominating image processing tasks, this proposal aims to modernize the design part of CNN models. ConvNeXt is structured based on ResNet [21], a standard CNN design. Figure 2 shows the structure of the ConvNeXt Block, which is a simple network such as Residual Block in DRUNet, which incorporates the activation function ReLU [22] between 3 × 3 convolutional layers, but rather incorporates Depthwise Conv, Pointwise Conv, and Layer Normalization [23], which will be described later. In addition, GELU [24] is used for the activation function instead of ReLU. Another major difference compared to the ResidualBlock in DRUNet is the number of blocks per scale. While DRUNet employs four Residual Blocks at any layer regardless of the scale, the number of blocks is changed for each layer in the proposed model by changing the ConvNeXt Block from 3 → 3 → 9 → 3 following the Swin Transformer. As a result of above modification, the number of parameters was significantly reduced from 32.64M to 18.46M, while maintaining the noise removal performance.

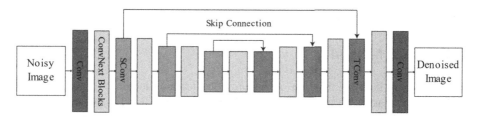

Fig. 1. Proposed network structure.

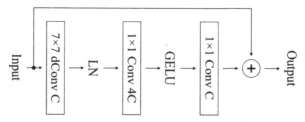

Fig. 2. Structure of ConvNeXt Block.

3 Noise2Noise

In general, when training a model for image restoration tasks, a dataset is created by pairing a noise-free image with a noise-infected image on the same background. However, it is often difficult to obtain noise-free images due to time and monetary costs. To solve this problem, Noise2Noise [19] is a method that can learn a transformation from a degraded image to a correct image using only noise images. In general, the strategy for estimating the unknown value z is to minimize the error from the measured value y based on some loss function L, i.e., to find z with the smallest mean deviation as shown in Eq. (1).

$$z = \text{argmin} \mathbb{E}_y \{L(x, y)\} \tag{1}$$

where z takes the arithmetic mean when L2 loss is adopted, and the median when L1 loss is adopted. Formulating the training with the input x and target pair y, and applying the conditional probability formula, we obtain Eq. (2).

$$\theta = \text{argmin} \mathbb{E}_x \{\mathbb{E}_{y|x} L(f_\theta(x), y)\} \tag{2}$$

where in the L2 loss, the training is performed so that the average value of multiple inference candidates is output. Using this fact, even if the target pair is $\hat{y}$ with noise added, if the expected value of the target distribution $\mathbb{E}\{p(\hat{y}|x\}$ satisfies $\mathbb{E}\{p(\hat{y}|x\} = \mathbb{E}\{p(y|x\}$, the learning can be performed as well as the case where the target does not contain any noise.

4 Proposed Method

Figure 3 shows the flow diagram of our proposed learning method. In our proposed method, two datasets are used for training. First, we use SIDD [17], which is widely used as a dataset for real noise reduction. This is used as the pre-trained model. The model is then re-trained using only the noise images captured by the actual device, depending on the device and the environment in which it is installed. By using Noise2Noise in the re-training process, it is possible to train only with images that contain noise. Through these procedures, it is possible to construct a network model that is suitable for the actual environment in which it will be used. The proposed method has a problem that when the number of training images for re-training is small, the network overfits and the results deteriorate. Therefore, in addition, the datasets used for re-training must be actually taken and collected, which incurs additional costs, and there are cases in which sufficient image collection is not possible. Therefore, in addition to the basic rotation and inversion, we apply three data extensions: NoiseSurrogate [25], RGB Permutation and Blend [26], which have been shown to be effective in the image restoration task, are used as data expansion methods.

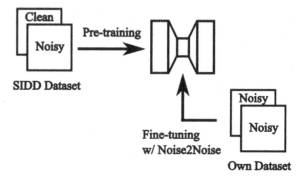

Fig. 3. Overview of our proposed learning method.

5 Experimental Results

In this section, we describe the dataset used for re-training with Noise2Noise and the settings used for training. For the dataset, we used images taken by surveillance cameras that are actually in use. No clean images without noise were collected, however, only images containing noise were used. The dataset consists of a total of 20 different imaging conditions, using 10 different backgrounds and 2 different exposure conditions. For each shooting condition, 10 frames of video were taken, and each frame was treated as an image, making a total of 100 pairs as the dataset for re-training. The resolution of the images is Full-HD, which is lower than that for the pre-training, however, relatively high resolution images have been taken. Figure 4 shows an example of images actually used for re-training. Table 1 shows the settings for pre-training and re-training. The patch size, batch size, weight decay, loss function, and initial learning rate are different from those for the pre-training. For the patch size, we follow H. Touvron et al. [28]. However, the batch size is reduced to reduce the learning time and computational cost. For the loss function of L2 loss, which outputs the average value of inferred images, is used according to the Noise2Noise theory.

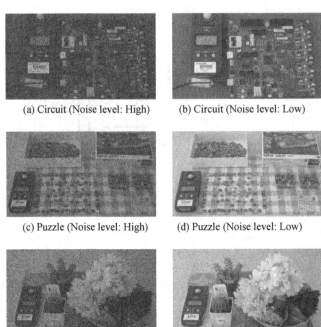

(a) Circuit (Noise level: High)   (b) Circuit (Noise level: Low)

(c) Puzzle (Noise level: High)   (d) Puzzle (Noise level: Low)

(e) Flower (Noise level: High)   (f) Flower (Noise level: Low)

Fig. 4. Example of re-training images.

Table 1. Experimental conditions for re-training.

Parameters	Pre-training	Re-training
Patch size	128	192
Batch size	16	14
Optimization function	AdamW [27]	
Weight decay	$1e^{-4}$	$1e^{-6}$
Loss function	Charbonnier loss	L2 loss
Initial learning rate	$1e^{-4}$	$1e^{-6}$
Learning decrease rate	Half per 200,000 iterations	

Table 2. Experimental results (PSNR [dB]).

Test Images	Sheet music	Spray can	Trump card
Noise2Noise [19]	24.92	26.37	25.38
SwinIR [16]	14.68	14.74	14.99
Restormer [29]	20.07	19.68	19.81
Proposed method	**25.26**	**26.59**	**25.59**

Table 3. Experimental results (SSIM).

Test Images	Sheet music	Spray can	Trump card
Noise2Noise [19]	0.440	0.453	0.434
SwinIR [16]	0.166	0.137	0.162
Restormer [29]	0.428	0.423	0.423
Proposed method	**0.456**	**0.464**	**0.456**

To confirm the effectiveness of our proposed method, we compare the models trained by our proposed method with those trained by Noise2Noise without pre-training, using the dataset for re-training. As in the previous section, an objective evaluation of PSNR and SSIM is conducted using the frame-averaged image as the ideal image, and a subjective evaluation is conducted focusing on noise reduction performance and texture preservation. Tables 2 and 3 show the results of PSNR and SSIM for the test images, and Figs. 5 and 6 show the results of noise reduction for the two test images. In Tables 2 and 3, we confirmed that PSNR and SSIM were higher than those of the other two models. In addition, the subjective evaluation also showed that the blur around the texture was slightly reduced. In these results, compared to the model using Noise2Noise alone, the model with pre-training using an open dataset as in our proposed method improves both objective and subjective evaluation results, confirming the effectiveness of the pre-training.

(a) Noisy
(PSNR: 12.17 [dB], SSIM: 0.095)

(b) Averaging image

(c) SwinIR [16]
(PSNR: 14.74 [dB], SSIM: 0.137)

(d) Restormer [29]
(PSNR: 19.68 [dB], SSIM: 0.425)

(e) Pre-trained model
(PSNR: 21.18 [dB], SSIM: 0.435)

(f) Proposed method
(PSNR: 26.54 [dB], SSIM: 0.449)

Fig. 5. Original image and restored images (Spray can image)

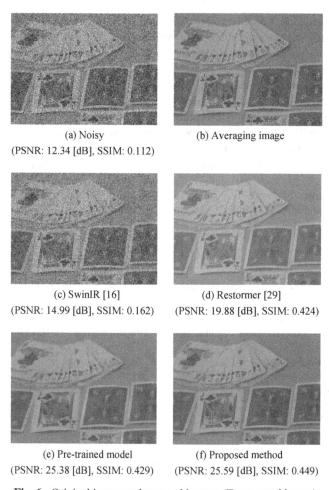

(a) Noisy
(PSNR: 12.34 [dB], SSIM: 0.112)

(b) Averaging image

(c) SwinIR [16]
(PSNR: 14.99 [dB], SSIM: 0.162)

(d) Restormer [29]
(PSNR: 19.88 [dB], SSIM: 0.424)

(e) Pre-trained model
(PSNR: 25.38 [dB], SSIM: 0.429)

(f) Proposed method
(PSNR: 25.59 [dB], SSIM: 0.449)

Fig. 6. Original image and restored images (Trump card image)

6 Conclusion

In this paper, with the aim of improving the practicality, we have investigated a learning method that does not require clean and noiseless images using Noise2Noise, thereby significantly reducing the cost of dataset creation. In order to further reduce the burden of dataset collection, we proposed a learning flow in which the models are pre-trained using open datasets and then re-trained using Noise2Noise, which not only further improves the results but also reduces the number of images with real noise required for re-training. This learning method makes it possible to create a dataset without collecting clean, noise-free images and does not require a large number of images, which greatly facilitates model construction and thus contributes significantly to improving the practicality of the model. As for the performance of the models, we confirmed that the possibility of using images obtained by actual shooting devices as the dataset allows us to create models that show better results than those trained on open datasets. The output images after denoising were confirmed to have a clear improvement in performance, as the background contrast and blurring around characters were eliminated. In addition, we confirmed the improvement of the results compared to the models trained only with Noise2Noise by using the open dataset as a pre-training model and following the procedure of re-training.

Future work includes the development of a learning method that does not significantly degrade performance even when the number of images for re-training is further limited, as well as a more lightweight and high-performance model. Specifically, we should refer to the fusion model of CNN and Transformer proposed by Zhang et al. [30]. We will also consider new modules to improve the compatibility between DRUNet and ConvNeXt.

Acknowledgment. This work was supported by Telecom Advanced Technology Research Support Center and JSPS KAKENHI Grant Number JP22K12072.

References

1. Zhang, K., et al.: Plug-and-play image restoration with deep denoiser prior. IEEE Trans. Pattern Anal. Mach. Intell. **44**, 6360–6376 (2021)
2. Buades, A., Coll, B., Morel, J.-M.: A non-local algorithm for image denoising. In: IEEE International Conference on Computer Vision and Pattern Recognition (CVPR), vol. 2, pp. 60–65 (2005)
3. Dabov, K., Foi, A., Katkovnik, V., Egiazarian, K.: Image denoising by sparse 3-D transform-domain collaborative filtering. IEEE Trans. Image Process. **16**(8), 2080–2095 (2007)
4. Buades, A., Coll, B., Morel, J.-M.: Nonlocal image and movie denoising. Int. J. Comput. Vis. **76**(2), 123–139 (2008)
5. Mairal, J., Bach, F., Ponce, J., Sapiro, G., Zisserman, A.: Non-local sparse models for image restoration. In: IEEE International Conference on Computer Vision (ICCV), pp. 2272–2279 (2009)
6. Elad, M., Aharon, M.: Image denoising via sparse and redundant representations over learned dictionaries. IEEE Trans. Image Process. **15**(12), 3736–3745 (2006)
7. Dong, W., Zhang, L., Shi, G., Li, X.: Nonlocally centralized sparse representation for image restoration. IEEE Trans. Image Process. **22**(4), 1620–1630 (2013)
8. Rudin, L.I., Osher, S., Fatemi, E.: Nonlinear total variation based noise removal algorithms. Physica D: Nonlinear Phenom. **60**(1), 259–268 (1992)
9. Osher, S., Burger, M.: An iterative regularization method for total variation based image restoration. Multiscale Model. Simul. **4**(2), 460–489 (2005)
10. Weiss, Y., Freeman, W.T.: What makes a good model of natural images? In: IEEE Conference on Computer Vision and Pattern Recognition (CVPR), pp. 1–8 (2007)
11. Lan, X., Roth, S., Huttenlocher, D., Black, M.J.: Efficient belief propagation with learned higher-order Markov random fields. In: Leonardis, A., Bischof, H., Pinz, A. (eds.) ECCV 2006. LNCS, vol. 3952, pp. 269–282. Springer, Heidelberg (2006). https://doi.org/10.1007/11744047_21
12. Li, S.Z.: Markov Random Field Modeling in Image Analysis. Springer, London (2009). https://doi.org/10.1007/978-1-84800-279-1
13. Roth, S., Black, M.J.: Fields of experts. Int. J. Comput. Vis. **82**(2), 205–229 (2009)
14. Gu, S., Zhang, L., Zuo, W., Feng, X.: Weighted nuclear norm minimization with application to image denoising. In: IEEE International Conference on Computer Vision and Pattern Recognition (CVPR), pp. 2862–2869 (2014)

15. Zhang, K.: Beyond a Gaussian denoiser: residual learning of deep CNN for image denoising. IEEE Trans. Image Process. **26**(7), 3142–3155 (2017)
16. Liang, J., Cao, J., Sun, G., Zhang, K., Van Gool, L., Timofte, R.: SwinIR: image restoration using swin transformer. In: IEEE International Conference on Computer Vision (ICCV), pp. 1833–1844 (2021)
17. Abdelhamed, A., Lin, S., Brown, M.S.: A high-quality denoising dataset for smartphone cameras. In: IEEE Conference on Computer Vision and Pattern Recognition (CVPR), pp. 1692–1700 (2018)
18. Plotz, T., Roth, S.: Benchmarking denoising algorithms with real photographs. In: IEEE International Conference on Computer Vision and Pattern Recognition (CVPR), pp. 1586–1595 (2017)
19. Lehtinen, J.: Noise2Noise: learning image restoration without clean data. In: IEEE International Conference on Machine Learning (ICML), pp. 2965–2974 (2018)
20. Liu, Z., Mao, H., Wu, C.Y., Feichtenhofer, C., Darrell, T., Xie, S.: A ConvNet for the 2020s. In: IEEE International Conference on Computer Vision and Pattern Recognition (CVPR), pp. 11976–11986 (2022)
21. He, K., Zhang, X., Ren, S., Sun, J.: Deep residual learning for image recognition. In: IEEE International Conference on Computer Vision and Pattern Recognition (CVPR), pp. 770–778 (2016)
22. Krizhevsky, A., Sutskever, I., Hinton, G.E.: ImageNet classification with deep convolutional neural networks. In: Advances in Neural Information Processing Systems, pp. 1097–1105 (2012)
23. Ba, J.L., Kiros, J.R., Hinton, G.E.: Layer normalization. arXiv: 1607.06450 (2016)
24. Hendrycks, D., Gimpel, K.: Gaussian error linear units (GELU). arXiv: 1606.08415 (2016)
25. Calvarons, A.F.: Improved Noise2Noise denoising with limited data. In: IEEE International Conference on Computer Vision and Pattern Recognition (CVPR), pp. 796–805 (2021)
26. Yoo, J., Ahn, N., Sohn, K.: Rethinking data augmentation for image super-resolution: a comprehensive analysis and a new strategy. In: IEEE International Conference on Computer Vision and Pattern Recognition (CVPR), pp. 8375–8384 (2020)
27. Loahchilov, I., Hutter, F.: Decoupled weight decay regularization. In: IEEE International Conference on Learning Representations (ICLR) (2019)
28. Touvron, H., Vedaldi, A., Douze, M., Jégou, H.: Fixing the train-test resolution discrepancy. In: Neural Information Processing Systems (2019)
29. Zamir, S.W., Arora, A., Khan, S., Hayat, M., Khan, F.S., Yang, M.: Restormer: efficient transformer for high-resolution image restoration. In: IEEE International Conference on Computer Vision and Pattern Recognition (CVPR), pp. 5728–5739 (2022)
30. Zhang, K., et al.: Practical blind denoising via Swin-Conv-UNet and data synthesis. arXiv: 2203.13278 (2022)

Automating Kernel Size Selection in MRI Reconstruction via a Transparent and Interpretable Search Approach

Alan Okinaka[1], Gulfam Saju[2], and Yuchou Chang[2(✉)]

[1] Physics Department, Ursinus College, 601 E Main St, Collegeville, PA 19426, USA
[2] Computer and Information Science Department, University of Massachusetts Dartmouth, 285 Old Westport Road, Dartmouth, MA 02747, USA
ychang1@umassd.edu

Abstract. GeneRalized Autocalibrating Partial Parallel Acquisition (GRAPPA) is a clinical Magnetic Resonance Imaging (MRI) reconstruction method. The kernel size in GRAPPA directly controls the image quality and the optimal kernel size can be manually selected through comparing multiple reconstructed images. However, the optimal kernel size is often impractical to be manually selected in clinical settings. To resolve this issue, we propose an automated kernel size selection method utilizing grid search, which maintains GRAPPA's transparent and interpretable nature in a linear interpolation process. This strategy redefines kernel size selection as an exhaustive search problem and tests all potential kernel sizes within a predefined hyperparameter space. Experimental results, evaluated through both qualitative and quantitative metrics, demonstrate the effectiveness of our method in consistently identifying the optimal kernel size. The proposed approach significantly enhances the efficiency and utility of GRAPPA reconstruction for ensuring high image quality pivotal in accurate clinical diagnoses and treatment plans.

Keywords: Magnetic Resonance Imaging · Clinical Imaging · Grid Search

1 Introduction

GeneRalized Autocalibrating Partial Parallel Acquisition (GRAPPA) [1] is a renowned method utilized in clinical imaging, specifically within the field of Magnetic Resonance Imaging (MRI). One of the distinguishing features of GRAPPA is its use of Autocalibration Signals (ACS) data, which enables the system to estimate interpolation coefficients. This characteristic eliminates the necessity for external training data, making GRAPPA an efficient and self-sufficient method for accelerating imaging speed. When comparing GRAPPA to deep learning-based MRI reconstruction methods [3], a significant advantage becomes apparent: GRAPPA employs a linear interpolator, making it transparent and interpretable. This transparency ensures that GRAPPA's workings can be thoroughly analyzed, providing a clear understanding of how the imaging results are achieved. Consequently, GRAPPA's use in clinical MRI continues to be a preferred choice for many practitioners due to its blend of efficiency, autonomy, and interpretability.

© The Author(s), under exclusive license to Springer Nature Switzerland AG 2023
G. Bebis et al. (Eds.): ISVC 2023, LNCS 14362, pp. 420–430, 2023.
https://doi.org/10.1007/978-3-031-47966-3_33

While GRAPPA offers several advantages, it also presents certain challenges, particularly related to kernel size optimization [2]. Generally, kernel size, which directly influences the quality of the reconstructed image, is manually optimized in GRAPPA. However, in practical, fast-paced clinical settings, manual selection and adjustment of the kernel size are often infeasible, leading to a potential compromise in the quality of the reconstructed images. This limitation underscores the need for an automated approach to kernel size selection. By automatically searching for the optimal kernel size, the imaging process could become more streamlined and efficient. Moreover, it would ensure consistently high image quality, vital for accurate clinical diagnoses and treatment plans, making the overall process more suited to the demanding needs of clinical applications.

In the context of GRAPPA's image reconstruction process, the selection of the optimal kernel size, which directly impacts the resultant image quality, can be redefined as a search problem. Considering GRAPPA's linear and transparent nature, the method used to find the optimal kernel size should similarly be interpretable. In this regard, grid search as a straightforward and exhaustive exploration of all combinations of predefined hyperparameters may be a suitable choice. Its simplicity lies in systematically testing all potential kernel sizes until the best one is identified, contributing significantly to achieving optimal image quality. Through its simple principle of testing all combinations in a predefined hyperparameter grid, grid search could be an efficient solution for automatic kernel size selection in GRAPPA, especially considering its linear and interpretable nature. This shift from manual selection to automated kernel size determination via grid search can substantially improve the efficacy and convenience of GRAPPA in clinical settings.

In this study, we introduce an innovative approach for automatic kernel size selection in the GRAPPA imaging method. Our proposed method is designed with a focus on achieving the highest possible quality in reconstructed images, therefore significantly enhancing the effectiveness and utility of GRAPPA in clinical imaging applications. The structure of the paper is as follows: the first part provides an introduction, setting the context and presenting the problem at hand. This is followed by the second part, where we discuss related works and the current landscape of solutions. The third section delves into the details of our proposed method for automatic kernel size selection. In the fourth section, we present the experimental results that demonstrate the efficacy of our proposed method, followed by the fifth and final section which provides a conclusion, summarizing our findings and their implications for GRAPPA imaging and potentially highlighting future avenues for further research.

2   Related Work

Functioning as a linear parallel MRI reconfiguration, GRAPPA [1] addresses the inverse issue by resolving a set of linear equations. Additionally, GRAPPA reconstruction can be depicted as

$$S_j(k_y - m\Delta k_y) = \sum_{l=1}^{L} \sum_{b=0}^{N_b-1} n(j, b, l, m) S_l(k_y - bA\Delta k_y) \tag{1}$$

In the formula, the weights used in the linear combination are shown by $n(j, b, l, m)$. N_b represents the number of blocks and A represents the acceleration factor in the reconstruction. Index l and b count through the individual coils and individual reconstruction blocks respectively [4]. The initial regression evaluation in GRAPPA can be substituted with other linear or nonlinear techniques to approximate the linear or nonlinear correlation [5–9] between the undersampled points and their adjacent captured points. A more precise calculation of the missing k-space data can be achieved, surpassing the original GRAPPA technique. As a result, reduced artifacts and an enhanced signal-to-noise ratio (SNR) in the reconfigured images can be secured.

As per machine learning theory, the generalization error is broken down into three components:

$$E = bias^2(x) + var(x) + \varepsilon^2 \qquad (2)$$

which represent bias, variance, and noise, respectively. Variance tends to increase as a larger number of features are employed to learn a linear or nonlinear mapping from raw to reconstructed data. The quality of the reconstruction may be subject to the Bias-Variance Tradeoff (BVT) [10] when a linear or kernel-based learning approach is utilized. Owing to BVT, concurrently reducing bias and variance poses a challenge. Ensemble methods are commonly adopted to lessen variance while maintaining low bias, thereby enhancing quality and stability. Diversity, an essential element for a successful ensemble method, signifies the difference among multiple individual learners. A collective result derived from a group of diverse learners is theoretically assured to accomplish a T-factor error reduction, given that the learners are independent [11], where T represents the ensemble size. Ensemble learning is not a single algorithm, but it accomplishes the learning task by creating and merging multiple diverse learning methods, striving for stable and accurate results. These multiple learning methods are viewed as the individual base or component learners, which can be assembled into homogeneous or heterogeneous ensembles. In the context of MRI reconstruction, diversity can be observed in the different sets of parameters used by a reconstruction method or the distinct reconstruction strategies. To search for the best reconstruction quality, a search algorithm is needed with optimal kernel size selection.

3   Proposed Method

3.1   Influence of Kernel Sizes on Image Quality

We assume each interpolator is a learner in machine learning and needs to be trained using original ACS data. Since multiple interpolators use different kernel sizes for convolution, they are trained with multiple different views, respectively. As shown in the figure below, a small and a large kernel containing small and larger numbers of neighboring k-space data points are used by these two interpolators for interpolating the target k-space signals. Each neighboring k-space data point represents one feature for interpolating the target signal: 6 features (6 black dots) for the small kernel (small view) and 16 features (16 black dots) for the large kernel (large view). Each view represents a feature set. In the calibration step of GRAPPA, two learners trained from these two views have different generalization performance, so that one learner is more accurate and another one less accurate. This observation is also consistent with Reference [2], which showed that the optimal view (optimal kernel size) needs to be manually observed and selected (Fig. 1).

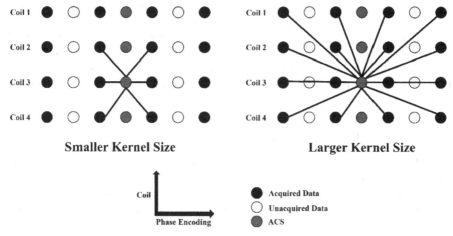

Fig. 1. Different kernel sizes for interpolating missing k-space data in the GRAPPA method. A larger kernel size contains more parameters in the interpolation process while a smaller kernel size includes fewer parameters in the interpolation. BVT is applied to different kernel sizes. An optimal kernel size is searched for to obtain an optimal quality of a reconstructed image.

In the interpolator size determination process, overfitting (interpolation size is too large) and underfitting (interpolation size is too small) problems may appear. For different k-space datasets, the optimal interpolator sizes have also deviated, so manual determination case-by-case is also time-consuming and infeasible in clinical settings. Quantitatively determining an interpolator's accuracy (e.g., using quantitative metrics like NMSE, SSIM, or PSNR) for the whole k-space is difficult without using the fully sampled k-space data. The proposed method cannot determine an interpolator's absolute value of accuracy but try to use the difference between two interpolators' accuracy for reducing the underfitting and overfitting issues.

3.2 Analysis of Kernel Size in GRAPPA Reconstruction

The association between acquired and unacquired k-space data can be divided into two categories: linear and nonlinear relationships. Commonly used in clinical routines, GRAPPA [1] operates as a linear relationship approach that establishes a linear correlation within auto-calibration signals (ACS), followed by utilizing this correlation to recover missing data in peripheral k-space. The linear shift-invariant property enhances the interpretability of GRAPPA, surpassing that of nonlinear relationship techniques. Thus, the impact of reconfiguration parameters, such as the size of the interpolation kernel on the quality of the image, can be quickly discerned. Deep learning uses nonlinear relationship strategies that offer intricate associations between acquired and unacquired k-space data. These strategies excel over their linear counterparts by reducing artifacts and noise. The interpretability of intricate networks, however, remains elusive despite their high accuracy, a result of the accuracy-interpretability trade-off [10] in machine learning theory. Unstable image reconstruction [13] might also occur during deep learning-based MRI reconfiguration, and it becomes challenging to determine the factors responsible for inconsistent performance. Alterations within the training and testing domains can potentially impede generalization performance, consequently impairing image quality [8]. The ability to have consistent and interpretable MRI reconfigurations could assure medical practitioners and patients of the reliability of learning-based medical imaging methodologies [12]. The resilience of reconstruction when employing the low acceleration factor typically surpasses that of reconstruction using the high acceleration factor.

3.3 Grid Search for Optimal Kernel Size

GRAPPA is a renowned parallel MRI reconstruction technique, where the kernel size plays a pivotal role in determining the quality of the reconstruction of missing k-space data. Optimizing this parameter is crucial, and one efficient and systematic approach to do this is through the utilization of the grid search method [14, 15]. Grid search is a hyperparameter tuning technique that offers an exhaustive search over a manually specified subset of hyperparameter values. In the context of GRAPPA, we aim to identify the optimal kernel size that will lead to the best possible reconstruction of the missing k-space data. To initiate this process, we first establish a set of possible kernel sizes that can be adjusted and scrutinized. The range and increments of this set must be chosen carefully, bearing in mind that a larger range or smaller increments will result in a more comprehensive search but will also demand more computational resources. Once this predefined set of kernel sizes is established, we proceed with the iterative process of k-space reconstruction. For each kernel size in the set, the GRAPPA algorithm is employed to perform a reconstruction of an undersampled k-space. The kernel size essentially determines how many neighboring k-space lines are used to estimate the missing k-space data. The choice of kernel size is a critical balance – a smaller kernel might lead to a less accurate estimation due to limited data, while a larger kernel could introduce errors due to the assumption of linearity over a larger region. One reconstruction process with a selected kernel size can be shown in Fig. 2.

Following the reconstruction process in Fig. 2, the performance of each reconstruction is then evaluated. This evaluation involves objective quantitative metrics that assess the quality of the reconstruction against a known ground truth or a fully sampled data set. We used the fully sampled k-space-based reconstruction as the ground truth for evaluating all reconstructed images by different kernel sizes. In this case, we leveraged metrics such as the Normalized Mean Square Error (NMSE), Structural Similarity Index Measure (SSIM), and Peak Signal-to-Noise Ratio (PSNR). NMSE provides a measurement of the overall error in the reconstruction. SSIM, on the other hand, assesses the perceived change in structural information, offering insight into the visibility of the artifacts, while PSNR measures the peak noise error. Each of these metrics brings a unique perspective to the evaluation, and together, they provide a comprehensive understanding of the reconstruction performance. Upon completion of this evaluation for each kernel size in the predefined set, we find ourselves in a position to select the kernel size that yields the

Fig. 2. One reconstruction using a selected kernel size by GRAPPA. ACS data are used as the target or labeled data in this training process of the reconstruction. Once the reconstruction is completed, its performance metrics are evaluated in comparison to the reference image with full sampling. Missing k-space data are interpolated using the estimated kernel coefficients. Next reconstruction selects another kernel size from the pre-defined set and repeats the three steps above. Note that only ACS data are used for grid search because ACS data represent the real acquired data from an MRI scanner.

best performance. This optimal kernel size is typically chosen based on a compromise among the NMSE, SSIM, and PSNR values, as the perfect balance between these metrics often leads to the most satisfactory reconstruction results.

The proposed grid search method provides a systematic and robust approach to identifying the optimal kernel size for the GRAPPA algorithm. This technique takes advantage of the benefits of exhaustive search and cross-validation to yield a kernel size that enhances the reconstruction quality of missing k-space data. However, it's important to remember that while this method may provide the best solution within the predefined range, it might not be the absolute optimal solution. Regular refinements and reconsiderations of the range of kernel sizes, as well as advancements in algorithmic design and hardware capabilities, may lead to further optimization of the GRAPPA algorithm.

3.4   The Effects of Search Space on Reconstruction Quality

Grid search isn't without its limitations. In some cases, grid search may fail to identify the best optimal kernel size due to inadequacies in the pre-established set of kernel sizes or the increments chosen. If these predetermined choices do not encapsulate the true optimal value, the grid search will, quite understandably, be unable to locate it. To counteract this drawback and bolster the reconstruction performance, one of the first steps could be to refine the search space. This might involve either broadening the range of possible kernel sizes under consideration or reducing the increment steps between the values in the search grid. Tuning these aspects would permit a more detailed exploration of potential kernel sizes and increase the probability of stumbling upon the optimal value.

Refining the search space may not always be sufficient, and the conventional grid search might need to be substituted with more sophisticated methods. Two such alternatives could be adaptive grid search [16] and random search [17]. An adaptive grid search method brings a certain dynamism to the process - it identifies promising regions within the grid and narrows down the search to that region, thereby improving the efficiency and effectiveness of the search. On the other hand, a random search method provides a solution to the exhaustive nature of grid search. By selecting random combinations of hyperparameters for evaluation, it can sometimes uncover optimal values that might be overlooked in a regular grid search. The influence of human expertise [2] can be utilized in this process. Particularly for something as specialized as MRI reconstruction, the experience of an MRI technologist could be invaluable. Their experience and intuition about the plausible range of optimal kernel sizes could help in defining the search space more accurately and efficiently.

While grid search remains a powerful tool in hyperparameter tuning, its effectiveness is dependent on various factors, such as the defined search space and the increment steps. In situations where it falls short, alternative methods like adaptive grid search [16] and random search [17], and the application of human expertise [2], can offer more nuanced and effective strategies to locate the best kernel size for the GRAPPA algorithm. Ultimately, the goal is to enhance the reconstruction performance, and sometimes that means going beyond the conventional methodologies and embracing more flexible and sophisticated techniques.

4 Experimental Results

4.1 Reconstruction Datasets

Two datasets are used to evaluate the reconstruction performance of the proposed grid search-based GRAPPA method. The first dataset was acquired on a GE 3T scanner (GE Healthcare, Waukesha, WI) with an 8-channel head coil. In the first dataset, a uniform water phantom was scanned using a gradient echo sequence (TE/TR = 10/100 ms, 31.25 kHz bandwidth, matrix size = 256×256, FOV = 25 cm^2). The third set of coronary brain data was acquired using a 2D gradient echo sequence (slice thickness = 3.0 mm, matrix size = 256×256, FOV = 24×24 cm^2, and TE/TR = 2.29/100 ms).

4.2 Reconstruction Performance

The phantom dataset was subject to undersampling by an outer reduction factor of 5, with the ACS lines set at 30. The block number for the interpolation kernel size was established at 2, and the column values varied in a range from 3 to 35, using only odd numbers. These 17 distinct kernel sizes facilitated the creation of a diversified search space for the recovery of k-space data. Subsequently, we applied the grid search to identify the best reconstruction quality. In Fig. 3, we present the reconstructed images produced by using manual selection (3 columns) and automatic determination by grid search (17 columns), respectively. It is seen that the reconstruction generated through the optimal kernel size searched surpasses the reconstructions by manual selection in terms of quality. This method notably suppresses noise and aliasing artifacts, leading to clearer images. In terms of quantitative metrics, the reconstruction utilizing grid search demonstrated commendable performance with an NMSE of 0.903095e–04, PSNR:4.358909e + 01, and SSIM: 9.540220e-01. Grid search-based reconstruction reinforces its capacity for efficient noise and artifact suppression. For the reconstruction using 3 columns manually selected, NMSE:1.221693e–03, PSNR:3.655454e + 01, and SSIM: 7.769426e-01.

Moreover, Fig. 4 portrays the NMSE values generated from individual reconstructions based on all columns (indicated by the green curve). A bias-variance trade-off can

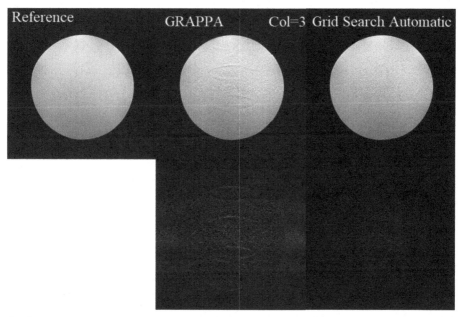

Fig. 3. Phantom reconstruction using the optimal kernel size by grid search. For each reconstruction, the k-space data is recovered by using an interpolation kernel size. For the kernel sizes, the block number is set as 2, and column numbers range from 3 to 35. Manually selected column number 3 is used to show the reconstructed phantom images. Optimal kernel size is identified in the grid search process and it is used to reconstruct missing k-space data and final image.

be observed with a "U" shape. When less parameters are used in a smaller kernel size and more parameters are used in a larger kernel size, NMSE errors are high. On the bottom of the "U" shape, optimal kernel size (in this dataset, the kernel size of 2 blocks by 17 columns is optimal) can be obtained.

In the second dataset, we employed 30 ACS lines and the outer reduction factor 6 for undersampling k-space data. In the search space of columns 9 to 23, grid search can identify the best quality of image reconstruction with kernel size 2 blocks by 9 columns. From the different maps shown in Fig. 5, the optimal kernel size-based reconstruction has less noise than other reconstructed images. The quantitative metric values are shown in Table 1. It is seen that the kernel size identified by the grid search has the lowest value of NMSE and the highest values of PSNR and SSIM. The grid search can effectively find the GRAPPA reconstruction kernel size with the best quality in this search space with 8 kernel sizes.

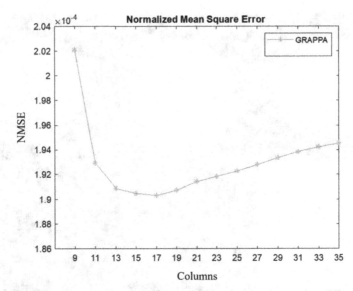

Fig. 4. Bias-variance tradeoff curve for the GRAPPA reconstructions using different columns ranging from 9 to 35. The optimal kernel size-based GRAPPA reconstruction has the lowest NMSE errors which locate at the bottom of the "U" shape.

Table 1. Quantitative Metric Values for Evaluating Reconstructions of Coronary Brain Data.

Kernel Size	NMSE	PSNR	SSIM
2 × 9	**1.491039e-01**	**4.137814e + 01**	**9.525026e-01**
2 × 11	1.568932e-01	4.118346e + 01	9.493362e-01
2 × 13	1.678597e-01	4.092436e + 01	9.451885e-01
2 × 15	1.818892e-01	4.061941e + 01	9.400285e-01
2 × 17	1.983778e-03	4.028633e + 01	9.343896e-01
2 × 19	2.185512e-03	3.991481e + 01	9.277394e-01
2 × 21	2.442428e-03	3.949184e + 01	9.197368e-01
2 × 23	2.738180e-03	3.905595e + 01	9.110834e-01

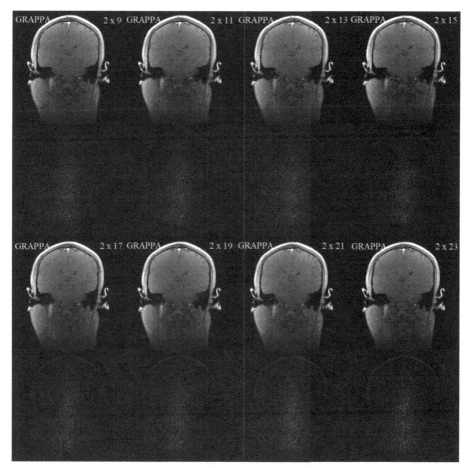

Fig. 5. A coronary brain image reconstruction results using different kernel sizes. The proposed grid search method can identify the best reconstruction quality in a search space.

5   Conclusion

In conclusion, we have introduced a grid search approach to automate the identification of the optimal GRAPPA reconstruction quality. Our proposed methodology has demonstrated its effectiveness in discerning the optimal kernel size. This has been substantiated through experiments on in-vivo MRI datasets, which affirm the method's ability to accurately pinpoint the best kernel size within a predefined search space. As a future course of action, we aim to enhance the search space by leveraging prior knowledge, thereby refining and optimizing the outcomes of clinical MRI even further.

Acknowledgment. This work was supported by the National Science Foundation under Grant No. 2050972.

References

1. Griswold, M.A., et al.: Generalized autocalibrating partially parallel acquisitions (GRAPPA). Magn. Reson. Med. **47**(6), 1202–1210 (2002)
2. Blaimer, B., et al.: Comparison of phase-constrained parallel MRI approaches: analogies and differences. Magn. Reson. Med. **75**(3), 1086–1099 (2016)
3. Hammernik, K., Schlemper, J., Qin, C., Duan, J., Summers, R.M., Rueckert, D.: Systematic evaluation of iterative deep neural networks for fast parallel MRI reconstruction with sensitivity-weighted coil combination. Magn. Reson. Med. **86**(4), 1859–1872 (2021)
4. Wang, Z., Wang, J., Detre, J.A.: Improved data reconstruction method for GRAPPA. Magn. Reson. Med. **54**(3), 738–742 (2005)
5. Wang, H., et al.: Improving GRAPPA reconstruction using joint nonlinear kernel mapped and phase conjugated virtual coils. Phys. Med. Biol. **64**(14), 14NT01 (2019)
6. Chang, Y., Liang, D., Ying, L.: Nonlinear GRAPPA: a kernel approach to parallel MRI reconstruction. Magn. Reson. Med. **68**(3), 730–740 (2012)
7. Chang, Y., Saritac, M.: Group feature selection for enhancing information gain in MRI reconstruction. Phys. Med. Biol. **67**(4), 045011 (2022)
8. Chang, Y., Nakarmi, U.: Parallel MRI reconstruction using broad learning system. In: 43rd Annual International Conference of the IEEE Engineering in Medicine and Biology Society (EMBC), 31 October–4 November (2021)
9. Chang, Y., Pham, H.A., Li, Z.: A dual-interpolator method for improving parallel MRI reconstruction. Magn. Reson. Imaging **92**, 108–119 (2022)
10. Belkin, M., Hsu, D., Ma, S., Mandal, S.: Reconciling modern machine-learning practice and the classical bias–variance trade-off. Proc. Natl. Acad. Sci. **116**(32), 15849–15854 (2019)
11. Zhou. Z.H.: Ensemble Methods: Foundations and Algorithms, 1st edn. Chapman and Hall/CRC (2012). ISBN-10: 1439830037
12. Hasani, N., et al.: Trustworthy artificial intelligence in medical imaging. PET Clinics **17**(1), 1–12 (2022)
13. Antun, V., Renna, F., Poon, C., Adcock, B., Hansen, A.C.: On instabilities of deep learning in image reconstruction and the potential costs of AI. Proc. Natl. Acad. Sci. U.S.A. **117**(48), 30088–30095 (2020)
14. Gowriswari, S., Brindha, S.: Hyperparameters optimization using gridsearch cross validation method for machine learning models in predicting diabetes mellitus risk. In: International Conference on Communication, Computing and Internet of Things (IC3IoT) (2022)
15. Ranjan, G.S.K., Verma, A.K., Radhika, S.: K-nearest neighbors and grid search CV based real time fault monitoring system for industries. In: IEEE 5th International Conference for Convergence in Technology (I2CT) (2019)
16. Wang, W., Wang, S., Zhang, Z.: Improved adaptive grid interactive multiple model algorithm based on maneuverability division. In: IEEE 5th Advanced Information Technology, Electronic and Automation Control Conference (IAEAC) (2021)
17. Jahedbozorgan, M., Amjadifard, R.: Sunshine: a novel random search for continuous global optimization. In: The 1st Conference on Swarm Intelligence and Evolutionary Computation (CSIEC) (2016)

Segmentation and Identification of Mediterranean Plant Species

Parminder Kaur[1][(✉)], Daniela Gigante[2], Marco Caccianiga[3],
Simonetta Bagella[4], Claudia Angiolini[5,6], Manolo Garabini[7], Franco Angelini[7],
and Paolo Remagnino[1]

[1] Department of Computer Science, Durham University,
Stockton Road, Durham DH1 3LE, UK
{parminder.kaur,paolo.remagnino}@durham.ac.uk

[2] Department of Agricultural, Food and Environmental Sciences,
University of Perugia, Borgo XX giugno 74, 06121 Perugia, Italy
daniela.gigante@unipg.it

[3] Department of Biosciences, Università Sdegli Studi di Milano,
Via Celoria 26, 20133 Milan, Italy
marco.caccianiga@unimi.it

[4] Department of Chemical, Physical, Mathematical and Natural Science,
Università di Sassari, Via Piandanna 4, 07100 Sassari, Italy
bage@uniss.it

[5] Department of Life Sciences, Università degli studi di Siena,
Via PA. Mattioli 4, 53100 Siena, Italy
claudia.angiolini@unisi.it

[6] NBFC, National Biodiversity Future Center, Palermo, Italy

[7] Centro di Ricerca "Enrico Piaggio" and Dipartimento di Ingegneria
dell'Informazione, Università di Pisa, Largo Lucio Lazzarino 1, 56126 Pisa, Italy

Abstract. Recently, object recognition and image segmentation have gained much attention in the computer vision field and image processing for effective object localisation and identification. Researchers have applied semantic segmentation and instance segmentation in diverse application areas. However, the least research has been performed in natural habitat monitoring or plant species identification in natural environments/surroundings. For this study, we composed a real image dataset from four habitats: forests, dunes, grasslands, and screes from various locations in Italy. Habitat expert botanists annotated the data using bounding box annotations which have been further utilised to generate the plant species masks using the recently proposed Segment Anything Model (SAM) for segmentation, localisation, and identification tasks. Extensive experimentation has been performed on habitat data with bounding boxes and masks using YOLOv8 detection and segmentation models. Comparative analysis of models, model training with different train data percentages, and the importance of masks over bounding boxes have been studied and discussed.

Keywords: Deep learning · Object identification · Plant species recognition · Instance segmentation · Habitat monitoring

G. Bebis et al. (Eds.): ISVC 2023, LNCS 14362, pp. 431–442, 2023.
https://doi.org/10.1007/978-3-031-47966-3_34

1   Introduction

Natural habitats play a vital role in the survival of humans, flora and fauna. So, they are required to be monitored and preserved for the existence of life on Earth. Although artificial intelligence is being utilised in several applications nowadays, monitoring of natural habitats is still performed chiefly through field observations by human experts, especially terrestrial habitats [1]. There are several existing challenges for monitoring the conservation status of natural habitats defined according to the Habitats Directive (92/43/EEC), such as:(1) human operators are the only practical options for monitoring; (2) human involvement provides a significant amount of subjectivity in this process, and this lessens the consistency and comparability of relevés; and (3) each habitat monitoring can be done during a limited period in a year, so with an increase in number of habitats, more number of professional surveyors are required. So, to overcome these challenges, the latest deep learning techniques can be utilised to automate the whole habitat monitoring process or to assist human experts in the field.

Lately, deep classification, detection and segmentation architectures have been widely utilised in various fields, including plant image classification, plant or leaf disease detection, plant phenotyping, and habitat monitoring through satellite images. Recently, automatic habitat or environment monitoring has been carried out using remote sensing images [25]. For instance, a NaturaSat software tool has been introduced to monitor habitats using satellite images in [13]. There are multiple public datasets available for plant/leaf recognition and plant/leaf disease detection. As an exemplar, PlantCLEF [5] organises a challenge yearly for plant specie identification by providing massive image data comprising several plant types. However, there is a scarcity of plant image data taken in the field in its habitat and annotated by human experts. Motivated by the above issues, we composed real image data of target species such as typical species (TS), characteristic species (CS), alien species (AS) and early warning species (EWS) from four habitats: forests, dunes, grasslands, and screes. The presence of TS and CS indicates favourable habitat conservation status, while the existence of EWS and AS is not a good sign for habitat health [1].

This article mainly focuses on monitoring the conservation status of natural habitats by identifying the target species in the four habitats to assist humans in assessing the habitat conservation status. After collecting images from the four habitats, they are annotated by the domain experts in their respective habitats for plant localisation and identification. We utilise the Segment Anything Model (SAM) [11] for converting bounding boxes to segmentation masks as they provide a precise understanding of the plant's shape, size, and position. Bounding box annotation in itself is an expensive task, and polygon annotation is even more complex and time-consuming if done manually, especially in the case of plants due to their complex shapes, growth in groups, and mixing up with other plants and backgrounds. However, SAM made this job more accessible by introducing a framework which can be used to retrieve appropriate segment masks as per the given bounding boxes. Then the YOLOv8 detection and segmentation models have been utilised to analyse their performance on this novel plant species data and to answer an essential question of whether the expensive polygon annotation is required or the results are almost the same even with bounding box annotation.

Contributions

The major contributions of this study are as follows:

1. To overcome the annotated data scarcity of plant species, we collected data from four habitats: forests, dunes, grasslands, and screes and ground truth generation using bounding box annotations by botanists.
2. Proposed a pipeline for plant species identification and monitoring the health of natural habitats using state-of-the-art YOLOv8 segmentation model and SAM [11].
3. To analyse whether the polygon annotation (segment mask) performs better than bounding box annotation for plant species localisation and recognition.

The rest of the article is organised as follows: Sect. 2 presents the related literature in plant-related tasks, YOLOv8, and SAM, Sect. 3 provides a brief introduction to SAM, YOLOv8, and the proposed framework, Sect. 4 demonstrates all the experimentation and the obtained results, and Sect. 5 concludes the study.

2   Related Work

Researchers are mostly utilising miscellaneous deep learning approaches for plant identification due to their better performance over traditional approaches and improved accuracy in other application areas [2]. Authors in [22] have fine-tuned the pre-trained self-supervised vision transformer (ViT) on ImageNet data for plant image identification and secured a first place in PlantCLEF2022 [5] challenge. After experimentation, it has been shown that the data can be utilised to pre-train a model for plant disease recognition or other plant-related tasks. In [17], authors have introduced a new dataset consisting of 100 ornamental plant species collected from the Beijing Forestry University campus. They implemented a 26-layer ResNet model for plant identification. A lightweight deep convolutional neural network, Ayur-PlantNet, is introduced in [14] for 40 Ayurvedic plant species classification. First, plant segments are retrieved from the images and then further classified for identification.

Tea bud and leaf target detection have been performed by YOLOv8 in [21] to improve the accuracy of tea-picking robots in locating tea bud picking points in complex environment. Authors in [26] have utilised the YOLOv8 segmentation model for jujube fruit instance segmentation. Different YOLO models are compared to find the best segmentation model for the required task. The proposed YOLOseg-Jujube is robust, fast, has less computation cost, can identify jujube fruit ripeness stages, and is even accessible for real-time low-power device applications. An optimised version of YOLOv8 has been proposed in [10] by incorporating Simulated Annealing (SA) for finding the optimal solution of the loss function in the last layer of CNN to apply in crop prevention from diseases and insect pests. After experimentation, it has been found that the modified version of YOLOv8 outperforms YOLOv7 in disease and pest identification.

The Segment Anything Model (SAM) has been exploited in various application areas for multiple purposes. The SAM's performance has been tested on a substantial medical dataset in [7] and found that it shows better results in prompt mode (prompt points and bounding boxes for mask generation) rather than everything mode (mask generation for all objects). In digital pathology, SAM showed excellent segmentation performance for large connected objects; however, unsatisfying performance for dense instance segmentation even after providing several prompts [3]. Authors in [20] have proposed Leaf Only SAM by merging post-processing steps with SAM to segment potato leaves. Leaf Only SAM is compared with Mask RCNN (finetuned on a small potato leaf dataset), and Mask RCNN outperformed Leaf Only SAM. The advantage of Leaf Only SAM is that no annotated data and extra training are required, so it can be utilised in that scenario. Authors in [24] have proposed a novel Inpaint Anything (IA) framework by integrating SAM and image inpainting.

3   Proposed Methodology

This section briefly introduces SAM and YOLOv8, and the proposed pipeline for localisation and identification of plant species. The bounding box annotations are transformed to segment masks using SAM, and then species are recognised using YOLOv8.

3.1   Segment Anything Model (SAM)

Segment Aything Model (SAM) is a foundation model for image segmentation which has been recently proposed by Meta [11]. It has been trained with 1 billion masks on 11 million images and has a splendid zero shot segmentation capability. SAM utilises an MAE [6] pre-trained Vision Transformer (ViT) [4] with minimal adaptations to process high resolution inputs. It was tested on 23 datasets to evaluate its zero shot transfer potential and it showed excellent results. Given an image as input to SAM, it segments the whole image and automatically generates masks. It also provides an option of providing a prompt for mask generation as per requirement. These prompts include prompt points, bounding box coordinates, or a combination of both. We can also specify prompts for adding or removing the mask area to generate the exact mask shape.

3.2   You Only Look Once (YOLO)

YOLO (You Only Look Once) was initially proposed by Joseph Redmon and it was the first model to detect the bounding boxes and predict the class probabilities by processing the image in one go [15]. The object detection models before YOLO were remodelling the classification models to perform detection. However, in YOLO, they framed the object detection problem as a regression problem to spatially separated bounding boxes and associated class probabilities. Afterwards, multiple improved YOLO versions were introduced by various researchers, and the YOLO models transformed the computer vision field. They have been applied in miscellaneous research areas and found to be quite efficient. YOLO models are pre-trained on massive datasets such as ImageNet and COCO. So, the pre-trained model weights can be easily used to further train the model on custom datasets with less number of instances and obtain good results. These models can produce high accuracy with small model sizes, and they are faster to train as well [16].

The latest version of the YOLO series is YOLOv8, which was proposed by the Ultralytics team in the early 2023 [18]. It is an open-source state-of-the-art model distributed under the General Public License [8]. Glenn Jocher introduced YOLOv5 after minor changes in the YOLOv3 model [9]. YOLOv8 is the further improved version of YOLOv5. The significant changes incorporated in YOLOv8 are anchor-free detection, mosaic augmentation, and updates in the convolution blocks used in the model, such as replacing the C3 module with the C2f module. The YOLOv8 architecture and major changes are shown in [19].

3.3   Framework

Figure 1 illustrates the step-by-step procedure followed for plant species identification and localisation. Firstly, the plant species images are collected from four habitats. Habitat expert botanists annotate the images with bounding box annotations using the Labelbox tool [12], which are then exported as a single JSON file per habitat. Each JSON file is converted to the YOLO object detection annotation format text files corresponding to each image in the dataset. YOLOv8 object detection model is trained using this transformed dataset which is then capable of predicting bounding boxes along with species class and confidence score on test images. The bounding boxes from the YOLO detection data format are utilised to generate masks using the Segment Anything Model (SAM), which are then saved in the TXT file (along with class information) corresponding to each image which can be directly provided to YOLOv8 segmentation model for training. The trained segmentation model can predict the bounding boxes and masks along with class and confidence scores on given query images.

4   Experimental Analysis

4.1   Dataset

The dataset consists of images comprising the selected target species from four habitats: forests, dunes, grasslands, and screes. Figure 2 shows the sample images of one species from each habitat. Each species name is mentioned under the corresponding image. Human experts have composed the data by visiting the

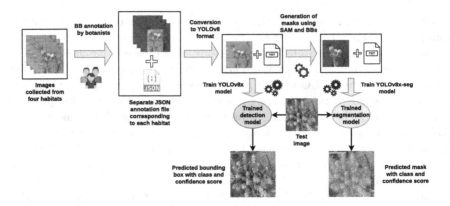

Fig. 1. Proposed pipeline for plant species detection, segmentation, and localisation

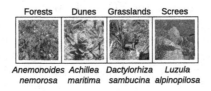

Fig. 2. Sample data from all habitats

habitat locations and doing field operations at the exact time of the year as per plant blooming. The collected images are annotated by botanists using bounding box annotations around the appropriate plant species in the image using the LabelBox tool [12]. Table 1 shows the target plant species considered for the experimentation from respective habitats. The number of training, validation and testing data instances are displayed in Table 2. The train, validation, and test splits are 70, 20, and 10.

Table 1. Various plant species from four habitats

Dunes	Forests	Grasslands	Screes
Carpobrotus acinaciformis	*Anemonoides nemorosa*	*Asphodelus macrocarpus*	*Luzula alpinopilosa*
Achillea maritima	*Corydalis cava*	*Dactylorhiza sambucina*	*Geum reptans*
Calamagrostis arenaria	*Doronicum columnae*	*Orchis morio*	*Oxyria digyna*
Eryngium maritimum			*Cerastium pedunculatum*
Pancratium maritimum			*Cerastium uniflorum*
Thinopyrum junceum			*Leucanthemopsis alpina*
			Ranunculus glacialis
			Saxifraga bryoides

Table 2. Training, testing and validation data splits considered for the experiments

Habitat/Split	Train	Val	Test	Total
Grasslands	645	185	92	922
Forests	765	217	110	1092
Screes	428	123	61	612
Dunes	424	121	60	605
All habitats	2262	646	323	3231

4.2 Evaluation Metrics

The typical evaluation metrics for object detection and segmentation have been chosen for evaluating the model performance, such as precision, recall, F1 score, confusion matrix, mAP50, and mAP50-95 [23]. mAP50 depicts the mean Average Precision at an IoU (Intersection over Union) threshold of 0.5 and mAP50-95 over IoU thresholds of 0.5–0.95 in steps of 0.05. The results section also displays bar charts, PR, and F1 score curves for performance visualisation.

4.3 Model Training

YOLOv8 detection and segmentation models have been trained for 200 epochs with batch size 8 and image size 640x640. Model training is performed on default YOLOv8 hyper-parameter values. All the experimentation has been performed on Intel Core i9 24-Core Processor (Up to 5.8 GHz) and 12 GB NVIDIA GEFORCE RTX 3060 GPU.

4.4 Results

All the results are obtained on test data only, and test data splits (number of instances) are mentioned in Subsect. 4.1. The highest values are highlighted in bold wherever required. YOLOv8x segmentation model has been exploited for its better performance than other versions for all the individual segmentation experimentation. Table 3 compares YOLOv8x object detection and segmentation models on all habitats and considers all classes of each habitat. *Inst.* represents that particular class's total number of instances. The segmentation (box or mask) results are better in the case of forests and grasslands; however, the detection results (only bounding box) are better for dunes and screes. There could be multiple reasons behind these results (dunes and screes): (1) Dunes and screes data have less number of instances and more classes (plant species) than forests and grasslands; (2) Most of the images contain a single large focused plant, so easier to represent with a bounding box as it almost covers the whole image; (3) SAM could not properly generate masks for dunes and screes. Table 4 presents the performance metric values for bounding boxes and masks obtained using the yolov8x segmentation model trained on all habitats data.

Table 3. Comparison of object detection and segmentation model results on all habitats

Classes	Inst.	Precision			Recall			mAP50			mAP50-95		
		Detect	Segment		Detect	Segment		Detect	Segment		Detect	Segment	
		Box	Box	Mask	Box	Box	Mask	Box	Box	Mask	Box	Box	Mask
Forests	552	0.741	**0.812**	0.794	0.708	**0.741**	0.718	0.755	**0.778**	0.751	0.431	**0.605**	0.495
Dunes	78	**0.871**	0.809	0.676	**0.753**	0.52	0.438	**0.799**	0.604	0.488	**0.628**	0.454	0.232
Grasslands	740	0.768	**0.791**	0.777	0.752	**0.764**	0.739	0.787	**0.813**	0.773	0.366	**0.549**	0.439
Screes	100	**0.825**	0.438	0.421	**0.504**	0.496	0.48	**0.571**	0.417	0.395	**0.379**	0.259	0.227

Table 4. Yolov8x segmentation model performance metrics for all habitats

Classes	Inst.	Bounding box				Mask			
		Prec	Rec	mAP50	mAP50-95	Prec	Rec	mAP50	mAP50-95
All	1470	0.735	0.604	0.645	0.469	0.616	0.581	0.576	0.35
Asphodelus macrocarpus	463	0.806	0.692	0.782	0.502	0.723	0.693	0.696	0.364
Dactylorhiza sambucina	174	0.874	0.799	0.854	0.577	0.785	0.787	0.829	0.528
Orchis morio	103	0.764	0.835	0.847	0.613	0.695	0.845	0.837	0.484
Anemonoides nemorosa	227	0.866	0.858	0.909	0.652	0.775	0.817	0.15	0.444
Corydalis cava	99	0.611	0.333	0.426	0.277	0.568	0.394	0.436	0.245
Doronicum columnae	226	0.92	0.956	0.973	0.888	0.897	0.96	0.977	0.811
Carpobrotus acinaciformis	15	0.905	0.639	0.873	0.698	0.788	0.667	0.783	0.349
Achillea maritima	17	0.73	0.765	0.847	0.631	0.551	0.765	0.658	0.406
Calamagrostis arenaria	8	0.605	0.75	0.669	0.537	0.466	0.656	0.521	0.246
Eryngium maritimum	13	0.767	0.692	0.747	0.559	0.656	0.769	0.655	0.445
Pancratium maritimum	11	0.8	0.727	0.658	0.38	0.317	0.364	0.249	0.124
Thinopyrum junceum	14	0.6	0.357	0.463	0.384	0.563	0.37	0.478	0.242
Luzula alpinopilosa	6	0.832	0.825	0.755	0.548	0.784	0.833	0.755	0.47
Geum reptans	20	0.595	0.35	0.426	0.253	0.53	0.35	0.406	0.233
Oxyria digyna	5	0.606	0.327	0.323	0.217	0.636	0.363	0.268	0.208
Cerastium pedunculatum	12	0.592	0.486	0.37	0.205	0.325	0.333	0.281	0.109
Cerastium uniflorum	7	0.943	0.571	0.582	0.416	0.884	0.571	0.582	0.358
Leucanthemopsis alpina	13	0.586	0.231	0.248	0.146	0.311	0.154	0.208	0.141
Ranunculus glacialis	17	0.791	0.588	0.807	0.664	0.695	0.672	0.806	0.59
Saxifraga bryoides	20	0.511	0.3	0.338	0.237	0.365	0.25	0.286	0.211

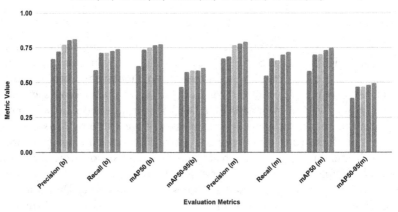

Fig. 3. Comparison of evaluation metrics at different train data percentages on forests

Figure 3 shows the segmentation model's performance when trained on different train percentages of training data on forests, keeping the validation and test data the same. The train samples are picked randomly manually from the whole train data portion for each training. All metrics have the highest values when the model is trained on 100% of train data. Figure 4 demonstrates the comparison of different YOLOv8 segmentation model versions on all habitat data for all classes in the form of a bar chart. Figure 5 shows the mask F1 plot for all the habitats

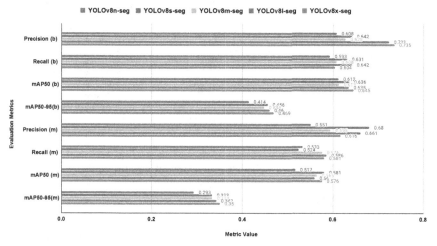

Fig. 4. Comparison of YOLOv8 segmentation models on all habitat test data

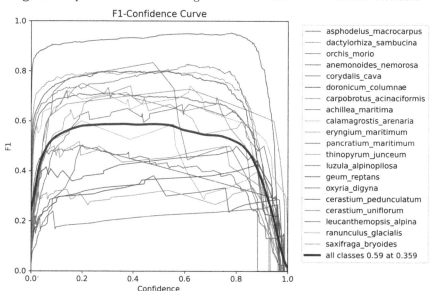

Fig. 5. Test data mask F1 plot for all habitats data

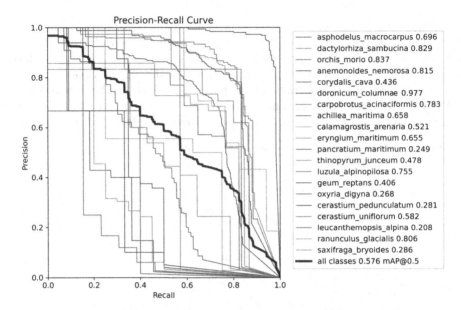

Fig. 6. Test data mask PR curve for all habitats data

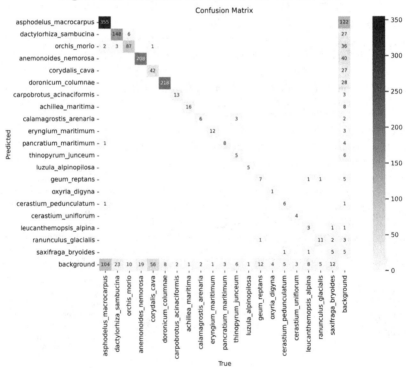

Fig. 7. Confusion matrix for all habitats data

data obtained using YOLOv8x segmentation model, and Fig. 6 demonstrates the mask Precision-Recall (PR) curve. The confusion matrix obtained from all habitat test data is displayed in Fig. 7. It can be visualised in the confusion matrix that the high number of test instances are predicted as "background", and the actual "background" is indicated as different plant species. So, the model is getting confused between the background and the actual plant, which is evident in this complex application (plants resemble the background).

5 Conclusion

In this paper, we have experimented on real plant species image data collected from four habitats: forests, dunes, grasslands, and screens. Botanists annotated the images using bounding box annotations. The bounding boxes are used as a prompt to SAM to retrieve corresponding masks. The YOLOv8 object detection and segmentation model has been compared to analyse whether the segment masks or polygon annotation provide better results than the bounding boxes. After extensive experimentation, we got mixed results. For two habitats (dunes and screes), detection metric values are higher; for the other two, segmentation metric values are higher (forests and grasslands). Even for forest and grassland segmentation, mostly the box evaluation metrics have higher values than the mask metrics. It can be inferred that SAM can be utilised for generating masks if required; however, it will not certainly provide an appropriate localisation with an exact plant species shape due to their complex nature and similar background. More experiments are also performed to compare different versions of the YOLOv8 segmentation model and train the model with diverse percentages of train data. Presently, we are collecting more data (images and videos) via field operations and using a robot which we will utilise further for future experimentation, and also try to automate the monitoring of habitats using the robot entirely.

Acknowledgement. This research was supported by Grant agreement No. 101016970, European Union's Horizon 2020 Research and Innovation Programme - ICT-47-2020.

References

1. Angelini, F., et al.: Robotic monitoring of habitats: the natural intelligence approach. IEEE Access (2023)
2. Arya, S., Sandhu, K.S., Singh, J., Kumar, S.: Deep learning: as the new frontier in high-throughput plant phenotyping. Euphytica **218**(4), 47 (2022)
3. Deng, R., et al.: Segment anything model (SAM) for digital pathology: assess zero-shot segmentation on whole slide imaging. arXiv preprint arXiv:2304.04155 (2023)
4. Dosovitskiy, A., et al.: An image is worth 16×16 words: transformers for image recognition at scale. arXiv preprint arXiv:2010.11929 (2020)
5. Goëau, H., Bonnet, P., Joly, A.: Overview of plantCLEF 2022: image-based plant identification at global scale. In: CLEF 2022-Conference and Labs of the Evaluation Forum, vol. 3180, pp. 1916–1928 (2022)

6. He, K., Chen, X., Xie, S., Li, Y., Dollár, P., Girshick, R.: Masked autoencoders are scalable vision learners. In: Proceedings of the IEEE/CVF Conference on Computer Vision and Pattern Recognition, pp. 16000–16009 (2022)
7. Huang, Y., et al.: Segment anything model for medical images? arXiv preprint arXiv:2304.14660 (2023)
8. Jocher, G.: Ultralytics YOLOv8 github (2023). https://github.com/ultralytics/ultralytics
9. Jocher, G., et al.: ultralytics/YOLOv5: v7. 0-YOLOv5 SOTA realtime instance segmentation. Zenodo (2022)
10. Kang, J., Zhao, L., Wang, K., Zhang, K., et al.: Research on an improved YOLOv8 image segmentation model for crop pests. Adv. Comput. Signals Syst. **7**(3), 1–8 (2023)
11. Kirillov, A., et al.: Segment anything. arXiv preprint arXiv:2304.02643 (2023)
12. Labelbox: Labelbox (2023). https://labelbox.com
13. Mikula, K., et al.: Naturasat—a software tool for identification, monitoring and evaluation of habitats by remote sensing techniques. Remote Sens. **13**(17), 3381 (2021)
14. Pushpa, B., Rani, N.: Ayur-PlantNet: an unbiased light weight deep convolutional neural network for Indian ayurvedic plant species classification. J. Appl. Res. Med. Aromatic Plants **34**, 100459 (2023)
15. Redmon, J., Divvala, S., Girshick, R., Farhadi, A.: You only look once: unified, real-time object detection. In: Proceedings of the IEEE Conference on Computer Vision and Pattern Recognition, pp. 779–788 (2016)
16. Redmon, J., Farhadi, A.: YOLOv3: an incremental improvement. arXiv preprint arXiv:1804.02767 (2018)
17. Sun, Y., Liu, Y., Wang, G., Zhang, H., et al.: Deep learning for plant identification in natural environment. Comput. Intell. Neurosci. **2017** (2017)
18. Ultralytics Team: Ultralytics YOLOv8 docs (2023). https://docs.ultralytics.com/
19. Ultralytics: Ultralytics YOLOv8 (2023). https://github.com/ultralytics/ultralytics/issues/189
20. Williams, D., MacFarlane, F., Britten, A.: Leaf only SAM: a segment anything pipeline for zero-shot automated leaf segmentation. arXiv preprint arXiv:2305.09418 (2023)
21. Xu, F., Li, B., Xu, S.: Accurate and rapid localization of tea bud leaf picking point based on YOLOv8. In: Meng, X., Chen, Y., Suo, L., Xuan, Q., Zhang, Z.K. (eds.) BDSC 2023. CCIS, vol. 1846, pp. 261–274. Springer, Singapore (2023). https://doi.org/10.1007/978-981-99-3925-1_17
22. Xu, M., Yoon, S., Jeong, Y., Lee, J., Park, D.S.: Transfer learning with self-supervised vision transformer for large-scale plant identification. In: International Conference of the Cross-Language Evaluation Forum for European Languages, pp. 2253–2261. Springer (2022)
23. Yan, B., Fan, P., Lei, X., Liu, Z., Yang, F.: A real-time apple targets detection method for picking robot based on improved YOLOv5. Remote Sens. **13**(9), 1619 (2021)
24. Yu, T., et al.: Inpaint anything: segment anything meets image inpainting. arXiv preprint arXiv:2304.06790 (2023)
25. Yuan, Q., et al.: Deep learning in environmental remote sensing: achievements and challenges. Remote Sens. Environ. **241**, 111716 (2020)
26. Zhao, H., et al.: Jujube fruit instance segmentation based on yolov8 method. Available at SSRN 4482151 (2023)

Exploiting Generative Adversarial Networks in Joint Sensitivity Encoding for Enhanced MRI Reconstruction

Gulfam Saju[1], Alan Okinaka[2], and Yuchou Chang[1]([✉])

[1] Computer and Information Science Department, University of Massachusetts Dartmouth, 285 Old Westport Road, Dartmouth, MA 02747, USA
ychang1@umassd.edu
[2] Physics Department, Ursinus College, 601 E Main St, Collegeville, PA 19426, USA

Abstract. In this paper, we propose a novel approach for improving the quality of Parallel Magnetic Resonance Imaging (pMRI) reconstructions by incorporating the power of Generative Adversarial Networks (GANs). We integrate the Joint Sensitivity Encoding (JSENSE) technique with a GAN for parallel magnetic resonance imaging (MRI). The innovation lies in refining the JSENSE iterative reconstruction process using a GAN which effectively addresses the persistent challenge of low signal-to-noise ratio (SNR) and artifact degradation. While JSENSE offers improved reconstruction in rapid scanning or under-sampled acquisitions, images often exhibit noise and aliasing artifacts when the reduction factor is high. To resolve this problem, we deployed a GAN within the JSENSE framework for image-to-image translation and transforming noisy and artifact-ridden images into high-quality ones. Our GAN model, trained on paired sets of clean and noisy MRI images, performs noise and artifact removal after each JSENSE reconstruction iteration. Comparative evaluations with standard JSENSE and other contemporary techniques, such as CG-SENSE indicate significant improvement in the quality of the proposed method. Our approach achieved superior Structural Similarity Index Measure (SSIM) and lower Normalized Mean Squared Error (NMSE) with increased reduction factors and demonstrated its effectiveness in high-quality MRI reconstruction.

Keywords: Magnetic Resonance Imaging · MRI reconstruction · Generative Adversarial Network · Parallel MRI

1 Introduction

Due to the non-invasive characteristics and superior ability to differentiate soft tissues, Magnetic Resonance Imaging (MRI) serves as a potent tool in both medical practice and scientific research. However, high-quality image reconstruction from MRI data is a challenging task, especially when the data is undersampled. Parallel Magnetic Resonance Imaging (pMRI) is a clinical solution that accelerates the imaging process by undersampling k-space data while exploiting spatial sensitivity profiles of multiple receiver coils [1].

© The Author(s), under exclusive license to Springer Nature Switzerland AG 2023
G. Bebis et al. (Eds.): ISVC 2023, LNCS 14362, pp. 443–451, 2023.
https://doi.org/10.1007/978-3-031-47966-3_35

Joint Sensitivity Encoding (JSENSE) [2], an advanced iterative method, has been used for pMRI reconstruction. This technique jointly estimates the sensitivity maps of the multiple coils and reconstructs the image. However, JSENSE reconstructions often introduce noise and artifacts, especially in situations of rapid scanning with undersampled acquisitions. In particular, background phase variations existing in coil sensitivities can contribute to noise in parallel MRI reconstructions [23]. Though optimized phase distribution could potentially minimize this noise [23], it remains a challenge due to the difficulty in modeling different origins of phase variation. Furthermore, as the reduction factor is increased to accelerate the acquisition process, the level of noise also increases. These constraints limit its applicability in clinical settings for further accelerating imaging speed.

Advancements in deep learning have initiated a paradigm shift in many fields, including medical imaging. Generative Adversarial Networks (GANs) [3] have emerged as a powerful tool for image-to-image translation tasks, demonstrating promising results in noise reduction and artifact removal. Notably, the Cycle-Consistent Generative Adversarial Network (CycleGAN) [4] model has been effective in such applications, given its capacity to learn a mapping between the distributions of different image domains without the need for explicitly paired training data.

This work bridges the gap between traditional parallel imaging reconstruction techniques and deep learning methodologies. We propose a novel method that integrates the CycleGAN model within the JSENSE reconstruction loop. In this framework, JSENSE acts as the initial image constructor from undersampled k-space data, while Cycle-GAN refines these initial reconstructions by transforming the noisy and aliasing artifact images into cleaner ones. Our model exploits the strengths of both techniques, and we observe a significant enhancement in the quality of reconstructed MRI images while also potentially facilitating faster pMRI protocols. The aim of this research is two-fold: to provide a novel technique for improved JSENSE reconstruction and to illustrate the potential of combining traditional imaging methodologies with advanced Deep Learning [5] techniques. Traditional methods tend to struggle with reconstructing noise-free images at high reduction factors, whereas our methods demonstrate significant performance improvement even under such conditions. The results demonstrate that our proposed method yields significant improvements in the quality of reconstructed MRI images over standard JSENSE and other existing techniques.

The rest of the paper is organized as the following: Section 2 describes the related work section, which provides an overview of the traditional parallel MRI technique and implementation of GAN in MRI reconstruction. Section 3 describes our proposed method, which integrates CycleGAN into the JSENSE reconstruction loop. Section 4 presents our experimental setup, including the datasets used, CycleGan training details, the performance metrics adopted, and the experimental results. The paper is concluded in Sect. 5 with the conclusion section.

2   Related Work

Parallel MRI enhances the speed of image acquisition by employing multiple receiver coils, each providing a unique perspective of the scanned object. Parallel Imaging reconstruction techniques such as Sensitivity Encoding (SENSE) [6] have been pivotal in enhancing imaging speed. The SENSE method performs image reconstruction based on the sensitivity profiles of each individual coil. It reduces scan times, but high reduction factors can lead to noise amplification, known as "g-factor noise. "JSENSE [2] goes a step further by jointly estimating the sensitivity maps and the image reconstruction. Deep learning methodologies have outperformed conventional techniques in numerous medical imaging applications in recent years. Various deep learning architectures, particularly Convolutional Neural Networks (CNNs) and Generative Adversarial Networks (GANs), have been applied to MRI reconstruction tasks for accelerated and artifact-free reconstruction [7–9].

Generative Adversarial Networks (GANs) have increasingly been utilized in MRI reconstruction due to their exceptional ability to mimic prior information for generative tasks. Various methods have been proposed to enhance their effectiveness. Shitrit et al. [10] introduced a technique that reconstructs missing k-space data from undersampled information employing a GAN framework. Yang et al. [11] incorporated the U-Net structure into the generator of DAGAN. Moreover, Mardani et al. [12] proposed a unique approach that combined Compressed Sensing algorithms with GANs and enforced reconstruction constraints through a cyclic loss. Furthermore, Shaul et al. [13] devised a two-stage GAN architecture - KIGAN, capable of estimating missing k-space data and rectifying motion artifacts in MR images. Li et al. [14] developed SEGAN to recover MR image structure, leveraging local and global information. In recent developments, Murugesan et al. [15] fused global and local contextual information in their GAN-based model, Recon-GLGAN. Deora et al. [16] proposed a framework rooted in GANs that underscored the importance of maintaining intricate texture nuances within reconstructed MR images, achieved via the application of a patch-oriented discriminator and an SSIM-oriented loss function. Gulfam et al. [21] proposed an improved JSENSE method utilizing an unrolled deep network prior to replace the initial reconstruction. Another study by Gulfam et al. [22] introduced a novel approach by integrating the JSENSE method with an untrained neural network (UNN) without needing external training data. Inspired by these advances and aiming to tackle the noise and artifact challenges in JSENSE reconstructions, our work introduces a novel integration of JSENSE and GAN in the MRI reconstruction process. This unique approach aims to enhance the quality of reconstructions by exploiting the capabilities of GANs to perform image-to-image translation and noise and artifact removal, achieving superior results.

3 Methods

3.1 Problem Formulation

Joint Sensitivity Encoding (JSENSE) is an advanced iterative technique utilized for multichannel image reconstruction in MRI [2]. The method works by simultaneously estimating the sensitivity maps and the reconstructed image, which substantially improves the quality of the final image, particularly in instances of undersampled acquisition. The JSENSE method can be expressed as a system of linear equations that represent the multichannel acquisition process:

$$y_i = E(c_i)x + n_i, i = 1, 2, \ldots, N \tag{1}$$

here, y_i is the acquired data from the i th coil, $E(c_i)$ is the encoding operator, which includes the Fourier transform, and the coil sensitivity encoding, x is the image to be reconstructed, n_i is the noise in the i th coil, and N is the total number of coils.

The JSENSE method involves an iterative process that alternates between two main steps: image reconstruction and sensitivity estimation. In the image reconstruction step, the coil sensitivities are assumed to be known, and the image is estimated by solving the optimization problem:

$$\min_{x} \sum_{i=1}^{N} ||E(c_i)x - y_i||^2 + \lambda R(x) \tag{2}$$

where, λ is a regularization parameter that controls the trade-off between data fidelity and prior knowledge, $R(x)$ is a regularization term that encodes prior knowledge about the image, such as its sparsity in a certain transform domain. In the sensitivity estimation step, the coil sensitivities are estimated by fitting a model to the data. This iterative process is repeated for a number of iterations, with the aim of gradually improving the accuracy of both the image and the coil sensitivities.

3.2 Proposed Method

With the problem formulation, we propose a new method that leverages the power of Generative Adversarial Networks (GANs) within the framework of the JSENSE reconstruction technique. This is achieved by introducing a CycleGAN [4] model into the JSENSE iterative reconstruction process for improving image quality reconstructed, mainly focusing on noise and artifact reduction. The primary focus of this integration is to improve the JSENSE reconstruction quality. Our approach consists of a refined JSENSE reconstruction step where a CycleGAN model is employed for image refinement. This refinement stage takes place within each iteration of the JSENSE reconstruction process, as shown in Fig. 1.

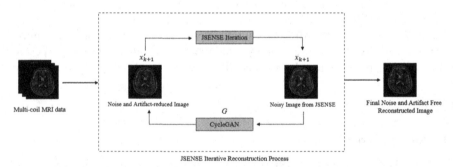

Fig. 1. Framework of the proposed CycleGAN-assisted JSENSE method. The figure demonstrates how CycleGAN is incorporated into the JSENSE iterative reconstruction process.

The first step of the JSENSE iterative process remains the same where the image is reconstructed by solving the following optimization problem:

$$x_{k+1} = \underset{x}{argmin} ||E(c_k) + y||^2 + \lambda R(x) \tag{3}$$

where x_{k+1} represents the estimated image at $(k + 1)$ th iteration, $E(c_k)$ is the encoding operation involving the Fourier transform and the estimated coil sensitivity c_k, y represents the acquired data from the multiple coils, and λ and $R(x)$ has the same definition.

Once the image x_{k+1} is estimated, it is then passed through the CycleGAN model, which acts as a refinement tool to produce a noise and artifact-reduced version of the image. We denote this refined image as $x\prime_{k+1}$ as:

$$x'_{k+1} = G(x_{k+1}) \tag{4}$$

here, G represents the generator of the CycleGAN model. Finally, the sensitivity estimation step is adjusted to incorporate this refined image, $x_{k+1}\prime$. The coil sensitivities are now estimated by minimizing the discrepancy between the encoding of the refined image and the acquired data:

$$c_{k+1} = \underset{c}{argmin}||E(c)x_{k+1}\prime + y||^2 \tag{5}$$

In this way, the refinements achieved by the CycleGAN model are effectively incorporated into the JSENSE iterative process. The improved image quality obtained through this refinement should lead to a more accurate estimation of coil sensitivities in the subsequent iterations, thereby enhancing the overall reconstruction quality. The process is repeated until a pre-specified stopping criterion is met.

4   Experimental Setup and Results

4.1   Datasets and Training Details

For training the CycleGAN model, a unique dataset was utilized that comprised 630 paired brain slice images. Each pair included an artifact and noisy image and its corresponding fully sampled and noise-free version. The noisy data was generated using JSENSE reconstruction to serve as a robust comparative measure, allowing the model to learn the necessary transformations for effective noise and artifact removal. This training dataset was extracted from an open-source fMRI [20] brain dataset obtained using a 3T Philips scanner with a 16-coil system. Key parameters for this procedure included a repetition time of 2000 ms, an echo time of 30 ms, and a matrix size of $768 \times 396 \times 16 \times 16$. Oversampling in the readout was managed by transitioning from k-space to an image, with the focus on the central 256×256 region. For assessing and testing the proposed method's performance, we used two different brain slices which were not included in the training dataset. The brain slices were extracted from the same fMRI open-source dataset package.

Training of the CycleGAN model was performed utilizing the Adam optimizer with a learning rate of 0.0002, β_1 set to 0.5, and β_2 set to 0.999. We adopted a batch size of 1, considering the substantial size and complexity of the MRI images. As for the loss functions, we applied a combination of adversarial loss, cycle consistency loss, and identity loss in line with the original CycleGAN settings. The model was trained for 200 epochs, where the first 100 epochs utilized a linearly decaying learning rate, and a constant learning rate was applied for the remaining epochs. The experiments were performed on a desktop equipped with an Intel Core i7 processor, 64 GB RAM, and NVIDIA Quadro P2200 GPU. MATLAB was used for the JSENSE reconstruction and initial training dataset preparation. Python 3.8, along with PyTorch 1.4, was utilized for CycleGAN model implementation, training, and evaluation. When local resources were insufficient, Google Colab's GPU acceleration was employed.

4.2 Results

In this study, we aimed to investigate the effectiveness of the proposed JSENSE-CycleGAN integrated method for MRI reconstruction. To provide a comprehensive analysis, we conducted a comparative study, juxtaposing the performance of our novel approach against two established methods: CG-SENSE [24] and the conventional JSENSE [2].

Figure 2 presents the comparative results of the MRI reconstruction for the first brain slice across the three methods, where the outer reduction factor was set to 4, and Auto-calibration Signal (ACS) lines constituted 12% for all methods. In terms of quantitative performance metrics, the Structural Similarity Index Measure (SSIM) and Peak Signal-to-Noise Ratio (PSNR) were used. For the CG-SENSE method, SSIM and PSNR values of 0.7030 and 30.9016 were recorded, respectively. The JSENSE method yielded slightly different scores, with SSIM at 0.7025 and PSNR at 31.1765. Our proposed JSENSE-CycleGAN approach demonstrated a significant improvement reaching an SSIM value of 0.9230 and a PSNR of 33.7876, indicating a higher structural similarity and signal clarity in the reconstructed images. It is seen that our method successfully reduced noise and artifacts in the reconstructed image.

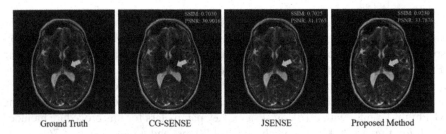

| Ground Truth | CG-SENSE | JSENSE | Proposed Method |

Fig. 2. Comparative MRI reconstruction results of the first brain slice using CG-SENSE, JSENSE, and our proposed JSENSE-CycleGAN approach. All methods employed an outer reduction factor of 4 and 12% ACS lines. The arrows in the figure clearly show that our method provides enhanced structural similarity and signal clarity and significantly reduces noise and artifacts.

Figure 3 presents the MRI reconstruction results of a second brain slice, using an outer reduction factor of 4 and 12% ACS lines. The SSIM and NMSE values for the CG-SENSE method were 0.6989 and 0.0339, respectively, while the JSENSE method recorded 0.6561 and 0.0394. However, our JSENSE-CycleGAN approach significantly outperformed both, with an SSIM of 0.8955 and NMSE of 0.0171, demonstrating superior structural preservation and lower reconstruction errors. Figure 3 also shows the regions of interest extracted from the reconstructed brain slices of each method. A visual examination of these regions underscores the superiority of the proposed JSENSE-CycleGAN approach since it exhibits lower noise and fewer artifacts than both the CG-SENSE and JSENSE methods.

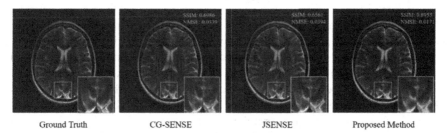

| Ground Truth | CG-SENSE | JSENSE | Proposed Method |

Fig. 3. MRI reconstruction comparison for a different brain slice using CG-SENSE, JSENSE, and the proposed JSENSE-CycleGAN method under the same reduction factor and ACS line conditions. The regions of interest from each method's output highlight the lower noise and fewer artifacts produced by our approach, corroborating the superior SSIM and lower NMSE values.

Figure 4 provides a performance analysis of our proposed JSENSE-CycleGAN method under varying reduction factors. Specifically, the reduction factors employed are 2, 4, and 5. The corresponding SSIM values achieved for these reduction factors are 0.9598, 0.9230, and 0.9089, respectively. These results, derived from the first brain slice, clearly show that despite increasing the reduction factor, our method maintains a high SSIM value, indicating consistent performance in preserving the structural fidelity of the reconstructed image.

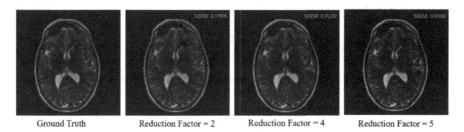

| Ground Truth | Reduction Factor = 2 | Reduction Factor = 4 | Reduction Factor = 5 |

Fig. 4. Performance of our proposed method using different reduction factors (2, 4, 5) on the first brain slice. The SSIM values indicate our method's ability to maintain high structural fidelity even as the reduction factor increases.

5 Conclusion

Our study has highlighted the novel JSENSE-CycleGAN integration for improving parallel MRI reconstruction. A marked improvement was delivered over traditional methods such as CG-SENSE and JSENSE. The efficacy of our approach is evident in its superior performance, substantiated by higher SSIM values across different reduction factors, and signifies superior preservation of structural fidelity in the reconstructed images. Additionally, the compelling visual quality of the output, characterized by a significant reduction in noise and artifacts, underlines the remarkable strength and adaptability of our proposed method. It sets a challenging precedent for future methodologies in MRI reconstruction.

While this integration between JSENSE and CycleGAN is promising, it opens new dimensions for future exploration. Future research directions may include the integration of other advanced deep learning architectures, such as 3D convolutional neural networks or transformer models [17], to handle more complex imaging scenarios. Additionally, the applicability of the proposed method could be extended to other MRI modalities, such as Diffusion Tensor Imaging (DTI) [18] or Functional MRI (fMRI) [19], further broadening the impact of this work. Furthermore, the use of more sophisticated loss functions or training strategies to improve the GAN's performance can be considered. Lastly, an in-depth investigation into the effects of varying the ACS lines and the reduction factor on the quality of the reconstructed images could provide deeper insights into the optimal parameters for our proposed method.

Acknowledgment. This work was supported by the National Science Foundation under Grant No. 2050972.

References

1. Larkman, D.J., Nunes, R.G.: Parallel magnetic resonance imaging. Phys. Med. Biol. **52**(7), R15 (2007)
2. Ying, L., Sheng, J.: Joint image reconstruction and sensitivity estimation in SENSE (JSENSE). Magn. Reson. Med. Official J. Int. Soc. Magn. Reson. Med. **57**(6), 1196–1202 (2007)
3. Goodfellow, I., et al.: Generative adversarial networks. Commun. ACM **63**(11), 139–144 (2020)
4. Zhu, J.Y., Park, T., Isola, P., Efros, A.A.: Unpaired image-to-image translation using cycle-consistent adversarial networks. In: Proceedings of the IEEE International Conference on Computer Vision, pp. 2223–2232 (2017)
5. LeCun, Y., Bengio, Y., Hinton, G.: Deep learning. Nature **521**(7553), 436–444 (2015)
6. Pruessmann, K.P., Weiger, M., Scheidegger, M.B., Boesiger, P.: SENSE: sensitivity encoding for fast MRI. Magn. Reson. Med. Official J. Int. Soc. Magn. Reson. Med. **42**(5), 952–962 (1999)
7. Laino, M.E., Cancian, P., Politi, L.S., Della Porta, M.G., Saba, L., Savevski, V.: Generative adversarial networks in brain imaging: a narrative review. J. Imaging **8**(4), 83 (2022)
8. Pal, A., Rathi, Y.: A review and experimental evaluation of deep learning methods for MRI reconstruction. J. Mach. Learn. Biomed. Imaging, 1 (2022)
9. Saju, G., Li, Z., Abiri, R., Liu, T., Chang, Y.: Incorporating untrained neural network prior in PROPELLER imaging. In: ISMRM Scientific Meeting & Exhibition (Vol. 4038) (2023)
10. Shitrit, O., Riklin Raviv, T.: Accelerated magnetic resonance imaging by adversarial neural network. In: Cardoso, M.J., (eds.) et al. DLMIA/ML-CDS -2017. LNCS, vol. 10553, pp. 30–38. Springer, Cham (2017). https://doi.org/10.1007/978-3-319-67558-9_4
11. Yang, G., et al.: DAGAN: Deep de-aliasing generative adversarial networks for fast compressed sensing MRI reconstruction. IEEE Trans. Med. Imaging, **37**(6), 1310–1321 (2017)

12. Mardani, M., et al.: Deep generative adversarial neural networks for compressive sensing MRI. IEEE Trans. Med. Imaging **38**(1), 167–179 (2018)
13. Shaul, R., David, I., Shitrit, O., Raviv, T.R.: Subsampled brain MRI reconstruction by generative adversarial neural networks. Med. Image Anal. **65**, 101747 (2020)
14. Li, Z., Zhang, T., Wan, P., Zhang, D.: SEGAN: structure-enhanced generative adversarial network for compressed sensing MRI reconstruction. In: Proceedings of the AAAI Conference on Artificial Intelligence, vol. 33, no. 01, pp. 1012–1019 (2019)
15. Murugesan, B., Vijaya Raghavan, S., Sarveswaran, K., Ram, K., Sivaprakasam, M.: Recon-GLGAN: a global-local context based generative adversarial network for MRI reconstruction. In: Knoll, F., Maier, A., Rueckert, D., Ye, J.C. (eds.) MLMIR 2019. LNCS, vol. 11905, pp. 3–15. Springer, Cham (2019). https://doi.org/10.1007/978-3-030-33843-5_1
16. Deora, P., Vasudeva, B., Bhattacharya, S., Pradhan, P. M.: Structure preserving compressive sensing MRI reconstruction using generative adversarial networks. In: Proceedings of the IEEE/CVF Conference on Computer Vision and Pattern Recognition Workshops, pp. 522–523 (2020)
17. Shamshad, F., et al.: Transformers in medical imaging: a survey. Med. Image Anal. **88**, 102802 (2023)
18. Le Bihan, D., et al.: Diffusion tensor imaging: concepts and applications. J. Magn. Reson. Imaging: Official J. Int. Soc. Magn. Reson. Med. **13**(4), 534–546 (2001)
19. DeYoe, E.A., Bandettini, P., Neitz, J., Miller, D., Winans, P.: Functional magnetic resonance imaging (FMRI) of the human brain. J. Neurosci. Methods **54**(2), 171–187 (1994)
20. The OpenfMRI dataset. OpenfMRI. https://www.openfmri.org/dataset/
21. Saju, G., Li, Z., Abiri, R., Liu, T., Chang, Y.: Improving JSENSE using an initial reconstruction with an unrolled deep network prior. In: ISMRM Scientific Meeting & Exhibition (Vol. 4037) (2023)
22. Saju, G., Li, Z., Abiri, R., Liu, T., Chang, Y.: Joint estimation of coil sensitivity and image by using untrained neural network without external training data. In: ISMRM Scientific Meeting & Exhibition, vol. 3893 (2023)
23. Chang, Y., Saju, G., Yu, J., Abiri, R., Li, Z., Liu, T.: Suppressing MRI background noise via modeling phase variations. In: ISMRM Scientific Meeting & Exhibition, vol. 2031 (2023)
24. Pruessmann, K.P., Weiger, M., Börnert, P., Boesiger, P.: Advances in sensitivity encoding with arbitrary k-space trajectories. Magn. Reson. Med. Official J. Int. Soc. Magn. Reson. Med. **46**(4), 638–651 (2001)

Multisensory Modeling of Tabular Data for Enhanced Perception and Immersive Experience

Shamima Yasmin[1]([⊠])[iD] and Chowdhury Q. Jamal[2]

[1] Eastern Washington University, Spokane, WA 99202, USA
syasmin@ewu.edu
[2] University of Waterloo, Waterloo, ON N2L 3G1, Canada
cyjamal@uwaterloo.ca

Abstract. Multisensory visualization incorporating sight, sound, and touch can substantially enhance user interest and perception compared to unimodal vision-only applications. In a music-enhanced heatmap, color-coded rectangular bars become audibly distinct as they are assigned auditory parameters (i.e., pitch, tempo, and so on) depending on the data range. While navigating with a haptic device, music-enhanced bars in a heatmap would respond with varying audio feedback. Bars can be further assigned tangible properties (i.e., friction or stiffness) depending on variable values. This paper investigates the efficacy of immersive multimodal visualization that considers enhanced user experience. Research findings showed that a multimodal approach is more effective in improving overall user experience and engagement than traditional unimodal vision-based experience. If enhanced with virtual reality (VR), multi-sensory visualization can provide an immersive experience as users interact with and explore large datasets in a life-size environment. In addition, multimodal strategies can create a diverse, accessible, and inclusive environment.

Keywords: Multimodal systems · Virtual reality · Human-computer interaction · Haptics · Information visualization · Multivariate data · Visualization techniques and methodologies

1 Introduction

Simulated learning environments that incorporate multiple senses (i.e., audio, visual, and touch) have proven to be highly effective for specific learnings and have been successfully used for training soldiers, medical professionals, technicians, people needing special assistance, and more [1,2]. Sight, sound, fantasy, and interactive approach of a video game work as incentives to keep players' interest awake and induce them to continue playing. Video games become more enjoyable as players become part of the virtual environment (VE) by putting on VR headsets. Research findings continue to argue for a game-based approach and its multimodal and immersive components as foundational motivational tools for effective learning [3, 4]. User's spatial perception and proprioception were recommended to be used in visualization experiences by incorporating other senses, i.e., sound and touch [5].

Multisensory modeling can define data or objects with multiple sensory channels to enrich users' perception levels. A VR-enhanced multisensory data visualization application makes the overall environment immersive and engaging so that users can be motivated to dig deeper into the content than a unimodal vision-only application. With the enhanced realism of VR, multisensory mapping creates a diverse and inclusive platform for data exploration and analysis.

2   Background

Incorporating different senses in visual representations is not new. In visualization, audio integration was done in two ways: verbal and non-verbal. Verbal mode guides users in visual displays [6]. Verbal modalities help the blind and visually impaired (BVI) process visual information by navigating data tables via keyboard interactions.

Non-verbal or non-speech audio feedback is called sonification. Data variables were mapped to auditory variables, such as pitch, tempo, and more. For example, higher-pitched sounds represented higher values of variables and vice versa. Sonification of data tables provided an inclusive approach to making information accessible to the BVI [7–10]. Sonification in audio-visual data representations helped sighted users notice subtle differences, which could not be identified with unimodal visual feedback [11]. Scientific visualization, where data variations are highly irregular for visual differentiation, sonification improved user perception [12]. The recently developed technique Soniscope [13] performed audio-visual mapping of data to a scatter plot, allowing sighted users to interactively select regions with a mouse to get an overview of the dataset.

End effectors such as Touch haptic devices allowed users to touch, feel, and grab virtual objects by moving the device handle and were widely used to explore tangible graphs, charts, maps, and more by the BVI along with speech-based audio integration [14, 15]. With sonification, users could get a quick overview of bar charts during haptic navigation [5]. Ultraleap's ultrasound-based technology used several ultrasound transducers that created pressures in users' hands so they could feel 3D shapes in mid-air with their hands [16]. Compared to end effector-type haptic devices, Ultraleap's haptic technology has limited force feedback capability to explore virtual objects and their underlying physical properties (i.e., stiffness, friction, elasticity, and so on).

Simple 3D bar charts of different sizes (i.e., room-scale, table-scale, and hand-scale) were explored with VR integration, and comparisons in user experience were made with the hand-scale physical representations [17]. Cordeil et al. [18] introduced ImAxes (Immersive Axes), a sophisticated VR-enhanced multidimensional visualization tool that allowed users to walk around in virtual space to interact and manipulate data axes and create interesting visualizations such as 3D circular parallel coordinate plots, scatter plot matrices, and so on from existing data sets. 2D plots arranged in a grid called 'small multiples display' were explored in an immersive 3D space [19]. Grid cells represented by 3D shelves were explored in VR that could be further arranged in a flat, semi-circular, or circular fashion, letting users interactively grab and move shelf posts as needed. "DataHop" [20] made very good use of space in VR to allow users to arrange data horizontally or vertically using their preferred layouts. TimeTables [21], a VR-based visualization system for spatiotemporal data exploration arranged multiple space-time cubes on virtual tabletop maps to let users drill down in time to get in-depth information, i.e., energy consumption in different areas or individual buildings on campus. With "DataHop" and "TimeTables", users could be teleported for closer inspection and analysis of data.

Most non-VR desktop-based multimodal data visualization techniques were developed to help people with special needs access information. VR-enhanced multimodal VEs were reported to enhance user experience in games and similar applications. However, as discussed, interactivity and vastness, not multimodality, were emphasized in existing VR data visualization. Research findings demonstrate higher user perception and engagement with multimodal techniques. Both learners and educators preferred the audio-visual mode to unimodal visual learning materials [22]. VR visualization has been recommended to discover and understand meaningful patterns hidden in data [23]. Sight, sound, and touch in VR together could make data discovery more enjoyable.

This research incorporates multimodality in data visualization. In addition to the vision-only presentation, data can be explored by combining additional senses, i.e., audio and touch with the option for VR integration. Research findings demonstrated users' preference for an interactive multimodal data visualization compared to a unimodal vision-only demonstration.

3   The Proposed Approach

This research explores multimodality in data visualization for enhanced user experience and immersion. Different components of the proposed approach are explained below.

3.1   Modality Preferences with the Option for VR Integration

Users were provided with several options to explore data tables. The two-circle Venn diagram in Fig. 1a demonstrates this. The left side of the Venn diagram shows the non-VR option, where data can be visualized with the traditional vision-only mode or multiple modes, i.e., audio-visual or audio-visual-haptic. With the unimodal vision-only option, color variations demonstrated variations in the values of variables as shown in Fig. 1b and Fig. 1c. Colorful bars in the data table were sonified in the audio-visual mode and variations in data were also represented by varying acoustic parameters (i.e., pitch, tempo, and more). With the audio-visual-haptic option, in addition to visual and audio feedback, as discussed, bars in the data table demonstrated variations in surface friction that could be perceived during haptic navigation. Interactive data discovery via sight, sought, and touch could be further enriched with VR integration as shown by the right side of the Venn diagram in Fig. 1a. All three senses can be used together to enrich the visualization experience. If there's cognitive overload with multiple senses or VR integration, users could remove the headset to explore the non-VR versions using fewer sense(s).

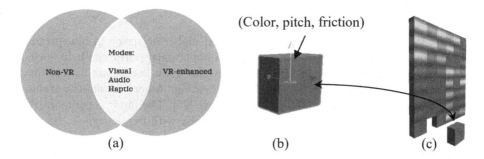

(a)   (b)   (c)

Fig. 1. (a) A two-circle Venn diagram showing different modality options to visualize data in non-VR or VR-enhanced platforms. (b) A multisensory rectangular bar was assigned different sensory parameters (i.e., color, pitch, and friction). (c) A multisensory heatmap made of multisensory rectangular bars each with distinct sensory parameters.

3.2 Continuity in Presentations and Ease of Navigation

Data arranged on a line or curve are more perceptible than those not on the line or curve [24]. Continuous and organized presentations provide faster navigation and comparison as eyes do not need to move far between objects and ears do not get confused. In the same way, faster haptic navigation can be guaranteed when presentations are organized and continuous, limiting extra movements of fingers and hands. In continuous presentations, scalability works better as data can be presented in chunks whenever needed to be zoomed in without causing sensory disruptions. Heatmaps present variables in a contiguous fashion, providing better comparison, navigation, and scalability. Hence, a heatmap was chosen for multimodal presentations of tabular data. Each bar in the heatmap was represented by a rectangular block (Fig. 1b). Bars were stacked row-wise and column-wise, as shown in Fig. 1c to facilitate haptic navigation.

3.3 Multisensory Mapping and Sensory Synchronization

3D rectangular bars were the building blocks in a multisensory heatmap (Fig. 1c). Different sensory parameters assigned to 3D rectangular bars in a heatmap are shown in Fig. 1b. These are further detailed below.

Visual. The red-green color pair was chosen for visual feedback. Red colors demonstrated high values while green showed low values. In-between values were different combinations of red and green according to variable values. Variable values were normalized before mapping to RGB (0 to 1) color components. The normalized value was directly assigned to the red component, while the normalized value was subtracted from 1 to calculate the value of the green component. The blue component was set to zero.

Audio. Users with higher musicality exhibited higher accuracy in interpreting sonified data tables [11]. Irrespective of musicality, popular music can help novice users understand subtle tonal differences produced by variations in auditory parameters. Popular music was used for sonification. Among acoustic parameters, the pitch was reported as the most intuitive [25]. The pitch, a comparative high-low measure of sound changing logarithmically with frequency, can be varied within a narrow range to avoid shrill or dull output. The normal pitch value is 1f. To produce meaningful sound, the pitch was varied between 0.5f to 3f.

Haptic. The haptic display was demonstrated by the surface friction that ranged between 0 to 1. A frictional value of '0' represented a friction-free smooth surface, whereas '1' demonstrated a very rough surface. In-between values demonstrated different mixtures of roughness and smoothness.

Sensory synchronization is important to strengthen the overall effect in multi-sensory modeling. An ascending pitch or friction was perceived as a higher value, while a descending pitch or friction was perceived as a lower value, corresponding to reddish and greenish regions in the visual representation, respectively. The reddish part of the model produced high values for pitch and friction, green areas generated low pitch and friction, and in-between areas generated medium values for the sensory parameters. Table 1 demonstrates synchronization among different sensory parameters. For ease of sensory mapping, normalized values were directly assigned to friction ranging from 0 to 1. The corresponding pitch was calculated as 3 times the normalized value. A constant pitch of 0.5f was assigned for values less than the threshold value, i.e., 0.2f.

Table 1. Synchronization among different sensory parameters, i.e., color, pitch, and friction

Variable (Normalized)	Visual (Color)			Audio (Sonification)	Haptic
	Red (r)	Green (g)	Blue (b)	Pitch	Friction
0 to 1f	0 to 1f	0 to 1f	0f	0.5f to 3f	0 to 1f
value	value	1-value	0	if (value > .2f) pitch = 3xvalue; else pitch = 0.5f;	value

3.4   Diversity and Inclusion

The design principle does not follow the "one size fits all" policy. Users' modality preferences and the choice for VR integration may vary. The proposed approach allows a user to choose the option that suits them the best. The design principle values user emotion [26]. With sonification, the data table becomes a sounding instrument as the users navigate it with a haptic device. Audio integration in multisensory modeling can reflect users' cultural backgrounds and emotions and can be effectively used to incorporate diversity and inclusion in data visualization. Virtual touch creates a special bond between users and data to prompt users to dive deep into the embedded content. With the proposed approach, each user can develop a personalized application version.

4   Implementation and Results

The project used Unity3d for its implementation. Audio integration is simple with Unity. An Oculus Quest 2 VR headset was used for VR integration. The Unity interface provides an easy plug-in for haptic devices and VR headsets. Humans interact with their surroundings via kinesthetic force feedback. End-effector-type haptic devices demonstrated kinesthetic force feedback during user interaction. These devices are lightweight and can easily be plugged into computers and laptops. 3D systems' 'Touch' haptic device (www.3dsystems.com) was used to interact with objects in VR and non-VR options. Figure 2 (top left) demonstrates the device setup. As the program started, a CSV file was read, and a colorful heatmap was displayed. Figure 2 (right) demonstrates a heatmap representation of a data table with 6 variables (i.e., proficiency in reading, math, writing, percent of graduation in SAT, pupil-staff ratio, and drop-outs) and ten observations. The data is about educational statistics in twenty states of the United States. The color variation shows variation in variable values, i.e., red represents a high value, and green demonstrates a low value. Each rectangular bar in a heat map was assigned a color, pitch, and friction depending on variable values so that each bar could be distinct visually, audibly, and haptically from another. Users could touch and feel each bar in the data table with a haptic device. The reddish bars felt rough, the greenish ones generated a smooth feeling, and bars with mixed colors felt neither very rough nor smooth. A piece of music with varying pitches was played as bars in the heatmap were touched with the haptic device. The pitch increased with the values of variables and vice versa. When the user touched a bar, it was highlighted; the corresponding row and column were also emphasized. For example, the highlighted bar in the heatmap in Fig. 2 represents math proficiency in Wisconsin. As the "Display Variable" button was clicked with the haptic cursor by pressing the first stylus button, variable values allowed users to dig deep into data.

4.1   User Interaction with Different Buttons

Users interacted with buttons with the haptic cursor. As the haptic cursor neared a button, that button was selected and next, the first stylus button was pressed to

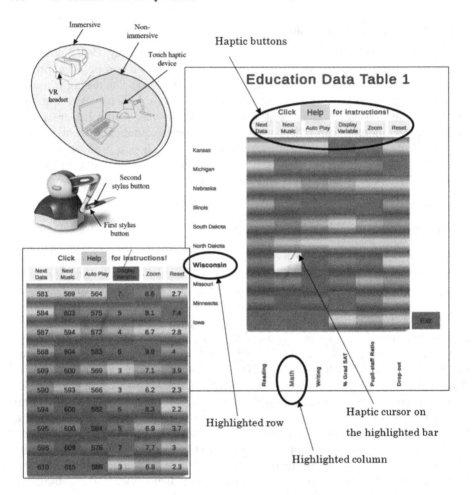

Fig. 2. (Left top) The boundaries between immersive (VR) and non-immersive (non-VR) VEs have been outlined. A VR headset is added to immerse users in the VE. A "Touch" haptic device is used to interact with objects both in VR and non-VR modes. The first and second stylus buttons in a 'Touch' haptic device are shown. (Right) A multimodal heatmap that incorporates three senses: sight, sound, and touch. Variations in values are visualized with color-coded rectangular bars: red represents higher values and green lower values. As users navigate data tables with a haptic device, they can feel variations in friction and pitch of music; both friction and pitch increase with values of variables and vice versa. As the haptic cursor touches a bar in the heatmap, the bar is highlighted with the corresponding row and column. (Bottom left) The "Display Variable" button displays values of variables as the haptic cursor toggles it on with the press of the first stylus button. (Color figure online)

perform an action. New data tables could be uploaded with the "Next Data" button. Similarly, users could choose different music by selecting the "Next Music" button. The current implementation allowed users to choose music from a few

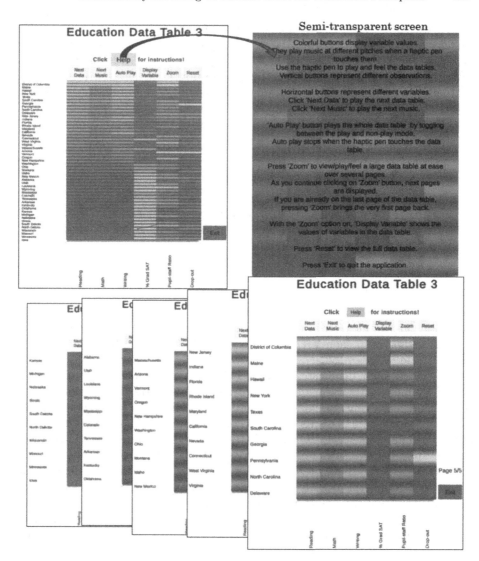

Fig. 3. (Top left) A multimodal heatmap with 50 observations shown on one page. (Top right) The 'Help' button shows user interaction details on a semi-transparent background on the top of the heatmap when toggled on. (Bottom) In 'Zoom' mode, the same data table expands over 5 pages with 10 observations per page.

options: Shady Dave's "My love" on piano tone, "Can't help falling in" on violin, "Jingle bells" on piano, and "My heart will go on" on violin.

The "Auto Play" button toggled between playing the data table column-wise starting from the first row and stopping playing. This is called the audio-visual mode. Each cell of the data table played for 5 s. The "Zoom" button displayed ten rows per page and helped explore large datasets page by page. This has been demonstrated in Fig. 3. As the user continued pressing the "Zoom"' button, the next page with the page number was displayed. After the last page, the zoom button brought the first page back. The "Display Variable" button showed the values of variables and worked when the zoom option was turned on. The "Reset"' button showed the default visualization of the complete data table on one page. The "Help"' button provided user interaction details on a semi-transparent plane shown in Fig. 3 and the application would exit with the "Exit" button.

5   Evaluation

Thirteen sighted subjects (10 males, two females, and one from the LGBTQ+ group) within the age range of 20 to 55 volunteered to participate in the user study. Five participants had prior experience using "Touch" haptic devices. All participants except one had experience with VR headsets.

5.1   Study Design

With the proposed approach, users evaluated the following options to explore modalities and immersion in data visualization: 1) unimodal vision-only (non-VR), 2) audio-visual (non-VR), 3) audio-visual-haptic (non-VR), and 4) audio-visual-haptic (VR).

Recent research demonstrated that enhanced engagement and immersion offered by multimodality made users quite oblivious to time and surroundings [11]. Though the time to explore a multisensory display was longer than the vision-only mode, participants reported completing tasks faster with the multi-modal version. Wang et al. [26] ignored objective evaluation in data visualization as time was opted out as an evaluation criterion in preference for subjective components such as creativity in visualization and users' emotional experience with data. Considering the overall aspect of multisensory visualization, subjective measures were emphasized to evaluate user experience.

Likert scales are deemed most appropriate for subjective evaluation. A Likert scale ranging from 1 (poor) to 5 (excellent) was used. While evaluating user experience for different options stated above, the following metrics were considered: immersion, engagement, interactivity, cognition, confidence, and satisfaction. Before rating their experience with different data visualization options, participants were asked to consider a few questions: Did a multimodal VE make them more engaged with the content or cause distractions? Was multimodal visualization a better option for in-depth data exploration than the vision-only mode? Did they enjoy the playfulness in visualization as they made datasets respond by interacting with them? Did multimodality help them identify variations in visualization (i.e., high, medium, and low values) more accurately than the unimodal option? Did they feel more confident with multimodality and VR enhancement than the unimodal non-VR mode? Did redundant senses in a multimodal display increase their confidence and reduce mental workload? Which option offered the utmost satisfaction, i.e., comfort and relaxation? The user experience scores for different visualization options were expected to reflect answers to these questions.

5.2 Procedure

As mentioned, the user study emphasized user experience with multimodality and VR in tabular data visualization. Before the user study, participants were briefed on the application and its use. Next, participants were asked to fill out the demographic form. During the evaluation, participants were asked to differentiate variables using different modes and identify high, medium, and low variable values with different sensory parameters (i.e., color, pitch, and friction), value range (i.e., maximum and minimum values for variables) based on representations in different modes. Interactions with data tables or buttons, both in VR and non-VR, were all performed with a "Touch" haptic device.

As the program started, a data table with six variables and ten observations appeared. Participants explored the data table using different modes and options. They chose different music for the auditory display. Clicking on the "Next Data" button uploaded the next data table comprising six variables and 20 observations. The third data table included six variables and 50 observations. Using the "Zoom" button, the second and third data tables could be explored in detail as this option displayed 10 rows per page.

Participants spent 15 min to one hour in total exploring the data tables in different modes. At the end of the study, participants were asked to fill out a Likert scale-based questionnaire to reflect their experience with different options. Any comments or suggestions for future improvements were encouraged.

5.3 Results and Analysis

All statistical analyses were conducted using R. The effect of modes and immersion on user preference was investigated. Likert scale datasets are considered ordinal or ranked. The normality of data distribution was checked using the Shapiro-Wilk test (significance level at $\alpha = 0.05$). As the normality of data was not confirmed for all options in the results, therefore, the Friedman test (a nonparametric method) for repeated measures was conducted for paired data sets. The null hypothesis considered there was no difference in user experience with multimodality and immersion whereas the alternate hypothesis considered a significant difference in user experience with variations in modality and immersion. The results are shown in Fig. 4.

Overall, the Friedman test showed a significant difference in user experience with modality and VR. The null hypothesis was rejected ($\chi^2_{Friedman} = 12.33$, p $= 0.00632 < 0.01$, $\hat{W}_{kendall} = 0.32$, $CI_{95\%} = [0.17, 1.0]$, $n_{pairs} = 13$). The p-value showed strong evidence against the null hypothesis. Kendall's coefficient of concordance $\hat{W}_{kendall}$ with a value of 0.32 with 95% confidence interval measured the effect size as fair. However, the global Friedman test did not show which options significantly differed. Hence, post-hoc analysis with Durbin-Conover tests was

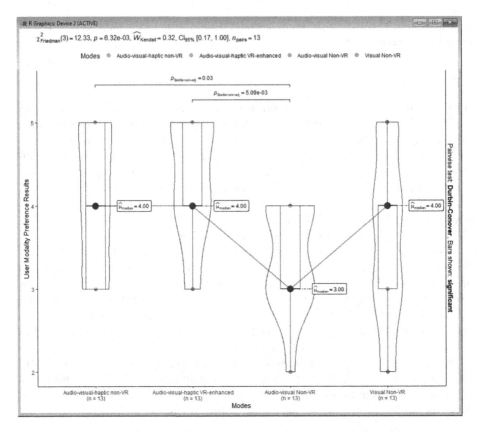

Fig. 4. Friedman test results summary with the Durbin-Conover posthoc pairwise test results with Bonferroni p-value correction for multiple pairwise comparisons.

conducted with a Bonferroni correction for multiple comparisons. A significant difference was found between the following modes: audio-visual (non-VR) versus audio-visual-haptic (non-VR) (p = 0.03 < 0.05) and audio-visual (non-VR) versus audio-visual-haptic (VR-enhanced) (p = 0.00509 < 0.01).

Among all four options, the VR-enhanced audio-visual-haptic mode was preferred by most users followed by the non-VR audio-visual-haptic mode. The unimodal vision-only (non-VR) version took third place while users least appreciated the audio-visual (non-VR) mode. Regarding VR-enhanced audio-visual-haptic mode, one participant commented, *"The VR version really brought it all together. The A+V+T (audio-visual-haptic) version was cool, especially the touch, but when immersed in the VR, the touch felt a lot better to me".*

Some participants reported audio integration as a distraction. Some suggested, *"I'm not sure how I would do this but maybe implementing different sounds for each roughness like a guitar for rough and flute for smooth could be interesting".* One participant jotted down, *"I feel the auditory is (typically) less precise and thus less viable than touch. ...it is easier to notice data dif-*

ferences through touch. I believe auditory elements may be improved by using chords instead of whole song segments to make it less chaotic and more immediately differentiable". Lack of user intervention and precision in audio feedback might have made the audio-visual mode the least popular. However, another participant preferred sound to vision as they wrote, *"I had a hard time telling the differences of levels via color. I relied on sound for that."* Different participants had different preferences and levels of perception.

In addition, most participants preferred audio to be used with touch to make the sense of touch more profound as one commented, *"I really enjoyed the correlation between pitch and texture".* This has been reflected in another participant's comment cited below who ranked both immersive and non-immersive versions of audio-visual-haptic mode as excellent.

"The study was most interesting when closing my eyes or not paying attention visually. I could scrub through the data and feel the differences in roughness and have a general idea of the gradient of how the color changed through the charts. However, as soon as audio was introduced, the reddest part of the chart stuck out, and I was able to remember exactly where the reddest parts were. Through just audio and no touch, however, I was not able to tell what the color gradient looked like despite understanding that very well through touch. The visuals were not that engaging, however, the touch and audio were, but in different ways. I would have had to read the labels on the charts more carefully for the visuals to become more engaging. Note: after thinking about it some more, the combination of haptics and audio could have been the cause for the impactful experience, not just audio like I originally thought".

When asked about the scope for diversity and inclusion, participants commented positively. Below are some related comments from participants.

"I think something like this could be turned into a really cool learning tool for mentally challenged individuals/impaired individuals".

"I think this type of program would be amazing, especially for disabled children".

6   Conclusion and Future Work

Findings from this research supported user appreciation for multimodal visualization of tabular data. Though most participants preferred VR-enhanced immersive data visualization, no significant difference was noted between the VR-enhanced audio-visual-haptic mode and its non-VR version. As discussed in the background section, most existing research demonstrated user preference for the audio-visual mode compared to the vision-only option. We received different user feedback; the audio-visual mode received fewer positive responses than the visual mode and was least appreciated among all options. Some existing research [12] recommended combining several acoustic parameters i.e., frequency, timbre, and more for distinct audio feedback, which would be tested in the future implementation. However, as users' scores, comments, and different features for different options were compared and analyzed, the low appreciation of the audio-visual mode could be attributed to the non-interactive nature of the audio-visual mode in the current implementation. Therefore, it can be concluded that interactivity plays a crucial role in multimodal data visualization and should be integrated wherever possible. The current implementation used red and green colors to represent high and low values. Users will be allowed to choose colors for the high and low values from a color palette to visualize the heatmap with different color combinations. The future version would allow users to upload their favorite tones. With the zoom option on, the current version of the multimodal heatmap scrolls vertically allowing users to explore each observation in detail. Datasets with many variables will be tested with the options for horizontal scrolling. The future implementation will make necessary modifications in the interface such as incorporating speech-based guidance to include the BVI in the evaluation.

References

1. Whitehead, A., Johnson, H., Nixon, N., Welch, J.: Exergame effectiveness: what the numbers can tell us. In: Proceedings of the 5th ACM SIGGRAPH Symposium on Video Games (Sandbox 2010), pp. 55–62 (2010)
2. Lecuyer, A., Mobuchon, P., Megard, C., Perret, J., Andriot, C., Colinot, J.-P.: HOMERE: a multimodal system for visually impaired people to explore virtual environments. In: Proceedings on IEEE Virtual Reality, pp. 251–258 (2003)
3. Plassr, J.-L., Homer, B.-D., Kinzer, C.-K.: Foundations of game-based learning. Educ. Psychol. **50**(4), 258–283 (2015)
4. Farber, M.: Gamify Your Classroom: A Field Guide to Game-based Learning. Peter Lang Publishing (2015)
5. Yu, W., Brewster, S.: Comparing two haptic interfaces for multimodal graph rendering. In: Proceedings on HAPTICS 2002, pp. 3–9 (2002)
6. Zong, J., Lee, C., Lundgard, A., Jang, J., Hajas, D., Satyanarayan, A.: Rich screen reader experiences for accessible data visualization. Comput. Graph. Forum (Proc. EuroVis) **41**(3) (2022)
7. Brewster, S.-A., Wright, P.-C., Edwards, A.: An evaluation of earcons for use in auditory human-computer interfaces. In: Proceedings on CHI 1993, pp. 222–227 (1993)
8. Alty, J.: Communicating graphical information to blind users using music. In: Proceedings on CHI 1998, pp. 574–581 (1998)
9. Ramloll, R., Brewster, S., Yu, W., Riedel, B.: Using non-speech sounds to improve access to 2D tabular numerical information for visually impaired users. In: Blandford, A., Vanderdonckt, J., Gray, P. (eds.) People and Computers XV–Interaction without Frontiers, pp. 515–529. Springer, London (2001). https://doi.org/10.1007/978-1-4471-0353-0_32
10. Kildal, J., Brewster, S.: Explore the matrix: browsing numerical data tables using sound. In: Proceedings on ICAD 2005 (2005)
11. Rönnberg, N.: Musical sonification supports visual discrimination of color intensity. Behav. Inf. Technol. **38**(10), 1028–1037 (2019)
12. Kramer, G.: Mapping a single data stream to multiple auditory variables: a subjective approach to creating a compelling design. In: Proceedings of 3rd International Conference on Auditory Display. Santa Fe Institute (1996)

13. Enge, K., Rind, A., Iber, M., Höldrich, R., Aigner, W.: Towards multimodal exploratory data analysis: SoniScope as a prototypical implementation. In: Proceedings of the EuroVis 2022 (2022)
14. Ramloll, R., Yu, W., Brewster, S., Riedel, B., Burton, M., Dimigen, G.: Constructing sonified haptic line graphs for the blind student: first steps. In: Proceedings of the fourth international ACM conference on Assistive technologies (Assets 2000). Association for Computing Machinery, New York (2000)
15. Roberts, J., Franklin, K., Cullinane, J.: Virtual haptic exploratory visualization of line graphs and charts. In: Proceedings of SPIE - The International Society for Optical Engineering (2002)
16. Sand, A., Rakkolainen, I., Isokoski, P., Kangas, J., Raisamo, R., Palovuori, K.: Head-mounted display with mid-air tactile feedback. In: Proceedings of the 21st ACM Symposium on Virtual Reality Software and Technology (VRST 2015), pp. 51–58. Association for Computing Machinery, New York (2015)
17. Danyluk, K., Ulusoy, T., Wei, W., Willett, W.: Touch and beyond: comparing physical and virtual reality visualizations. IEEE Trans. Vis. Comput. Graph. **28**(04), 1930–1940 (2022)
18. Cordeil, M., Cunningham, A., Dwyer, T., Thomas, B.-H., Marriott, K.: ImAxes: immersive axes as embodied affordances for interactive multivariate data visualization. In: Proceedings of UIST 2017, pp. 71–83(2017)
19. Liu, J., Prouzeau, A., Ens, B., Dwyer, T.: Design and evaluation of interactive small multiples data visualisation in immersive spaces. In: Proceedings of IEEE Conference on Virtual Reality and 3D User Interfaces (VR), pp. 588–597 (2020)
20. Hayatpur, D., Xia, H., Wigdor, D.: DataHop: spatial data exploration in virtual reality. In: Proceedings of UIST 2020, Virtual Event, USA, pp. 818–828 (2020)
21. Zhang, Y., Ens, B., Satriadi, K., Prouzeau, A., Goodwin, S.: TimeTables: Embodied exploration of immersive spatio-temporal data. In: Proceedings of IEEE on Conference Virtual Reality and 3D User Interfaces (VR), Christchurch, New Zealand, pp. 599–605 (2022)
22. Tomlinson, B., Walker, B., Moore, E.: Auditory display in interactive science simulations: description and sonification support interaction and enhance opportunities for learning. In: Proceedings on CHI 2020, pp. 1–12 (2020)
23. Donalek, C., et al: Immersive and collaborative data visualization using virtual reality platforms. In: Proceedings on IEEE International Conference on Big Data, pp. 609–614 (2014)
24. Borgo, R., et al.: Glyph-based visualization: foundations, design guidelines, techniques and applications. In: Sbert, M., Szirmay-Kalos, L. (eds.) Proceedings of Eurographics 2013 - State of the Art Reports. The Eurographics Association (2013)
25. Wang, R., Jung, C., Kim, Y.: Seeing through sounds: mapping auditory dimensions to data and charts for people with visual impairments. Comput. Graph. Forum **41**(3), 71–83 (2022)
26. Wang, Y., et al.: An emotional response to the value of visualization. IEEE Comput. Graphics Appl. **39**, 8–17 (2019)

Coping with Bullying Incidents by the Narrative and Multi-modal Interaction in Virtual Reality

Lu-Hua Ma, En-Chen Chen$^{(\boxtimes)}$ ⓘ, and Tsai-Yen Li$^{(\boxtimes)}$ ⓘ

Department of Computer Science, National Chengchi University, Taipei, Taiwan
leochen819@gmail.com, li@nccu.edu.tw

Abstract. Bullying poses a significant threat to students' well-being, causing enduring psychological and physical harm. Traditional teaching falls short in preparing students to confront and counteract bullying. This study introduces a VR-based approach, immersing users in bullying scenarios, allowing them to select responses leading to diverse outcomes. Employing multi-modal interaction through gestures and voice commands enhances immersion and user engagement. This method facilitates multidimensional engagement, fostering a tangible sense of presence. The system was assessed with twelve university students who underwent pre-interview evaluations of their bullying awareness. Results highlight the potential of virtual reality simulations as an educational tool, enabling effective bullying coping strategies. Participants praised the natural and fluid multi-modal interaction, along with the captivating interactive narrative, leading to repeated system engagement. Combining multi-modal interactions and VR-based bullying scenarios not only deepened participants' comprehension of bullying but also equipped them with vital coping skills. In conclusion, this study showcases the promise of VR simulations and multi-modal interactions in educating students about bullying, empowering them to navigate such challenges adeptly.

Keywords: Bullying · Immersion · Multi-modal Interaction · Virtual Reality

1 Introduction

Campus bullying profoundly impacts students, hindering their growth and well-being. It involves repeated aggression within schools, encompassing physical, verbal, or relational acts. A power imbalance is pivotal, as influential individuals target weaker peers with harmful actions. Bullying takes forms like physical assaults, name-calling, rumors, exclusion, and online attacks, causing immediate distress and emotional harm. This jeopardizes the educational environment's safety and support. Preventing bullying is vital; schools must raise awareness, teach empathy, set anti-bullying policies, and offer support. Cultivating a culture of kindness and acceptance fosters safe spaces for all students to thrive.

The development of virtual reality (VR) technology has aided in this regard. By immersing users in a safe and believable world, VR allows users to emotionally connect with characters, cultures, histories, and ongoing stories [1]. VR technology enhances

G. Bebis et al. (Eds.): ISVC 2023, LNCS 14362, pp. 466–479, 2023.
https://doi.org/10.1007/978-3-031-47966-3_37

storytelling by immersing users in believable worlds and fostering emotional connections. VR's realism, immersion, and motivation make it a powerful medium. As campus bullying's severity warrants effective mediums, VR scenarios aim to educate students on bullying and response strategies, reducing harm through empathy and behavior change.

Storytelling is a life-prevalent form of communication and experience sharing, allowing people to convey thoughts or emotions. As a new narrative medium, VR has shown the potential to deliver better learning outcomes than other media [2] and generate higher levels of empathy, immersion, and story engagement [3]. In terms of interactive storytelling in virtual reality, users often take on an "active" role in the narrative context, as opposed to the "passive" role in most other traditional narrative media [4]. Users engage with the system in scenarios, shaping storylines. VR and interactive design enhance authentic experiences, enabling diverse coping strategies against bullying. We aimed to explore whether VR interactive storytelling and multimodal interactions deepen bullying comprehension, attitude change, and coping skills acquisition. Pre- and post-experience interviews assess changes while evaluating immersive multimodal interactions in VR bullying scenarios to inform future interactive approaches.

2   Related Work

2.1   Definition of School Bullying

Furlong, Michael, and Gale Morrison pointed out that school bullying is a long-standing issue in schools, referring to malicious bullying behavior among students [5]. Dan Olweus provided a more specific description of school bullying, stating that it involves a student being repeatedly bullied or harassed by one or more students over a prolonged period, and the bullied student cannot resist due to weaker power [6]. Amra and Agarwal identified several factors contributing to bullying, including culture, systems, family, emotional aspects, the need for security, and excessive self-awareness [7].

A research survey in [8] found that students who experience multiple forms of bullying simultaneously have more difficulty choosing strategies to seek help from others. This may be explained by their fear of retaliation from the bullies after disclosing the incidents to someone else. Additionally, they often feel ashamed of how their peers perceive them, leading them to suffer in silence [9, 10]. Kanetsuna [11] compared the results of help-seeking behaviors among students in Japan and English-speaking countries, revealing that the main reasons for not seeking help were fears that the bullying would worsen, lack of trust in others, and lack of confidence. Therefore, despite the standard advice to seek help, there may be better choices in practice than this strategy.

Consequently, students need a tool to help them cope with bullying. Research shows that without a sense of physical and emotional safety, students struggle to overcome fear and anxiety and voluntarily explore new challenges [12]. For example, an increased sense of security and self-worth in the classroom motivates students' learning, self-discipline, willingness to take risks, and ability to handle mistakes effectively [13]. Bullying affects learning; a safe simulation is essential. Users learn to cope by experiencing bullying scenarios within a narrative context. Storytelling is integral to bullying simulations. Players can assume different roles and experience bullying through various methods

[14]. Role-playing facilitates the development of socio-emotional skills, personal identity, and awareness of social rules [15]. Role-playing aids students in understanding bullying by adopting various perspectives, fostering empathy, and practicing resolution methods. This enhances empathy, perspective-taking, and knowledge, which is crucial for bullying prevention and intervention [16]. VR is an aid tool for comprehending bullying, offering safe scenarios to explore responses and consequences. The immersive experience transforms attitudes and strategies, incorporating school and support roles to enhance understanding of intervention possibilities.

2.2 Using VR as a Narrative Medium

Mandal states that virtual reality is an absorbing, interactive, computer-mediated experience in which individuals perceive and interact with synthetic (simulated) environments through special human-machine interface devices as if they were real [17]. With the widespread use of virtual reality technology, a new trend has emerged: delivering stories through virtual reality. Virtual reality makes users feel present in a virtual world; they are directly placed in a scene as if they are part of the story, resulting in heightened emotional responses to the narrative [18]. Stories facilitate communication, share experiences, and serve cognitive, emotional, and expressive functions. They aid learning through pre-scripted narratives or personal storytelling by enhancing cognitive processes like planning, reconstruction, and summarization of abstract concepts. Furthermore, narratives have an emotional function, using artistic genres such as literature, drama, film, and plot-based media like games to engage users, enhance immersion, and apply them in interactive media and virtual reality production [19]. Research shows that users experience a higher sense of immersion, greater empathy towards the story's characters, and increased engagement when experiencing interactive narrative scenarios through virtual reality compared to using smartphones [3].

Interactive narrative has become one of the most compelling applications of combining narrative and virtual reality. Interactive narrative refers to users creating or influencing a dramatic story plot through actions, assuming a role in a fictional world, issuing commands to computer-controlled characters, or directly manipulating the fictional world state [20]. In such games, players participate and influence the story through interaction with the game, bound by a set of rules and overseen by the game designer, who provides the story structure and game elements [21]. Immersing users into the story and engaging them emotionally and cognitively [22], as Riedl and Bulitko point out, aims to make users believe they are an integral part of an unfolding story and that their actions have meaningful consequences within that story [20]. Research has found that electronic games' immersive and interactive experiences can enhance the conveyance of narratives or similar experiences to users [23, 24].

Ivanov and Ramos designed a bullying intervention system for young girls with two interactive scenarios [25]. In the school hallway scenario, the student attempts to attend class but encounters another girl who blocks her path and bullies her. All interactions in the virtual environment are from a first-person perspective, as acting from a first-person perspective has been shown to facilitate learning in virtual environments [26]. By allowing users to experience bullying behavior from different perspectives and understanding the thoughts and feelings of others, the game promotes learning about bullying. Research suggests that if sufficient scene design and interactivity are provided, bullying simulations in virtual reality environments can be viable for fostering student empathy [16].

2.3 Multimodal Interaction in Virtual Reality

VR interactive narrative scenarios effectively create a compelling bullying experience, making it a suitable tool for users. In real-life interactions, humans use gestures and language to communicate with others or objects. If interactions in VR scenarios are designed to incorporate gestures along with voice, it can enhance the user's immersion and sense of presence. VR system development has started to utilize multiple ways of sensing as input systems, known as multimodal interaction. Multimodal interaction allows users to provide natural interactions simultaneously using two or more input channels. Information between different modalities possesses complementary and redundant features, and the combination of gestures and sound can more intuitively express the user's intentions [27]. Several studies have also shown that when provided with multimodal interaction, users strongly prefer using multimodal interfaces compared to experiencing only a single sense [28, 29].

When considering VR interactive design, the primary interaction methods include user-menu interaction, user-object interaction, and user input, such as text or selection [30]. Through menu-based interaction, users can make choices from visual lists of dialogues or actions [31]. On the other hand, in interactive narratives where users interact with characters but cannot respond through their actions, users are limited to interacting through a mouse and keyboard. This interactive method's lack of extensive physical expression somewhat diminishes the user's gaming experience [32]. As VR gesture recognition technology has matured, researchers have begun to incorporate gesture recognition into the interaction design of VR narrative games. Gestures are postures or movements of the upper limbs that users can employ to express their interactive intentions and convey corresponding interactive information [33]. Users can send simple commands to the system through gestures, such as selection, movement, and deletion, or express more complex intentions, such as switching the current interactive scene, controlling virtual objects, or performing virtual actions. Current gesture input methods can be categorized as wearable sensor-based, touch device-based, and computer vision-based input [27]. Comparative studies between the traditional controller and gesture-based interaction in VR experiences have found that using gestures for tasks provides a more natural and smooth experience while increasing the sense of presence [34].

VR simulating bullying cultivates empathy, reducing real-life bullying. Traditional VR scenarios involve menu-based interactions, teaching bullying coping via different choices. Immersion and user experience benefit from voice and gesture recognition for natural interactions. Multimodal VR interactions enhance immersion, focusing on bullying contexts. A study targeting young girls designed a bullying intervention using voice recognition and text-based options for natural interaction [25]. Based on combining gesture and speech recognition to enhance VR experiences, fostering authenticity and effective knowledge transmission in bullying scenarios. Natural interactions boost presence and engagement, improving overall effectiveness in addressing bullying. Designing immersive interactive narratives based on gesture and speech recognition allows users to engage with characters and objects, driving the storyline.

3 Objectives and System Design

We adopted verbal bullying and relational bullying as behaviors of bullying. Through VR, users can experience being bullied from the victim's perspective in a first-person narrative. Users can simulate real-life bullying situations and practice their responses. The storyline also simulates possible consequences in the real world, allowing users to understand appropriate ways to respond to real-life situations.

3.1 Objectives

This study devised a VR interactive narrative system to address high school bullying, aiding students in comprehending bullying scenarios and effective coping strategies. The system was developed according to education expert's insights. To assess effectiveness, user feedback through questionnaires and interviews gauged system usage and understanding of bullying coping strategies. This evaluation process aimed to determine the system's impact on students' grasp of real-life bullying challenges and how to counteract them.

3.2 Experiment Design

Materials. We used the Oculus Quest 2 for the headset device of VR in the experiment. The headset was connected to a PC with an Intel Core i7-4790, 16 GB RAM, NVIDIA GeForce RTX 2060, and a 1-TB HDD.

The Setting of the Story. In addition to the experimental design and storytelling, this study focused on the interactive effects and visual presentation in VR technology. The VR scenario's content was developed using the Unity3D game engine. For the models, some of the 3D scenes and object models were sourced from the internet, and Maya was used for detailed processing. Some models were created using Maya, while the character models were obtained from Maximo.

In terms of the story setting, we aimed to make users feel close to reality. Therefore, we referenced the most common times and locations of bullying incidents. The most common places for bullying are classrooms and restrooms, while the most frequent times are during recess, after school, and lunchtime [35]. Thus, the story is set in a classroom after school. The story takes place in a classroom involving two classmates who bully the user, along with an observer. Within the class, a small group of students frequently mocked and gave the user derogatory nicknames. The user felt uncomfortable and injustice in their mind. The user needed to make choices and act to break free from this verbal and relational bullying, as shown in Fig. 1(a). The research scenario provided users with options to ignore or tolerate bullying. Still, based on previous discussions with interviewees, the scenario also included a continuous bullying approach to make users understand that ignoring or tolerating was not an effective coping strategy. Regarding other correct approaches, the study suggests feeling discomfort to the bully. However, the scenario also incorporated random outcomes due to the uncertainty of the bully's behavior. The bully might stop the bullying as a result, or they might continue their bullying behavior. Therefore, the victim might eventually have to file a complaint with a teacher or the bullying prevention committee. The study also aimed to present how teachers and the bullying prevention committee handle such complaints, encouraging users to be courageous in filing complaints in the future, as shown in Fig. 1(b).

(a)   (b)

Fig. 1. (a) The scenarios of bullying and (b) The Bullying Prevention Committee

Interaction Design in VR. The interactive design included gesture and voice interactions. We designed relevant voice responses based on the storyline and interview results for different coping strategies for voice interaction. We utilized the Unity Microphone API and Audio Source for voice recording. The recorded voice was stored and uploaded to the cloud for real-time speech recognition. This allowed users to engage in voice conversations with characters in the scenario. Specific keywords could trigger the development of decision tree-based storylines according to the game settings. Regarding gesture interaction, considering that the bullying scenarios primarily involved verbal interactions, the physical interactions mainly revolved around counterattacks. Therefore, in the design, a fist gesture represents an attitude of revenge. Additionally, the system is also designed for humorous responses to compromise. The motion for this type of response involves raising the thumb, indicating the user's more relaxed and funnier attitude.

Interactive feedback was facilitated through visual icons in the design, ensuring users understood their interactions with the system. A yellow icon signaled interaction availability, red indicated recognition failure, and green showed successful recognition, as shown in Fig. 2. When the icons for interactive feedback appeared, they would be fixed in front of the user's eyes and move along with the user's perspective remaining in front of the user's eyes.

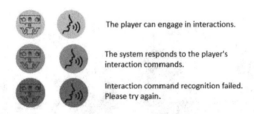

Fig. 2. Interactive feedback design in the VR system

Procedure. First, there was a pre-experimental interview before the VR experience, which primarily aimed to understand the participants' bullying experiences and took approximately 15 min. The participants proceeded to the VR experience, which lasted about 20 min. After completing the VR experience, a post-experience questionnaire was given to gather feedback on the participants' experience, which took approximately 10 min. Finally, a semi-structured interview was conducted with the participants to inquire about their bullying experiences within the scenario, which took 15 to 20 min. The entire experiment was expected to take about 1 h to complete, as shown in Fig. 3. After the experiment, the results of the questionnaires and interviews were analyzed separately to gain insights into the system's user experience.

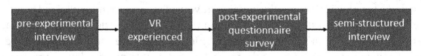

Fig. 3. The Experimental Procedure

Responsive Strategies for Bullying. According to the study on response strategies to bullying, the most successful approaches are (1) informing teachers or adults and (2) seeking help from peers [11]. On the other hand, unsuccessful strategies include (1) retaliating, (2) complying with the bully, and (3) displaying helplessness. Additionally, the study in [36] considered humorous responses proposed for verbal bullying have gained widespread support, including humor as a response strategy in the research design. Furthermore, based on recommendations from expert interviews, a serious informing approach was also added to the response strategies. Considering these, we have categorized the response strategies into the following five types: retaliation, seeking help from teachers, displaying helplessness, humorous responses, and serious informing.

The study identified successful and unsuccessful bullying response strategies, including informing teachers, seeking help from peers, retaliation, compliance, and humor. A VR scenario involving three episodes addresses campus bullying. Users choose gestures like making a fist or seeking help, leading to varied outcomes. The scenario aims to educate users on effective coping with bullying through interactive and branching storylines, offering an immersive experience to comprehend the consequences of their choices when dealing with bullies, as shown in Fig. 4.

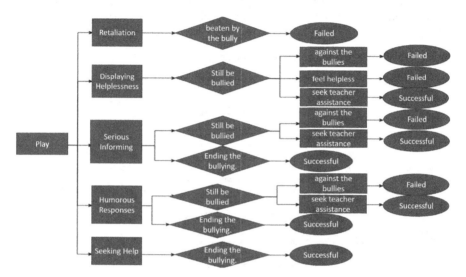

Fig. 4. The Decision Tree of the Storyline

4 Experimental Results

4.1 Participants

The study obtained approval from the Chengchi University Ethics Committee and screened participants for emotional well-being. Twelve students participated, receiving information about the process and providing informed consent. Pre-test interviews, post-experience surveys, and semi-structured interviews were conducted. The analysis focused on system operation and storytelling based on participants' feedback before and after the experience.

4.2 Analysis of Questionnaire Results

This study analyzed the system's operational aspects, storytelling experience and functionality, and immersion by conducting a questionnaire survey to gather user feedback. Respondents mention their degree of agreement or disagreement based on the 5 points of the Likert scale (1 - Strongly disagree, 2 - Disagree, 3 - Neutral, 4 - Agree, 5 - Strongly agree) for a series of statements about their attitude.

About the Operation of the System. The questionnaire evaluates users' experience with multimodal interaction involving gestures and voice during storytelling, as shown in Table 1. Scores for intuitive and smooth interactions were consistently high, favoring the combination of gestures and voice. However, lower scores were seen for the first and seventh questions. Participants' feedback indicated a disconnect when unable to interact with a taken notebook initially, impacting expectations. Multiple branching paths caused shifts between character interaction and accessing menus via gestures, making the experience feel more like a game system. This emphasizes aligning user expectations and minimizing disruptions for an enhanced VR experience.

Table 1. The survey of operations in the VR

Questions	Mean	S.D
1、 I find using gesture recognition for operations to be intuitive.	4.33	0.98
2、 I feel that using gesture recognition for operations is smooth.	4.42	0.67
3、 I feel that the hand on the screen is my own hand.	4.67	0.49
4、 I feel that speech recognition accurately translates my words.	4.58	0.90
5、 I find speech recognition to be very smooth.	4.33	0.98
6、 I feel that using voice and speaking to NPCs can simulate real-life conversations with other people.	4.42	0.67
7、 I feel that interacting with NPCs using gestures and voice is just like real-life interaction..	4.17	0.83
8、 I feel that I enjoy the interaction method that combines gestures and voice.	4.75	0.62

Analysis and Discussion of Storytelling Experience. This questionnaire focuses on inquiring about participants' narrative experience in the game, as shown in Table 2.

Table 2. The survey of the story experience and VR design

Questions	Mean	S.D
1、 I feel that I can understand the content of the story.	4.75	0.45
2、 I feel that I had been bullied by the characters in the scenes.	4.08	0.90
3、 I feel that I can empathize with the feeling of being bullied.	4.25	0.62
4、 I feel that the progression of the story is smooth.	4.42	0.90
5、 I feel it can happen in real life that the situations in the story are scenarios of bullying.	4.58	0.67
6、 I feel that the virtual characters were interacting with me.	4.08	1.16
7、 I feel that I had influenced the development of the storyline.	4.58	0.90

The survey focused on story experience and VR design, with participants generally rating above four on average. This suggests their comprehension of the narrative and belief in influencing its direction through interactive storytelling. However, one question received a lower score due to Participant 3's perspective. Having encountered severe bullying, this participant deemed the depicted bullying milder and didn't feel personally bullied. The interview revealed that their unique background shaped this perception, showcasing the subjectivity of experiences. Nonetheless, the narrative managed to evoke emotions linked to past incidents, despite differing severity interpretations. The results affirmed participants' understanding of the narrative's realism and empowerment to shape it. Participant 3's insight underscored the significance of acknowledging individual variances and experiences when crafting immersive storytelling in virtual reality. It highlighted how personal histories influence perceptions, and despite varied interpretations, the narrative could trigger emotional resonance based on each person's memories and feelings.

Analysis of the Immersive VR Experience. This questionnaire aimed to investigate the overall immersion experienced by participants in the VR, as shown in Table 3. In the immersion section, curiosity about the storyline's progression received the highest score. While some participants expressed excitement and anger, others found depicted bullying behavior relatively mild, causing slight discomfort. The game minimized violent visual scenes to manage emotional responses, opting for verbal cues. Some participants observed the portrayed bullying to lack significant threats, minimizing worry. Generally, the immersion was influenced by perceived severity. Milder bullying scenes lessened the emotional impact, preventing excessive discomfort or worry for participants. The findings highlight the importance of balancing immersive experiences while considering emotional responses to varying levels of bullying intensity.

Table 3. The survey of immersion in the VR.

Questions	Mean	S.D
1. I feel that my emotions follow the development of the storyline.	3.92	1.08
2. I'm curious to know how the story will unfold.	4.92	0.29
3. I would worry about whether I can successfully overcome the bullying.	3.67	1.37
4. I feel so immersed in the storyline that I even want to have direct conversations with the virtual characters.	4.17	1.11
5. I find the operations in the scenario to be easily familiar.	4.83	0.39
6. I feel that interacting in the VR is like interacting in the real world.	4	1.13
7. During the experience, I didn't notice what was happening in the real world.	4.17	0.94
8. I feel like I had disconnected from the real world.	3.42	0.90
9. During the experience, I felt that the story setting was the only thing I cared about.	4.17	0.94
10. I feel that the gameplay time went by quickly.	4.5	0.80

4.3 Analysis of the Interview

Following the VR experience, interviews and observations revealed intriguing insights:

1. Users tended to experiment boldly with strategies in the VR scenario that might differ from real-life situations. The simulation enabled participants to overcome real-world constraints and try diverse approaches, boosting their courage to confront fear.
2. Most participants felt the sensation of being bullied during the scenario. Emotional responses like grievance and anger indicated that the designed bullying behavior fostered empathy and resonance, connecting with their own emotions.
3. Post-experience, users grasped the proper ways to respond to bullying. Participants comprehended conveyed coping techniques, distinguishing effective and ineffective strategies through various interactive outcomes. Additional response strategies were learned, contributing to a mindset shift that helped them remain composed in similar situations.
4. Users expressed interest in revisiting the system. Most willingly replayed the game, highlighting the appeal of interactive storytelling combined with bullying design. This combination enhanced the system's replayability value.
5. Users believed that VR experiences featuring interactive bullying storytelling were beneficial for adolescents to understand bullying. This approach was considered more effective than traditional lectures or videos, leaving a profound impression on adolescents. The fusion of VR, interactive storytelling, and bullying education demonstrated the potential to impart impactful knowledge about bullying to young audiences.

5 Discussions and Limitations

The study observed that participants had encountered bullying as victims in the past, often responding passively or seeking help. In the VR scenario, participants initially chose retaliatory approaches, suggesting that VR allowed bold behavior. The system suggested responses based on outcomes, enabling experiential learning from different perspectives. To improve interactions, future iterations should offer more object and character engagement, enhancing the tutorial system for clearer options. The VR scenario resonated with participants who related it to past experiences, illustrating the potential of VR storytelling to evoke emotional responses. Tailoring narratives to diverse backgrounds and perspectives is crucial.

Due to the relatively small sample size in this study, caution is needed when drawing conclusions about correlations. Based on participant feedback, immersion is revealed as a subjective experience influenced by background, interpretation, and expectations. Considering the application of research results from college students to young people, it is crucial to emphasize understanding the storyline and environmental support. Further design and planning of bullying and coping strategies suitable for different age groups, especially considering adaptation to real-life scenarios at different developmental stages, should be a priority, along with enhancing coping skills appropriately.

6 Conclusion and Future Work

The study aimed to compare campus bullying coping strategies and integrate successful approaches into a VR system combining multimodal interaction and interactive story-telling. The goal was to provide a natural, immersive experience by simulating real-life interactions through gestures and speech. System development focused on gesture and speech recognition for enhanced user experience. Immersion aimed to help users understand verbal and relational bullying and various response outcomes for effective real-life applications.

VR bullying scenarios were effective for simulation-based instruction, offering users a secure platform to engage in simulated responses confidently. VR facilitated detachment from reality and interactive engagement in the virtual environment. However, limitations were noted due to gesture design, resulting in misinterpreted actions or lack of interaction options. Future designs could involve user input to refine gesture and interaction elements. Diverse bullying scenarios were desired by participants, suggesting the need to encompass multiple types across learning stages, deepening understanding of bullying dynamics and responses. The study aimed to develop a versatile VR system to eliminate campus bullying in different age groups, promoting positive learning experiences. The hope is for increased attention on bullying issues, leading to educational designs that offer comprehensive insight, ultimately alleviating the impact of bullying on young lives. Future designs should incorporate participant feedback to improve portrayal and immersion. The study underscores the value of experiential VR learning in understanding bullying dynamics and coping strategies.

References

1. Nadan, T., Alexandrov, V., Jamieson, R., Watson, K.: Is virtual reality a memorable experience in an educational context? Int. J. Emerg. Technol. Learn. (iJET) **6**(1), 53–57 (2011)
2. Calvert, J., Abadia, R.: Impact of immersing university and high school students in educational linear narratives using virtual reality technology. Comput. Educ. **159**, 104005 (2020)
3. Bindman, S.W., Castaneda, L.M., Scanlon, M., Cechony, A.: Am I a bunny? The impact of high and low immersion platforms and viewers' perceptions of role on presence, narrative engagement, and empathy during an animated 360 video. In: Proceedings of the 2018 CHI Conference on Human Factors in Computing Systems, pp. 1–11 (2018)
4. Aylett, R.S., Louchart, S., Dias, J., Paiva, A., Vala, M.: FearNot! – an experiment in emergent narrative. In: Panayiotopoulos, T., Gratch, J., Aylett, R., Ballin, D., Olivier, P., Rist, T. (eds.) IVA 2005. LNCS (LNAI), vol. 3661, pp. 305–316. Springer, Heidelberg (2005). https://doi.org/10.1007/11550617_26
5. Furlong, M., Morrison, G.: The school in school violence: definitions and facts. J. Emot. Behav. Disord. **8**(2), 71–82 (2000)
6. Gredler, G.R., Olweus, D.: Bullying at School: What We Know and What We Can Do, 140 p. Blackwell Publishing, Malden (1993). $25.00 Wiley Online Library, 2003
7. Amra, R., Agarwal, S.: Contributing factors leading bullying among children (2019)
8. Skrzypiec, G., Slee, P., Murray-Harvey, R., Pereira, B.: School bullying by one or more ways: does it matter and how do students cope? Sch. Psychol. Int. **32**(3), 288–311 (2011)
9. Naylor, P., Cowie, H.: The effectiveness of peer support systems in challenging school bullying: the perspectives and experiences of teachers and pupils. J. Adolesc. **22**(4), 467–479 (1999)

10. Naylor, P., Cowie, H., del Rey, R.: Coping strategies of secondary school children in response to being bullied. Child Psychol. Psychiatry Rev. **6**(3), 114–120 (2001)
11. Kanetsuna, T., Smith, P.K., Morita, Y.: Coping with bullying at school: children's recommended strategies and attitudes to school-based interventions in England and Japan. Aggressive Behav.: Off. J. Int. Soc. Res. Aggression **32**(6), 570–580 (2006)
12. Ekstrom, R.B., Goertz, M.E., Pollack, J.M., Rock, D.A.: Who drops out of high school and why? Findings from a national study. Teach. Coll. Rec. **87**(3), 356–373 (1986)
13. Brooks, R.B.: Creating a positive school climate: strategies for fostering self-esteem, motivation, and resilience. In: Educating Minds and Hearts: Social Emotional Learning and the Passage into Adolescence, pp. 61–73 (1999)
14. Marietta, G., Viola, J., Ibekwe, N., Claremon, J., Gehlbach, H.: Improving relationships through virtual environments: How seeing the world through victims' eyes may prevent bullying. In: Annual Meeting of American Educational Research Association, Chicago, IL (2015)
15. Rosselet, J.G., Stauffer, S.D.: Using group role-playing games with gifted children and adolescents: a psychosocial intervention model. Int. J. Play Ther. **22**(4), 173 (2013)
16. Oyekoya, O., Urbanski, J., Shynkar, Y., Baksh, A., Etsaghara, M.: Exploring first-person perspectives in designing a role-playing VR simulation for bullying prevention: a focus group study. Front. Virtual Reality **2**, 672003 (2021)
17. Mandal, S.: Brief introduction of virtual reality & its challenges. Int. J. Sci. Eng. Res. **4**(4), 304–309 (2013)
18. Shin, D.: Empathy and embodied experience in virtual environment: to what extent can virtual reality stimulate empathy and embodied experience? Comput. Hum. Behav. **78**, 64–73 (2018)
19. Roussou, M.: The interplay between form, story, and history: The use of narrative in cultural and educational virtual reality. In: Balet, O., Subsol, G., Torguet, P. (eds.) ICVS 2001. LNCS, vol. 2197, pp. 181–190. Springer, Heidelberg (2001). https://doi.org/10.1007/3-540-45420-9_20
20. Riedl, M.O., Bulitko, V.: Interactive narrative: an intelligent systems approach. AI Mag. **34**(1), 67 (2013)
21. Ostrin, G., Frey, J., Cauchard, J.R.: Interactive narrative in virtual reality. In: Proceedings of the 17th International Conference on Mobile and Ubiquitous Multimedia, pp. 463–467 (2018)
22. Green, M.C., Jenkins, K.M.: Interactive narratives: processes and outcomes in user-directed stories. J. Commun. **64**(3), 479–500 (2014)
23. Sundar, S.S., Oh, J., Kang, H., Sreenivasan, A.: How does technology persuade? SAGE Handb. Persuas. Dev. Theory Pract. 388 (2012)
24. Gorini, A., Capideville, C.S., De Leo, G., Mantovani, F., Riva, G.: The role of immersion and narrative in mediated presence: the virtual hospital experience. Cyberpsychol. Behav. Soc. Netw. **14**(3), 99–105 (2011)
25. Ivanov, L., Ramos, N.: "Bully": a virtual reality environment for anti-bullying education. In: The Thirty-Third International Flairs Conference (2020)
26. Lindgren, R.: Generating a learning stance through perspective-taking in a virtual environment. Comput. Hum. Behav. **28**(4), 1130–1139 (2012)
27. Yang, L., Huang, J., Feng, T., Hong-An, W., Guo-Zhong, D.: Gesture interaction in virtual reality. Virtual Reality Intell. Hardw. **1**(1), 84–112 (2019)
28. Oviatt, S.: Mulitmodal interactive maps: designing for human performance. Hum.-Comput. Interact. **12**(1–2), 93–129 (1997)
29. Cohen, P.R., Oviatt, S.L.: The role of voice input for human-machine communication. Proc. Natl. Acad. Sci. **92**(22), 9921–9927 (1995)
30. Wall, E.S.: An empirical study of virtual reality menu interaction and design. Mississippi State University (2021)

31. McCoy, J., Treanor, M., Samuel, B., Wardrip-Fruin, N., Mateas, M.: Comme il faut: a system for authoring playable social models. In: Proceedings of the AAAI conference on artificial intelligence and interactive digital entertainment, vol. 7, no. 1, pp. 158–163 (2011)

32. Piplica, A., DeLeon, C., Magerko, B.: Gestural interactions for interactive narrative co-creation. In: Proceedings of the AAAI Conference on Artificial Intelligence and Interactive Digital Entertainment, vol. 8, no. 2, pp. 26–31 (2012)

33. Mitra, S., Acharya, T.: Gesture recognition: a survey. IEEE Trans. Syst. Man Cybern. Part C (Appl. Rev.) **37**(3), 311–324 (2007)

34. Wu, H., Wang, Y., Qiu, J., Liu, J., Zhang, X.: User-defined gesture interaction for immersive VR shopping applications. Behav. Inf. Technol. **38**(7), 726–741 (2019)

35. Haddon, L., Vincent, J.: European children and their carers' understanding of use, risks and safety issues relating to convergent mobile media. Report D4, vol. 1 (2014)

36. Gibbs, T.J.: Teacher perceptions of school violence prevention strategies. Ohio University (2014)

Author Index

Printed in the United States
by Baker & Taylor Publisher Services